The GREAT ATLAS of Italian WINES

Alessandro Avataneo · Vittorio Manganelli

The GREAT ATLAS of Italian WINES

The definitive tool for understanding,
choosing, and discussing
Italian wines with expertise

Rizzoli
NEW YORK

New York · Paris · London · Milan

CONTENTS

INTRODUCTION

There are over 18 million acres of vineyards in the world, and 1.7 million of them are in Italy. The country has the fourth-largest vineyard acreage in the world after Spain, France, and China, but ranks first in terms of the range of grape varieties grown. In Italy, there are 255,000 winegrowers and 45,000 winemakers, including more than 500 cooperative wineries, producing around 1.3 billion gallons of wine annually. Working on an average number of five labels per producer, this comes out to over two hundred thousand different labels each year. France, Italy, and Spain supply half of the 7.8 billion gallons of wine consumed globally. This sounds like a lot but is just one-sixth of worldwide annual beer production, of which nearly 48 billion gallons are consumed each year across the globe.

Twenty years ago, there were 891,000 wineries in Italy. Growing grapes and producing wine is no easy task. Taking care of our bodies and celebrating with friends, drinking conscientiously in the knowledge that whatever we are consuming will not harm us since it does not contain hazardous chemicals and that no compromises were made by whoever produced it, means not being satisfied with a hydroalcoholic solution derived from grapes but rather practicing an age-old ritual, which is precisely why we wrote this book. The intoxication it can bring is only one aspect of wine. Our focus is on the complex cultural object that expresses human creativity.

The aim of this Great Atlas is to provide a complete, up-to-date and detailed picture of Italian wine production: a work of reference for those who are already familiar with wine, and a mine of information for those who want to explore the amazing variety of areas, *terroirs*, grape varieties, and types of wine that characterize the Italian peninsula.

This book is radically different from a typical guide linked to point scores and advertising. It is a scientific text with a reader-friendly slant, in which wine is described from several perspectives: geographical, historical, sensory, anthropological, and cultural.

The characteristics of the different production areas and the grape varieties grown there are all fully illustrated and explained through the combination and composition of texts, maps, and lists of producers of note who have shown the most qualitative continuity over time, combined with infographics of the sensory archetypes of the main designations. Finally, the book includes a selection of two hundred and seventy-five labels that best represent the geography and contemporary history of Italian wine, in a post-pandemic world shaken by climate change and the crisis of raw materials.

The selected wines are the result of two lifetimes of testing and structured degustation. To arrive at this comprehensive selection, we blind-tasted them, together with colleagues, experts, ordinary consumers, and young students of various geographical origins, then compared the results of our tastings with the descriptions in the major national and international wine guides, in search of a broad and rigorous point of view that was neither provincial, factious, self-referential, or over-flattering. We celebrate the best Italian wines, all the while knowing that the ideal wine does not exist, but rather is the one you chase from one glass to the next, in a continuous search for amazement, surprises, harmonies, and discoveries. Wine is alive, it evolves, and it changes continuously: there is no perfect wine, but there are perfect circumstances in which to open a certain wine, and in the best cases it is the wine that makes a situation memorable, because every good bottle always contains a story made up of life, vine, and wine, as well as good conversation and the story of the person drinking it.

Buon viaggio.

....

GUIDE TO THE REFERENCES

The wines we have selected represent the excellence of Italian production: they are certainly good, and all have a story to tell.

The Atlas describes the characteristics of each region's main Designations (DOCG and DOC), highlighting the most important producers and wines in each area, where the main criterion is consistent quality regardless of vintage. There is a special section at the end of each chapter listing the recommended wines that fall outside the designations but which are classified by the producer as IGT or White, Red, Rosé, or Spumante wines. There are 1580 wineries in total, all identified on the corresponding maps.

The price indications are the average found in wine shops and on store websites. One dollar sign, $, indicates bottle prices below $25, two $$ those from $25 to $49, three $$$ those from $50 to $99, four $$$$ those up to $199, and five $$$$$ those over $200.

Taking into account the differences in the world market due to distribution costs and excise duties, $ = cheap, $$ medium-low, $$$ medium-high, $$$$ high, $$$$$ very high.

The ten parameters used in the infographics are described below. The values range from 1 = poor, not very present or very low, to 5 = very present or very high, with 3 indicating a quantitatively average value.

This method makes it possible to visually represent the identity of a wine, overcoming the limits of a subjective and, as such, questionable judgment. In general, the more uniform and broad the graph, the more balanced the components of a wine; a jagged graph, on the other hand, highlights a wine that is peculiar and angular, but no less good or with less personality. The graph represents the archetype, i.e., the sensory synthesis to which all wines of a given type tend.

WINEGLASSES

Readers will find, next to the name of each Designation described, illustrations of certain wineglasses, relating to the types of production according to each specific regulation. The color of the wine contained in the traditional glasses indicates white, red, or rosé wines; the flute symbolizes spumante, and the smaller glass represents sweet wines and/or passito wine.

White   Red   Rosé   Spumante   Sweet/passito

DESCRIPTION OF THE PARAMETERS

Aromas
The aromatic intensity of the wine, perceived first through the nostrils and then retronasally.

Astringency
The dry, astringent sensation resulting mainly from the presence of tannin. In white wines and sweet wines, where no significant tannin component is present, astringency is replaced by **minerality** and **sweetness** respectively.

Complexity
The presence of multiple characteristics that add up to create rich and varied aromas and flavors, the opposite of banality. In a great wine, complexity can coexist with a high drinkability that makes it accessible.

Drinkability
The ease of tasting, the smoothness, the reduced presence of tannic and acidic contrasts, but also sweetness, which would make the flavor difficult.

Freshness
On the taste level, it is provided by acids and salts, while on the nose it comes mainly from citrus and menthol aromas.

Fruitiness
Indicates the presence of aromas reminiscent of fruit (white, yellow, or red). It is the dominant scent in rather simple and straightforward wines.

Harmony
The balanced relationship, both on the nose and in the mouth, between the components, without the clear dominance of any one element.

Longevity
The ability of a wine to evolve positively in the bottle over the years. It is generally believed to reach 40–50 years in reds, 20–30 in whites, and many more in fortified wines.

Minerality
In white wines, the complex hints are reminiscent of flint, rubbed matchstick, iodine, and hydrocarbons.

Mouth
The impact on palate and tongue. The density, the texture, the fullness, the richness of the sequence of tactile sensations and the gustatory length.

Structure
The strength of the taste architecture, given mainly by polyphenols, different types of alcohol, and mineral salts. It is measured by the fixed residue parameter, the minimum level of which is established in the regulations of the individual designations.

Sweetness
This is given by the perceptible presence of residual sugars, i.e., not transformed into alcohol during fermentation, which can vary from anywhere between 0 and 1 ounce per quart.

Piedmont

It is one of the most recognized and celebrated food and wine regions in Italy, owing its success to the diverse landscapes and native grape varieties that have found their *genius loci* here. There is a particular affinity with Nebbiolo, a difficult grape variety, and it has become apparent that only in these *terroirs* can it express its complexity.

In 1965, the average Italian consumed 110 liters of wine per year. Today, it is less than half of that. In fifty years, wine has gone from being something consumed every day to a symbol of conviviality and status—in some cases even a fashion object and a collectable. Yet in celebrating Italian wine, we must not forget that the scenario today also originates from a tragedy, which took place in the town of Narzole, northwest of Cuneo, on March 17, 1986. This was a month before the Chernobyl disaster. Following incidents where wine was adulterated with methanol, twenty-three people died and dozens lost their sight. It turned out that this adding of industrial alcohol to wine was a widespread practice, not only in the Langhe. Two producers ended up in prison while others got away with emptying their tanks into rivers and streams. The victims would never be compensated. It was time for a change.

Following in the footsteps of Luigi Veronelli, who had already published his catalogue of Italy's best wines in 1961, the first Vini d'Italia guide was published in 1988. It was edited by Gambero Rosso and the newly founded Slow Food movement, the association based in Bra, in the Langhe, which was to become something of an ambassador of good, healthy, and sustainable food and wine. In this way, the spark that revolutionized an entire sector of the Italian economy was ignited in Piedmont, transforming the land of evil, as it was called by Beppe Fenoglio, into a food and wine region capable of attracting visitors and investments from all over the world.

In Barolo, a winegrowing area in the province of Cuneo, a new generation of producers clashed with old traditions. Inspired by the example of Burgundy, they introduced practices such as thinning-out in the vineyard, and innovations such as the use of barriques for aging, with the aim being to obtain wines of an ever higher quality. Elio Altare, Giorgio Rivetti, and Roberto Voerzio lead the line of modernists, while on the other side are traditionalists such as Bartolo Mascarello, Beppe Rinaldi, and Bruno Giacosa. Their contrasting approaches create vitality and diversity of expression, and they all strive for excellence. The Barolo received top scores from magazines such as *Wine Spectator* and *Wine Advocate*, and in just a few years, in some cases reached unaffordable prices, as in the case of Monfortino and some of the reserves of the finest crus. In Barbaresco, it is Angelo Gaja who achieved world fame with his wines, leading the way for two generations of producers.

Piedmont is the only Italian region that activated a cru system in the 1980s, which led in 2010 to the recognition of one hundred and seventy vineyards in Barolo and sixty-six in Barbaresco. These are the MGAs (*Menzioni Geografiche Aggiuntive*, or Additional Geographical Indications), the recognition that the quality of wine is given not only by the hand of man but by the *terroir*, the synthesis of natural and human elements that make up the cultural identity of a territory.

When the concept of the *terroir* was not yet codified, the wisest farmers would clamber to the top of the hills in winter, after a heavy snowfall, to see on which *bricchi* the snow melted first. This is how they identified the best *sorì*, which in dialect means "exposed to the midday sun."

The region offers a great diversity of landscapes and soils. The climate, until a few years ago temperate—the 45th parallel passes through Turin—is changing, with less snow and little rain. What was once the exception—the scorching summer of 2003—has become a constant, from 2015 onward, with increasingly hot and dry vintages that yield increasingly alcoholic wines.

The hill systems surround the central plain where the Po flows, and are in turn surrounded by the Alpine arc where all its tributaries are born. The hills of the Langhe were formed between one hundred and sixty million years ago. On these primordial rocks, successive layers of clay alternating with others of sandstone and limestone, more porous and draining, accumulated. This mineral complexity, combined with the variety of microclimates in the area, allows Nebbiolo to express a range of nuances on these marls that is more precise and identifiable than in any other area.

Farther north on the left bank of the Tanaro is a long canyon, which in the past was a gigantic waterfall from which the river spilled to end up in the bed where it flows today. It cuts diagonally across the wild lands of the Roero, where vines still alternate with orchards and woods. These hills are steeper, sandier, and crumblier than those of Barolo and Barbaresco, are rich in fossils and marine sediments, because they were submerged until three million years ago, and produce more delicate Barbera and Nebbiolo than the more structured Langhe and Monferrato.

The lands of northern Piedmont, on the other hand, are of morainic origin: during the retreat of the glaciers twenty thousand years ago, enormous quantities of gravel, stones, sand, and clay accumulated on the remains of ancient volcanoes to form more rounded hills, interspersed with lakes and streams. In these areas, Nebbiolo expresses a fresher and more mineral character than in the Langhe.

In Carema, on the border with Valle d'Aosta, Nebbiolo is still cultivated on terraces built by the ancient Romans. Other indigenous reds have been growing in Piedmont for centuries and are well worth tasting, such as the intense and fruity Dolcetto, the austere and spicy Grignolino del Monferrato, and the jaunty and delicate Verduno Pelaverga.

Piedmont is also a land of whites: to the south, from the 820 to the 2,940 feet of Mombarcaro, lies Alta Langa, a land of hazelnuts and dry, sharp, sparkling wines. In the Canavese, the fresh and floral Erbaluce; in the Novi Ligure area, the more elegant and mineral Gavi, while in the Roero there is the soft and exotic Arneis.

In the far southeast of the region, in the Colli Tortonesi area, Timorasso has been rediscovered and set in stone since the 1980s under the ancient Roman name of Tortona, Derthona. Lastly, there are the 24,710 acres of Moscato, for one hundred million bottles of Asti and Moscato d'Asti sparkling wine that employ three thousand seven hundred companies. Piedmont's 113,231 acres of vineyards produce 5% of Italian wine—2.26 million hectoliters—for 1.24 billion euros in revenue, 11% of the value of national production.

....

MAIN VINES GROWN IN THE REGION

Arneis

With a few exceptions, wines made from Arneis grapes were once recognized by their sour and straightforward character, hence the name of the grape, which in Piedmontese dialect indicates a lively and mischievous individual. This grape has long been neglected, despite the fact that its origin dates back at least six hundred years, probably from the toponym Reneysium, today Bricco Renesio, near Canale. It was traditionally planted between the rows of Nebbiolo vines, so as to attract birds, to prevent them from eating the red berries, which were already more prized at the time. On the other hand, if vinified skillfully, protecting it from oxidation and preserving the tropical harmony it releases after fermentation, Arneis gives freshness and exoticism, with notes of grapefruit, citron, lime, sage, papaya, broom, and hawthorn. There is even tomato leaf, typical of Sauvignon, with passion fruit and a soft, delicately almond finish that acquires fullness with a few years of aging, without fading. Today Arneis is part of the Roero DOCG and Langhe DOC Arneis.

Barbera

"Barbera, Barbera, we are all your children," are words still sung in Piedmontese taverns, and a sip of good Barbera is enough to grasp the meaning of the hymn. Its origins are uncertain: it was already being cultivated in the Middle Ages under the generic name of gray grape, but it was in 1798 that Giuseppe Nuvolone Pergamo, Count of Scandaluzza, mentioned it in the Calendario Georgico della Società Agraria di Torino. Beloved by winegrowers because it grows well even in less fertile land, so much so that it covers one-third of Piedmont's acres under vine, it has become the second most cultivated grape variety in Italy after Sangiovese, and is the most widely grown Italian grape variety abroad. The wine made from Barbera grapes is lively and crisp: it enchants with its intense, impenetrable red color, with purple, almost blue reflections, and it makes the mouth pop from gluttony, like diving into a field of blackberries and blueberries amid cherries and wild mint. If vinified incorrectly, the impact is rustic and vinous, or exaggerated by too much wood or alcohol. But if everything is in balance, Barbera expresses opulence in harmony, refinement in the violence of the fruit. To be consumed between five and fifteen years in the DOCG Nizza, Barbera

The DOCGs

- Alta Langa
- Asti/Moscato d'Asti
- Barbaresco
- Barbera d'Asti
- Barbera del Monferrato Superiore
- Barolo
- Brachetto d'Acqui/Acqui
- Canelli
- Dogliani
- Dolcetto di Diano d'Alba/Diano d'Alba
- Dolcetto di Ovada Superiore/Ovada
- Erbaluce di Caluso /Caluso
- Gattinara
- Gavi/Cortese di Gavi
- Ghemme
- Nizza
- Roero
- Ruché di Castagnole Monferrato
- Terre Alfieri

The DOCs

- Alba
- Albugnano
- Barbera d'Alba
- Barbera del Monferrato
- Boca
- Bramaterra
- Calosso
- Canavese
- Carema
- Casorzo/Malvasia di Casorzo d'Asti
- Cisterna d'Asti
- Colli Tortonesi
- Collina Torinese
- Colline Novaresi
- Colline Saluzzesi
- Cortese dell'Alto Monferrato
- Coste della Sesia
- Dolcetto d'Acqui
- Dolcetto d'Alba
- Dolcetto d'Asti
- Dolcetto di Ovada
- Fara
- Freisa d'Asti
- Freisa di Chieri
- Gabiano
- Grignolino d'Asti
- Grignolino del Monferrato Casalese
- Langhe
- Lessona
- Loazzolo
- Malvasia di Castelnuovo Don Bosco
- Monferrato
- Nebbiolo d'Alba
- Piemonte
- Pinerolese
- Rubino di Cantavenna
- Sizzano
- Strevi
- Valli Ossolane
- Valsusa
- Verduno Pelaverga/ Verduno

d'Asti and Barbera del Monferrato Superiore DOCG, and in the DOCs Barbera d'Alba, Barbera del Monferrato, Colli Tortonesi, Gabiano, Langhe, Monferrato, and Pinerolese.

Bonarda

Widespread in Piedmont and Oltrepò Pavese—and also cultivated in Argentina—it has small, sweet grapes with low tannin content from which simple, medium-bodied, vinous, and slightly aromatic wines are produced, to be drunk young. It must be present in a minimum percentage of 85% in the DOC of the same name (→ Lombardy), while it may be present in smaller percentages in other designations, such as Pinerolese DOC, together with Nebbiolo, Freisa, or Barbera.

Brachetto del Piemonte

Present in Brachetto d'Acqui or Acqui DOCG, it is one of the few red grape varieties that produces an aromatic, delicate, low-alcohol wine with hints of violets and wild roses. Cultivated in the Acqui Terme area since the time of the ancient Romans, today it is mostly produced in sweet and sparkling versions, but can also be vinified dry, with some pleasant results.

Cortese

A grape inventoried for the first time in 1614 in the cellars of the castle of Casale Monferrato, in the province of Alessandria, and today widespread also in the province of Asti, where it appears in designations such as Colli Tortonesi and Monferrato. It can also be found in Oltrepò Pavese, in Lombardy, and in Veneto, on the shores of Lake Garda, for a total of about 7,413 cultivated acres. From it comes Gavi or Cortese di Gavi DOCG, a famous Piedmontese white wine, appreciated for its dry and light character, with delicate and fresh almond and white flower aromas. Its neutral and refreshing character, with pleasant citrine notes, makes it suitable for fish, so much so that it is traditionally requested in restaurants in nearby Liguria.

Croatina

Originally from the Valle del Versa, in Rovescala, Oltrepò Pavese, it is now cultivated in the provinces of Cuneo, Alessandria, and in the designations of Northern Piedmont, where it is generally accompanied by Nebbiolo. Some producers vinify it in purity, such as Christoph Künzli, in Boca, from a centuries-old vineyard, or Walter Massa, who in the Colli Tortonesi produces a pure version with a chalky flavor and aromas of plum and bergamot.

Dolcetto

An indigenous Piedmontese wine that is very popular in the provinces of Cuneo and Asti, it is the everyday wine par excellence, especially in the taverns of the province of Cuneo: intense, dry, and fruity, with a beautiful violet color and easy to drink thanks to its pleasant taste of cherry and berries, with hints of licorice, plum, and hazelnut in the best cases. It ripens almost a month earlier than Nebbiolo and is more resistant to the cold, but proves difficult to vinify because it tends to be vinous and bitter, due to its low acidity and excessive tannin; this is why delicate extractions and short fermentations generally produce the best results. In Piedmont, it is produced in the Diano DOCG and the Alba, Asti, Acqui, Ovada,

and Ormeasco di Pornassio DOCs, on the border with Liguria. The most important DOCG is Dogliani, where a Campo de Vin Dolzet in Pianezzo is mentioned for the first time in an ordinance of August 1593, issued by the municipality to regulate the grape harvest.

Erbaluce

In any challenge for the most beautiful names ever given to a grape variety, Erbaluce would be on the podium, born of the thirst of a transcendentalist poet like Walt Whitman. In the past it was called Elbalus, *albaluce*, or dawn light, because its ripe berries glow orange and coral pink at first light. An ancient vine, already known in Roman times, it has found its ideal *terroir* in the Canavese, Biellese, and Novarese areas, in particular along the shores of Lake Viverone and on the Serra d'Ivrea. This is Europe's largest morainic amphitheater, a remnant of debris from the last ice age. Erbaluce di Caluso or Caluso DOCG wines can be dry white, sweet, or sparkling. In the best dry versions, freshness and verticality are complemented by a discreet complexity of white-fleshed fruit, while in the sparkling version there is a characteristic bread crust taste. In the rare passito versions, the grape harvest may be delayed until March to allow the botrytis time to take root, the berries to dehydrate and develop; with aging in barriques, aromas of acacia honey, apricots, figs, walnuts, almonds, cocoa, and saffron, balanced between heady sweetness and refreshing slight sourness develop.

Favorita

Favorita is the name of Vermentino in the Roero (→ Vermentino in Sardinia). Widespread as a table grape in the early twentieth century, it has now become, along with Arneis, the other most widely grown white grape in the area, and produces simple, light wines that are best drunk young.

Freisa

One of the most widespread grape varieties in Piedmont since the early sixteenth century. A descendant of Nebbiolo and Viognier, but complicated to vinify because it is rather acidic and tannic, in the most successful versions it produces essences of red and black berry fruit, spices of pepper and cinnamon, with a clean and persistent finish. In general, there is such a wide range of alternative vinifications as to generate more confusion than variety, including dry, sweet, sparkling, or even frothy "freisa," refined in steel or wood, vinified pure or almost pure. Examples of this are the DOC wines Freisa d'Asti, Freisa di Chieri, and Langhe Freisa, or blended with other vines, as in the DOC wines Canavese Red, Colli Tortonesi Rosso, Monferrato Freisa, and Pinerolese Freisa.

Grignolino

It has been cultivated in Monferrato for at least eight hundred years, where it was known as Barbesino, Barbisino, or Grignolerii, while today it is part of the DOC Grignolino d'Asti and Grignolino del Monferrato. Its name derives from a synecdoche, because the *grignòle*, in Asti dialect, are the grape seeds, which in Grignolino berries are found in greater quantity than in other grapes and for this reason bring more tannin to the wine. When the acidic and astringent side is kept at bay, Grignolino can be a convincing wine: fresh, delicate, and austere, pale red in color with orange and garnet highlights, and with a recognizable aromatic profile of alpine herbs and flowers, roses, wild strawberries, and currants, combined with a slightly bitter spiciness of pepper and cloves that closes on a dry, savory finish.

Moscato Bianco

White Muscat has been cultivated in Piedmont for centuries, particularly in the Canelli area, today it occupies almost a quarter of the region's vineyard area. It is an aromatic grape variety, i.e. a vine whose wine has the same aromas as the grape berry. The Greek origin and spread of Muscat throughout the Mediterranean is confirmed by genetic analyses, which recognize two ancient table grapes—Axina, cultivated today in Sardinia, and Heptakilo or Eftakoilo, in Greece—as the ancestors of Muscat. Other Muscats descended from the white Muscat, such as Moscato Giallo or Moscato Rosa from Trentino, although the name Muscat, with its variations in several languages, is used to indicate at least two hundred distinct and often unrelated varieties. It derives from a Persian word from the fifth century BC, indicating a particular musk fragrance with medicinal properties, extracted from the glands of musk deer. The name later changed to the Greek *moskos* and the Latin *muscus*. Pliny the Elder called it an Apiana vine because he had observed that bees were attracted to it, and in the encyclopedia *On the Properties of Things*, the Franciscan Bartolomeo Anglico first mentions, around 1230, a wine "extracted from Muscat grapes." The success of Muscat transformed Canelli's landscape and economy. Its Wine Cathedrals wind their way underground for 12.5 miles and are such an advanced work of engineering that they deserve UNESCO protection as World Heritage Sites, together with the winegrowing landscapes of Langhe, Monferrato, and Roero. The two types of DOCG are Asti and Moscato d'Asti. There is also a small Muscat-based DOC, in Loazzolo, where enchanting Passiti wines are produced. Because of its low alcohol content, Muscat is often the first wine one tastes in one's life: a teaspoon is enough to be inebriated with refreshing scents of musk, citrus, yellow and white flowers, and aromas of sage and cedar that expand to orange, peach, and apricot as it withers.

Nebbiolo

Cases of elective affinity between *terroir* and varietal vinified in purity are rare, and the resulting wines are precious: Rieslings in Moselle, Pinot Noir and Chardonnay in Burgundy, Sangiovese in Montalcino, Tempranillo in Rioja, Syrah in the Rhone valley, Cabernet Franc in the Loire, and a few others. In Piedmont, Nebbiolo has been cultivated for eight hundred years, and here it has developed the ability to express all the nuances of a specific *terroir*. As in Burgundy, the Langhe is also the result of an extreme parcellation of vineyards, which would not exist without this grape variety. From the designations of the south—Barolo, Barbaresco, and Roero—to those of the north—Gattinara, Ghemme, Boca, Sizzano, Fara, Bramaterra, Lessona, and Carema—Nebbiolo is a mystery. It needs to suffer on difficult terrain to give its best. It ripens late, and more than any other native vine is capable of extracting the identity of a single hill and making it recognizable. Many debate the organoleptic differences between Barolo and Barbaresco. The truth is that it is not easy to distinguish them in a blind tasting. However, with experience, wanting to generalize, one can recognize in Barolo a more severe structure, less friendly than Barbaresco, which is finer

and more harmonious, especially in the first years. The world of Barolo is wide and multifaceted: from the classicism of Cannubi to the balsamic traits of Monforte, from the power of Serralunga to the refinement of Castiglione Falletto, to the delicacy of La Morra, each commune and each vineyard convey a unique bouquet of scents, which also vary according to the general climatic trend of the year and the microclimates of the individual valleys and hills. They are protected by the Alpine chain and caressed by the mild and humid currents of the Ligurian Sea, so much so that, for wine lovers, an evening in company to debate and train both nose and palate on the different nuances of a battery of great Nebbiolos is always well spent. In the most solemn and articulated versions, a Nebbiolo in the fullness of its expression—therefore between nine and twenty-five years of age—conveys a sumptuous, almost perturbing beauty, because it invites the senses to perceive all the kaleidoscopic poetry of which the wine is capable: roses, violets, licorice, sour cherries, raspberries, blueberries, blackberries, thyme, pine needles, camphor, eucalyptus, tobacco, undergrowth, leather, tar, and chocolate. On a tactile level, the highest degree of complexity and balance between tannins and acidity triggers a long sequence of suggestions that stimulate every corner of the mouth, between sensations of freshness, velvet, and vibrant intensity, and a long symphonic finish.

Pelaverga Piccolo

Vinified in purity in the small Verduno Pelaverga DOC, it produces light, pale red wines with delicate aromas of roses and wild strawberries and a dry, spicy flavor that is irresistibly pleasant on the palate.

Timorasso

It is first mentioned in a document from 1209, in Tortona. Until the early twentieth century it was one of the most appreciated and widespread vines in the province of Alessandria, then replaced by the more robust Cortese after the advent of Phylloxera. Rediscovered at the end of the 1980s by a handful of producers, led by Walter Massa, Timorasso has regained its rightful place among the best Italian native vines, within the Colli Tortonesi DOC, for its resilience in aging and for the complexity of its aromatic bouquet, which ranges from floral to mineral, with accents of flint, ginger, honey, lime, almond, and lemon, and with aging acquires an oxidative and brackish creaminess, cloaked in candied orange.

Uva Rara

Not to be confused with Bonarda dell'Oltrepò Pavese, it is so called not because of its scarcity (*uva rara* literally means "rare grapes"), but because of the small number of grapes per bunch. It is mainly used to soften Nebbiolo in northern Piedmont appellations and to bring structure, alcohol, and acidity to the wines in which it participates.

Vespolina

Also known as Balsamina, Ughetta, Nespolina, Massana, Cinerina, or Inzaga, Vespolina appears in Giorgio Gallesio's Pomona Italiana, under the name Vitis Circumpadana, and spread in the area between Novara, Biella, and Vercelli from the nineteenth century onward. Despite its good spiciness, tannin, and acidity, it is rarely vinified as a single variety in the DOC Colline Novaresi and Coste della Sesia appellations, while it is often found in northern Piedmont appellations as a complement to its ancestor, Nebbiolo.

Barolo DOCG

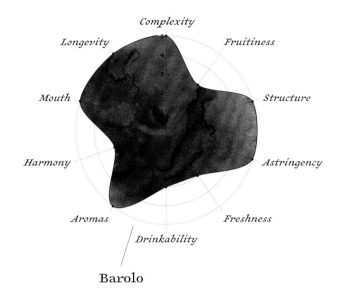

Barolo

While "Nebbiolo" wine was spoken and written about in Piedmont as far back as the thirteenth century, it was only from the mid-nineteenth century that the name "Barolo" wine became established because that was the period in which production techniques were refined, thanks to the foresight of Juliette Colbert di Maulévrier, wife of Marquis Carlo Tancredi Falletti di Barolo, and Camillo Benso Count of Cavour, who owned land in Grinzane, later to become Grinzane Cavour. The technicians they called upon, the Frenchman Louis Oudart and especially General Francesco Staglieno, established the rules for the production of this new wine, making it very similar to what is tasted around the world today. But, although the new Barolo was immediately appreciated in many European courts, it was phylloxera that destroyed most of the European vineyards between the nineteenth and twentieth centuries, and the two world wars that prevented its true success. This came, in essence, only from the 1980s onward, when American critics put Barolo on a par with the great wines of Bordeaux and when dozens of new, small producers joined the very few names that had hitherto made its history, such as Marchesi di Barolo, Fontanafredda, Giuseppe Mascarello, Pio Cesare, Giuseppe Conterno, Massolino, and Giuseppe Rinaldi. Those were the years in which Elio Grasso, Conterno Fantino, Elio Altare, the Revello brothers, Giovanni Corino, Davide Rosso, to name but a few of the creators of the Barolo *nouvelle vague*, entered the scene.

Immediately afterward, at the end of the last century, a heated debate began, fortunately almost overcome, pitting the traditionalists, led by charismatic producers such as Bartolo Mascarello and Giuseppe Rinaldi, against the modernists, supported with conviction by dozens of young producers led by the example of Elio Altare and Roberto Voerzio. The waning of contention does not mean that there has been a generalized meeting of minds toward identical working systems in the vineyard and cellar: what is certain is that the so-called traditionalists propose ever sharper and more elegant selections, while among the modernists, the hint of wood deriving from aging in barriques has faded almost everywhere.

This is a unique wine, characterized by the refinement and complexity of its aromas (from tar to violets, from truffles to currants) and the rare power of taste, quite alcoholic (often around 14.5% by volume), capable of improving in the bottle for decades.

From 5,244 acres under vine spread over the eleven municipalities of Serralunga d'Alba, Monforte d'Alba, Castiglione Falletto, Novello, Barolo, La Morra, Cherasco, Verduno, Grinzane Cavour, Diano d'Alba, and Roddi, the almost three hundred producers produce about fourteen million bottles per year.

—

Producers and their trademark and signature wines:

1. Anna Maria ABBONA, Farigliano
   Barolo Bricco San Pietro ($$)
2. Marziano ABBONA, Dogliani
   Barolo Cerviano-Merli ($$)
   Barolo Ravera ($$)
3. Fratelli ALESSANDRIA, Verduno
   Barolo Monvigliero ($$$)
   Barolo Gramolere ($$$)
4. Gianfranco ALESSANDRIA, Monforte d'Alba
   Barolo San Giovanni ($$)
5. Elio ALTARE, La Morra
   Barolo Arborina ($$$$)
   Barolo Cerretta Riserva Vigna Bricco ($$$$)
6. AZELIA, Castiglione Falletto
   Barolo Bricco Fiasco ($$$)
   Barolo Cerretta ($$$$)
   Barolo Margheria ($$$)
   Barolo San Rocco ($$$)
7. BEL COLLE, Verduno
   Barolo Monvigliero ($$)
8. BERSANO, Nizza Monferrato
   Barolo Badarina ($$)
9. Enzo BOGLIETTI, La Morra
   Barolo Brunate ($$$)
   Barolo Arione ($$$)
   Barolo Case Nere ($$$)
10. Giacomo BORGOGNO & Figli, Barolo
    Barolo Liste ($$$)
    Barolo Cannubi ($$$)
    Barolo Riserva ($$$$)
11. Chiara BOSCHIS, Barolo
    Barolo Cannubi ($$$)

12. BRANDINI, La Morra
Barolo Cerretta ($$$)
Barolo R56 ($$$)
13. Giacomo BREZZA e Figli, Barolo
Barolo Sarmassa Riserva Vigna Bricco ($$$)
Barolo Cannubi ($$)
14. BROCCARDO, Monforte d'Alba
Barolo Ravera ($$)
15. BROVIA, Castiglione Falletto
Barolo Brea Vigna Ca' Mia ($$$)
Barolo Villero ($$$)
16. Comm. G.B. BURLOTTO, Verduno
Barolo Acclivi ($$$$$)
Barolo Monvigliero ($$$$$)
17. Alberto BURZI, La Morra
Barolo Capalot Vecchie Viti ($$$)
18. CA' ROMÉ, Barbaresco
Barolo Cerretta ($$)
19. Giovanni CANONICA, Barolo
Barolo Paiagallo ($$$$)
20. CASA E. DI MIRAFIORE, Serralunga d'Alba
Barolo Lazzarito ($$$)
21. CASCINA FONTANA, Monforte d'Alba
Barolo ($$$)
22. CASTELLO DI VERDUNO, Verduno
Barolo Riserva Monvigliero ($$$)
23. CAVALLOTTO – Tenuta Bricco Boschis,
Castiglione Falletto
Barolo Bricco Boschis ($$$)
Barolo Bricco Boschis Riserva
Vigna San Giuseppe ($$$$)
24. CERETTO, Alba
Barolo Prapò ($$$)
Barolo Bricco Rocche ($$$$)
25. Michele CHIARLO, Calamandrana
Barolo Cerequio Riserva ($$$)
26. Domenico CLERICO, Monforte d'Alba
Barolo Ginestra Ciabot Mentin ($$$)
Barolo del comune di Serralunga d'Alba
Aeroplanservaj ($$$)
Barolo Ginestra Pajana ($$$)
27. Elvio COGNO, Novello
Barolo Ravera Bricco Pernice ($$$)
Barolo Ravera Riserva Vigna Elena ($$$$)
28. Giacomo CONTERNO, Monforte d'Alba
Barolo Riserva Monfortino ($$$$$)
Barolo Arione ($$$$$)
Barolo Cerretta ($$$$$)
Barolo Francia ($$$$$)
29. Paolo CONTERNO, Monforte d'Alba
Barolo Riserva Ginestra ($$$$)
30. CONTERNO FANTINO, Monforte d'Alba
Barolo Ginestra Vigna Sorì Ginestra ($$$)
31. CORDERO DI MONTEZEMOLO, La Morra
Barolo Enrico VI ($$$)

32. Giovanni CORINO, La Morra
Barolo Giachini ($$)
Barolo Riserva ($$$)
33. Renato CORINO, La Morra
Barolo Rocche dell'Annunziata ($$$)
Barolo Roncaglie Stefano Corino ($$)
34. DAMILANO, Barolo
Barolo Cannubi Riserva 1752 ($$$$)
35. Giacomo FENOCCHIO, Monforte d'Alba
Barolo Bussia Riserva 90 Dì ($$$)
Barolo Bussia ($$)
36. FIGLI LUIGI ODDERO, La Morra
Barolo Vigna Rionda ($$$$)
Barolo Rocche Rivera ($$$)
37. FONTANAFREDDA, Serralunga d'Alba
Barolo Fontanafredda Vigna La Rosa ($$$)
38. GAJA, Barbaresco
Barolo Sperss ($$$$$)
39. Ettore GERMANO, Serralunga d'Alba
Barolo Riserva Lazzarito ($$$)
Barolo Vignarionda ($$$$)
Barolo Prapò ($$$)
40. Bruno GIACOSA, Neive
Barolo Falletto Riserva Vigna Le Rocche ($$$$$)
41. Elio GRASSO, Monforte d'Alba
Barolo Gavarini Chiniera ($$$)
Barolo Ginestra Casa Maté ($$$)
42. Bruna GRIMALDI, Grinzane Cavour
Barolo Badarina ($$)
43. LA SPINETTA CAMPÈ, Grinzane Cavour
Barolo Campè ($$$$)
44. Giovanni MANZONE, Monforte d'Alba
Barolo Gramolere ($$)
Barolo Bricat ($$)
45. Paolo MANZONE, Serralunga d'Alba
Barolo Meriame ($$)
Barolo Riserva ($$$)
46. Mario MARENGO, La Morra
Barolo Brunate ($$)
Barolo Bricco delle Viole ($$)
47. Bartolo MASCARELLO, Barolo
Barolo ($$$$$)
48. Giuseppe MASCARELLO e Figlio, Monchiero
Barolo Monprivato Riserva Cà d' Morissio ($$$$$)
Barolo Monprivato ($$$$)
49. MASSOLINO, Serralunga d'Alba
Barolo Riserva Vigna Rionda ($$$$)
Barolo Margheria ($$$)
Barolo Parafada ($$$)
50. Fratelli MONCHIERO, Castiglione Falletto
Barolo Rocche di Castiglione ($$)
51. Giulia NEGRI – Serradenari, La Morra
Barolo Serradenari ($$$)

The Barolo MGAs

Barolo was the first Italian wine to make an organic and detailed use of the Additional Geographical Indication, or MGA (*Menzioni Geografiche Aggiuntive*), which was later defined by the Ministry of Agriculture as UGA, or *Unità Geografiche Aggiuntive* (Additional Geographical Units).

Until 2009, each producer had the right to call his Barolo by the name of a vineyard, which derived mostly from tradition but also from the family's imagination. But with the institution of the MGAs, the one hundred and eighty toponyms were defined, in addition to the eleven communal indications. These were, for instance, Barolo of the commune of Monforte d'Alba, of the commune of La Morra, and so forth, to which a winery can refer. Since 2010, a winery can use to indicate, with the appropriate documentation, that the grapes for its wine originate exactly from that cru, to a quantity of at least 85%. It goes without saying that the use of MGAs is optional, and that excellent products can also be made by blending grapes from different vineyards, as best demonstrated—to give just one example—by the Barolo of the Bartolo Mascarello winery.

The new regulations then provide that the name of the MGA may be followed by the name of a vineyard (or vineyards), of lesser extension, provided it is registered and officially approved by the Piedmont Region. In the list in parentheses are some that have achieved well-deserved fame, and others will no doubt follow as the situation evolves.

Within these one hundred and eighty MGAs, no quality levels have been established, so the French choice, which differs from area to area, of establishing hierarchies between the crus of the same area has so far been avoided: all MGAs are thus on the same level.

This is a choice that not all experts fully accept, since centuries of history have shown that the Nebbiolo grape merchants of the Barolo area were, and still are, well aware of the qualitative differences between the various vineyards.

Given that the situation is both workable and rapidly evolving—just think of the exploits of the MGA Ravera in the last ten years, for example—and by restricting oneself to an indication of what in France would be called Grand Cru, or Premier Cru, the results highlighted over the last sixty years by the sector's leading connoisseurs make it possible to indicate the twenty-six most valuable MGAs. The lodestones of judgment, as it were, are Renato Ratti's 1971 *Carta del Barolo* and Carlo Petrini's 1990 *Atlas of the Great Vineyards of the Langhe*, as well as Alessandro Masnaghetti's *Barolo MGA* volumes, the first edition of which was published in 2015. Since there is still insufficient evidence, the MGA indication of the municipalities of Cherasco, Diano d'Alba, Grinzane Cavour, and Roddi has been avoided in this book. In parentheses, the area planted with Nebbiolo da Barolo grapes is indicated in acres.

BAROLO
(37 MGAs in total, 165 acres at grade one)
- Brunate (20 acres → see also La Morra)
- Bussia (5 acres → see also Monforte d'Alba)
- Cannubi (94 acres, also including those of Cannubi Muscatel, Cannubi Valletta, Cannubi Boschis, Cannubi San Lorenzo)
- Cerequio (1.5 acres → see also La Morra)
- Ravera (16 acres → see also Novello)
- Sarmassa (30 acres; wines: Bricco, Merenda)

CASTIGLIONE FALLETTO
(20 MGAs in total, 124 acres at grade one)
- Bricco Boschis (30 acres. San Giuseppe vineyard)
- Fiasco (15 acres)
- Monprivato (15 acres)
- Rocche di Castiglione (17 acres → see also Monforte d'Alba)
- Villero (47 acres)

LA MORRA
(39 MGAs in total, 174 acres at grade one)
- Arborina (12 acres)
- Brunate (42 acres → see also Barolo)
- Cerequio (55 acres → see also Barolo)
- Rocche dell'Annunziata (64 acres. Rocchette vineyard)

MONFORTE D'ALBA
(11 MGAs in total, 423 acres at grade one)
- Bussia (306 acres. Bofani, Cicala, Colonnello, Mondoca, Pianpolvere, Romirasco vineyards → see also Barolo)
- Ginestra (77 acres. Del Gris, Pajana, Sorì Ginestra vineyards)
- Mosconi (37 acres)
- Rocche di Castiglione (2.5 acres → see also Castiglione Falletto)

NOVELLO
(7 MGAs in total, 127 acres at grade one)
- Ravera (127 acres. Elena vineyard → see also Barolo)

SERRALUNGA D'ALBA
(39 MGAs in total, 261 acres at grade one)
- Arione (8.5 acres)
- Badarina (32 acres)
- Cerretta (64 acres)
- Falletto (15 acres)
- Francia (22 acres)
- Lazzarito (54 acres. La Delizia vineyard)
- Margheria (15 acres)
- Ornato (15 acres)
- Prapò (13.5 acres)
- Vignarionda (21 acres)

VERDUNO
(7 MGAs in total, 47 acres at grade one)
- Monvigliero (47 acres)

52. ODDERO PODERI E CANTINE, La Morra
Barolo Riserva Vignarionda ($$$$)
Barolo Bussia Riserva Vigna Mondoca ($$$)
Barolo Rocche di Castiglione ($$$)

53. PARUSSO, Monforte d'Alba
Barolo Bussia Riserva ($$$$)

54. PECCHENINO, Dogliani
Barolo Le Coste di Monforte ($$)

55. PIO CESARE, Alba
Barolo Ornato ($$$$)
Barolo Pio ($$$)

56. Luigi PIRA, Serralunga d'Alba
Barolo Vigna Rionda ($$$)

57. PODERE ROCCHE DEI MANZONI,
Monforte d'Alba
Barolo Big 'd Big ($$$)

58. PODERI ALDO CONTERNO,
Monforte d'Alba
Barolo Bussia Riserva Granbussia ($$$$$)
Barolo Bussia Romirasco ($$$$)

59. PODERI COLLA, Alba
Barolo Bussia Dardi Le Rose ($$)

60. PODERI LUIGI EINAUDI, Dogliani
Barolo Cannubi ($$$)
Barolo Terlo Vigna Costa Grimaldi ($$)

61. Guido PORRO, Serralunga d'Alba
Barolo Vigna Rionda ($$$)
Barolo Lazzairasco ($$)

62. Ferdinando PRINCIPIANO, Monforte d'Alba
Barolo Boscareto ($$$)
Barolo Ravera di Monforte ($$)

63. RATTI, La Morra
Barolo Rocche dell'Annunziata ($$$)

64. RÉVA, Monforte d'Alba
Barolo Cannubi ($$$$)
Barolo Ravera ($$$)

65. Fratelli REVELLO, La Morra
Barolo Conca ($$)
Barolo Rocche dell'Annunziata ($$$)

66. Michele REVERDITO, La Morra
Barolo Badarina ($$$)

67. Giuseppe RINALDI, Barolo
Barolo Brunate ($$$$$)
Barolo Bussia ($$$$$)
Barolo Tre Tine ($$$$$)

68. ROAGNA, Barbaresco
Barolo Pira Vecchie Viti ($$$$$)
Barolo Rocche di Castiglione ($$$$)

69. Giovanni ROSSO, Serralunga d'Alba
Barolo Vignarionda Ester Canale Rosso ($$$$$)
Barolo Serra ($$$)
Barolo Cerretta ($$$)

70. Luciano SANDRONE, Barolo
Barolo Aleste (former Cannubi Boschis) ($$$$)
Barolo Le Vigne ($$$)
Barolo Vite Talin ($$$$$)

71. Giorgio SCARZELLO e Figli, Barolo
Barolo Sarmassa Vigna Merenda ($$$)

72. Paolo SCAVINO, Castiglione Falletto
Barolo Bric dël Fiasc ($$$)
Barolo Riserva Rocche dell'Annunziata ($$$$$)

73. TERRE DEL BAROLO – Arnaldo Rivera,
Castiglione Falletto
Barolo Vignarionda ($$$)

74. G.D. VAJRA, Barolo
Barolo Bricco delle Viole ($$$)
Barolo Cerretta Luigi Baudana ($$$)

75. Mauro VEGLIO, La Morra
Barolo Arborina ($$$)
Barolo Riserva Rocche dell'Annunziata ($$$)
Barolo Castelletto ($$$)

76. VIETTI, Castiglione Falletto
Barolo Riserva Villero ($$$$$)
Barolo Rocche di Castiglione ($$$$)
Barolo Ravera ($$$$)
Barolo Lazzarito ($$$$)

77. VITE COLTE, Barolo
Barolo del comune di Barolo Essenze ($$)

78. Roberto VOERZIO, La Morra
Barolo Brunate ($$$$$)
Barolo Cerequio ($$$$$)

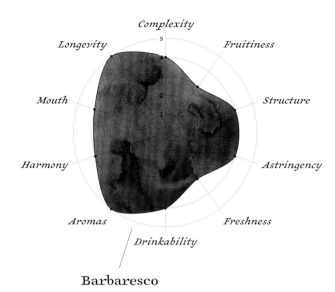

Barbaresco

Barbaresco DOCG

The name "Barbaresco" originated at the end of the nineteenth century, and before that in previous centuries it was more generically referred to as "Nebbiolo," sometimes combined with the grapes of the same name from the Barolo area. The production zone was precisely defined first by the DOC regulations in 1966, and then by the DOCG guidelines in 1980, and includes the entire municipalities of Barbaresco, Neive, and Treiso, joined by the hamlet of San Rocco Seno d'Elvio in the municipality of Alba. Always in friendly competition with Barolo for first place among Piedmontese wines, it has too often been considered its younger sibling, whereas it rightfully has its own charm and personality that make it one of the world's great wines: elegance of bouquet, remarkable structure, decades of longevity. Barolo is often a little more powerful, rigid, and tannic than Barbaresco, but this does not detract from its importance and qualities. Sixty-six *Menzioni Geografiche Aggiuntive* (MGA, or Additional Geographical Indications)—the first in Italy—were approved in 2007, which can be used on labels by producers to indicate their most prized vineyards. Below are those that, in view of the production history of numerous wineries, have received the highest critical acclaim. For the municipality of Barbaresco these include: Asili, Faset, Martinenga, Montefico, Montestefano, Ovello, Pajé, Pora, Rabajà, Rio Sordo, Roncaglie, Ronchi; for the municipality of Neive: Albesani, Basarin, Bricco di Neive, Cottà, Currà, Gallina; for the municipality of Treiso: Ausario, Manzola, Pajoré, Rizzi, Rombone, San Stunet, Valeirano. Average annual production is close to five million bottles, most of which are exported.

—

Producers and their trademark and signature wines:

1. Marco e Vittorio ADRIANO, Alba
    Barbaresco Basarin ($$)
2. BEL COLLE, Verduno
    Barbaresco Pajoré ($$)
3. Olek BONDONIO, Barbaresco
    Barbaresco Roncagliette ($$$)
4. Piero BUSSO, Neive
    Barbaresco Albesani Borgese ($$$)
    Barbaresco Gallina ($$$)
5. CA' DEL BAIO, Treiso
    Barbaresco Pora ($$$)
    Barbaresco Riserva Asili ($$$$)
    Barbaresco Asili ($$$)
6. CA' ROMÉ, Barbaresco
    Barbaresco Maria di Brün ($$$)
7. CANTINA DEL PINO, Barbaresco
    Barbaresco Ovello ($$)
    Barbaresco Albesani ($$)
8. CASCINA DELLE ROSE, Barbaresco
    Barbaresco Rio Sordo ($$$)

9. CASCINA LUISIN, Barbaresco
    Barbaresco Rabajà ($$$)
10. CASCINA MORASSINO, Barbaresco
    Barbaresco Ovello ($$)
    Barbaresco Morassino ($$)
11. CASCINA ROCCALINI, Barbaresco
    Barbaresco Roccalini ($$)
12. CASTELLO DI NEIVE, Neive
    Barbaresco Albesani Riserva Vigna Santo
    Stefano ($$$)
13. CERETTO, Alba
    Barbaresco Asili ($$$$)
14. Fratelli CIGLIUTI, Neive
    Barbaresco Serraboella ($$$)
15. Giuseppe CORTESE, Barbaresco
    Barbaresco Rabajà ($$)
16. GAJA, Barbaresco
    Barbaresco Sorì Tildin ($$$$$)
    Barbaresco Costa Russi ($$$$$)
    Barbaresco Sorì San Lorenzo ($$$$$)
17. Bruno GIACOSA, Neive
    Barbaresco Riserva Asili ($$$$$)
    Barbaresco Rabajà ($$$$)
18. LA SPINETTA, Castagnole delle Lanze
    Barbaresco Gallina ($$$$)
19. MARCHESI DI GRÉSY, Barbaresco
    Barbaresco Martinenga Riserva
    Camp Gros ($$$$)
    Barbaresco Martinenga Gaiun ($$$)
20. MURA MURA, Montegrosso d'Asti
    Barbaresco Starderi ($$$)
21. Fiorenzo NADA, Treiso
    Barbaresco Rombone ($$$)
    Barbaresco Montaribaldi ($$$)

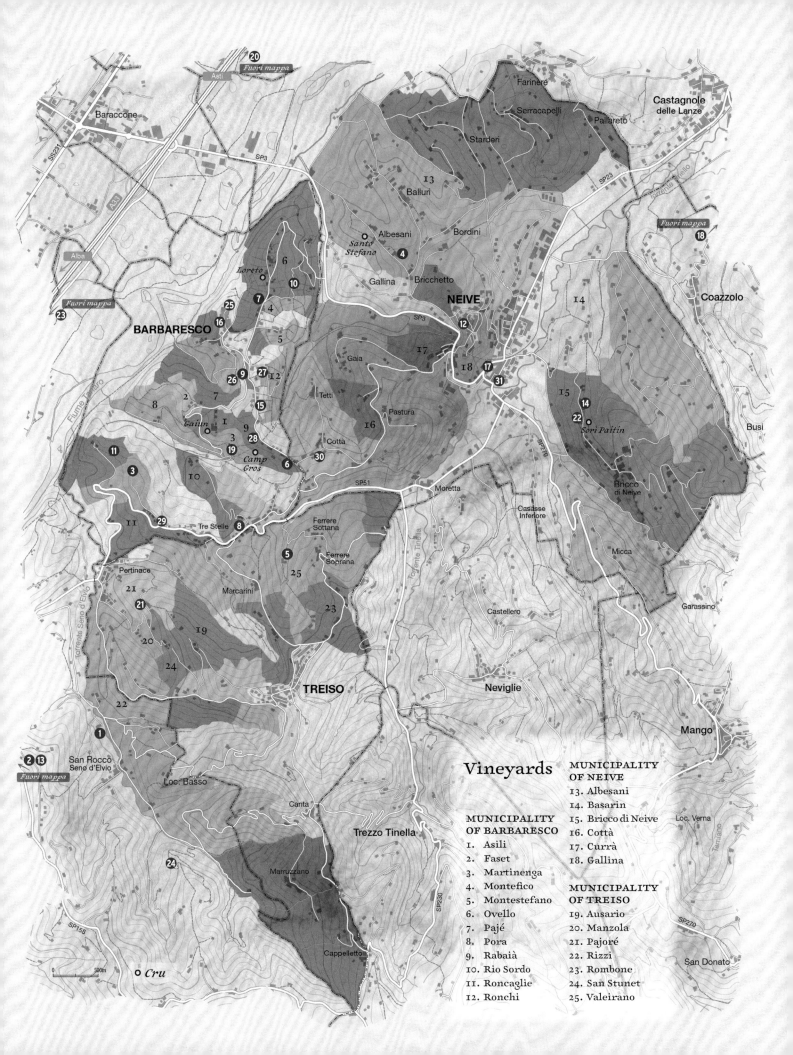

Vineyards

MUNICIPALITY OF BARBARESCO

1. Asili
2. Faset
3. Martinenga
4. Montefico
5. Montestefano
6. Ovello
7. Pajé
8. Pora
9. Rabaià
10. Rio Sordo
11. Roncaglie
12. Ronchi

MUNICIPALITY OF NEIVE

13. Albesani
14. Basarin
15. Bricco di Neive
16. Cottà
17. Currà
18. Gallina

MUNICIPALITY OF TREISO

19. Ausario
20. Manzola
21. Pajoré
22. Rizzi
23. Rombone
24. San Stunet
25. Valeirano

○ *Cru*

0   500m

22. PAITIN, Neive
Barbaresco Sorì Paitin Riserva
Vecchie Vigne ($$$)
Barbaresco Serraboella Sorì Paitin ($$)
23. PIO CESARE, Alba
Barbaresco Il Bricco ($$$)
24. PODERI COLLA, Alba
Barbaresco Roncaglie ($$)
25. PRODUTTORI DEL BARBARESCO, Barbaresco
Barbaresco Riserva Montefico ($$$)
Barbaresco Riserva Montestefano ($$$)
Barbaresco Riserva Asili ($$$)
Barbaresco Riserva Ovello ($$$)
26. ROAGNA, Barbaresco
Barbaresco Crichët Pajé ($$$$$)
Barbaresco Asili Vecchie Viti ($$$$$)
27. Albino ROCCA, Barbaresco
Barbaresco Ovello Vigna Loreto ($$$)
Barbaresco Ronchi ($$$)
Barbaresco Angelo ($$$)
28. Bruno ROCCA, Barbaresco
Barbaresco Rabajà ($$$)
Barbaresco Riserva Currà ($$$$)
Barbaresco Maria Adelaide ($$$$)
29. SOCRÉ, Barbaresco
Barbaresco Riserva Roncaglie ($$$)
Barbaresco Pajoré ($$$)
30. SOTTIMANO, Neive
Barbaresco Currà ($$$)
Barbaresco Pajoré ($$$)
Barbaresco Cottà ($$$)
31. Francesco VERSIO, Neive
Barbaresco ($$$)

Langhe DOC

Established in 1994 to bring the few grape varieties in the area that did not have a DOC, it can bear the stamp of fourteen grape varieties, such as Langhe Nascetta or Langhe Dolcetto, or be made in the Langhe Bianco, Langhe Rosso, and Langhe Rosato versions, in the Langhe and Roero areas, with all seventy-four varieties authorized in Piedmont. The best results so far have come from white wines made from Viognier, Riesling, Sauvignon, and Chardonnay grapes, along with reds from Barbera and Nebbiolo. Some twenty-two-million bottles are produced annually, driven by the growing success of Langhe Nebbiolo, which alone exceeds seven million bottles.

—

Producers and their trademark and signature wines:

1. Marziano ABBONA, Dogliani
Langhe Cinerino (Viognier) ($)
2. Elio ALTARE, La Morra
Langhe Rosso Larigi (Barbera) ($$$)
Langhe Rosso Giàrborina (Nebbiolo) ($$$)
Langhe Rosso La Villa (Barbera, Nebbiolo) ($$$)
3. ASCHERI, Bra
Langhe Bianco Montalupa (Viognier) ($$)
4. BURLOTTO Comm. G.B., Verduno
Langhe Sauvignon Dives ($)
5. Domenico CLERICO, Monforte d'Alba
Langhe Arte (Barbera; Nebbiolo) ($$)
6. CONTERNO FANTINO, Monforte d'Alba
Langhe Monprà (Barbera, Nebbiolo) ($$)
Langhe Chardonnay Bastia ($$)
7. GAJA, Barbaresco
Langhe Chardonnay Gaia e Rey ($$$$$)
8. Ettore GERMANO, Serralunga d'Alba
Langhe Riesling Hérzu ($)
9. MARCHESI DI GRÉSY, Barbaresco
Langhe Chardonnay Grésy ($$)
10. Fiorenzo NADA, Treiso
Langhe Rosso Seifile (Barbera, Nebbiolo) ($$)
11. PARUSSO, Monforte d'Alba
Langhe Sauvignon Rovella ($$)
12. PIO CESARE, Alba
Langhe Chardonnay Piodilei ($$)
13. Giovanni ROSSO, Serralunga d'Alba
Langhe Nebbiolo Ester Canale Rosso ($$$$)
14. SOCRÉ, Barbaresco
Langhe Chardonnay Paint It Black ($)

Nebbiolo d'Alba DOC

The area of production is Roero, where the Valmaggiore hill is famous, and that part of the Langhe including Diano d'Alba *in primis* where Barolo and Barbaresco cannot be produced. Note how the use of 100% Nebbiolo grapes is compulsory—while in the Langhe Nebbiolo drops to 85%—and how there are Spumante and Spumante Rosé versions, made with the Martinotti Method or with the Metodo Classico, offered by a growing number of wineries. In the best versions it already has considerable elegance and fine harmony in the first years after the harvest. Approximately five million bottles per year are produced.

—

Producers and their trademark and signature wines:

15. BRICCO MAIOLICA, Diano d'Alba
    Nebbiolo d'Alba Superiore Cumot ($)
16. Giacomo GRIMALDI, Barolo
    Nebbiolo d'Alba Vigna Valmaggiore ($)
17. HILBERG-PASQUERO, Priocca
    Nebbiolo d'Alba Sul Monte ($$)
18. LE CECCHE, Diano d'Alba
    Nebbiolo d'Alba ($)
19. Luciano SANDRONE, Barolo
    Nebbiolo d'Alba Valmaggiore ($$)

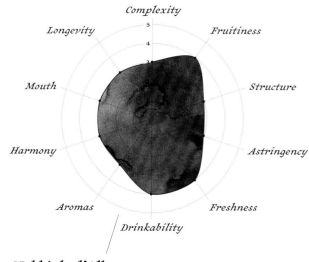

Nebbiolo d'Alba

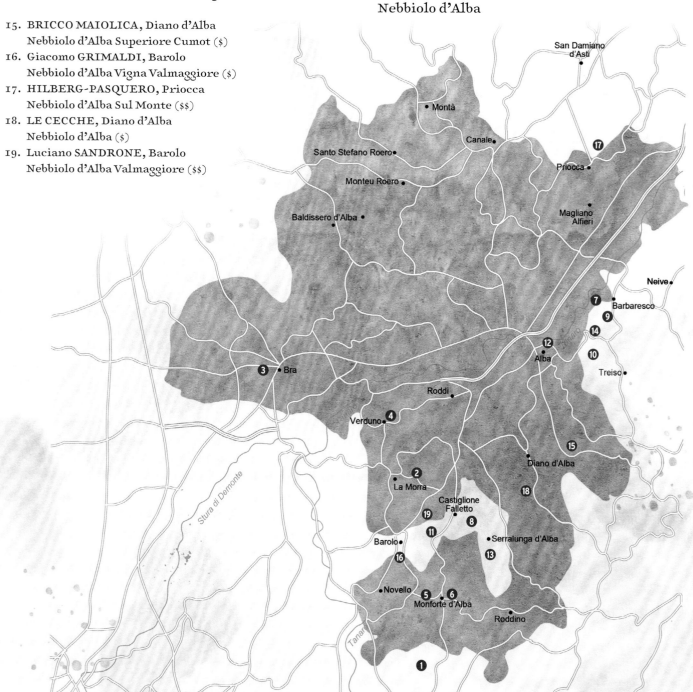

Carema DOC

It is produced exclusively in the medieval municipality of Carema, on the border with Valle d'Aosta, on small vineyard terraces that make up one of Italy's most stunning winegrowing landscapes, with a path called *Il sentiero dei vigneti*, or the Vineyard Trail, that we highly recommend to wine tourists. Made from Nebbiolo grapes, for at least 85%, it is slightly more austere and vegetal than Nebbiolo from warmer areas, presenting a splendid and complex personality. The many small estates make it difficult to develop wine in the municipality, but in recent years wineries have opened up that we hope to highlight in future editions. Total annual production is just over seventy thousand bottles.

—

Producers and their trademark and signature wines:

1. CANTINA DEI PRODUTTORI NEBBIOLO DI CAREMA, Carema
Carema Riserva ($)
2. FERRANDO, Ivrea
Carema Etichetta Bianca ($$$)
Carema Etichetta Nera ($$$)
3. MURAJE, Carema
Carema Sumié ($$$)

Boca DOC

Less than one hundred thousand bottles per year are produced of this tiny designation relating to five municipalities of Upper Piedmont in the province of Novara, including Boca, in which the predominant Nebbiolo, at 70 to 90%, is joined by Vespolina and *uva rara*. Aged for a minimum of thirty-four months, at least eighteen in wood after the harvest. Particular aromas, characterized by ripe fruits well contrasted by balsamic hints.

—

Producers and their trademark and signature wines:

4. BARBAGLIA, Cavallirio
Boca ($$)
5. CANTINE DEL CASTELLO CONTI, Maggiora
Boca Il Rosso delle Donne ($$$)
6. Davide CARLONE, Grignasco
Boca Adele ($$)
7. LE PIANE, Boca
Boca ($$$)

Bramaterra DOC

A small, prized DOC from Upper Piedmont, based mainly on Nebbiolo grapes at a ratio of 50 to 80%, with Croatina up to 30% and the potential addition of *uva rara* and Vespolina. Just one hundred forty thousand bottles per year of this important wine are produced, very multifaceted in its aromas, which range from lavender to rose and damp soil, with considerable body and excellent smoothness, also thanks to the contribution of soft Croatina.

—

Producers and their trademark and signature wines:

8. Odilio ANTONIOTTI, Sostegno
Bramaterra ($$)
9. COLOMBERA & GARELLA, Masserano
Bramaterra Cascina Cottignano ($$)
10. LE PIANELLE, Brusnengo
Bramaterra ($$)
11. NOAH, Brusnengo
Bramaterra ($$)
12. TENUTE SELLA, Lessona
Bramaterra I Porfidi ($$)

Coste della Sesia DOC

The hills around Gattinara and Lessona are also mainly dedicated to Nebbiolo, Vespolina, and *uva rara*, in blends with varying percentages. Just one hundred fifty thousand bottles are produced each year, and there is no shortage of surprising wines.

—

Producers and their trademark and signature wines:

8. Odilio ANTONIOTTI, Sostegno
Coste della Sesia Nebbiolo ($)
13. CASTELLO DI CASTELLENGO, Cossato
Coste della Sesia Nebbiolo Castellengo ($$)
10. LE PIANELLE, Brusnengo
Coste della Sesia Rosso Al Forte ($)
14. PROPRIETÀ SPERINO, Lessona
Coste della Sesia Uvaggio ($$)
12. TENUTE SELLA, Lessona
Coste della Sesia Rosso Orbello ($)

Colline Novaresi DOC

The hills around Ghemme and Borgomanero are the realm of Nebbiolo grapes—also known here as Spanna—Vespolina, and *uva rara*, sometimes bringing with it excellent results. About 1.5 million bottles are produced annually, almost half of which is Colline Novaresi Nebbiolo.

—

Producers and their trademark and signature wines:

15. Francesco BRIGATTI, Suno
    Colline Novaresi Nebbiolo MötZiflon ($)
16. IOPPA, Romagnano Sesia
    Colline Novaresi Vespolina Mauletta ($)
17. VIGNETI VALLE RONCATI, Briona
    Colline Novaresi Spanna Runcà ($)

Fara DOC

A very small DOC that today grows on just 15 acres, cultivated with 50 to 70% Nebbiolo, joined mainly by Vespolina and *uva rara*, in the municipalities of Fara and Briona. The result is a classic Nebbiolo from Upper Piedmont, slightly fresher and smoother than the more famous appellations. Only thirty thousand bottles are produced per year.

—

Producers and their trademark and signature wines:

18. Gilberto BONIPERTI, Barengo
    Fara Bartön ($$)
19. IL CHIOSSO, Gattinara
    Fara ($)

Gattinara DOCG

Made from at least 90% Nebbiolo grapes grown within the Gattinara municipality alone, it deserves the fame it has earned, even abroad, as it is a very complex wine, suitable for aging even for decades in the bottle, with a fine harmony of taste thanks to its good acidity and nonaggressive tannins. Just over five hundred thousand bottles are produced per year, and growing.

—

Producers and their trademark and signature wines:

20. ANTONIOLO, Gattinara
    Gattinara Riserva Osso San Grato ($$$)
    Gattinara Riserva ($$)
    Gattinara Riserva San Francesco ($$$)
21. BIANCHI, Sizzano
    Gattinara ($)
22. Paride IARETTI, Gattinara
    Gattinara Vigna Valferana ($$)
    Gattinara Pietro ($$)
23. NERVI CONTERNO, Gattinara
    Gattinara Vigna Valferana ($$$$)
    Gattinara Vigna Molsino ($$$$)
    Gattinara ($$$)
24. TORRACCIA DEL PIANTAVIGNA, Ghemme
    Gattinara ($$)
25. Giancarlo TRAVAGLINI, Gattinara
    Gattinara Riserva ($$)
    Gattinara Tre Vigne ($$)

Ghemme DOCG

In the municipalities of Ghemme and Romagnano Sesia, only 125 acres are dedicated to the production of this prestigious appellation of Upper Piedmont, from at least 85% Nebbiolo grapes. A remarkable wine, at times slightly more rustic and acidic than the other Piedmontese DOCGs based on Nebbiolo, of great charm and suitable for long aging in glass. The annual bottles produced are about two hundred fifty thousand.

—

Producers and their trademark and signature wines:

26. ANTICHI VIGNETI DI CANTALUPO, Ghemme
    Ghemme Collis Breclemae ($$)
15. Francesco BRIGATTI, Suno
    Ghemme Oltre il Bosco ($$)

27. CHIOVINI & RANDETTI, Sizzano
    Ghemme ($)
19. IL CHIOSSO, Gattinara
    Ghemme ($)
16. IOPPA, Romagnano Sesia
    Ghemme Santa Fé ($$)
    Ghemme Balsina ($$)
28. Tiziano MAZZONI, Cavaglio d'Agogna
    Ghemme Ai Livelli ($$)
    Ghemme dei Mazzoni ($$)
29. MIRÙ, Ghemme
    Ghemme ($)
30. ROVELLOTTI, Ghemme
    Ghemme Chioso dei Pomi ($)
24. TORRACCIA DEL PIANTAVIGNA, Gattinara
    Ghemme Vigna Pelizzane ($$)

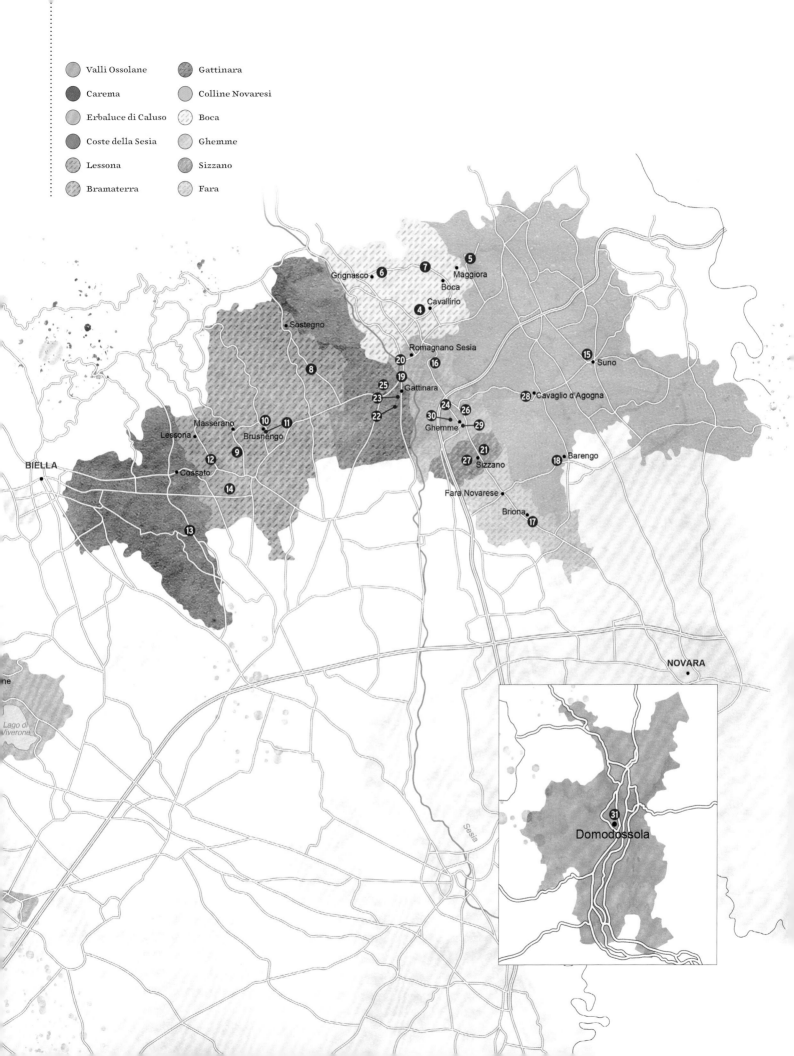

Valli Ossolane
Carema
Erbaluce di Caluso
Coste della Sesia
Lessona
Bramaterra

Gattinara
Colline Novaresi
Boca
Ghemme
Sizzano
Fara

Grignasco
6
7
5
Maggiora
Boca
4
Cavallirio
Sostegno
Romagnano Sesia
8
20
16
15
Suno
19
25
Gattinara
28
Cavaglio d'Agogna
23
24
Masserano
10
11
22
30
26
Lessona
9
Ghemme
29
Brusnengo
12
21
18
Barengo
Cossato
27
Sizzano
14
Fara Novarese
13
Briona
17

BIELLA

Lago di
Viverone

NOVARA

Domodossola
31

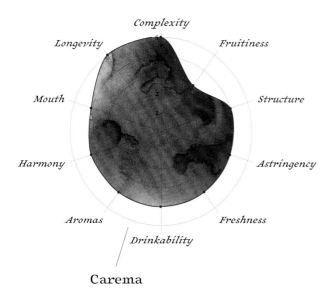

Carema

Gattinara

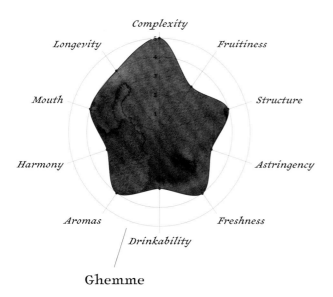

Ghemme

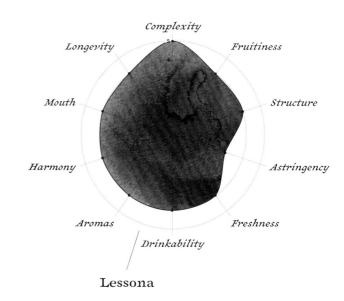

Lessona

Lessona DOC

It is made exclusively in the municipality of Lessona, where about 50 acres are cultivated with DOC status, and is made with at least 85% Nebbiolo grapes, which are also called *Spanna* here, which may be supplemented with Vespolina and *uva rara*. It is a complex wine, in which at times nuances of iron can be detected, endowed with a significant and welcome savoriness. Suitable for long aging, it has a mandatory minimum maturation of twenty-two months (at least twelve in wood) from the harvest. Approximately eighty-five-thousand bottles per year are produced.

—

Producers and their trademark and signature wines:

11. NOAH, Brusnengo
Lessona ($$)
14. PROPRIETÀ SPERINO, Lessona
Lessona ($$$)
12. TENUTE SELLA, Lessona
Lessona Omaggio a Quintino Sella ($$)
Lessona San Sebastiano allo Zoppo ($$)

Sizzano DOC

The production of this small but pleasant DOC wine exclusively for the municipality of the same name, in the province of Novara, has now been reduced to 15 acres and thirty thousand bottles per year. The constituent grapes are Nebbiolo, at between 50 and 70%, and Vespolina and/or *uva rara* for the remainder, while maturation in the cellar must be at least twenty-two months, sixteen in wood, from the date of the harvest.

—

Producers and their trademark and signature wines:

21. BIANCHI, Sizzano
Sizzano ($)
27. CHIOVINI & RANDETTI, Sizzano
Sizzano ($$)

Valli Ossolane DOC

A very small and heroic DOC in Upper Piedmont, on the extreme northern hills of Novarese and Vercellese territory in Verbano province. It centers on the cultivation of Nebbiolo, which in the fourteenth century was *prunent*, but excellent results are also obtained here with other local grapes, such as Croatina, and with Merlot. Annual production is close to seventy thousand bottles, which are well worth tasting.

—

Producer and its trademark and signature wines:

31. CANTINE GARRONE, Domodossola
Valli Ossolane Nebbiolo Superiore Prünent ($$)
Valli Ossolane Rosso Cà d' Maté (Nebbiolo, Croatina) ($)
Valli Ossolane Rosso Tarlap (Merlot) ($)

Roero DOCG

Established in 2004, it is one of the rare Italian DOCGs in which white and red grapes coexist: Arneis for Roero Bianco, or Roero Arneis, and Nebbiolo for Roero, or Roero Rosso. On the same scenic, sandy hills of the nineteen municipalities of this area on the orographic left of the Tanaro River, in the province of Cuneo, you can therefore find Nebbiolo grapes, generally in the highest and most ventilated parts, and Arneis, in the rows of vines below. For both types there is a Riserva version, with a minimum maturation of sixteen months for the Bianco and thirty-two months—at least six in wood—for the Rosso. The characteristic that has made the fortune of Roero made from Arneis grapes certainly lies in the freshness of the aromas, which range between grapefruit, tomato leaf, and broom in a strongly variegated and captivating whole. For Roero from Nebbiolo grapes, it should be noted that the high percentage of sand present in the vineyards enriches the olfactory component and softens the tannic thrust typical of the variety. In 2017, the Consorzio di Tutela Roero, in the wake of Barolo and Barbaresco, added one hundred thirty-four MGAs (Additional Geographical Indications) to the regulations, useful information regarding the best vineyards in the area. Overall annual production is growing, exceeding seven million bottles, largely of Roero Bianco, 60% of which is exported.

—

Producers and their trademark and signature wines:

1. Giovanni ALMONDO, Montà
    Roero Arneis Bricco delle Ciliegie ($)
    Roero Bric Valdiana ($$)
    Roero Arneis Le Rive del Bricco delle Ciliegie ($)
2. Pierangelo CAREGLIO, Baldissero d'Alba
    Roero Arneis Savij ($)
3. CASCINA CA' ROSSA, Canale
    Roero Riserva Mompissano ($$)
    Roero Valmaggiore Vigna Audinaggio ($$)
4. Matteo CORREGGIA, Canale
    Roero Riserva Ròche d'Ampsèj ($$)
5. Stefanino COSTA, Montà
    Roero Arneis Sarun ($)
    Roero Gepin ($)
6. DELTETTO, Canale
    Roero Riserva Braja ($)
    Roero Arneis San Michele ($)
7. LE MORE BIANCHE, Magliano Alfieri
    Roero Arneis Ironia ($)
8. MALVIRÀ, Canale
    Roero Arneis Renesio ($)
    Roero Riserva Vigna Mombeltramo ($$)
    Roero Riserva Trinità ($$)
9. MARSAGLIA, Castellinaldo d'Alba
    Roero Brich d'America ($)
10. MONCHIERO CARBONE, Canale
    Roero Arneis Cecu d'la Biunda ($)
    Roero Riserva Printi ($$)
    Roero Riserva Renesio Incisa ($$)
    Roero Riserva Bricco Genestreto ($$)
11. Angelo NEGRO, Monteu Roero
    Roero Riserva Sudisfà ($$)
    Roero Arneis 7 Anni ($$)
12. Alberto OGGERO, Santo Stefano Roero
    Roero Bianco ($)
    Roero Rosso ($)
13. Marco PORELLO, Canale
    Roero Arneis Camestrì ($)
    Roero Torretta ($)
14. VALFACCENDA, Canale
    Roero Riserva Valmaggiore ($$)
    Roero Bianco Riserva Loreto ($)

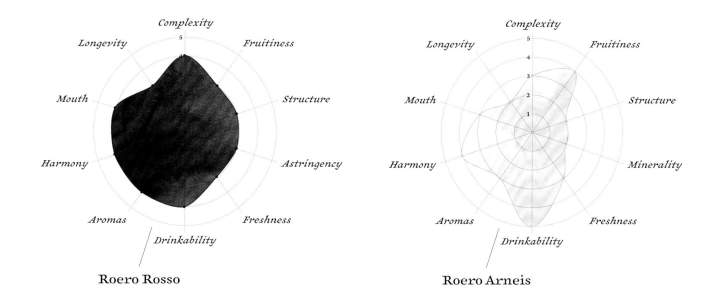

Roero Rosso

Roero Arneis

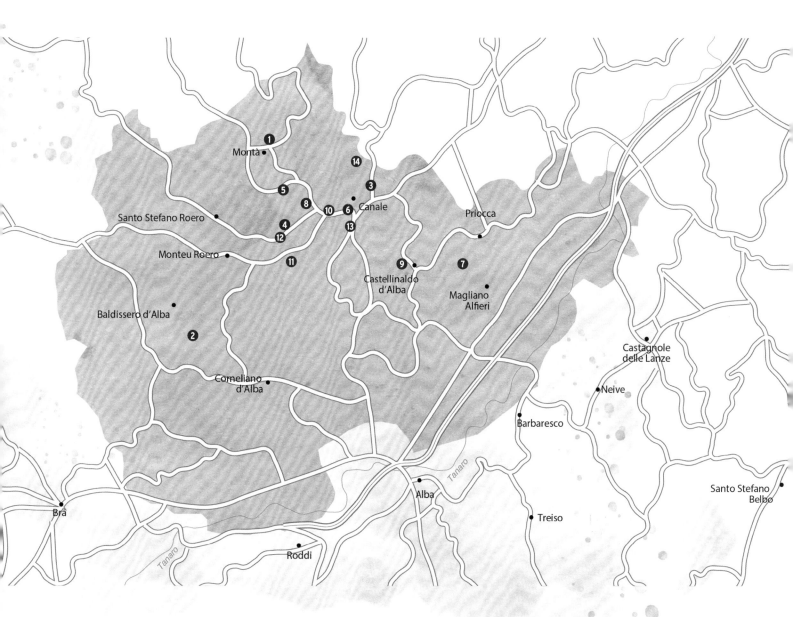

Barbera d'Alba DOC

Endowed with remarkable olfactory intensity, often with notes of plum, Barbera d'Alba is characterized by a palate with little tannin and considerable acidity, often blunted by aging in wood. It does not have the same aging capacity as Barolo or Roero Rosso, but offers great taste satisfaction even more than ten years after harvest. The Superiore specification is permitted if it is matured for at least one year before sale. It is produced, with certain success also internationally, on over 3,950 acres cultivated in fifty-four municipalities both in the Langhe and Roero, with annual production close to twelve million bottles.
—

Producers and their trademark and signature wines:

1. Gianfranco ALESSANDRIA, Monforte d'Alba
    Barbera d'Alba Vittoria ($$)
2. BRICCO MAIOLICA, Diano d'Alba
    Barbera d'Alba Superiore Vigna Vigia ($)
3. BROVIA, Castiglione Falletto
    Barbera d'Alba Sorì del Drago ($)
4. CA' VIOLA, Dogliani
    Barbera d'Alba Bric du Luv ($)
5. CASA E. DI MIRAFIORE, Serralunga d'Alba
    Barbera d'Alba Superiore ($)
6. CASCINA MUCCI, Roddino
    Barbera d'Alba Superiore ($)
7. Fratelli CIGLIUTI, Neive
    Barbera d'Alba Vigna Serraboella ($)
8. Giacomo CONTERNO, Monforte d'Alba
    Barbera d'Alba Vigna Francia ($$$)
9. Giovanni CORINO, La Morra
    Barbera d'Alba Ciabot dù Re ($)
10. Renato CORINO, La Morra
    Barbera d'Alba Pozzo ($$)
11. Matteo CORREGGIA, Canale
    Barbera d'Alba Marun ($)
12. HILBERG-PASQUERO, Priocca
    Barbera d'Alba Superiore ($$)
13. LE CECCHE, Diano d'Alba
    Barbera d'Alba ($)
14. MONCHIERO CARBONE, Canale
    Barbera d'Alba MonBirone ($$)
15. PODERI ALDO CONTERNO, Monforte d'Alba
    Barbera d'Alba Conca Tre Pile ($$)
16. Paolo SCAVINO, Castiglione Falletto
    Barbera d'Alba Affinato in Carati ($$)
17. Fratelli SEGHESIO, Monforte d'Alba
    Barbera d'Alba Superiore La Chiesa ($$)
18. G.D. VAJRA, Barolo
    Barbera d'Alba Superiore ($$)
19. VIETTI, Castiglione Falletto
    Barbera d'Alba Scarrone Vigna Vecchia ($$)
20. Roberto VOERZIO, La Morra
    Barbera d'Alba Riserva Vigneto Pozzo dell'Annunziata ($$$$$)

Barbera d'Asti

Nizza

Barbera d'Alba

Po

51 • Gabiano

Casale
Monferrato

Cerrina Monferrato •

Ozzano
Monferrato

Serralunga di Crea •

37
41
39 • Rosignano Monferrato
54

Moncucco
Torinese •

• Castelnuovo
Don Bosco

43 • Grazzano Badoglio

56

40 • Vignale Monferrato

Po

• Castagnole Monferrato

53

ASTI

ALESSANDRIA

21 • Rocchetta Tanaro

Montà •

29 27

San Martino
Alfieri

35

• Incisa Scapaccino

nto Stefano Roero

14 Canale

28

Novi

11

Priocca

12

24 Vinchio

49

33

Monteu Roero •

Agliano
Terme •

34

45 31

aldissero d'Alba •

Magliano
Alfieri

Castagnole
delle Lanze

50 44

Nizza Monferrato

Capriata
d'Orba

Neive 23

26

30

• Calamandrana

38

Barbaresco •

25

Calosso

46

• Castelletto d'Orba

Bra •

Alba

7

32

47
Canelli

22 • Alice Bel Colle

Roddi

55

Castiglione Tinella

52 • Strevi

Neviglie

Verduno •

Grinzane
Cavour

Santo
Stefano Belbo

42

20

2

48

Prasco •

La Morra •

10

5

• Diano d'Alba

Bubbio •

Ovada

• Tagliolo Monf

9 3 19

18

16

13

Rodello •

• Montelupo Albese

Loazzolo •

36 15

Castiglione Falletto

Barolo •

Serralunga d'Alba

Novello •

17

6

1

8

Roddino

Monforte d'Alba

Monchiero

4

Dogliani •

• Bossolasco

Farigliano

Barbera d'Asti DOCG

Slightly more impetuous than Barbera d'Alba, it has suffered for decades from a reputation as a facile and atypical wine, something that was at times also due to scandals where it was illegally blended with wines from Southern Italy. Partly in order to remedy this image, the producers decided to promote the transition from DOC to DOCG, which took place in 2008, bolstered by the worldwide success that Braida had achieved since 1982 with its expensive and prestigious Bricco dell'Uccellone label. A red wine of fine drinkability, always with good acidity on the palate, decisive in its fruity aromas, certainly suitable for aging in wood, and capable of maturing in the bottle for a few years. Almost thirty million bottles are produced annually from 8,650 acres of vines in one hundred sixty-seven municipalities—one hundred sixteen in the province of Asti, and fifty-one in the province of Alessandria, for the most part the same as those in the Monferrato DOC area.

—

Producers and their trademark and signature wines:

21. BRAIDA, Rocchetta Tanaro
 Barbera d'Asti Bricco dell'Uccellone ($$$)
 Barbera d'Asti Bricco della Bigotta ($$$)
22. CANTINA ALICE BEL COLLE, Alice Bel Colle
 Barbera d'Asti Superiore Alix ($)
23. Gianni DOGLIA, Castagnole delle Lanze
 Barbera d'Asti Superiore Genio ($)
24. Roberto FERRARIS, Agliano Terme
 Barbera d'Asti Nobbio ($)
25. LA MORANDINA, Castiglione Tinella
 Barbera d'Asti Zucchetto ($)
26. LA SPINETTA, Castagnole delle Lanze
 Barbera d'Asti Superiore Bionzo ($$)
27. LA TANARELLA, San Martino Alfieri
 Barbera d'Asti Rosso Mini ($)
28. LAIOLO REGININ, Vinchio
 Barbera d'Asti La Mora ($)
29. MARCHESI ALFIERI, San Martino Alfieri
 Barbera d'Asti Superiore Alfiera ($$)
 Barbera d'Asti La Tota ($)
 Barbera d'Asti Carlo Alfieri ($$$)
30. SCAGLIOLA, Calosso
 Barbera d'Asti Superiore Sansì Selezione ($$)
31. SCARPA, Nizza Monferrato
 Barbera d'Asti Superiore La Bogliona ($$)
32. TENUTA IL FALCHETTO, Santo Stefano Belbo
 Barbera d'Asti Superiore Bricco Paradiso ($)
33. TENUTA OLIM BAUDA, Incisa Scapaccino
 Barbera d'Asti Superiore Le Rocchette ($)
19. VIETTI, Castiglione Falletto
 Barbera d'Asti La Crena ($$)

34. VILLA TERLINA, Agliano Terme
 Barbera d'Asti Monsicuro ($$)
35. VINCHIO VAGLIO, Vinchio
 Barbera d'Asti Superiore Sei Vigne Insynthesis ($$)
36. VITE COLTE, Barolo
 Barbera d'Asti Superiore La Luna e i Falò ($)

Barbera del Monferrato DOC

A DOC generally dedicated to the freshest, fruitiest, and most immediate wines produced in two hundred and sixteen municipalities in the provinces of Asti and Alessandria, from at least 85% Barbera grapes. Most of the aging takes place in steel only and the wine is marketed a few months after the harvest. There is also a Frizzante version. About six million bottles per year are produced.

—

Producers and their trademark and signature wines:

37. Paolo ANGELINI, Ozzano Monferrato
 Barbera del Monferrato First ($)
38. TACCHINO, Castelletto d'Orba
 Barbera del Monferrato Albarola ($)
39. VICARA, Rosignano Monferrato
 Barbera del Monferrato Volpuva ($)

Barbera del Monferrato Superiore DOCG

Like Barbera d'Asti, Barbera d'Asti from Monferrato has also chosen to have its own DOCG, to differentiate itself from the easier DOC version and to offer itself on the market as an important and structured wine, fresh to the palate but suitable for a certain aging. This is well demonstrated by some productions made in Monferrato Casalese, and the obligatory time spent in wood of at least six months. Approximately three hundred fifty thousand bottles are produced per year.

—

Producers and their trademark and signature wines:

40. Giulio ACCORNERO e Figli, Vignale Monferrato
    Barbera del Monferrato Superiore
    Bricco Battista ($$)
41. CASTELLO DI UVIGLIE, Rosignano Monferrato
    Barbera del Monferrato Superiore Le Cave ($)
42. GAGGINO, Ovada
    Barbera del Monferrato Superiore Ticco ($)
43. SULIN, Grazzano Badoglio
    Barbera del Monferrato Superiore Ornella ($$)

....

Nizza DOCG

Labelled as a subzone of Barbera d'Asti Superiore since 2013, Nizza was established as an autonomous DOCG thanks to the recognition, by critics and the market, of the value of Barbera-based wines in this area, which includes eighteen municipalities around the town of Nizza Monferrato. Moreover, the Nizza Producers' Association has already started the procedure for the recognition of the MGAs, or Additional Geographical Indications. The minimum aging before marketing is eighteen months, at least six in wood, with thirty and twelve in the case of the Riserva. A particularly powerful and structured type of wine, sometimes considerably enriched by time in barrels, capable of maturing for years in the bottle. Production, which is constantly growing, exceeds 1.3 million bottles per year.

—

Producers and their trademark and signature wines:

44. BERSANO, Nizza Monferrato
    Nizza Riserva Generala ($$)
45. CASCINA LA BARBATELLA, Nizza Monferrato
    Nizza La Vigna dell'Angelo ($$)
    Nizza La Vigna dell'Angelo Riserva ($$)
46. Michele CHIARLO, Calamandrana
    Nizza Riserva La Court ($$)
47. COPPO, Canelli
    Nizza Pomorosso ($$)
24. Roberto FERRARIS, Agliano Terme
    Nizza Libertà ($)
48. ISOLABELLA DELLA CROCE, Loazzolo
    Nizza Augusta ($)
49. LA GIRONDA, Nizza Monferrato
    Nizza Le Nicchie ($)
50. SETTE, Nizza Monferrato
    Nizza ($)
33. TENUTA OLIM BAUDA, Incisa Scapaccino
    Nizza Riserva Bauda ($$)

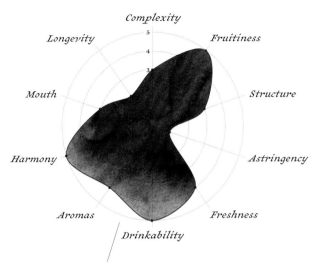

Barbera d'Alba

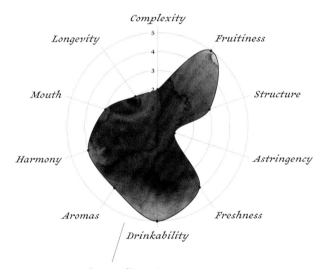

Barbera d'Asti

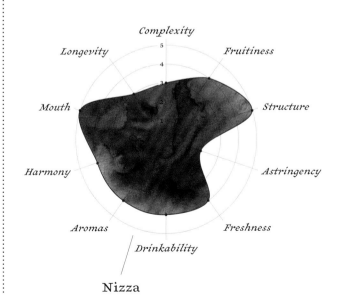

Nizza

Gabiano DOC

A DOC that would seem to be illogical, since it comes from less than 2.5 acres planted with 90 to 95% Barbera grapes, in the Monferrato Casalese in the province of Alessandria. However, here we suggest a winery that offers a version of particular value. About fifty thousand bottles are produced annually.
—

Producer and its trademark and signature wine:

51. CASTELLO DI GABIANO, Gabiano
    Gabiano Riserva A Matilde Giustiniani ($$)

....

Brachetto d'Acqui or Acqui DOCG

One of the rare aromatic red wines—compared by some to a Muscat in red clothing—it is characterized by hints of rose, musk, and violet, sweet and low in alcohol. Almost three million bottles are produced annually, often as Spumante and more rarely as Passito.
—

Producer and its trademark and signature wine:

52. MARENCO, Strevi
    Brachetto d'Acqui Pineto ($)

....

Ruché di Castagnole Monferrato DOCG

Pepper, rose, wild strawberries, and geranium are the aromas most perceived in this red that is always appetizing and barely astringent in the mouth. A wine of easy drinkability, never too demanding even when aged in wood, which is attracting more and more attention among consumers. A little over one million bottles are produced annually from 308 acres of vines.
—

Producer and its trademark and signature wines:

53. FERRARIS AGRICOLA, Castagnole Monferrato
    Ruché di Castagnole Monferrato Clàsic ($)
    Ruché di Castagnole Monferrato Vigna del Parroco ($)

Monferrato DOC

A vast DOC, stretching from the right bank of the River Po to the Ligurian Apennines, embracing the territories of two hundred and twenty-nine municipalities in the provinces of Asti and Alessandria. It is used by producers as a DOC for experimentation, especially in relation to the creation of blends between typical local grapes, such as Barbera and Cortese, with international vines, from Merlot to Cabernet Sauvignon and Pinot Noir, but there is no lack of valid productions in purity, as demonstrated by the recommended Chardonnay. Production is close to seven million bottles per year, of rather variable quality.
—

Producers and their trademark and signature wines:

54. BONZANO VINI, Rosignano Monferrato
    Monferrato Rosso Hosteria (Pinot Noir, Barbera) ($)
45. CASCINA LA BARBATELLA, Nizza Monferrato
    Monferrato Rosso Sonvico
    (Barbera, Cabernet Sauvignon) ($$)
55. PRUNOTTO, Alba
    Monferrato Rosso Mompertone (Barbera; Syrah) ($)
56. TENUTA SANTA CATERINA, Grazzano Badoglio
    Monferrato Bianco Silente delle Marne
    (Chardonnay) ($$)

....

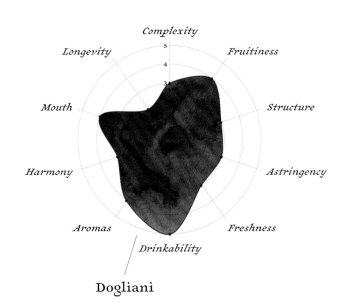

Dogliani

Dogliani DOCG

In the confused Piedmontese panorama of designations dedicated to the Dolcetto grape, the Dogliani DOCG is the one that has established itself with most certainty, even though it encompasses very different production styles, which in cellar aging envisage only steel or large barrels, cement or amphorae. For the Superiore version, at least one year of aging in the cellar after the harvest is required. However, it remains a wine of magnificent drinkability, ready for consumption a few months after the harvest but able to improve for three or four years in the bottle, where it dilutes its own, albeit fascinating, fruity impetuosity and reduces the astringent component due to the good presence of tannin. Dolcetto grape wine has always been the favorite lunch companion of the Langhe producers because, as Bruno Giacosa used to say, "while eating, you cannot drink anything better." Almost three million bottles per year are produced.

—

Producers and their trademark and signature wines:

1. Anna Maria ABBONA, Farigliano
   Dogliani Superiore Majoli ($)
   Dogliani Superiore San Bernardo ($)
2. Marziano ABBONA, Dogliani
   Dogliani Papà Celso ($)
3. CASCINA CORTE, Dogliani
   Dogliani Superiore Pirochetta Vecchie Vigne ($)
4. CHIONETTI, Dogliani
   Dogliani Briccolero ($)
5. PECCHENINO, Dogliani
   Dogliani Superiore Sirì d'Jermu ($)
   Dogliani Superiore Bricco Botti ($)
6. PODERI LUIGI EINAUDI, Dogliani
   Dogliani Superiore Tecc ($)
7. SAN FEREOLO, Dogliani
   Dogliani Superiore Valdibà ($)
   Dogliani Superiore Vigneti Dolci ($)

Dolcetto d'Alba DOC

Once a renowned Langhe DOC, today it faces many critical issues: changing consumer tastes, the vine's susceptibility to attacks by flavescenza dorata, the Dogliani DOCG becoming an increasingly strong point of reference, and the fact that it is a wine that is not very profitable and less and less loved by producers than the other types in this prestigious winegrowing area. Nevertheless, on an organoleptic level, its aromas of black fruits and its good grip make it an ideal companion for pasta or rice dishes. Close to seven million bottles are produced per year, and declining.

—

Producers and their trademark and signature wines:

8. AZELIA, Castiglione Falletto
   Dolcetto d'Alba Bricco dell'Oriolo ($)
9. Franco BOASSO – Gabutti, Serralunga d'Alba
   Dolcetto d'Alba ($)
10. BROVIA, Castiglione Falletto
    Dolcetto d'Alba Vignavillej ($)
11. CA' VIOLA, Dogliani
    Dolcetto d'Alba Barturot ($)
12. MARCHESI DI GRÉSY, Barbaresco
    Dolcetto d'Alba Monte Aribaldo ($)
13. Fratelli MOSSIO, Rodello
    Dolcetto d'Alba Bricco Caramelli ($)
14. Luciano SANDRONE, Barolo
    Dolcetto d'Alba ($)
15. G.D. VAJRA, Barolo
    Dolcetto d'Alba Coste&Fossati ($)

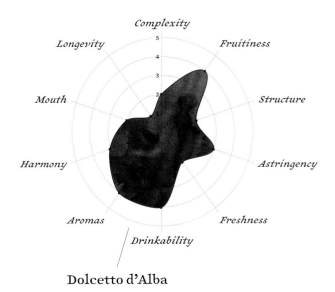

Dolcetto d'Alba

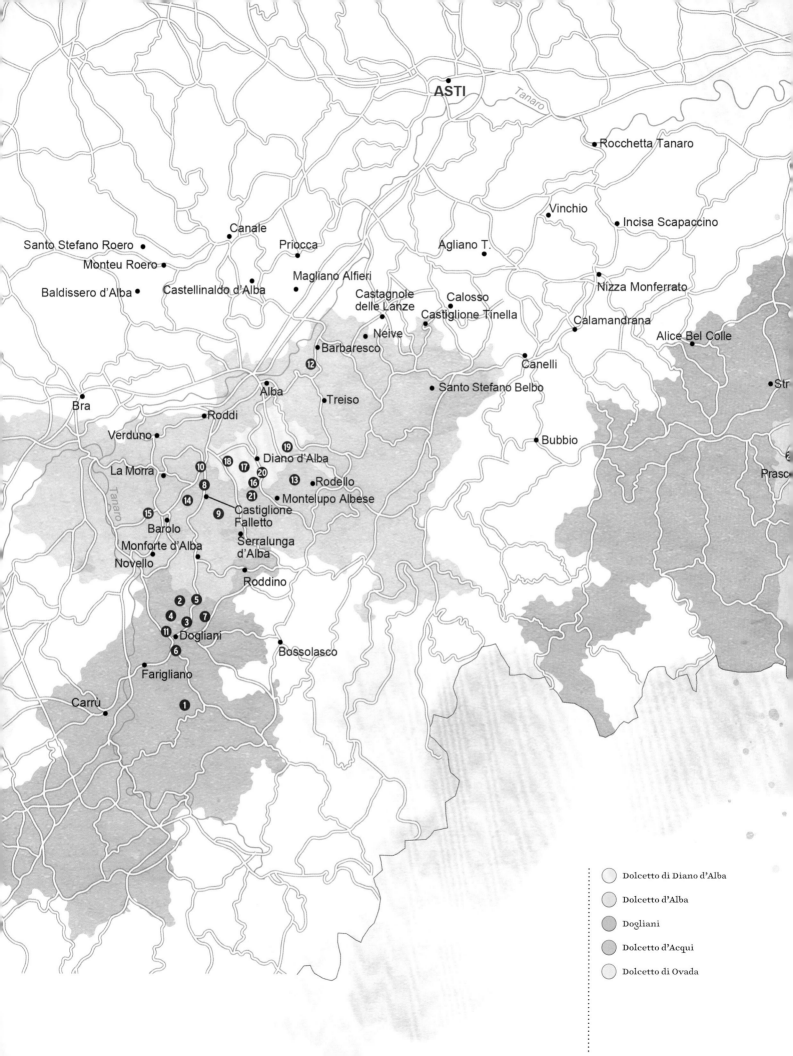

ASTI

Tanaro

• Rocchetta Tanaro

• Vinchio
• Incisa Scapaccino

Santo Stefano Roero •
• Canale
Priocca •
Monteu Roero •
• Agliano T.
• Nizza Monferrato
Baldissero d'Alba •
Castellinaldo d'Alba •
Magliano Alfieri •
Castagnole delle Lanze
• Calosso
Castiglione Tinella •
• Calamandrana
• Alice Bel Colle
❶❷ Neive •
Barbaresco •
• Canelli
• Str
⓬
Bra •
Alba
• Treiso
• Santo Stefano Belbo
Prasc
• Roddi
Verduno •
• Bubbio
⓳
⓲ ⓱ • Diano d'Alba
La Morra •
❿ ⓴
❽ ⓰
⓭ • Rodello
⓮
❾ ⓫ Castiglione
• Montelupo Albese
⓯ Falletto
Barolo •
Monforte d'Alba •
Serralunga
d'Alba
Novello •
• Roddino
❷ ❺
❹ ❼
• Bossolasco
⓫ ❸
❻ Dogliani
Farigliano
Carrù •
❶

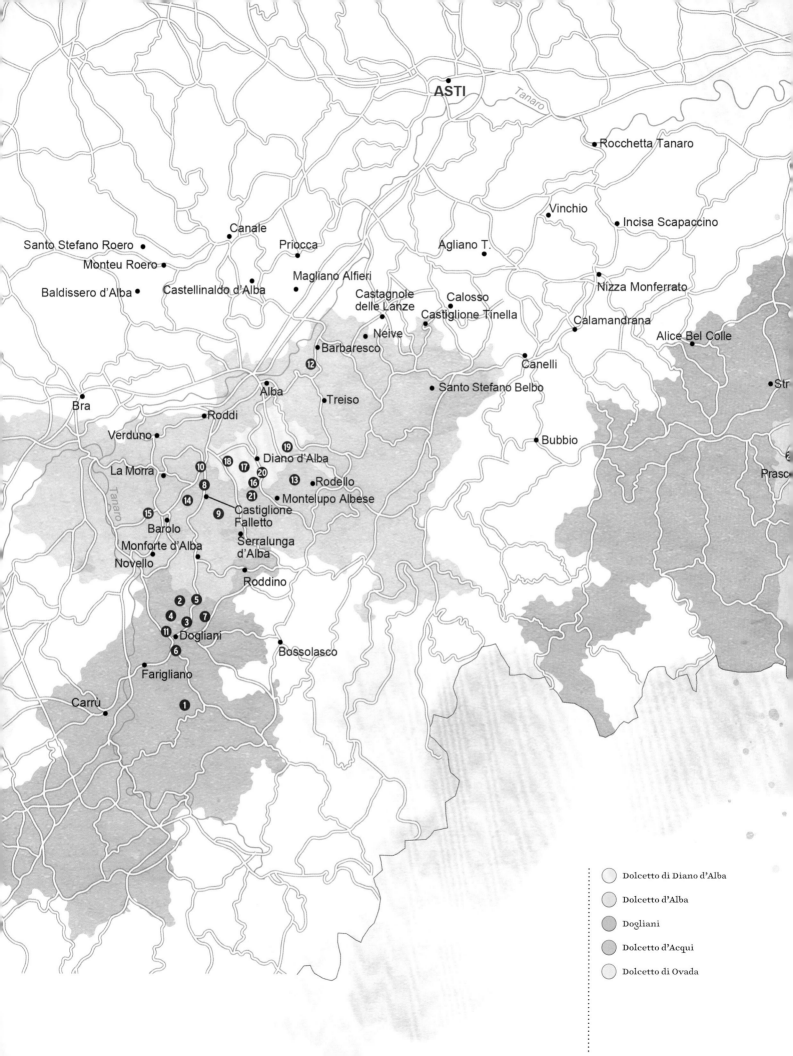

Dolcetto di Diano d'Alba
Dolcetto d'Alba
Dogliani
Dolcetto d'Acqui
Dolcetto di Ovada

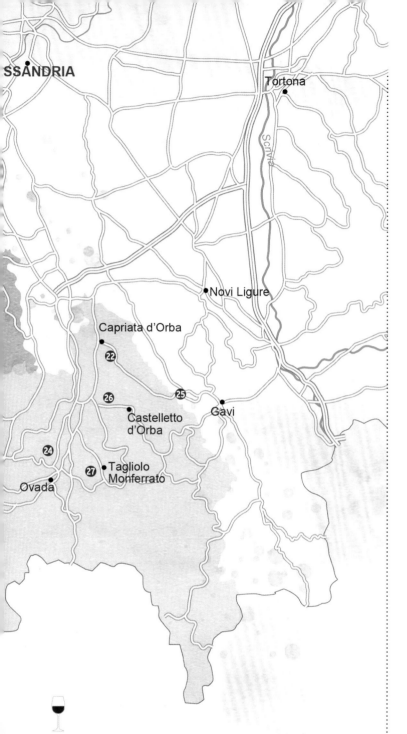

SSANDRIA

Tortona

Scrivia

Novi Ligure

Capriata d'Orba

22

26   25

Castelletto   Gavi
d'Orba

24

27   Tagliolo
     Monferrato

Ovada

Dolcetto di Diano d'Alba or Diano d'Alba DOCG

The area of Diano d'Alba, along with Rodello and Montelupo Albese, has always been famous for the quality of its Dolcetto grapes, even if this does not mean that there was a need for a new autonomous DOCG, in 2010, which has in any case found some worthy interpreters. It should be noted that the producers of Dolcetto di Diano d'Alba had in some ways anticipated the birth of the MGA and the UGA back in the 1980s, when they had identified seventy-six *sorì*, a term in the local dialect used to indicate particularly well-exposed vineyards, sometimes shown on the label. Around one million bottles are produced annually.

—

Producers and their trademark and signature wines:

16. Fratelli ABRIGO, Diano d'Alba
    Diano d'Alba ($)
17. Giovanni ABRIGO, Diano d'Alba
    Dolcetto di Diano d'Alba Superiore Garabei ($)
    Dolcetto di Diano d'Alba Sorì dei Crava ($)
18. Claudio ALARIO, Diano d'Alba
    Dolcetto di Diano d'Alba Sorì Pradurent ($)
    Dolcetto di Diano d'Alba Sorì Costa Fiore ($)
19. BRICCO MAIOLICA, Diano d'Alba
    Dolcetto di Diano d'Alba ($)
20. CORTINO – Produttori Dianesi, Diano d'Alba
    Diano d'Alba Superiore Sorì Santa Lucia ($)
21. LE CECCHE, Diano d'Alba
    Diano d'Alba ($)

....

Dolcetto di Ovada Superiore or Ovada DOCG
Dolcetto di Ovada DOC

Slightly more powerful, astringent, and richer than the Dolcetto made in the Langhe. It is easy to find freshness and smoothness in the DOC version, more depth, fleshiness, and length in the DOCG version, which was established in 2008 without great commercial success. It is often refined in wood. About 2.2 million bottles of DOC and one hundred and eighty thousand of DOCG are produced annually.

—

Producers and their trademark and signature wines:

22. CASCINA GENTILE, Capriata d'Orba
    Ovada Riserva Le Parole Servon Tanto ($)
23. Davide CAVELLI, Prasco
    Ovada Bricco La Zerba ($)
24. GAGGINO, Ovada
    Ovada Convivio ($)
25. IL ROCCHIN, Gavi
    Dolcetto di Ovada ($)
26. TACCHINO, Castelletto d'Orba
    Dolcetto di Ovada Superiore Du Riva ($)
    Dolcetto di Ovada ($)
27. TENUTA ALEMANNI, Tagliolo Monferrato
    Dolcetto di Ovada Superiore Ansé ($)

Grignolino d'Asti DOC and Grignolino del Monferrato Casalese DOC

These two wines, based on the Grignolino grape variety of the same name, are regaining ground among consumers thanks to vinifications that are increasingly attentive to creating a harmony of taste that is not easy to achieve, due to considerable astringency on the palate. The aromas recall red fruits and flowers, together with an omnipresent, delicate, and pleasant hint of spices. In both designations—the first relating to the province of Asti, the second to that of Alessandria—interesting and valid experiments are being conducted to present Grignolino on the market after a few years of aging in the cellar. Annual production is 1.5 million bottles for the Asti version, six hundred thousand for the Casalese version.

—

Producers and their trademark and signature wines:

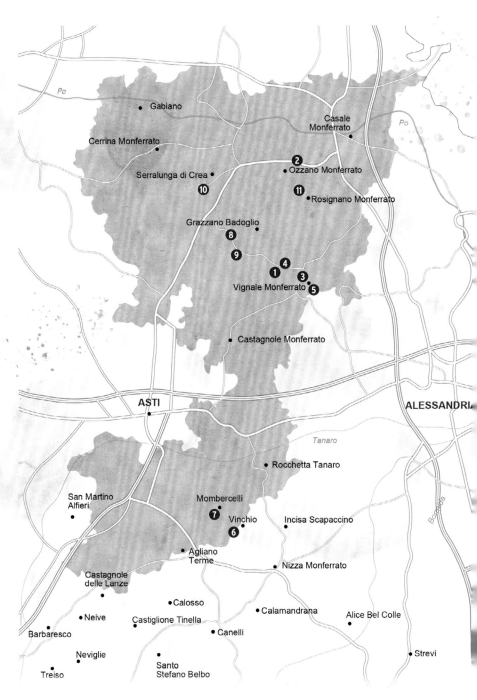

1. Giulio ACCORNERO e Figli, Vignale Monferrato
    Grignolino del Monferrato Casalese Bricco del Bosco ($)
    Grignolino del Monferrato Casalese Monferace Bricco del Bosco ($$)
2. Paolo ANGELINI, Ozzano Monferrato
    Grignolino del Monferrato Casalese Monferace Golden Arbian ($$)
3. Oreste BUZIO, Vignale Monferrato
    Grignolino del Monferrato Casalese ($)
4. Marco CANATO, Vignale Monferrato
    Grignolino del Monferrato Casalese Celio ($)
5. GAUDIO – Bricco Mondalino, Vignale Monferrato
    Grignolino del Monferrato Casalese Bricco Mondalino ($)
6. LAIOLO REGININ, Vinchio
    Grignolino d'Asti L'Intruso ($)
7. Luigi SPERTINO, Mombercelli
    Grignolino d'Asti ($)
8. SULIN, Grazzano Badoglio
    Grignolino del Monferrato Casalese ($)
9. TENUTA SANTA CATERINA, Grazzano Badoglio
    Grignolino d'Asti Monferace ($$)
10. TENUTA TENAGLIA, Serralunga di Crea
    Grignolino del Monferrato Casalese Monferace ($$)
11. VICARA, Rosignano Monferrato
    Grignolino del Monferrato Casalese .G ($)

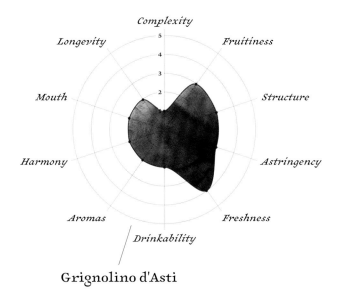

Grignolino d'Asti

Verduno Pelaverga
or Verduno DOC

A seductive DOC wine made from the small Pelaverga grape, characterized by a pale ruby color, aromas of pepper, rose, and wild strawberry, and a fresh, slightly tannic palate that is easy to drink. Produced exclusively in Verduno and, to a small extent, in La Morra and Roddi, in recent years it has been enjoying a well-deserved rediscovery, undoubtedly favored by its promotion at the Castello di Verduno restaurant. Today, it amounts to 75 acres under cultivation and about two hundred thousand bottles per year are produced.

—

Producers and their trademark and signature wines:

1. Fratelli ALESSANDRIA, Verduno
    Verduno Pelaverga Speziale ($)
2. Comm. G.B. BURLOTTO, Verduno
    Verduno Pelaverga ($)
3. CASTELLO DI VERDUNO, Verduno
    Verduno Basadone ($)
4. Gian Luca COLOMBO – Segni di Langa, Roddi
    Verduno Pelaverga ($)

Verduno Pelaverga

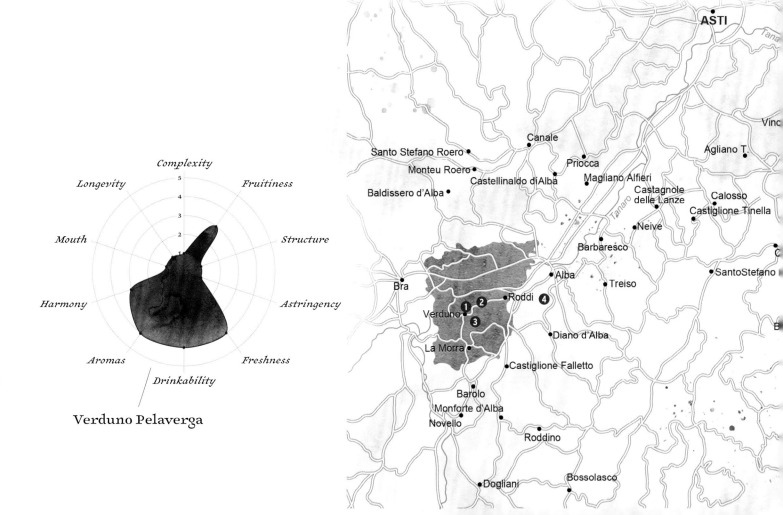

Freisa d'Asti DOC

In the Monferrato region, it is considered a wine suitable for almost all meals, having red flower aromas, good freshness of flavor, and a drinkability that is never too demanding, even when—as is the case in the Superiore versions mentioned—it is aged in wood. An average of 1.2 million bottles per year are produced from 420 acres of vineyards.

—

Producers and their trademark and signature wines:

1. CASCINA GILLI, Castelnuovo Don Bosco
    Freisa d'Asti Superiore Arvelé ($)
2. TENUTA SANTA CATERINA, Grazzano Badoglio
    Freisa d'Asti Superiore Sorì di Giul ($)

Freisa di Chieri DOC

A red wine traditionally loved by the inhabitants of Turin, it deserves to be known elsewhere for its drinkability, with taste elements that recall certain characteristics of both Nebbiolo and Barbera. Approximately four hundred thousand bottles per year are produced, also in less significant Dolce, Frizzante, and Spumante versions.

—

Producer and its trademark and signature wine:

3. BALBIANO, Andezeno
    Freisa di Chieri Superiore Federico I
    Il Barbarossa ($)

Albugnano DOC

A small, growing DOC, which takes its name from the municipality of Albugnano, also known as "the balcony of Monferrato" thanks to the splendid panorama. It is thus located in the province of Asti, but you can still breathe the air of the Turin hills. A wine with a good structure, moderately astringent and very fruity, suitable for aging for a few years. About fifty acres, at least 85% cultivated with Nebbiolo, yield approximately one hundred seventy thousand bottles per year.

Malvasia di Castelnuovo Don Bosco DOC

With a color poised between rosé and cherry, it offers the intense aromatic notes typical of the Malvasia di Schierano grape and is normally offered with a considerable residual sugar content, as the regulations state that the alcohol content cannot exceed 7% by volume. The small production area—around 125 acres, from which about five hundred thousand bottles are produced annually—is in a hilly area in the province of Asti, just behind the Collina Torinese.

—

Producer and its trademark and signature wine:

1. CASCINA GILLI, Castelnuovo Don Bosco
    Malvasia di Castelnuovo Don Bosco ($)

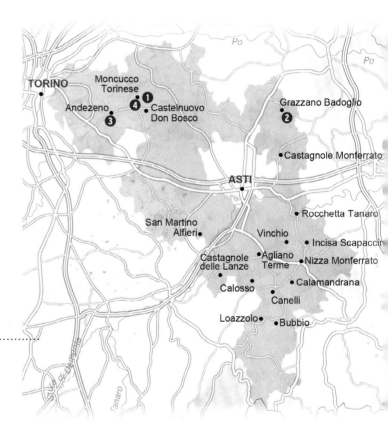

—

Producers and their trademark and signature wines:

1. CASCINA GILLI, Castelnuovo Don Bosco
    Albugnano Superiore Notturno ($)
4. Mario MOSSO, Moncucco Torinese
    Albugnano Superiore Parlapà ($)

Erbaluce di Caluso
or Caluso DOCG

In past centuries, the Canavesano, an area north of Turin, with small parts in the provinces of Biella and Vercelli, was famous above all for its Passito made from the Erbaluce grape. As consumer tastes changed, however, the still and sparkling versions became more and more popular, which were also successful due to the good acidic vein naturally present in the grape variety. The still version, as it used to be called, is characterized by nuances of herbs, citrus fruits, and plums, followed by a savory and pleasant drinkability. Aging in wood is rare, as in the 13 Mesi by Favaro. The Spumante, again made from 100% Erbaluce grapes, must be made with the Metodo Classico, remaining in the bottle on the lees for at least thirty-six months. The total annual production of the three types is close to two million bottles.

—

Producers and their trademark and signature wines:

1. CIECK, San Giorgio Canavese
   Erbaluce di Caluso Passito Alladium ($)
   Erbaluce di Caluso Vigna Misobolo ($)
   Erbaluce di Caluso Brut Nature M. Cl. ($)
2. FAVARO, Piverone
   Erbaluce di Caluso Tredicimesi ($)
   Erbaluce di Caluso Le Chiusure ($)
3. FERRANDO, Ivrea
   Erbaluce di Caluso Cariola ($)
4. LA MASERA, Piverone
   Erbaluce di Caluso Anima d'Annata ($)
   Erbaluce di Caluso Macaria ($)
5. ORSOLANI, San Giorgio Canavese
   Erbaluce di Caluso La Rustìa ($)
   Caluso Passito Sulé ($)
   Caluso Extra Brut Cuvée
   Tradizione M. Cl. ($)

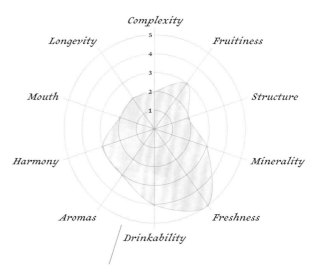

Erbaluce di Caluso

Gavi or Cortese di Gavi DOCG

A famous Piedmontese white, also appreciated abroad for its aromas of white and yellow flowers, sometimes slightly citrusy, with a palate of good freshness and overall harmony. Usually aged in cement or steel, but well adapted to a delicate passage in wood and able to improve in the bottle for several years, offering refined notes of hydrocarbons. With one hundred ninety wineries associated with the Consortium of the same name in 2021, about thirteen million bottles are produced annually, 80% of which are exported, from 3,955 acres of vineyards in eleven municipalities in the province of Alessandria, including Gavi, Bosio, Novi Ligure, and Tassarolo.

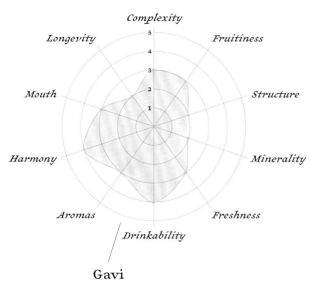

Gavi

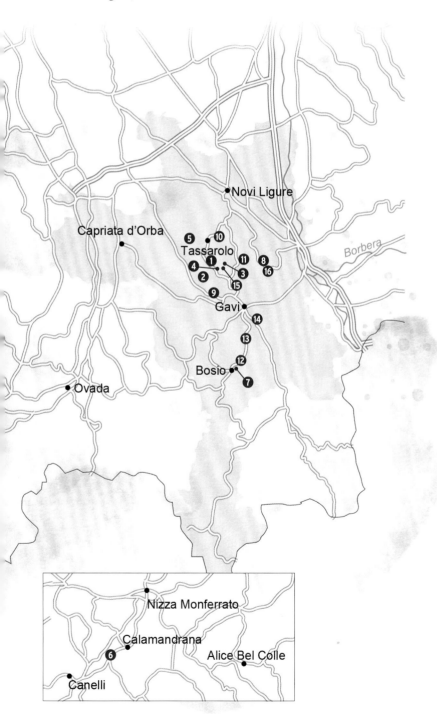

—

Producers and their trademark and signature wines:

1. Cinzia BERGAGLIO, Tassarolo
   Gavi del comune di Gavi Grifone delle Roveri ($)
2. Nicola BERGAGLIO, Gavi
   Gavi del comune di Gavi Rovereto Minaia ($)
   Gavi del comune di Gavi ($)
3. BROGLIA – Tenuta La Meirana, Gavi
   Gavi del comune di Gavi Bruno Broglia ($)
4. CASTELLARI BERGAGLIO, Gavi
   Gavi Pilin ($)
5. CASTELLO DI TASSAROLO, Tassarolo
   Gavi del comune di Tassarolo Marchesi Spinola ($)
6. Michele CHIARLO, Calamandrana
   Gavi Fornaci ($)
7. LA CAPLANA, Bosio
   Gavi del comune di Gavi ($)
8. LA GHIBELLINA, Gavi
   Gavi del comune di Gavi Altius ($)
9. LA GIUSTINIANA, Gavi
   Gavi del comune di Gavi Montessora ($)
10. LA MESMA, Gavi
    Gavi del comune di Gavi Etichetta Gialla ($)
    Gavi Riserva Vigna della Rovere Verde ($)
11. LA RAIA, Novi Ligure
    Gavi Riserva Vigna della Madonnina ($)
    Gavi Pisé ($)
12. LA SMILLA, Bosio
    Gavi del comune di Gavi ($)
13. Giordano LOMBARDO, Gavi
    Gavi del comune di Gavi San Martino ($)
•   Franco MARTINETTI, Torino
    Gavi Minaia ($$)
14. PRODUTTORI DEL GAVI, Gavi
    Gavi del comune di Gavi GG ($)
15. TENUTA SAN PIETRO, Tassarolo
    Gavi del comune di Tassarolo San Pietro ($)
16. VILLA SPARINA, Gavi
    Gavi del comune di Gavi Monterotondo ($$)

Colli Tortonesi DOC

It is still the red Barbera grape variety that is most widely cultivated on this beautiful hilly strip in the province of Alessandria. But it is the Timorasso white wine that has attracted the attention of consumers over the last thirty years, with a success that has led to major Langhe wineries investing in the area, including La Spinetta, Roagna, Borgogno, and Vietti. It is a white wine suitable both for delicate aging in wood and long maturation in the bottle, where it first develops pleasant notes of white flowers, peach, and citrus fruits, then mineral and slightly chalky hints. The taste is savory but also rather thick and enveloping, robust as it were. Approximately 2.3 million bottles of Colli Tortonesi are produced annually, including about nine hundred thousand of the white Timorasso, with plans soon to dedicate a cultivation of no less than 865 acres to this grape and the specific name of a subzone, called Derthona. Valter Massa, acknowledged as the architect of the rebirth of Timorasso since 1987, has opted for the, perhaps temporary, exit from the DOC, so it is listed at the end of the region.

—

Producers and their trademark
and signature wines:

1. Luigi BOVERI, Costa Vescovato
    Colli Tortonesi Timorasso Derthona
    Filari di Timorasso ($$)
    Colli Tortonesi Timorasso Derthona ($)
2. Giovanni DAGLIO, Costa Vescovato
    Colli Tortonesi Timorasso Derthona Cantico ($)
3. LA COLOMBERA, Tortona
    Colli Tortonesi Timorasso Il Montino ($$)
    Colli Tortonesi Timorasso Derthona ($)
4. Claudio MARIOTTO, Tortona
    Colli Tortonesi Timorasso Pitasso ($$)
    Colli Tortonesi Timorasso Cavallina ($$)
    Colli Tortonesi Barbera Poggio del Rosso ($)
•   Franco MARTINETTI, Turin
    Colli Tortonesi Timorasso Martin ($$)
5. Carlo Daniele RICCI, Costa Vescovato
    Colli Tortonesi Timorasso San Leto ($$)
6. VALLI UNITE, Costa Vescovato
    Colli Tortonesi Timorasso San Vito ($)
7. VIGNE MARINA COPPI, Castellania
    Colli Tortonesi Timorasso Fausto ($$)

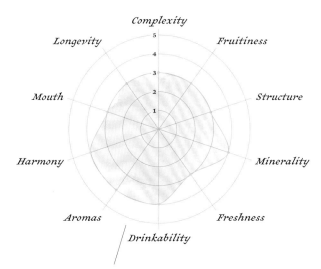

Colli Tortonesi Timorasso

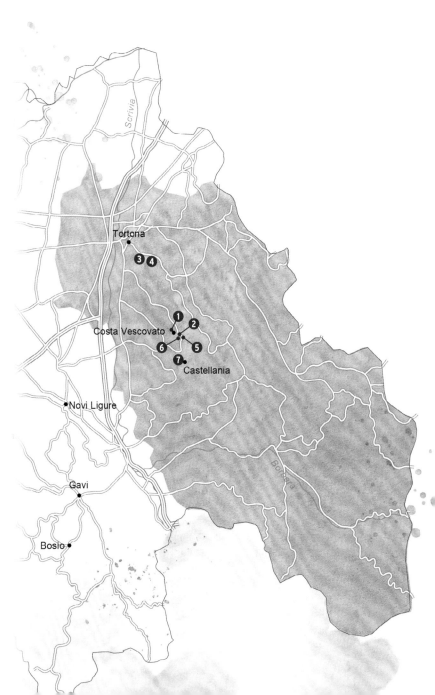

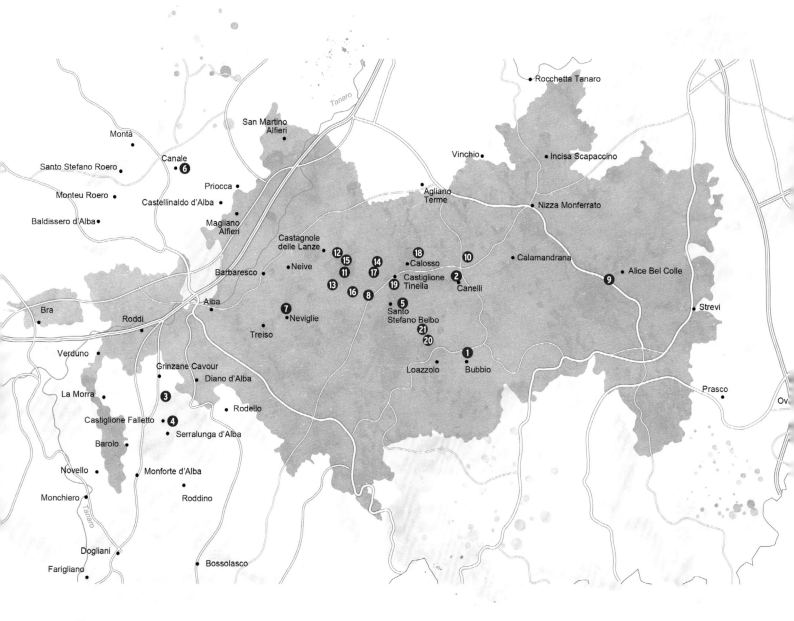

Alta Langa DOCG

A vast DOCG that geographically is not limited just to the highest part of the Langhe but also embraces vast territories in the province of Cuneo and parts of Asti and Alessandria, at an average altitude of between 820 and 1,805 feet. The DOCG is exclusively for sparkling wine, also rosé, made with the Metodo Classico—that is, with refermentation in the bottle—for at least thirty months, or thirty-six in the case of the Riserva, using no less than 90% Pinot Noir and/or Chardonnay grapes. Contrary to what is usually the case in the world of "bubbly," the indication of the year of production of the grapes is always mandatory. The taste objective is to offer rather dry and sharp sparkling wines, for which the Pas Dosé version is widely used. The production development that followed the issue of the DOCG in 2011 has been remarkable, so much so that production has already exceeded 2.8 million bottles per year, with estimates for further growth even in the areas planted with vines, now close to 988 acres.

Producers and their trademark and signature wines:

1. COLOMBO – Cascina Pastori, Bubbio
   Alta Langa Brut Rosé Riserva ($)
2. CONTRATTO, Canelli
   Alta Langa Pas Dosé Blanc de Noirs For England ($$)
   Alta Langa Extra Brut Blanc de Blancs For England ($$)
3. FONTANAFREDDA, Serralunga d'Alba
   Alta Langa Brut Nature Blanc de Noir Riserva Vigna Gatinera ($$)
4. Ettore GERMANO, Serralunga d'Alba
   Alta Langa Blanc de Noir Pas Dosé Riserva ($$)
5. MARCALBERTO, Santo Stefano Belbo
   Alta Langa Extra Brut Millesimo ($$)
6. Enrico SERAFINO, Canale
   Alta Langa Blanc de Noirs Pas Dosé Riserva Zero ($$)
   Alta Langa Pas Dosé Riserva Zero 140 ($$$$)

Asti and Moscato d'Asti DOCG

A single DOCG that includes two types: Asti and Moscato d'Asti, both made exclusively from the white Muscat grape. It is a unique and inimitable wine thanks to the individual nature of this grape, enchanting for its aromas of cedar, sage, lavender, and banana, sweet but also with an excellent acidic freshness on the palate. With a few exceptions, it can be said that Asti is the favorite product of the large wineries, which often offer it at very low prices, as a classic accompaniment to *panettone*, for instance, while Moscato d'Asti is a type to which dozens of quality artisans successfully dedicate themselves. Processing takes place in autoclaves, and the obligatory alcohol content is between 6 and 8% by volume for Asti, and between 4.5 and 6.5% by volume for Moscato d'Asti, which is slightly sweeter on the palate and has less froth. Moscato is therefore corked, as if it were a still wine, while the classic sparkling wine cork is used for the Asti bottle. There exists a note of controversy with this wine due to a possible similarity with Prosecco, so in 2017 the Asti Secco type was also included in the specifications, with higher alcohol content and, obviously, lower residual sugar content. Extra particular, albeit at little more than amateur level, is the production with the Metodo Classico, of which the Contratto label is worth mentioning. In 2023 the creation of the new autonomous Canelli DOCG was approved, the fruit of muscat grapes grown in seventeen municipalities. Production is based on vineyards spread over fifty-two municipalities in the provinces of Asti, Cuneo, and Alessandria, cultivated by no less than three thousand seven hundred winegrowers on a surface area of 25,200 acres, exceeding one hundred million bottles per year, sixty of which are Asti and forty-two are Moscato d'Asti.

—

Producers and their trademark and signature wines:

7. BERA, Neviglie
   Moscato d'Asti Canelli ($)
8. CA' D' GAL, Santo Stefano Belbo
   Moscato d'Asti Canelli Sant'Ilario ($)
   Moscato d'Asti Vite Vecchia ($$)
9. CANTINA ALICE BEL COLLE, Alice Bel Colle
   Asti 12 Mesi M. Cl. ($)
10. CASCINA BARISÉL, Canelli
    Moscato d'Asti Canelli ($)
11. CAUDRINA, Castiglione Tinella
    Moscato d'Asti La Galeisa ($)
2. CONTRATTO, Canelli
   Asti Spumante De Miranda M. Cl. ($)
12. Gianni DOGLIA, Castagnole delle Lanze
    Moscato d'Asti Casa di Bianca ($)
13. FERRERO, Santo Stefano Belbo
    Moscato d'Asti Teresina ($)
14. LA MORANDINA, Castiglione Tinella
    Moscato d'Asti Canelli ($)
15. LA SPINETTA, Castagnole delle Lanze
    Moscato d'Asti Bricco Quaglia ($)

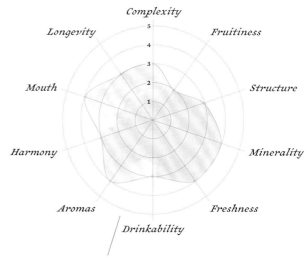

Alta Langa Pas Dosé

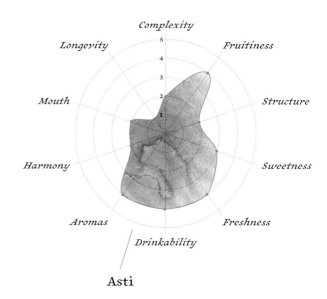

Asti

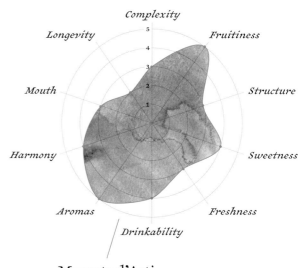

Moscato d'Asti

16. MONGIOIA, Santo Stefano Belbo
    Moscato d'Asti Canelli Moscata Anfora ($)
17. Elio PERRONE, Castiglione Tinella
    Moscato d'Asti Sourgal ($)
18. SCAGLIOLA, Calosso
    Moscato d'Asti Volo di Farfalle ($)
19. TENUTA IL FALCHETTO, Santo Stefano Belbo
    Moscato d'Asti Canelli Ciombo ($)

....

Loazzolo DOC

Made from dried, and possibly botyrized, white Muscat grapes (this is the process that occurs when a grape fungus reduces the concentration of water in the fruit, thus increasing its sugar content). It is a persuasive and charming sweet wine, always very intense in its multifaceted aromaticity, produced exclusively in the municipality of the same name in the province of Asti, at an altitude of around 1,312 feet. It can only be marketed two years after the harvest and must be aged for at least six months in small casks of less than 250 liters. It is one of the smallest DOC wines in Italy, of which only forty thousand bottles per year are produced, mostly in small sizes.

—

Producers and their trademark and signature wines:

20. BORGO MARAGLIANO, Loazzolo
    Loazzolo ($$)
21. FORTETO DELLA LUJA, Loazzolo
    Loazzolo Piasa Rischei ($$)

....

Piemonte DOC

A spillover DOC, owing its status also due to the abolition of the *Indicazioni Geografiche Tipiche* (Typical Geographical Indications) throughout the region and generally lacking in particular merit, with many grapes in all vinification styles, especially in the Spumante and Frizzante versions, from Piedmont Pinot-Chardonnay Spumante Brut to Piedmont Chardonnay-Sauvignon. But the good news is that there is no shortage of fine exceptions. More than thirty-five million bottles are produced annually.

—

Producers and their trademark and signature wines:

- COLOMBO – Cascina Pastori, Bubbio
  Piemonte Pinot Nero Apertura ($)

- COPPO, Canelli
  Piemonte Chardonnay Monteriolo ($$)
- ISOLABELLA DELLA CROCE, Loazzolo
  Piemonte Pinot Nero Bricco del Falco ($$)
- Albino ROCCA, Barbaresco
  Piemonte Cortese La Rocca ($)
- Paolo SARACCO, Castiglione Tinella
  Piemonte Moscato d'Autunno ($)

....

Pinerolese DOC

A small, heroic appellation reserved for red and rosé wines made at the foot of the Cottian Alps, mainly from Barbera, Bonarda dell'Oltrepò Pavese, Dolcetto, and Freisa grapes, but also from local vines that are now in danger of extinction, such as those used in Ramìe, for at least 60%, as well as Avanà, Avarengo, Chatus, and Becuet. Just over one hundred twenty thousand bottles are produced each year.

—

Producers and their trademark and signature wines:

- Daniele COUTANDIN, Perosa Argentina
  Pinerolese Ramìe ($$)
- LE MARIE, Barge
  Pinerolese Rosso Debarges ($)
  Pinerolese Rouge de Lissart ($)

....

Recommended wines outside the DOC/DOCG designations:

- BORGO MARAGLIANO, Loazzolo
  Giuseppe Galliano Brut Nature M. Cl. ($)
  Giuseppe Galliano Brut Rosé M. Cl. ($)
- Ezio CERRUTI, Castiglione Tinella
  Sol Passito (Moscato) ($$)
- IULI, Cerrina Monferrato
  Malidea (Nebbiolo) ($$)
  Barabba (Barbera) ($$)
- MARCALBERTO, Santo Stefano Belbo
  Marcalberto Blanc de Blancs
  Pas Dosé M. Cl. (Chardonnay) ($$)
- PODERE ROCCHE DEI MANZONI, Monforte d'Alba
  Valentino Brut Zero M. Cl. (Chardonnay) ($$)
- VIGNETI MASSA, Monleale
  Derthona Costa del Vento (Timorasso) ($$)
  Derthona Montecitorio (Timorasso) ($$)
  Derthona Sterpi (Timorasso) ($$)

CONTRATTO

Via Giuliani 56
Canelli (Asti)
contratto.it
Year of establishment: 1867
Owner: the Rivetti family
Average number of bottles
produced per year: 170,000

The historic Contratto winery, equipped with underground cellars of unparalleled charm, was acquired in 2011 by the Rivetti family, famous for Barbaresco, Barolo, and Moscato. Since then, a production revolution has been underway, based first and foremost on the establishment of a vineyard estate in the Alta Langa. The 104 acres, cultivated organically and destined to grow, already guarantee a production that has once again placed the name Contratto at the top of Italian sparkling wine production.

ALTA LANGA PAS DOSÉ BLANC DE NOIRS FOR ENGLAND

First year of production: 1920
Average number of bottles produced per year: 15,000
Grape variety: Pinot Noir

The soft pressing of the grapes gives rise to a soft rosé color, with aromas characterized above all by notes of citrus fruits and currants that come from the wine's forty months on the lees. The taste has matter and above all vivacity; it is taut and dry, with ringing acidity, energetic and persistent. A brilliant execution of Alta Langa DOCG.

ENRICO SERAFINO

Corso Asti 5
Canale (CN)
enricoserafino.it
Year of establishment: 1878
Owner: Krause Group
Average number of bottles produced per year: 350,000

The acquisition by Kyle Krause in 2015 led to the decision to have its own vineyards, especially in the Alta Langa, where the important sector dedicated to seven types of Metodo Classico sparkling wine was born, with a total of 148 acres under cultivation. Equally important is the commitment to revitalize Serafino's historical tradition of vinifying the red grapes typical of the Langhe and Roero, as demonstrated by the five labels already dedicated to Barolo, the two to Barbaresco, and the two to Roero DOCG. There have been numerous awards for the sparkling, not to mention the great reds.

ALTA LANGA PAS DOSÉ BLANC DE NOIRS RISERVA ZERO

First year of production: 2004
Average number of bottles produced per year: 22,000
Grape variety: Pinot Noir

The Riserva Zero is the one on which the company focuses most strongly to express its idea of Alta Langa DOCG: Pinot Noir grapes from a single harvest, maturation of over five years on the lees, no added sugar. The result is a wine with white flowers and yellow fruit in evidence, with a memory of yeast that leads toward the minerality of chalk and flint. An electrifying palate, lively, taut, and fresh but devoid of aggression thanks to the softness of the bubbles, of absolute refinement.

PIERO BUSSO

Via Albesani 8
Neive (CN)
bussopiero.com
Year of establishment: 1948
Owner: the Busso family
Average number of bottles produced per year: 45,000

Piero Busso immediately made a name for himself in the world of quality wine thanks to incisive wines—never too woody but vivid and fresh, sometimes even with a touch of healthy rusticity, as in the case of Barbaresco Gallina Viti Vecchie. In thirty years he and his entire family have built a small, functional, and prestigious winery that can count on a surface area of 25 acres of vines, which have long been cultivated organically.

BARBARESCO ALBESANI BORGESE

First year of production: 1979
Average number of bottles produced per year: 3,000
Grape variety: Nebbiolo

The vast Albesani area includes the excellent location of the Vigna Borgese, which is found just above the famous Santo Stefano cru and yields rather severe wines with good tannicity, suitable for long aging. It was here that Piero Busso made his first bottles in 1979, which were to take their present official name of Albesani Borgese from 2007. A wine that is always very direct and energetic on the palate, with aromas of red flowers and a touch of citrus, with a pleasant mineral background of damp earth and a touch of pine resin.

CA' DEL BAIO

Via Ferrere 33
Treiso (CN)
cadelbaio.com
Year of establishment: 1891
Owner: the Grasso family
Average number of bottles produced per year: 140,000

Giulio Grasso—with the increasingly active collaboration of his three daughters—has always been an expert winemaker, and in the last twenty years has also worked to organize a wine cellar capable of producing prestigious labels. The success has grown year after year and has taken Ca' del Baio to the top quality level of the designation. The Pora is accompanied by four other Barbaresco labels, all from 69 acres of property: the balsamic Asili, also in the powerful Riserva version, the fruity Vallegrande, soon also Riserva, and the juicy Autinbej.

BARBARESCO PORA

First year of production: 2004
Average number of bottles produced per year: 2,500
Grape variety: Nebbiolo

Profound olfactory complexity, in which persuasive mentholated notes and violet petals, affable hints of tar, and tantalizing undergrowth fruits combine. The taste is of rare clarity, rich in pulp but also authoritative austerity, extremely refined, persistent, and with prestigious balance. The fine fruit of an important cru.

CERETTO
Località San Cassiano 34
Alba (CN)
ceretto.com
Year of establishment: 1937
Owner: the Ceretto family
Average number of
bottles produced per year:
1,050,000

Great wines from great
vineyards: from Prapò to
Bricco Rocche in Barolo, from
Asili to Gallina in Barbaresco,
propulsive centers set in the
395 acres of property cultivated
organically or biodynamically.
Oenological style devoted to
elegance and finesse, without
invasive hints of wood or
exaggerated concentrations,
always crisp and pure. The
winery is also famous for the
works of art that enrich some
of its properties: the Barolo
Chapel by Sol LeWitt and
David Tremlett in the Brunate
vineyard, *Il Cubo* on the Bricco
Rocche, and *L'Acino* on the
Bernardina estate.

BARBARESCO ASILI
First year of production: 1974
Average number of bottles produced
per year: 5,000
Grape variety: Nebbiolo

The wine that has made the winery known
throughout the world, always endowed with
fascinating balsamic and undergrowth fruit
notes, with a palate that represents perfect
harmony, never very astringent and always
fresh, of such enjoyable drinkability that it
almost makes one forget the rare complexity
it possesses. It improves in the bottle for at
least thirty years.

GIUSEPPE CORTESE
Strada Rabajà 80
Barbaresco (CN)
cortesegiuseppe.it
Year of establishment: 1971
Owner: the Cortese family
Average number of bottles
produced per year: 65,000

This small winery has built a
vast reputation thanks to the
faithful interpretation given
to its 22 acres of vineyards,
consisting of the celebrated
Rabajà and the simpler
Trifolera, on the hill opposite.
The former produces the
Barbaresco of the same name,
also in the magnificent Riserva
version, while the latter
produces Barbera and Dolcetto
d'Alba, Langhe Nebbiolo, and
the immediate Chardonnay
Scapolin. A well-deserved
success for Giuseppe Cortese, a
great winemaker, and his sons,
who firmly believe that strict
adherence to tradition is the
best way to guarantee a great
future for Barbaresco.

BARBARESCO RABAJÀ
First year of production: 1978
Average number of bottles produced
per year: 17,000
Grape variety: Nebbiolo

After a month of fermentation in cement
and maturation of almost two years in
used Slavonian oak barrels, a Barbaresco of
superlative complexity is born, rich in its
aromas of red flowers and black fruits to
which a hint of tar and eucalyptus is added
with age. The flavor is powerful, with lively
acidity and moderate tannicity, juicy, and
agile with carefully curated elegance. It is
pure and bewitching.

GAJA
Via Torino 18
Barbaresco (CN)
Year of establishment: 1859
Owner: the Gaja family
Average number of bottles
produced per year: 350,000

Elegance and longevity are the
main qualities highlighted
by wine critics regarding the
wines of this world-famous
name. Equally important is the
care taken in the cultivation
of the vineyards, which have
grown to 227 acres and are
still growing, with prestigious
consultations with specialists
aimed at obtaining excellent
grapes not treated with
synthetic chemicals. Among
the most famous labels are the
rare Barbaresco selections—
Sorì Tildin, Sorì San Lorenzo
(to which an interesting
volume by Edward Steinberg
is dedicated), and Costa
Russi—together with Barolo
Sperss. Superlative wines,
dedicated to an audience with
spending power.

BARBARESCO SORÌ TILDIN
First year of production: 1970
Average number of bottles produced
per year: 12,000
Grape variety: Nebbiolo

The Barbaresco Sorì Tildin, offered as a
Langhe Nebbiolo between 1996 and 2013,
is one of the labels that symbolizes the
refinement and ability to improve over
decades that is typical of Gaja wines. The
aromas are decidedly floral and spicy, vivid
and sharp, with roses always in evidence and
a hint of toasty wood in the early years of the
bottle. The flavor is enveloping but rich in
freshness, barely marked by the astringency
of the tannins and a reminder of pine resin,
of absolute charm.

BRUNO GIACOSA
Via XX Settembre 52
Neive (CN)
brunogiacosa.it
Year of establishment: 1900
Owner: Bruno Giacosa
Average number of bottles
produced per year: 400,000

Bruno Giacosa was a
profound connoisseur of the
Langhe vineyards, a skillful
winemaker, a firm believer in
the tradition of quality, and
the first producer to receive
an honorary degree from the
University of Gastronomic
Sciences in Pollenzo. To the 44
acres of his own property, from
which the famous red labels
for the Riserva versions of
Barolo Le Rocche del Falletto
and Barbaresco Asili are also
made, he has always combined
grapes purchased from trusted
vine growers, thus building
a name that has become a
worldwide oenological legend.

BARBARESCO RISERVA ASILI
First year of production: 1967
Average number of bottles produced
per year: 12,000
Grape variety: Nebbiolo

The long fermentation of the grapes on the
skins and maturation in large barrels add
a touch of austerity to the typical finesse
of the Asili cru. The aromas highlight
currant and raspberry, wilted rose petals,
and mentholated herbs in a combination of
rare and seductive complexity. The palate
is full of tension and vitality, with good
freshness and silky tannins, considerable
volume, and a finish of rigorous elegance.
An unforgettable, much sought-after, and
therefore now rather expensive wine.

MARCHESI DI GRÉSY
Strada della Stazione 21
Barbaresco (CN)
marchesidigresy.com
Year of establishment: 1797
Owner: the Asinari di
Grésy family
Average number of bottles
produced per year: 200,000

In forty years, Alberto di Grésy
has managed to build, on the
strength of a centuries-old
company history, a winery
whose name has become
a symbol of classicism and
refinement in the world of
Barbaresco. Thirty of the
total eighty-six acres of the
suggestive amphitheater,
which are completely planted
with vines of Martinenga,
are dedicated to this wine,
in which the Gaiun and
Camp Gros crus stand out for
qualitative performance. The
other three estates give rise to
an articulated offer of labels in
which local and French grapes
are blended, with a place of
honor constantly reserved
for Dolcetto d'Alba Monte
Aribaldo, among the most
established of the type.

BARBARESCO MARTINENGA
RISERVA CAMP GROS
First year of production: 1978
Average number of bottles produced
per year: 7,500
Grape variety: Nebbiolo

Presented as Barbaresco Riserva from 2010,
it has enchanting longevity qualities, so it
is advisable to consume it even many years
after the harvest. It opens on notes of red
fruits and flowers, including raspberry and
violet, followed by spicy and mineral hints
of licorice and tar. The palate is of confidant
harmony, persuasive, very elegant, slightly
tannic, and with good acidic freshness,
enhanced by fine hints of pine resin.

PRODUTTORI DEL
BARBARESCO
Via Torino 54
Barbaresco (CN)
produttoridelbarbaresco.com
Year of establishment: 1958
Owner: the fifty cooperative
societies of the Produttori del
Barbaresco
Average number of bottles
produced per year: 580,000

This winery is world-famous for
its excellent wines and for having
demonstrated how cooperation
can combine with the logic of
the market and give adequate
remuneration to the vine growers
who bring their grapes here.
After an initial attempt in 1894
by Domizio Cavazza, the true
putative father of Barbaresco, and
the cessation of activity during
the Fascist period, Produttori del
Barbaresco was reborn in 1958
and since then has continued on a
virtuous path that has brought it
to its current size and quality. By
choice of statute, the winery makes
wine exclusively from Nebbiolo
grapes, offered in Langhe Nebbiolo,
a basic Barbaresco, and nine fine
Riserva versions deriving from a
total of 277 acres, indicating for
each vineyard the names of the
growers who produce the grapes.

BARBARESCO RISERVA OVELLO
First year of production: 1967
Average number of bottles produced
per year: 19,000
Grape variety: Nebbiolo

It is difficult to choose, so high is the level,
between the prestigious names of the
crus from which the Barbaresco Riserva
are born: Asili, Montefico, Montestefano,
Muncagota, Ovello, Pajè, Pora, Rabajà, and
Rio Sordo. Ovello is consistently among the
most awarded by wine guides thanks to the
richness of flavor that it offers after three
years of maturation in large casks: currants,
raspberries, and cherries are at the center
of the fine range of aromas, then the palate
is powerful and with excellent tension but
not astringent, pleasantly fresh, with a
persuasive finish of sweet spices.

FIORENZO NADA
Località Rombone, Via
Ausario 12/C
Treiso (CN)
nada.it
Year of establishment: 1921
Owner: the Nada family
Average number of bottles
produced per year: 45,000

Bruno Nada was a young
teacher when he decided, in
1982, to start making wine
from grapes grown in his
family's vineyards. It was an
immediate success, thanks to
an elegant and refined style, in
which small woods played as
decisive a role as the thinning
of the grapes in the rows. The
Barbaresco Rombone was
later joined by those of the 25
organic acres of the Manzola
and Montaribaldi vineyards,
without forgetting that the
exquisite Seifile, one of the
most award-winning Langhe
Rosso ever, was born here, the
fruit of old Barbera vines with
a touch of Nebbiolo.

BARBARESCO ROMBONE
First year of production: 1982
Average number of bottles produced
per year: 3,500
Grape variety: Nebbiolo

In the latest vintages, the wood is less
perceptible than it used to be, and leaves
ample room for the fruity notes and
austerity of flavor typical of the Rombone di
Treiso cru. The aromas turn toward currant
and raspberry, joined by a whiff of orange
and pine resin. There is a taste of exemplary
harmony, barely marked by tannins, fresh
and lively, with a finish of perfect elegance in
which red rose petals are noticeable. Incisive,
balanced, and important.

ALBINO ROCCA
Strada Ronchi 18
Barbaresco (CN)
albinorocca.com
Year of establishment: 1940
Owner: the Rocca family
Average number of bottles
produced per year: 100,000

Angelo Rocca brought the
winery created by his father
Albino to international
prominence, leaving his
daughters an oenological
legacy based on beautiful
vineyards and a famous name.
Today, Monica, Daniela,
and Paola not only continue
but grow the business,
restructuring the cellar and
creating new prestigious
labels, including a splendid
Barbaresco dedicated to their
father Angelo. The twelve
red wines—the fruit of 44
acres planted with Nebbiolo,
Barbera, and Dolcetto—are
joined by three white wines, in
which the complex Piedmont
Cortese La Rocca stands out
for its personality.

BARBARESCO OVELLO VIGNA
LORETO
First year of production: 1990
Average number of bottles produced
per year: 2,700
Grape variety: Nebbiolo

Born in a small vineyard with seventy-year-
old vines and matured for two years in large
casks, it offers a fine olfactory complexity
and a well-structured body. The nose is filled
with violet petals enlivened by smoke and a
faint citrus touch; the flavor is captivating,
with good overall balance and discreet
freshness right up to the refined tarry touch
on the finish.

BRUNO ROCCA
Strada Rabajà 60
Barbaresco (CN)
brunorocca.it
Year of establishment: 1978
Owner: the Rocca family
Average number of bottles produced per year: 75,000

Francesco Rocca has taken the reins and, together with his ever-active father, Bruno, leads both the agronomic and vinification side of the business, with skills now equal to his enthusiasm and desire to experiment. The 37 acres of the estate are cultivated with the utmost respect for the environment, while the wines, somewhat characterized by the invasive elegance of the barriques in the first years of the winery's activity, now accurately show the distinctive character of each cru. The Rabajà is joined by other world-famous "feathered" labels, notably the Barbaresco Currà, also in the prized Riserva version, and the rare Maria Adelaide.

BRUNO ROCCA

Barbaresco
Rabajà®

BARBARESCO RABAJÀ
First year of production: 1978
Average number of bottles produced per year: 7,000
Grape variety: Nebbiolo

Cherries, blackberries, and many red petals impose themselves on a slightly licorice and smoky base, in a persuasive and profound whole. The taste is rich in substance, soft overall, and with a good alcohol content, just fresh and slightly resinous in the refined finish. A label that has made the history of the new Barbaresco.

GIANFRANCO ALESSANDRIA
Località Manzoni 13
Monforte d'Alba (CN)
gianfrancoalessandria.com
Year of establishment: 1986
Founder: the Alessandria family
Average number of bottles produced per year: 55,000

Gianfranco Alessandria was a convinced participant in the movement that, starting in the 1980s, gave birth to the new image of Barolo, mainly through the reduction of grape yields in the vineyard and the adoption of small French types of wood for maturation in the cellar. Although it has only 20 acres under vine, it has become famous not only for its Barolo San Giovanni, but also for its exquisite Barbera d'Alba Vittoria, to which it combines small batches of excellent Langhe Nebbiolo and juicy Dolcetto d'Alba.

BARBERA D'ALBA VITTORIA
First year of production: 1995
Average number of bottles produced per year: 4,500
Grape variety: Barbera

A modern and elegant style, based on a remarkable concentration of flavor and ample roasted aromas. Ripe plums and spices precede fine hints of smoke and tar, then the palate expresses itself with strength and envelopment, without ever losing a pleasant acidic backbone. The prototype of the new, award-winning Barbera d'Alba.

SOTTIMANO
Località Cottà 21
Neive (CN)
sottimano.it
Year of establishment: 1975
Owner: the Sottimano family
Average number of bottles produced per year: 90,000

Father Rino and son Andrea Sottimano are playing a leading role in the growing success of Barbaresco on the international markets, thanks to strict selections in the vineyard and elegant winemaking, in which new types of wood often contribute to the aromatic and taste intensity. The 49 acres cultivated organically are spread over five important Barbaresco crus—Currà, Cottà, Pajorè, Fausoni, Basarin—and give rise to as many labels, joined by the Riserva version.

SOTTIMANO

BARBARESCO
DENOMINAZIONE DI ORIGINE CONTROLLATA E GARANTITA

CURRÁ

2019

ESTATE BOTTLED BY / IMBOTTIGLIATO ALL'ORIGINE DA
Azienda Agricola Sottimano - Neive - ITALIA
PRODUCT OF ITALY / PRODOTTO IN ITALIA

NET CONT. 750 ML. ALC. 14% BY VOL.   75 CL ℮ 14% VOL.
CONTIENE SOLFITI - CONTAINS SULFITES - ENTHÄLT SULFITE - INNEHÅLLER SULFITER - L519

BARBARESCO CURRÀ
First year of production: 1994
Average number of bottles produced per year: 3,000
Grape variety: Nebbiolo

The Currà vineyard guarantees, in addition to the classic fruity aromas, a refreshing characteristic reminiscent of pine resin and eucalyptus, to which are added the sweet spices deriving from maturation in wood. The flavor is particularly rich and sustained, sinuous, barely astringent, and overall austere, enlivened by an exquisite final citrus note. The refinement of Barbaresco.

CA' VIOLA
Borgata San Luigi 11
Dogliani (CN)
caviola.com
Year of establishment: 1991
Owner: Giuseppe Caviola
Average number of bottles produced per year: 90,000

Fresh out of school, Beppe Caviola began vinifying small batches of grapes in the garage of his family home in Montelupo Albese. Since then, it has been a crescendo of successes, well represented by his career as wine consultant for prestigious companies all over Italy and his new charming company headquarters in Dogliani. The acquisition of new vineyards has gone hand in hand, both in Alta Langa for the production of Riesling and an important plot in the Sottocastello cru in Novello for Barolo, arriving today at a total vineyard area of 44 acres cultivated organically.

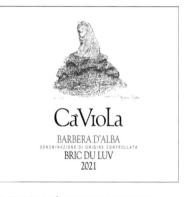

BARBERA D'ALBA BRIC DU LUV
First year of production: 1991
Average number of bottles produced per year: 5,000
Grape variety: Barbera

The company's entire line is of established quality, but Barbera d'Alba remains the wine of the heart, the one with which Beppe Caviola made his name and the one he continues to vinify with the same passion as thirty years ago. A delicate passage in wood adds a hint of smoke to the very fruity aromas, with plums in evidence; the flavor is vivid, snappy, rich in substance but light and sinuous, with refined freshness and unparalleled drinkability.

AZELIA

Via Alba-Barolo 143
Castiglione Falletto (CN)
azelia.it
Year of establishment: 1920
Owner: Luigi Scavino
Average number of bottles
produced per year: 85,000

Luigi Scavino and his son
Lorenzo confidently lead a
winery known and appreciated
for wines that are always rich
and elegant, thanks both to
very old vineyards and the
skillful use of wood. The 39.5
acres under vine are located
in Castiglione Falletto—
cru Bricco Fiasco—and in
Serralunga d'Alba—cru San
Rocco, Margheria, Bricco
Voghera, Cerretta—and are
among the most prestigious
in the Barolo area. Also worth
tasting is the always splendid
Dolcetto d'Alba Bricco
dell'Oriolo, from Montelupo
Albese.

BAROLO SAN ROCCO

First year of production: 1995
Average number of bottles produced
per year: 6,000
Grape variety: Nebbiolo

Born in a small cru rich in history in
Serralunga d'Alba, it is characterized by
finesse and power, showing Luigi Scavino's
skills in the use of fermentation barrels,
here particularly delicate in their aromatic
contribution. The aromas are classic,
with black and red fruits such as cherries
and blueberries accompanied by a barely
noticeable spiciness. The sip is powerful,
voluminous, energetic thanks to the pulp
and the important tannic component, with a
finish on tones of eucalyptus and licorice.

GIACOMO BREZZA E FIGLI

Via Lomondo 4
Barolo (CN)
brezza.it
Year of establishment: 1885
Owner: the Brezza family
Average number of bottles
produced per year: 95,000

Enzo Brezza has made small
but significant adjustments
to the historical winemaking
approach of the house, taking
particular care of the perfect
cleaning of the large barrels
and the organic cultivation of
the 49 acres of the property.
The vineyards cover several
communes in the Langhe and
extend as far as the other side
of the Tanaro River, in the
Roero, but the heart is in the
commune of Barolo with the
three prized crus of Sarmassa,
Cannubi, and Castellero. A
very well-cared-for traditional
style.

BAROLO SARMASSA RISERVA VIGNA BRICCO

First year of production: 2011
Average number of bottles produced
per year: 2,500
Grape variety: Nebbiolo

After a long time spent fermenting on the
skins, two years in a Slavonian oak cask, and
an additional two years in the bottle, this
fine selection comes to the market offering
a clear expression of red fruit accompanied
by a balsamic nuance. The flavor is warm,
not heavy, almost slender, lively, with
important but not scratchy tannins, fresh
and harmonious. A few bottles, presented
as Barolo Bricco Sarmassa since 1979 and
since 2011 as Riserva Vigna Bricco, interpret a
great vineyard at its best.

GIACOMO BORGOGNO & FIGLI

Via Gioberti 1
Barolo (CN)
borgogno.com
Year of establishment: 1761
Owner: the Farinetti
family
Average number of bottles
produced per year: 270,000

The Farinetti family took over
this historic winery in 2008,
preserving the winemaking
style linked to the strictest
tradition and innovating
greatly in the offer of labels,
thanks to the acquisition of
vineyards in the Tortonese
area for the production of
Timorasso, in San Marzano
Oliveto for Nizza and for
Barbera d'Asti, on the slopes
of the Sicilian volcano for
Etna. At the forefront is
always Barolo, from the
prestigious Cannubi, Liste,
and Fossati vineyards, the
jewel in the crown of the 106
acres of organically cultivated
property.

BAROLO RISERVA

First year of production: 1921
Average number of bottles produced
per year: 20,000
Grape variety: Nebbiolo

It is made from selected grapes from the
different crus and matured for four years
in large Slavonian oak barrels, with a
brief pause in cement before bottling. The
aromas are crisp and open on floral hints
of violets and roses, joined by small berries
and licorice; the palate is of pleasant acidity,
incisive but not biting in the tannins, of rare
harmony. It has just turned a century old,
an interpretation of tradition at the highest
level.

BROVIA

Frazione Garbelletto, via
Alba-Barolo 145
Castiglione Falletto (CN)
brovia.net
Year of establishment: 1863
Owner: Elena Brovia, Alex
Sanchez
Average number of bottles
produced per year: 70,000

It is not enough to have
excellent vineyards, to work
them well, to use quality
barrels: if this were the case,
many of the 14 million bottles
of Barolo produced each
year would be very good.
What is needed, instead, is
that sensitivity made up of a
thousand and one details that
the Brovias manage to pay
attention to in every Barolo
production, from Villero to
Brea Vigna Ca' Mia to Rocche
di Castiglione. High quality is
also offered with the Barbera
d'Alba Sorì del Drago and with
the Dolcetto d'Alba Vignavillej,
the fruit of a total of 39.5 acres
cultivated organically.

BAROLO VILLERO

First year of production: 1991
Average number of bottles produced
per year: 6,000
Grape variety: Nebbiolo

Matured in large wood, it demonstrates at
the highest level the historically recognized
qualities of the Villero cru: red flowers and
black fruits, delicate sweet spices enlivened
by a hint of eucalyptus, an undertone of
damp earth to give grit and complexity. The
palate is remarkably structured, with very
dense but not overpowering tannins, full
of fruity pulp, moderately acidic, very long,
sharp.

COMM. G.B. BURLOTTO

Via Vittorio Emanuele 28
Verduno (CN)
burlotto.com
Year of establishment: 1850
Owners: Marina Burlotto,
Fabio Alessandria
Average number of bottles
produced per year: 90,000

One of Barolo's most
prestigious historic wineries,
founded by Giovan Battista
Burlotto, began winning
medals at international wine
competitions in 1886. Today,
Fabio Alessandria continues
along that path, in turn
reaping often stellar scores
on both sides of the ocean.
The 39.5 acres under vine
give rise to important Barolo
offerings: Monvigliero (in
Verduno), Cannubi (in Barolo),
and Castelletto (in Monforte
d'Alba) are joined by the prized
Acclivi, a blend of all the crus
in the commune of Verduno.

BAROLO MONVIGLIERO

First year of production: 1982
Average number of bottles produced
per year: 7,500
Grape variety: Nebbiolo

It matures for a good three years in casks,
after the grapes grown on the 5 acres
dedicated to this label have been vinified as
whole clusters, hence not destemmed, and
macerated for two months in a submerged
vat. This technique adds some vegetal
notes to the classic aromas of small red
fruits, which are joined by mineral notes of
cinchona and fresh hints of citrus. The taste
is sinuous, well marked by a slight tannicity,
refined, enveloping, and prestigious.

DOMENICO CLERICO

Località Manzoni 22/A
Monforte d'Alba (Cuneo)
domenicoclerico.com
Year of establishment: 1976
Owner: Giuliana Viberti
Average number of bottles
produced per year: 120,000

Domenico Clerico was a
great innovator: he put the
vineyard first and wanted
winemaking in the cellar to
be such as to make Barolo
one of the great wines of the
world, a concept that fifty
years ago was anything but
taken for granted. He was
therefore one of the first in
the Langhe to equip himself
with rotomacerators and
barriques, to express his idea
of a long-lived and at the
same time enjoyable wine a
few years after the harvest,
with immediate international
success. Giuliana Viberti
continues the approach
desired by her husband with
equal decision and skill, with
59 acres cultivated organically
in prestigious locations.

BAROLO GINESTRA CIABOT MENTIN

First year of production: 1982
Average number of bottles produced
per year: 6,000
Grape variety: Nebbiolo

It is no longer just barriques, but also
large barrels for the winery's flagship
Barolo, whose grapes come from the highly
prized Ginestra cru of Monforte d'Alba,
famous both for its power of flavor and
for the balsamic aromas that characterize
it. Blueberries and blond spices complete
the picture, followed by a palate of precise
harmony, long and fascinating, with little
astringency and beautiful freshness. One of
the great Langa classics.

CAVALLOTTO - TENUTA BRICCO BOSCHIS

Via Alba-Monforte 102
Castiglione Falletto (CN)
cavallotto.com
Year of establishment: 1928
Owner: the Cavallotto
family
Average number of bottles
produced per year: 95,000

Alfio Cavallotto is a careful
interpreter of the Nebbiolo
grapes that grow on his
62 acres, where he applies
cultivation that is not only
organic but totally respectful
of the environment, so much
so that he prefers to defend the
vines with herbal infusions
rather than copper. In the
cellar, he carries out long
maturations in large Slavonian
oak barrels to preserve the
purity of the grapes, obtaining
a Barolo with a decidedly
traditional style, even a
little gruff and closed in the
first years, endowed with a
persuasive complexity that
grows for decades in the
bottle.

BAROLO BRICCO BOSCHIS RISERVA VIGNA SAN GIUSEPPE

First year of production: 1968
Average number of bottles produced
per year: 9,000
Grape variety: Nebbiolo

The aromas constantly lead to violets and
small berries, with various spicy nuances
and fine hints of eucalyptus and pine resin.
The palate is austere and voluminous, with
an invigorating acidity and tannins that are
always present but never aggressive until a
rich finish in which blackberries and licorice
emerge. Classicism.

ELVIO COGNO

Via Ravera 2
Novello (CN)
elviocogno.com
Year of establishment: 1990
Owners: Nadia Cogno,
Valter Fissore
Average number of bottles
produced per year: 110,000

Valter Fissore, oenological
heir to the great cellar master
who was his father-in-law
Elvio Cogno, has built a
splendid cellar, surrounded
by his 37 acres of vines in
different positions of the ever
more famous Ravera cru. The
production is centered on
Barolo, proposed in four fine
versions all united by a rare
technical precision, always
crisp and clean, never rustic,
woody, or too concentrated,
interpreting the most refined
classicism of the Nebbiolo
grape.

BAROLO RAVERA BRICCO PERNICE

First year of production: 2005
Average number of bottles produced
per year: 4,000
Grape variety: Nebbiolo

It matures for thirty months in a large
Slavonian oak cask and expresses in finesse
the most typical personality of Barolo
from this area: never too tannic, never
too spicy, and never lacking in freshness,
always very fruity and always vivid on a
rich, multifaceted palate. Small red berries
are joined by violet petals, then the palate
is sinuous and incisive without becoming
astringent, with a drinkability that is as
complex as it is pleasant.

GIACOMO CONTERNO
Località Ornati 2
Monforte d'Alba (CN)
Year of establishment: 1900
Owner: Roberto Conterno
Average number of bottles
produced per year: 60,000

Roberto Conterno has
managed to avoid being
conditioned by the heavy
inheritance he received from
his father Giovanni, who had
handed him a Monfortino
already firmly established in
the pantheon of the world's
great wines. He has proceeded
to make acquisitions that
have significantly broadened
the oenological offering. In
addition to the purchase
of the Nervi winery in
Gattinara, there are now
also vineyards—42 acres in
total—in the Arione and
Cerretta crus, with results
that are themselves worthy of
praise. Magnificent vineyards,
large barrels, careful attention
to every detail, splendid
classicism, a legendary name.

BAROLO RISERVA MONFORTINO
First year of production: 1924
Average number of bottles produced per
year: 10,000
Grape variety: Nebbiolo

Now reserved for collectors or very wealthy
enthusiasts, Monfortino is always a
great wine, only released in the vintages
considered perfect by Roberto Conterno,
who, for example, decided not to produce
the highly celebrated 2016 vintage. Matured
for about five years in large barrels, it is the
quintessence of Barolo's clearest aromas, from
rose to currant, eucalyptus to leather, violet
to spice. The palate is austere and powerful,
rich in soft tannins, enveloping, and very
long, with a finish that elegantly repeats the
entire olfactory spectrum. It may not be the
best Barolo in every vintage, but it is always a
masterpiece.

ETTORE GERMANO
Località Cerretta 1
Serralunga d'Alba (CN)
germanoettore.com
Year of establishment: 1975
Owner: Sergio Germano
Average number of bottles
produced per year: 170,000

Sergio Germano's first
work experience was as
an agronomist, but it was
not long before he showed
brilliant skills as a cellarman,
first making Barolo then his
multi-award-winning Langhe
Riesling Hérzu, and finally
Metodo Classico sparkling
wines, including several Alta
Langa DOCG productions.
There are five labels of Barolo:
in addition to the Lazzarito
Reserve, the one from
Serralunga d'Alba, the Prapò,
the Cerretta, and, since 2010,
the area's most famous cru, the
Vignarionda. A level of quality
of rare pleasantness across the
entire range, which originates
from 49.5 acres organically
cultivated.

BAROLO RISERVA LAZZARITO
First year of production: 2003
Average number of bottles produced
per year: 5,500
Grape variety: Nebbiolo

It is the fruit of very old Nebbiolo vines in
this exciting Riserva Lazzarito, persuasive
on the nose thanks to notes of dried violets
and currants, against a refined balsamic and
licorice background. The taste demonstrates
the greatness of this cru at its best, rich
as it is with soft and caressing tannins,
powerful but also fresh and with a very long
persistence. The aging of at least two years
in large oak barrels helps to highlight the
fruity purity of this great Barolo.

RENATO CORINO
Frazione Annunziata,
Borgata Pozzo 49/A
La Morra (CN)
renatocorino.it
Year of establishment: 2005
Owner: the Corino family
Average number of bottles
produced per year: 50,000

There are only red grapes in
the scenic winery and the 20
acres under vine of Renato
Corino and his son Stefano,
with Nebbiolo in evidence in
five versions of Barolo. The
oenological style is devoted
to elegance, avoiding any
rusticity or roughness, also
thanks to the intervention of
small French barrels during
the maturation of the wines.
The award-winning Rocche
dell'Annunziata, Riserva, and
Arborina have recently been
joined by the refined Barolo
Roncaglie, which bears the
name of the young author,
Stefano Corino, on its label.
Other medals also came from
the complex Barbera d'Alba
Pozzo.

BAROLO ROCCHE
DELL'ANNUNZIATA
First year of production: 2005
Average number of bottles produced
per year: 4,500
Grape variety: Nebbiolo

It is made in small wood and in one of
the most famous crus of the entire Barolo
area, renowned for the innate elegance
and harmony it brings to its grapes,
always characterized by a delicious
balsamic nuance. The aromas are complex
amidst memories of red fruits and sweet
spices, with a delicate smokiness in the
background. The sip is enveloping and well-
balanced, incisive but not astringent, with
acidic freshness right through to the long
finish where a hint of licorice is appreciated.

ELIO GRASSO
Località Ginestra 40
Monforte d'Alba (CN)
eliograsso.it
Year of establishment: 1928
Owner: the Grasso family
Average number of bottles
produced per year: 95,000

Moving from banker to
winegrower, Elio Grasso
has invented not only a new
profession but also a passion
that has led him to notable
achievements, including the
construction of a new wine
cellar of great charm. In the
splendid tunnel dedicated to
fermentation, large barrels are
increasingly taking the place
of barriques. Today, it is his
son Gianluca who presides
over the vinification of the
grapes from the family's 44.5
acres, in which the Barolo
offerings Ginestra Casa Maté,
Gavarini Chiniera, and Riserva
Rüncot stand out.

BAROLO GINESTRA CASA MATÉ
First year of production: 1978
Average number of bottles produced
per year: 20,000
Grape variety: Nebbiolo

Abandoning the woody modernity of its
early years, Casa Maté matures in Slavonian
oak, shows a strict adherence to classic
canons and succeeds in fully expressing the
splendid personality of one of the Langhe's
most celebrated vineyards, Ginestra. In
the aromas, the mint and eucalyptus
notes typical of this hillside appear in the
forefront, together with classic red flowers
and dried violets. Silky tannins, savoriness,
and structure make for an unforgettable
taste.

MARIO MARENGO

Località Serradenari 2/A
La Morra (CN)
Year of establishment: 1899
Owner: Mario Marengo
Average number of bottles
produced per year: 35,000

The cellar is spacious, suitable
for storing both the French
barriques and the numerous
steel tanks in which the
vinification of the different
plots of the 17 acres of vines,
located between Barolo,
Castiglione Falletto, and
Vezza d'Alba, takes place. The
oenological style is secure
and precise, playing on the
balance between the power of
the Nebbiolo grapes and the
delicate spiciness of oak. Few
bottles, prestigious quality.

BAROLO BRUNATE

First year of production: 1974
Average number of bottles produced
per year: 7,000
Grape variety: Nebbiolo

The barely noticeable wood and classic
Brunate violet give precise elegance to
aromas that include spices, underbrush
fruits, and a gentle touch of tar. The palate
has dense tannins that are quite sensitive
in the first few years of bottle aging, and
is important and dense, with a refined
balsamic finish. A refined and convincing
modernity.

GIUSEPPE MASCARELLO E FIGLIO

Via Borgonuovo 108
Monchiero (CN)
mascarello1881.com
Year of establishment: 1881
Owner: the Mascarello
family
Average number of bottles
produced per year: 60,000

A winery that in over a
century of activity has
become a point of reference
for lovers of traditional
Barolo, complex only thanks
to the expressiveness of the
Nebbiolo grapes, never refined
thanks to small barrels or
exaggerated concentrations.
The small production comes
from 30 acres under vine
and includes the main types
of Langa, but it is obviously
Barolo that occupies the scene:
Monprivato is joined by the
unobtainable and expensive
Riserva Cà d'Morissio, the
sumptuous Villero, and the
fruitier Perno Vigna Santo
Stefano, all of rare purity and
faithful to the model dictated
by classicism.

BAROLO MONPRIVATO

First year of production: 1970
Average number of bottles produced
per year: 18,000
Grape variety: Nebbiolo

This famous label was born on 15 acres of
the splendid Monprivato cru in Castiglione
Falletto, of which Mauro Mascarello is the
sole interpreter. The aging in large casks
leaves ample room for complex aromas of
small fruits and red flowers, not without an
austerity of great classicism in which vegetal
hints of roots and minerals of damp earth
can be detected. The flavor is of moderate
power, delicate in its tannicity, refreshing in
its acidity enlivened by a touch of savoriness,
and splendid in its slightly balsamic finish.

BARTOLO MASCARELLO

Via Roma 19
Barolo (CN)
Year of establishment: 1918
Owner: Maria Teresa
Mascarello
Average number of bottles
produced per year: 30,000

Maria Teresa Mascarello has
not let herself be intimidated
by the weight of the legacy left
to her in 2005 by her father
Bartolo, acknowledged as the
most cultured winemaker in
Langa, the most farsighted
defender of the purity of Barolo
against the Americanophile
temptations deriving from the
use of small French woods,
and the progressive enemy of
the political right. Famous and
rare is the label he designed
in colored pencils, bearing
the words "no barrique, no
Berlusconi"—and as, finally,
an excellent Barolo vinemaker.
The result is that the small
production continues at an
excellent level, with even more
refined and harmonious tones.
Barolo is flanked by small, valid
productions of Barbera d'Alba,
Langhe Nebbiolo, and Dolcetto
d'Alba.

BAROLO

First year of production: 1918
Average number of bottles produced
per year: 19,000
Grape variety: Nebbiolo

In keeping with tradition, Barolo is made
from small plots in several fine vineyards:
Cannubi (2.5 acres), Rocche dell'Annunziata
(3 acres), Bussia Monrobiolo (1 acre),
San Lorenzo (0.7 acres), Ruè (1.2 acres).
Refinement takes place in large French
oak barrels, which give free rein to the
expression of the grapes: cinchona, violets,
roses, leather, and a hint of licorice that
increases with the years in the bottle; the
taste is always very well-balanced, not
astringent, lively, and fresh, with a finish of
balsamic tones.

MASSOLINO

Piazza Cappellano 8
Serralunga d'Alba (CN)
massolino.it
Year of establishment: 1896
Owner: the Massolino
family
Average number of bottles
produced per year: 360,000

A solid centuries-old tradition
that also shines in terms of
dynamism, as demonstrated
by the slow but continuous
increase in the area under
vines and owned, which has
now reached 123.5 acres thanks
to the latest acquisitions in
the Parussi cru in Castiglione
Falletto, and even in the
Barbaresco area in the Albesani
cru. The wines are all of
great classicism and extreme
stylistic refinement, so much
so that they have made this
winery an indispensable
reference point in the elite of
Langhe producers.

BAROLO RISERVA VIGNA RIONDA

First year of production: 1982
Average number of bottles produced
per year: 8,000
Grape variety: Nebbiolo

It is the perfect interpretation of the
characteristics of this celebrated cru,
considered by many to be the most
emblematic of the entire Barolo area:
power, complexity, balance, and refinement.
Matured in large casks, the nose highlights
fresh herbs combined with small fruits
against a background of pine and eucalyptus
resin. The taste is rich and textural, endowed
with enchanting tannins that are never
aggressive, sinuous and multifaceted, very
long, with hints of licorice in a joyful finish.
A wine as expensive and precious as the
vineyard that makes it.

ODDERO PODERI E CANTINE
Frazione Santa Maria 28
La Morra (CN)
oddero.it
Year of establishment: 1878
Owner: Mariacristina Oddero
Average number of bottles produced per year: 80,000

A prestigious winery steeped in history, it has vineyards in some of the most renowned crus in the Barolo area, from Brunate to Monvigliero, from Rocche di Castiglione to Bussia and Vignarionda, for a total of 89 acres under vine, including the Gallina cru in Barbaresco. The oenological style remains strictly classic, rather severe, with maceration on the skins lasting close to thirty days and the use of large barrels. The owner's results represent a fine overview of the MGAs of the Barolo area.

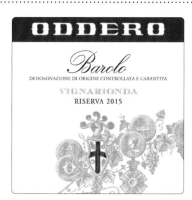

BAROLO RISERVA VIGNARIONDA
First year of production: 1985
Average number of bottles produced per year: 3,000
Grape variety: Nebbiolo

Born on just under 2.5 acres of the most sought-after and prestigious vineyard in the entire Barolo designation, it matures for forty months in Austrian oak and is put on the market seven years after the harvest. Extraordinary olfactory complexity, with black currants and blackberries combined with a dark spiciness of rare charm and a mentholated touch. Superlative on the palate, as powerful and rich in tannins and acidity as it is silky and enveloping. An expensive bottle, capable of improving for decades.

GIOVANNI ROSSO
Via Roddino 10/1
Serralunga d'Alba (CN)
giovannirosso.com
Year of establishment: 1960
Owner: Davide Rosso
Average number of bottles produced per year: 250,000

Davide Rosso has given an impetus and a new face to his father's winery, building a cellar equipped with a heliport and functional winemaking rooms. The grapes come from ten estate vineyards, as well as from the purchase of a few batches of grapes from neighboring vintners, for a total of 52 acres, with the Vigna Rionda, Serra, and Cerretta crus creating the most important Barolo selections. The approach to the wines is one of assured classicism, with an articulation, harmony, and balance that has few equals.

BAROLO VIGNARIONDA ESTER CANALE ROSSO
First year of production: 2007
Average number of bottles produced per year: 2,000
Grape variety: Nebbiolo

A wine that has quickly become an oenological legend, expensive and sought-after not so much for the small number of bottles made as for the grace, elegance, complexity, and absolute pleasantness that Davide Rosso manages to extract from his small portion of the magical Vigna Rionda. An unparalleled blend of power and delicacy.

LUCIANO SANDRONE
Via Pugnane 4
Barolo (CN)
sandroneluciano.com
Year of establishment: 1978
Owner: the Sandrone family
Average number of bottles produced per year: 95,000

Luciano Sandrone, who passed away in January 2023, was an indispensable point of reference in the history of modern Barolo: he started out in his home garage and immediately made people appreciate his sensitivity as a cellarman, capable of carefully interpreting even the most difficult vintages, a very modern interpreter of the aromatic purity and harmonious taste balance of Barolo. Six labels are produced on the estate's 67 acres and in the large new cellar, all of them very well cared for and the fruit of typical Langhe vines: Nebbiolo, Barbera, Dolcetto. The famous Cannubi Boschis (now Aleste) and Le Vigne were joined in 2013 by Barolo Vite Talin, as rich in personality as it is rare.

BAROLO ALESTE
First year of production: 2013
Average number of bottles produced per year: 9,800
Grape variety: Nebbiolo

Luciano Sandrone has always believed that the ideal format for maturing Barolo is the *tonneau*, and it is in these French casks that Aleste (an acronym derived from his grandchildren Alessia and Stefano) stays for thirty months. This is the new name given since 2013 to Barolo Cannubi Boschis, the wine that has created the winery's worldwide fame since 1985. Rich in red fruits, violets, and sweet spices, on the palate it is of superior harmony, always very expressive, and never astringent, rich but not concentrated, of refined elegance. An unforgettable Barolo.

PAOLO SCAVINO
Via Alba-Barolo 157
Castiglione Falletto (CN)
paoloscavino.com
Year of establishment: 1921
Owner: the Scavino family
Average number of bottles produced per year: 180,000

Enrico Scavino brought this splendid winery to international fame and continues to offer, together with his daughters Enrica and Elisa, bottles that make the history of modern Barolo. The 79 acres of vineyards are located in some of the most strategic and famous crus of the area, including Rocche dell'Annunziata—from which an award-winning Riserva is produced—Prapò, Ravera, Cannubi, and Monvigliero, together with Bric dël Fiasc, from which the flagship wine of the house comes. The company's production philosophy focuses on refinement.

BAROLO BRIC DËL FIASC
First year of production: 1978
Average number of bottles produced per year: 12,000
Grape variety: Nebbiolo

The position of the vineyard (MGA Fiasco di Castiglione Falletto) favors the harmonious union of the more powerful and tannic traits of the vineyards in the Serralunga d'Alba area, with the softer and fruitier ones typical of La Morra, in a taste balance of absolute quality. The aromas open on small berries of undergrowth and bay leaves, well supported by hints of juniper and violets; the palate is of absolute precision, crisp and balanced, slightly fresh and delicately astringent, very long. A marvel of pleasantness and complexity.

VIETTI

Piazza Vittorio Veneto 5
Castiglione Falletto (CN)
vietti.com
Year of establishment: 1873
Owner: the Krause Group
Average number of bottles
produced per year: 400,000

A winery founded at the end
of the nineteenth century by
Carlo Vietti, which became
famous in the 1960s thanks
to the production of the
first single-vineyard Barolo
wines. It has definitively
established itself in the elite
of the big international names
in the last thirty years, as a
result of the oenological and
organizational skill of Luca
Currado Vietti. In 2016, the
American Krause Group took
over ownership, confirming
the production approach
and proceeding with the
acquisition of important
new vineyards, not only in
the Barolo area but also in
Barbaresco and the Colli
Tortonesi.

BAROLO RISERVA VILLERO

First year of production: 1982
Average number of bottles produced
per year: 3,500
Grape variety: Nebbiolo

Always known as a top-quality vineyard,
especially for the structural power that
manifests itself on the palate, the Villero
Riserva proposed by Vietti is enriched with
very dense aromas of fruit, from plums
to blueberries, and refined notes of dark
spices, in a prestigious complexity that is
found intact in the finish. The expensive
bottle is embellished with designer labels
in a series that began in 1982 with Gianni
Gallo and has continued with images from
famous international designers, from Robert
Cunningham to Renzo Piano.

VIGNETI MASSA

Piazza G. Capsoni 10
Monleale (AL)
Year of establishment: 1879
Owner: the Massa family
Average number of bottles
produced per year: 150,000

Tireless prophet and evocative
promoter of the Timorasso
grape, Walter Massa has
reconstructed the image of the
Colli Tortonesi and convinced
his fellow winemakers to focus
on this white, which in just
a few years has conquered
wine critics, now often being
included among the most
important Italian wines. In the
cellar, the fruit of 74 acres of
property like Barbera, Freisa,
and Moscato are also vinified
with conviction, but there is no
doubt that the spotlights are
on the labels proposed with
the toponym of Derthona,
the ancient Tortona: Costa
del Vento, Montecitorio, and
Sterpi , capable of improving
in glass for decades.

DERTHONA COSTA DEL VENTO

First year of production: 1987
Average number of bottles produced
per year: 6,500
Grape variety: Timorasso

Born as Colli Tortonesi DOC, Walter Massa's
Costa del Vento is a very multifaceted white
wine from Timorasso grapes, endowed
with that personality which, after a few
years of aging in the bottle, is often
summarized with the word "mineral," in
this case meaning aromas of chalk and
hydrocarbons. The structure is savory, rich,
and harmonious, as befits a label that is
leading the oenological renaissance of an
entire area.

MARZIANO ABBONA

Borgata San Luigi 40
Dogliani (CN)
abbona.com
Year of establishment: 1970
Owner: Marziano Abbona
Average number of bottles
produced per year: 330,000

The goal that Marziano
Abbona set himself fifty years
ago has been achieved: to build
a splendid cellar in which the
great wines of the Langhe
are made, with Barolo in first
place, Dogliani DOCG as a
great expression of his native
land, then an articulated
range of all local types, from
Langhe Nebbiolo to Barbera
d'Alba, closing the circle with
a successful white, Cinerino.
The 148 acres are cultivated
organically and from here
twenty labels are born that are
always clear and of exquisite
workmanship, headed by the
Barolos Cerviano-Merli and
Ravera along with Papà Celso.

DOGLIANI PAPÀ CELSO

First year of production: 1975
Average number of bottles produced
per year: 38,000
Grape variety: Dolcetto

Marziano Abbona has found his recipe to
get out of the confusion between those who
want Dolcetto grapes to give concentrated
and woody wines, and those who want them
nicely drinkable: Papà Celso ages only in
steel and does not give up offering richness
and complexity, enhancing those fruity
characteristics so typical of Dogliani. There
are blackberries and plums, then refreshing
herbs to give elegance and articulation.
Great grip on the palate, suffused in the
tannins, and lively in the acidity, silky and
long, of rare pleasantness. The reference
point for wines from Dolcetto grapes.

FAVARO

Strada Chiusure 1/bis
Piverone (TO)
Year of establishment: 1992
Owner: the Favaro family
Average number of bottles
produced per year: 20,000

This small winery has
become famous thanks to
the production of rich and
persuasive Erbaluce di Caluso
DOCG, far from that biting
acidity that was once the
main characteristic of this
typology. After a few years
of experimentation, which
began by paying particular
attention to reducing the
yields in the vineyard, the
first acknowledgments from
critics and the market began
in 1996, with a success that has
continued to grow. The two
white labels—Le Chiusure
and 13 Mesi—are joined by
tiny productions based on
Nebbiolo, Freisa, and Syrah
made from the 8.5 acres of the
property.

ERBALUCE DI CALUSO
TREDICIMESI

First year of production: 2002
Average number of bottles produced
per year: 2,000
Grape variety: Erbaluce

Most of the wine matures in concrete, while
the rest stays in French wood that is not
new: after thirteen months the two lots
are assembled, with a result of confidant
harmony. The aromas range from peach to
rosemary, on a stimulating tropical citrus
base. The palate remains fresh and savory as
is required by the Erbaluce grapes, with the
final addition of honeyed and floral aromas
that give a pleasant sensation of complexity
and elegance.

ANTONIOLO

Corso Valsesia 27
Gattinara (VC)
Year of establishment: 1948
Owner: the Antoniolo
family
Average number of bottles
produced per year: 70,000

A prominent name not only in upper Piedmont but nationally, thanks to rigorous qualitative choices starting from the processing of the 37 acres of vineyards, which are then vinified and offered separately for fifty years. The production is centered on the Nebbiolo grape, with the aim of achieving elegance and complexity without the excessive contribution of the aging woods, thus also preserving the peculiarities deriving from the mineral characteristics of the soils of the area. The three versions of Gattinara Riserva are constantly included in the top of the regional qualitative lists.

GATTINARA RISERVA OSSO SAN GRATO

First year of production: 1974
Average number of bottles produced per year: 3,500
Grape variety: Nebbiolo

It is also elegant in the slightly fresher and more vegetal notes that distinguish Nebbiolo from upper Piedmont, with rhubarb joining black fruits and a hint of citrus peel of considerable complexity. The taste is powerful, without glyceric softness, with beautiful tannins, and perceptible acidity, with a finish that gives a gentle hint of tar in an articulated whole well harmonized by the three years of aging in cask.

GIANCARLO TRAVAGLINI

Via delle Vigne 36
Gattinara (VC)
travaglinigattinara.it
Year of establishment: 1958
Owner: Cinzia Travaglini
Average number of bottles produced per year: 230,000

Cinzia Travaglini, together with her family, today manages the business founded and enabled by her father Giancarlo with ability and innovative spirit, an absolute point of reference, and not only for its significant production, of the whole of upper Piedmont. The 136 acres of property are dedicated to the Nebbiolo grape, which gives rise to six labels among which, in addition to those dedicated to the three Gattinara productions, there also stands out a curious version in the Metodo Classico, the Nebolè.

GATTINARA RISERVA

First year of production: 1958
Average number of bottles produced per year: 25,000
Grape variety: Nebbiolo

Intense notes of juniper and licorice dominate the aromatic spectrum, yet not without a mineral contribution of wet earth and a hint of dried citrus. In the mouth there is no shortage of acidity and sapidity typical of upper Piedmont, but the taste sensation is overall warm and rather enveloping, robust, moderately tannic, and incisive up to the delicious finish marked by fresh hints of pine resin.

NICOLA BERGAGLIO

Frazione Rovereto 59
Gavi (AL)
Year of establishment: 1946
Owner: the Bergaglio
family
Average number of bottles produced per year: 150,000

A classic family farm, a demonstration that results can be obtained by intelligently applying the traditional knowledge relating to both the countryside and the cellar, integrated only by those operational precautions that are allowed by simple and noninvasive technology. The 49 acres of property are cultivated exclusively with Cortese grapes and give rise to three labels, all aged in steel only: the complex Gavi from the municipality of Gavi Rovereto Minaia, the floral Gavi from the municipality of Gavi Rovereto, and the more immediate Gavi. A constant of quality established over time, appreciated internationally.

GAVI DEL COMUNE DI GAVI ROVERETO MINAIA

First year of production: 1987
Average number of bottles produced per year: 75,000
Grape variety: Cortese

It is the recognized standard-bearer of the appellation, capable of improving for decades in the bottle, offered at a decidedly affordable price. The nose is articulated on notes of white flowers on a background of almond and medicinal herbs; the taste is full of strength, juicy, always slightly fresh, and almost sapid, captivating in its simple richness. Over the years, very fine notes of flint open up, completing the variegated expression of one of the most interesting whites of Piedmont.

VILLA SPARINA

Frazione Monterotondo 56
Gavi (AL)
villasparina.it
Year of establishment: 1974
Owner: the Moccagatta
family
Average number of bottles produced per year: 650,000

In fifty years the Moccagattas have built a splendid establishment, aimed not only at wine production but also at welcoming and accommodating tourists. The 161 acres of vineyards are largely dedicated to the Cortese grape, from which various labels are born: from Gavi aged for ten years to the Metodo Classico, from the immediate Gavi of the municipality of Gavi to the Monterotondo complex. Among the productions in red, the Barbera del Monferrato Superiore Rivalta stands out.

GAVI DEL COMUNE DI GAVI MONTEROTONDO

First year of production: 1997
Average number of bottles produced per year: 10,000
Grape variety: Cortese

The importance of this Gavi derives more from the strict selection of the grapes than from the cellar techniques, where a small part of the wine is aged in wood and then joined to the remainder that has rested in steel only. The aromas are of ripe white fruits, pears in particular, and orange peels, on a slightly spicy background. The flavor is of good freshness, well balanced, endowed with important fruity pulp, and enriched in the finish by hints of medicinal herbs. It is also suitable for aging in the bottle for a few years.

ELIO ALTARE
Frazione Annunziata 51
La Morra (CN)
elioaltare.com
Year of establishment: 1976
Owner: the Altare family
Average number of bottles
produced per year: 70,000

Elio Altare set the standard,
handing down not only
knowledge but also trust
and pride to many young
winemakers who, in the 1980s,
approached winemaking and
opened cellars that have become
famous throughout the world.
There are two maxims to which
he is particularly attached: his
"Gentlemen, the barrique is not
a passing fad" and that of Oscar
Wilde, "Tradition is a successful
innovation." A master in the
treatment of the barrels and in
maturation in wood as much as
in the sustainable cultivation
of his 27 acres, he continues to
create memorable labels both
in the DOCG Barolo—from
Arborina to the Riserva Cerretta
Vigna Bricco to the rare Brunate
and Cannubi—and in the DOC
Langhe—Giarborina, The Villa,
and Larigi.

LANGHE ROSSO LARIGI
First year of production: 1989
Average number of bottles produced
per year: 2,500
Grape variety: Barbera

The quintessence of the Barbera vine, in
a version that manages to express three
characteristics that this cultivar does not
always have: elegance, complexity, and
longevity. The notes of small black fruits
predominate, from blackberry to cherry,
accompanied by delicate spices and a refined
note of smoke. The mouth maintains
excellent freshness; it is vivid and dynamic
even if rich in substance and alcohol, of rare
elegance and absolute pleasantness.

CAUDRINA
Strada Brosia 21
Castiglione Tinella (CN)
caudrina.it
Year of establishment: 1970
Owner: Romano Dogliotti
Average number of bottles
produced per year: 180,000

Romano Dogliotti, after
learning the production
techniques from his father
Redento, took over the
company in 1997, with the
important collaboration of
the whole family. Always
passionate about Moscato,
however, he also wanted
to devote himself to red
wines, achieving remarkable
goals, especially with Nizza
Montevenere. From the 62
acres of vineyards, together
with the Moscato d'Asti La
Galeisa and La Caudrina,
the Asti La Selvatica was
born, which boasts the label
created by the famous distiller
Romano Levi in 1993.

MOSCATO D'ASTI LA GALEISA
First year of production: 1989
Average number of bottles produced
each year: 15,000
Grape variety: Moscato Bianco di
Canelli

Irresistible aromas of grapefruit, orange,
raisins, and sage blend with white flowers
and a mineral touch of chalk in a very
intense and absolutely pleasant swirl. As
per the style of the house, the sweetness is
present but not overwhelming, the acidity is
lively and sinuous, the bubbles delicate and
appetizing.

CA' D' GAL
Strada Vecchia di
Valdivilla 1
Santo Stefano Belbo (CN)
cadgal.it
Year of establishment: 1990
Owner: Alessandro Boido
Average number of bottles
produced per year: 80,000

Alessandro Boido is the
cantor of the rich, dense, and
fascinating Moscato that is
born in the vineyard before in
the cellar, far from that idea
of a sweet sparkling wine
that in past years has been
the fortune—but also the
curse—of an entire area. Its 32
acres of vines, often advanced
in years, have low yields and
allow for a considerable sugar
concentration, which is then
managed by creating different
types, from the famous
Moscato d'Asti Vigna Vecchia
to Lumine to Sant'Ilario, with
a small space dedicated to Asti.

MOSCATO D'ASTI CANELLI
SANT'ILARIO
First year of production: 2014
Average number of bottles produced
per year: 12,000
Grape variety: Moscato Bianco di
Canelli

The aromas are captivating, deep, and very
intense, characterized by a sweet swirl of
tropical fruits, citrus fruits, and peaches
combined with fresh hints of sage and mint:
the maximum of olfactory expressiveness.
The mouth is soft and delicately sugary
but also decidedly acidic, with a fine
effervescence that enhances freshness
and drinkability. An exquisite tasting for
everyone, instructive even for those who
have doubts about low-alcohol sweet wines.

MICHELE CHIARLO
Strada Statale Nizza-
Canelli 99
Calamandrana (AT)
michelechiarlo.it
Year of establishment: 1956
Owner: the Chiarlo family
Average number of
bottles produced per year:
1,100,000

An imposing winery that from
the beginning set itself the
intention of enhancing the
native Piedmontese vines,
soon becoming a prestigious
name in the field of wines
based on both Barbera (Nizza
Montemareto, Nizza La Court
Vigna Veja, Nizza La Court)
and Nebbiolo (Barolo Cerequio
Riserva, Barolo Cerequio,
Barolo Cannubi, Barbaresco
Asili, Barbaresco Faset). In
the 247 acres of vineyards
owned, there are also whites,
in particular Gavi and Moscato
d'Asti. A precious Piedmontese
wine institution, enriched by
the Art Park La Court and the
Palás Cerequio, both worth
visiting.

NIZZA RISERVA LA COURT
First year of production: 1996
Average number of bottles produced
per year: 16,000
Grape variety: Barbera

Labeled as Barbera d'Asti Superiore until
2014, today it represents an essential
reference within the young DOCG Nizza. It
is characterized on the nose by dark fruits
such as plums and soft balsamic hints,
then the sip unfolds ample, structured, and
elegant, balanced by the beautiful freshness
typical of the vine, up to a finish in which
fine spicy and fruity hints emerge, from
cocoa with black cherry. A precise expression
of the vitality and grandeur of the Barbera
grape variety.

TENUTA OLIM BAUDA
Regione Prata 50
Incisa Scapaccino (AT)
tenutaolimbauda.it
Year of establishment: 1961
Owner: the Bertolino
family
Average number of bottles
produced per year: 200,000

In sixty years of activity,
the winery has built a
solid reputation as a great
interpreter of the Barbera
vine, available in four different
versions: Barbera d'Asti DOC,
Barbera d'Asti Superiore
DOCG, Nizza DOCG, and
Nizza Riserva Bauda DOCG.
The other labels of the house,
all worth tasting, mainly
include the Grignolino and
Freisa d'Asti reds, together
with the white Gavi and
Moscato d'Asti. The 74 acres
of vineyards, organically
farmed, coalesce in the hill that
surrounds the beautiful villa
where the winery is based.

NIZZA RISERVA BAUDA
First year of production: 2015
Average number of bottles produced
per year: 14,000
Grape variety: Barbera

The aging in wood lasts thirty months and
gives just a few spicy facets to a wine that is
characterized by ample aromas of red fruits,
from plums to blackberries, and by a palate
that is powerful and structured but at the
same time fresh, dynamic, and an excellent
reflection of the original characteristics of
the grape. Of enjoyable drinkability and a
great interpretation of the Barbera grape.

MONCHIERO CARBONE
Via Santo Stefano Roero 2
Canale (CN)
monchierocarbone.com
Year of establishment: 1990
Owner: Francesco
Monchiero
Average number of bottles
produced per year: 210,000

Francesco Monchiero's project
is ambitious and farsighted:
to demonstrate that the Roero
area is able to offer red and
white wines of international
significance, through the labels
of his cellar on the one hand
and by bringing together all
the producers in a collective
protection consortium on the
other. Its bottles are born from
74 acres of vineyards and from
continuous experimentation in
winemaking, with amphorae
that are combined with French
and Austrian barrels, giving
results that have already been
recognized and awarded by
international critics. Roero
Bianco and Roero Rosso
dominate the stage, but a
well-deserved space is firmly
occupied by the persuasive
Barbera d'Alba MonBirone.

ROERO RISERVA RENESIO INCISA
First year of production: 2016
Average number of bottles produced
per year: 3,500
Grape variety: Arneis

The wine that points the way for the precise
interpretation of Roero Bianco Riserva, a
recently established typology. No longer
just the classic and immediate aromas of
white fruits and herbs typical of the Arneis
grape, but references to almond, sage, and
linden, in a combination of confidant and
homogeneous elegance also favored by
partial aging in wood. The first taste never
hides the acidity but integrates it with
enveloping softness, deriving from the rich
fruity substance. The Roero Bianco Riserva
of the future.

GIOVANNI ALMONDO
Via San Rocco 26
Montà (CN)
giovannialmondo.com
Year of establishment: 1978
Owner: Domenico Almondo
Average number of bottles
produced per year: 140,000

Domenico Almondo is a
well-known protagonist
of the Roero winemaking
renaissance: he graduated in
agriculture in 1980 and he
immediately distinguished
himself—through his famous
Bricco delle Ciliegie—for the
enhancement of the Arneis
grape, demonstrating the
complexity and longevity of
this type. Equally valid are the
results, achieved today thanks
to the active participation of
his children, with the Nebbiolo
grape of the Bric Valdiana, which
has contributed to revitalizing
the red version of the Roero
DOCG. The new cellar welcomes
the grapes of 57 acres, cultivated
with organic methods.

ROERO ARNEIS LE RIVE DEL
BRICCO DELLE CILIEGIE
First year of production: 2014
Average number of bottles produced
per year: 3,500
Grape variety: Arneis

A small and always valid selection of grapes
carefully chosen to create the spearhead of
the company. The vinification takes place
mainly in steel, limiting the contact with
wood to 10%. In the aromas there are many
white flowers and wild herbs, while the
palate is solid and incisive, not very acidic
but enlivened by a tasty touch of sapidity. An
interpretation that makes the most of the
potential of the Arneis grape.

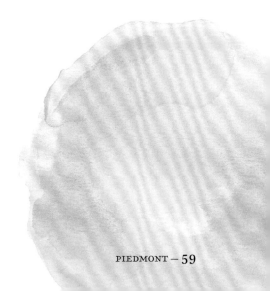

Valle d'Aosta

The wines of the Valle d'Aosta, a small region nestled between France, Switzerland, and Piedmont, whose seventy-four municipalities are home to one hundred and thirty thousand inhabitants, of which thirty-four thousand live in the capital Aosta, are increasingly appreciated around the world.

From an oenological point of view, Valle d'Aosta occupies a leading position among the Italian regions that have come to the fore in recent years in terms of production and overall quality.

The framework in which these brilliant results are set remains for the moment characterized by decidedly limited quantitative dimensions: just over 1,235 acres under vine and two million bottles per year, produced by sixty-seven wineries. And it is this last number that guarantees certain prospects of further growth for the sector: while until thirty years ago the production came almost entirely from the six community wine cellars strongly desired by the Autonomous Region of Valle d'Aosta, today these receive only 50% of the local grapes, and there are more and more young people who are beginning to make wine themselves and open new companies, united by the objective of respect and rigorous interpretation of the territory.

The blossoming of regional oenology has finally allowed, in 2022, for the birth of a new official body from which we expect not only promotional activities but also the reorganization of the production and regulatory panorama of the sector: the Consortium of Wines of Valle d'Aosta.

Large numbers of bottles can never be expected, but it is certain that the recovery of old vineyards is proceeding and that new plantings are also springing up at fairly high altitudes, given that the rise in temperatures now makes it possible to obtain excellent ripening of vines planted even above 1,640 to 1,968 feet. It is interesting to note that the classification of vineyards defines 5% as lowland, 35% as hillside, and 60% as mountainous.

Mountain wines are the fruit of truly heroic cultivation, in which freshness, vitality, and dynamism are the distinguishing features of all the vines grown. Among those selected, the productions that will emerge in the next few years based on Petite Arvine and Fumin grapes are to be followed with particular attention.

The DOC

● Valle d'Aosta / Vallée d'Aoste

With the following geographic indications:

– Blanc de Morgex et de La Salle
– Enfer d'Arvier
– Torrette
– Nus
– Chambave
– Arnad-Montjovet
– Donnas

MAIN VINES GROWN IN THE REGION

Chardonnay
→ International Grape Varieties

Cornalin
Its name derives from the dogwood, a wild shrub that grows in these forests. Also known as Corniola or Brolbanc and widespread in the Aosta Valley and Canton Valais—where it is called Humagne Rouge—it is cultivated from Arnad to Arvier, up to an altitude of 2,295 feet. Its elaborate genetic pedigree sees it descended from Prié, a Valle d'Aosta variety that is the ancestor of Mayolet, which when crossed with Petit Rouge produces Rouge du Pays, a vine cultivated in Switzerland under the name of Cornalin, which is the progenitor of the Valle d'Aosta Cornalin. It usually appears in blends together with other indigenous varieties such as Petit Rouge or Fumin, and enriches wines with aromas of black fruits, notes of bark and spices, a bright red color with violet hues, a full body, low acidity, and pleasant tannin.

Fumin

An ancient vine cultivated exclusively in Valle d'Aosta, with an intense and penetrating color, it owes its name to the smoky gray of the bloom that covers the ripe berries, forming a thin veil of wax that protects them from parasites and solar radiation, while preserving their moisture. Identified for the first time in 1836, in Lorenzo Gatta's *Saggio sulle viti e sui vini della Valle d'Aosta*, it is prized by winegrowers for its resistance to frost and for the consequent possibility of cultivating it in vineyards facing north, on the orographic left of the Dora. Fumin-based wines are rich in aromas of undergrowth and berries: blueberries, blackberries, mulberries, and juniper. The strong, fragrant character softens with age, adding hints of leather, spices, tobacco, and licorice to the bouquet on the finish. It is vinified both in blends and on its own.

Mayolet

A rare, almost extinct vine, indigenous to the Valle d'Aosta, where it is mentioned as early as 1787 between Saint-Vincent and Arvise, it is used to complement other grapes for its contribution in terms of alcohol content and smoothness.

Muscat

→ International Grape Varieties

Neyret

A descendant of the Petit Rouge, not to be confused with the Piedmontese Neretto variety, it appeared in Aosta as early as 1587. Described by Lorenzo Gatta as Neyret di Saint-Vincent, it disappeared due to phylloxera and was rediscovered in recent years, it is used in *coupage* with other local varieties to increase alcohol and color. Vinified in purity, it is striking for its intense dark red with violet hues and its taste of black currants and vegetal hints of earth and Asian spices.

Petit Rouge

Belonging to the Oriou family of vines, the basis of Torrette—one of the most popular wines in the region—it is an ancient indigenous variety that produces spicy wines with a characteristic perfume of violets and dried rosehips, accompanied by herbaceous notes of currants, blueberries, and raspberries, with a touch of blood oranges and bitter almonds on the finish.

Petite Arvine

Wisteria, peonies, hawthorn, violets, yellow plums, rennet apples, passion fruits, tangerines, grapefruits, and rhubarb: such is the aromatic richness of Petite Arvine, the region's most representative white grape variety, with an articulated potential that gives crystal-clear, vibrant, fresh, balanced, persistent wines with a distinct flavor. Imported from Valais, where it was already cultivated in the seventeenth century, it has found another *terroir* of choice in Valle d'Aosta.

Pinot Gris

→ International Grape Varieties

Pinot Noir

→ International Grape Varieties

Syrah

→ International Grape Varieties

......

Valle d'Aosta / Vallée d'Aoste DOC

This is a regional DOC, created in 1985, and it is subdivided into several categories. There is the indication of a grape variety, such as Pinot Noir, Pinot Gris, Pinot Blanc, Chardonnay, Petite Arvine, or Fumin, a toponym, like Chambave, Donnas, or Nus, or a type, like White. In this mountainous region, where the vines are often cultivated on terraces laboriously carved out of the rock, the producers' preference is for white varieties. There is, however, no lack of significant results with Pinot Noir, Fumin, and, increasingly, also with Nebbiolo.

There are seven subareas in the valley, designated according to the wine most representative of each area: Blanc de Morgex et de La Salle, Enfer d'Arvier, Torrette, Nus, Chambave, Arnad-Montjovet, Donnas.

An examination of the most widely used local grape varieties shows us that significant results have been achieved in recent years with Valle d'Aosta Petite Arvine, rich in aromatic herbs against a background of citrus fruits, with a powerful and enveloping feel, albeit with considerable acidity. Fumin is also enjoying a period of success thanks to its aromas of small black fruits and a palate in which a once less sought-after freshness is now appreciated. A note on the persuasive Vallée d'Aoste Nus Malvoisie: the variety is actually Pinot Gris, as captivating and soft in its aromas of white fruits, honey, and dried flowers as it is incisive and direct on the palate.

Of scenic importance, set between 2,950 and 3,935 feet above sea level on the slopes of Mont Blanc, this area dedicated to Blanc de Morgex et de La Salle is the only subzone in the Upper Valley where the Prié Blanc grape still produces both white wines and fine sparkling wines. The local Cave Mont Blanc, which has almost eighty conferring members, is the best example of this.

Almost all of the region's production, made by sixty-seven wineries of very different sizes, is included in the DOC, with an overall output that slightly exceeds two million bottles.

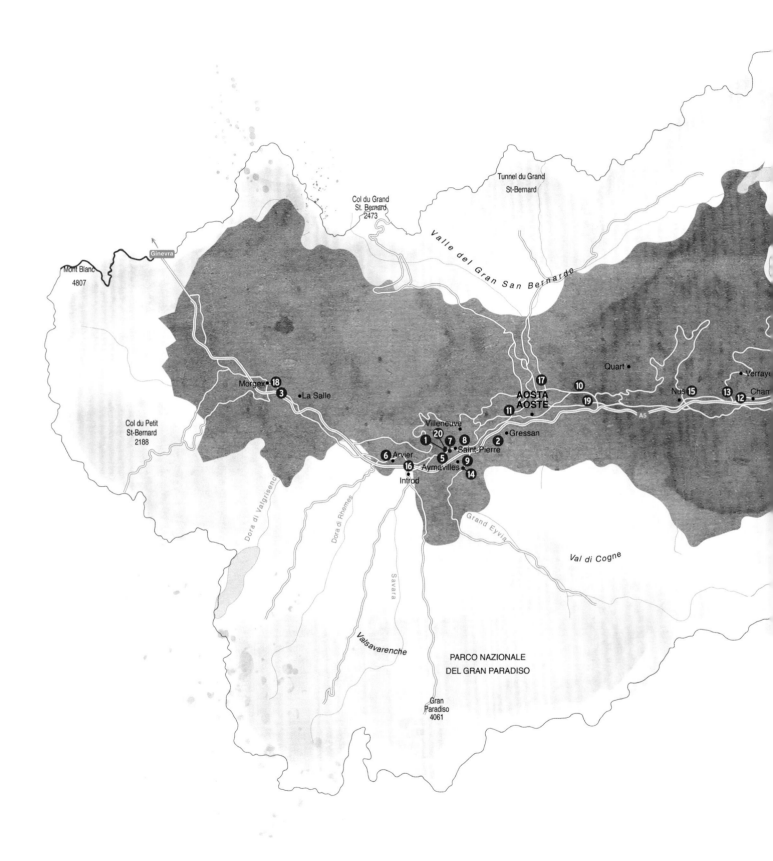

Mont Blanc
4807

Ginevra

Col du Grand
St. Bernard
2473

Tunnel du Grand
St-Bernard

Valle del Gran San Bernardo

Col du Petit
St-Bernard
2188

Morgex • **18**
3 • La Salle

Quart •

Verraye

17
10
AOSTA
AOSTE
11
19

Nus **15**
13
12
Cham

A5

Villeneuve
1 **20**
7 **8**
2 • Gressan
Saint-Pierre
6 • Arvier
5 •
9
Aymavilles •
16 •
14
Introd

Dora di Valgrisenc

Dora di Rhemes

Savara

Grand Eyvia

Val di Cogne

Valsavarenche

PARCO NAZIONALE
DEL GRAN PARADISO

Gran
Paradiso
4061

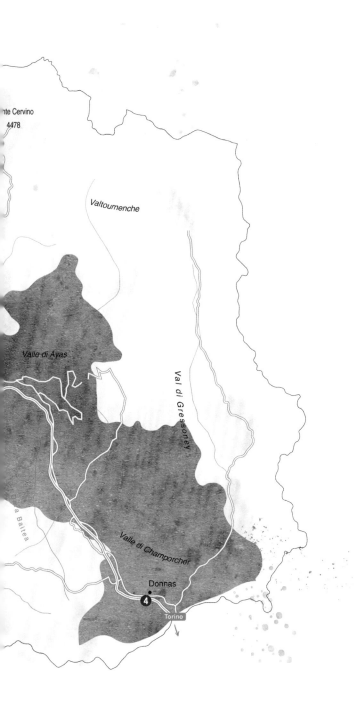

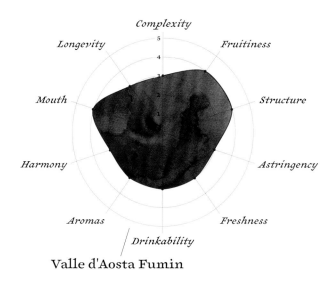

Valle d'Aosta Fumin

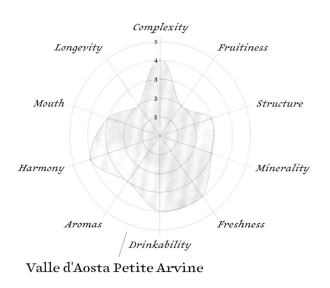

Valle d'Aosta Petite Arvine

Producers and their trademark and signature wines:

1. ANSELMET, Villeneuve
   Vallée d'Aoste Pinot Noir Semel Pater ($$$)
   Vallée d'Aoste Pinot Noir Tradition ($$)
   Vallée d'Aoste Chardonnay Mains et Coeur ($$$)
   Vallée d'Aoste Le Prisonnier (40% Petit Rouge,
   35% Cornalin, 20% Fumin, 5% Mayolet) ($$$)
2. CAVE GARGANTUA, Gressan
   Vallée d'Aoste Pinot Noir Pierre ($$$)
3. CAVE MONT BLANC DE MORGEX
   ET LA SALLE, Morgex
   Vallée d'Aoste Blanc de Morgex
   et de La Salle La Piagne ($)
4. CAVES DE DONNAS, Donnas
   Vallée d'Aoste Donnas ($)
5. CHÂTEAU FEUILLET, Saint-Pierre
   Vallée d'Aoste Petite Arvine ($)
6. COENFER, Arvier
   Valle d'Aosta Enfer d'Arvier Clos de l'Enfer
   (Petit Rouge) ($$)
7. DI BARRÒ, Saint-Pierre
   Vallée d'Aoste Torrette Superieur ($)
8. DI FRANCESCO-GASPERI, Saint-Pierre
   Vallée d'Aoste Petite Arvine ($)
9. Didier GERBELLE, Aymavilles
   Vallée d'Aoste Rouge L'Aïné (Neyret) ($$)
   Vallée d'Aoste Petit Rouge Vigne Plan ($)
10. GROSJEAN VINS, Quart
    Vallée d'Aoste Fumin Vigne Rovettaz ($$)
    Vallée d'Aoste Chardonnay Le Vin de Michel ($$)
11. INSTITUT AGRICOLE RÉGIONAL, Aosta
    Vallée d'Aoste Petite Arvine ($)
    Vallée d'Aoste Fumin ($)
12. LA CROTTA DI VEGNERON, Chambave
    Vallée d'Aoste Chambave Moscato
    Passito Prieuré ($)
    Vallée d'Aoste Fumin Esprit Follet ($)
13. LA VRILLE, Verrayes
    Vallée d'Aoste Chambave Muscat Flétri ($$)
    Vallée d'Aoste Fumin ($$)
    Vallée d'Aoste Chambave Muscat ($)
14. LES CRÊTES, Aymavilles
    Valle d'Aosta Chardonnay Cuvée Bois ($$)
    Valle d'Aosta Petite Arvine Fleur ($)
    Valle d'Aosta Fumin ($)
    Valle d'Aosta Nebbiolo Sommet ($$)
15. LES GRANGES, Nus
    Vallée d'Aoste Nus Malvoisie ($)
16. LO TRIOLET, Introd
    Vallée d'Aoste Pinot Gris ($)
    Vallée d'Aoste Rouge Coteau Barrage
    (Syrah, Fumin) ($)
    Vallée d'Aoste Fumin ($$)

17. Elio OTTIN, Aosta
    Vallée d'Aoste Petite Arvine ($)
    Vallée d'Aoste Pinot Noir L'Emerico ($$)
    Vallée d'Aoste Fumin ($$)
18. Ermes PAVESE, Morgex
    Vallée d'Aoste Blanc de Morgex et de La Salle
    Pas Dosé Pavese XLVIII ($$)
19. ROSSET TERROIR, Quart
    Vallée d'Aoste Syrah 870 ($$)
    Vallée d'Aoste Chardonnay 770 ($$)

Recommended wines outside the DOC/DOCG designations:

20. LA PLANTZE, Villeneuve
    Ferox (Sauvignon Blanc) ($)
19. ROSSET TERROIR, Quart
    Sopraquota 900 (Petite Arvine,
    Altre Uve Bianche) ($$)

ANSELMET

Frazione Vereytaz 30
Villeneuve (AO)
maisonanselmet.it
Year of establishment: 2007
Owner: Giorgio Anselmet
Average number of bottles
produced per year: 80,000

Curiosity and passion have
led the Anselmet family first
to experiment and then to
perfect numerous indigenous
and international varieties,
resulting in a production of
twenty-two labels from their
27 acres. The most famous
and award-winning are,
in addition to the recently
presented Mains et Coeur, the
refined Chardonnay Elevé en
Fût de Chêne and the Pinot
Noir Semel Pater, among
the most convincing in Italy.
Characteristic of the entire line
is the taste-olfactory precision,
always crisp and refined, at the
top of regional production.

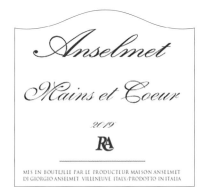

VALLÉE D'AOSTE CHARDONNAY MAINS ET COEUR

First year of production: 2016
Average number of bottles produced
per year: 2,000
Grape variety: Chardonnay

Born at an altitude of 2,625 feet, this wine
possesses an olfactory freshness of herbs
and white flowers that combines with the
notes of hazelnuts, butter, and spices typical
of barrique-aged Chardonnay. The palate is
rich and enveloping with a lingering touch
of acidity, while the finish is of rare richness,
with white fruits, rosemary, and a hint of
vanilla adding complexity. An example of
harmony and balance at the highest level.

LES CRÊTES

Strada Regionale 20, 50
Aymavilles (AO)
lescretes.it
Year of establishment: 1989
Owner: the Charrère
family
Average number of bottles
produced per year: 225,000

Constantine Charrère built
the success of the region's
largest private winery
by adding vineyard after
vineyard year after year, up
to the current 59 acres spread
over six municipalities. Fame
came early, thanks to the
Chardonnay Cuvée Bois—
presented here—but there
are many labels that have
gained deserved fame, from
the Petite Arvine Fleur to the
Fumin, and from the Pinot
Noir Reveil to the more recent
Nebbiolo Sommet. Elena and
Eleonora Charrère now lead a
high-quality operation, which
is still growing.

VALLE D'AOSTA CHARDONNAY CUVÉE BOIS

First year of production: 1993
Average number of bottles produced
per year: 25,000
Grape variety: Chardonnay

Enchanting complexity in this Chardonnay
capable of improving for years in the bottle.
The aromas range from tropical fruit and
notes from the toasting of the barrels,
from white fruits to honey. The flavor is
absolutely elegant, rich, and smooth, with a
slight touch of acidity and astringency from
the oak that make it even more persistent
and complete.

LO TRIOLET

Frazione Junod 7
Introd (AO)
lotriolet.it
Year of establishment: 1993
Owner: Marco Martin
Average number of bottles
produced per year: 55,000

In just a few years, Marco
Martin has gained confidence,
increasing both an initially
limited production and his
ability to interpret the region's
most representative grape
varieties, from Petite Arvine
to Fumin and Pinot Noir.
On his 12 acres of vines, to
which he adds grapes from
a few neighboring growers,
he cultivates twelve different
varieties, among which a Pinot
Gris stands out, a grape of
which he has proved to be the
best interpreter in the valley.

VALLÉE D'AOSTE PINOT GRIS

First year of production: 1993
Average number of bottles produced
per year: 12,000
Grape variety: Pinot Gris

This Vallée d'Aoste Pinot Gris is rich and
immediate in its aromas of officinal herbs,
white flowers, and citrus fruits. It is lively
and fresh on the palate, with a splendid
savory grip, also thanks to a touch of
savoriness and a remarkable persistence.
Reasonably priced and highly enjoyable.

ROSSET TERROIR

Località Torrent de
Maillod 4
Quart (AO)
rosseterroir.it
Year of establishment: 2001
Owner: Nicola Rosset
Average number of bottles
produced per year: 50,000

A dynamic and ambitious
winery, always on the lookout
for new vineyards and new
winemaking techniques, with
a solid production capacity in
a beautiful, newly renovated
facility. The 25 acres planted
with vines include the varieties
that are best adapted to the
altitudes in Valle d'Aosta, from
Petite Arvine to Pinot Gris,
from Pinot Noir to Cornalin,
from Fumin to Chardonnay,
with outstanding results also
with Syrah.

SOPRAQUOTA 900

First year of production: 2018
Average number of bottles produced per
year: 5,500
Grape varieties: Petite Arvine, other grapes

The name refers to the altitude of the vineyards
in the commune of Villenueve where the grapes
are grown and already indicates the wine's
most outstanding characteristics: freshness and
great personality. Aging takes place in different
containers—amphorae, wood, and steel—allowing
a refined aromatic development rich in herbs and
citrus fruits. The palate is splendid, enjoying the
delicate contrast between acidity and softness,
between alcohol and sapidity.

Lombardy

Dotted with large lakes and artistic cities such as Mantua, Bergamo, Como, Cremona, and Brescia, the Lombardy of Franciacorta, Valtellina, and Chiaretto, all of which are clearly growing, is the region with the most UNESCO-listed sites in Italy—eleven out of fifty-three—and the second highest GDP in Europe, but it is also one of the most polluted.

A vast region with a surface area of 9,212 square miles and no less than ten million inhabitants, where the capital Milan is rapidly gaining international recognition thanks to the energy with which it operates in various sectors, from fashion to design to finance. Regional wine production is fairly stable, with a slight downward trend due to the contraction of the total area under vine, and is close to 37 million gallons per year, or 3% of the national total. There are five Designations of Controlled and Guaranteed Origin and twenty-one DOC wines, covering more than 60% of Lombardy's wine production.

Since this area stretches from north to south, between the Swiss border and the Po Valley, and enjoys a high presence of lakes, production is clearly differentiated between the mountain area, which covers 40% of the territory, the hilly area (13%), and the flat area (47%). In the highest part, in Valtellina, we find excellent red wines based on Nebbiolo grapes, with the Sforzato di Valtellina and Valtellina Superiore DOCGs leading the sector. This is a strip of terraced vineyards bearing fruit along 1,550 miles of stone walls between 985 and 2,300 feet above sea level, in a landscape created by mankind over the centuries with such distinctive and fascinating results as to be designated a UNESCO World Heritage site.

Descending towards the Po River, below Lake Iseo (also called Sebino) in the province of Brescia, one encounters the hills of Franciacorta, where the production of *bollicine* or "bubbly," the term preferred by local producers to indicate their sparkling wines, prevails. Significant agronomic investments now guarantee a solid production base of Chardonnay and Pinot Noir grapes—joined by smaller portions of Pinot Blanc and, more recently, of the local Erbamat grape variety—while the cellars are equipped with the most refined technologies for Metodo Classico production.

It is nonetheless a young area that has exploded in the last twenty years, with wine critics constantly emphasizing how the search for a precise physiognomy of the various types produced is still underway: one year, the progress made in the soft Satèn, which gains in structure and richness of flavor, is highlighted, while the following year the greater acidity of the Pas Dosé versions and the gradual abandonment of the softer, more appealing characteristics are exalted. This is furthering the general recognition of an excellent level of quality, as well testified by the long list of recommended producers.

Heading further toward the plain, one enters the vast Oltrepò Pavese area, an articulated hill system with 27,180 acres of vineyards dedicated to both red and white grapes. The red Croatina,

Barbera, and Uva Rara grapes achieve the best results in soils with a good presence of clay and limestone, while Pinot Noir and white grapes are mainly grown on soils with a greater presence of sand.

In addition to the fresh and incisive reds, with Bonarda leading the way, and evidence of a rich "red" past, thanks primarily to Buttafuoco, the still versions made from Pinot Noir or Rhine Riesling grapes, as well as the sparkling wines made with the Metodo Classico, which has had its own independent DOCG since 2007, receive the most critical acclaim.

At the opposite end of the region, in an almost flat area that enjoys a happy temperate climate due to the presence of Lake Garda, we find the Lugana DOC area, currently undergoing brilliant productive development thanks to local and international consumer appreciation. The Riviera del Garda Classico DOC is smaller in size but steadily increasing in the area bordering the highest part of the lake, proving to be a devoted home of rosé wines capable of responding to the growing market demand for this delicate type.

Passo dello Stelvio
2757

Passo di Foscagno
2291

Passo di Gavia
2621

Mese

Valchiavenna

Monte Disgrazia
1678

VALTELLINA

Tirano
Villa di Tirano
Ponte in
Valtellina
Tresivio
Bianzone
SONDRIO
Chiuro   Teglio

Adda

Adamello
3554

Abbazia
di Piona

Lago
di Como

Capo di Ponte

Val Camonica

Passo
della Presolana
1297

Campo dei Fiori
1276

Lago
Maggiore

VARESE

Svizzera

COMO

Brianza

LECCO

Val Brembana

Darfo
Boario Terme

Lago
d'Iseo

Lago
d'Idro

Riviera del Garda

Lago di Garda

Lago
di Varese

A8

A9

La Valletta
Brianza

VALCALEPIO

Scanzorosciate

BERGAMO

Trescore
Balneario

GARDA
BRESCIANO

MONZA

Provaglio
d'Iseo

Monticelli Brusati

Capriolo

Adro

Corte Franca

Muscoline

San Felice del Benaco

Puegnago del Garda
Manerba del Garda

Polpenazze
del Garda

A4

Erbusco

Passirano

Gussago

Moniga del Garda
Padenghe sul Garda

Torino

Coccaglio

Cazzago
San Martino

Botticino

Bedizzole

Sirmione

A58

A35

FRANCIACORTA

BRESCIA

Lonato
del Garda

Desenzano del Garda

A4

Peschiera del Garda

Venezia

Abbazia di
Morimondo

LUGANA

Adda

MILANO

Capriano
del Colle

Pozzolengo

GARDA COLLI
MANTOVANI

Mella

Certosa
di Pavia

LODI

Chiese

Serio

Brennero

A22

Ticino

PAVIA

San Colombano
al Lambro

A1

Oglio

CREMONA

A21

Torino

MANTOVA

A7

Po

Roma

Po

Genova

OLTREPÒ
PAVESE

Canneto
Pavese

Cigognola

San Damiano
al Colle

Santa Giuletta

Torricella Verzate

Casteggio

Pietra
de' Giorgi

Rovescala

Corvino San Quirico

Mornico Losana

Calvignano

Oliva
Gessi

Eremo di
Sant'Alberto
di Butrio

Passo
del Penice
1149

MAIN VINES GROWN IN THE REGION

Barbera and Bonarda
→ Piedmont

Chardonnay, Pinot Noir, Pinot Blanc → International Grape Varieties

Croatina

In Lombardy, it is mainly used together with Vespolina, Barbera, or Uva Rara to give fragrance and smoothness to Bonarda wine from the Oltrepò Pavese, not to be confused with the Bonarda grape variety, an indigenous Piedmontese grape. In purity, it is rarely vinified due to its low acidity and slender body, but in the best versions the aromas of ripe red fruit are lively and the flavor soft and harmonious. Also used in blends in the Buttafuoco and San Colombano DOC wines.

Erbamat

An almost extinct grape variety, typical of the Brescia area, also known as Albamatto or Erbamatto, it has been known since the sixteenth century as one of the most prized white varieties in the area between Lake Garda and Lake Iseo. It owes its curious name to the grass-green color of its berries and is genetically identical to Verdealbara, a local Trentino grape that is also almost extinct. It can be found in blends with Trebbiano Valtènesi (white Verdicchio), while it has slightly aromatic characteristics if vinified on its own. It has made a comeback, especially in Metodo Classico Franciacorta sparkling wines, thanks to its late ripening, as it withstands the heat and brings freshness and delicate aromas to the wine.

Erbanno

It belongs to the heterogeneous group of Schiava vines, with which it should not be confused, however, because it is genetically different. It is known by numerous synonyms, including Schiava Lombarda, Schiava Nera, and Slept, which in the local dialect means "enslaved, domesticated." A grape variety with strong dyeing properties, it presents itself in the glass with a dense purple-red color. The nose smells of blackberries, cherries, and plums accompanied by notes of pepper and cloves. The palate is juicy, light, and snappy.

Groppello

So called because its compact grapes appear to be knotted—*grop* in local dialect means "knot." Groppello or Groppello Gentile was mentioned in 1299 by Pier de' Crescenzi as Pignolo, and the wine it produced was so prized that it was exported to Germany as early as the sixteenth century. Originally grown on the Brescia side of Lake Garda, in Valtènesi, it is mainly used as a base for Chiaretto, in combination with Sangiovese, Marzemino, and Barbera. The wines are cherry pink in color, with fresh aromas of wisteria, violet and lavender, raspberry and currant, and a good balance of softness and acidity in the mouth. In purity, there is a certain savoriness, accompanied by spicy notes and a slightly bitter finish.

Marzemino → Trentino

The DOCGs

- Franciacorta
- Oltrepò Pavese Metodo Classico
- Scanzo / Moscato di Scanzo
- Sforzato di Valtellina / Sfursat di Valtellina
- Valtellina Superiore

The DOCs

- Bonarda dell'Oltrepò Pavese
- Botticino
- Buttafuoco dell'Oltrepò Pavese / Buttafuoco
- Capriano del Colle
- Casteggio
- Cellatica
- Curtefranca
- Garda
- Garda Colli Mantovani
- Lambrusco Mantovano
- Lugana
- Oltrepò Pavese
- Oltrepò Pavese Pinot Grigio
- Pinot Nero dell'Oltrepò Pavese
- Riviera del Garda Classico
- San Colombano al Lambro / San Colombano
- San Martino della Battaglia
- Sangue di Giuda dell'Oltrepò Pavese / Sangue di Giuda
- Terre dei Colleoni / Colleoni
- Valcalepio
- Valtellina Rosso / Rosso di Valtellina

Nebbiolo → Piedmont

In Lombardy, Nebbiolo is included in the precious designations of Valtellina Rosso—a ready, flowing wine—Valtellina Superiore—where it is often harvested overripe—and Sfursat, a dry red from dried grapes. These are heroic, extreme variations of an extraordinary, difficult, and complex grape variety, which over the centuries has trained itself to live in the cold and find ideal exposures in a favorable microclimatic island amidst mountains verging on 13,125 feet in height. In the Superiore versions, fruit preserved in spirit, mountain herbs, sweet spices, and black pepper animate a wine of strong impact and character; in the Sfursat, the bouquet explodes toward Mediterranean flowers and spices, with balsamic nuances and a long finish of dehydrated black plum.

Trebbiano di Soave
→ Verdicchio in Marche

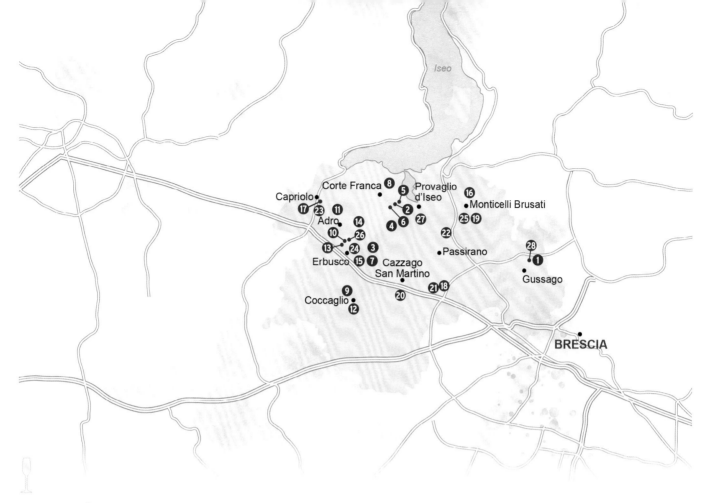

Franciacorta DOCG

It is the first Italian DOCG, from 1995, which is dedicated exclusively to sparkling wine made with the Metodo Classico from Chardonnay, Pinot Noir, and Pinot Blanc grapes. If twenty years ago there were those who noted abundant fruity notes and a certain softness of taste in Franciacorta, it can be truthfully said that today there are many wineries that have adopted a more dry style, where the aromas remind one of bread crust and yeast while the flavor is decidedly acidic, sometimes even aggressively thanks to the bubbles. This is all in relation to the different types envisaged and the relative residual sugar content: ranging from Dosage Zero (or Pas Dosé or Dosage Zéro: between 0 and 3 g/l) to demi-sec (between 33 and 50 g/l), passing through extra Brut (between 0 and 6 g/l), Brut (no more than 12 g/l, the most widespread version), extra dry (between 12 and 17 g/l), and Sec (or dry, between 17 and 32 g/l). Wine critics reward the two driest types, Dosage Zero and Extra Brut, where the producer has to rely solely on the richness of the grapes without resorting to extra sugar. More softness is found in the fruity Satèn type (called Crémant until 1994, when the European Union ruled that this term was exclusively French), where the *prise de mousse* takes place with less sugar and a consequent maximum pressure of only five atmospheres. The minimum bottle aging on the lees is eighteen months for Franciacorta, twenty-four for Rosé and Satèn, thirty for vintage wines, and sixty for Riserva. The vast majority of wines does not indicate the vintage on the label, and may therefore be the result of blends of different vintages, while 12% are vintage wines. Production comes from 6,400 acres under vine and exceeds twenty million bottles per year, 15% of which are exported.

—

Producers and their trademark and signature wines:

1. Andrea ARICI – Colline della Stella, Gussago
   Franciacorta Dosaggio Zero Nero ($$)
2. BARONE PIZZINI, Provaglio d'Iseo
   Franciacorta Extra Brut Animante ($)
   Franciacorta Satèn ($$)
   Franciacorta Brut Naturae ($$)
3. BELLAVISTA, Erbusco
   Franciacorta Brut Teatro alla Scala ($$)
   Franciacorta Extra Brut Pas Operé ($$$)
   Franciacorta Extra Brut Riserva
   Vittorio Moretti ($$$$)
4. Guido BERLUCCHI, Corte Franca
   Franciacorta Extra Brut Riserva Extrême Palazzo Lana ($$$)
   Franciacorta Nature 61 ($$)
5. BERSI SERLINI, Provaglio d'Iseo
   Franciacorta Extra Brut ($$)
6. BOSIO, Corte Franca
   Franciacorta Extra Brut Boschedòr ($$)
7. CA' DEL BOSCO, Erbusco
   Franciacorta Dosage Zéro Riserva
   Annamaria Clementi ($$$$)
   Franciacorta Satèn Vintage Collection ($$$)
   Franciacorta Extra Brut Rosé Riserva
   Annamaria Clementi ($$$$)

8. CASCINA CLARABELLA, Corte Franca
    Franciacorta Non Dosato Èssenza ($)
9. CASTELLO BONOMI, Coccaglio
    Franciacorta Dosage Zéro ($$)
    Franciacorta Satèn ($$)
10. CAVALLERI, Erbusco
    Franciacorta Collezione Grandi Cru ($$)
    Franciacorta Pas Dosé ($$)
11. CONTADI CASTALDI, Adro
    Franciacorta Zèro ($)
12. CORTE FUSIA, Coccaglio
    Franciacorta Brut ($)
13. DERBUSCO CIVES, Erbusco
    Franciacorta Dosaggio Zero Riserva
    Decem Annis ($$)
    Franciacorta Brut Le Millésime ($$)
14. FERGHETTINA, Adro
    Franciacorta Dosaggio Zero Riserva 33 ($$)
    Franciacorta Extra Brut Eronero ($$)
15. Enrico GATTI, Erbusco
    Franciacorta Brut ($)
    Franciacorta Nature ($$)
16. LA MONTINA, Monticelli Brusati
    Franciacorta Dosaggio Zero Riserva Baiana ($$)
17. LANTIERI DE PARATICO, Capriolo
    Franciacorta Brut Arcadia ($$)
18. LE MARCHESINE, Passirano
    Franciacorta Dosaggio Zero Riserva Secolo Novo ($$)
19. LO SPARVIERE, Monticelli Brusati
    Franciacorta Extra Brut ($)
20. 1701, Cazzago San Martino
    Franciacorta Rosé Dosaggio Zero ($$)
21. MONTE ROSSA, Cazzago San Martino
    Franciacorta Brut Cabochon ($$$)
    Franciacorta Brut Blanc de Blancs P. R. ($)
22. MOSNEL, Passirano
    Franciacorta Extra Brut EBB ($$)
    Franciacorta Parosé Rosé Pas Dosé ($$)
    Franciacorta Satèn Brut ($$)
23. RICCI CURBASTRO, Capriolo
    Franciacorta Extra Brut ($)
    Franciacorta Satèn ($)
24. UBERTI, Erbusco
    Franciacorta Extra Brut Comarì del Salem ($$)
    Franciacorta Dosaggio Zero Riserva Sublimis ($$)
25. VILLA, Monticelli Brusati
    Franciacorta Extra Brut Extra Blu ($$)
26. VILLA CRESPIA, Adro
    Franciacorta Brut Millè ($)
27. Chiara ZILIANI, Provaglio d'Iseo
    Franciacorta Satèn Millesimato Ziliani C ($)

Curtefranca DOC

As the name implies, the DOC is relative to Franciacorta country and envisages only two types, Bianco and Rosso, which is the one most widely produced. The composition of Rosso is strictly Bordeaux: Cabernet Franc and/or Carmenère for at least 20%, Merlot for no less than 25%, and Cabernet Sauvignon between 10 and 35%. Approximately ninety thousand bottles are produced annually.

—

Producer and its trademark and signature wine:

28. CASTELLO DI GUSSAGO, Gussago
    Curtefranca Rosso Pomaro ($$)

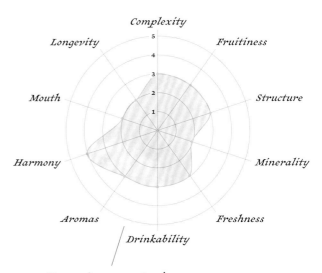

Franciacorta Satèn

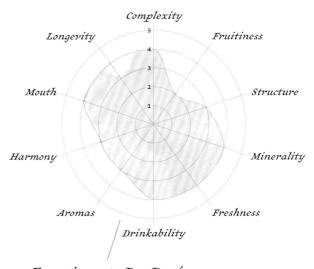

Franciacorta Pas Dosé

Valtellina Rosso
or Rosso di Valtellina DOC

This is the freshest and most immediate version of Valtellina Superiore DOCG, made from at least 90% Nebbiolo, or Chiavennasca, grapes and marketable as early as six months after the harvest. For the most part, no drying and no wood are involved in a wine simply devoted to pleasant drinkability. Less than four hundred thousand bottles are produced annually.

—

Producers and their trademark and signature wines:

1. ASCESA, Tresivio
   Rosso di Valtellina ($)
2. Marcel ZANOLARI, Bianzone
   Rosso di Valtellina L'Essenziale ($)

Sforzato di Valtellina
or Sfursat di Valtellina DOCG

The Valtellina is a fascinating area in the province of Sondrio, north of Lake Como, where Nebbiolo (here called Chiavennasca) also gives splendid results in this version, which is the result of drying the grapes in special rooms for a period that can range from a few weeks to a few months, so that about 30% of the water contained in the grapes evaporates. But fear not—this is not a passito wine: the concentration concerns the power and envelopment in the mouth, together with the expansion of the typical aromas of Nebbiolo while the perfect drinkability is given by both the sustained acidity and the absence of residual sugars. The regulations require at least twenty-four months of aging in the cellar, no less than twelve in wood, and an alcohol content of at least 14%. A sumptuous wine, among the greats of Italy, produced annually in about three hundred thousand bottles.

—

Producers and their trademark and signature wines:

3. Sandro FAY, Teglio
   Sforzato di Valtellina Ronco del Picchio ($$)
4. NINO NEGRI, Chiuro
   Sforzato di Valtellina Sfursat 5 Stelle ($$$)
   Sforzato di Valtellina Sfursat Carlo Negri ($$)
5. Mamete PREVOSTINI, Mese
   Sforzato di Valtellina Albareda ($$$)
6. RAINOLDI, Chiuro
   Sfursat di Valtellina Fruttaio Ca' Rizzieri ($$)
   Sfursat di Valtellina ($$)
7. TRIACCA, Villa di Tirano
   Sforzato di Valtellina San Domenico ($$)
   Sforzato di Valtellina Il Monastero ($$)

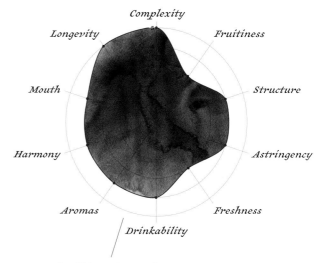

Valtellina Superiore

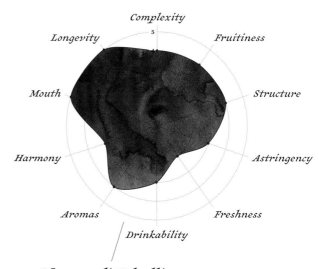

Sforzato di Valtellina

Valtellina Superiore DOCG

Mese •

Lago di Mezzola

Lago di Como

Also born on the astonishing terraces that characterize Valtellina is this DOCG that, unlike Sforzato, is not always made from grapes subjected to drying in the *fruttaio*, but also from a more or less considerable over-ripening of the grapes on the vine. The grape is always Nebbiolo, at a minimum of 90%, and the areas of cultivation can be indicated on the label: Maroggia, Sassella, Grumello, Inferno, and Valgella. The minimum aging in the cellar after the harvest is twenty-four months, with thirty-six for the Riserva, at least twelve in wood, for a complex wine with great structure, tannicity slightly blunted by the delayed harvest, and always good freshness. Over two million bottles are produced annually.
—

Producers and their trademark and signature wines:

8. AR.PE.PE., Sondrio
   Valtellina Superiore Sassella Riserva Rocce Rosse ($$$)
   Valtellina Superiore Sassella Stella Retica ($$)
   Valtellina Superiore Inferno Fiamme Antiche ($$)
9. COOPERATIVA AGRICOLA TRIASSO E SASSELLA, Sondrio
   Valtellina Superiore Sassella Sassi Solivi ($)
10. DIRUPI, Ponte in Valtellina
    Valtellina Superiore Dirupi ($$)
    Valtellina Superiore Inferno Guast ($$)
11. Luca FACCINELLI, Chiuro
    Valtellina Superiore Grumello Tell ($)
3. Sandro FAY, Teglio
   Valtellina Superiore Valgella Riserva Carterìa ($$)
12. Giorgio GIANATTI, Montagna in Valtellina
    Valtellina Superiore Grumello San Martino ($$)
13. LA PERLA – Marco Triacca, Teglio
    Valtellina Superiore La Mossa ($)
14. Alberto MARSETTI, Sondrio
    Valtellina Superiore Grumello Vigna Le Prudenze ($$)

15. Pietro NERA, Chiuro
    Valtellina Superiore Inferno Riserva ($$)
4. NINO NEGRI, Chiuro
   Valtellina Superiore Sassella Le Tense ($)
   Valtellina Superiore Inferno Carlo Negri ($)
5. Mamete PREVOSTINI, Mese
   Valtellina Superiore Sassella San Lorenzo ($$)
6. RAINOLDI, Chiuro
   Valtellina Superiore Inferno Riserva ($$)
   Valtellina Superiore Grumello Riserva ($$)
16. TENUTA SCERSCÉ, Tirano
    Valtellina Superiore Inferno Flammante ($$)

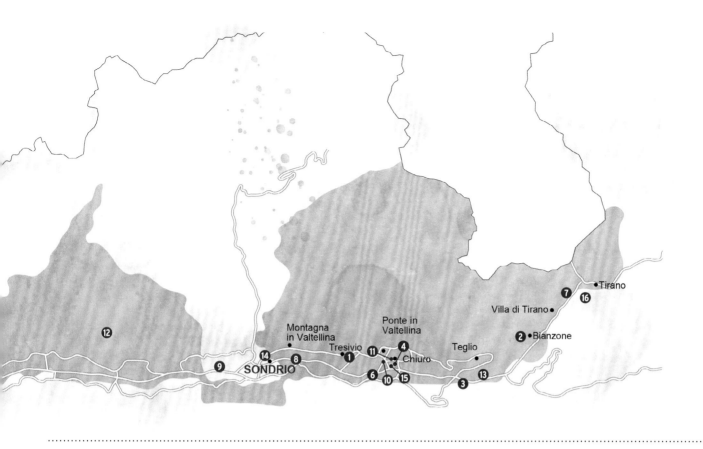

Pinot Nero dell'Oltrepò Pavese DOC

This appellation is exclusively intended for still red wines made from at least 95% Pinot Noir grapes. In the best versions, it is a wine that maintains the finesse and gracefulness typical of Pinot Noir from cooler areas, guaranteeing rich, harmonious drinkability. A growing DOC, today produced in over 1.5 million bottles annually.

—

Producers and their trademark and signature wines:

1. CONTE VISTARINO, Rocca de' Giorgi
   Pinot Nero dell'Oltrepò Pavese Pernice ($$)
   Pinot Nero dell'Oltrepò Pavese Tavernetto ($)
2. CORDERO SAN GIORGIO, Santa Giuletta
   Pinot Nero dell'Oltrepò Pavese Partù ($)
3. FRECCIAROSSA, Casteggio
   Pinot Nero dell'Oltrepò Pavese Giorgio
   Odero ($$)
4. TENUTA MAZZOLINO, Corvino San Quirico
   Oltrepò Pavese Pinot Nero Noir ($$)

Oltrepò Pavese DOC

A DOC that covers a vast hilly strip of the province of Pavia and includes no less than thirty-six different types. The main grape varieties from which the area's production success was born are red Barbera, Pinot Noir, and Croatina on the one hand, and Riesling on the other. The creation of autonomous DOC and DOCG for some types, including Oltrepò Pavese Metodo Classico DOCG, Pinot Nero dell'Oltrepò Pavese DOC, and Buttafuoco dell'Oltrepò Pavese DOC, has restricted the expressive potential of this DOC designation, which nonetheless often remains a valid witness to grapes and vinification that live up to its name. Over twenty million bottles are produced per year.

—

Producers and their trademark and signature wines:

5. CA' DI FRARA, Mornico Losana
   Oltrepò Pavese Riesling Riserva Oliva ($)
3. FRECCIAROSSA, Casteggio
   Oltrepò Pavese Rosso Anamari ($$)
6. ISIMBARDA, Santa Giuletta
   Oltrepò Pavese Riesling Renano Vigna Martina Le Fleur ($)
   Oltrepò Pavese Riesling Renano Vigna Martina ($)
7. TRAVAGLINO, Calvignano
   Oltrepò Pavese Riesling Renano Riserva Campo della Fojada ($)
8. Bruno VERDI, Canneto Pavese
   Oltrepò Pavese Rosso Riserva Cavariola ($$)
   Oltrepò Pavese Bonarda Vivace Possessione di Vergombera ($)

Oltrepò Pavese Metodo Classico DOCG

The specifications state that Metodo Classico and Metodo Classico Rosé must be made from at least 70% Pinot Noir grapes, with the possible addition of Chardonnay, Pinot Gris, and Pinot Blanc, rising to 85% when the Pinot Noir specification is added. The great success of this grape in Oltrepò has been known for centuries, so much so that many Metodo Classico producers in neighboring regions have used it, and in part continue to do so today. Precisely because of the high presence of Pinot Noir, it is a particularly fruity and always rather rich type of bubbly on the palate. Both the Riserva type, with at least forty-eight months on the lees, and the change of the DOCG name to Oltrepò Metodo Classico are in the process of being approved. Annual production, which is growing, exceeds 1.6 million bottles.

—

Producers and their trademark and signature wines:

9. BALLABIO, Casteggio
   Oltrepò Pavese Metodo Classico Pinot Nero Dosaggio Zero Farfalla Cave Privée ($$$)
10. CALATRONI, Santa Maria della Versa
    Oltrepò Pavese Metodo Classico Pinot Nero Pas Dosé Rosé ($$)
    Oltrepò Pavese Metodo Classico Pinot Nero Extra Brut Rosé NorEma ($)
11. CASTELLO DI CIGOGNOLA, Cigognola
    Oltrepò Pavese Metodo Classico Pinot Nero Pas Dosé Moratti Cuvée dell'Angelo ($$)
12. PICCOLO BACCO DEI QUARONI, Montù Beccaria
    Oltrepò Pavese Metodo Classico Pinot Nero Brut Nature Rosé PBQ ($)

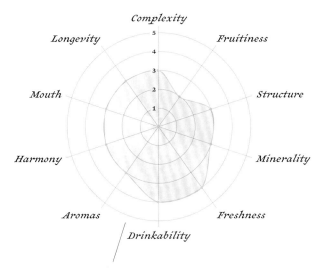

Oltrepò Pavese Metodo Classico Pas Dosé

13. SCUROPASSO, Pietra de' Giorgi
    Oltrepò Pavese Metodo Classico Cruasé Roccapietra ($)
8. Bruno VERDI, Canneto Pavese
   Oltrepò Pavese Metodo Classico Pinot Nero Extra Brut Vergomberra ($)

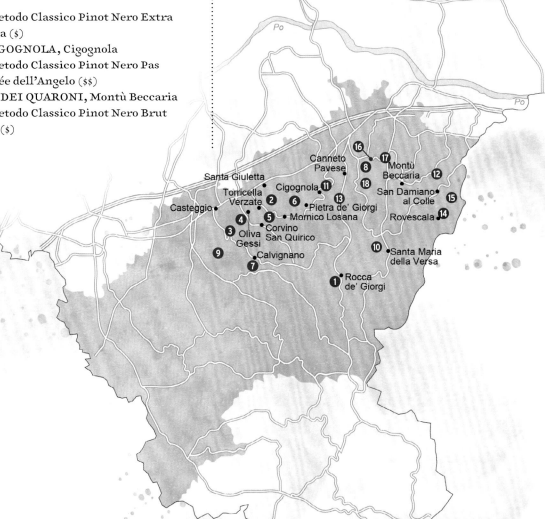

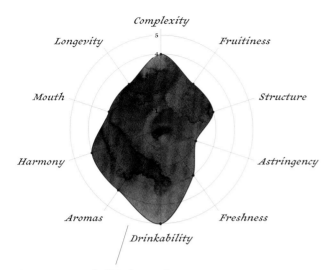

Pinot Nero dell'Oltrepò Pavese

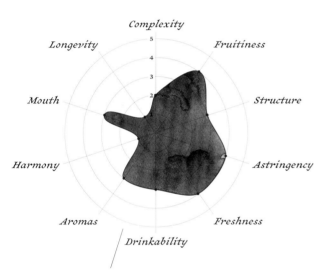

Bonarda dell'Oltrepò Pavese

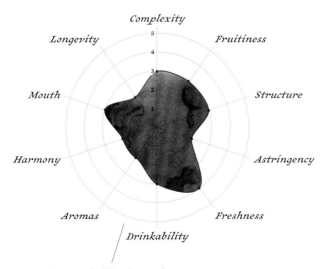

Buttafuoco dell'Oltrepò Pavese

Bonarda dell'Oltrepò Pavese DOC

It comes from the Croatina grape at a mix of at least 85%, with possible inclusion of Barbera, Vespolina, and Uva Rara, and it is a wine characterized not only by its rather lively ruby red color but also by its immediate and pleasant drinkability, both in the still and sparkling versions. The aromas are always very fruity, while the flavor is characterized by acidity and a good tannic component. Over twenty million bottles are produced each year.

—

Producers and their trademark and signature wines:

14. Fratelli AGNES, Rovescala
    Bonarda dell'Oltrepò Pavese Frizzante
    Campo del Monte ($)
15. MARTILDE, Rovescala
    Bonarda dell'Oltrepò Pavese ($)

Buttafuoco dell'Oltrepò Pavese or Buttafuoco DOC

Made from Barbera, at 25 to 65%, and Croatina, at 25 to 65%, with the possible addition of *uva rara* and Vespolina up to 45%, this red fruit-rich wine is often described as "crispy" due to its vitality, freshness, and consistency in an almost overwhelming taste. Approximately sixty thousand bottles per year are produced.

—

Producers and their trademark and signature wines:

16. FIAMBERTI, Canneto Pavese
    Buttafuoco Storico Vigna Sacca del Prete ($$)
    Buttafuoco Storico Vigna Solenga ($$)
17. Andrea PICCHIONI, Canneto Pavese
    Buttafuoco Bricco Riva Bianca ($$)
    Buttafuoco Solinghino ($)
18. Francesco QUAQUARINI, Canneto Pavese
    Buttafuoco Vigna La Guasca ($)

Riviera del Garda Classico DOC

This DOC covers a vast area in the province of Brescia, where numerous white and red grapes are cultivated. However, success is mainly derived from the Valtènesi subzone and its Chiaretto version. The prevailing cultivar is Groppello, which is rarely used exclusively by itself, but is always able to bring good freshness, moderate tannicity, and aromas not just of red fruits but also spices. The regulations state that a minimum of 30% Groppello may be blended with Marzemino, Barbera, and Sangiovese grapes—each at no more than 25%—in addition to any other types envisaged for the Lombardy region. The overall production of the DOC exceeds three million bottles per year, of which over two million are Valtènesi Chiaretto.

—

Producers and their trademark and signature wines:

1. Giovanni AVANZI, Manerba del Garda
   Riviera del Garda Classico Valtènesi Chiaretto Rosavero ($)
2. CANTRINA, Bedizzole
   Riviera del Garda Classico Valtènesi Chiaretto ($)
3. CASCINA BELMONTE, Muscoline
   Riviera del Garda Classico Valtènesi Chiaretto Costellazioni ($)
4. COSTARIPA, Moniga del Garda
   Riviera del Garda Classico Valtènesi Chiaretto RosaMara ($)
   Riviera del Garda Classico Valtènesi Chiaretto Molmenti ($$)
5. LE CHIUSURE, San Felice del Benaco
   Riviera del Garda Classico Valtènesi Chiaretto ($)
6. LE GAINE, Bedizzole
   Riviera del Garda Classico Groppello ($)
7. PASINI SAN GIOVANNI, Puegnago del Garda
   Riviera del Garda Classico Valtènesi Lettera C ($$)
   Riviera del Garda Classico Valtènesi Il Valtènesi ($)
8. SINCETTE, Polpenazze del Garda
   Riviera del Garda Classico Groppello ($)
9. TURINA, Moniga del Garda
   Riviera del Garda Classico Valtènesi Chiaretto Setamora ($)

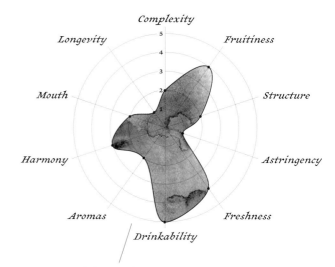

Riviera del Garda Classico
Valtènesi Chiaretto

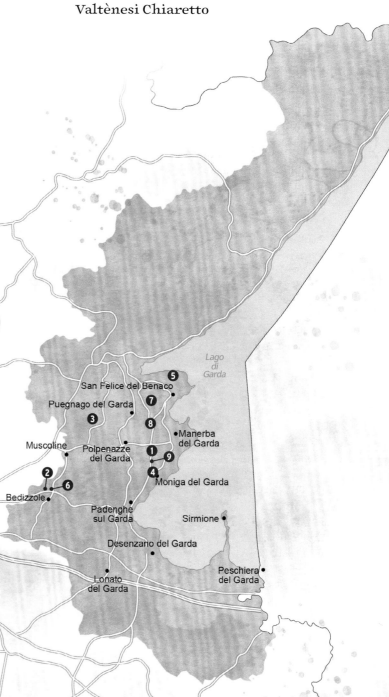

Lugana DOC

We are south of Lake Garda, in an area that includes part of the province of Brescia, in Lombardy, and a smaller part of the province of Verona, in Veneto. The grape used is Trebbiano di Soave, also known as Trebbiano di Lugana or Turbiana, from a vine recognized in the National Catalogue of Vine Varieties of the Ministry of Agricultural Policies that has close genetic affinities with Verdicchio. It has many organoleptic similarities with this, particularly on the fresh palate, while the aromas are more fruity and often citrusy. In recent decades, Lugana has grown particularly strongly, from twelve million bottles in 1990 to the current total of twenty-five million. There are also the highly renowned Superiore and Riserva types, often aged in wood, as well as Spumante and Vendemmia Tardiva.

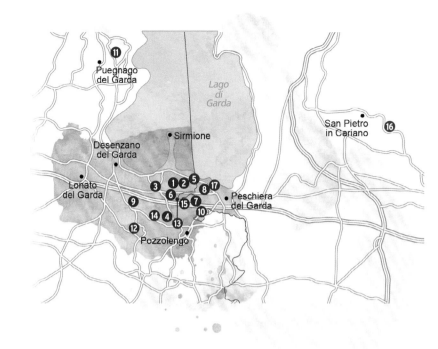

—

Producers and their trademark and signature wines:

1. CÀ DEI FRATI, Sirmione
   Lugana Brolettino ($)
2. CA' LOIERA, Sirmione
   Lugana Riserva del Lupo ($)
3. CÀ MAIOL, Desenzano del Garda
   Lugana Riserva Fabio Contato ($$)
   Lugana Molin ($)
4. CITARI, Desenzano del Garda
   Lugana Conchiglia ($)
5. CORTE SERMANA, Peschiera del Garda (Veneto)
   Lugana Riserva Sermana ($)
6. LA RIFRA, Desenzano del Garda
   Lugana Riserva Il Bepi ($)
7. LA SANSONINA, Peschiera del Garda (Veneto)
   Lugana Fermentazione Spontanea ($)
8. LE MORETTE, Peschiera del Garda (Veneto)
   Lugana Benedictus ($)
   Lugana Riserva ($)
9. MONTONALE, Desenzano del Garda
   Lugana Orestilla ($)
   Lugana Montunal ($)
10. OTTELLA, Peschiera del Garda (Veneto)
    Lugana Riserva Molceo ($)
11. PASINI SAN GIOVANNI, Puegnago del Garda
    Lugana Riserva Busocaldo ($)
12. PERLA DEL GARDA, Lonato del Garda
    Lugana Superiore Madonna della Scoperta ($)
    Lugana Riserva Madre Perla ($)
13. PILANDRO, Desenzano del Garda
    Lugana Arilica ($)

14. SELVA CAPUZZA, Desenzano del Garda
    Lugana Selva ($)
    Lugana Menasasso ($)
15. TENUTA ROVEGLIA, Pozzolengo
    Lugana Riserva Vigne di Catullo ($)
    Lugana Limne ($)
16. TOMMASI, San Pietro in Cariano (Veneto)
    Lugana Riserva Le Fornaci ($)
17. ZENATO, Peschiera del Garda (Veneto)
    Lugana Riserva Sergio Zenato ($$)

Lugana Riserva

Botticino DOC

Produced on less than 75 acres in the municipalities of Botticino, Rezzato, and Brescia, it is made from a blend of Barbera, at a minimum of 30%, Marzemino, at a minimum of 20%, Sangiovese, with a minimum of 30%, Slave Gentile, at a minimum of 10%, and any other red grapes, at no more than 10%. The result is a wine particularly rich in aromas, with spices, violets, and red fruits in evidence and with a good acidic structure, suitable for aging in glass for a few years. One hundred forty thousand bottles are produced annually.

—

Producer and its trademark and signature wines:

1. NOVENTA, Botticino
    Botticino Gobbio ($$)
    Botticino Colle degli Ulivi ($)

○ Botticino
● Capriano del Colle

Capriano del Colle DOC

A small hill DOC in the province of Brescia that makes various types of wines, among which the Rosso stands out. The grape blends required by regulations are very particular: Marzemino, to at least 40%, Merlot, to at least 20%, and Sangiovese, at a minimum of 10%. Aromas of violets and field herbs precede a fresh and soft taste, not very tannic and easy to drink. Just over thirty thousand bottles per year are produced.

—

Producer and its trademark and signature wine:

2. LAZZARI, Capriano del Colle
    Capriano del Colle Rosso
    Riserva degli Angeli ($)

Valcalepio DOC

The DOC territory covers a beautiful area of the Bergamo hills, on the fringes of Lake Iseo, and includes a white version, a Moscato Passito, and Valcalepio Rosso, made exclusively from Merlot and Cabernet grapes, which after three years of aging, one of which in wood, can avail itself of the Riserva designation, as in the case presented here. Approximately one million bottles per year are produced.

—

Producer and its trademark and signature wine:

1. MEDOLAGO ALBANI, Trescore Balneario
    Valcalepio Rosso Riserva I Due Lauri ($)

San Colombano al Lambro or San Colombano DOC

A small denomination, once popular in Milanese *trattorie*, made in the territory of five municipalities straddling the provinces of Milan (where San Colombano al Lambro is located), Lodi, and Pavia. There is also a white version, but it is the Rosso that deserves the most attention: it is mainly made from Croatina and Barbera grapes and is fresh and juicy, but also capable of long bottle aging. Three hundred fifty thousand bottles are produced annually.

—

Producer and its trademark and signature wine:

2. Antonio PANIGADA - Banino,
    San Colombano al Lambro
    San Colombano Rosso Banino Tranquillo ($)

Scanzo or Moscato di Scanzo DOCG

One of Italy's smallest DOCGs, derived 100% from the aromatic black berry grape of the same name, from which it draws impressive olfactory complexity and decades of evolutionary capacity. It must have a grape-to-wine yield of no more than 30% and an aging of at least two years. Production is around forty thousand bottles per year.

—

Producers and their trademark and signature wines:

3. BIAVA, Scanzorosciate
    Moscato di Scanzo ($$$)
4. Sereno MAGRI, Scanzorosciate
    Moscato di Scanzo ($$)

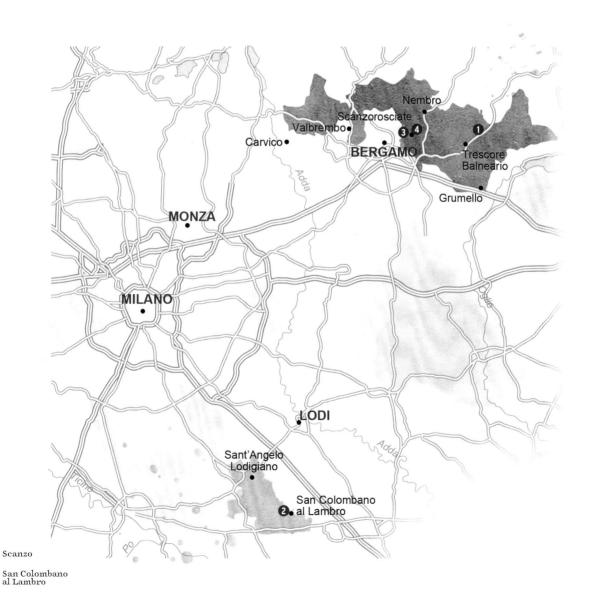

Scanzo

San Colombano
al Lambro

Recommended wines outside the DOC/DOCG designations:

1. Fratelli AGNES, Rovescala
   Loghetto (Croatina) ($)
2. BISI, San Damiano al Colle
   Roncolongo (Barbera) ($)
3. Alessio BRANDOLINI, San Damiano al Colle
   Note d'Agosto Pinot Noir Rosé Extra Brut M. Cl. ($)
4. CANTINA CONCARENA, Capo di Ponte
   Mat (Riesling Renano, Sauvignon) ($)
5. GIORGI, Canneto Pavese
   Top Zero Nature M. Cl. (Pinot Noir) ($)
6. I GESSI – Defilippi, Oliva Gessi
   MariaCristina Pas Dosé Rosé M. Cl. (Pinot Noir) ($)
7. LA COSTA, La Valletta Brianza
   San Giobbe (Pinot Noir) ($)
   Serìz (Merlot, Syrah) ($)
8. MONSUPELLO, Torricella Verzate
   Brut M. Cl. (Pinot Noir) ($)
   Nature M. Cl. (Pinot Noir) ($)
9. Andrea PICCHIONI, Canneto Pavese
   Arfena (Pinot Noir) ($)
10. PRATELLO, Padenghe sul Garda
    Khaos Groppello Anfora ($$)
11. SINCETTE, Polpenazze del Garda
    Le Zalte (Cabernet Sauvignon, Cabernet Franc, Merlot) ($$)
12. Enrico TOGNI REBAIOLI, Darfo Boario Terme
    Rebaioli Cavalier Enrico (Merlot) ($)
    San Valentino (Erbanno) ($)

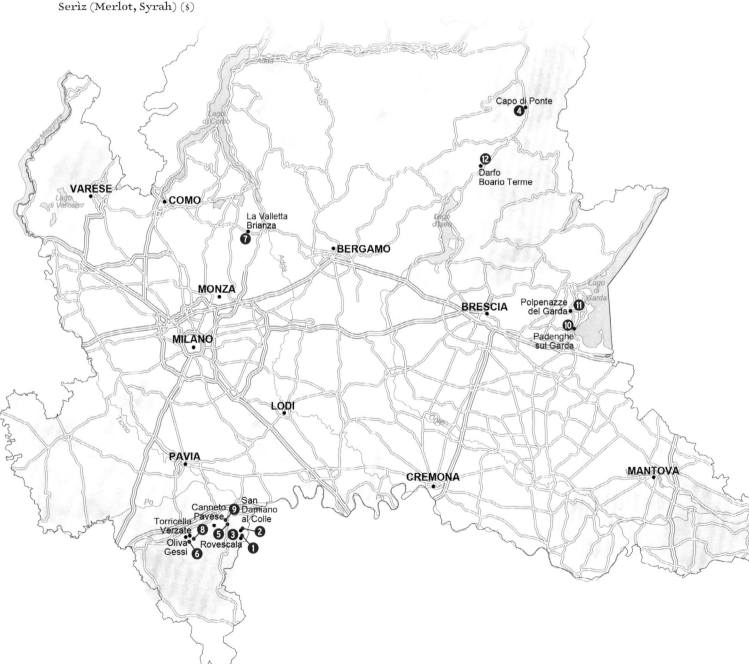

BELLAVISTA

Via Bellavista 5
Erbusco (BS)
bellavistawine.it
Year of establishment: 1977
Owner: the Moretti family
Average number of
bottles produced per year:
1,500,000

Vittorio Moretti, with the
valuable collaboration of
oenologist Mattia Vezzola,
has created a winery of
notable prestige, capable of
offering a line of labels all
marked by the highest quality.
At the heart of this success
lie the estate's 502 acres,
where only the two typical
Franciacorta grape varieties,
Pinot Noir and Chardonnay,
are cultivated with great care
under an organic system.
The Terra Moretti group
today owns three wineries
in Tuscany (Petra, Teruzzi,
and Acquagiusta), two in
Franciacorta (Bellavista and
Contadi Castaldi), and Sella &
Mosca in Sardinia.

FRANCIACORTA EXTRA BRUT PAS OPERÉ

First year of production: 1981
Average number of bottles produced
per year: 20,000
Grape varieties: Chardonnay (70%),
Pinot Noir (30%)

The first fermentation takes place partly in
stainless steel and partly in wood. The wine
then rests in the bottle on the lees for four
years, achieving an olfactory complexity that
includes citrus and tropical notes, medicinal
herbs, hazelnut, and white flowers; the
flavor is incisive and compelling, savory and
fresh, dry to the close on notes of thyme and
cedar. The soul of Franciacorta.

CA' DEL BOSCO

Via A. Zanella 13
Erbusco (BS)
cadelbosco.com
Year of establishment: 1968
Owners: the Zanella
family and Gruppo
Vinicolo Santa Margherita
Average number of bottles
produced per year: 800,000

There is high quality on
all the labels on offer, with
the selections known as
Annamaria Clementi and
Vintage Collection becoming
highly sought-after by wine
enthusiasts all over the world.
This is the fruit of the objective
set by the farsighted Maurizio
Zanella back in the 1970s,
proceeding since then with
continuous technological
improvements and the
expansion of the vineyard
surface area, which has now
reached 618 acres, cultivated
organically. At the top of
Italian sparkling.

FRANCIACORTA DOSAGE ZÉRO RISERVA ANNAMARIA CLEMENTI

First year of production: 1979
Grape varieties: Chardonnay, Pinot
Noir, Pinot Blanc

After initially maturing in wood and after
eight years of bottle aging, it presents
aromas of prestigious elegance reminiscent
of flowers and white fruits, bread crust,
and stimulating spices such as ginger.
The mouth is voluminous and enveloping
but equally sinuous and articulate, with a
swirling finish in which attractive hints of
citrus and yeasts follow one another. The
grape content varies depending on seasonal
trends, averaging between 55% and 75% for
Chardonnay and between 10% and 25% for
both Pinot Noir and Pinot Blanc.

FERGHETTINA

Via Saline 11
Adro (BS)
ferghettina.it
Year of establishment: 1991
Owner: the Gatti family
Average number of bottles
produced per year: 500,000

The production philosophy
laid down by Roberto Gatti
tends to create sparkling
wines endowed with great
natural complexity: long stays
on the lees, avoiding recourse
to maturing in wood for the
base cuvées. The adoption
of organic farming in the
cultivation of the 494 acres
of vineyards, divided into
ninety plots that are then
vinified separately, also goes
in this direction. In addition
to Dosaggio Zero Riserva 33,
there are seven labels of the
various types of Franciacorta
made from Chardonnay and
Pinot Noir grapes, joined by
the two still productions,
Curtefranca Bianco and Rosso.

FRANCIACORTA DOSAGGIO ZERO RISERVA 33

First year of production: 2004
Average number of bottles produced
per year: 8,000
Grape variety: Chardonnay

The eighty-four months spent on the lees
lend a rare and pleasant freshness and
olfactory complexity that highlights oranges
and lemons, together with white-fleshed
fruit set against a floral background. The
flavor is intense and full, almost creamy
but very rich in acidity and savoriness,
of superlative elegance. Great proof of a
Franciacorta made from pure Chardonnay
grapes.

MOSNEL

Frazione Camignone, Via
Barboglio 14
Passirano (BS)
mosnel.com
Year of establishment: 1836
Owner: the Barzanò
family
Average number of bottles
produced per year: 250,000

Brothers Giulio and Lucia
Barzanò represent the fifth
generation of a family that was
one of the first to believe in
Franciacorta's predisposition
toward sparkling wines, and
that has gradually endowed
itself with an important
vineyard estate, today
consisting of 104 acres under
organic management. The
wine offering, which includes
the main types of the DOCG,
from Nature to Pas Dosé to
Brut to Riserva, has recently
been enriched by the fine
Riedizione line, which offers
selections aged for more than
ten years.

FRANCIACORTA SATÈN BRUT

First year of production: 1996
Average number of bottles produced
per year: 35,000
Grape variety: Chardonnay

A portion of the base wine matures in
barriques, which contributes to a soft,
creamy note on the palate that combines
well with the vitality provided by the
effervescence and reappearance of lively
citrus tones on the finish. The aromas are
articulated and include sweet hints of
peach and brioche bread combined with
stimulating spicy and herbaceous hints. A
fine and always reliable testimony to the
Satèn typology.

UBERTI

Località Salem, via E. Fermi 2
Erbusco (BS)
ubertivini.it
Year of establishment: 1793
Owner: the Uberti family
Average number of bottles produced per year: 180,000

Silvia Uberti oversees both the 62 acres of vineyards and cellar operations, where seven types of Franciacorta DOCG are made, having achieved particular fame thanks to the Salem Comarì, the Sublimis Dosaggio Zero, the Extra Brut Dequinque, and the Satèn Magnificentia. A dynamic winery, increasingly committed to safeguarding the environment and preserving biodiversity.

FRANCIACORTA EXTRA BRUT COMARÌ DEL SALEM
First year of production: 1981
Average number of bottles produced per year: 6,500
Grape varieties: Chardonnay (80%), Pinot Blanc (20%)

Produced on a single plot from old vines, the must ferments partly in steel and partly in barriques, then begins its aging period on the lees for no less than sixty months. The aromas are intense and range from white flowers to pastries, in a combination of remarkable elegance. The palate is smooth and flowing, endowed with an acidic freshness that does not detract from the fruity substance and gives dynamism. A great Franciacorta classic.

ZENATO

Via San Benedetto 8
Peschiera del Garda (VR)
zenato.it
Year of establishment: 1960
Owner: the Zenato family
Average number of bottles produced per year: 2,000,000

The company's soul remains tied to Lugana, although it is Valpolicella—where there is a second active vinification cellar—that brings a new propulsive thrust already rich in recognition. To this, one must add the independent production of Sansonina, which is dedicated to both Lugana and Garda red wines, and which brings the total area under vine to a good 544 acres. The Riserva presented must therefore be joined by a vast array of labels, among which the Amarone della Valpolicella Classico, the Lugana Santa Cristina, and the Garda Merlot Sansonina enjoy particular fame.

LUGANA RISERVA SERGIO ZENATO
First year of production: 1993
Average number of bottles produced per year: 31,000
Grape variety: Trebbiano di Lugana

The aim is to make a wine that expands the personality of Trebbiano di Lugana to the highest level, which is the reason for its long maturation, partially in large wood, and prolonged bottle aging before release. The result is of great complexity, with white flowers combined with citrus nuances and a touch of sweet almond. The palate is appreciated for its silky smoothness veined with savoriness and an elegant spicy finish. A champion of the type.

CONTE VISTARINO

Frazione Scorzoletta 82
Rocca de' Giorgi (PV)
contevistarino.it
Year of establishment: 1674
Owner: Ottavia Giorgi Vimercati di Vistarino
Average number of bottles produced per year: 380,000

The production is rich in labels and ranges from the Metodo Classico to still whites, from Buttafuoco to Sangue di Giuda, but it is the still and red vinified Pinot Noir that has given fame and prestige to this historic winery. Five versions of this type are presented, led by Pernice, Tavernetto, and Bertone, and there are increasingly important projects involving the winery's 494 acres of vineyards and research into the best-known grape variety of the Oltrepò Pavese.

PINOT NERO DELL'OLTREPÒ PAVESE PERNICE
First year of production: 1997
Average number of bottles produced per year: 6,500
Grape variety: Pinot Noir

Violets and currants are in the foreground, followed by more mature notes of tar and smoke from aging in small wood for a year. The flavor is varied, encompassing both an enveloping and silky aspect given by the alcohol and the softness of the tannins, and a fresh component, particularly through the citrusy hints of the elegant finish. It perfectly embodies the qualities of the great Pinot Noir of the Oltrepò Pavese.

FRECCIAROSSA

Via Vigorelli 141
Casteggio (PV)
frecciarossa.com
Year of establishment: 1919
Owner: the Odero Radici family
Average number of bottles produced per year: 80,000

The winery, combining perseverance and conviction, has focused on the validation of the red grapes of the Oltrepò, particularly Pinot Noir, also keeping an eye on the potential of Croatina, Barbera, Uva Rara, and Vespolina. The oenological offer derives from 52 organically cultivated acres and includes all types of production, from the Metodo Classico to still whites, but the notoriety acquired in over a century of activity was born and continues to grow with the still reds, in particular with Giorgio Odero and Carillo, from pure Pinot Noir, and with the Anamari blend.

PINOT NERO DELL'OLTREPÒ PAVESE GIORGIO ODERO
First year of production: 1989
Average number of bottles produced per year: 6,000
Grape variety: Pinot Noir

Crisp berries combine with notes of dark spices and an elegant hint of eucalyptus. The flavor is important and enveloping, even more structured than the aromas suggest, with good acidity softened by the alcohol and passage in large wood for a year. At the pinnacle of Italian Pinot Noir.

MONSUPELLO

Via San Lazzaro 5
Torricella Verzate (PV)
monsupello.it
Year of establishment: 1893
Owner: the Boatti family
Average number of bottles
produced per year: 310,000

Pierangelo Boatti is
increasingly convinced of
the importance of adopting
a production philosophy
based on the use of Pinot
Noir, vinification of the bases
in steel only, and the almost
exclusive use of grapes from
his own 124 acres of vineyards.
The production—with
Brut, Brut Rosé, and Blanc
de Blancs Extra Brut at the
forefront, as well as Nature—is
characterized by elegant and
lively wines, free of softness
and sweetness, endowed with
incisive bubbles and powerful
taste. The winery that has
brought the sparkling wines of
Oltrepò Pavese to fame.

NATURE

First year of production: 1982
Average number of bottles produced
per year: 70,000
Grape varieties: Pinot Noir (90%),
Chardonnay (10%)

The aromas are among the most classic,
with pan brioche and hazelnut in evidence,
combined with refined citrus notes. The
good alcohol content—around 13% by
volume—and the very slight residual
sugar—just under 3 grams (0.1 ounce)—
contribute to the harmony and structure,
without in any way detracting from a
flavor that is decidedly dry, vigorous, and
refreshingly savory. Fineness and energy at
the highest level.

AR.PE.PE.

Via del Buon Consiglio 4
Sondrio
arpepe.com
Year of establishment: 1984
Owner: the Pelizzatti
Perego family
Average number of bottles
produced per year: 100,000

The winery's history began in
1864, but it was in 1984 that,
thanks to the efforts of Arturo
Pelizzatti Perego, the current
company structure took shape.
The mainstay of production
is represented by "mountain"
Nebbiolo, proposed in eleven
labels largely related to the
three main designations of
Valtellina: Sassella, Grumello,
and Inferno. The 37 acres
planted with vines are
managed without the aid of
chemical pesticides and the
wines are characterized by
long cellar stays, first in wood
and then in the bottle, to be
placed on the market only
when taste harmony has been
achieved.

VALTELLINA SUPERIORE SASSELLA RISERVA ROCCE ROSSE

First year of production: 1984
Average number of bottles produced
per year: 12,000
Grape variety: Nebbiolo

The grapes of the Rocce Rosse Reserve
are grown in one of the most evocative,
panoramic, and heroic vineyards in the
entire valley, then the wine matures in wood
and cement for forty months. It presents
an aromatic symphony based on red and
black fruits, against a background of good
ripeness reminiscent of citrus marmalade
and not without refreshing balsamic notes.
The flavor is vigorous, well-balanced, and
free of harshness. An archetypal Nebbiolo
from the Alps.

NINO NEGRI

Via Ghibellini 3
Chiuro (SO)
ninonegri.net
Year of establishment: 1897
Owner: Gruppo Italiano
Vini
Average number of bottles
produced per year: 800,000

The winery that made the
history of modern Valtellina
winemaking, first under
the leadership of Carlo and
Nino Negri, then under the
guidance of Gruppo Italiano
Vini through the figure of
Angiolino Maule.
The group owns 86 acres, but
the bulk of the grapes come
from 309 acres of historic vine
growers who are supported
and assisted in the continuous
maintenance and renovation
of the splendid vine terraces
typical of this area. The great
classic represented by the
Sfursat 5 Stelle is accompanied
by other productions of
absolute importance, from
Sforzato di Valtellina and
Valtellina Superiore dedicated
to Carlo Negri, to Grumello
Sassorosso and Sassella Le
Tense.

SFORZATO DI VALTELLINA SFURSAT 5 STELLE

First year of production: 1983
Average number of bottles produced
per year: 25,000
Grape variety: Nebbiolo

The grapes, 100% Nebbiolo, are dried for a
few weeks to obtain a concentration of the
substances in the berries—alcohol, minerals,
sugars, aromas—then the wine is matured
in French wood of different sizes for two
years. The result is a powerful and elegant
red wine, rich and multifaceted, with aromas
ranging from small berries to dark cherries
against a background of lively balsamicity;
the flavor is full-bodied but always agile and
remarkably persistent. A great expression of
the Nebbiolo grape.

RAINOLDI

Via Stelvio 128
Chiuro (SO)
rainoldi.com
Year of establishment: 1925
Owner: Aldo Rainoldi
Average number of bottles
produced per year: 185,000

This historic winery with
commercial traditions is
now increasingly involved in
finding new vineyards of its
own, which have now reached
30 acres and are productively
added to the grapes purchased
from long-standing suppliers.
The winery's fame is linked
above all to Sforzato di
Valtellina, and in particular
to the superlative Ca' Rizzieri
selection, but Aldo Rainoldi
has amply demonstrated its
excellence, with Valtellina
Superiore as well.

VALTELLINA SUPERIORE GRUMELLO RISERVA

First year of production: 2007
Average number of bottles produced per
year: 5,000
Grape variety: Nebbiolo

It originates in the Grumello subzone, at an
altitude of around 1,800 feet, so it is always
endowed with fine acidity and a touch of
savoriness. It matures for eighteen months in
oak and displays aromas of both red fruits and
citrus fruits, in a refined smoky and balsamic
setting. The palate is fresh, not very astringent,
very rich in flesh, and endowed with a long,
elegant finish with hints of medicinal herbs.

Veneto

Based on the names alone of a few places, it is easy enough to grasp the exceptional historical, cultural, and scenic nature of this region: Venice, Verona, Padua, Vicenza, the Dolomites, and Lake Garda. Veneto produces 20% of Italian wine.

The beauty of the cities and variety of Veneto's scenery characterize one of Italy's most powerful and productive regions, fourth in terms of size but first in terms of wine production, with almost 247,000 acres under vine and a phenomenon—Prosecco DOC—that makes no secret of its desire to reach the target of one billion bottles per year.

The thirty DOC and fourteen DOCG wines are articulated in a remarkable geological variety that characterizes very different places—which specific native vines have chosen as their *terroir* of choice—along with the main international vines that began to spread in these lands at the beginning of the nineteenth century. Within this great outdoor arena, Valpolicella's fame is strengthened, firmly establishing itself with Amarone, Recioto, and the Ripasso version in the consumption of many European countries and the New World. Even the Romans extolled the wine produced by the Reti, the inhabitants of these areas, and Pliny the Elder tells of the tradition of drying the grapes in use at the time.

In the Middle Ages, Verona and Venice were recognized centers of production and trade, and in the sixteenth century, Padua spread viticulture to the Euganean Hills. During this period, the Garganega grape took root in Soave, and Corvina in Valpolicella. Today, the white-wine soul of the region is revealed in Soave wine, originating from no less than 17,300 acres, partly of volcanic origin, in the province of Verona. It is one of Italy's most famous whites and, especially in the versions that make use of the Classico, Colli Scaligeri, and Superiore mentions, is showing a good ability to improve in the bottle for more than ten years.

Other valid productions for still white wines can be found throughout the region, starting with Custoza DOC, but regional wine production is now conditioned by the success of Prosecco DOC, a simple and pleasant wine without ambition, produced in nine provinces between Veneto and Friuli. Valuable and tantalizing productions, again from Glera grapes, can be found in the Conegliano Valdobbiadene Prosecco DOCG, where the hilly soils and non-massive agriculture offer a flash of vitality and personality to the most widely produced type of sparkling wine in the world.

Only 20% of Veneto's vineyards are now dedicated to red grapes, with qualitative results that nonetheless place this region among the most appreciated in Italy. The credit for this goes above all to Amarone, which is increasingly abandoning the image of a very alcoholic and somewhat sweet red wine in favor of a lively and multifaceted wine, capable of preserving its fruity crispness for decades. Corvina, Corvinone, and Rondinella grapes also give us the fresher and more immediate Bardolino, which with its Chiaretto version is making a name for itself in the general growth of rosé wine consumption.

The Merlot and Cabernet Sauvignon vines, present here for two centuries after being imported from Bordeaux, yield highly significant results, albeit in limited quantities, in both the Euganean Hills and the Berici Hills, with some significant encroachment in the Lison-Pramaggiore DOC. In the Piave area, these grapes, which are well present and enjoy interesting success, are accompanied by the impetuous personality of Raboso, which now enjoys its own Malanotte DOCG. The sweet wine scenario is very articulated, opening with the red Recioto della Valpolicella, continuing with the whites Recioto di Soave and Gambellara, and finishing up with an exciting interpretation of the Muscat grape, the Fior d'Arancio.

The results of all this are a productive reality that sees the annual production of close to 290 million gallons, together with thirty-six community wine cellars, involved in almost thirty thousand farms, with an average area under vine of just over 7 acres. The average grape yield per acre is among the highest in Italy: 6.5 tons.

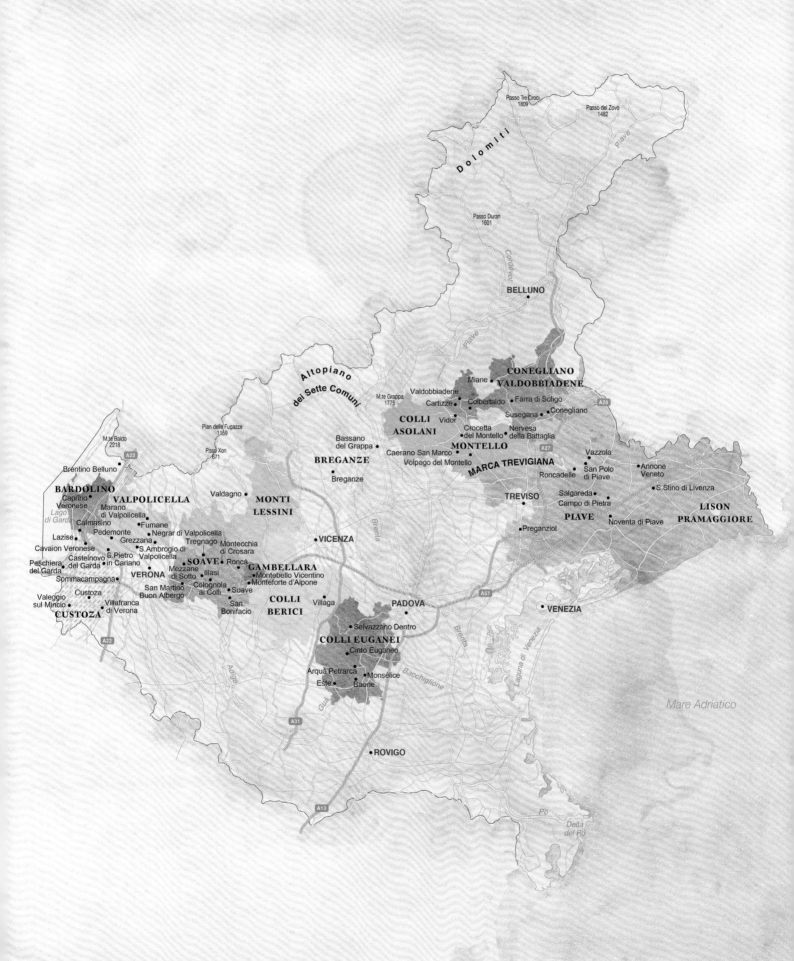

Passo Tre Croci
1809

Passo del Zovo
1482

D o l o m i t i

Piave

Passo Duran
1601

Cordévol

Piave

BELLUNO

CONEGLIANO
VALDOBBIADENE
Miane

Valdobbiadene
Cartizze   Colbertaldo   Farra di Soligo
COLLI   Vidor   Susegana   Conegliano
M.te Grappa   **ASOLANI**   Crocetta   Nervesa
1775   del Montello   della Battaglia

Altopiano
del Sette Comuni

Plan delle Fugazze
1159

Bassano
del Grappa   **MONTELLO**
BREGANZE   Caerano San Marco
P.sso Xon   Volpago del Montello   **MARCA TREVIGIANA**
671
Breganze   Vazzola

M.te Baldo   San Polo
2218   Roncadelle   di Piave   Annone
Veneto

Bréntino Belluno   **TREVISO**   S.Stino di Livenza
Salgareda

BARDOLINO   Valdagno   Campo di Pietra   **LISON**
Caprino   **PIAVE**   **PRAMAGGIORE**
Veronese   **VALPOLICELLA**   **MONTI**   Noventa di Piave
Marano   **LESSINI**
Lago   di Valpolicella
di Garda   Fumane   Preganziol
Calmasino   Pedemonte   Negrar di Valpolicella
Lazise   Grezzana   Tregnago   **VICENZA**
Cavaion Veronese   S.Ambrogio di   Montecchia
Valpolicella   di Crosara   Brenta
Castelnovo   S.Pietro   Ronca
Peschiera   del Garda   in Cariano   **SOAVE**
del Garda   Mezzane   **GAMBELLARA**
Sommacampagna   **VERONA**   di Sotto   Illasi   Montebello Vicentino
San Martino   Colognola   Monteforte d'Alpone
Custoza   Buon Albergo   ai Colli   Soave   **PADOVA**
Valeggio   **COLLI**
sul Mincio   Villafranca   San   **BERICI**   Villaga   **VENEZIA**
CUSTOZA   di Verona   Bonifacio
Laguna di Venezia

Adige   **COLLI EUGANEI**
Selvazzano Dentro

Cinto Euganeo

Bacchiglione

Arquà Petrarca   Monsélice
Este   Baone

Gua

Mare Adriatico

ROVIGO

Po

Delta
del Po

MAIN VINES GROWN IN THE REGION

Cabernet Sauvignon, Cabernet Franc, Carmenère, Merlot

→ International Grape Varieties
Widely used in Veneto, often in Bordeaux blends, in the designations Colli Berici, Colli Euganei, Breganze, Montello, Lison, and Piave.

Corvina, Corvinone, Rondinella, Molinara, Oseleta

In order of importance, the constituent grape varieties of the reds of the Amarone, Recioto della Valpolicella, and Bardolino Superiore DOCGs, of Valpolicella, and of Bardolino DOC. Together, they create one of Italy's great red wines—Amarone della Valpolicella—characterized by special processing involving a long drying period. The concentration of matter is such as to produce a wine of impressive structure and impact, immediately recognizable for its opulence, with a dense and soft taste and intense aromas of black cherry, blackberry, black currant, dehydrated plum, caramel, cocoa, cinnamon, and coffee, with a balsamic final sensation.

The Corvina is first mentioned by Alessandro Peccana in his 1627 treatise *De' problemi del bever freddo*. These vines, the product of an ornithologist's imagination, bear the names of the birds that traditionally eat them, but may also be so called because the juice of the berries has a raven color. Corvinone, despite its coarse name, is elegant and fine, less alcoholic, and more acidic than Corvina, and complex on the nose. The Rondinella completes the aromatic range, contributing to the overall harmony of the wine with good fruit, discreet acidity, and flavor.

The Molinara, or mill grape, so called because the bloom makes it look as if it were covered in flour, maintains a balance between acidity and tannins and thus adds flavor and fragrance, but the color is drab and the body light. In contrast, Oseleta can surprise with its dense tannic texture, color intensity, concentrated fruit, and a spicy note of nutmeg and clove. In Bardolino Superiore, these vines yield wines that are fresher and more immediate than Amarone because the grapes are not dried.

Durella

Also known as Cina, Cagnina, and Rabiosa, this is a grape with sharp acidity, suitable for making sparkling wine. It is used in the Lessini Durello DOC and to produce sparkling wines with a light body and hints of pan brioche, toasted hazelnut, and minerality characteristic of the volcanic *terroir* of origin.

The DOCGs

- Amarone della Valpolicella
- Bagnoli Friularo/ Friularo di Bagnoli
- Bardolino Superiore
- Colli Asolani Prosecco/Asolo Prosecco
- Colli di Conegliano
- Colli Euganei Fior d'Arancio/Fior d'Arancio Colli Euganei
- Conegliano Valdobbiadene Prosecco/ Conegliano Prosecco/ Valdobbiadene Prosecco
- Lison
- Montello Rosso/ Montello
- Piave Malanotte/ Malanotte del Piave
- Recioto della Valpolicella
- Recioto di Gambellara
- Recioto di Soave
- Soave Superiore

The DOCs

- Arcole
- Asolo Montello/ Montello Asolo
- Bagnoli di Sopra/ Bagnoli
- Bardolino
- Breganze
- Chiaretto di Bardolino
- Colli Berici
- Colli Euganei
- Corti Benedettine del Padovano
- Custoza
- Delle Venezie/ Beneškíh Okolišev
- Gambellara
- Garda
- Lessini Durello/ Durello Lessini
- Lison-Pramaggiore
- Lugana DOC (→ Lombardy)
- Merlara
- Monti Lessini
- Piave/Vini del Piave
- Prosecco
- Riviera del Brenta
- San Martino della Battaglia
- Soave
- Valdadige/Etschtaler
- Valdadige Terradeiforti/ Terradeiforti
- Valpolicella
- Valpolicella Ripasso
- Venezia
- Vicenza
- Vigneti della Serenissima/ Serenissima

Garganega

Mentioned for the first time in 1304 by Pietro de' Crescenzi in his agricultural treatise *Ruralium Commodorum Libri XII,* in Veneto it is found in the Soave and Gambellara designations, often together with Trebbiano, Friulano, and Cortese. It is a late-ripening, vigorous, and very productive plant and therefore requires special care in vineyard management. Rooted in the volcanic *terroirs* formed by basaltic rocks, tuff, and limestone of Soave and Gambellara—between the provinces of Verona and Vicenza—it prefers cool but well-irradiated slopes, from which it produces pleasant, well-structured wines, recognizable by a wide range of floral and citrus fragrances together with hints of elder, pear, white peach, apple, and lime.

Glera

Of Istrian origin, where it is known by the name of Teran Bijeli and related to the Zilavka of Bosnia-Herzegovina, it is the grape that forms the basis of the Prosecco designation and was cultivated in the village of Prosecco, near Trieste, as far back as the fourteenth century. To visualize the reach of its extension today in the Veneto region, one has to imagine a square with 185 miles on each side; the intentions are to grow another 245 acres in the coming years. The resulting wine has good acidity and different levels of dryness depending on whether it is Dry, Extra Dry, or Brut; the palate does not seek complexity but ease of drinking. The nose in the best cases refers to a pleasant bouquet of white flowers, accompanied by tropical and citrus scents. With refinement, the typical bread crust and a hint of aniseed and honey appear.

Raboso Piave and Raboso Veronese

Traditionally cultivated in the Piave designations, they are so called because of the acidic and astringent—angry—character of the wines they produce. Vinified in both red and dry and sweet versions as spumante or rosé. In the recent Malanotte DOCG, from the Raboso Piave, even surlier than its Veronese cousin, one can obtain complex and consistent reds, played on a seductive combination of dark fruit—Morello cherry and plum—and exotic fruit—dates, figs, and sultanas—with a dark chocolate and rhubarb finish, which respects the freshness of the vine but is rounded off by a small percentage of grapes left to dry for a month before being vinified.

Tai Rosso

→ Grenache in International Grape Varieties

Vespaiola

Exclusive to the province of Vicenza, it is blended in Breganze Bianco, Vicenza Bianco, and Gambellara, but is at its best in Breganze Torcolato, an intense and persistent passito with floral and honeyed notes.

Valpolicella DOC and Valpolicella Ripasso DOC

While for many decades Valpolicella DOC was considered the poor relation of Amarone by consumers and producers alike, the situation has qualitatively changed in the last twenty years, and one can now taste with satisfaction a red wine that is not overly concentrated but not lacking in structure, and has an enjoyable drinkability. The aromas are rich in small red fruits, often clear and elegant thanks to careful vinification, sometimes delicately accompanied by the spiciness of the aging wood. The taste is smooth and incisive with good articulation, lively, soft tannins, and pleasant freshness. Valpolicella Ripasso DOC, in which the wine is refermented for a few days in contact with the marc used to produce Amarone and Recioto, thus gaining in aromas and taste matter, is increasingly in demand on the market. The annual production of Valpolicella DOC is twenty million bottles with a good thirty-five million bottles of Valpolicella Ripasso DOC.

—

Producers and their trademark and signature wines:

1. BENEDETTI – Corte Antica, Sant'Ambrogio di Valpolicella
   Valpolicella Classico Superiore ($)
2. BERTANI, Grezzana
   Valpolicella Classico Superiore Ognisanti di Novare ($)
3. BRIGALDARA, San Pietro in Cariano
   Valpolicella Superiore Case Vecie ($)
4. CA' LA BIONDA, Marano di Valpolicella
   Valpolicella Classico Superiore CasalVegri ($)
5. CORTE ADAMI, Soave
   Valpolicella Superiore ($)
6. CORTE SANT'ALDA, Mezzane di Sotto
   Valpolicella Ca' Fiui ($)
7. Romano DAL FORNO, Illasi
   Valpolicella Superiore Monte Lodoletta ($$$$)
8. I CAMPI, Illasi
   Valpolicella Superiore ($)
9. LA DAMA, Negrar di Valpolicella
   Valpolicella Classico Superiore Ca' Besi ($)
10. LA GIUVA, Verona
    Valpolicella Superiore Il Rientro ($)
11. MONTE DALL'ORA, San Pietro in Cariano
    Valpolicella Classico Superiore San Giorgio Alto ($$)
    Valpolicella Classico Superiore Camporenzo ($)
12. Marco MOSCONI, Illasi
    Valpolicella Superiore ($)
13. ROCCOLO GRASSI, Mezzane di Sotto
    Valpolicella Superiore ($$)

14. SECONDO MARCO, Fumane
Valpolicella Classico Superiore Ripasso ($$)
15. SPERI, San Pietro in Cariano
Valpolicella Classico Superiore Sant'Urbano ($)
16. TENUTA SANT'ANTONIO, Colognola ai Colli
Valpolicella Superiore La Bandina ($)
17. VILLA SPINOSA, Negrar di Valpolicella
Valpolicella Classico Superiore Ripasso Jago ($)
18. Pietro ZANONI, Verona
Valpolicella Superiore ($)

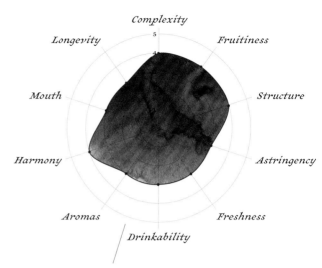

Valpolicella Classico Superiore

Amarone della Valpolicella DOCG

The grapes giving life to Amarone are twofold: Firstly, 45% to 95% Corvina, possibly substituted by up to 50% Corvinone grapes. The latter is a vine in its own right that is slightly more acidic and less alcoholic than Corvina, to which it is genetically related. Then there is Rondinella, accounting for 5% to 30%, possibly with up to 25% further use of authorized grapes. The production area consists of the entire foothills of the province of Verona. Amarone can be Classico if the vineyards are located in the municipalities of Negrar, Marano, Fumane, Sant'Ambrogio, and San Pietro in Cariano, or bear the indication Valpantena when the grapes are grown in the similarly named valley. The production process of this wine, which has been famous for centuries but only named as such for the last few decades, involves placing the grapes in crates after harvesting, or else on racks in well-ventilated fruit lofts for a period of one hundred and twenty days, during which they lose half their weight. These grapes, which are very concentrated and sugary, are then pressed and aged for at least two years in wood. The result is a great wine that tends to be dry, decidedly alcoholic, often close to 16% by volume, rich in aromas of ripe fruit and spices, from sultanas to licorice, soft and dense. Over eighteen million bottles are produced annually and exported all over the world.

Producers and their trademark and signature wines:

19. Stefano ACCORDINI, Fumane
Amarone della Valpolicella Classico Acinatico ($$)
20. ALLEGRINI, Fumane
Amarone della Valpolicella Classico Riserva Fieramonte ($$$$$)
Amarone della Valpolicella Classico ($$$)
21. Lorenzo BEGALI, San Pietro in Cariano
Amarone della Valpolicella Classico Riserva Monte Ca' Bianca ($$$)
2. BERTANI, Grezzana
Amarone della Valpolicella Classico ($$$)
3. BRIGALDARA, San Pietro in Cariano
Amarone della Valpolicella Classico ($$$)
22. Luigi BRUNELLI, San Pietro in Cariano
Amarone della Valpolicella Classico Riserva Campo Inferi ($$$)
4. CA' LA BIONDA, Marano di Valpolicella
Amarone della Valpolicella Classico Vigneti di Ravazzòl ($$$)
23. CORTE RUGOLIN, Marano di Valpolicella
Amarone della Valpolicella Riserva Monte Danieli ($$$)
6. CORTE SANT'ALDA, Mezzane di Sotto
Amarone della Valpolicella Valmezzane ($$$)
24. Valentina CUBI, Fumane
Amarone della Valpolicella Classico Morar ($$$)
25. DAL CERO Family – Tenuta Corte Giacobbe, Roncà
Amarone della Valpolicella ($$$)
7. Romano DAL FORNO, Illasi
Amarone della Valpolicella Vigneto di Monte Lodoletta ($$$$$)

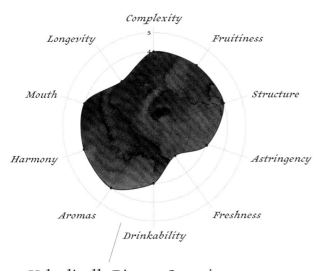

Valpolicella Ripasso Superiore

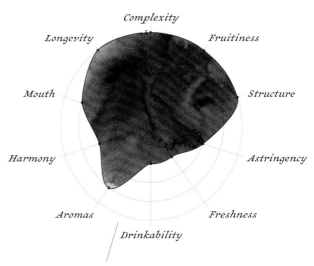

Amarone della Valpolicella

26. GUERRIERI RIZZARDI, Bardolino
Amarone della Valpolicella Classico Riserva Villa
Rizzardi ($$)

27. LE RAGOSE, Negrar di Valpolicella
Amarone della Valpolicella Classico Caloetto ($$$)

28. MASI, Sant'Ambrogio di Valpolicella
Amarone della Valpolicella Classico Campolongo di
Torbe ($$$$)
Amarone della Valpolicella Classico Costasera ($$)

29. Roberto MAZZI e Figli, Negrar di Valpolicella
Amarone della Valpolicella Classico Punta di Villa ($$$)

30. MONTE DEI RAGNI, Fumane
Amarone della Valpolicella Classico ($$$$)

31. MONTE ZOVO – Famiglia Cottini, Caprino Veronese
Amarone della Valpolicella ($$)

12. Marco MOSCONI, Illasi
Amarone della Valpolicella ($$$)

32. MUSELLA, San Martino Buon Albergo
Amarone della Valpolicella ($$)

33. NOVAIA, Marano di Valpolicella
Amarone della Valpolicella Classico Riserva Le Balze ($$$)

34. Giuseppe QUINTARELLI, Negrar di Valpolicella
Amarone della Valpolicella Classico Riserva ($$$$$)
Amarone della Valpolicella Classico ($$$$$)

13. ROCCOLO GRASSI, Mezzane di Sotto
Amarone della Valpolicella ($$$)

35. SANTI, Illasi
Amarone della Valpolicella Classico Proemio ($$)

14. SECONDO MARCO, Fumane
Amarone della Valpolicella Classico Riserva Fumetto
($$$$$)

15. SPERI, San Pietro in Cariano
15 della Valpolicella Classico Sant'Urbano ($$)

36. David STERZA, Fumane
Amarone della Valpolicella Classico ($$)

37. TEDESCHI, San Pietro in Cariano
Amarone della Valpolicella Riserva Maternigo ($$$$)
Amarone della Valpolicella Classico Capitel Monte
Olmi ($$$)

16. TENUTA SANT'ANTONIO, Colognola ai Colli
Amarone della Valpolicella Campo dei Gigli ($$$)
Amarone della Valpolicella Riserva Lilium Est ($$$$)

38. TOMMASI, Pedemonte
Amarone della Valpolicella Classico Riserva De Buris
($$$$$)

39. VENTURINI, San Pietro in Cariano
Amarone della Valpolicella Classico CampoMasua ($$)

40. VIGNETI DI ETTORE, Negrar di Valpolicella
Amarone della Valpolicella Classico ($$$)

17. VILLA SPINOSA, Negrar di Valpolicella
Amarone della Valpolicella Classico Albasini ($$$)

41. VIVIANI, Negrar di Valpolicella
Amarone della Valpolicella Classico Della Casa dei
Bepi ($$$)

42. Pietro ZARDINI, San Pietro in Cariano
Amarone della Valpolicella Classico Riserva Leone
Zardini ($$$)

43. ZÝMĒ, San Pietro in Cariano
Amarone della Valpolicella Classico Riserva La
Mattonara ($$$$$)

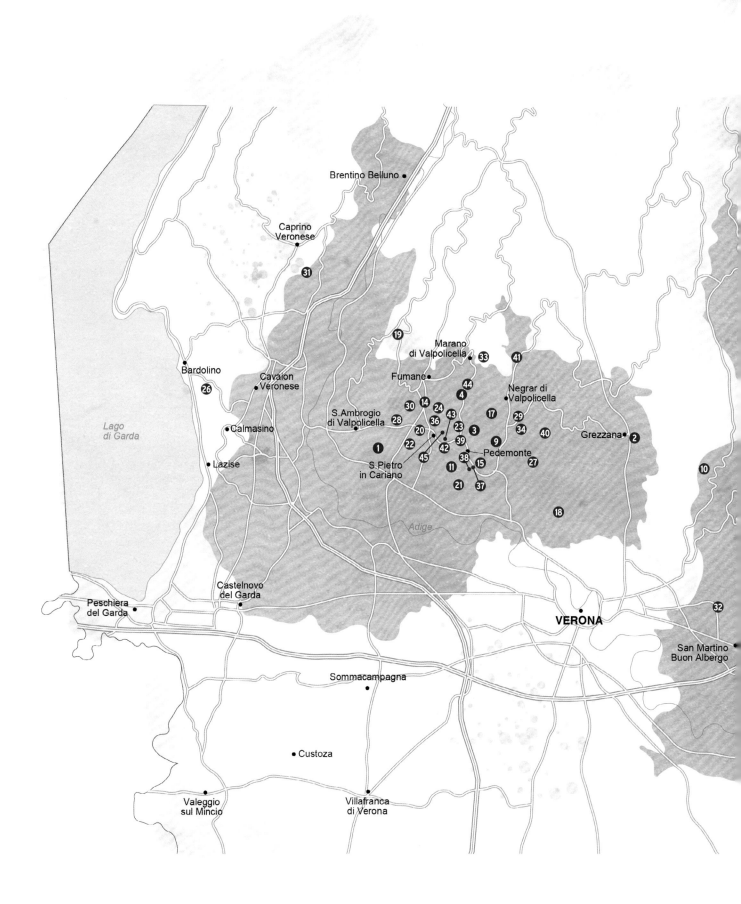

Brentino Belluno •

Caprino
Veronese •

㉛

⑲

Marano
di Valpolicella
• Fumane •   ㉝   ㊶

• Bardolino   ㊹   Negrar di
                    Cavaion   ④   Valpolicella
⑯   Veronese   ㉚ ⑭   •
                              S.Ambrogio   ㉘ ⑭⑳⑭   ⑰   ㉙
                              di Valpolicella ㉘   ㊱ ㊸   ㉞
• Calmasino   ⑳   ㉓ ③   ㊵
                                            ㊷ ㊴   ⑨   Grezzana • ②
Lago   ①   ㉒   ㊷   Pedemonte
di Garda   ㊺   ㊳⑮   ㉗
                              S.Pietro   ⑪ ㉑ ㊲
• Lazise   in Cariano   ⑩

                                                                  ⑱

Castelnovo
del Garda •

Peschiera   VERONA
del Garda •   ㉜

                                                              San Martino
                                                              Buon Albergo •

                    Sommacampagna
                    •

              • Custoza

Valeggio   Villafranca
sul Mincio •   di Verona •

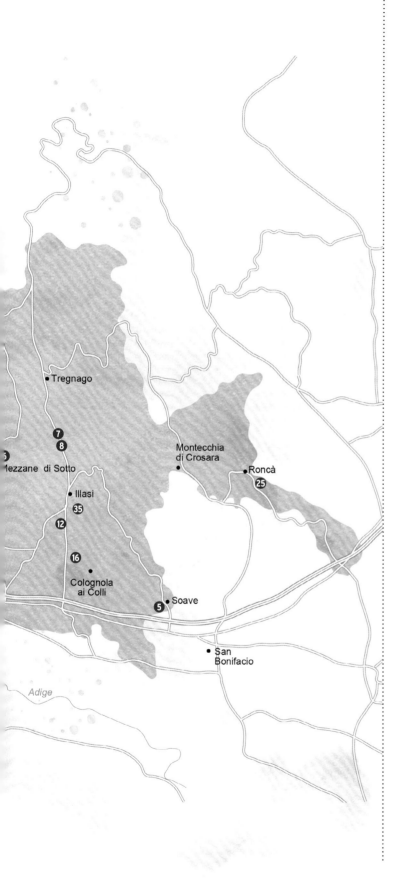

• Tregnago

Mezzane di Sotto

⑦
⑧

Montecchia
di Crosara

• Illasi

㉟

⑫

⑯

Colognola
ai Colli

⑤ • Soave

• Roncà

㉕

• San
Bonifacio

Adige

Recioto della Valpolicella DOCG

The same grapes used to make Amarone are dried for a period of three to four months, with a 40% yield in wine: the result is a Recioto della Valpolicella—a DOCG since 2010—rich in fruit aromas from ripe black cherry to walnuts to cherries in alcohol, spicy and powerful, in which, thanks to the early arrest of fermentation, not all the sugar has been transformed into alcohol. The minimum alcohol content is 12% by volume, with a minimum potential residual alcohol content of at least 50 grams (1.8 ounces) of unfermented sugar, so as to guarantee a certain sweetness of flavor. Approximately four hundred thousand bottles per year are produced, often in small sizes.

—

Producers and their trademark and signature wines:

44. ANTOLINI, Marano di Valpolicella
    Recioto della Valpolicella Classico ($)
21. Lorenzo BEGALI, San Pietro in Cariano
    Recioto della Valpolicella Classico ($$)
28. MASI, Sant'Ambrogio di Valpolicella
    Recioto della Valpolicella Classico Amandorlato
    Mezzanella ($$$)
45. RUBINELLI VAJOL, San Pietro in Cariano
    Recioto della Valpolicella Classico ($$)
41. VIVIANI, Negrar di Valpolicella
    Recioto della Valpolicella Classico ($$$)

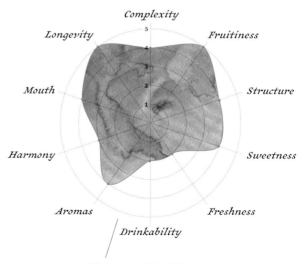

Recioto della Valpolicella

Soave DOC and Soave Superiore DOCG and Recioto di Soave DOCG

As occurred in other historical areas of Italian wine production, from Chianti to the Langhe of Barolo, the 1970s and early 1980s coincided with a period in which many producers were dedicated to quantity rather than quality, causing a decline in the image of important designations. But it was in the eighties that the concept and desire for the redemption of Italian wine strongly emerged, with many wineries, new and old, beginning to make stunning improvements that are still ongoing. The creation of the Soave Superiore DOCG (2001) also moved in this direction but proved to be of little use and is therefore scarcely used today. A fundamental step for the certification of the territory occurred in 2019 when, after years of research, thirty-three Additional Geographical Units were officially recognized, indicating the toponyms of the most famous production areas, to which the names of the vineyards recognized by the Veneto Region can be added. Fruit and white flowers, and often even citrus and mineral notes—some speak of "gunpowder"—characterize the aromas, while the flavor is one of good harmony, fresh but not acidic, and flowing. Today's figures say that production is close to fifty-six million bottles per year, ten of which can use the Classico or Colli Scaligeri specification. Almost 80% of these are exported due to mostly moderate prices. The small and refined Recioto di Soave DOCG, from dried grapes, is limited to three hundred and thirty thousand bottles per year. The grapes used are Garganega (at least 70%), with Trebbiano di Soave and Chardonnay for the remainder.

—
Producers and their trademark and signature wines:

1. CA' RUGATE, Montecchia di Crosara
    Soave Classico Monte Fiorentine ($)
    Soave Classico Monte Alto ($)
2. COFFELE, Soave
    Soave Classico Ca' Visco ($)
    Recioto di Soave Classico Le Sponde ($ $)
3. FILIPPI, Soave
    Soave Colli Scaligeri Vigne della Brà ($)
    Soave Colli Scaligeri Castelcerino ($)
4. GINI, Monteforte d'Alpone
    Soave Classico La Froscà ($)
    Soave Classico Contrada Salvarenza Vecchie Vigne ($)
5. I CAMPI, Illasi
    Soave Classico Campo Vulcano ($)
6. I STEFANINI, Monteforte d'Alpone
    Soave Superiore Classico Monte di Fice ($)
7. INAMA, San Bonifacio
    Soave Classico Foscarino I Palchi Grande Cuvée ($$)
    Soave Classico Carbonare ($)
8. LA CAPPUCCINA, Monteforte d'Alpone
    Soave Classico Monte Stelle ($)
9. LE BATTISTELLE, Monteforte d'Alpone
    Soave Classico Roccolo del Durlo ($)
10. MONTE TONDO, Soave
    Soave Superiore Classico Foscarin Slavinus ($)
11. PIEROPAN, Soave
    Soave Classico Calvarino ($)
    Soave Classico La Rocca ($$)
12. PRÀ, Monteforte d'Alpone
    Soave Classico Monte Grande ($)
    Soave Classico Staforte ($)
13. SUAVIA, Soave
    Soave Classico Monte Carbonare ($)
14. TAMELLINI, Soave
    Soave Classico Le Bine de Costìola ($)
15. TENUTA SANT'ANTONIO, Colognola ai Colli
    Soave Vecchie Vigne ($)
16. Agostino VICENTINI, Colognola ai Colli
    Soave Superiore Il Casale ($)

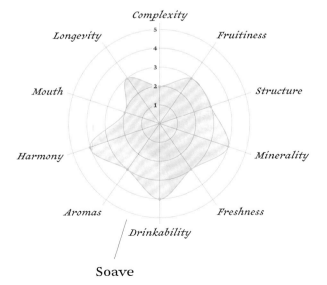

Soave

Gambellara DOC and Recioto di Gambellara DOCG

At least 80% Garganega grapes are used to produce it in four municipalities in the province of Vicenza. It is a wine that, in the still version, is convincingly and pleasantly drinkable thanks to clear floral aromas and a taste that is always fresh with acidity. Recioto di Gambellara is also produced in the same area, in small quantities, and in 2008 obtained its own DOCG, which includes the Classico and Spumante types. Overall production is close to two million bottles per year.

—

Producers and their trademark and signature wines:

17. CAVAZZA, Montebello Vicentino
    Recioto di Gambellara Classico Capitel ($)
18. DAL MASO, Montebello Vicentino
    Gambellara Ca' Fischele ($)

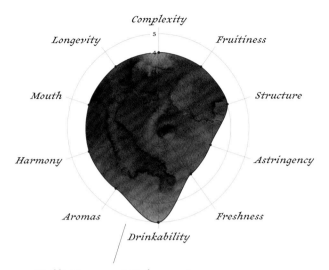

Colli Euganei Cabernet

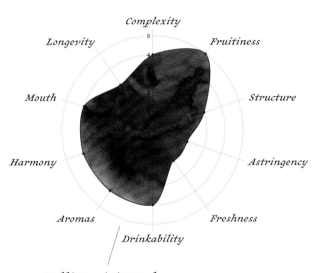

Colli Berici Merlot

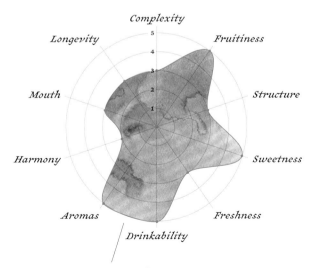

Colli Euganei Fior d'Arancio

Colli Euganei DOC

The DOC covers a hilly area spread over seventeen municipalities in the province of Padua and includes twenty-six different types, made from white and red grapes. The versions that have established themselves with the most assurance, and not only on the Italian market, are those using Merlot, Cabernet Sauvignon, and Carmenère. Colli Euganei Rosso, which is very widespread, is made from Merlot (40 to 80%), Cabernet Sauvignon, and/or Franc and/or Carmenère (20 to 60%), possibly with Raboso for no more than 10% and at least two years of aging in the cellar for the Riserva versions. Elegant olfactory hints of small red fruits predominate, the most frequently mentioned being blackberries and cherries, sometimes with citrus or slightly balsamic touches, and the spiciness of the aging wood, with a dense but always responsive taste. A total of over five million bottles are produced annually.

—

Producers and their trademark and signature wines:

1. CA' LUSTRA – Zanovello, Cinto Euganeo
    Colli Euganei Merlot Sassonero ($)
    Colli Euganei Cabernet Girapoggio ($)
2. CA' OROLOGIO, Baone
    Colli Euganei Rosso Calaóne ($)
3. CONTE EMO CAPODILISTA – La Montecchia, Selvazzano Dentro
    Colli Euganei Rosso Villa Capodilista ($$)
4. IL FILÒ DELLE VIGNE, Baone
    Colli Euganei Merlot Casa del Merlo ($$)
    Colli Euganei Cabernet Riserva Borgo delle Casette ($$)
5. IL MOTTOLO, Arquà Petrarca
    Colli Euganei Rosso Serro ($)
    Colli Euganei Carmenère Vignànima ($$)
6. VIGNALTA, Arquà Petrarca
    Colli Euganei Rosso Gemola ($$)
    Colli Euganei Merlot Riserva ($)

Colli Berici DOC

In this vast hilly area in the province of Treviso, numerous red and white varieties are cultivated, both local and international (from Sauvignon to Tai and Pinot Noir), but the area's success derives above all from the successful growth here of Bordeaux varieties. These are Merlot, Cabernet Sauvignon and Franc, and

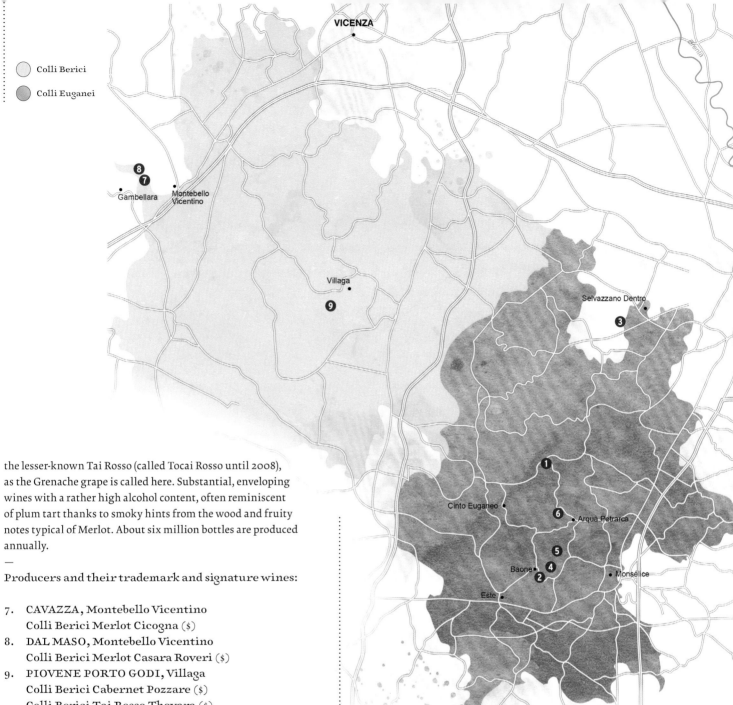

Colli Berici

Colli Euganei

the lesser-known Tai Rosso (called Tocai Rosso until 2008), as the Grenache grape is called here. Substantial, enveloping wines with a rather high alcohol content, often reminiscent of plum tart thanks to smoky hints from the wood and fruity notes typical of Merlot. About six million bottles are produced annually.

—

Producers and their trademark and signature wines:

7. CAVAZZA, Montebello Vicentino
   Colli Berici Merlot Cicogna ($)
8. DAL MASO, Montebello Vicentino
   Colli Berici Merlot Casara Roveri ($)
9. PIOVENE PORTO GODI, Villaga
   Colli Berici Cabernet Pozzare ($)
   Colli Berici Tai Rosso Thovara ($)

Colli Euganei Fior d'Arancio or Fior d'Arancio Colli Euganei DOCG

In the Euganean Hills, yellow Muscat has been cultivated for centuries and has therefore earned its own independent DOCG, which also includes a Spumante and a passito version. And it is precisely the latter that wins during tastings, thanks to aromas

of orange blossom, lavender, apricot, and Mediterranean scrub, followed by a soft, sweet taste in the mouth with no lack of fresh and acidic elements to create a harmony of sensations. A total of more than one million bottles are produced each year, of reduced size in the case of the passito.

—

Producers and their trademark and signature wines:

1. CA' LUSTRA – Zanovello, Cinto Euganeo
   Colli Euganei Fior d'Arancio Passito ($)
3. CONTE EMO CAPODILISTA – La Montecchia,
   Selvazzano Dentro
   Colli Euganei Fior d'Arancio Passito Donna Daria ($)
6. VIGNALTA, Arquà Petrarca
   Colli Euganei Fior d'Arancio Passito Alpianae ($$)

Bardolino and Chiaretto di Bardolino DOC and Bardolino Superiore DOCG

Produced in sixteen municipalities in the province of Verona, Bardolino DOC, with slight differences in the Superiore DOCG version, is made from Corvina grapes at between 35% and 95%, with the possible intervention of Corvinone for no more than 20%, Rondinella at between 5% and 40%, and other varieties for no more than 20%. Given the ampelographic composition, comparing it with Amarone would be natural, but in this area, a different wine has been created, one with good alcohol content and rich in spices, but fresher and more immediate, from grapes that are not dried and to be consumed within a few years of the harvest. The popular Chiaretto type—corresponding to a rosé—has had its own official name since 2021, changing from Bardolino Chiaretto to Chiaretto di Bardolino. Seventeen million bottles of Bardolino and nine million of Chiaretto di Bardolino are produced annually, a figure that is growing.

—

Producers and their trademark and signature wines:

1. CASARETTI, Calmasino
   Bardolino La Rocca ($$)
2. CORTE GARDONI, Valeggio sul Mincio
   Bardolino Superiore Pràdicà ($)
3. LE FRAGHE, Cavaion Veronese
   Chiaretto di Bardolino Traccia di Rosa ($)
   Bardolino Classico Brol Grande ($)
4. LE TENDE, Lazise
   Bardolino Classico ($)
5. LE VIGNE DI SAN PIETRO, Sommacampagna
   Bardolino ($)
6. Marcello MARCHESINI, Lazise
   Bardolino Classico ($)
7. Giovanna TANTINI, Castelnuovo del Garda
   Chiaretto di Bardolino ($)
8. VIGNETI VILLABELLA, Calmasino
   Bardolino Classico Chiaretto Villa Cordevigo ($)
   Bardolino Montebaldo Morlongo ($)

Custoza DOC

It is cultivated in nine municipalities in the province of Verona, and the grapes it is made from are Trebbiano Toscano (10 to 45%), Garganega (20 to 40%), and Tai (formerly Tocai Friulano, at 5 to 30%), with the possible addition of other grapes (such as Malvasia, Cortese, Chardonnay, etc.) for no more than 30%. With considerable variability deriving from the cultivars used, on the nose Custova is a wine rich in white fruit, citrus fruits, and fresh, almost balsamic notes, while the palate is quite consistent and often endowed with considerable savoriness. It deserves to be aged in glass. Thirteen million bottles are produced each year.

—

Producers and their trademark and signature wines:

9. CANTINA DI CUSTOZA, Sommacampagna
   Custoza Superiore Custodia ($)
10. CAVALCHINA, Sommacampagna
    Custoza Superiore Amedeo ($)
2. CORTE GARDONI, Valeggio sul Mincio
   Custoza Mael ($)
11. GORGO, Custoza
    Custoza San Michelin ($)
    Custoza Superiore Summa ($)
12. MENEGOTTI, Villafranca di Verona
    Custoza Superiore Elianto ($)
13. MONTE DEL FRÀ, Sommacampagna
    Custoza Superiore Cà del Magro ($)
14. Albino PIONA, Villafranca di Verona
    Custoza Superiore Campo del Selese ($)

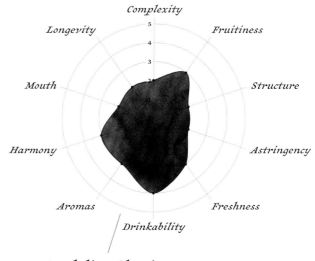

Bardolino Classico

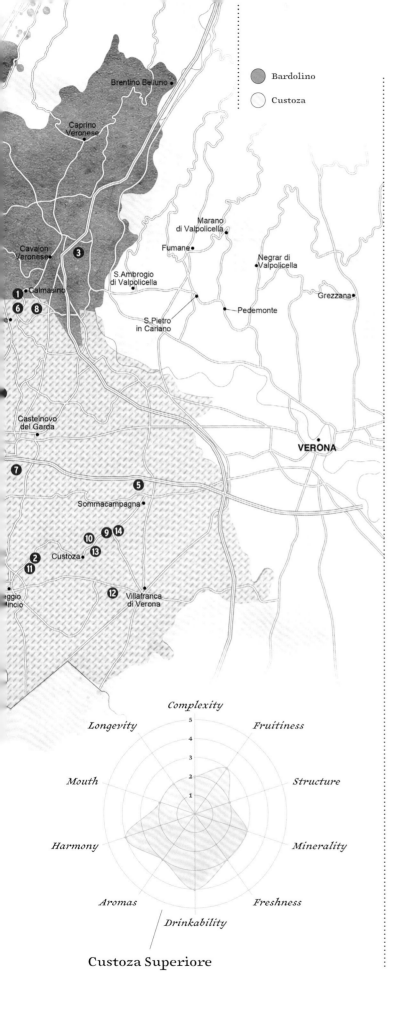

Bardolino

Custoza

Prosecco DOC

Italy's most exported DOC wine, in demand all over the world, that in twenty years has proved capable of creating a true production revolution not only in Veneto but also in Friuli-Venezia Giulia, the two regions where the six hundred million bottles are produced annually. The typologies, in addition to the basic Prosecco, include the Spumante and Frizzante versions, made from at least 85% Glera grapes, as well as the recently discussed Spumante Rosé, in which Pinot Noir, vinified in red, must make up between 10% and 15%. These are mostly wines with simple white fruit aromas, drinkable and very cheap, so wine critics take little interest in them and suggest focusing on the DOCG versions of Glera. We recommend two of them, rich in personality.

—

Producers and their trademark and signature wines:

1. BIANCAVIGNA, Conegliano
    Prosecco Brut ($)
2. GREGOLETTO, Miane
    Prosecco Treviso Frizzante Sui Lieviti ($)

Colli Asolani Prosecco or Asolo Prosecco DOCG

The production area covers seventeen municipalities in the province of Treviso, at an altitude between 330 and 1,500 feet, and the grape is called Glera, which up until 2009 was called Prosecco. The latter makes up for at least 85%. It is produced by refermentation in autoclaves, more rarely in bottles, and has a minimum alcohol content of 10.5% by volume, or 11 in the case of Superiore. The aromas lead to apple, pear, and yellow flowers, sometimes with fresher notes reminiscent of citrus fruits. Compared to Valdobbiadene DOCG, some experts suggest there is a greater savoriness on the palate. About twenty-five million bottles are produced, of varying levels of quality.

—

Producers and their trademark and signature wines:

3. BELE CASEL, Caerano di San Marco
    Asolo Prosecco Superiore Vecchie Uve ($)
4. CASE PAOLIN, Volpago del Montello
    Asolo Prosecco Superiore Col Fondo Sui Lieviti
    Brut Nature ($)

Custoza Superiore

Conegliano Valdobbiadene Prosecco or Conegliano Prosecco or Valdobbiadene Prosecco DOCG

This DOCG wine originates from fifteen hillside municipalities in the province of Treviso and represents the qualitative apex of Prosecco, headed by the famous and fascinating area dedicated to Superiore di Cartizze. This consists of 265 acres worked by no less than one hundred and forty owners, resulting in an annual production of almost one and a half million bottles. It is made from at least 85% Glera grapes and also includes the Frizzante and Superiore types, and is allowed to bear the names of municipalities or hamlets after the specification "Rive di..." The Superiore is the type most appreciated by experts: a wine with a very rich bouquet of white fruit, such as apple and pear, often joined by delicate notes of citrus and Mediterranean herbs. Its strong point is certainly on the palate, always smooth and flowing, never lacking a touch of savoriness that counteracts the residual sugars. Remember that in the widespread Brut type, there are between 5 and 12 g/l (0.18 and 0.42 oz/qt)—which thus builds a joyful drinkability responsible for its fortune worldwide. In 2009, forty-three MGAs (Menzioni Geografiche Aggiuntive - Additional Geographical Mentions) were instituted, which here are called *Rive*, meaning "steeply sloping terrain." Twelve relate to the names of municipalities and thirty-one to the names of hamlets, imposing stricter quality criteria than the DOCG. Just over one hundred million bottles are produced per year—compared to over six hundred million for Prosecco DOC—80% of which are exported.

Producers and their trademark and signature wines:

5. **ADAMI**, Vidor
   Valdobbiadene Prosecco Superiore Rive di Colbertaldo Asciutto Vigneto Giardino ($)
   Valdobbiadene Prosecco Superiore Extra Brut Rive di Farra di Soligo Col Credas ($)
6. **ANDREOLA**, Farra di Soligo
   Valdobbiadene Prosecco Superiore Brut Rive di Refrontolo Col del Forno ($)
1. **BIANCAVIGNA**, Conegliano
   Conegliano Valdobbiadene Prosecco Superiore Extra Brut Millesimato Rive di Ogliano ($)
7. **BISOL 1542**, Valdobbiadene
   Valdobbiadene Prosecco Superiore Dry Millesimato Rive di Campea ($)

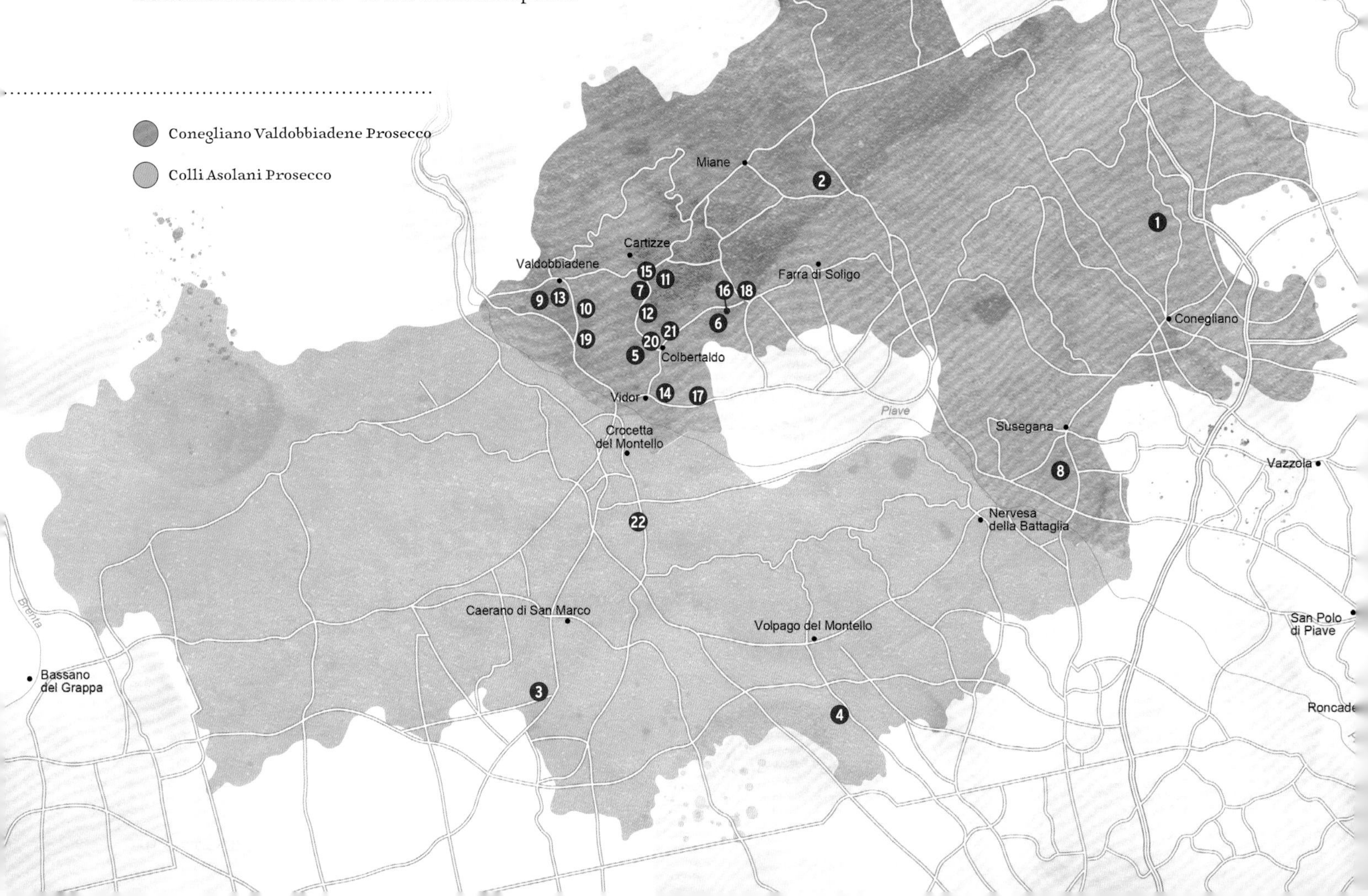

Conegliano Valdobbiadene Prosecco

Colli Asolani Prosecco

8. BORGOLUCE, Susegana
    Valdobbiadene Prosecco Superiore Extra Brut
    Rive di Collalto ($)
9. BORTOLOMIOL, Valdobbiadene
    Valdobbiadene Prosecco Superiore Brut
    Millesimato Ius Naturae ($)
    Valdobbiadene Prosecco Superiore Brut Nature
    Millesimato Rive San Pietro di Barbozza Grande
    Cuvée del Fondatore Motus Vitae ($)
10. CA' DEI ZAGO, Valdobbiadene
    Valdobbiadene Prosecco Frizzante a
    Rifermentazione Spontanea in Bottiglia ($)
11. CASA COSTE PIANE, Valdobbiadene
    Valdobbiadene Prosecco Frizzante ...
    Naturalmente ($)
12. Silvano FOLLADOR, Valdobbiadene
    Valdobbiadene Prosecco Superiore Brut
    Nature ($)
13. Nino FRANCO, Valdobbiadene
    Valdobbiadene Prosecco Superiore Brut Nodi ($)
    Valdobbiadene Proseccco Superiore Dry Primo
    Franco ($)
14. LA TORDERA, Vidor
    Valdobbiadene Prosecco Superiore Extra Brut
    Rive di Guia Otreval ($)
15. LE COLTURE, Valdobbiadene
    Valdobbiadene Prosecco Superiore Brut Rive di
    Santo Stefano Gerardo ($)
    Valdobbiadene Superiore di Cartizze Dry ($)
16. MEROTTO, Farra di Soligo
    Valdobbiadene Prosecco Superiore Brut
    Millesimato Rive di Col San Martino Cuvée del
    Fondatore Graziano Merotto ($)
    Valdobbiadene Prosecco Superiore Extra Dry
    Millesimato Castè ($)
17. MIOTTO, Colbertaldo
    Valdobbiadene Prosecco Superiore Extra Brut
    Rive di Colbertaldo De Rive ($)
18. MONGARDA, Farra di Soligo
    Conegliano Valdobbiadene Prosecco Superiore
    Extra Dry ($)
19. RUGGERI, Valdobbiadene
    Valdobbiadene Prosecco Superiore Extra Dry
    Millesimato Giustino B. ($)
    Valdobbiadene Prosecco Superiore Brut
    Millesimato Vecchie Viti ($)
    Valdobbiadene Superiore di Cartizze Brut ($)
20. SORELLE BRONCA, Vidor
    Valdobbiadene Prosecco Superiore Brut Rive di
    Rua Particella 181 ($)
21. SPAGNOL – Col del Sas, Vidor
    Conegliano Valdobbiadene Prosecco
    Superiore Extra Brut Quindici16 ($)
22. VILLA SANDI, Crocetta del Montello
    Valdobbiadene Prosecco Superiore di Cartizze
    Brut La Rivetta ($)

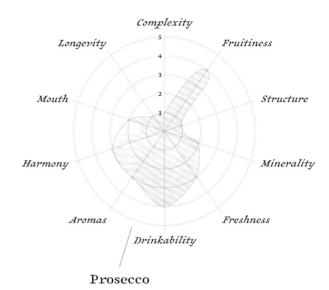

Prosecco

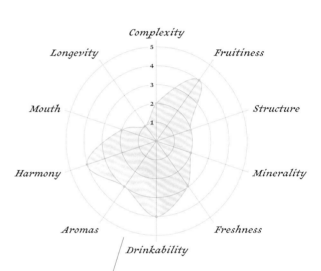

Conegliano Valdobbiadene
Prosecco Extra Dry

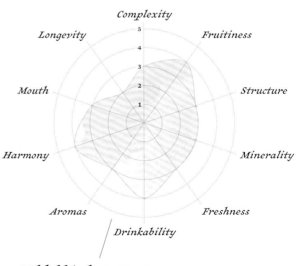

Valdobbiadene Prosecco
Superiore di Cartizze Brut

Asolo Montello or Montello Asolo DOC and Montello Rosso or Montello DOCG

Both the DOC and DOCG areas include the hilly territory of Asolo and eighteen other municipalities in the province of Treviso, north of Venice. The area has also proved suitable for the use of international cultivars, with significant results in the vinification of red grapes. While the DOC—called Montello-Colli Asolani until 2019—encompasses seventeen different types, also from white grapes, the DOCG is reserved for Rosso. With minimal differences in the production regulations, both Asolo Montello Rosso DOC and Montello Rosso DOCG must be made from Cabernet Sauvignon grapes (at 40 to 70%, or 50 to 70% in the case of the Venegazzù subzone); and then Merlot and/or Cabernet Franc and/or Carmenère from 30% to 60%, which is reduced to 30 to 50% for Venegazzù. These are clear Bordeaux-style red wines, rich in blackberry and medicinal herb aromas, long, soft, and silky on the palate. About six hundred and fifty thousand bottles per year are produced, seventy thousand of which are DOCG.

—

Producers and their trademark and signature wines:

1. CASE PAOLIN, Volpago del Montello
   Montello – Colli Asolani Rosso San Carlo ($$)
2. LOREDAN GASPARINI, Volpago del Montello
   Montello – Colli Asolani Venegazzù Superiore
   Capo di Stato ($$$)
3. SERAFINI & VIDOTTO, Nervesa della Battaglia
   Montello – Colli Asolani Il Rosso dell'Abazia ($$)

Piave or Vini del Piave DOC and Piave Malanotte or Malanotte del Piave DOCG

A vast designation that includes part of the provinces of Treviso and Venice, where mostly red grapes of Bordeaux origin are grown (from Merlot to Cabernet Sauvignon), to which the traditional Raboso is added, as well as white grapes ranging from Tai al Verduzzo to Chardonnay. Of particular interest is the Piave Malanotte, recognized as DOCG in 2010, which is made from Piave Raboso grapes—a decidedly acidic and tannic cultivar—and Veronese Raboso—slightly softer and less surly—after drying the bunches in percentages varying from 15% to 30%. The result is a wine rich in ripe fruit and spicy hints with a powerful, vital, and fresh first taste thanks to its considerable acidity. Two million bottles of Piave DOC are produced annually; one hundred sixty thousand bottles of them are Malanotte del Piave DOCG.

—

Producers and their trademark and signature wines:

4. BONOTTO DELLE TEZZE, Vazzola
   Piave Malanotte ($$)
5. CA' DI RAJO, San Polo di Piave
   Piave Malanotte Notti di Luna Piena ($)
6. Giorgio CECCHETTO, Vazzola
   Piave Malanotte Gelsaia ($$)
   Piave Raboso ($)
7. TESSÈRE, Noventa di Piave
   Piave Malanotte ($)

Asolo Montello
and Montello Rosso

Piave and Piave
Malanotte

Lison and Lison-
Pramaggiore

Farra di Soligo

Colbertaldo

Vidor

Piave

Crocetta
del Montello

Caerano di San Marco

❷ Volpago del Mc

❶

Bassano
del Grappa

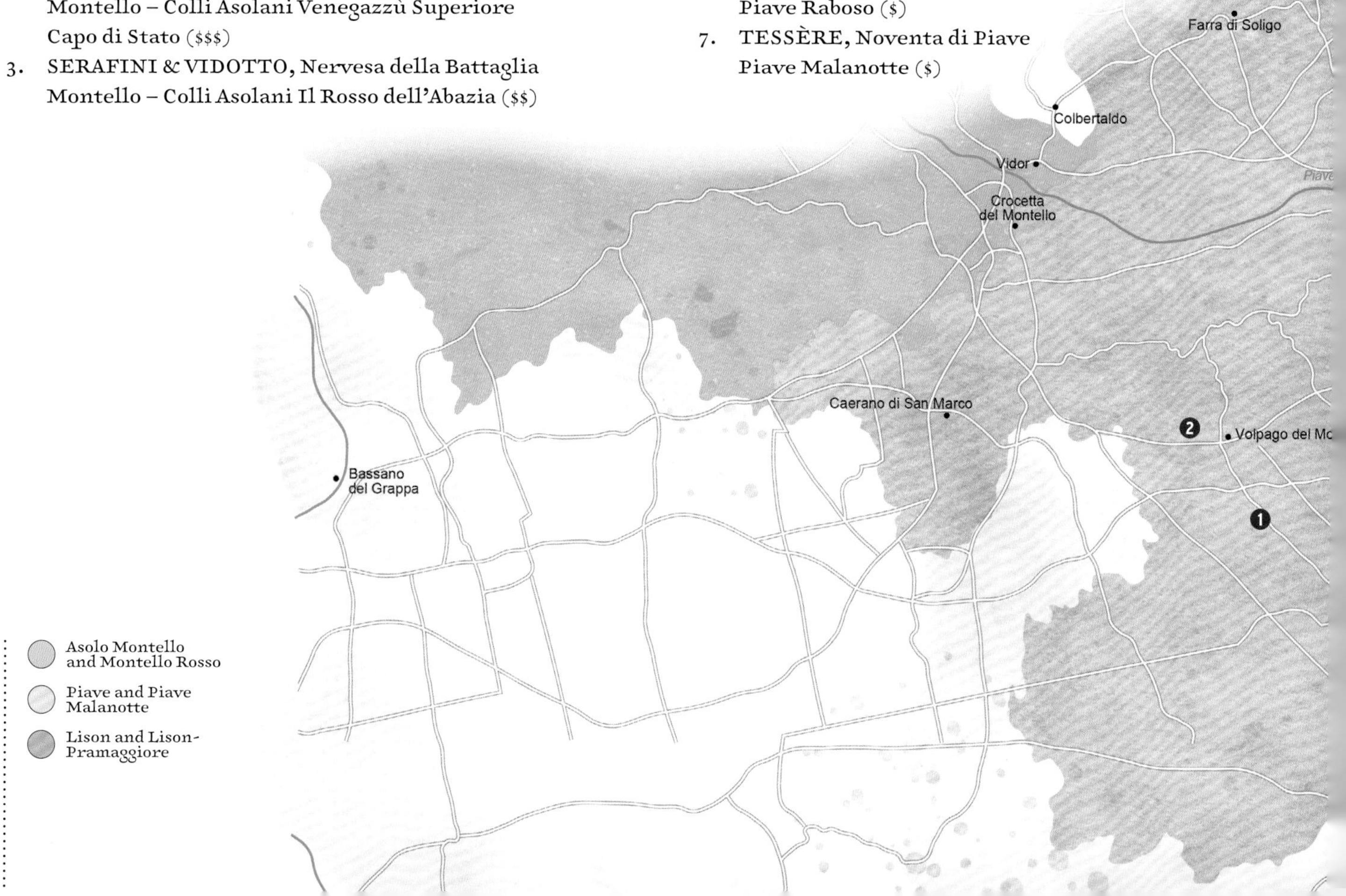

Lison-Pramaggiore DOC and Lison DOCG

An interregional DOC and DOCG that spans three provinces, Venice and Treviso in Veneto and Pordenone in Friuli-Venezia Giulia, it is based on local grapes (such as Refosco dal Peduncolo Rosso) or international grapes (Merlot, Malbec), with the Cabernet Franc, Cabernet Sauvignon, and Pinot Gris types necessarily produced in Friuli territory. The DOCG, on the other hand, is only for white wine produced with at least 85% Tai, formerly known as Tocai Friulano. The Lison-Pramaggiore Bianco is made with at least 50% Friulano, and the Rosso with no less than 50% Merlot. Overall production is close to two million bottles per year; the DOCG does not exceed three hundred fifty thousand.

—

Producers and their trademark and signature wines:

8. BOSCO DEL MERLO, Pravisdomini (Friuli)
    Lison Pramaggiore (Venezia DOC since 2019)
    Refosco dal Peduncolo Rosso Riserva Roggio dei
    Roveri ($)
9. MOSOLE, San Stino di Livenza
    Lison Pramaggiore Merlot Ad Nonam ($$)
10. MULIN DI MEZZO, Annone Veneto
    Lison Classico ($)

Montello Rosso

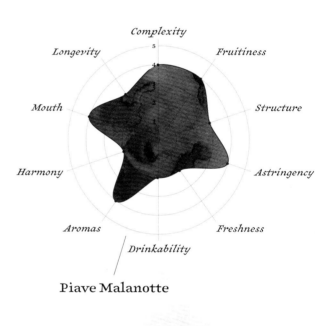

Piave Malanotte

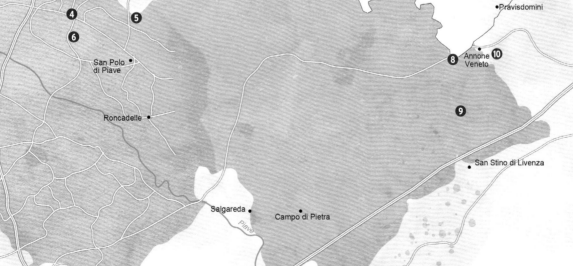

Breganze DOC

The territory of this DOC spans thirteen municipalities in the province of Vicenza and includes numerous types, based on local and international grapes. These include two selections that have been on the crest of the wave for years: a Torcolato, made from dried Vespaiola grapes, and a spicy Cabernet with notes of licorice. Annual production is close to two million bottles.

—

Producers and their trademark and signature wines:

1. MACULAN, Breganze
    Breganze Torcolato ($)
2. VIGNETO DUE SANTI, Bassano del Grappa
    Breganze Cabernet Due Santi ($$)

Lessini Durello or Durello Lessini DOC

A DOC was created in 2011 to regulate the flourishing sparkling wine production of the Lessini Mountains area, which consists of no less than 70,000 acres between the provinces of Verona and Vicenza. There is also a Charmat Method version, defined as Lessini Durello, but the most relevant products come from the elaboration using the Metodo Classico, called Monti Lessini, of the Durella grapes (at minimum 85%), known for their fruity scents and, above all, their sharp acidity, after a period of at least thirty-six months on the lees. A total of over three million bottles are produced per year.

—

Producers and their trademark and signature wines:

3. CASA CECCHIN, Montebello Vicentino
    Lessini Durello Extra Brut Nostrum M. Cl. ($)
4. DAL CERO Family – Tenuta Corte Giacobbe, Roncà
    Lessini Durello Extra Brut Riserva Cuvée
    Augusto M. Cl. ($$)
5. DAL MASO, Montebello Vicentino
    Lessini Durello Pas Dosé Riserva M. Cl. ($)
6. FONGARO, Roncà
    Lessini Durello Brut Riserva M. Cl. ($$)

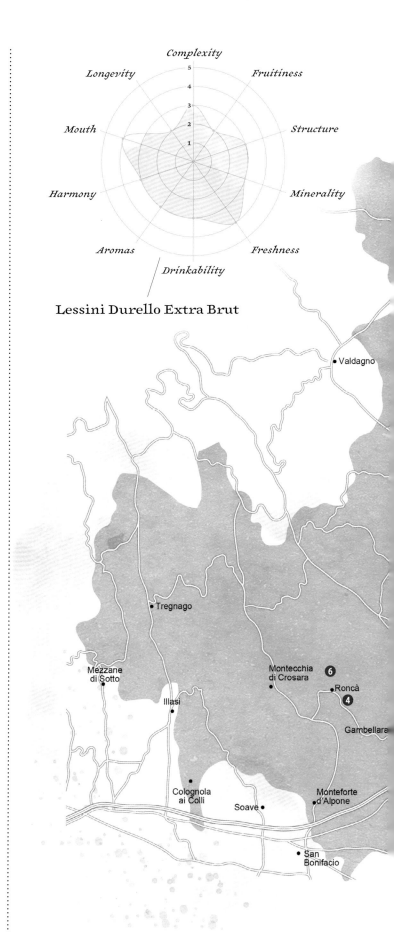

Lessini Durello Extra Brut

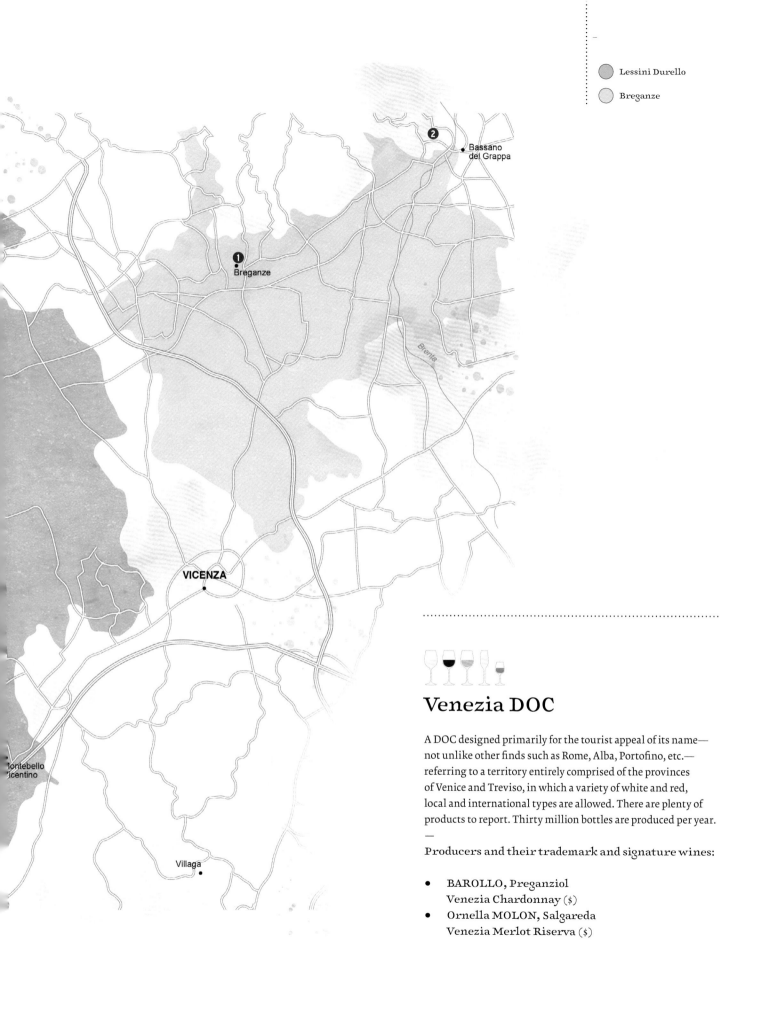

Venezia DOC

A DOC designed primarily for the tourist appeal of its name—
not unlike other finds such as Rome, Alba, Portofino, etc.—
referring to a territory entirely comprised of the provinces
of Venice and Treviso, in which a variety of white and red,
local and international types are allowed. There are plenty of
products to report. Thirty million bottles are produced per year.
—
Producers and their trademark and signature wines:

- BAROLLO, Preganziol
  Venezia Chardonnay ($)
- Ornella MOLON, Salgareda
  Venezia Merlot Riserva ($)

Recommended wines
outside the DOC/DOCG designations:

1. ALLEGRINI, Fumane
   La Poja (Corvina) ($$$)
2. ANSELMI, Monteforte d'Alpone
   Capitel Croce (Garganega) ($)
   I Capitelli (Garganega) ($)
   Capitel Foscarino (Garganega, Chardonnay) ($)
3. BAROLLO, Preganziol
   Frank! (Cabernet Franc) ($)
4. BORIN VINI E VIGNE, Monselice
   Zuàn Giovanni Borin (Cabernet Sauvignon,
   Syrah, Merlot) ($)
5. CA' OROLOGIO, Baone
   Relógio (Carmenère, Cabernet Franc) ($$)
6. CA' RUGATE, Montecchia di Crosara
   Studio (Trebbiano di Soave, Garganega) ($)
7. Italo CESCON, Roncadelle
   Madre (Manzoni Bianco) ($$)
8. CONTE EMO CAPODILISTA – La Montecchia,
   Selvazzano Dentro
   Baòn (Cabernet Sauvignon, Merlot) ($)
9. Nino FRANCO, Valdobbiadene
   Grave di Stecca (Glera) ($)
10. GARBOLE, Tregnago
    Hurlo (Corvina...) ($$$$$)
11. LA BIANCARA, Montebello Vicentino
    Pico (Garganega) ($)
12. MACULAN, Breganze
    Fratta (Cabernet Sauvignon, Merlot) ($$$)
    Crosara (Merlot) ($$$)
13. MASARI, Valdagno
    Masari (Cabernet Sauvignon, Merlot) ($)
14. MOSOLE, San Stino di Livenza
    Hora Prima (Chardonnay, Tai, Sauvignon) ($)
15. ROENO, Brentino Belluno
    Riesling Renano Collezione di Famiglia ($$)
16. SUTTO, Campo di Pietra
    Campo Sella (Merlot) ($$)

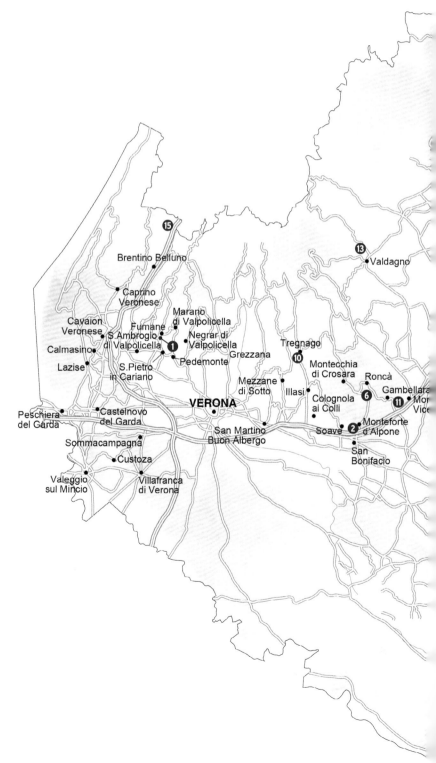

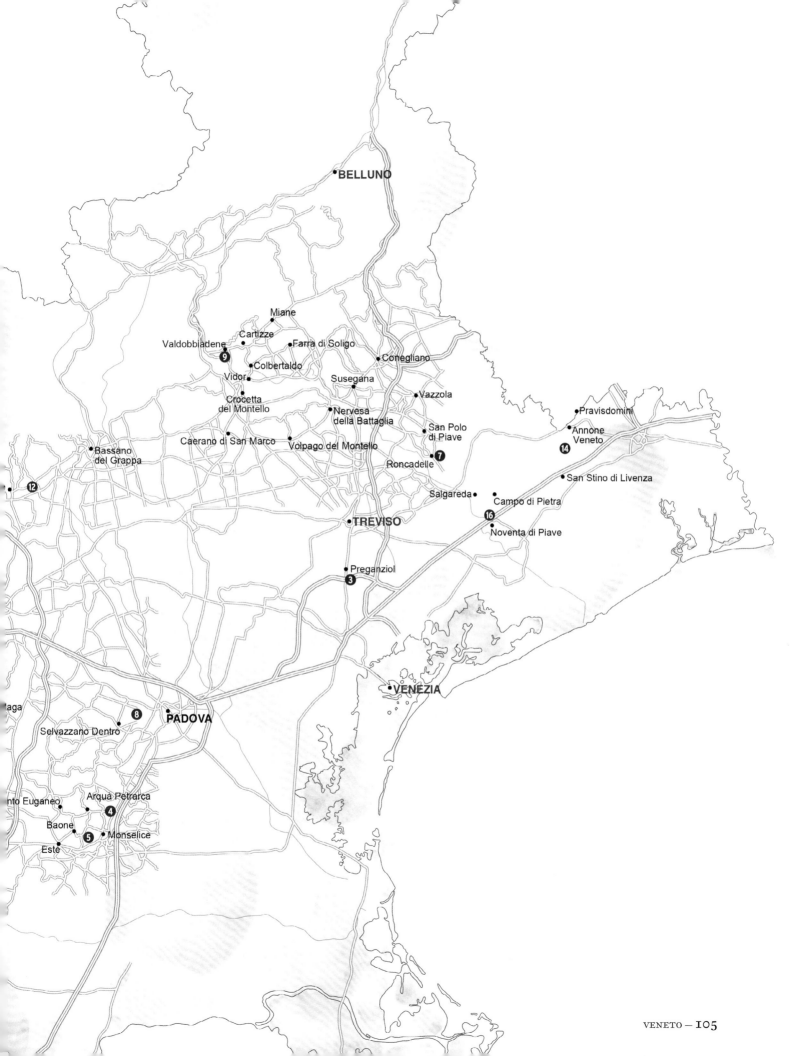

BELLUNO

Miane

Cartizze

Valdobbiadene
Farra di Soligo
9
Colbertaldo
Conegliano
Vidor
Susegana
Crocetta
del Montello
Vazzola
Nervesa
della Battaglia
San Polo
di Piave
Pravisdomini
Caerano di San Marco
Annone
Veneto
Volpago del Montello
14
Bassano
del Grappa
Roncadelle
7
12
San Stino di Livenza
Salgareda
Campo di Pietra
16
TREVISO
Noventa di Piave

Preganziol
3

VENEZIA

aga
8
PADOVA
Selvazzano Dentro

Arquà Petrarca
nto Euganeo
4
Baone
5 Monselice
Este

ALLEGRINI
Via Giare 5
Fumane (VR)
allegrini.it
Year of establishment: 1854
Owner: the Allegrini
family
Average number of
bottles produced per year:
1,300,000

This famous winery has two
main strengths: the large
vineyards and the winemaking
methods. In fact, the 370
acres of estate vineyards are
home to true grand crus of
Valpolicella, such as La Grola
and Fieramonte, while in the
cellar, withering and wood are
used to guarantee complexity,
power, and freshness at the
same time. The results are of
a consistently high standard,
with labels appreciated
throughout the world, among
which La Poja, made solely
from Corvina grapes, and
Amarone della Valpolicella
Classico Riserva Fieramonte
consistently excel.

AMARONE DELLA VALPOLICELLA CLASSICO
First year of production: 1958
Average number of bottles produced
per year: 120,000
Grape varieties: Corvina (45%),
Corvinone (45%), Oseleta (5%),
Rondinella (5%)

Matured in small new wood barrels for
eighteen months, it opens with refined spicy
tones well contrasted by intense small black
fruits; the flavor is confident and of great
impact, strong with a soft alcoholic content
but also dry thanks to the low residual
sugar, with a pleasant savoriness and a long
finish that recalls a touch of roasting.

ROMANO DAL FORNO
Frazione Cellore, località
Lodoletta 1
Illasi (VR)
info@dalfornoromano.it
Year of establishment: 1983
Owner: Romano Dal Forno
Average number of bottles
produced per year: 45,000

The best way—not only
because of the lack of a
company website—to get to
know this famous operation
is to be accompanied by
Romano Dal Forno on a tour
of the vineyards and among
the barrels. Seeing those few
isolated bunches of grapes,
you will discover what is
meant by low yields, while the
cellar will demonstrate that
a great wine is also the result
of persistent and attentive
care from vinification through
to bottling. Excellence made
Amarone, an emblem of
Valpolicella.

AMARONE DELLA VALPOLICELLA VIGNETO DI MONTE LODOLETTA
First year of production: 1983
Average number of bottles produced
per year: 25,000
Grape varieties: Corvina (60%),
Rondinella (20%); Croatina, Oseleta

The most evident merit of this great label
lies in its balance and harmony: on the nose,
warm notes of cocoa and cherries in alcohol
blend with hints of aromatic herbs and
citrus fruits, the palate is never too soft—
although very rich and enveloping—thanks
to the presence of well-blunted tannins
and a thread of acidity that accompanies
the entire flavor. The price lives up to its
celebrity status. Purity in complexity.

BERTANI
Via Asiago 1
Grezzana (VR)
bertani.net
Year of establishment: 1857
Owner: Bertani Domains
Average number of
bottles produced per year:
1,700,000

The evocative historic cellars
are the best testimony to the
entrepreneurial ability and
farsightedness of a company
that has earned itself leading
status not only in Valpolicella
but in the Italy of quality wine.
Successful selections from
Valpolicella are accompanied
by safe productions from
Valpantena, the Soave area,
and Garda thanks to a vineyard
area that has reached 495 acres.
The refinement of classicism.

AMARONE DELLA VALPOLICELLA CLASSICO
First year of production: 1958
Average number of bottles produced
per year: 90,000
Grape varieties: Corvina (80%),
Rondinella (20%)

This is the winery's most awarded and highly
celebrated label, the result of careful aging
in wood for up to seven years. The crisp
aromas of spices are joined by a red fruit as
ripe as it is persuasive and lively, the flavor is
elegant, powerful, not at all astringent, and
magnificently supported by a vein of acidity
right through to the long finish full
of macerated flowers. Timeless greatness.

GIUSEPPE QUINTARELLI
Via Cerè 1
Negrar (VR)
vini@giuseppequintarelli.it
Year of establishment: 1924
Owner: the Quintarelli
family
Average number of bottles
produced per year: 60,000

The cellar has been elegantly
restructured but the style
of the wines is unchanged,
linked to the teachings of
Giuseppe Quintarelli that have
taken this name to the top of
national oenology. Wines of
great purity and enormous
structure, rich in personality
and vitality, inimitable. The
common characteristics of the
few labels proposed include
long maturation in the cellar
and marketing reserved
exclusively for the best
vintages, to which we must
add the difficult availability
and resulting prices. In
addition to the wine presented
here, the estate's 30 acres
produce the not-to-be-missed
Amarone Riserva, Cabernet
Alzero, and Recioto.

AMARONE DELLA VALPOLICELLA CLASSICO
First year of production: 1961
Average number of bottles produced
per year: 14,000
Grape varieties: Corvina (55%),
Rondinella (30%); Cabernet, Croatina,
Nebbiolo, Sangiovese

A wine that is very respectful of the
variability of each vintage, but always
characterized by elegance and austerity.
The aromas are reminiscent of rose petals
and violets together with the dark tones of
blackberries and ink; the flavor is imposing
thanks to the fruity flesh, delicately
astringent, well warmed by the alcohol,
and of rare gustative length. A legend, as
such sought after throughout the world, of
Veneto oenology.

SECONDO MARCO

Via Campolongo 9
Fumane (VR)
secondomarco.it
Year of establishment: 2008
Owner: Marco Speri
Average number of bottles
produced per year: 85,000

In just a few years, Marco Speri has shown that he is capable of proposing his own way of understanding Valpolicella, based above all on his own idea of viticulture that—in his 42 acres—is not only organic but also careful to allow each plant to capture as much light and air as possible. The oenological offer is closely linked to the territory's classic grape varieties, so that, in addition to the Riserva whose label is presented, one can also taste Amarone, Recioto, Ripasso, and Valpolicella Classico. A winery that can look to the future with confidence.

AMARONE DELLA VALPOLICELLA CLASSICO RISERVA FUMETTO

First year of production: 2008
Average number of bottles produced per year: 3,000
Grape varieties: Corvina (55%), Rorvinone (35%), Rondinella (10%)

Fumetto immediately convinced all wine critics on its first release. Matured for seven years in large wood, it presents itself with distinct notes of red flowers, a beautiful base of ripe black fruit, and a spicy touch reminiscent of cocoa. The structure is particularly incisive, delicately astringent, and ennobled by the elegance of a finish in which balsamic nuances unite with citrus memories.

TEDESCHI

Frazione Pedemonte, via
G. Verdi 4/A
San Pietro in Cariano (VR)
tedeschiwines.com
Year of establishment: 1630
Owner: the Tedeschi
family
Average number of bottles
produced per year: 500,000

Siblings Antonietta, Riccardo, and Sabrina Tedeschi have added to the historic and much-appreciated crus within the Valpolicella Classica area—Monte Olmi, La Fabriseria, and Lucchine—with other vineyards in Maternigo, in the municipality of Tregnago, from which they have immediately obtained excellent qualitative results. The overall production, which originates from 119 acres of estate vineyards, is thus today driven by four labels of Amarone della Valpolicella DOCG, joined by eight reds based on the area's classic grapes (mainly Corvina, Corvinone, and Rondinella) and a single white, Soave DOC. Classicism made Amarone.

AMARONE DELLA VALPOLICELLA RISERVA MATERNIGO

First year of production: 2016
Average number of bottles produced per year: 6,000
Grape varieties: Corvina (40%), Corvinone (40%), Rondinella (20%)

A result so remarkable that it deserved the label on its first release, welcomed by wine critics as a new benchmark for Valpolicella. Matured for four years in large Slavonian oak casks, it combines ripe aromas of cocoa and chocolate with fresher hints of undergrowth fruits and refined balsamic notes. The robust and structured palate combines youthful aspects of tannins, acidity, and citrus fruits with enveloping creamy sensations.

SPERI

Frazione Pedemonte, via
Fontana 14
San Pietro in Cariano (VR)
speri.com
Year of establishment: 1874
Owner: the Speri family
Average number of bottles
produced per year: 400,000

A historic family-run winery that has chosen to represent the classicism of Valpolicella through just five labels, all made exclusively from the area's typical red grapes. The estate's 148 acres of vineyards are organically farmed and find their most striking expression in the panoramic Sant'Urbano vineyard, cultivated with the traditional pergola system and interspersed with olive trees.

AMARONE DELLA VALPOLICELLA CLASSICO SANT'URBANO

First year of production: 1958
Average number of bottles produced per year: 100,000
Grape varieties: Corvina and Corvinone (70%), Rondinella (25%), Molinara (5%)

The grapes are dried for over three months in the drying loft that dominates the Sant'Urbano vineyard, then the wine is matured first in French tonneaux and then in large Slavonian oak casks. This gives rise to aromas of cherries in alcohol, cocoa, and sultanas that are finely enlivened by vegetal hints; the flavor is rich and powerful, silky and enveloping, not without dynamic citrus touches. A wine that best expresses the vitality and complexity of the great Amarone.

TENUTA SANT'ANTONIO

Via Ceriani 23
Colognola ai Colli (VR)
tenutasantantonio.it
Year of establishment: 1995
Owner: the Castagnedi
family
Average number of bottles
produced per year: 800,000

An ever-youthful wine cellar in which there is a great desire to experiment, as demonstrated by the Télos project that aims to produce increasingly uncontaminated wines, with just as much care taken to constantly offer labels of indisputable quality. From 272 acres of estate vineyards come three Amarone products: the Campo dei Gigli, the rare Riserva Lilium Est, and the Antonio Castagnedi selection. These are joined by three versions of Valpolicella and three of Soave DOC, completing a range that places Tenuta Sant'Antonio at the top of Italian oenology.

AMARONE DELLA VALPOLICELLA CAMPO DEI GIGLI

First year of production: 1995
Average number of bottles produced per year: 15,000
Grape varieties: Corvina and Corvinone (70%), Rondinella (20%); Croatina, Oseleta

Matured for three years in French wood, it offers a contrast between the fresh balsamic notes and a warm cocoa reminder, in a complexity to which spices, blackberries, and violets contribute, in a whole of great finesse and articulation. The taste is very important and rich, never yielding, and always well articulated, newly fresh, and very long.

ZÝMĒ

Via Ca' del Pipa 1
San Pietro in Cariano (VR)
zyme.it
Year of establishment: 2003
Owner: Celestino Gaspari
Average number of bottles
produced per year: 140,000

Celestino Gaspari, thanks to
work experiences that have
seen and continue to see
him present in numerous
Valpolicella cellars (most
notably that of Giuseppe
Quintarelli), is a competent
and refined interpreter of the
peculiarities of the Corvina
grape, which he presents not
only in his Riserva version but
also in an always successful
Amarone della Valpolicella
Classico. In his 82 acres under
vine, he is also a skillful
and curious experimenter,
as he demonstrates with
labels such as Harlequin
(made from fifteen different
grape varieties), Cabernet, or
Syrah. Zýmē (yeast, in Greek)
perfectly demonstrates that
one can innovate without
neglecting tradition.

AMARONE DELLA VALPOLICELLA CLASSICO RISERVA LA MATTONARA

First year of production: 2001
Average number of bottles produced
per year: 4,000
Grape varieties: Corvina (40%),
Corvinone (30%), Rondinella (15%);
Oseleta, Croatina

An Amarone made from grapes naturally
dried for three months, fermented in cement
without added yeasts, and then matured for
nine years in casks: a marvel of richness and
pleasantness. The aromas reveal ripe red fruits
and refreshing balsamic hints against a broadly
spiced background. The flavor is of bewitching
complexity, with an austerity just softened by
the slight residual sugar, very long, with an
elegantly licorice-like finish. A highly sought-
after selection, and as such rather expensive,
produced only in the best vintages.

VIGNALTA

Via Scalette 23
Arquà Petrarca (PD)
vignalta.it
Year of establishment: 1980
Owners: Lucio Gomiero,
Paolo Guzzo, Luciano
Salvagnin
Average number of bottles
produced per year: 240,000

This is a leading name in the
Euganean Hills, famous above
all for the elegance of its reds
made from grapes from beyond
the Alps (primarily Cabernet
Franc and Sauvignon, Merlot,
and Carmenère, but there is also
a production based on Syrah
and another on Pinot Noir
grapes). In addition to the award-
winning Gemola, there are thus
nine other labels that vary in
complexity and richness, but
which well represent the mastery
achieved by Vignalta both in
the vineyard, where the 86 acres
have recently been converted
to organic farming, and in the
cellar processes. Another wine
that has brought Lucio Gomiero
great fortune is the fragrant
and bewitching Colli Euganei
Fior d'Arancio Passito Alpianae,
which is well worth trying.

COLLI EUGANEI ROSSO GEMOLA

First year of production: 1991
Average number of bottles produced
per year: 20,000
Grape varieties: Merlot (70%),
Cabernet Franc (30%)

Small black fruits, blueberry tart, balsamic
notes, and sweet spices in this complex
and persuasive red, aged in medium-sized
French wood for two years. On the palate,
it is of great harmony, not very astringent
thanks to the well-melted tannins in the
fruity pulp, enveloping, and very persistent.

CONTE EMO CAPODILISTA – La Montecchia

Via Montecchia 16
Selvazzano Dentro (PD)
lamontecchia.it
Year of establishment: 1100
Owner: the Emo
Capodilista family
Average number of bottles
produced per year: 130,000

The magnificent estate is an
inescapable point of reference
for wine tourists, thanks to 74
acres of vineyards interspersed
with woods on which the
welcoming family villa stands.
In addition to its Fior d'Arancio
Passito, the winery is also
famous for the Colli Euganei
Rosso Villa Capodilista, but all
its reds from Cabernet Franc,
Cabernet Sauvignon, and
Merlot grapes are of interest
as well. A centuries-old history
that continues to feed on a
passion for fine viticulture.

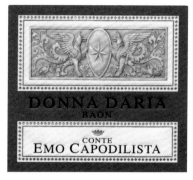

COLLI EUGANEI FIOR D'ARANCIO PASSITO DONNA DARIA

First year of production: 2000
Average number of bottles produced
per year: 4,000 (375 ml) (12.7 fl oz)
Grape variety: Moscato Giallo

The grapes are dried for over two months
to achieve the ideal sugar concentration,
then matured in steel only to preserve intact
the intense and attractive aromas of citrus
fruits, candied fruit, honey, and herbs.
The taste is particularly complex and of a
persuasive sweetness well diluted by a long
finish refreshed by orange peel.

MONTE DEL FRÀ

Strada Custoza 35
Sommacampagna (VR)
montedelfra.it
Year of establishment: 1958
Owner: the Bonomo
family
Average number of
bottles produced per year:
1,000,000

The company's vineyards
have exceeded 494 acres and
production has diversified
over time, focusing on
three main types: reds from
Valpolicella, whites from the
Custoza, Lugana, and Soave
designations, and Bardolino
Chiaretto. In order to achieve
the best production efficiency,
the Bonomo family decided
to use two autonomous
processing cellars: one in
Custoza and one in San Pietro
in Cariano. The labels grouped
in the line called Monte del
Frà are characterized by a fine,
almost didactic adherence
to the characteristics of the
different territories.

CUSTOZA SUPERIORE CÀ DEL MAGRO

First year of production: 1988
Average number of bottles produced
per year: 60,000
Grape varieties: Garganega,
Trebbiano, Cortese, Incrocio Manzoni

The strong component of flowers and white
fruit is well counterbalanced by the vital
presence of freshly cut grass and spices. The
palate is nicely enveloping and structured,
endowed with savoriness and a long finish
that combines refined mineral notes and
soft hints of chamomile. Cà del Magro is a
well-deserved standard-bearer for the best
Custoza.

MACULAN

Via Castelletto 3
Breganze (VI)
maculan.net
Year of establishment: 1946
Owner: the Maculan family
Average number of bottles
produced per year: 600,000

Fausto Maculan has always
believed in the Breganze
region's affinity for Bordeaux
grape varieties, demonstrated
by his famous labels mostly
based on Cabernet Sauvignon
and Merlot, without shying
away from experimenting with
Chardonnay, Sauvignon, and
even Pinot Noir. The success of
his approach is guaranteed by
no less than 99 acres of exquisite
vineyards, meticulous grape
selection, and aging in wood to
provide prestigious elegance. A
winery that ranks among the top
producers in the country.

FRATTA

First year of production: 1977
Average number of bottles produced
per year: 7,000
Grape varieties: Cabernet Sauvignon,
Merlot

The barrel aging adds a delicate smoky and
spicy hint to a substantial base of small red
and black fruits, ranging from blackberry
to raspberry to blueberry. The flavor is rich
in both balsamic freshness and delicate
tannins, as well as soft fruity pulp, until a
sumptuous finish with notes of cocoa and
licorice. A great classic.

SERAFINI & VIDOTTO

Via L. Carrer 8/12
Nervesa della Battaglia
(TV)
serafinievidotto.it
Year of establishment: 1986
Owner: Francesco
Serafini, Antonello
Vidotto, the Farinetti
family
Average number of bottles
produced per year: 200,000

The winery led by Antonello
Vidotto and Francesco
Serafini, both technicians of
proven ability, quickly became
famous for the elegance of the
company's flagship product,
Rosso dell'Abazia, the fruit
of Bordeaux grapes that have
found their ideal environment
on the Asolo hills. Over the
years, however, production
has expanded to include new
productions such as the red
Recantina, Manzoni Bianco,
and, increasingly, Asolo
Superiore Extra Dry Bollicine
di Prosecco. The prestigious
winery is surrounded by 62
acres of estate vineyards.

MONTELLO - COLLI ASOLANI IL ROSSO DELL'ABAZIA

First year of production: 1988
Average number of bottles produced per
year: 21,000
Grape varieties: Cabernet Sauvignon
(40%), Cabernet Franc (40%), Merlot
(20%)

A grape that is very articulate in its aromas and
persuasive on the palate. The aromas contain
medicinal herbs, blackberries and blueberries,
plums and cherries, balsamic traits, and a
background of spices with a hint of vanilla. The
palate is superlative for the balance among the
components: the tannins are barely noticeable,
the alcohol gives a balanced contribution
of warmth, and the hint of acidity leads to a
lingering finish of exquisite elegance. The
gustatory finesse of Colli Asolani.

NINO FRANCO

Via G. Garibaldi 147
Valdobbiadene (TV)
ninofranco.it
Year of establishment: 1919
Owner: Primo Franco
Average number of
bottles produced per year:
1,000,000

A name of international
prestige included in the
wine lists of the world's
most famous restaurants,
which has made the Glera
vine its oenological mission,
dedicating itself with
increasing success. From its
own vineyards, worked with
painstaking care, comes not
only Grave di Stecca but also
the prestigious Conegliano
Valdobbiadene Superiore
Nodi and Vigneto della Riva
di San Floriano. However,
quality is spread over all seven
of the white labels, from the
immediate and drinkable
Rustico to the Sassi Bianchi,
from the inimitable Superiore
di Cartizze to the famous
Primo Franco, vintage since
1983.

GRAVE DI STECCA

First year of production: 2007
Average number of bottles produced
per year: 12,000
Grape variety: Glera

It originates from the single vineyard of the
same name, enriched by the presence of the
splendid Villa Barberina and the striking
stone walls that surround it. In its youth, it
bewitches with fragrant aromas of fruit and
white flowers, then slight mineral notes join
in; the flavor is lively thanks to the bubbles,
but also enveloping and persuasively soft.
This is due not only to the careful selection
of the grapes but also to cellar techniques
that tend to allow the grape's personality to
express itself at the highest level through long
stays on the lees accompanied by continuous
batônnage. The height of Glera's personality.

CA' RUGATE

Via Pergola 36
Montecchia di Crosara
(VR)
carugate.it
Year of establishment: 1986
Owner: the Tessari family
Average number of bottles
produced per year: 700,000

Michele Tessari has gradually
given impetus to a winery that
began in Soave and today also
occupies an important space
in Valpolicella, in addition to
having made acquisitions in
Lessini Durello, thus reaching
222 acres of organically
cultivated vineyards. While
Monte Fiorentine is the most
famous label, not to be missed
is the complexity of Studio,
in which the predominant
Trebbiano di Soave is blended
with Garganega, with partial
aging in wood. Also aged in
oak is the rich and persuasive
Soave Monte Alto. Reliability
and pleasantness across the
entire range.

SOAVE CLASSICO MONTE FIORENTINE

First year of production: 1988
Average number of bottles produced
per year: 55,000
Grape variety: Garganega

This is a label that knows no letup and that,
year after year, has earned a top position
in the varied world of Soave Classico. The
absolute merit of Monte Fiorentine is its
ability to improve for years in the bottle,
combining the initial aromas of flowers
and white fruits with hints of minerals and
withered petals.

GINI

Via G. Matteotti 42
Monteforte d'Alpone (VR)
ginivini.com
Year of establishment: 1980
Owner: the Gini family
Average number of bottles
produced per year: 200,000

One of the great names in Soave with some splendid vineyards where, thanks to the volcanic component of the soil, there are still many vines that were not affected by the arrival of phylloxera at the beginning of the twentieth century. The area under vine, which is organically managed, spans 148 acres and is mostly dedicated to the Garganega grape, but the first bottles of red grapes from Valpolicella are more than interesting. A family history, handed down through fifteen generations of winegrowers, today enhanced and revitalized by productions of assured quality.

SOAVE CLASSICO CONTRADA SALVARENZA VECCHIE VIGNE
First year of production: 1990
Average number of bottles produced per year: 10,000
Grape variety: Garganega

The images of these "Old Vines" give a good idea of the sensory quality that can be achieved in the grapes produced from these hundred-year-old vines. The aromas are very complex and include fresh elements reminiscent of tropical and citrus fruits, sweet contributions reminiscent of ripe white fruit and honey, and mineral hints leading to flint over the years. The palate is broad and rich, with softness diluted by a nuance of tannin resulting from aging in wood. An emblem of Soave, a label awarded by wine critics all over the world.

INAMA

Località Biacche 50
San Bonifacio (VR)
inama.wine
Year of establishment: 1965
Owner: Stefano Inama
Average number of bottles
produced per year: 500,000

A winery that year after year, starting with the first bottlings in 1991, has grown not only in numbers but also in quality and the definition of a precise company style, based on olfactory and taste richness as well as a rare elegance in all the labels produced.
The 153 acres of property include an area dedicated to white grapes in the Soave area—where the famous Sauvignon Vulcaia also originates—and vineyards in the Berici Hills, destined for reds, among which important results based on Carmenère, Merlot, and Cabernet Sauvignon stand out.

SOAVE CLASSICO FOSCARINO I PALCHI GRANDE CUVÉE
First year of production: 2019
Average number of bottles produced per year: 6,000
Grape variety: Garganega

First produced in 2019, it is a novelty that has contributed to the recent qualitative reawakening of the Soave area, focusing the critical spotlight on the potential of the Garganega grape. Matured for six months in barrels of varying sizes, it shows fruit and white flowers followed by a hint of sweet spices; the palate is both powerful and elegant, with the rich fruity flesh well balanced by the savoriness and citrus component, in a combination of rare harmony. A great interpretation of the Foscarino cru.

PIEROPAN

Via G. Camuzzoni 3
Soave (VR)
pieropan.it
Year of establishment: 1880
Owner: the Pieropan family
Average number of bottles
produced per year: 520,000

The deservedly most famous winery—in Italy and abroad—of the Soave designation, brought to success by the farsightedness of Leonildo Pieropan, who in his wines sought to combine taste quality with respect for the environment. Even the splendid new wine cellar was designed to allow noninvasive processing and to enhance the surrounding landscape. The fruit of 173 acres of organically cultivated land, in addition to the Soave Classico Calvarino, the La Rocca selection, and the more straightforward Soave Classico are also of great value. Also of particular interest is the recent Calvarino 5 project (seven thousand bottles, outside the DOC), which combines the grapes of five consecutive harvests aged in vitrified cement for a good ten years, demonstrating the evolutionary potential of the Garganega grape.

SOAVE CLASSICO CALVARINO
First year of production: 1971
Average number of bottles produced per year: 55,000
Grape varieties: Garganega (70%), Trebbiano di Soave (30%)

Matured for a year in cement, on the nose it combines fresh scents reminiscent of white fruit, sage, and elderflower with fine hints of almonds and a nuance of chalk and flint; the palate is pleasantly dry, rather savory, with good volume and tasty drinkability. Of timeless classicism.

PRÀ

Via della Fontana 31
Monteforte d'Alpone (VR)
vinipra.it
Year of establishment: 1983
Owner: Graziano Prà
Average number of bottles
produced per year: 360,000

Graziano Prà is a landmark in the area and one of the protagonists in the rediscovery of Soave, interpreted for forty years with a stylistic purity that consistently guarantees richness and tasty drinkability. The famous Monte Grande is accompanied by three other labels from Soave and three more recent reds from Valpolicella, grown on 91 acres of organically cultivated land. Whites that are apparently simple, vital, and slender, always crisp and full of personality, excellent representatives of the territory.

SOAVE CLASSICO MONTE GRANDE
First year of production: 1988
Average number of bottles produced per year: 18,000
Grape varieties: Garganega (70%), Trebbiano di Soave (30%)

The delicate passage in large French casks gives a touch of creaminess to the palate and a whiff of sweet spices to the nose, but the notes of yellow flowers and citrus fruits typical of Garganega always dominate, and with a few years in the bottle, are complemented by fine mineral hints. Pleasantness and drinkability, combined with a friendly cost, make Monte Grande a prestigious representative of the best Soave.

SUAVIA

Frazione Fittà, via Centro 14
Soave (VR)
suavia.it
Year of establishment: 1982
Owner: the Tessari family
Average number of bottles
produced per year: 180,000

Only white grapes—
Garganega and Trebbiano
di Soave—are found in the
Tessari sisters' 44 acres of
organically farmed vineyards.
The winery's objective is to
best express the characteristics
of these soils where the legacy
left by volcanic eruptions
is still alive, maturing the
wines in steel only, in more or
less prolonged contact with
the yeasts. The production
includes six labels of certain
value, from the more
immediate Soave Classico
to the meditative Recioto di
Soave Acinatium, passing
through the multi-award-
winning Massifitti, a pure
Trebbiano di Soave.

SOAVE CLASSICO MONTE CARBONARE

First year of production: 1986
Average number of bottles produced
per year: 30,000
Grape variety: Garganega

It presents an enchanting array of flowers
and white fruits to which, after a few years
in the bottle, increasingly intense mineral
hints are added ranging from flint to sulfur.
The palate is splendidly linear and easy to
drink, not without an enveloping touch of
creaminess and joyful freshness. Offered at
moderate prices, it is a sure reference in the
world of Soave Classico.

MONTE DALL'ORA

Località Castelrotto, Via
Monte dall'Ora 5
San Pietro in Cariano (VR)
montedallora.com
Year of establishment: 1995
Owners: Carlo Venturini
and Alessandra
Zantedeschi
Average number of bottles
produced per year: 40,000

A small winery established with
the intention of demonstrating
how high quality can be
achieved through the deepest
respect for nature. The 32
biodynamically cultivated
acres contain, in fact, not only
vines but also fruit plants and
vegetables to ensure the widest
biodiversity, while in the cellar,
the direct expressiveness of the
grapes is favored, relying on
spontaneous fermentation and
little use of sulfur dioxide. The
six red wines on offer are typical
of the area, from Amarone to
Recioto, and the company's
success is due above all to the
three versions of Valpolicella
Classico, which are particularly
lively and rich in personality. A
reality worth knowing.

VALPOLICELLA CLASSICO SUPERIORE SAN GIORGIO ALTO

First year of production: 2015
Average number of bottles produced
per year: 4,000
Grape varieties: Corvina (60%),
Corvinone (20%), Rondinella (20%)

It enchants with its frankness and
essentiality, devoid as it is of sugary
presences and withered notes in favor of
freshness, delicacy, and taste tension. The
aromas, in addition to the classic red fruit,
highlight hints of spices and eucalyptus,
then the flavor captivates with its joyful
drinkability, devoid of astringency and
woody hints, with contained alcohol and
delicate acidity. The purity of Valpolicella.

RUGGERI

Via Prà Fontana 4
Valdobbiadene (TV)
ruggeri.it
Year of establishment: 1950
Owner: Rotkäppchen-
Mumm Sektkellereien
Average number of
bottles produced per year:
1,600,000

The Bisol family has a decades-
long history of success in
the world of Valdobbiadene
Prosecco and is committed
to research to achieve both
longer-lived plantings—
through the Vecchie Viti
project—and eco-sustainable
agriculture—with the Zero
Impact objective. An operation
that concerns both the 79
acres of property, including an
important plot in the Cartizze
area, and the more than one
hundred historical vintners.
In addition to Giustino B., the
Valdobbiadene Superiore Brut
and Extra Dry and the Cartizze
Brut and Dry both stand out
with continuity in the vast and
qualified production.

VALDOBBIADENE PROSECCO SUPERIORE EXTRA DRY MILLESIMATO GIUSTINO B.

First year of production: 1995
Average number of bottles produced
per year: 55,000
Grape variety: Glera

The nose is crisp and articulate with apple,
grapefruit, and a touch of almond, while the
palate adds a vein enlivened by a touch of
savoriness to the more classic creaminess
of the bubbles. A timeless classic of the
designation.

ROCCOLO GRASSI

Via San Giovanni di Dio 19
Mezzane di Sotto (VR)
roccolograssi.it
Year of establishment: 1996
Owner: Marco and
Francesca Sartori
Average number of bottles
produced per year: 52,000

The Sartori siblings' small
company has made a great
name for itself among
Valpolicella wine lovers thanks
to painstaking work that tends
to preserve the characteristics
of the territory in each label,
avoiding any forcing in the 37
acres of vineyard and overly
invasive wood in the new
winery. Dedication to a project
that has led them to excel not
only with Amarone but, even
more so, with Valpolicella
Superiore, which has always
been among the most typical
and expressive DOC wines.
The four red wines are
accompanied by an equally
well-made Soave and Recioto
di Soave.

VALPOLICELLA SUPERIORE

First year of production: 1996
Average number of bottles produced
per year: 34,000
Grape varieties: Corvina (60%),
Rondinella (20%), Corvinone (15%),
Croatina (5%)

Red flowers and small black fruits combine
with delicate spiciness to create a rich and
crisp olfactory expression. On the palate, the
pleasantly soft contribution of the alcohol
is perceptible, well refreshed by both the
acidity and a delicately balsamic closure.
An important and articulate Valpolicella
Superiore, a benchmark of the type.

Trentino-Alto Adige

The region consists of two autonomous provinces,
Bolzano and Trento, which differ in many respects—historical,
linguistic, social, and landscape—including orography and viticulture.
It therefore makes sense to examine the two areas separately.

Trentino
—

For almost three thousand years, the course of the Adige River has been the central point of reference for viticulture in Trentino, which, however, includes quite different territories dedicated to distinct varieties. Arriving from the south, one finds the vast Vallagarina, where the indigenous Marzemino grape gives its best, albeit accompanied by excellent results from Bordeaux grapes. Continuing toward Trento are vast vineyards dedicated to what has become the area's wine vocation, Metodo Classico sparkling wine, made primarily from Chardonnay grapes. Climbing northward we reach the scenic Val di Cembra, full of terraced vineyards on stone walls that reach altitudes of over 2,295 feet, and give the best results with Müller-Thurgau. On the orographic right of the Adige is the Campo Rotaliano, an extensive plain dedicated to the Teroldego grape.

The general scenario of vineyards includes 32% on the valley floor, 39% in the hills, and 29% in the mountains, with the highest percentage in Italy of areas registered as Designations of Controlled Origin: over 90%. There are just under six thousand vine growers, with an average surface area close to 3.7 acres, while the fourteen communal wine cellars harvest 80% of Trentino grapes. Overall, white grapes make up 75% of the 25,200 acres of vine-growing areas, mostly used in the famous Trento DOC, which is dedicated exclusively to sparkling wine, so much so that the Trentodoc Protection Institute regulates over sixty wineries.

Alto Adige
—

South Tyrol is one of the areas most appreciated and envied, but not imitated, by the Italians, who find it remarkable in terms of tidiness, visitor-friendliness, care for the landscape, urban centers, and respect for the environment. This, in addition to being a producer of white wines that have won ample space on wine lists and wine shop shelves in every region of Italy. This is an image shared the world over, as demonstrated by the ever-growing success of tourism.

Viticulture developed here more than two millennia ago and gradually established itself over the following centuries thanks to the distinct character of its white wines, mainly on the mountainous slopes of the valleys carved by the Adige and Isarco Rivers, which join near Bolzano. The mountainous aspect of the area makes one think of great altitudes; they do in fact exceed 6,560 feet in the Alpine part, but Bolzano is at 860 feet and Trento at 636, thus enjoying a continental type of climate that allows for excellent grape growing. It is the Vinschgau Valley, in the northwest of the area, and the Eisack Valley, in the northeast, that benefit from cooler temperatures, and it is here that the sharpest and most acidic wines are born. Viticulture takes place between 720 and 3,280 feet above sea level, with red grapes mainly planted below 1,475 feet, reaching a cultivated area of close to 14,825 acres. The classification of the vineyards is almost equal: 33% valley floor, 36% hillside, and 31% mountains.

The white varieties are the predominant ones, with Pinot Gris, Pinot Blanc, Chardonnay, Sauvignon, and Gwürztraminer in first place, while Riesling is gaining more and more ground and fame. Among the red types, on the other hand, the historic Lagrein and Schiava are prevalent, held somewhat in the shadows by the success of grapes of French origin, Pinot Noir above all, but also Cabernet Sauvignon and Merlot.

Land ownership is very fragmented, with the average for the almost five thousand farms being a mere 2.5 acres. This has favored, since the end of the nineteenth century, the birth and brilliant development of community wine cellars that receive 65% of the local grapes, and that now work with twelve associations rightly recognized as models of excellence in global cooperation. This has not prevented the growth of more than two hundred private cellars of much smaller and increasingly award-winning production sizes.

A rich and strongly evolved winegrowing history, marked by—to name just two essential factors—the introduction of Riesling, Chardonnay, and Pinot Noir grapes ordered two centuries ago by John of Habsburg-Lorraine, Archduke of Austria, and the increasingly qualified work of the agronomic and oenological technicians who have trained and continue to train, since 1874, at the Institute of San Michele all'Adige.

This will culminate in the welcome definition, in 2022, of eighty-four Additional Geographical Units within the production specifications of the Alto Adige DOC, allowing wine enthusiasts to know in detail the qualitatively most important territories in the area.

Passo di Resia/
Reschen Pass
1504

Passo di Monte Giovio/
Jaufen Pass
2094

Brennero

A22

Varna/Vahrn

Bressanone/Brixen

VALLE ISARCO

Naturno/Naturns

Merano/Meran

VAL VENOSTA

Castelbello-Ciardes/
Kastelbell-Tschars

Chiusa/Klausen

Passo dello Stelvio/
Stilfser Joch
2757

PARCO NAZIONALE
DELLO STELVIO
NATIONALPARK
STILFSERJOCH

TERLANO

Nalles/Nals

SANTA
MADDALENA

Terlano/Terlan

Andriano/Andrian

Passo di Falzarego
2117

BOLZANO/BOZEN

Fiè allo Scillar/
Völs am Schlern

Cornaiano/Girlan

Appiano sulla Strada del Vino/
Eppan an der Weinstraße

Passo Pordoi
2239

Lago di
Santa Giustina

Caldaro sulla Strada del Vino/
Kaltern an der Weinstraße

Termeno sulla Strada del Vino/
Tramin an der Weinstraße

CALDARO

Noce

Ora/Auer

Cortaccia sulla Strada del Vino/
Kurtatsch an der Weinstraße

Montagna/Montan

VAL DI FIEMME

Egna/Neumarkt

Magrè sulla Strada del Vino/
Margreid an der Weinstraße

Cortina sulla Strada del Vino/
Kurtinig an der Weinstraße

Passo Rollei
1970

Avisio

Salorno sulla Strada del Vino/
Salum an der Weinstraße

TEROLDEGO
ROTALIANO

Mezzocorona

Cima d'Asta
2847

Faedo

Mezzolombardo

Cembra Lisignano

San Michele all'Adige

Lago di
Molveno

Pressano

Lavis

Brenta

TRENTO

VALSUGANA

Madruzzo

Chiese

Lasino

Sarca

Brenta

Rovereto

Isera

Lago di
Garda

A22

Ala

Monte Baldo
2218

Avio

Modena

The DOCs – Trentino

- Casteller
- Delle Venezie - Beneškіh Okolišev
- Lago di Caldaro / Caldaro - Kaltersee / Kalterer
- Teroldego Rotaliano
- Trentino
- Trento
- Valdadige / Etschtaler
- Valdadige Terradeiforti / Terradeiforti

The DOCs – Alto Adige

- Alto Adige / dell'Alto Adige - Südtirol / Südtiroler
- Lago di Caldaro / Caldaro - Kalterersee / Kalterer
- Valdadige

MAIN VINES GROWN IN THE REGION

Cabernet Sauvignon / Merlot / Pinot Noir

These are the international red grapes that are most used in Alto Adige → International Grape Varieties

Chardonnay / Pinot Noir / Pinot Meunier

These are the international grapes used for the sparkling Trentodoc → International Grape Varieties

Gewürztraminer (Savagnin) / Grüner Veltliner / Müller-Thurgau / Pinot Blanc / Pinot Gris / Riesling / Sauvignon / Sylvaner

These are the international white grapes most used in Alto Adige → International Grape Varieties

Kerner

A crossbreed of Schiava Grossa and Riesling, and for this reason considered semi-indigenous, Kerner, created in 1929 by August Herold, is widespread in Germany but reaches expressive heights in Alto Adige in the Valle Isarco, where it is cultivated up to 2,950 feet above sea level, as the plants can withstand spring frosts thanks to their late blossoming. Due to its marked acidity and intense aromas of apple, citrus, and tropical fruits, it is also suitable for sparkling winemaking.

Lagrein

A descendant of Pinot Noir and related to Syrah and Teroldego, it thrives on chalky, draining soils. In South Tyrol, it has been considered indigenous since it was first mentioned at the Abbey of Muri-Gries in 1318 when documents urged that Weiss Lagrein (white Lagrein), be given to the thirsty poor and the church. In 1370, Holy Roman Emperor Charles IV decreed that Lagreiner was the best wine in the area. Today, it is vinified in delicate, fresh rosé wines, or in a *dunkel* version, a more concentrated red wine of medium complexity, tasty and rustic, dry and tannic on the palate, which best expresses the varietal bouquet of violets, red currants, and blackberries. If aged in wood, it may present a rounder and more harmonious body.

Marzemino

Although there are archaeological investigations that hypothesize ancient origins in Asia Minor, and a slow approach to Italy thanks to trade routes developed over the centuries, the reconstruction of the genetic pedigree shows that Marzemino is not descended from the Turkish Merzifon Karasi but has its origins in northern Italy. A cousin of the Lagrein grape variety, by common descent from Teroldego, it was first officially mentioned in the preparation of a banquet in 1409 in honor of Pope Gregory XII, when a "Marzemino di Gradiscutta," a hamlet of Varmo in the province of Udine, was served. Since then, Marzemino has spread throughout Lombardy, Emilia, and Veneto, but it is in Trentino, in Vallagarina, between Isera and Volano, that it has found its elective *terroir*. It prefers poor, clayey, or basaltic soils, well exposed and sheltered from the wind. In its most successful versions, it reveals nuances of violets, mint, roots, and small red fruits. In the mouth, it is fragrant, spicy, and slightly balsamic with a soft finish of cinnamon and almond.

Nosiola

Trentino's only indigenous white grape variety, it is descended from the Raetica, the most widespread white grape in Roman times, and is related to the Rèze, an ancient variety cultivated in the Swiss Alps. In the dry version, it displays a pungent character with an aromatic sequence that shows a pleasant contrast between the acidity of grapefruit, the freshness of unripe apple, and more delicate nuances of lime and broom, ending with a hint of hazelnut—hence the name of the grape variety. Traditionally cultivated in the Valle dei Laghi between Trento and Lake Garda, since the seventeenth century, Nosiola has also been used to produce the extremely rare Vino Santo. This is the result of slowly drying the grapes on special racks called *arèle*, where they can lose up to 80% of their mass and be affected by Botrytis Cinerea, which develops its particular aromatic profile.

Schiava / Schiava Grigia / Schiava Gentile / Schiava Grossa

A family of genetically different vines, but identified by the name Schiava due to their cultivation on the pergola or using other supports, thus making it not as free as the bush vine. Common characteristics of these vines are high productivity, fairly early ripening, and the ability to adapt well to different types of environments. The vine always expresses a kaleidoscope of fragrant, bright aromas of violets, fresh red fruit, blueberries, citron, tangerine, almond, and cassis, which harmonize in a wine with a good structure and fine tannic texture, never too astringent, with a juicy, relaxed, enveloping, and drinkable taste. The legend that it originated from Georgia via Slovenia is not to date confirmed by any genetic affinity with modern Caucasian varieties.

Teroldego Rotaliano

It was mentioned for the first time in a sales contract of 1480 in Cognola, near Trento, and Tiroler Gold, "the gold of the Tyrol" as Trentino wine was called at the court of Vienna, is the main indigenous red grape variety, which finds its ideal territory in the Piana Rotaliana. Vinified in stainless steel, it gives ready, pomegranate-colored wines with fruity and vinous notes. Aged in wood, it takes on a deep ruby color with purple highlights and develops aromas of rose, cherry, currant, blueberry, raspberry, and blackberry, accompanied by a balsamic accent and a finish of almond and licorice. The palate is full, vigorous, fleshy, dry but not astringent, low in alcohol, and rather acidic.

Trento DOC

One of the rarer DOCs, and the first ever that, in 1993, was dedicated exclusively to the production of sparkling wines made using the Metodo Classico, i.e., by refermentation, in the bottle, of wines made from Chardonnay and/or Pinot Blanc, and/or Pinot Noir and/or Pinot Meunier grapes, in the white or rosé types. The minimum period in contact with yeasts is fifteen months, rising to thirty-six for the Riserva. There are small and understandable territorial variations with respect to the Trentino DOC: here vineyards are cultivated at altitudes above 2,625 feet and seventy-four municipalities are involved. The sparkling wine tradition began in the early twentieth century, thanks in particular to the work of Giulio Ferrari, and since then has steadily increased, reaching the current thirteen million bottles per year. Sensory characteristics vary greatly depending on the producer and type, but Trento generally tends to be fresher, more floral, and more austere than Franciacorta, the sparkling wine with which comparisons are normally made, which is characterized by hints of yeast and ripe white fruit.

—

Producers and their trademark and signature wines:

1. ABATE NERO, Trento
   Trento Brut Riserva Cuvée dell'Abate ($$)
   Trento Brut Domini ($$)
2. Nicola BALTER, Rovereto
   Trento Pas Dosé Riserva Balter ($$)
3. BOSSI FEDRIGOTTI, Isera
   Trento Brut Riserva Conte Federico ($)
4. CAVIT, Trento
   Trento Brut Altemasi Riserva Graal ($$)
   Trento Pas Dosé Altemasi ($$)
5. CESARINI SFORZA, Trento
   Trento Brut Riserva Aquila Reale ($$)
6. DORIGATI, Mezzocorona
   Trento Brut Riserva Methius ($$)
7. ETYSSA, Trento
   Trento Extra Brut Cuvée n. 5 ($$)
8. FERRARI – Fratelli Lunelli, Trento
   Trento Extra Brut Riserva del Fondatore Giulio Ferrari ($$$$)
   Trento Extra Brut Riserva Perlé Nero ($$$)
   Trento Brut Rosé Riserva del Fondatore Giulio Ferrari ($$$$$)
9. LETRARI, Rovereto
   Trento Dosaggio Zero Riserva ($)
   Trento Brut 976 Riserva del Fondatore ($$$)
10. MASO MARTIS, Trento
    Trento Brut Riserva Madame Martis ($$$)
    Trento Brut Blanc de Blancs ($)
11. MOSER, Trento
    Trento Brut Nature ($$)
12. ROTARI, San Michele all'Adige
    Trento Brut Riserva Flavio ($$)

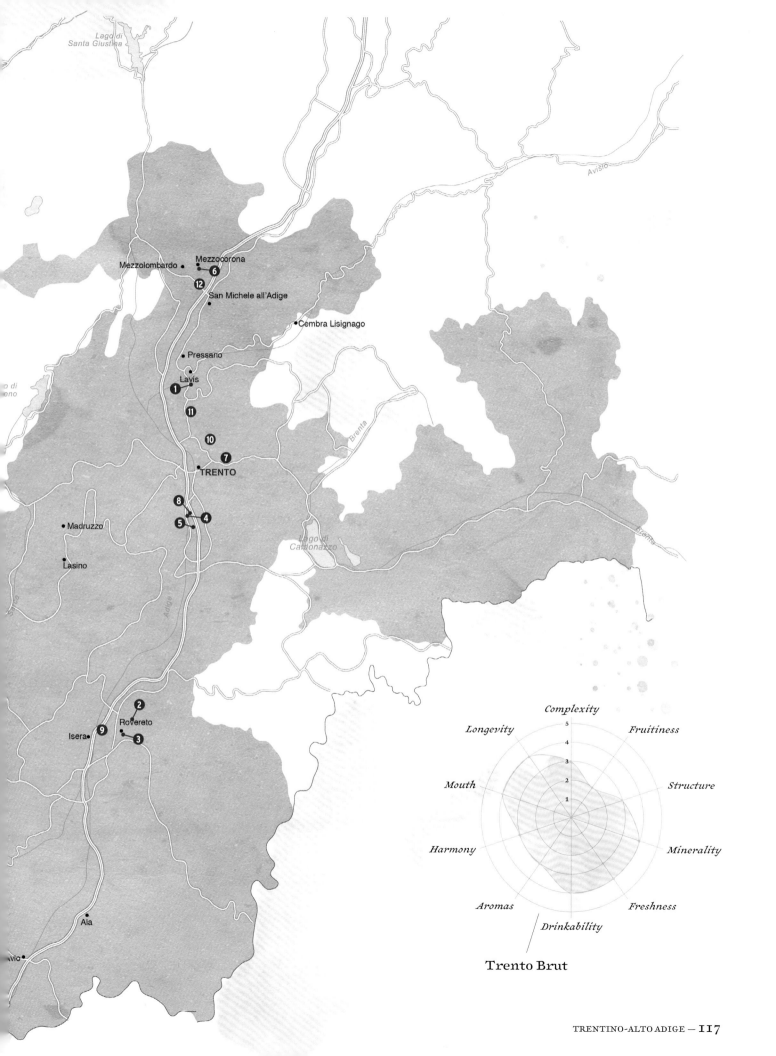

Mezzolombardo •
Mezzocorona
6
12
• San Michele all'Adige
• Cembra Lisignago
• Pressano
Lavis
1
11
10
7
TRENTO
8
4
5
• Madruzzo
• Lasino
• Lago di Calionazzo
2
Rovereto
Isera • **9**
3
Ala •
vio •

Complexity
Longevity
5
Fruitiness
4
3
Mouth
2
Structure
1
Harmony
Minerality
Aromas
Freshness
Drinkability

Trento Brut

Trentino DOC

In seventy-two municipalities in the Province of Trento, at altitudes ranging from 230 to 2,295 feet, twenty-nine types of wine can be produced based on different grape varieties, with possible specifications (Riserva or Liquoroso) and subareas. There are some territorial restrictions for Vino Santo—for which the grape yield in wine must not exceed 30%—and Marzemino. There are several dozen wine specifications allowed on the label, with results of particular value especially from Gewürztraminer, Müller-Thurgau, and Nosiola (from which Vino Santo is made) among the whites, and Pinot Noir and Marzemino among the reds. More than eighty million bottles are produced annually.

—

Producers and their trademark and signature wines:

1. BELLAVEDER, Faedo
   Trentino Pinot Nero Riserva Faedi ($$)
2. Lorenzo BONGIOVANNI, Avio
   Trentino Marzemino ($)
3. CANTINA LAVIS, Lavis
   Trentino Chardonnay Diaol ($)
4. CORVÉE, Cembra Lisignago
   Trentino Müller Thurgau Viàch ($)
   Trentino Pinot Nero Àgole ($$)
5. MASO CANTANGHEL, Lavis
   Trentino Pinot Nero Vigna Cantanghel ($$)
6. MASO FURLI, Lavis
   Trentino Gewürztraminer ($)
7. MASO GRENER, Lavis
   Trentino Pinot Nero Vigna Bindesi ($)
8. PISONI, Lasino
   Trentino Vino Santo ($$)
9. TENUTA MASO CORNO, Ala
   Trentino Pinot Nero Riserva Santa Maria ($$)
10. VALLAROM, Avio
    Trentino Marzemino ($)

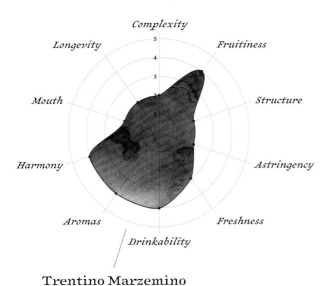

Trentino Marzemino

Teroldego Rotaliano DOC

The vast area covering 2,970 acres lying on the Campo Rotaliano, almost on the border with Alto Adige, has been known for its wine production since Roman times, there being mention of the Teroldego grape since the fifteenth century. It is here, at an altitude of just 655 to 820 feet, that the most characteristic red wine of Trentino, Teroldego Rotaliano, is produced in the territory of three municipalities. It is an apparently simple wine with a ruby-purple color, very rich in red fruit (from raspberry to blueberry), and suitable for drinking when young. It can, however, be pleasantly surprising after a few years in the bottle, especially if aged in wood, thanks to a good astringent component that enlivens and prolongs the taste. There are also Rosato (or Kretzer), Superiore, and Superiore Riserva types. Over six million bottles are produced annually.

—

Producers and their trademark and signature wines:

11. CANTINA ROTALIANA, Mezzolombardo
    Teroldego Rotaliano Superiore Riserva ($)
12. DE VESCOVI ULZBACH, Mezzocorona
    Teroldego Rotaliano Vigna Le Fron ($$)
    Teroldego Rotaliano Vigilius ($$)
13. Marco DONATI, Mezzocorona
    Teroldego Rotaliano Bagolari ($)
14. DORIGATI, Mezzocorona
    Teroldego Rotaliano Riserva Diedri ($$)
15. Andrea MARTINELLI, Mezzocorona
    Teroldego Rotaliano ($)
16. MEZZACORONA, Mezzocorona
    Teroldego Rotaliano Superiore Riserva Musivum ($$)
17. Roberto ZENI – Schwarzhof, San Michele all'Adige
    Teroldego Rotaliano Riserva Pini ($$)

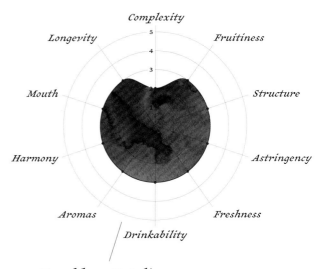

Teroldego Rotaliano

Lago di Santa Giustina

Noce

Avisio

Lago di Molveno

Lago di Garda

Sarca

Lago di Caldonazzo

Brenta

Mezzocorona
Mezzolombardo
Faedo
San Michele all'Adige
Cembra Lisignago
Pressano
Lavis
TRENTO
Madruzzo
Lasino
Calliano
Isera
Rovereto
Ala
Avio

13
15
11 12 16
14
17 1
7
6
3 5
4
8
9
2 10

Trentino

Teroldego Rotaliano

Alto Adige or dell'Alto Adige / Südtirol or Südtiroler DOC

The DOC covers the territory of the province of Bolzano, where vine cultivation was already widespread before the arrival of the Romans, in a hilly area characterized by the valleys of the Adige and Isarco Rivers. Wine critics are unanimous in defining South Tyrol as one area where white wine producers are making the most intense efforts to achieve high quality, to define the potential of each individual vineyard, and to adopt increasingly environmentally sustainable winegrowing methods. The results are visible, with a DOC that now sells in excess of forty million bottles per year worldwide. While still widespread, Pinot Gris is not at the top of the white wine awards, which are firmly occupied by Sauvignon, Chardonnay, Pinot Blanc, Gewürztraminer (or aromatic Traminer), and the less cultivated Riesling and Müller-Thurgau. In the field of reds, simple Lagrein and Schiava lead the ranking of the most-planted grape varieties, but it is Pinot Noir that creates the most celebrated selections, followed by important Cabernet Sauvignon–based offerings and, more rarely, Merlot. Within the hundred or so subdivisions envisaged by the regulations, based on different grape varieties and different vinification methods, and after an initial list of wineries using the all-encompassing Alto Adige DOC, we thought it useful to highlight the most relevant individual sub-areas. These include Santa Maddalena, Terlano, Valle Isarco, and Valle Venosta, with their own peculiarities to discover.

—

Producers and their trademark and signature wines:

1. ANSITZ WALDGRIES, Bolzano
   Alto Adige Sauvignon Myra ($)
   Alto Adige Lagrein Riserva Mirell ($$)
2. BARON WIDMANN, Cortaccia
   Alto Adige Sauvignon ($)
3. CANTINA ANDRIANO, Andriano
   Alto Adige Sauvignon Andrius ($$)
4. CANTINA BOLZANO, Bolzano
   Alto Adige Grieser Lagrein Riserva Prestige ($$)
   Alto Adige Lagrein Riserva Taber ($$)
5. CANTINA CALDARO, Caldaro
   Alto Adige Sauvignon Quintessenz ($)
6. CANTINA COLTERENZIO, Appiano
   Alto Adige Chardonnay Lafóa ($$)
   Alto Adige Cabernet Sauvignon Lafóa ($$$)
   Alto Adige Sauvignon Lafóa ($$)
7. CANTINA CONVENTO MURI-GRIES, Bolzano
   Alto Adige Lagrein Riserva Vigna Klosteranger ($$$)
   Alto Adige Lagrein Riserva Abtei Muri ($$)
8. CANTINA GIRLAN, Appiano
   Alto Adige Pinot Nero Riserva Curlan ($$$)
   Alto Adige Pinot Noir Riserva Trattmann ($$)
   Alto Adige Schiava Gschleier Alte Reben ($)

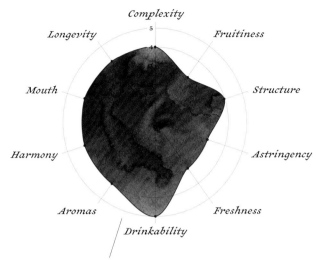

Alto Adige Cabernet Sauvignon

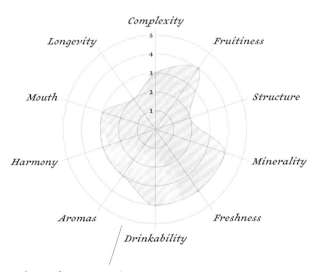

Alto Adige Sauvignon

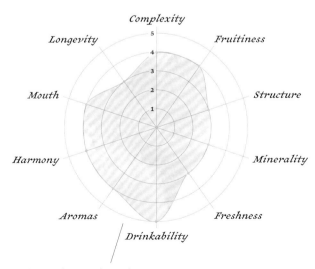

Alto Adige Chardonnay

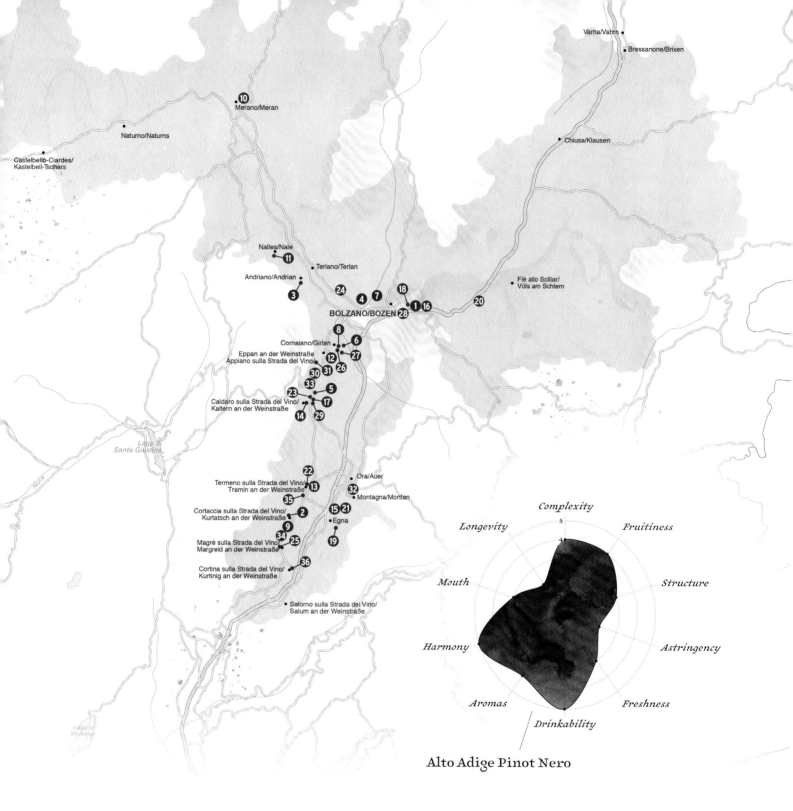

Alto Adige Pinot Nero

9. CANTINA KURTATSCH, Cortaccia
    Alto Adige Cabernet Sauvignon Riserva Freienfeld ($$)
    Alto Adige Chardonnay Riserva Freienfeld ($$)
    Alto Adige Gewürztraminer Riserva Brenntal ($$)
10. CANTINA MERANO, Merano
    Alto Adige Pinot Nero Riserva Zeno ($$)
11. CANTINA NALS MARGREID, Nalles
    Alto Adige Pinot Bianco Sirmian ($)
    Alto Adige Chardonnay Riserva Baron Salvadori ($$)
    Alto Adige Pinot Grigio Punggl ($)

12. CANTINA ST. MICHAEL EPPAN, Appiano
    Alto Adige Bianco Appius (Chardonnay, Pinot Gris,
    Sauvignon Blanc, Pinot Blanc) ($$$$)
    Alto Adige Sauvignon Sanct Valentin ($$)
    Alto Adige Pinot Nero Sanct Valentin ($$)
    Alto Adige Pinot Bianco Sanct Valentin ($$)
13. CANTINA TRAMIN, Termeno
    Alto Adige Gewürztraminer Nussbaumer ($$)
    Alto Adige Gewürztraminer Vendemmia Tardiva
    Terminum ($$)

14. CASTEL SALLEGG, Caldaro
Alto Adige Merlot Riserva Nussleiten ($$)
15. Peter DIPOLI, Egna
Alto Adige Sauvignon Voglar ($)
Alto Adige Merlot-Cabernet Iugum ($$)
16. ERBHOF UNTERGANZNER – Josephus Mayr, Bolzano
Alto Adige Lagrein Riserva ($$)
17. ERSTE+NEUE, Caldaro
Alto Adige Sauvignon Puntay ($)
18. GLÖGGLHOF – Franz Gojer, Bolzano
Alto Adige Lagrein Riserva ($$)
19. GOTTARDI, Egna
Alto Adige Pinot Nero Riserva ($$$)
20. GUMPHOF – Markus Prackwieser, Fiè allo Sciliar
Alto Adige Sauvignon Riserva Renaissance ($$)
Alto Adige Weissburgunder Riserva Renaissance ($$)
21. Franz HAAS, Montagna
Alto Adige Pinot Nero Schweizer ($$)
Alto Adige Sauvignon ($)
22. J. HOFSTÄTTER, Termeno
Alto Adige Pinot Nero Riserva Mazon ($$)
Alto Adige Pinot Bianco Barthenau Vigna S. Michele ($$)
23. KLOSTERHOF, Varna
Alto Adige Weissburgunder Acapella ($)
24. KORNELL, Terlano
Alto Adige Bianco Aichberg ($$)
Alto Adige Merlot Riserva Staffes ($$)
25. Alois LAGEDER, Magrè
Alto Adige Chardonnay Löwengang ($$$)
Alto Adige Cabernet Sauvignon Cor Römigberg ($$$)
26. Lorenz MARTINI, Appiano
Alto Adige Spumante Pas Dosé Riserva Comitissa M.
Cl. (Pinot Blanc, Chardonnay, Pinot Nero) ($$)
27. Ignaz NIEDRIST, Appiano
Alto Adige Sauvignon Porphyr & Kalk ($)
28. NUSSERHOF – Heinrich Mayr, Bolzano
Alto Adige Lagrein Riserva ($$)
29. RITTERHOF, Caldaro
Alto Adige Gewürztraminer Auratus ($$)
30. ST. QUIRINUS, Caldaro
Alto Adige Sauvignon Quirinus ($)
31. STROBLHOF, Appiano
Alto Adige Pinot Nero Riserva ($$)
32. TENUTA PFITSCHER, Montagna
Alto Adige Lagrein Riserva Griesfeld ($$)
33. TENUTA UNTERHOFER THOMAS, Caldaro
Alto Adige Sauvignon Mirum ($)
34. TIEFENBRUNNER, Cortaccia
Alto Adige Müller Thurgau Feldmarschall von Fenner ($$)
Alto Adige Sauvignon Riserva Rachtl ($$$)
35. Elena WALCH, Termeno
Alto Adige Chardonnay Riserva Vigna Castel Ringberg ($$)
Alto Adige Bianco Grande Cuvée Beyond the Clouds ($$$)
36. Peter ZEMMER, Cortina sulla Strada del Vino
Alto Adige Pinot Grigio Giatl ($$)

Alto Adige sottozona Santa Maddalena / Südtirol St. Magdalener DOC

In the area to the northeast of the city of Bolzano, the grape variety used is called Schiava, which yields wines rich in ruby-red color and fruity aromas, followed by an impression on the palate that has the advantage of enjoyable drinkability. It is never too astringent, with harmonious freshness and an almond finish. It is aged in steel and with delicate maturation in wood. Approximately 1.5 million bottles are produced each year.

—

Producers and their trademark and signature wines:

1. CANTINA BOLZANO, Bolzano
Alto Adige Santa Maddalena Classico Moar ($)
2. ERBHOF UNTERGANZNER – Josephus Mayr, Bolzano
Santa Maddalena Classico Heilmann ($)
3. GLÖGGLHOF – Franz Gojer, Bolzano
Alto Adige Santa Maddalena Vigna Rondell ($)
4. GRIESBAUERHOF, Bolzano
Alto Adige Santa Maddalena Classico Isarcus ($)
5. PFANNENSTIELHOF–JohannesPfeifer,Bolzano
Alto Adige Santa Maddalena Classico Annver ($)
6. ROTTENSTEINER, Bolzano
Alto Adige Santa Maddalena Classico Vigna Premstallerhof Select ($)
7. THURNHOF – Andreas Berger, Bolzano
Alto Adige Santa Maddalena ($)
8. UNTERMOSERHOF GEORG RAMOSER, Bolzano
Alto Adige Santa Maddalena Classico Hub ($)

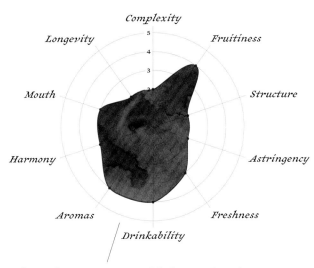

Alto Adige Santa Maddalena Classico

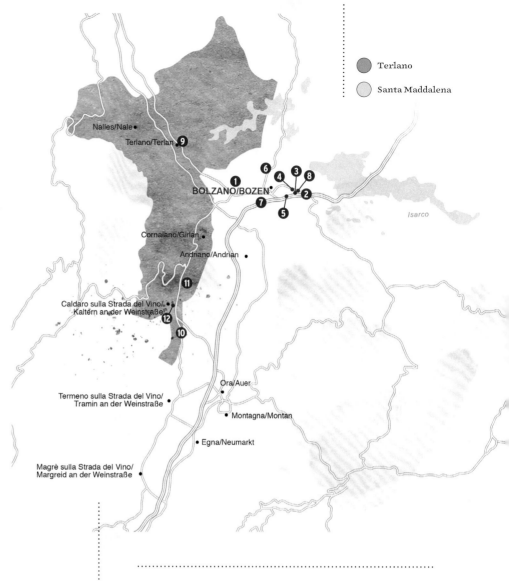

Terlano
Santa Maddalena

Alto Adige sottozona Terlano / Südtirol Terlaner DOC

A number of white cultivars are used here, among which Pinot Blanc, Sauvignon, and Chardonnay historically excel, and may be labeled as such if at least 85% of the grapes are present. Production exceeds 1.6 million bottles per year.

—

Producers and their trademark and signature wines:

9. CANTINA TERLANO, Terlano
    Alto Adige Terlano Pinot Bianco
    Riserva Vorberg ($$)
    Alto Adige Terlano Riserva
    Nova Domus ($$)
    Alto Adige Terlano Rarity ($$$$)
10. MANINCOR, Caldaro
    Alto Adige Terlano
    Sauvignon Tannenberg ($$)
    Alto Adige Terlano
    Pinot Bianco Eichhorn ($$)
    Alto Adige Terlano
    Chardonnay Sophie ($$)

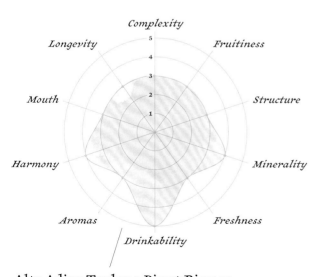

Alto Adige Terlano Pinot Bianco

Lago di Caldaro or Caldaro / Kalterersee or Kalterer DOC

A DOC dedicated only to red wine, based at least 85% on Schiava grapes of the Grossa, Gentile, or Grigia biotypes and grown in twelve municipalities in the province of Bolzano. This is where the area is located that can boast the title of Classico; the wines are also grown in eight municipalities in the province of Trento. It plays a lot on immediate pleasantness, usually aged in steel or large wooden barrels, and is to be consumed slightly chilled. Production reaches three million bottles per year.

—

Producers and their trademark and signature wines:

11. CANTINA CALDARO, Caldaro
    Lago di Caldaro Classico Superiore
    Quintessenz ($)
12. CASTEL SALLEGG, Caldaro
    Lago di Caldaro Scelto Classico Superiore
    Bischofsleiten ($)

Alto Adige sottozona Valle Isarco / Südtirol Eisacktal or Eisacktaler DOC

In a rather cool area, where the wines produced are rich in flavor and aroma, those from Sylvaner to Riesling and from Grüner Veltliner to Kerner enjoy a special place. Vinification without the use of wood is favored. Production is close to two million bottles per year.

—

Producers and their trademark and signature wines:

1. ABBAZIA DI NOVACELLA, Varna
   Alto Adige Valle Isarco Sylvaner Praepositus ($)
   Alto Adige Valle Isarco Riesling Praepositus ($)
   Alto Adige Valle Isarco Grüner Veltliner Praepositus ($)
2. CANTINA VALLE ISARCO, Chiusa
   Alto Adige Valle Isarco Kerner Aristos ($)
   Alto Adige Valle Isarco Grüner Veltliner Aristos ($)
3. GAFFER VON FELDENREICH, Ora
   Alto Adige Valle Isarco Kerner ($)
4. KÖFERERHOF – Günther Kerschbaumer, Varna
   Alto Adige Valle Isarco Sylvaner ($)
   Alto Adige Valle Isarco Sylvaner Riserva ($ $)
   Alto Adige Valle Isarco Pinot Grigio ($)
   Alto Adige Valle Isarco Riesling ($)
5. KUENHOF – Peter Pliger, Bressanone
   Alto Adige Valle Isarco Riesling Kaiton ($)
   Alto Adige Valle Isarco Sylvaner ($)
   Alto Adige Valle Isarco Veltliner ($)
6. STRASSERHOF, Varna
   Alto Adige Valle Isarco Sylvaner ($)
7. TASCHLERHOF – Peter Wachtler, Bressanone
   Alto Adige Valle Isarco Sylvaner ($)
   Alto Adige Valle Isarco Riesling ($)

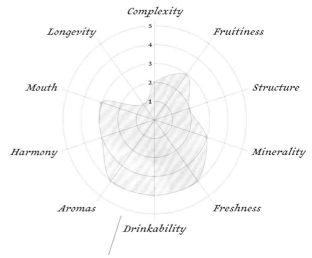

Alto Adige Valle Isarco Sylvaner

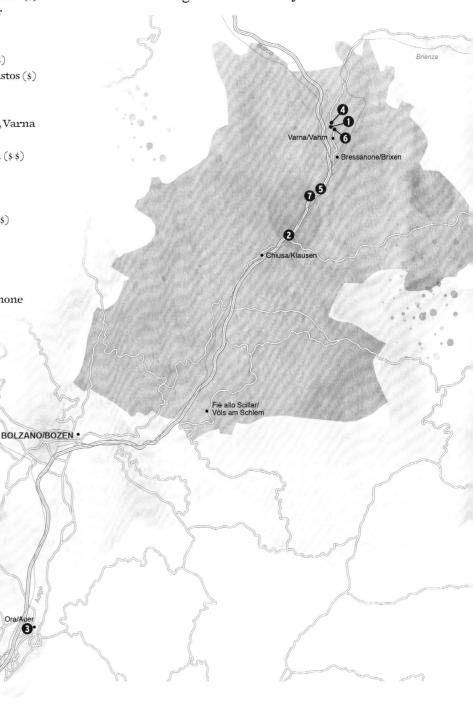

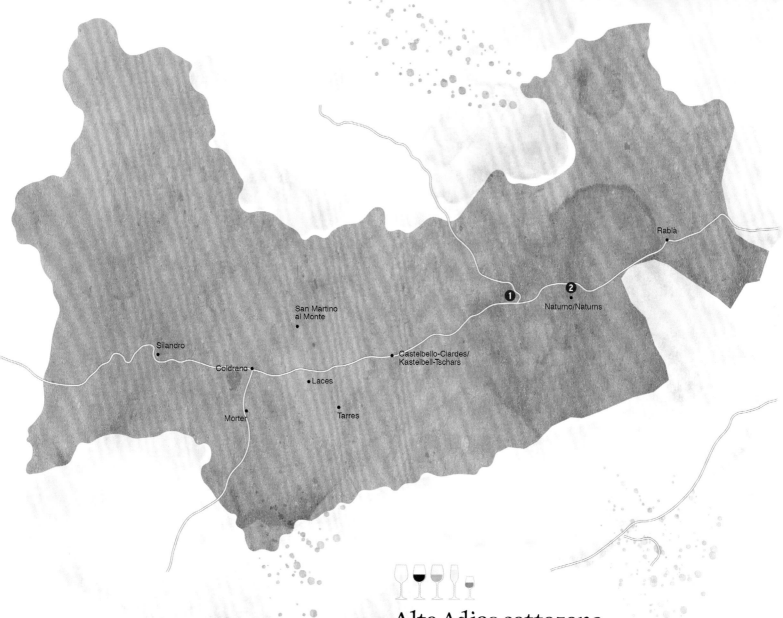

Alto Adige sottozona Valle Venosta / Südtirol Vinschgau DOC

This is the most eastern area in the province of Bolzano and has become famous for its Riesling, rich in aromas ranging from tropical fruit to flint, while the palate is vibrant, dry—with excellent acidity—tart, and free of fatness. Aging takes place in steel. Over two million bottles per year are produced.

—

Producers and their trademark and signature wines:

1. CASTEL JUVAL – UNTERORTL, Castelbello-Ciardes
   Alto Adige Valle Venosta Riesling Windbichel ($$)
   Alto Adige Valle Venosta Riesling Unterortl ($)
2. FALKENSTEIN – Franz Pratzner, Naturno
   Alto Adige Val Venosta Riesling ($)
   Alto Adige Val Venosta Pinot Bianco ($)

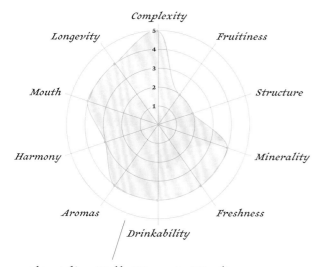

Alto Adige Valle Venosta Riesling

Recommended wines outside the DOC/DOCG designations:

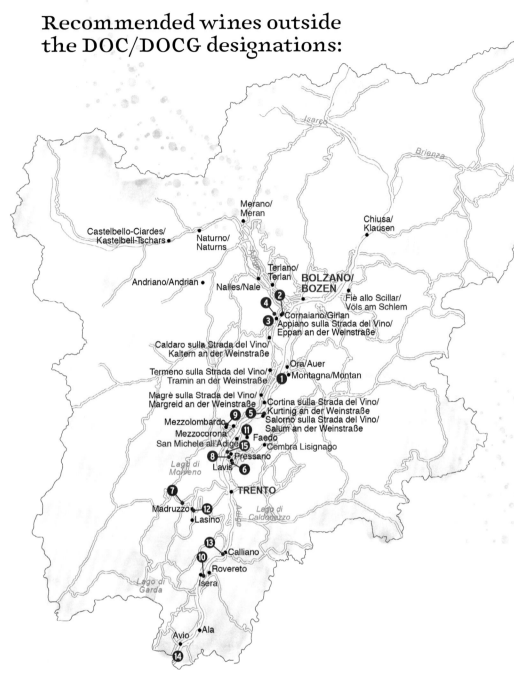

Merano/Meran

Chiusa/Klausen

Castelbello-Ciardes/Kastelbell-Tschars

Naturno/Naturns

Terlano/Terlan

BOLZANO/BOZEN

Andriano/Andrian

Nalles/Nale

Fiè allo Scillar/Völs am Schlem

2

4

Cornaiano/Girlan

3

Appiano sulla Strada del Vino/Eppan an der Weinstraße

Caldaro sulla Strada del Vino/Kaltern an der Weinstraße

Ora/Auer

Termeno sulla Strada del Vino/Tramin an der Weinstraße

1

Montagna/Montan

Magrè sulla Strada del Vino/Margreid an der Weinstraße

Cortina sulla Strada del Vino/Kurtinig an der Weinstraße

9

5

Salorno sulla Strada del Vino/Salum an der Weinstraße

Mezzolombardo

11

Faedo

Mezzocorona

15

Cembra Lisignago

San Michele all'Adige

8

Pressano

Lago di Molveno

Lavis

6

7

TRENTO

Madruzzo

12

Lago di Caldonazzo

Lasino

13

Calliano

10

Rovereto

Isera

Lago di Garda

Avio

Ala

14

ALTO ADIGE

1. Franz HAAS, Montagna
   Manna (Riesling Renano, Chardonnay, Gewürztraminer, Kerner, Sauvignon) ($$)
2. HARTMANN DONÀ, Appiano
   Donà Rouge (Schiava, Pinot Noir, Lagrein) ($$)
3. HOF GANDBERG – Thomas Niedermayr, Montagna
   Souvignier Gris ($$)
4. TENUTA ABRAHAM, Appiano
   Abraham Art Pinot Noir ($$$)
5. TENUTA DORNACH – Patrick Uccelli, Salorno
   Pinot Nero ($)

TRENTINO

6. CANTINA LAVIS, Lavis
   Maso Franch (Incrocio Manzoni) ($)
7. CANTINA TOBLINO, Madruzzo
   Largiller (Nosiola) ($$)
8. CESCONI, Lavis
   Olivar (Pinot Bianco, Chardonnay, Pinot Grigio) ($)
9. FORADORI, Mezzolombardo
   Granato (Teroldego) ($$$)
   Nosiola Fontanasanta ($$)
10. LONGARIVA, Rovereto
    Graminé (Pinot Grigio) ($)
11. POJER & SANDRI, Faedo
    Nosiola ($)
    Rosso Faye (Cabernet Sauvignon, Merlot, Lagrein) ($$)
12. PRAVIS, Lasino
    L'Ora (Nosiola) ($)
13. Eugenio ROSI, Calliano
    Esegesi (Cabernet Sauvignon, Merlot) ($$)
14. SAN LEONARDO, Avio
    San Leonardo (Cabernet Sauvignon, Cabernet Franc, Carmenère, Merlot) ($$$)
    Villa Gresti di San Leonardo (Merlot, Carmenère) ($$)
15. VIGNAIOLO FANTI, Pressano
    Isidor (Incrocio Manzoni) ($)

CANTINA COLTERENZIO / SCHRECKBICHL

Località Cornaiano,
Strada del Vino 8
Appiano / Eppan (BZ)
colterenzio.it
Year of establishment: 1960
Owner: the 300 members
of the Colterenzio
cooperative
Average number of
bottles produced per year:
1,900,000

The numerous members cultivate small plots, totaling 740 acres, in locations allowing the best possible expression of the territorial vocation of the fourteen different grape varieties used for vinification. The most famous products are included in the Lafóa line (comprising Sauvignon, Chardonnay, Gewürztraminer, and Cabernet Sauvignon) and in the Cru line, but it can safely be said that for more than thirty years, quality has been well spread across the entire range.

ALTO ADIGE SAUVIGNON LAFÓA

First year of production: 1993
Average number of bottles produced per year: 60,000
Grape variety: Sauvignon

Matured partly in wood and partly in steel, it is characterized above all by its lovely acidic freshness and the almost total absence of residual sugars, so that the flavor is always taut and lively, barely harmonized by the memory of oak. The nose is graceful, set on beautiful notes of tomato leaf and sage, never pungent. A Sauvignon of rare finesse and very pleasant.

CANTINA CONVENTO MURI-GRIES

Piazza Gries 21
Bolzano / Bozen
muri-gries.com
Year of establishment: 1845
Owner: the Convento dei
Benedettini di Muri-Gries
Average number of bottles
produced per year: 650,000

The Lagrein and Schiava grapes of this historic winery are located in the municipality of Bolzano, while the white grapes—especially Pinot Blanc and Chardonnay—and Pinot Noir are located in Appiano. They own a total of 86 acres, in addition to the grapes of local winegrowers, and produce nine quality labels, including the Terlano Pinot Bianco Riserva and Pinot Nero Riserva, as well as the now famous Klosteranger. A cellar as brilliant as the winery is fascinating.

ALTO ADIGE LAGREIN RISERVA VIGNA KLOSTERANGER

First year of production: 2014
Average number of bottles produced per year: 20,000
Grape variety: Lagrein

Lagrein can sometimes be simple and almost aggressive, even a little rustic and lacking the complexity expected of great wines. The farsighted project of winemaker Christian Werth, on the other hand, has succeeded in proving that it is possible to obtain a wine that, after long maturation in small wood, can be above all elegant and balanced. The aromas open on small berries and spices, while the palate rejoices in the balance between power and freshness, between velvety tannicity and juiciness. The revitalization and celebration of the best Lagrein.

CANTINA KURTATSCH / CORTACCIA

Strada del Vino 23
Cortaccia / Kurtatsch
(BZ)
kellerei-kurtatsch.it
Year of establishment: 1900
Owner: the 190 members
of the Cantina Kurtatsch
Average number of
bottles produced per year:
1,400,000

The 470 acres cultivated in the members' small vineyards enable the production of a range comprising dozens of labels, at the top of which are the selections included in the Terroir line. The grape varieties that have brought the greatest luster to the winery are those now historically best acclimatized in the valley, from Cabernet Sauvignon to Merlot, from Pinot Gris to Gewürztraminer, but equally interesting is the production of Schiava, from which the award-winning Sonntaler Alte Reben is made.

ALTO ADIGE CABERNET SAUVIGNON RISERVA FREIENFELD

First year of production: 1988
Average number of bottles produced per year: 8,000
Grape variety: Cabernet Sauvignon

After experimenting with oaks of various origins, the choice was made to mature the Freienfeld for two years first in French barriques and then in large wood, resulting in a wine so balanced that it fully convinced all the international critics. The aromas are rich in small black fruits and herbs, with a hint of licorice that emerges elegantly on the finish. The flavor is characterized by good acidity and limited astringency, with a balanced and very pleasant drinkability.

CANTINA ST. MICHAEL EPPAN

Via Circonvallazione 17
Appiano / Eppan (BZ)
stmichael.it
Year of establishment: 1907
Owners: the 330 members of
Cantina St. Michael-Eppan
Average number of
bottles produced per year:
2,500,000

A centuries-old history and international fortune that, in recent decades, has been closely linked to the figure of Hans Terzer, who has been working since 1977 both in the cellar and in the countryside to guarantee the highest quality of grapes and wines of absolute finesse. The numerous members cultivate 950 acres, working a great variety of grapes that are then distributed to different production lines, with the one dedicated to Sanct Valentin excelling in terms of celebrity and diffusion. There are also expensive and limited-edition versions aimed at highlighting the wines' great capacity for improvement in the bottle. Admirable overall quality.

ALTO ADIGE SAUVIGNON SANCT VALENTIN

First year of production: 1989
Average number of bottles produced per year: 145,000
Grape variety: Sauvignon

Delicate notes of tomato leaf and elderflower combine with peach and grapefruit, with a flavor of excellent substance, enveloping alcohol content and balanced freshness, right through to the elegant spicy finish. Soft but not opulent, fresh but not acidic, highly perfumed but barely aromatic: deservedly the company's best-known label.

CANTINA TRAMIN

Strada del Vino 144
Termeno / Tramin (BZ)
cantinatramin.it
Year of establishment: 1898
Owner: the 160 members
of Cantina Tramin
Average number of
bottles produced per year:
1,800,000

Cantina Tramin is now
known the world over thanks
to its centuries-old history
and the arrival at the helm
of the winery, in 1995, of
Will Stürz, considered an
oenologist of rare sensitivity
and competence. The
famous Nussbaumer is
flanked by other prestigious
Gewürztraminer labels,
in particular the rich Late
Harvest Terminum and the
award-winning Spätlese
Epokale. However, the
production range is much
broader, thanks in part to
the merger with the Cantina
Sociale di Egna in 1971, which
brought a dowry of new
vineyards, now totaling 667
acres. Valuable quality of the
entire range.

ALTO ADIGE GEWÜRZTRAMINER NUSSBAUMER

First year of production: 1990
Average number of bottles produced
per year: 72,000
Grape variety: Gewürztraminer

The aromas are very incisive and varied,
with exotic fruit, lavender, and rosewater in
the forefront against a background of citrus
and yellow spices. The palate is quite robust,
rich in juice and acidity, with a finish in
which refined hints of hydrocarbons appear
over time. The acknowledged archetype of
the best Italian Gewürztraminer, beyond
fashions.

ALOIS LAGEDER

Vicolo dei Conti 9
Magrè / Margreid (BZ)
aloislageder.eu
Year of establishment: 1823
Owner: the Lageder family
Average number of
bottles produced per year:
1,200,000

Alois Lageder passed on the
company baton to his son,
Clemens, after taking this
historic winery to the absolute
top of Italian quality. The
estate's 136 acres are farmed
using organic and biodynamic
methods, including vegetable
gardens and free-range oxen,
while other grapes come from
ninety historical contributors;
the result is over thirty labels
divided into three lines:
Classic Grapes, Compositions,
Masterpieces. Countless
awards have been received
internationally.

ALTO ADIGE CHARDONNAY LÖWENGANG

First year of production: 1983
Average number of bottles produced
per year: 50,000
Grape variety: Chardonnay

A wine that succeeds in smoothly
overcoming the risks of sweetness and
woodiness typical of many Chardonnays,
characterized by aromas in which field
grasses unite with citrus fruits and the
richness of flavor merges with the fresh
dynamism of acidity. Balance, finesse, and
vitality.

GUMPHOF - Markus Prackwieser

Località Novale di Presule,
Strada di Fiè 11
Fiè allo Sciliar / Völs am
Schlern (BZ)
gumphof.it
Year of establishment: 2000
Owner: Markus
Prackwieser
Average number of bottles
produced per year: 60,000

We are at the start of the Valle
Isarco, with steeply sloping
vineyards dominated by the
Sciliar Massif: it is here that
Markus Prackwieser harvests
the grapes for his 17 acres
from which he obtains his
ten labels, also using some
of his neighbors' grapes. The
grapes are the most typical
of the area: Sauvignon, Pinot
Blanc, and Traminer for the
whites, Pinot Noir and Schiava
for the reds. Immediate and
youthful are the wines of the
Mediaevum line, precise and
complex those of the Praesulis
line, superlative the Reserves
labeled Renaissance. Markus
Prackwieser is an artist of
winemaking.

ALTO ADIGE WEISSBURGUNDER RISERVA RENAISSANCE

First year of production: 2012
Average number of bottles produced
per year: 3,000
Grape variety: Pinot Blanc

A very articulate white, characterized on
the nose by white flowers on a slightly
smoky base. In the mouth, it is rich, soft, and
caressing, almost sweet in its fruity pulp
but taut and lively thanks to its freshness,
prestigiously persuasive, and very pleasant.
Small production, very high quality.

TIEFENBRUNNER - Schlosskellerei Turmhof

Frazione Niclara, Via
Castello 4
Cortaccia sulla Strada del
Vino / Kurtatsch an der
Weinstraße (BZ)
tiefenbrunner.com
Year of establishment: 1848
Owner: the
Tiefenbrunner family
Average number of bottles
produced per year: 700,000

Centuries of history had
already made the winery
famous, and with the latest
Tiefenbrunner generations,
it has been able to expand,
export, and achieve enviable
quality. In keeping with
tradition, the practice of
purchasing grapes from
small local winegrowers
continues, adding to the
69 acres of vines owned,
allowing the production of
twenty-seven labels. The best-
known include, in addition
to Feldmarschall, Sauvignon
Rachtl, Chardonnay Au, and
Pinot Noir Linticlarus.

ALTO ADIGE MÜLLER THURGAU FELDMARSCHALL VON FENNER

First year of production: 1974
Average number of bottles produced
per year: 9,000
Grape variety: Müller-Thurgau

It comes from a dedicated 7-acre vineyard at
an altitude close to 3,280 feet, then matures
for a year, partly in steel and partly in large
wood. The aromas are intense with delicate
aromaticity that guarantees finesse and
with clear notes of citrus fruits and yellow
spices; the flavor is incisive thanks to good
acidity, rich in substance, with an elegant
finish full of mineral notes in which the flint
stands out.

ABBAZIA DI NOVACELLA
Via Abbazia 1
Varna / Vahrn (BZ)
abbazianovacella.it
Year of establishment: 1142
Owners: Canonici
Regolari di Sant'Agostino
Average number of bottles
produced per year: 850,000

Centuries of experience in
cultivation have led the winery
to perfectly recognize the
potential of each individual
vineyard, in a vineyard park
that puts no less than 212 acres
at the disposal of the current
technical manager, Celestino
Lucin. The vocation of the
cool basin of Bressanone,
with vines cultivated between
1,970 and 2,950 feet above sea
level, is definitely made for
white wines, which reach their
maximum expressiveness
in the eight labels of the
Praepositus line. The historic
company headquarters is well
worth a visit.

**ALTO ADIGE VALLE ISARCO
RIESLING PRAEPOSITUS**
First year of production: 2007
Average number of bottles produced
per year: 12,000
Grape variety: Riesling

Yellow fruits such as peach and apricot
are at the forefront, while a refined hint
of hydrocarbons appears after a few years
in the bottle. The palate is substantial but
flowing, agile and direct thanks to the
good acid backbone, long and sharp with a
deliciously citrusy finish. The unparalleled
refinement of deep-sea Riesling.

KUENHOF - Peter Pliger
Via Lahner 12
Bressanone / Brixen (BZ)
kuenhof.com
Year of establishment: 1990
Owner: Peter Pliger
Average number of bottles
produced per year: 38,000

In his wines, Peter Pliger
expresses to perfection the
essentiality and measure
that comes from vineyards
perched on rocks, in not very
fertile areas. In this sense,
he severely limits the use of
wood, preferring the more
severe acacia to the generous
oak, and prefers steel, which
helps to avoid any hint of
softness and butteriness. From
15 acres planted with white
grapes, four pure and sober
labels of graceful exquisiteness
are born.

**ALTO ADIGE VALLE ISARCO
RIESLING KAITON**
First year of production: 1996
Average number of bottles produced
per year: 12,000
Grape variety: Riesling

The hints of hydrocarbons and flint are
best perceived after a few years in the
bottle, while the aromas of citrus and field
herbs, including mint, are immediate and
persistent. The flavor is bewitching, almost
cutting, with a touch of acidity that borders
on salinity, very tasty. A wine that has
contributed to the well-deserved fame of the
Valle Isarco.

**KÖFERERHOF - Günther
Kerschbaumer**
Via Pusteria 3
Varna / Vahrn (BZ)
koefererhof.it
Year of establishment: 1995
Owner: Günther
Kerschbaumer
Average number of bottles
produced per year: 85,000

One of the most popular
wineries not only in the Valle
Isarco but in the entire Alto
Adige. The award-winning
Alto Adige Valle Isarco
Sylvaner Reserve is joined by
labels from six other grape
varieties, yielding Veltliner,
Müller-Thurgau, Pinot Gris,
Kerner, Gewürztraminer, and
Riesling. The 25 acres of estate
vineyards, to which the grapes
of trusted suppliers are added,
are located quite high up, on
terraces between 2,130 and
2,460 feet above sea level: a
guarantee for both the good
acid component and aromatic
complexity favored by the
considerable temperature
fluctuations.

**ALTO ADIGE VALLE ISARCO
SYLVANER RISERVA**
First year of production: 2006
Average number of bottles produced
per year: 4,000
Grape variety: Sylvaner

Some of the grapes undergo a delicate
passage in wood, favoring the ideal fusion
of both the aromas and taste structure. The
two souls of the variety emerge on the nose:
on the one hand the fresh, citrusy, slightly
herbaceous and minty components, on the
other hand, slight mineral hints reminiscent
of flint. In the mouth, it is stimulatingly
drinkable, rather saline in a complex of true
harmony, with a finish that reveals refined
smoky hints.

CANTINA TERLANO
Via Silberleiten 7
Terlano / Terlan (BZ)
cantina-terlano.com
Year of establishment: 1893
Owner: the 143 members
of Cantina Terlano
Average number of
bottles produced per year:
1,500,000

Brought to international
notoriety thanks to the
extraordinary oenological
skills of Sebastian Stocker,
whose style is continued
today by Rudi Kofler, the
winery vinifies the grapes
processed on 470 acres,
making numerous separate
vinifications per vineyard.
The most famous production
line is Selection, in which,
among others, the award-
winning Sauvignon Quarz and
the even more famous Nova
Domus are found alongside
the Vorberg. A winery at the
pinnacle of quality, valid in
every label on offer.

**ALTO ADIGE TERLANO PINOT
BIANCO RISERVA VORBERG**
Year of establishment: 1993
Average number of bottles produced
per year: 55,000
Grape variety: Pinot Blanc

Matured in large wood, it has notes of white
fruit in the foreground, joined by a hint of
spice and a refined mineral hint of flint. The
palate is enveloping and soft, thanks to the
malolactic fermentation, and pleasantly dry,
being practically sugar-free, with a final hint
of savoriness. Impressive for its harmony
and complexity.

MANINCOR

Località San Giuseppe al
Lago 4
Caldaro / Kaltern (BZ)
manincor.com
Year of establishment: 1996
Owner: the Goëss-
Enzenberg family
Average number of bottles
produced per year: 350,000

A vast expanse for this private
winery, which has enjoyed
great success thanks to two
particularities: on the one
hand, the use of biodynamic
methods in all 124 acres of
the estate, and on the other
hand, the outstanding quality
of all sixteen labels on offer.
In addition to Sauvignon
Tannenberg, Pinot Blanc
Eichhorn, Chardonnay Sophie,
and Réserve della Contessa
from the Terlano subzone,
wine guides are fascinated by
both Pinot Noir wines from
the Mason vineyard.

ALTO ADIGE TERLANO SAUVIGNON TANNENBERG

First year of production: 2011
Average number of bottles produced
per year: 12,500
Grape variety: Sauvignon Blanc

The passage in wood is delicate, barely
perceptible, and is the background to
pleasant aromas of elder and tropical fruits.
This is followed by a taste that is elegant,
delicate, harmonious, and at the same time
impulsive, almost impetuous, thanks to the
absence of residual sugar and the acidulous
freshness. A national benchmark for
refinement and pleasantness.

FORADORI

Via D. Chiesa 1
Mezzolombardo (TN)
agricolaforadori.com
Year of establishment: 1939
Owner: Elisabetta
Foradori
Average number of bottles
produced per year: 180,000

Elisabetta Foradori is a tireless
experimenter: having joined
the company in 1984, she
has proven herself capable
of revaluing and making
the Teroldego grape variety
appreciated throughout the
world. She started first and
foremost from a streamlined
version of agriculture, like
the one found in her 74 acres
of biodynamically cultivated
land. Vinification processes
are carried out without the
addition of chemicals and
involve the use of cherry
and oak wood, as well as
amphorae, always respecting
the different personalities of
each vintage. The winery is a
member of the Renaissance
des Appellations association.

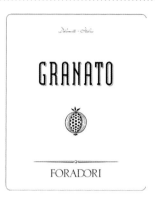

GRANATO

First year of production: 1986
Average number of bottles produced
per year: 20,000
Grape variety: Teroldego

A perfect demonstration of how the rich,
energetic, fruity, and somewhat impetuous
personality of Teroldego can be enhanced
without obscuring its more persuasive and
refined possibilities. Currants, cherries, and
blackberries in the aromas, good acidity,
restrained astringency, and a spicy finish on
the robust palate. The epitome of Teroldego
at its most enhanced.

CASTEL JUVAL - UNTERORTL

Frazione Juval 1/B
Castelbello Ciardes /
Kastelbell Tschars (BZ)
unterortl.it
Year of establishment: 1992
Owner: the Aurich,
& Reinhold Messner
families
Average number of bottles
produced per year: 35,000

Martin Aurich is not only a
lecturer in oenology, but also
a fine chiseler of vineyards
and wines, crafted with a
sensitivity that has brought
this small entity to the
forefront of the international
scene. The greatest successes
come from the Riesling,
but the Pinot Blanc and
Müller-Thurgau are also
deserved champions of
refreshing drinkability. A
sublime oenological mastery
based on just 12 acres of
organically cultivated land.

ALTO ADIGE VAL VENOSTA RIESLING WINDBICHEL

First year of production: 1994
Average number of bottles produced
per year: 2,500
Grape variety: Riesling

Born in a steep, rock-rich vineyard over
2,300 feet above sea level, it then matures
in steel only to preserve the clear mineral
and citrus aromas that also accompany the
savory finish on the palate. The flavor is vital
and stimulating, dry thanks to the very low
residual sugar and not very high alcohol
content, captivating.

SAN LEONARDO

Frazione Borghetto
sull'Adige, Località San
Leonardo
Avio (TN)
sanleonardo.it
Year of establishment: 1724
Owner: the Guerrieri
family
Average number of bottles
produced per year: 180,000

The estate has always
been characterized by the
production of important,
crisp reds, using French grape
varieties that have proved
to be at home in this area:
Cabernet Sauvignon, Merlot,
Carmenère. In the 111 acres
under vine, cultivated using
organic methods, there is also
room for pure white grapes,
Sauvignon and Riesling for
still wines, and Chardonnay
for the Metodo Classico. A
long history of prestige and
quality.

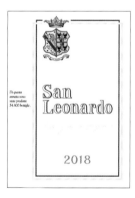

SAN LEONARDO

First year of production: 1982
Average number of bottles produced
per year: 70,000
Grape varieties: Cabernet Sauvignon
(60%), Carmenère (30%), Merlot
(10%)

A distinctly Bordeaux style in the grape
varieties and even more so in the maturation
in wood, which involves the long use of
small first, second, and third passage barrels.
The result is a San Leonardo of sure olfactory
elegance, with small berries and spices in
clear evidence, a delicate and multifaceted
taste, a little astringent and refined in a
finish where hints of cocoa, licorice, and
eucalyptus emerge. Among the great reds of
Italy for forty years.

DORIGATI
Via Dante 5
Mezzocorona (TN)
dorigati.it
Year of establishment: 1858
Owner: the Dorigati family
Average number of bottles produced per year: 100,000

This historic family, in addition to owning 15 acres of vines in the Campo Rotaliano, has always vinified grapes from trusted local growers. The most important production is centered on the Teroldego grape, from which, in addition to Diedri, the important Riserva Luigi is made, but an exquisite, award-winning Metodo Classico, Methius, is also deserving of fame. The company participates in the communication activities of the Teroldego Evolution association.

TEROLDEGO ROTALIANO RISERVA DIEDRI
First year of production: 1988
Average number of bottles produced per year: 10,000
Grape variety: Teroldego

A Teroldego with great personality, which adds both elegance from the fermentation in tonneaux, and a slightly austere character to the classic, intense fruity sensations typical of this grape. The Diedri thus achieves a fine complexity in which one can also perceive field grasses and a mineral reminder reminiscent of cinchona, which then expresses itself on the palate with a beautiful roundness favored by low tannins and a finish in which blueberries and eucalyptus appear. A splendid interpretation of the grape variety.

LETRARI
Via Monte Baldo 13
Rovereto (TN)
letrari.it
Year of establishment: 1976
Owner: the Letrari family
Average number of bottles produced per year: 150,000

Since the 1960s, Leonello, and later his daughter Lucia, have earned the respect not only of consumers but also of fellow Trentino producers for the fruity, fragrant style of their Trento wines offered in six versions. The 40 acres of estate vineyards produce primarily Metodo Classico sparkling wines from Chardonnay and Pinot Noir grapes, although there is no lack of red wines made from the traditional Marzemino and Teroldego varieties, as well as Bordeaux grapes that have long been typical of the area, such as Cabernet Franc and Merlot. A winery that has made a committed contribution to the success of Trentino sparkling wines.

TRENTO DOSAGGIO ZERO RISERVA
First year of production: 2004
Average number of bottles produced per year: 7,000
Grape varieties: Chardonnay (60%), Pinot Noir (40%)

The wine's sixty-month sojourn on the lees gives rise to a complexity in which the classic notes of hazelnut and bread crust are joined by the proverbial freshness of citrus fruits and herbs. The absence of added sugar ensures a consistently clean and solid structure, while the acidity adds drinkability and tonicity to the rich finish of green apple and mandarin. Consistently at the top of its type.

FERRARI
Via del Ponte di Ravina 15
Trento
ferraritrento.it
Year of establishment: 1902
Owner: the Lunelli family
Average number of bottles produced per year: 5,600,000

Italy's most famous winery for its Metodo Classico, with an excellent range that includes not only the Riserva del Fondatore but a number of world-renowned labels, all from the Trento DOC: from the Extra Brut Riserva Perlé Nero to the Brut Rosé Riserva del Fondatore Giulio Ferrari, from the Dosaggio Zero Perlé Cuvée Zero14 to the Brut Riserva Perlé Bianco. In keeping with tradition, a large portion of the grapes are purchased from historic vintners, while organic and biodynamic methods are being experimented with on the 247 acres of the estate. The Lunelli family has followed Giulio Ferrari's teachings to the full and realized his dreams.

TRENTO EXTRA BRUT RISERVA DEL FONDATORE GIULIO FERRARI
First year of production: 1972
Average number of bottles produced per year: 55,000
Grape variety: Chardonnay

Having spent more than a hundred months on the lees, it produces a Chardonnay of rare complexity with aromas ranging from bread crust to lime blossom, from light spices to smoky. The taste is both creamy and rich with lively acidity, in a flavor of rare and very long finesse. Fifty years at the top of Italian sparkling wine production.

Friuli-Venezia Giulia

The hills of the Collio and Friuli Colli Orientali DOC are an international symbol of quality white wines. The pebble-rich soils of the Isonzo area are in turn capable of expressing Chardonnay and Sauvignon, together with the very good Friulano. The arid and wild Karst area, characterized by limestone and iron-rich rocks, is highlighting the potential of the indigenous vines Vitovska and Malvasia Istriana.

The region's oenological reality is spread over a vast flat or gently undulating area from Pordenone to Udine, Friuli proper, joined by the small area in the provinces of Gorizia and Trieste, where high-quality wines are produced. There are over six thousand farms dedicated to viticulture, with an average surface area of just over 10 acres, while the six cooperative wine cellars operating in the area process a third of the total grapes.

The region's image is strongly linked to white wines, the fruit of both indigenous grapes such as Friulano (formerly Tocai) and Ribolla, without forgetting the increasingly popular Glera (formerly Prosecco), and the international Chardonnay and Sauvignon, which yield some of the most significant results here at a national level. However, the most widespread grape remains Pinot Gris, with no less than 19,300 acres and an international demand, especially from the United States, that shows no sign of diminishing.

Thanks to the rise of Prosecco, Friuli-Venezia Giulia has managed to avoid a production crisis and is one of the very few regions to see a continuous increase in the area under vine, which has now exceeded 66,700 acres resulting in an annual wine production of close to 53 million gallons. Of these, it is surprising that 30 percent are red wines containing the more than worthy fruits of Cabernet Sauvignon and Merlot. True masterpieces also originate from the local indigenous varieties, in particular Pignolo, Schioppettino, and Refosco dal Peduncolo Rosso, joined in the Karst by the scurvy Teran.

The oenological scenario is completed by two small Designations of Controlled and Guaranteed Origin dedicated to persuasive sweet wines made from dried grapes: Colli Orientali del Friuli Picolit, made from the grape of the same name, and Ramandolo, made from the Friulian Verduzzo.

The DOCGs

- Colli Orientali del Friuli Picolit
- Lison (→ Veneto)
- Ramandolo
- Rosazzo

The DOCs

- Carso DOC
- Collio Goriziano / Collio
- Delle Venezie - Beneškíh Okolišev
- Friuli / Friuli-Venezia Giulia
- Friuli Annia
- Friuli Aquileia
- Friuli Colli Orientali
- Friuli Grave
- Friuli Isonzo
- Friuli Latisana
- Lison-Pramaggiore DOC (→ Veneto)
- Prosecco (→ Veneto)

MAIN VINES GROWN IN THE REGION

Chardonnay
→ International Grape Varieties

Friulano (former Tocai)

Cultivated throughout the region, this is Sauvignonasse or Sauvignon Vert, a French grape variety originating in Gironde, introduced into Friuli in the nineteenth century under the name Tokai and later Tocai. Today, it is called Friulano, following a 1993 European agreement with Hungary to protect the name of the historic Tokaji area, where the famous sweet botrytized wine based on Furmint, Hàrzevelu, and Muscat Lunelu is produced, which has nothing to do with Friulian Tocai. Used to produce dry white wines with good alcohol content and fine vegetal and floral notes, when vinified as a single-varietal wine it has a golden color with greenish reflections and a complexity on the nose that ranges from aromatic herbs to fresh yellow-fleshed fruit—pear, peach, plum—through to notes of almond and flint. In the mouth, it is always full and flowing, soft and balanced, fresh on the entry and savory on the finish. It is part of the Collio, Friuli Colli Orientali, Friuli Isonzo, and Rosazzo Designations,

CADORE

CARNIA

Tarvisio

Tagliamento

Arzino

Meduna

Cellina

Duomo
Santa Maria
Assunta
in Gemona
Tarcento
Nimis
Ramandolo

FRIULI
COLLI
ORIENTALI

San Daniele
del Friuli

Povoletto
Torreano

Tagliamento

FRIULI GRAVE

UDINE

Cividale del Friuli

Premariacco
Prepotto

Ipplis
Dolegna del Collio

Buttrio
Corno di
Rosazzo

Manzano
San Floriano
del Collio

San Giovanni al Natisone
COLLIO
Oslavia

Cormons
GORIZIA

Capriva del Friuli
Mossa

Sacile
Moraro
San Lorenzo Isontino

PORDENONE
Farra d'Isonzo

Palmanova
Mariano del Friuli
ISONZO

Prata di Pordenone
Sagrado

LISON

LATISANA
Monfalcone

ANNIA
Cappella
Bresciani
Duino

Venezia
AQUILEIA
Aurisina

Aquileia
Sgonico

CARSO

TRIESTE

Laguna di Grado

Mare Adriatico

and is also cultivated in Lombardy—Garda Colli Mantovani—and Veneto—Colli Berici, Colli Euganei, and Lison Pramaggiore—where the vine is identified as Tai.

Malvasia Istriana / Malvazija istarska

Among the Malvasia varieties, the Istrian one cultivated in the Karst region produces some of the best results, and, in addition to its general freshness, is characterized by a hint of geranium and white musk on the nose, along with a certain sugary minerality reminiscent of dried apricot. Ampelographic studies have shown a clear difference with respect to Malvasia di Candia but genetic affinities with Malvasia delle Lipari or Malvasia di Sardegna, Malvasia Bianca Lunga, and Malvasia Nera di Brindisi. The wines vary greatly according to production style: from full and powerful to light and spicy, more pungent and refreshing thanks to notes of thyme, sage, and tarragon, never too bitter. With proper aging and processing that in some cases may involve over-ripening or drying of the grapes, the olfactory picture is enriched with touches of fresh rose, white peach, resin, caramel, and honey. In addition to the pure versions, it is often found in the company of other indigenous and international white varieties in Collio Goriziano and Friuli Colli Orientali.

Merlot
→ International Grape Varieties

Picolit

An ancient white grape variety from which the eponymous, extremely rare sweet wine is made from dried and botrytized grapes: Colli Orientali del Friuli Picolit. Already appreciated by the Doge of Venice at the end of the seventeenth century, in the eighteenth century it was one of the most sought-after wines in Europe, exported in precious Murano bottles and in direct competition with the already famous Hungarian Tokaji in the courts of France, England, Austria, Russia, and Holland. Forgotten in the nineteenth century due to low productivity and decimated by phylloxera, it was revived in the 1930s by the Perusini family of Rocca Bernarda. The name likely takes its cue both from the small bunches and the term Pecol, indicating the hilltops on which it was cultivated, given its late ripening. The color of the wine is bright gold, almost amber, with delicate but penetrating aromas of honey, wildflowers, dried figs, carob, sultanas, dates and apricots, beeswax, and herbs. In the mouth, acidity and sweetness are balanced in a dense, opulent, velvety, and dry mouthfeel, which closes on a very long finish with a characteristic almondy, balsamic, and mineral touch. Picolit can also be found in dry whites, in blends with other native or international varieties.

Pignolo

A red wine listed in the Friuli Colli Orientali and Friuli Isonzo DOCs, it originates in the hills of Rosazzo, in the province of Udine, where its presence has been documented for four hundred years. It develops small bunches, with berries so compact they look like pine cones—called *impignati* for this reason—from which it possibly derives its name. Decimated by phylloxera at the beginning of the last century and recovered in the 1980s from a few old vines found at the Abbey of Rosazzo, it has become the protagonist of a small rebirth, with well-deserved recognition for its qualities: on its own, it offers classic suggestions of cherry, strawberry, raspberry, blackberry jam, black currant, and ripe plum, to which aging adds fragrances of undergrowth, leather, and spices, with a hint of licorice. Alcohol, acidity, and tannin abound and soften with time, finding the right harmony and silkiness.

Pinot Blanc, Pinot Gris, Sauvignon
→ International Grape Varieties

Refosco dal Peduncolo Rosso

Widespread throughout the region, Refosco dal Peduncolo Rosso has a fine family history: the son of Marzemino and grandson of Teroldego, it is, in turn, the father of Corvina Veronese and grandfather of Rondinella, two grape varieties from Veneto present in Valpolicella and used in Amarone. The first documented sightings are in the early fifteenth century, on the Carso plateau. Since then, it has settled well in Friuli and in particular in the rainy Colli Orientali, thanks to its resistance to bad weather. Its high acidity, due to late ripening, is an element to be kept at bay, also through delayed harvests, long macerations, and aging in wood to extract all its full breadth, which leads to strong sensations of Asian spices, ripe red fruit, herbs, and undergrowth, and then truffles, chocolate, and tar. A grape that holds the potential for a great wine, succulent and deep.

Ribolla Gialla

It is widely used for orange wine in the Oslavia area, aged in amphorae, and in the Karst region. It is also found in Collio and Friuli Colli Orientali and is cultivated in Slovenia under the name Rebula. It is an ancient vine, present since the fourteenth century throughout Friuli and Istria, and was already mentioned in 1296 as Rabola in a dispute over the sale of wine between the bishop of Trieste and the monastery of San Giorgio Maggiore in Venice. In the whites, it is distinguished by its intense yellow color and floral freshness in which honeysuckle and jasmine are recognizable, while in the orange version, it develops a spicy and mineral complexity that is the result of vinification on the skins. Longer macerations, for months even, give the Ribolla an almost chewy density, remarkable persistence, and a unique olfactory sequence of wilted flowers, quince, dried apricot, candied orange peel and honey, turmeric and nutmeg, rhubarb, eucalyptus leaves and tobacco, and a refined touch of saffron, due to a special chemical compound extracted from the grapes.

Terrano

Typical of the Karst, it yields a wine with very dark violet colors—*ter* in German means tar—and vinous, fruity aromas. In the mouth, it is lively, fresh, and aromatic, a little rough and tannic but harmonious overall. It is also widespread in Emilia-Romagna under the name Cagnina, where it is enjoyed in a light, sparkling version shortly after the harvest.

Verduzzo Friulano

An ancient local variety used in Ramandolo DOCG, a sweet passito that extracts a fine acidity and hints of Mediterranean spices, acacia flowers, cedar, rosemary, mint, and hawthorn.

Vitovska

A blend of white Malvasia and Glera, it is grown on the rocky, limestone plateau of the Karst along the border between Trieste and Slovenia. Rediscovered by producers such as Edi Kante, Benjamin Zidarich, and Paolo and Walter Vodopivec, it undergoes lengthy aging in wood and experimentation in amphorae that yield surprising results. These are ancestral wines, played out on aromas of hay, sage, eucalyptus, peach, and apricot, featuring a herbaceous and brackish undertone, with licorice and cloves closing on a fresh and long iodine note.

Collio Goriziano or Collio DOC

With its 2,500 acres of hilly vineyards in the section of the province of Gorizia that borders on Slovenia, the Collio—whose name means "hill"—is the most famous Italian region for white wines, thanks to a commitment to quality that has developed steadily since the 1960s without any setbacks. Among the single-varietal wines, labels based on Ribolla Gialla, Pinot Blanc, Malvasia, Friulano, and Sauvignon have come into their own, but there is also a long tradition and great value provided by Collio Bianco, the fruit of a blend of mainly Friulano, Ribolla Gialla, and Malvasia. Considering the peculiarities of this small and prestigious area, and also given the more recent promotion of natural wines, macerated on the grape skins themselves and in amphorae, the Oslavia Producers' Association has proposed the institution of a new DOCG called Collio Ribolla di Oslavia, or Ribolla di Oslavia. When fermented in steel, the Ribolla Gialla del Collio yields a wine that is not particularly rich and complex, decidedly floral, fresh, slightly citrusy, lively, and savory. Aging can be done in amphorae and wood as well, while notes of aromatic herbs and honey develop, as the palate acquires volume and persistence. Annual production is around ten million bottles.

—

Producers and their trademark and signature wines:

1. Fausta BOLZICCO, Cormons
   Collio Ribolla Gialla ($)
2. BORGO CONVENTI, Farra d'Isonzo
   Collio Friulano ($)
   Collio Sauvignon ($)
3. Maurizio BUZZINELLI, Cormons
   Collio Malvasia ($)
4. CASTELLO DI SPESSA, Capriva del Friuli
   Collio Pinot Bianco Santarosa ($)
   Collio Sauvignon Segré ($)
5. Eugenio COLLAVINI, Corno di Rosazzo
   Collio Bianco Broy (Friulano, Chardonnay, Sauvignon) ($$)
6. COLLE DUGA, Cormons
   Collio Friulano ($)
   Collio Bianco (Friulano, Sauvignon, Chardonnay, Malvasia) ($)
   Collio Chardonnay ($)
7. DRAGA, San Floriano del Collio
   Collio Malvasia Miklus ($$)
8. I CLIVI, Corno di Rosazzo
   Collio Malvasia Vigna 80 Anni ($)
9. Edi KEBER, Cormons
   Collio Bianco (Friulano, Malvasia, Ribolla Gialla) ($)
10. LA CASTELLADA, Gorizia
    Collio Bianco della Castellada (Pinot Gris, Chardonnay, Sauvignon) ($$)
    Collio Friulano ($$)
11. LIVON, San Giovanni al Natisone
    Collio Friulano Manditocai ($$)
12. MUZIC, San Floriano del Collio
    Collio Bianco Stare Brajde (Friulano, Malvasia Istriana, Ribolla Gialla) ($)
    Collio Friulano Valeris ($)
13. Roberto PICECH, Cormons
    Collio Pinot Bianco ($)
14. PRIMOSIC, Gorizia
    Collio Friulano Skin ($$)
    Collio Chardonnay Gmajne ($$)
15. Doro PRINCIC, Cormons
    Collio Friulano ($)
    Collio Malvasia ($)
    Collio Pinot Bianco ($)

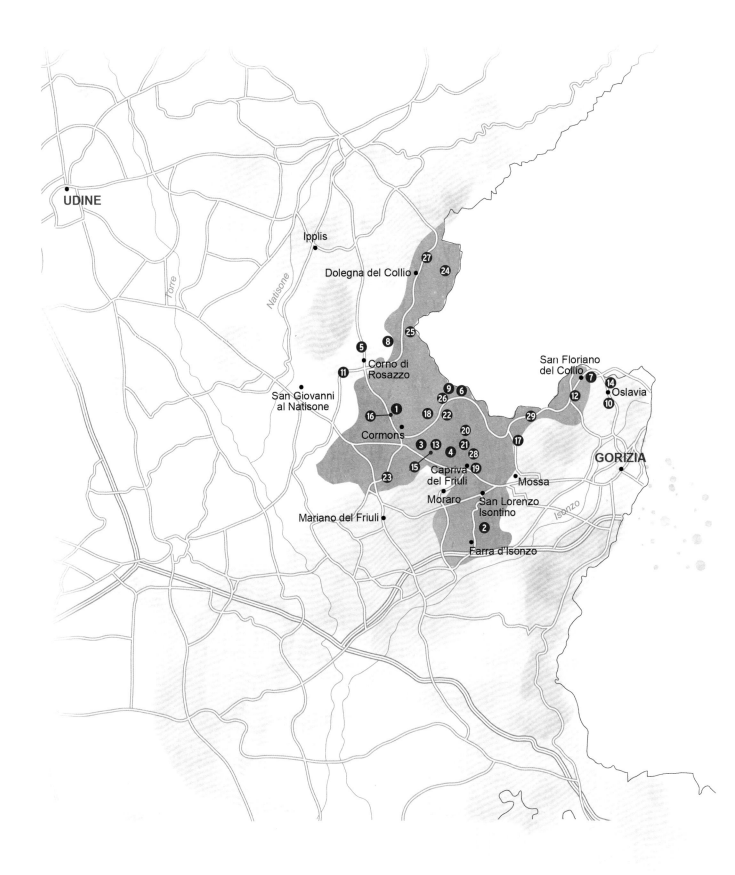

UDINE

Ipplis

Dolegna del Collio

27

24

25

8

5

Corno di
Rosazzo

11

San Giovanni
al Natisone

9   6

26

16   1

18   22

Cormons

20

3   13

4   28

21

15   19

23

Capriva
del Friuli

Moraro

San Lorenzo
Isontino

Mariano del Friuli

2

Farra d'Isonzo

San Floriano
del Collio

7

14

Oslavia

12

10

29

17

Mossa

GORIZIA

Natisone

Torre

Isonzo

16. RACCARO, Cormons
    Collio Friulano Vigna del Rolat ($)
    Collio Malvasia ($)
17. RONCO BLANCHIS, Mossa
    Collio Bianco Blanc di Blanchis
    (Friulano, Chardonnay, Sauvignon) ($)
    Collio Friulano ($)
18. RONCO DEI TASSI, Cormons
    Collio Bianco Fosarin
    (Pinot Blanc, Friulano, Malvasia) ($)
    Collio Malvasia ($)
    Collio Sauvignon ($)
19. RONCÙS, Capriva del Friuli
    Collio Bianco Vecchie Vigne
    (Malvasia Istriana, Friulano, Ribolla Gialla) ($$)
20. RUSSIZ SUPERIORE, Capriva del Friuli
    Collio Sauvignon Riserva ($$)
    Collio Pinot Bianco Riserva ($$)
    Collio Bianco Col Disôre ($$)
21. SCHIOPETTO, Capriva del Friuli
    Collio Friulano M Mario Schiopetto ($$$)
    Collio Friulano ($)
    Collio Pinot Bianco ($)
22. SIRK, Cormons
    Collio Bianco Martissima (Friulano, Ribolla
    Gialla, Malvasia) ($$)
23. TENUTA DI ANGORIS, Cormons
    Collio Bianco Langor Riserva Giulio Locatelli
    (Friulano, Sauvignon Blanc, Malvasia Istriana) ($)
24. TENUTA STELLA, Dolegna del Collio
    Collio Friulano ($)
25. TIARE, Dolegna del Collio
    Collio Sauvignon ($)
    Collio Friulano ($)
26. Franco TOROS, Cormons
    Collio Friulano ($)
    Collio Pinot Bianco ($)
27. VENICA & VENICA, Dolegna del Collio
    Collio Sauvignon Ronco delle Mele ($$)
    Collio Friulano Ronco delle Cime ($)
    Collio Pinot Bianco Tàlis ($)
28. VILLA RUSSIZ, Capriva del Friuli
    Collio Merlot Graf de La Tour ($$)
    Collio Sauvignon de La Tour ($$)
29. ZUANI, San Floriano del Collio
    Collio Bianco Vigne (Friulano, Chardonnay,
    Sauvignon, Pinot Gris) ($)

Collio Friulano

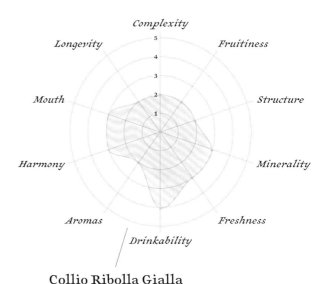

Collio Ribolla Gialla

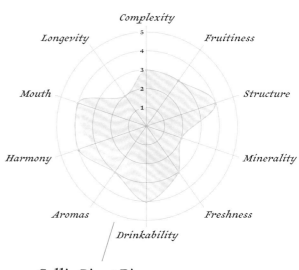

Collio Pinot Bianco

Friuli Colli Orientali DOC

The 5,000 acres under vine are spread across nineteen municipalities in the province of Udine, and include a considerable number of varieties, among which Merlot, Friulano, and Pinot Gris are widespread. Excellent results come from the white grapes—from Friulano to Pinot Blanc to Sauvignon and Chardonnay—but the most typical red of the area, Refosco dal Peduncolo Rosso, is also of great interest. The vineyards, located between 325 and 1,300 feet above sea level, are often terraced in the highest areas and also make a popular location for visitors. The total annual production of the DOC is around eight million bottles.

—

Producers and their trademark and signature wines:

1. AQUILA DEL TORRE, Povoletto
   Friuli Colli Orientali Refosco dal Peduncolo Rosso Riserva ($$)
   Friuli Colli Orientali Riesling At ($)
2. DORIGO, Premariacco
   Friuli Colli Orientali Sauvignon Ronc di Juri ($)
3. Livio FELLUGA, Cormons
   Friuli Colli Orientali Friulano ($)
4. GIGANTE, Corno di Rosazzo
   Friuli Colli Orientali Friulano Vigneto Storico ($)
   Friuli Colli Orientali Pignolo ($$)
5. I CLIVI, Corno di Rosazzo
   Friuli Colli Orientali Friulano San Pietro ($)
   Friuli Colli Orientali Bianco Galea ($)
6. LA VIARTE, Prepotto
   Friuli Colli Orientali Sauvignon Liende ($)
   Friuli Colli Orientali Friulano Liende ($)
7. LE DUE TERRE, Prepotto
   Friuli Colli Orientali Bianco Sacrisassi (Friulano, Ribolla Gialla) ($$)
   Friuli Colli Orientali Pinot Nero ($$)
8. LE VIGNE DI ZAMÒ, Manzano
   Friuli Colli Orientali Friulano Vigne 50 Anni ($$)
   Friuli Colli Orientali Chardonnay Ronco delle Acacie ($)
   Friuli Colli Orientali Pinot Bianco Tullio Zamò ($$)
9. MEROI, Buttrio
   Friuli Colli Orientali Refosco dal Peduncolo Rosso Vigna Dominin ($$$)
   Friuli Colli Orientali Rosso Nèstri (Merlot, Refosco) ($)
10. MIANI, Buttrio
    Friuli Colli Orientali Sauvignon Saurint ($$$$)
    Friuli Colli Orientali Rosso Miani (Merlot, Refosco, Cabernet Sauvignon, Cabernet Franc) ($$$$)
    Friuli Colli Orientali Ribolla Pettarin ($$$$)
11. Paolo RODARO, Cividale del Friuli
    Friuli Colli Orientali Malvasia ($)
    Friuli Colli Orientali Refosco dal Peduncolo Rosso Romain ($$)
12. RONCHI DI MANZANO, Manzano
    Friuli Colli Orientali Bianco Ellégri (Sauvignon, Friulano, Chardonnay, Picolit) ($)
    Friuli Colli Orientali Merlot Ronc di Subule ($)
13. RONCO DEL GNEMIZ, San Giovanni al Natisone
    Friuli Colli Orientali Sauvignon Sol ($$)
14. RONCO SEVERO, Prepotto
    Friuli Colli Orientali Merlot Artiùl ($$$$)
    Friuli Colli Orientali Pinot Grigio ($$)
15. Roberto SCUBLA, Ipplis
    Friuli Colli Orientali Bianco Pomèdes (Pinot Blanc, Friulano, Chardonnay, Riesling Renano) ($)
    Friuli Colli Orientali Verduzzo Friulano Passito Cràtis ($$)
16. SPECOGNA, Corno di Rosazzo
    Friuli Colli Orientali Bianco Identità (Friulano, Malvasia Istriana, Ribolla Gialla) ($$)
17. TORRE ROSAZZA, Manzano
    Friuli Colli Orientali Friulano ($)
    Friuli Colli Orientali Bianco Ronco delle Magnolie (Friulano, Pinot Blanc, Sauvignon, Ribolla Gialla) ($$)
18. TUNELLA, Premariacco
    Friuli Colli Orientali Bianco Biancosesto (Friulano, Ribolla) ($)
    Friuli Colli Orientali Sauvignon Col Matìss ($)
19. VIGNAI DA DULINE, San Giovanni al Natisone
    Friuli Colli Orientali Chardonnay Ronco Pitotti ($$)
20. VOLPE PASINI, Torreano
    Friuli Colli Orientali Sauvignon Zuc di Volpe ($)
    Friuli Colli Orientali Pinot Bianco Zuc di Volpe ($)
21. ZORZETTIG, Cividale del Friuli
    Friuli Colli Orientali Pinot Bianco Myò ($)

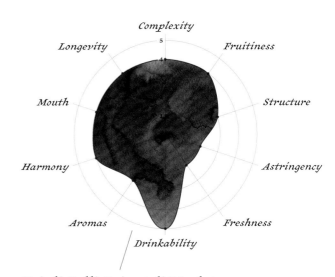

Friuli Colli Orientali Merlot

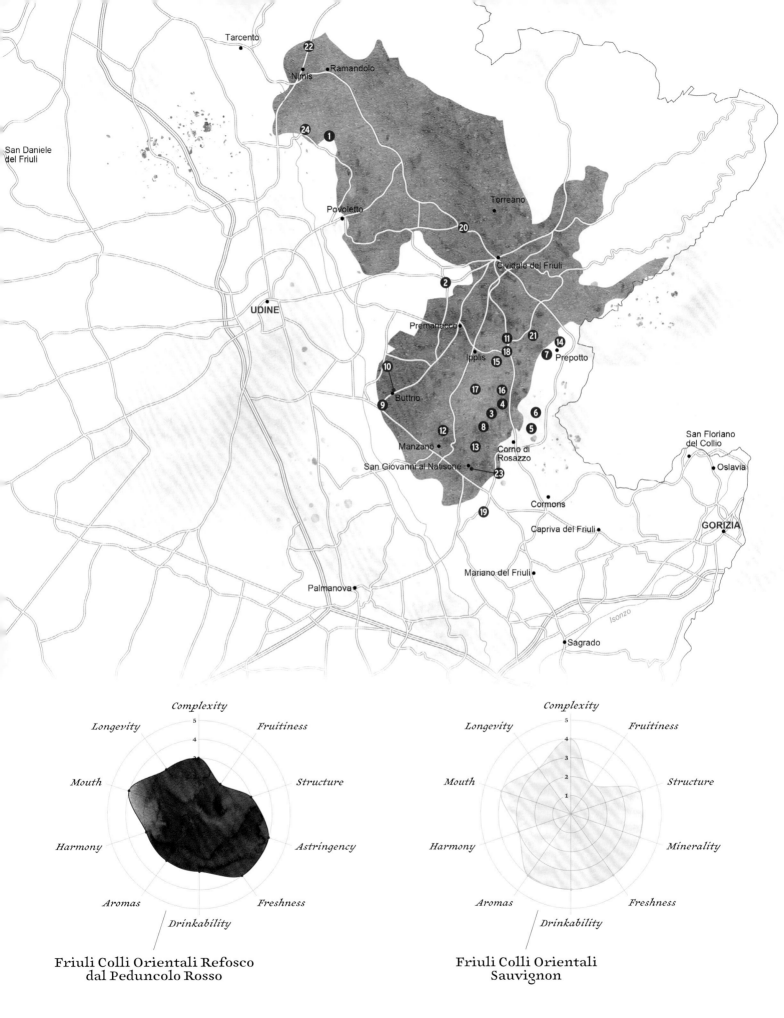

Friuli Colli Orientali Refosco
dal Peduncolo Rosso

Friuli Colli Orientali
Sauvignon

Rosazzo DOCG

The winemaking vocation of this small area, which lies in the municipal territories of Manzano, San Giovanni al Natisone, and Corno di Rosazzo in the province of Udine, has been known for centuries, thanks mainly to the work carried out by the monks at the Abbey of Rosazzo. The wine must consist principally of Friulano, at a minimum of 50%, Sauvignon from 20 to 30%, as well as Pinot Blanc, Chardonnay, Malvasia, and Ribolla Gialla grapes. This gives rise to wines rich in fruity aromas ranging from pear to grapefruit, and vegetable aromas ranging from sage to tomato leaf. There is always a fresh but important structure. Annual production is around sixty thousand bottles, and growing.

—

Producer and its trademark and signature wines:

3. Livio FELLUGA, Cormons
    Rosazzo Terre Alte ($$$)
    Rosazzo Abbazia di Rosazzo ($$)

Colli Orientali del Friuli Picolit DOCG

One of Italy's most distinctive sweet wines, rich in sugar thanks to the drying of the grapes, yet still with good acidity, it is made from the Picolit grape of the same name, with results that have garnered increasing fame over the centuries. The aromas are intense and at the same time delicate and elegant, ranging from wild flowers, ripe white fruits—especially peaches—and a hint of almond that can be detected on the finish. The reconstruction of the vineyards after the devastation by phylloxera limited its diffusion, so much so that today less than fifty thousand bottles per year are produced, in a small area between the provinces of Udine and Gorizia that has its epicenter around the Abbey of Rosazzo.

—

Producers and their trademark and signature wines:

23. ERMACORA, Ipplis
     Colli Orientali del Friuli Picolit ($$)
24. Marco SARA, Povoletto
     Colli Orientali del Friuli Picolit ($$)

Ramandolo DOCG

Another sweet pearl, this one made on several acres around the area of the hamlet of Ramandolo, near Nimis and Tarcento. This is in the province of Udine, and the wine comes only from dried grapes of Verduzzo Friulano with subsequent aging in wood. The aromas are highly appreciated, highlighting notes of apricots and honey, while the palate is offered a harmonious contrast between sweetness and freshness, enriched by a tannic touch typical of this grape. Total annual production is just over one hundred ten thousand bottles.

—

Producer and its trademark and signature wine:

22. IL RONCAT - Giovanni Dri, Nimis
     Ramandolo Il Roncat ($)

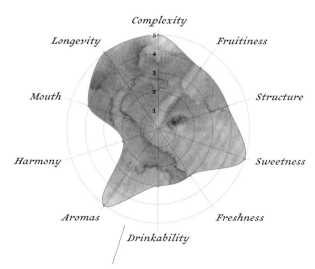

Friuli Colli Orientali Picolit

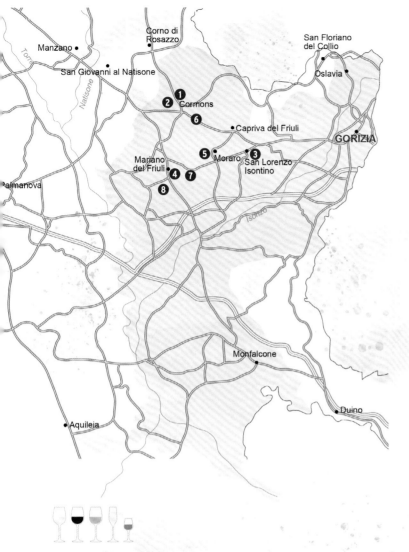

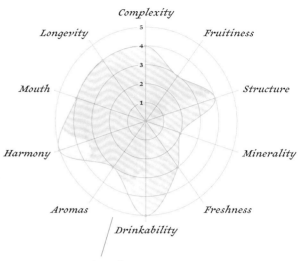

Isonzo Chardonnay

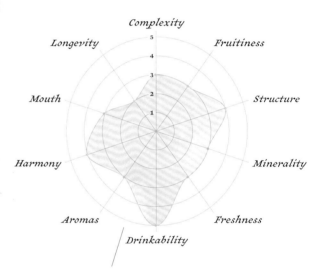

Isonzo Pinot Grigio

Friuli Isonzo DOC

The DOC area covers both flat land and rolling hills in the province of Gorizia, with a total of 2,000 acres under vine. In addition to the traditional local grapes, many international species are present here, with qualitative results that particularly reward the white types, starting with Friulano (formerly known as Tocai), Pinot Blanc, and Pinot Gris, and then Chardonnay and Sauvignon. Since this area is slightly warmer and lower than the neighboring Collio, the wines are slightly richer and more full-bodied, nevertheless capable of expressing great finesse and complexity. Annual production is just over five million bottles.

—

Producers and their trademark and signature wines:

1. BORGO SAN DANIELE, Cormons
    Friuli Isonzo Rive Alte Friulano ($)
    Friuli Isonzo Arbis Ròs (Pignolo) ($$)
2. DRIUS, Cormons
    Friuli Isonzo Friulano Sensar ($$)
    Friuli Isonzo Pinot Bianco ($)
3. LIS NERIS, San Lorenzo Isontino
    Friuli Isonzo Chardonnay Jurosa ($)
    Friuli Isonzo Pinot Grigio Gris ($)
    Friuli Isonzo Bianco Lis (Pinot Gris, Chardonnay, Sauvignon Blanc) ($$)

4. MASÙT DA RIVE, Mariano del Friuli
    Friuli Isonzo Chardonnay ($)
    Friuli Isonzo Pinot Bianco ($)
5. MURVA – Renata Pizzulin, Moraro
    Friuli Isonzo Sauvignon Blanc Teolis ($)
6. RONCO DEL GELSO, Cormons
    Friuli Isonzo Bianco Latimis (Friulano, Riesling, Pinot Blanc, Traminer) ($)
    Friuli Isonzo Rive Alte Pinot Grigio Sot lis Rivis ($)
7. TENUTA LUISA, Mariano del Friuli
    Friuli Isonzo Friulano I Ferretti ($)
8. VIE DI ROMANS, Mariano del Friuli
    Friuli Isonzo Sauvignon Blanc Vieris ($$)
    Friuli Isonzo Chardonnay ($$)
    Friuli Isonzo Sauvignon Blanc Piere ($$)

Carso DOC

A small DOC in a splendid area, comprising twelve municipalities in the provinces of Trieste and Gorizia, where one can quite rightly speak of "heroic" viticulture. (This is a general term used in Italian winemaking for a vineyard or rows of vines planted and growing on slopes, terraces, and hard-to-cultivate areas of land, often on hillsides.) Cultivation is mainly of white grapes, primarily Malvasia (with persuasive aromas of jasmine and wild flowers), but there is no shortage of red grapes, both the local Teran and Bordeaux. The average annual production of the Carso appellation is just over two hundred and eighty thousand bottles, with many quality producers preferring to offer wines without DOC status, as can be seen in the final list of the Friuli-Venezia Giulia region.

—

Producers and their trademark and signature wines:

1. CASTELVECCHIO, Sagrado
    Carso Malvasia Dileo ($)
2. KANTE, Duino Aurisina
    Carso Vitovska ($)

Friuli or Friuli Venezia Giulia DOC

A regional DOC introduced recently, in 2016, it covers a variety of municipalities in the four provinces of Friuli, although some experts reportedly felt it was surplus to requirements. There are twenty-one different types, the result of blends or use of single varieties. More than twenty million bottles a year are already marketed, and there is no lack of several versions of it.

—

Producers and their trademark and signature wines:

3. SIMON DI BRAZZAN, Cormons
    Friuli Pinot Grigio Traditiòn ($$)
4. VIGNETI LE MONDE, Prata di Pordenone
    Friuli Pinot Bianco ($)
    Friuli Cabernet Franc ($)

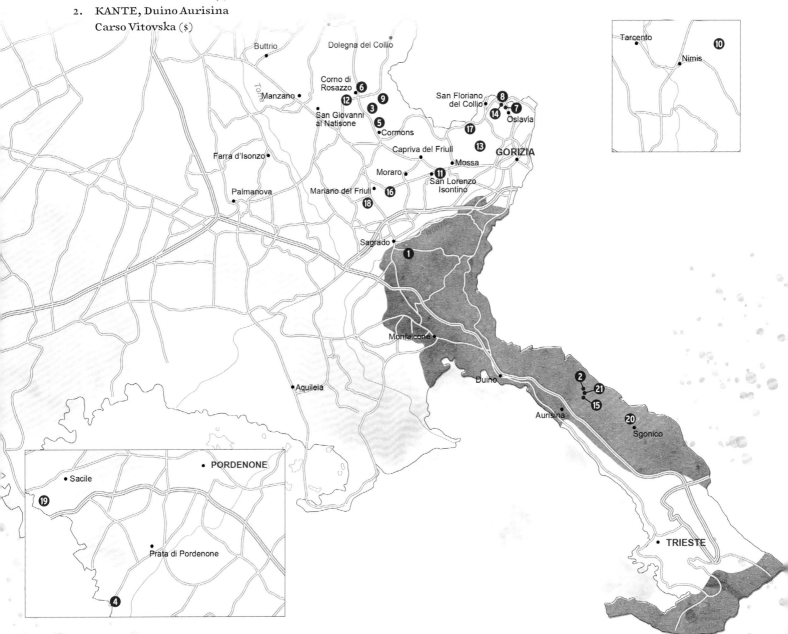

Recommended wines outside the DOC/DOCG designations:

Among the many producers who for all of their wines, or just for a few particular selections, have decided not to make use of the DOC and DOCG status, the Oslavia area stands out. In this small area close to the center of Gorizia, some wineries, led by Josko Gravner and Stanko Radikon, decided more than twenty years ago to apply the ancient technique of winemaking in amphorae—often followed by lengthy aging in wood—to the area's main grape variety. This is called Ribolla Gialla. Hence the rebirth of macerated whites, the so-called orange wines, which, thanks to their image of naturalness and purity, have also found their way to many wineries in other Italian regions.

5. BORGO SAN DANIELE, Cormons
   Arbis Blanc (Chardonnay, Pinot Blanc, Friulano, Altre Uve) ($$)
6. Eugenio COLLAVINI, Corno di Rosazzo
   Ribolla Gialla Brut ($)
7. GRAVNER, Gorizia
   Bianco Breg (Chardonnay, Sauvignon, Riesling Italico, Pinot Gris) ($$$)
   Ribolla Gialla ($$$)
8. IL CARPINO, San Floriano del Collio
   Ribolla Gialla ($$)
   Malvasia ($$)
9. JERMANN, Dolegna del Collio
   Vintage Tunina (Chardonnay, Sauvignon, Ribolla Gialla, Malvasia, Picolit) ($$)
   W... Dreams (Chardonnay) ($$)
   Capo Martino (Friulano, Picolit, Ribolla Gialla, Malvasia) ($$$)
2. KANTE, Duino Aurisina
   La Bora di Kante (Chardonnay) ($$$)
   Chardonnay ($)
10. LA RONCAIA, Nimis
    Eclisse (Sauvignon, Picolit) ($)
11. LIS NERIS, San Lorenzo Isontino
    Tal Lùc (Verduzzo, Riesling) ($$$)
12. LIVON, San Giovanni al Natisone
    Braide Alte (Chardonnay, Sauvignon, Picolit, Moscato Giallo) ($$)
13. Damijan PODVERSIC, Gorizia
    Kaplja (Chardonnay, Friulano, Malvasia Istriana) ($$)
    Ribolla Gialla ($$)
    Nekaj (Friulano) ($$)
14. RADIKON, Gorizia
    Ribolla ($$)
    Jakot (Friulano) ($$)
15. SKERK, Duino Aurisina
    Ograde (Vitovska, Malvasia, Sauvignon, Pinot Gris) ($$)
    Malvazija/Malvasia ($$)
    Vitovska ($$)

16. TENUTA LUISA, Mariano del Friuli
    Desiderium I Ferretti (Chardonnay, Friulano, Sauvignon) ($)
17. Franco TERPIN, San Floriano del Collio
    Ribolla Gialla ($$)
18. VIE DI ROMANS, Mariano del Friuli
    Dut'Un (Chardonnay, Sauvignon Blanc) ($$)
19. VISTORTA – Conte Brandolini D'Adda, Sacile
    Merlot Vistorta ($)
20. VODOPIVEC, Sgonico
    Solo MM (Vitovska) ($$$)
    Vitovska ($$)
21. ZIDARICH, Duino Aurisina
    Ruje (Merlot 85%, Terrano 15%) ($$$)
    V. Vitovska Collection ($$$)

Carso Vitovska

KANTE
Località Prepotto 1/A
Duino Aurisina (TS)
kante.it
Year of establishment: 1980
Owner: Edi Kante
Average number of bottles
produced per year: 70,000

Descending into the
atmospheric cellar carved
into the rock instantly
reveals both Edi Kante's
approach to oenology and
the underground soul of the
Karst, with its characteristic
stratification of rocks and
minerals. The name Edi Kante
has become world-famous as
the acknowledged balladeer
of this wild and pure area,
as well as the instigator of a
host of small, high-quality
producers who, following in
his footsteps, are enlivening a
winegrowing area as difficult
to work with as it was little
known a few decades ago.
In his 44 acres of vineyards,
Chardonnay and Sauvignon
have proved that they can
produce great wines just
as well as the indigenous
Vitovska.

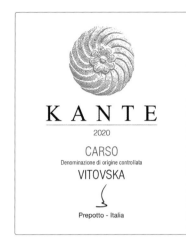

CARSO VITOVSKA
First year of production: 1980
Average number of bottles produced
per year: 12,000
Grape variety: Vitovska

A label in which the personality of this
rather shy grape is condensed to the highest
level, not very expansive, lacking in fatness,
but also endowed with a conquering
essentiality made up of articulate citrus and
herb nuances on the nose and a good pulp
furrowed by saline hints on the palate. The
exaltation of simplicity and purity made
wine.

DORO PRINCIC
Località Pradis 5
Cormons (GO)
Year of establishment: 1952
Owner: Sandro Princic
Average number of bottles
produced per year: 60,000

Doro Princic has become an
admired point of reference in
Collio for having been able,
without being specialized in
oenology, to create wines with
a strong personality, at times
slightly rustic but always
enthrallingly drinkable.
Sandro Princic, similarly
strong and expansively
energetic, has refined that
experience and today presents
a battery of six high-value
whites, among which, in
addition to Pinot Blanc,
Friulano and Malvasia are
always prized. Small quantities
of worthy Cabernet Franc and
Merlot, also grown on the
estate's 32 acres, complete the
range. An exemplary cellar.

COLLIO PINOT BIANCO
First year of production: 1962
Average number of bottles produced
per year: 15,000
Grape variety: Pinot Blanc

Matured in stainless steel only, it is clear
and intense, very rich in flowers and white
fruits, with pear in evidence; the palate
is particularly intense and enveloping,
endowed with a robustness that does not
prevent a pleasant acidic background, and
a finish in which a faint hint of almond
appears. The character and pleasantness of
Pinot Blanc.

EDI KEBER
Località Zegla 17
Cormons (GO)
edikeber.it
Year of establishment: 1957
Owner: the Keber family
Average number of bottles
produced per year: 50,000

Kristian Keber now heads the
company, which has centuries-
old Austrian origins and which
became famous thanks to his
father Edi, who created the
actual winery by transforming
the previous mixed
agricultural business and
concentrating on viticulture.
The first critical and market
successes came with the Tocai
label, but it wasn't long before
he became convinced that he
could achieve the height of the
territory's expression using
the area's three most typical
grapes all together: Friulano,
Ribolla Gialla, and Malvasia
Istriana. Hence the decision to
produce a single wine, Collio
Bianco.

COLLIO BIANCO
First year of production: 1993
Average number of bottles produced
per year: 45,000
Grape varieties: Friulano (70%),
Malvasia Istriana (15%), Ribolla
Gialla (15%)

From 30 biodynamically cultivated acres
comes a wine right at the top of the Italian
quality scale. The robust structure of Friulano
blends with the spicy aromatic contribution
of Istrian Malvasia and the acidic freshness of
Ribolla, building a wine rich in acacia flowers,
chamomile, and a hint of ginger. Delicate
maturation in cement concurs to make the
enchanting palate direct, lively, and juicy,
with excellent smoothness all the way to the
complex finish in which citrus hints combine
with a hint of almond.

RACCARO
Via San Giovanni 87
Cormons (UD)
raccaro.it
Year of establishment: 1928
Owner: the Raccaro
family
Average number of bottles
produced per year: 30,000

Dario Raccaro took over the
company reins in 1986 and
since then has consistently
demonstrated more than
brilliant skills, both in the
17 cultivated acres and in the
well-equipped cellar. The
wine produced is limited,
apart from Vigna del Rolat,
an award-winning Malvasia,
and an equally deserving
Collio Bianco, plus a handful
of bottles of Merlot. This is a
name that has reached the top
of Collio quality, with wines
endowed with impeccable
classicism and sparkling
personality.

COLLIO FRIULANO VIGNA
DEL ROLAT
First year of production: 2006
Average number of bottles produced
per year: 18,000
Grape variety: Friulano

Named after the winery's location, Rolat,
or oak forest, it is vinified, like all the house
whites, in steel only. It has a fine, typical
nose, characterized by white-fleshed fruit
and wildflowers on a hint of tomato leaf,
while the palate is rich and structured,
with notable pulpiness and good alcoholic
warmth combined with a refreshing acidic
note, leading to an attractive finish in which
citrus fruits and a touch of almond are
perceived. Among the great whites of Italy.

RONCO DEI TASSI
Località Monte 38
Cormons (GO)
roncodeitassi.it
Year of establishment: 1989
Owner: Fabio Coser
Average number of bottles
produced per year: 130,000

Fabio Coser is a well-known oenologist, a profound connoisseur, and admirer of the Collio vineyards. Hence the decision, in 1989, to open his own company, which has gradually expanded to its current 57 acres, with results that were immediately rewarded by the trade press. Bianco Fosarin is joined by six labels of precise execution and territorial fidelity, from Friulano to Sauvignon, from Malvasia to Ribolla Gialla, also leaving room for the important Cjarandon, based on Merlot and Cabernet Sauvignon. From 2021, a Family Collection will also be offered, including Malvasia, Sauvignon, and Pinot Blanc suitable for long bottle aging.

COLLIO BIANCO FOSARIN
First year of production: 1990
Average number of bottles produced per year: 12,000
Grape varieties: Pinot Blanc (40 to 50%), Friulano (30 to 40%), Malvasia (20%)

A classic and successful expression of Collio, in which wood-aged Pinot Blanc is joined by Friulano and Malvasia from steel alone. Fresh white flowers and hints of citrus fruits characterize a sharp and elegant nose, the palate is rich in flesh and well refreshed by the acidity, with a dynamic finish of fine personality. Small only in its friendly price, it is a great white of precision.

FRANCO TOROS
Località Novali 12
Cormons (UD)
vinitoros.com
Year of establishment: 1900
Owner: Franco Toros
Average number of bottles
produced per year: 60,000

The impetus toward the high quality of this wine cellar came from Franco Toros forty years ago, when he decided to renovate and expand the vineyards in order to create an all-round winery. A passionate cultivator of his own 30 acres, he has also proved himself equal to the task in terms of winemaking, deciding to offer seven monovarietal labels. Among these, in addition to the Friulano that we present here, the Pinot Gris, Sauvignon, and Pinot Blanc, together with the Merlot, the only red wine of the house, constantly stand out. A remarkable constancy of quality on all the labels.

COLLIO FRIULANO
First year of production: 2007
Average number of bottles produced per year: 15,000
Grape variety: Friulano

A label that could be described as didactic, meticulous as it is in telling the story of the personality of this symbolic grape of Friuli. The nose is clear white fruit, from pear to apple, with refined nuances of wild herbs; the palate is quite dense and rich in pulp, always with that acidic brushstroke that makes the taste stimulating and vivid. A high demonstration of the qualities of the Friulano grape in purity.

VILLA RUSSIZ
Via Russiz 4/6
Capriva del Friuli (GO)
villarussiz.it
Year of establishment: 1869
Owner: Fondazione Villa Russiz
Average number of bottles produced per year: 220,000

This historic and prestigious winery came to prominence in the nineteenth century, when Count Theodor de La Tour imported and planted French vines that have since become the winery's standard-bearers. The 111 acres under vine, now owned by a charitable foundation, also include the classic Collio grapes, from Friulano to Malvasia, with results of absolute value. A constant commitment to quality, crowned by international recognition.

COLLIO MERLOT GRÄF DE LA TOUR
First year of production: 1992
Average number of bottles produced per year: 4,500
Grape variety: Merlot

Exactly the Merlot that lovers of this grape variety expect: a well-contained oak contribution with a lively fruitiness, elegant spiciness, the typical plum tart in the background but also a stimulating touch of red currant. The tannins are soft and useful in creating depth and density, in an enveloping flavor that never tires.

VENICA & VENICA
Località Cerò 8
Dolegna del Collio (GO)
venica.it
Year of establishment: 1930
Owner: the Venica family
Average number of bottles produced per year: 300,000

International notoriety quickly arrived thanks to the elegance of the Sauvignon-based wines, but the level proposed by brothers Gianni and Giorgio Venica through their 99 acres of vineyards is similarly high with the other white varieties, starting with Pinot Blanc (Tàlis) and moving on to Friulano (Ronco delle Cime) via Malvasia (Pètris). Less well known but certainly of interest are the reds, especially those derived from the indigenous Refosco and Schioppettino. One of the most famous names in Italian white wine, characterized by valuable qualitative continuity.

COLLIO SAUVIGNON RONCO DELLE MELE
First year of production: 1995
Average number of bottles produced per year: 43,000
Grape variety: Sauvignon

The brief maturation of a small part of the wine in used wood guarantees a velvety touch and adds a spicy element to Italy's most famous Sauvignon. Peach and tomato leaf at first, then tropical and citrus fruits in the intense and decisive aromatic expression. The flavor is rigorous, solid, fresh, and almost saline, of impeccable elegance right through to the almondy finish. Sauvignon at the highest level.

LE DUE TERRE
Via Roma 68/B
Prepotto (UD)
Year of establishment: 1984
Owners: Silvana Forte,
Flavio and Cora Basilicata
Average number of bottles
produced per year: 18,000

A winery that was born
small and has decided to
remain small, to allow Flavio
Basilicata to personally care
for each plant on his 12-acre
property. To this vineyard
capacity, one must add
an oenological sensibility
allowing each of the five
produced labels to grow and
develop most purely and
directly, through spontaneous
fermentations and the use
of small wood and cement
for maturation. Wines full of
energy and solid quality.

FRIULI COLLI ORIENTALI BIANCO SACRISASSI
First year of production: 1992
Average number of bottles produced
per year: 6,000
Grape varieties: Friulano (70%),
Ribolla (30%)

The fifteen days' maceration on the skins
gives it an intense, bright gold color and
makes itself felt on the palate with a very
slight tannicity, while the two years in wood
give a delicate contribution of softness
to a palate that is decidedly lively and
appetizing. The citrus aromas are in fine
evidence on the nose and also return in the
enthralling finale in the taste, while the
flavor is devoted to an elegant freshness. A
splendid expression of the Colli Orientali
del Friuli.

LE VIGNE DI ZAMÒ
Località Rosazzo, Via
Abate Corrado 4
Manzano (UD)
levignedizamo.com
Year of establishment: 1978
Owner: the Zamò and
Farinetti families
Average number of bottles
produced per year: 300,000

The winemaking business
started in 1978 by Tullio
Zamò, who had adopted the
soon-to-be-famous name of
Vigne dal Leon, has continued
through the work of his sons
with successive acquisitions
that have led to the current
104 organically farmed acres of
property. Since 1996, the name
has been as we know it now, Le
Vigne di Zamò, and between
2010 and 2015 the brand was
taken over by Oscar Farinetti's
group without any change
in the company's vocation
for high quality. Many labels
have become famous, from
Pinot Blanc to Friulano No
Name, along with selections
of Merlot, Chardonnay, and
Friulano presented in the
Vigne Cinquant'Anni line.

FRIULI COLLI ORIENTALI CHARDONNAY RONCO DELLE ACACIE
First year of production: 2015
Average number of bottles produced
per year: 3,000
Grape variety: Chardonnay

A wine devoted to great pleasantness,
the fruit of an excellent vineyard, and an
oenological technique involving the use
of small French woods that are partially
renewed each year. In the aromas, sweet
notes of small pastries and medicinal
herbs, dried fruit, and orange peel coexist
in complete harmony; the taste is soft and
barely enlivened by the tannins released by
the oak, enveloping but not without a touch
of savoriness, with a fine finish on tropical
fruit.

TUNELLA
Via del Collio 14
Premariacco (UD)
tunella.it
Year of establishment: 1986
Owner: the Zorzettig
family
Average number of bottles
produced per year: 400,000

Most of the 173 acres of
vineyard are dedicated to white
grapes, which, in addition
to Biancosesto, are also used
to make some excellent
Friulano, Sauvignon Colmatìss,
and Pinot Gris: all have an
exceptional capacity to improve
for years in the bottle. Good
news also comes from the reds,
particularly with Pignolo, from
the vine of the same name,
and with Ronco della Torre,
in which the predominant
grape is Merlot. The winery is
technologically advanced and
stands out for the clear finesse
of its entire offering.

FRIULI COLLI ORIENTALI BIANCO BIANCOSESTO
First year of production: 2003
Average number of bottles produced
per year: 30,000
Grape varieties: Friulano, Ribolla
Gialla

It presents the fresh characteristics of both
grapes at their best, with some sweetness
on the nose and a certain roundness on
the palate resulting from maturation in
Slavonian oak barrels. The aromas range
between flowers and white fruits and a
whiff of honey, the palate is consistent and
multifaceted, favored in drinkability by a
persistent acidulous note and enchanting
in the finish where almond appears. This is
a great and typical expression of Bianco dei
Colli Orientali del Friuli, and what's more, it
is offered at an affordable price.

LIS NERIS
Via Gavinana 5
San Lorenzo Isontino (GO)
lisneris.it
Year of establishment: 1879
Owner: Alvaro Pecorari
Average number of bottles
produced per year: 400,000

Alvaro Pecorari marked the
winery's productive turning
point in 1981 when he set
himself the goal of making
the world aware of the
characteristics and merits of
Isonzo, a lesser-known DOC
compared to Collio and Colli
Orientali. In his vineyards,
which have now reached
an impressive 183 acres, he
has therefore worked with
methods considered cutting-
edge at the time, starting with
grassing, to recreate the most
suitable environment for the
development of his grapes.
The results are excellent across
the entire range, both with the
monovarietals, among which
the Chardonnay Jurosa, the
Friulano La Vila, and the Pinot
Gris stand out, and with the
blends, led by the Bianco Lis
and the Rosso Lis Neris. Wines
of great reliability and marked
personality, with a long life.

FRIULI ISONZO BIANCO LIS
First year of production: 1999
Average number of bottles produced
per year: 25,000
Grape varieties: Pinot Gris,
Chardonnay, Sauvignon

The percentage of the three grapes changes
according to the vintage, in order to always
allow the achievement of a style based on
both freshness and structure. Maturation
in barrels favors roundness and releases
slight hints of smoke and toasting, without
detracting from the contribution of the
grapes, based on citrus and floral notes on
the nose and a dynamic citrine vein in the
mouth. The perfect demonstration of the
company's ability to construct wines of
international value through the union of
different cultivars.

VIE DI ROMANS
Località Vie di Romans 1
Mariano del Friuli (GO)
viediromans.it
Year of establishment: 1900
Owner: the Gallo family
Average number of bottles
produced per year: 300,000

A symbol of Friulian quality
and run by Gianfranco Gallo
since 1978, the winery has
148 acres under vine and will
soon have a new cellar that
is even more important and
functional than the beautiful
current premises. The twelve
labels faithfully reflect the
different grape varieties and
vineyards of origin and are not
put on the market until two
years after the harvest, as they
are always rich and important
products that improve with
aging. Many productions
have won awards from wine
critics, from Piere—which is
presented—to Chardonnay Vie
di Romans, from Pinot Grigio
Dessimis to Bianco Dut'Un.
Wines rich in personality,
beautifully crafted.

FRIULI ISONZO SAUVIGNON
BLANC PIERE
First year of production: 1974
Average number of bottles produced
per year: 24,000
Grape variety: Sauvignon

Although the alcohol content is usually
above 14% by volume, it offers freshness and
vitality both on the nose and in the mouth.
The aromas are reminiscent of field grasses
and sage with a slight hint of tomato leaf,
along with persuasive peach notes. The
palate is of beautiful acidity and full of
tension, also favored by maturation in steel
only. Refinement made Sauvignon.

LIVIO FELLUGA
Frazione Brazzano, Via
Risorgimento 1
Cormons (GO)
liviofelluga.it
Year of establishment: 1956
Owner: the Felluga family
Average number of bottles
produced per year: 800,000

The estate created by Livio
Felluga in the last century is
now run by his family and has
reached 383 acres in size, with
vineyards in both Collio and
Colli Orientali. The estate's
vocation is for whites, among
which Terre Alte, Sauvignon,
Friulano, and Ribolla Gialla
stand out, but great care is also
afforded to reds, among which
the Sossò blend, Merlot, and
Pignolo Eremita stand out. The
labels with the Collio map in
the background have become a
worldwide symbol of quality.

ROSAZZO TERRE ALTE
First year of production: 1981
Average number of bottles produced
per year: 27,000
Grape varieties: Friulano, Pinot
Blanc, Sauvignon

The typical white fruit of Friulano is
didactically combined with the vegetal
freshness of Sauvignon and the pulpiness
of Pinot Blanc, creating a wine of rare
complexity and envelopment. Alcoholic
fermentation takes place in steel, with
malolactic fermentation and maturation
in oak, giving density and harmony to the
union of the three grape varieties. Terre
Alte now benefits from the Rosazzo DOCG,
established in 2011. With full merit, one
of the best-known and most appreciated
Italian whites.

GRAVNER
Frazione Oslavia, Località
Lenzuolo Bianco 9
Gorizia
gravner.it
Year of establishment: 1901
Owner: Josko Gravner
Average number of bottles
produced per year: 35,000

It is worth listening directly to
the voice of Josko Gravner—
best done in the cellar, but
there are also good accounts
on his website—about the
philosophical and human
process that has led him to be
the acknowledged bard of the
naturalness of wine, as well
as a profound seeker of the
maximum possible potential
of the grape, obtained both in
the countryside, on 44 acres
with standard-setting farming
systems and yields, and in
the cellar, where steel and
barriques have been banished
in favor of amphorae and large
barrels. Not easy wines, of
astonishing complexity.

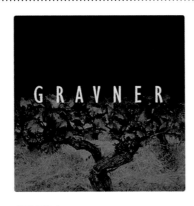

RIBOLLA
First year of production: 1998
Average number of bottles produced
per year: 20,000
Grape variety: Ribolla Gialla

After seven months of maceration in
amphorae on the skins and seven years
of maturation in large used barrels, the
Ribolla presents an antique gold color with
orange reflections, then the aromas move
between vegetal hints of medicinal herbs
and notes of ripe citrus. The flavor impresses
with consistency, salinity, tension, and
persistence, in an ensemble dominated by
acid freshness. Inimitable.

JERMANN
Frazione Ruttars, Località
Trussio 11
Dolegna del Collio (GO)
jermann.it
Year of establishment: 1880
Owner: the Antinori
family
Average number of bottles
produced per year: 900,000

A winery that has become
a worldwide symbol of the
quality of Friulian white
wines. Thanks to Vintage
Tunina, no doubt, but more
than appreciated results
have also been recorded with
Capo Martino (in which
Chardonnay and Sauvignon
are replaced by Friulian)
and with W... Dreams, a
spicy pure Chardonnay.
The estate's 420 acres of
vineyards are mainly located
in the Collio and Isonzo
areas, with a small offshoot
in Slovenia. Silvio Jermann
was the main architect of such
success and has remained
at the operational helm of
the company even since the
Florentine Antinori family
took over the majority
shareholding in 2021.

VINTAGE TUNINA
First year of production: 1975
Average number of bottles produced
per year: 55,000
Grape varieties: Chardonnay,
Sauvignon, Ribolla Gialla, Malvasia,
Picolit

This is the wine that has brought the
most visibility to the winery, endowed
with an admirable constancy of quality
characterized by persuasive hints of yellow
fruit, from apricots to peaches, and of
flowers, from lime to acacia, against a light
spicy background. The taste is always rich
and enveloping, slightly soft but lively and
responsive, of rare elegance. One of Italy's
most celebrated and appreciated whites.

Emilia-Romagna

The hyphen that joins the two large areas of this region indicates unity at the administrative level, but it is also a sign of division, signaling the profound winegrowing diversity of the two areas, with the rather flat Emilia region mainly dedicated to the production of sparkling and spumante wines, while the hills of Romagna are the realm of Sangiovese grapes and still white wines. The two areas will therefore be addressed separately, without forgetting what the people of Emilia and Romagna have in common: a unique savoir-faire and savoir-vivre that is admired the world over.

Emilia

—

The territory can be divided into three main areas: the vast area dedicated to Lambrusco, the Colli Piacentini, and the Colli Bolognesi.

The best-known sparkling red wine in the world has been protected, since 2021, by the Consorzio di Tutela del Lambrusco (Consortium for the Protection of Lambrusco), which is responsible for the promotion of wines born in an area of no less than 41,000 acres, reaching one hundred and seventy million bottles per year, forty-two of which are within the seven DOCs in which this vine is included.

Lambrusco, in its various types, is one of the wines most appreciated by Italian-American restaurants since the post–World War II period, thanks to its festive drinkability and low price. Since then, its success has continued, developing internationally also in northern European countries but always solidly based on consumption by families in northern Italy, especially thanks to the Lambrusco di Sorbara, Reggiano, and Lambrusco di Castelvetro Designations.

The 11,860 acres of vineyards in the Colli Piacentini are mainly located on the slopes of four beautiful valleys and are characterized by the presence of red grapes that are well represented by the Gutturnio DOC, which combines Barbera and Croatina grapes offered in both still and sparkling versions. The white type that has been most successful here is based on aromatic Malvasia di Candia, which can be offered both in fresh and never trivial sparkling versions, as well as sumptuous passito versions.

Finally, the Colli Bolognesi can boast a good presence of red grapes, especially Barbera and the Bordeaux varieties, but owe their fame to Pignoletto, from the grape of the same name, proposed in various versions that are always endowed with pleasant aromatic expressions.

Romagna

—

There are Sangiovese grapes for the reds and Albana for the whites, but that's not all: numerous local and even new-generation producers are proposing wines based on grapes historically present in the area, such as Trebbiano, Pagadebit, and Grechetto Gentile, alongside the reds Centesimino and Longanesi. At the same time, innovations in the cellar are advancing, with a growing number of companies beginning to experiment with the use of amphorae and maceration on the skins that now includes the white wines too.

The overall regional picture sees the presence of a vineyard park of over 128,500 acres, 67% of which are distributed in the plains, 32% in the hills, and 1% in the mountains. Total wine production averages close to 145.5 million gallons, produced by seventeen and a half thousand farms and thirty-one cooperative wineries.

MAIN VINES GROWN IN THE REGION

Albana

Widespread above all between Ravenna and Forlì, it is a very ancient grape, mentioned in 1303 by ampelographer Pietro de' Crescenzi, but already known in Roman times. The term "Albus" would thus refer to the Colli Albani, southeast of Rome. Recognized as the first DOCG dedicated to a white wine in Italy, it is appreciated in the dry versions for its pleasant simplicity, while in the trellis- or plant-dried version, the classic bouquet of candied fruit emerges.

Barbera, Croatina
(→ Piedmont and Lombardy)

Centesimino

An original indigenous Romagnolo grape, its diffusion resumed in the 1960s thanks to Pietro Pianori of Faenza, starting from some old vines in his garden that had escaped phylloxera.

The wines are fresh and fragrant, simple but not trivial, and endowed with irresistible drinkability thanks to the delicate harmony that the variety is able to express among notes of small red berries, wild meadow, and spices.

Grechetto (→ Umbria)

Lambrusco

An indigenous Emilia red wine par excellence, with ancestral origins that date back to Etruscan times. There is archaeological evidence that the peoples of these areas cultivated vines four thousand years ago, but the ancient *labrusche* vines—a term that

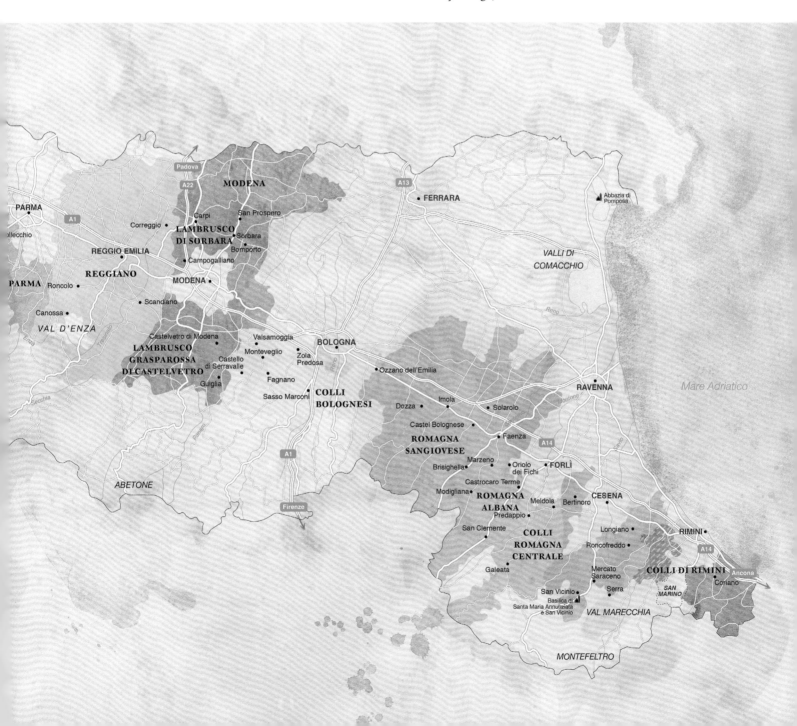

indicated all wild vines born spontaneously, and later domesticated—have no genetic relationship with today's Lambrusco, which is divided into several subvarieties: Barghi, Benetti, Grasparossa, Fiorano, Maestri, Marani, Montericco, Oliva, Pennini, Salamino, Viadanese, Vittona, and Lambrusco di Sorbara. Vinified and refermented in autoclaves or in the bottle, it leads to red wines, whether semi-sparkling or sparkling, that taste of violets, wild strawberries, and raspberries, with a dry and easy flavor, where it is possible to distinguish a more tannic and structured Lambrusco Grasparossa from a fresher and lighter Lambrusco di Sorbara.

Longanesi

In 1920, Aldo Longanesi found a vine clinging to an old oak tree on his farm in Boncellino—a hamlet of Bagnacavallo—in the province of Ravenna: it was the last Longanesi grape plant to survive phylloxera. Starting in the 1950s, the Longanesi family experimented with its vinification, until in 2000 the cultivar was entered into the National Register of Wine Grape Varieties. Today, the "Il Bagnacavallo" consortium protects the production of Bursôn wine, a monovarietal from Longanesi grapes, which surprises with its remarkable structure and intense aromas of black cherry, dried plum, and chocolate.

Malbo Gentile

A rare and ancient red grape, rediscovered in Emilia in the Colli di Scandiano e di Canossa DOC, whose wines recall blackberries, cherries, and ripe fruit, it produces fragrant and fresh wines.

Malvasia Bianca di Candia Aromatica

More complex and multifaceted than Malvasia Bianca di Candia, with grapes reminiscent of Muscat aromas, it is widespread in the provinces of Piacenza, Parma, and Reggio Emilia. In the Colli Piacentini, it is produced pure in sparkling, dry, and passito versions. The latter impresses with its luminous antique gold color, a balsamic explosion on the nose against a background of tea leaf, honey, and candied citrus fruit, and a brilliant freshness that supports the powerful sugar structure.

Melara, Santa Maria

Grapes from which the rare Vin Santo di Vigoleno in the Colli Piacentini is made. The name Melara recalls the vine's vocation for drying and the consequent production of sweet wines similar to honey, whose strong sugar concentration is well counterbalanced by a marked acidity. It is complemented by the Santa Maria grape, already mentioned in the eighteenth century, with notes of dried fruit and toasted hazelnuts.

Pignoletto, Rebola

Widespread and reported here in the Colli Bolognesi and Colli di Rimini, it is used to produce mostly semi-sparkling wines of a pale yellow color, defined by a bouquet of white-fleshed

The DOCG - Emilia
- Colli Bolognesi Pignoletto

The DOCs - Emilia
- Bosco Eliceo
- Colli Bolognesi
- Colli d'Imola
- Colli di Faenza
- Colli di Parma
- Colli di Scandiano e di Canossa
- Colli Piacentini
- Gutturnio
- Lambrusco di Sorbara
- Lambrusco Grasparossa di Castelvetro
- Lambrusco Salamino di Santa Croce
- Modena / di Modena
- Ortrugo dei Colli Piacentini / Ortrugo-Colli Piacentini
- Pignoletto
- Reggiano
- Reno

The DOCG - Romagna
- Romagna Albana

The DOCs - Romagna
- Colli di Rimini
- Colli Romagna Centrale
- Romagna

fruits such as pear and apple, accompanied by green tea and lavender, on a dry and rather harmonious palate. In a still version and with moderate aging in wood or steel, it offers more complexity and a savory note.

Pinot Noir → International Grape Varieties

Sangiovese → Tuscany
Also widespread in Romagna, where it is more rustic and vinous, moderately tannic, and more played on immediacy than the Tuscan versions.

Trebbiano → Tuscany
Widely used in the Romagna, Colli di Rimini, and Colli Romagna Centrale Designations.

Lambrusco di Sorbara DOC

It is produced in twelve municipalities in the province of Modena, mainly from the grape of the same name, which must be present at a minimum of at least 60%. It has garnered substantial critical acclaim in recent years, thanks above all to its notable acidity that, combined with the scarce presence of residual sugars, guarantees a lively and fresh taste. Along with this, the contribution of the bubbles created by the carbon dioxide is decisive. It is successfully produced both in the Frizzante version—often "frothed" in large steel containers—and in the Spumante Metodo Classico version. Its alcohol content is rather low, around 11%, and production is close to eighteen million bottles per year.

—

Producers and their trademark and signature wines:

1. CANTINA DELLA VOLTA, Bomporto
   Lambrusco di Sorbara Spumante Brut Rosé M. Cl. ($)
   Lambrusco di Sorbara Rimosso ($)
2. CANTINA DI CARPI E SORBARA, Carpi
   Lambrusco di Sorbara Secco Omaggio a Gino Friedmann ($)
3. CAVICCHIOLI, San Prospero
   Lambrusco di Sorbara Vigna del Cristo ($)
4. Cleto CHIARLI, Castelvetro di Modena
   Lambrusco di Sorbara Vecchia Modena Premium ($)
   Lambrusco di Sorbara del Fondatore ($)
5. Alberto PALTRINIERI, Bomporto
   Lambrusco di Sorbara Leclisse ($)
   Lambrusco di Sorbara Radice ($)

6. PODERE IL SALICETO, Campogalliano
   Lambrusco di Sorbara Falistra ($)
7. ZUCCHI, San Prospero
   Lambrusco di Sorbara Brut in Purezza Silvia Zucchi ($)
   Lambrusco di Sorbara Brut Rito ($)

Lambrusco Grasparossa di Castelvetro DOC

It is produced in fourteen municipalities in the province of Modena from Lambrusco Grasparossa grapes, which make up at least 85% of the wine. The color is a decidedly deep ruby red, at times with violet reflections, with slight astringency due to the good presence of tannin and an alcohol content at around 12%. The aromas are reminiscent of small red fruits and has no particular acidity. About sixteen million bottles per year are produced, with varying quality levels.

—

Producer and its trademark and signature wine:

8. FATTORIA MORETTO, Castelvetro di Modena
   Lambrusco Grasparossa di Castelvetro Secco Canova ($)

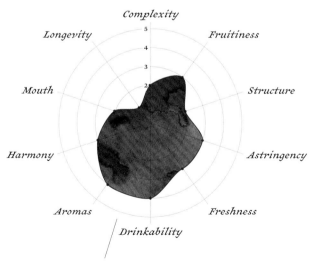

Lambrusco di Sorbara

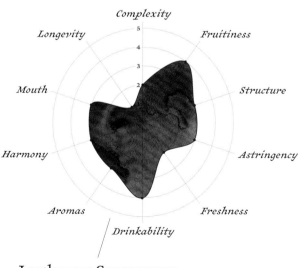

Lambrusco Grasparossa
di Castelvetro

Reggiano DOC

The production area includes the entire province of Reggio Emilia, with the obvious exclusion of land not suitable for vines. It can be made with the different types of Lambrusco grapes present locally: Marani, Salamino, Montericco, Maestri, di Sorbara, Grasparossa, Viadanese, Olive, and Barghi, all included at a minimum percentage of at least 85% overall. It is considered the easiest and most immediate type of Lambrusco, often offered with a certain residual sugar, endowed with fruity scents such as cherry and plum, as well as being sparkling, lively, and consistent to the palate. There are several brilliant examples of this, the best-selling type of Lambrusco, with over twenty-four million bottles produced annually.

—

Producers and their trademark and signature wines:

9. Ermete MEDICI, Reggio Emilia
    Reggiano Lambrusco Concerto ($)
    Reggiano Rosso Assolo ($)
10. VENTURINI BALDINI, Roncolo
    Reggiano Lambrusco Brut Rosato Cadelvento ($)

Colli Piacentini DOC

A vast area in which, among the fourteen types of wine listed in the local manufacturers regulations, the best-known results are achieved by the aromatic Malvasia and the sumptuous Vin Santo di Vigolen. These are made from the rare local grapes called Melara and Santa Maria. Notable results also come from the Sauvignon and Cabernet Sauvignon grapes. The most sought-after areas consist of 8,150 acres of vineyards distributed between Val Nure, Val d'Arda, Val Trebbia, and Val Tidone, between 500 and 1,475 feet above sea level. A revision of the production regulations is underway, which will also lead to the institution of a new DOCG for Malvasia. Annual production is close to thirteen million bottles.

—

Producers and their trademark and signature wines:

1. BARATTIERI, Albarola
   Colli Piacentini Vinsanto Val di Nure Albarola ($$$)
2. CANTINA VALTIDONE, Borgonovo Val Tidone
   Colli Piacentini Malvasia Frizzante 50 Vendemmie ($)
3. IL NEGRESE, Ziano Piacentino
   Colli Piacentini Malvasia Passito ($)
4. LA TOSA, Vigolzone
   Colli Piacentini Malvasia Sorriso di Cielo ($)
5. LURETTA, Gazzola
   Colli Piacentini Cabernet Sauvignon Corbeau ($$)
   Colli Piacentini Sauvignon I Nani e le Ballerine ($)
6. LUSENTI, Ziano Piacentino
   Colli Piacentini Malvasia Bianca Regina ($)
7. LUSIGNANI, Vernasca
   Colli Piacentini Vin Santo di Vigoleno ($$)

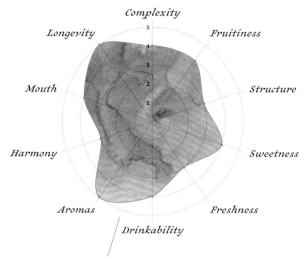

Colli Piacentini Vinsanto

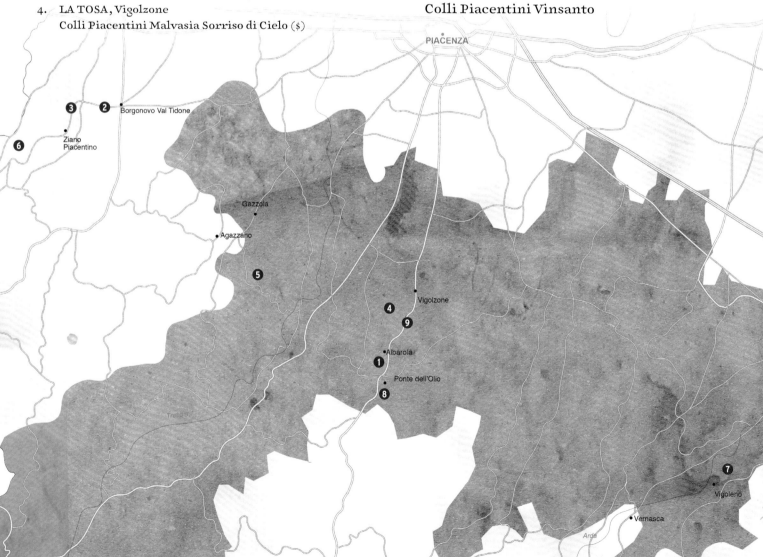

Gutturnio DOC

Up until 2010 it was included in the vast DOC of Colli Piacentini, and Gutturnio takes its name from the cup that the ancient Romans exchanged with toasts made at the end of dinner. It is made from a blend of Barbera, at 55–70%, and Croatina, at 30 to 45%, and is also vinified in a Frizzante version, but it is the Superiore and Riserva types that stand out, thanks to intense fruity aromas and an important, rich, and always fresh taste. A proposal for the institution of the Gutturnio DOCG is currently being drafted. Approximately twelve million bottles are produced annually from over 2,710 acres of vineyards.

—

Producers and their trademark and signature wines:

2. CANTINA VALTIDONE, Borgonovo Val Tidone
    Gutturnio Riserva Bollo Rosso ($)
4. LA TOSA, Vigolzone
    Gutturnio Superiore Vignamorello ($)
8. MARENGONI, Ponte dell'Olio
    Gutturnio Riserva Farosa ($)
9. ROMAGNOLI, Vigolzone
    Gutturnio Superiore Ape ($)

Colli Bolognesi Pignoletto DOCG

This is produced from at least 95% content of Pignoletto grapes, in eight municipalities in the province of Bologna, with a small stretch of additional land jutting into Savignano sul Panaro in the province of Modena. Very floral and lively wines, often citrusy and with vegetal notes, with good grip on the palate in all versions, which include two sparkling types, Frizzante and Spumante, and two still ones, Superiore and Classico Superiore. In the vast majority of cases, aging takes place in steel only. Just under two million bottles a year are produced.

—

Producers and their trademark and signature wines:

1. Floriano CINTI, Sasso Marconi
    Colli Bolognesi Pignoletto Frizzante ($)
2. CORTE D'AIBO, Monteveglio
    Colli Bolognesi Pignoletto Superiore Monte Freddo ($)
3. FATTORIE VALLONA, Fagnano
    Colli Bolognesi Pignoletto Superiore ($)
4. Alessandro FEDRIZZI, Castello di Serravalle
    Colli Bolognesi Pignoletto Frizzante Rifermentato in Bottiglia ($)
5. GAGGIOLI, Zola Predosa
    Colli Bolognesi Pignoletto Superiore P ($)
6. IL MONTICINO, Zola Predosa
    Colli Bolognesi Pignoletto Classico del Monticino ($)
7. MANARESI, Zola Predosa
    Colli Bolognesi Pignoletto Classico Superiore ($)
8. ORSI – Vigneto San Vito, Valsamoggia
    Colli Bolognesi Pignoletto Frizzante Sui Lieviti ($)

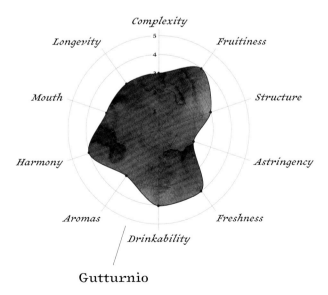

Gutturnio

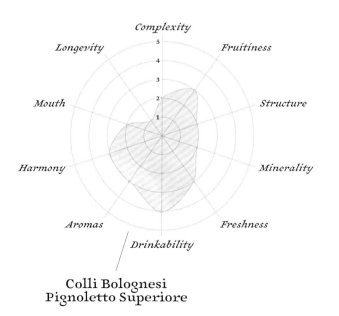

Colli Bolognesi
Pignoletto Superiore

Castelvetro di Modena

Valsamoggia

8

7 Zola
5 **6** Predosa

BOLOGNA

2 •Monteveglio

Guiglia •
Castello
di Serravalle
Fagnano• **3**

Ozzano dell'Emilia •

4

Sasso Marconi **1**

Reno

Panaro

Idice

Colli di Rimini DOC

Twenty-six municipalities in the province of Rimini are home to vineyards cultivated with Sangiovese and Trebbiano, which form the basis for Colli di Rimini Rosso and Bianco, but the most distinctive results come from Cabernet Sauvignon and the less common white Rebola. This is none other than Grechetto di Todi, also called Pignoletto in Emilia: it is persuasive, with rather subtle hints of white fruits and fresh vitality of flavor. Total production is around one million bottles per year.

—

Producers and their trademark and signature wines:

1. Enio OTTAVIANI, San Clemente
   Colli di Rimini Rebola ($)
2. PODERE DELL'ANGELO, Rimini
   Colli di Rimini Rebola Giulietta ($)
3. PODERE VECCIANO, Coriano
   Colli di Rimini Rebola Vigna La Ginestra ($)
4. SAN PATRIGNANO, Coriano
   Colli di Rimini Cabernet Sauvignon Montepirolo ($)

Colli Romagna Centrale DOC

A little-used DOC covering twenty-two municipalities in the province of Forlì-Cesena, in which local grapes (such as Trebbiano Romagnolo and Sangiovese) and international grapes (such as Cabernet Sauvignon and Chardonnay) coexist. Annual production is just sixty thousand bottles, mainly of red wines.

—

Producer and its trademark and signature wine:

5. PERTINELLO, Galeata
   Colli Romagna Centrale Sangiovese Pertinello ($)

Romagna DOC

A vast area, not always identical depending on the grape varieties used in the thirteen types envisaged, but which nonetheless is mainly Trebbiano—remembering that Romagna Albana has its own independent DOCG—and Sangiovese. It is precisely from the Romagna Sangiovese DOC that the best results come, making this type one of the most distinctive Italian reds. In addition to the obligation to age the Superiore and Riserva in the cellar for at least two years before marketing, the regulations provide for the possibility of naming one of the sixteen subzones, grouped under the Rocche di Romagna brand. This is a choice that may yield valid results in the years to come, considering the great variety of soil and climate conditions of this vast area. Many critics have attempted to define the characteristics that differentiate Romagna Sangiovese from Chianti: this is a warmer zone, hence with fuller-bodied wines that are slightly less acidic, but there are many climatic variables and several production styles that do not allow easy generalizations. Excellent results from fresh, young, immediate, and easy-drinking Romagna Sangiovese—as Villa Papiano and Villa Venti, among others, well demonstrate—and great satisfaction is also given by several examples of Superiore and Riserva, in the "Tuscan" style and suitable for medium to long bottle aging. Total annual production is thirty million bottles, of which, in terms of red wines only, twelve million are Romagna Sangiovese, one million are Sangiovese Riserva, and seven hundred thousand are Sangiovese Superiore Riserva, and growing.

—

Producers and their trademark and signature wines:

6. BALÌA DI ZOLA, Modigliana
   Romagna Sangiovese Riserva Modigliana Redinoce ($)
7. Stefano BERTI, Forlì
   Romagna Sangiovese Riserva Predappio Calisto ($)
   Romagna Sangiovese Superiore Bartimeo ($)
8. CA' DI SOPRA, Brisighella
   Romagna Sangiovese Marzeno ($)
9. Chiara CONDELLO, Predappio
   Romagna Sangiovese Riserva Predappio Le Lucciole ($$$)
10. Leone CONTI, Faenza
    Romagna Sangiovese Superiore Riserva ($)
11. COSTA ARCHI, Castel Bolognese
    Romagna Sangiovese Riserva Serra Il Beneficio ($)
    Romagna Sangiovese Riserva Serra Assiolo ($)
12. DREI DONÀ – Tenuta La Palazza, Forlì
    Romagna Sangiovese Superiore Riserva Pruno ($)
    Romagna Sangiovese Predappio Notturno ($)
13. FATTORIA NICOLUCCI, Predappio
    Romagna Sangiovese Superiore Riserva Predappio di Predappio Vigna del Generale ($$)

14. FATTORIA ZERBINA, Faenza
    Romagna Sangiovese Pietramora Riserva Marzeno ($)
15. Paolo FRANCESCONI, Faenza
    Romagna Sangiovese Superiore Limbecca ($)
16. GALLEGATI, Faenza
    Romagna Sangiovese Brisighella Corallo Rosso ($)
    Romagna Sangiovese Brisighella Riserva Corallo Nero ($)
17. I SABBIONI, Forlì
    Romagna Sangiovese Oriolo ($)
18. LA CASETTA DEI FRATI, Modigliana
    Romagna Sangiovese Modigliana Framonte ($)
19. LE ROCCHE MALATESTIANE, Rimini
    Romagna Sangiovese Superiore Sigismondo ($)
20. Giovanna MADONIA, Bertinoro
    Romagna Sangiovese Riserva Bertinoro Ombroso ($)
21. MUTILIANA, Modigliana
    Romagna Sangiovese Modigliana Acereta ($)
22. PALAZZONA DI MAGGIO, Ozzano dell'Emilia
    Romagna Sangiovese Superiore Ulziano ($)
23. PODERE LA BERTA, Brisighella
    Romagna Sangiovese Superiore Riserva Olmatello ($)
24. Noelia RICCI, Predappio
    Romagna Sangiovese Predappio Godenza ($)
    Romagna Sangiovese Predappio Il Sangiovese ($)
25. RONCHI DI CASTELLUCCIO, Modigliana
    Romagna Sangiovese Modigliana Ronco dei Ciliegi ($$)
26. TENUTA LA VIOLA, Bertinoro
    Romagna Sangiovese Bertinoro Il Colombarone ($)
27. TRERÈ, Faenza
    Romagna Sangiovese Superiore Riserva Amarcord
    d'un Ross ($)
28. VILLA PAPIANO, Modigliana
    Romagna Sangiovese Riserva Modigliana Vigna Probi ($)
29. VILLA VENTI, Roncofreddo
    Romagna Sangiovese Superiore Primo Segno ($)

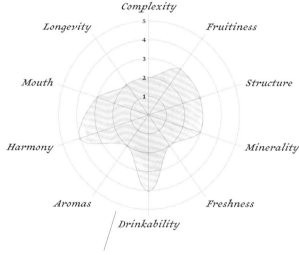

Romagna Albana Secco

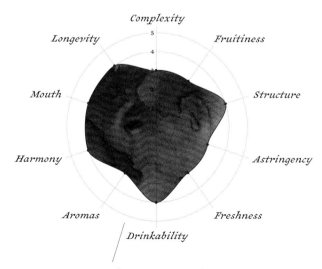

Romagna Sangiovese Superiore

Ozzano dell'Emilia

RAVENNA

22

Dozza
31   35
38

Imola

Solarolo

16

40

Castel Bolognese

11

36   27

Faenza

23

15

10 30

14

Brisighella

Marzeno

33 Oriolo
dei Fichi

17

FORLÌ

8

25

37

41

12

6 Modigliana

18

24   9   7

Castrocaro Terme

Bertinoro   26
32 20 34

CESENA

Meldola

21 28

13   Predappio

Longiano

29

Roncofreddo

5

Galeata

39

Mercato
Saraceno

San Vicinio

Serra

Romagna

Colli di Rimini

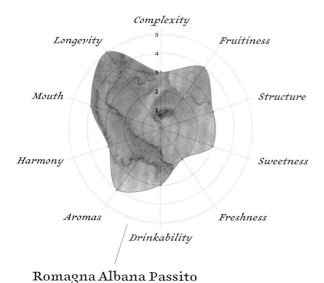

Romagna Albana Passito

Romagna Albana DOCG

It was the first Italian white wine to obtain DOCG status, in 1987, and then called Albana di Romagna. At least 95% of it is made from the Albana grape of the same name, which can be offered in Secco, Amabile, Dolce, Passito, and Passito Riserva versions. The production area includes over 2,000 acres in the provinces of Forlì-Cesena and Ravenna, with a small stretch of land in Emilia, in the province of Bologna. The aromas of the Secco version are reminiscent of yellow-fleshed fruit and white flowers; the taste is quite powerful, never too acidic but always fresh and remarkably drinkable. Results of absolute value are also obtained with the Passito, where persuasive notes of figs, dates, and honey reign supreme. Just under a million bottles per year are produced.

—

Producers and their trademark and signature wines:

30. ANCARANI, Faenza
Romagna Albana Secco Sânta Lusa ($)
31. Vittorio ASSIRELLI, Dozza
Romagna Albana Passito Piccolo Fiore ($)
32. BISSONI, Bertinoro
Romagna Albana Passito ($)
33. CANTINA SAN BIAGIO VECCHIO, Faenza
Romagna Albana Secco SabbiaGialla ($)
34. CELLI, Bertinoro
Romagna Albana Secco I Croppi ($)
35. FATTORIA MONTICINO ROSSO, Imola
Romagna Albana Secco Codronchio ($)
Romagna Albana Secco A ($)
14. FATTORIA ZERBINA, Faenza
Romagna Albana Passito Scacco Matto ($$)
Romagna Albana Passito Arrocco ($)
Romagna Albana Secco Bianco di Ceparano ($)
36. Stefano FERRUCCI, Castel Bolognese
Romagna Albana Passito Domus Aurea ($)
37. FONDO SAN GIUSEPPE, Brisighella
Romagna Albana Secco Fiorile ($)
16. GALLEGATI, Faenza
Romagna Albana Passito Riserva Regina di Cuori ($)
20. Giovanna MADONIA, Bertinoro
Romagna Albana Secco Neblina ($)
38. PODERI DELLE ROCCHE, Imola
Romagna Albana Secco Compadrona ($)
39. TENUTA SANTA LUCIA, Mercato Saraceno
Romagna Albana Secco Albarara ($)
40. TRE MONTI, Imola
Romagna Albana Secco Vitalba (€)
41. Marta VALPIANI, Castrocaro Terme
Romagna Albana Secco Madonna dei Fiori ($)

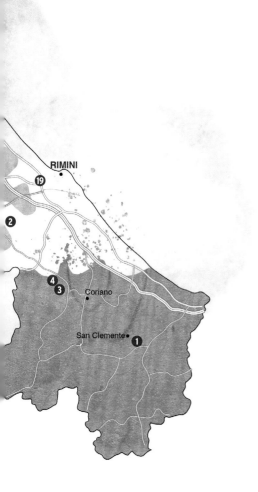

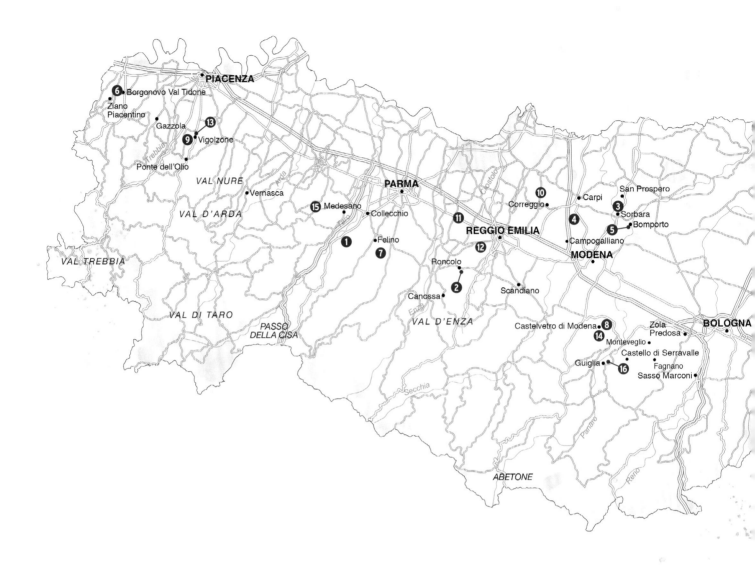

Colli di Parma DOC

A small hilly DOC offering several types of grapes, both white and red, with interesting results with the Barbera and Malvasia. Annual production close to one million bottles.

—

Producer and its trademark and signature wines:

1. MONTE DELLE VIGNE, Collecchio
    Colli di Parma Malvasia Callas ($)
    Colli di Parma Barbera Brusata ($)

Colli di Scandiano e di Canossa DOC

We are in the province of Reggio Emilia, where ample space is given over to Lambrusco vineyards. There is also a wine made from the ancient Malbo Gentile grape, very fragrant with notes of flowers and red fruit, rich in a beautiful ruby red color, and not lacking in tannin, with good persistence on the palate. About three hundred and fifty thousand bottles are produced annually, scattered across numerous white and red types.

—

Producer and its trademark and signature wine:

2. VENTURINI BALDINI, Roncolo
    Colli di Scandiano e di Canossa Malbo Gentile
    TERS ($)

Recommended wines outside the DOC/DOCG designations:

EMILIA

3. Francesco BELLEI & C., Bomporto
   Cuvée Brut M. Cl. (Chardonnay, Pinot Noir) ($)
   Lambrusco Ancestrale ($)
4. BERGIANTI – Terrevive, Carpi
   San Vincent (Lambrusco di Sorbara) ($)
5. CANTINA DELLA VOLTA, Bomporto
   Il Mattaglio Blanc de Noirs Brut M. Cl.
   (Pinot Noir) ($)
6. CANTINA VALTIDONE, Borgonovo Val Tidone
   Arvange Pas Dosé M. Cl.
   (Pinot Noir, Chardonnay) ($$)
7. Camillo DONATI, Felino
   Il Mio Lambrusco ($)
   Il Mio Malvasia ($)
8. Vittorio GRAZIANO, Castelvetro di Modena
   Lambrusco Fontana dei Boschi ($)
9. LA TOSA, Vigolzone
   L'Ora Felice (Malvasia di Candia Aromatica) ($$)
10. LINI 910, Correggio
    In Correggio Rosso Millesimato
    (Lambrusco Salamino) ($$)
11. Ermete MEDICI, Reggio Emilia
    Spumante Brut Rosso Granconcerto M. Cl.
    (Lambrusco Salamino) ($)
12. PODERE CIPOLLA – Denny Bini, Reggio Emilia
    Rosa dei Venti (Lambrusco Grasparossa,
    Malbo Gentile) ($)
13. ROMAGNOLI, Vigolzone
    Valluna (Barbera, Pinot Noir) ($)
    Il Pigro Dosaggiozero Extra Brut M. Cl. ($)
14. SAN POLO, Castelvetro di Modena
    Saio Rosso (Lambrusco) ($)
15. TENUTE VENTURINI FOSCHI, Medesano
    Gemma Malvasia ($)
16. TERRAQUILIA, Guiglia
    Il Nativo Ancestrale (Pignoletto, Trebbiano) ($)

ROMAGNA

17. Paolo FRANCESCONI, Faenza
    Vite in Fiore (Albana) ($)
18. SAN VALENTINO, Rimini
    Luna Nuova (Cabernet Franc) ($$)
19. VIGNE DEI BOSCHI, Solarolo
    Poggio Tura (Sangiovese) ($)

LA TOSA

Località La Tosa
Vigolzone (PC)
latosa.it
Year of establishment: 1980
Owner: the Pizzamiglio
family
Average number of bottles
produced per year: 120,000

The business of brothers
Stefano and Ferruccio
Pizzamiglio, which started
almost as a game more than
forty years ago, began to
take shape and develop with
increasing professionalism
and passion from 1984 onward,
soon becoming an essential
qualitative point of reference
in the Colli Piacentini. The 47
organically cultivated acres
contain mainly the area's
classic vines: Barbera and
Croatina for the reds, Malvasia
di Candia for the whites,
with a small area reserved
for Sauvignon and Cabernet
Sauvignon, used for the
ever-popular Luna Selvatica.
A company full of ideas and
oenological prowess.

Vignamorello La Tosa
Gutturnio
Denominazione di origine controllata
Superiore
Vino Biologico
Contiene solfiti · Contains sulfites · Enthält Sulfite
2021
Imbottigliato all'origine dall'azienda agricola 'La Tosa' di Ferruccio e Stefano Pizzamiglio, Vigolzone, Vigolzone - Italia Prodotto in Italia
0,75 l ℮ 14,5% vol.

GUTTURNIO SUPERIORE VIGNAMORELLO

First year of production: 1988
Average number of bottles produced
per year: 12,000
Grape varieties: Barbera (70%),
Bonarda (30%)

The grapes are harvested at an advanced
stage of ripeness to obtain open and
complex aromas, while the palate enjoys the
fine acidity typical of Barbera. After a few
months in wood, the nose picks up precise
notes of plum and cherry accompanied
by a hint of medicinal herbs; the flavor is
important and structured but constantly
maintains a vivid freshness, with a minimal
contribution from the tannic component.
The elegance and balance of Colli Piacentini.

CLETO CHIARLI

Via Belvedere 8
Castelvetro di Modena
(MO)
chiarli.it
Year of establishment: 2001
Owner: the Chiarli family
Average number of bottles
produced per year: 900,000

The family's vast vineyard area
spanning 247 acres allows for
the production of different
types of Lambrusco, both in
terms of grape origin—with
Grasparossa and Sorbara—
and processing techniques
including refermentation
in the bottle, the ancestral
method, and the Metodo
Classico. The Brut Maestro,
Vecchia Modena Premium,
and Grasparossa di Castelvetro
Vigneto Cialdini, exquisite
expressions of the world of
Lambrusco, along with the
Sorbara del Fondatore, have
been particularly praised by
critics.

LAMBRUSCO DI SORBARA DEL FONDATORE

First year of production: 1978
Average number of bottles produced
per year: 12,000
Grape variety: Lambrusco di Sorbara

Obtained by refermentation in the bottle,
on the nose it has a slight cloudiness due
to the presence of the spent yeasts, then
opens on varied aromas of small fresh fruits,
from strawberries to currants. The flavor
is smooth and drinkable but also has good
flesh, pleasantly dry and slightly savory.

CANTINA DELLA VOLTA

Via per Modena 82
Bomporto (MO)
cantinadellavolta.com
Year of establishment: 2010
Owner: Christian Bellei
Average number of bottles
produced per year: 110,000

Christian Bellei's passion
for sparkling wine is all-
consuming, so much so that
from his 40 acres of vines he
produces not only different
types of Lambrusco di Sorbara
but also sparkling wines based
on Chardonnay and Pinot
Noir. The most award-winning
labels from wine guides, in
addition to Brut Rosé, include
the more immediate Rimosso,
refermented in the bottle, and
the five different versions of
Mattaglio Metodo Classico.
High-level results across the
entire range.

LAMBRUSCO DI SORBARA SPUMANTE BRUT ROSÉ M. CL.

First year of production: 2010
Average number of bottles produced
per year: 35,000
Grape variety: Lambrusco di Sorbara

More than forty months on the lees create
a pale pink rosé with lustrous, energetic
bubbles. The aromas barely touch brioche
and focus on the vitality of fresh red berries,
with currants at the forefront. On first taste,
one is captivated by a crisp acidity that
persists until the finish, in which rose petals
also appear. The ultimate in pleasantness
and immediacy.

PALTRINIERI

Località Sorbara, Via
Cristo 49
Bomporto (MO)
cantinapaltrinieri.it
Year of establishment: 1926
Owner: Alberto Paltrinieri
Average number of bottles
produced per year: 190,000

The business was started
by Alberto Paltrinieri's
grandfather, who today
offers the original artisanal
characteristics, integrating
them with refinement and
expressiveness rivaled by few
in the Lambrusco area. From
45 organically cultivated
acres come seven labels made
from Lambrusco di Sorbara
grapes, made with autoclave
or bottle fermentation, but
also with the Metodo Classico.
Wines in which the passion
and expertise of the producer
are evident, along with the
outspoken personality of
Lambrusco di Sorbara.

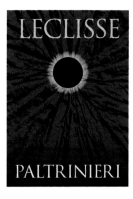

LAMBRUSCO DI SORBARA LECLISSE

First year of production: 2007
Average number of bottles produced
per year: 20,000
Grape variety: Lambrusco di Sorbara

It comes from old vines, the grapes of which
are pressed so delicately as to create a rather
pale onion skin color. The aromas are very
intense, lively, and articulate, proposing
strawberries, rose petals, and raspberries
along with a touch of white fruit; the palate
enjoys a bewitching acidity that transcends
into savoriness, as well as fine bubbles of
extreme pleasantness that lead to a berry
finish. An apparent simplicity that gives
great gustatory joy.

FATTORIA NICOLUCCI

Via Umberto I 21
Predappio (FC)
vininicolucci.com
Year of establishment: 1885
Owner: the Nicolucci
family
Average number of bottles
produced per year: 90,000

Alessandro Nicolucci uses
his oenological expertise to
propose wines that come
from environmentally
aware farming and that best
represent the characteristics
of the Predappio Alta area
while avoiding any technical
interventions that soften
the natural power of his
Sangiovese grapes. From 25
acres, all organically farmed,
he obtains red selections that
refuse barrique maturation
in favor of unroasted oak and
that can improve in glass for
many years.

ROMAGNA SANGIOVESE SUPERIORE RISERVA PREDAPPIO DI PREDAPPIO VIGNA DEL GENERALE

First year of production: 1980
Average number of bottles produced
per year: 20,000
Grape variety: Sangiovese

Born in a vineyard planted shortly after the
First World War, it matures for two years
in large barrels and offers refined aromas of
dark fruits such as cherry and blackberry,
against a backdrop of spices and cinchona;
the flavor is decisive, structured, and, in the
first few years in the bottle, even rigid due
to the presence of a tannic mass that then
evolves into complexity, always clear and
certainly pleasant. A great expression of
Sangiovese di Romagna.

FATTORIA ZERBINA

Località Marzeno, Via
Vicchio 11
Faenza (RA)
zerbina.com
Year of establishment: 1966
Owner: Cristina
Geminiani
Average number of bottles
produced per year: 170,000

Cristina Geminiani started
working in the family winery
in 1985 on the strength of
her oenological experience
and studies in France. She
immediately became famous
for her ability to offer sweet
wines made from grapes
attacked by botrytis cinerea,
such as Arrocco and Scacco
Matto. The winery is also
known for its Sangiovese-
based reds made from 82
organically farmed acres,
among which the Riserva
Pietramora and the modern
Marzieno excel. Small doses
of French grape varieties are
blended in with them.

ROMAGNA ALBANA PASSITO SCACCO MATTO

First year of production: 1987
Average number of bottles produced
per year: 3,700 (from 350 to 1,500 ml)
(12.7 to 50.7 fl oz)
Grape variety: Albana

Produced only in vintages characterized
by the regular development of noble rot, it
has an enchantingly deep and persuasive
bouquet, in which candied fruit and honey
combine with hints of spice. The palate
is rich, almost oily, and silky soft, with a
persistent acidulous note that harmonizes
and guarantees constant pleasantness. One
of Italy's great sweet wines.

VILLA PAPIANO

Via Ibola 24
Modigliana (FC)
villapapiano.it
Year of establishment: 2000
Owner: the Bordini family
Average number of bottles
produced per year: 50,000

Predominantly local vines
in the winery run by expert
oenologist Francesco Bordini,
with 25 acres cultivated using
organic and biodynamic
methods on the high slopes
of the Ibola Valley. Excellent
results are obtained,
in addition to the four
Sangiovese grape productions,
including the Vigna Probi
presented, along with the
whites Strada Corniolo, from
Trebbiano grapes, and Terra!,
based on Albana. A splendid
location and great respect for
the environment, leading to
wines rich in personality.

ROMAGNA SANGIOVESE RISERVA MODIGLIANA VIGNA PROBI

First year of production: 2001
Average number of bottles produced
per year: 12,000
Grape variety: Sangiovese

Born in a plot lying at an altitude of over
1,650 feet, this Riserva is matured in
both cement and large barrels. Probi is a
particularly fresh version of Sangiovese
di Romagna, rich on the nose with hints
of citrus and small red fruits; the mouth
is lively, with dense tannins that are not
very incisive, tonic, with a final recall of
medicinal herbs. Splendid drinkability in an
important wine.

TRE MONTI

Località Bergullo, Via
Lola 3
Imola (BO)
tremonti.it
Year of establishment: 1971
Owner: the Navacchia
family
Average number of bottles
produced per year: 200,000

In thirty years of business,
brothers Vittorio and David
Navacchia have helped Tre
Monti shine like a star in the
Romagna firmament, thanks
in part to an innovative spirit
that has led them to adopt
different aging methods, the
most notable of which include
the amphorae used for the
whites and the productions
without the addition of sulfur
dioxide. In addition to the
famous Vitalba, the winery
offers seventeen other labels,
which originate from 128
organically farmed acres,
among which the Romagna
Albana Vigna Rocca and
Trebbiano Piuttosto stand out.

ROMAGNA ALBANA SECCO VITALBA

First year of production: 2013
Average number of bottles produced
per year: 8,000
Grape variety: Albana

Careful use of Georgian amphorae combined
with first-rate, well-ripened grapes,
produces a version of Albana with a slightly
rosy, golden color and assured elegance. The
aromas range from yellow-fleshed fruit to
honey, from tea to aromatic herbs; the flavor
is persuasive, soft, and full-bodied but also of
great vitality and enjoyable freshness. A fine
interpretation of Romagna Albana.

Liguria

The centuries-old winegrowing tradition is based on indigenous grape varieties without allowing itself to be influenced by France and Piedmont, the two surrounding oenological giants. The exception is the multifaceted Vermentino, which yields excellent results both where the Ligurian territory begins to merge with Tuscany and on the Riviera di Ponente.

Compared to the Côte d'Azur, Liguria is appreciated for its wilder and more hidden aspects. Inhabited since Neolithic times, it became one of the most prosperous maritime republics thanks to the development of trade from Genoa and still retains its particular beauty and authentic character of life between the sea and the mountains. A map of the region shows a continuous arc of mountains and steep hills dropping into the sea from France to Tuscany, leaving no room for flat areas. The coastal areas are densely populated and the gradient of the slopes in the narrow valleys is often more than 30%, which is why all wine critics describe Ligurian vineyards as "heroic."

And this is the feeling one gets when visiting the terraced vineyards of Dolceacqua or the Cinque Terre, where the vines grow on terraces where work can only be done by hand, and where the grape harvest is carried out by carts running on rails as scenic as they are vertiginous. Viticulture in these areas is not just an agricultural expression but an ancestral philosophy of peasant resistance.

Starting from the French border, the narrow and long Riviera Ligure di Ponente offers attractive wines from the Rossese grape, the Dolceacqua, still little known due to its low overall production, but of great charm and pleasantness: it is the flagship in red of the Ligurian region.

Continuing toward Genoa, the almost unchallenged reign of white grapes begins, in particular Pigato and Vermentino, which in recent years have been showing definite signs of vitality and originality, after being limited, for a period, to producing wines to quench the thirst of hot tourists flocking to the Ligurian beaches in their millions during the summer.

Approaching the eastern part of the Ligurian arc are the famous Cinque Terre, offering several intoxicating examples of the potential of local white grapes, both in still whites and in the almost unobtainable Passiti.

The landscape in the Colli di Luni is at times less difficult and craggy, where the delicate aromaticity of the Vermentino grape offers some of its best interpretations on a national level.

The total wine production is close to 2.6 million gallons per year, processed by one thousand five hundred farms with an average size of close to 2.5 acres. It is interesting to note the elevation profile of the 3,950 cultivated acres: the land is 60% hilly and 10% flat, joined by 30% mountainous vineyards. Like other regions of Italy, Liguria too must live with a paradox: on the one hand, the beauty of its capital city, its villages where time seems to have stopped, and its nature reserves, such that 70% of the entire territory is still covered by forestland; and on the other hand, the general hydrogeological instability, with repeated flooding due to uncontrolled building development and soil sealing.

MAIN VINES GROWN IN THE REGION

Albarola

Also known as Bianchetta Genovese, it is rarely vinified in purity insofar as a fairly neutral variety, unless subjected to long macerations from which herbaceous and fruity aromas and a more energetic and enveloping structure can be extracted. Together with Bosco and Vermentino, it contributes to creating one of Italy's rarest and most sought-after passito wines, the legendary Cinque Terre Sciacchetrà.

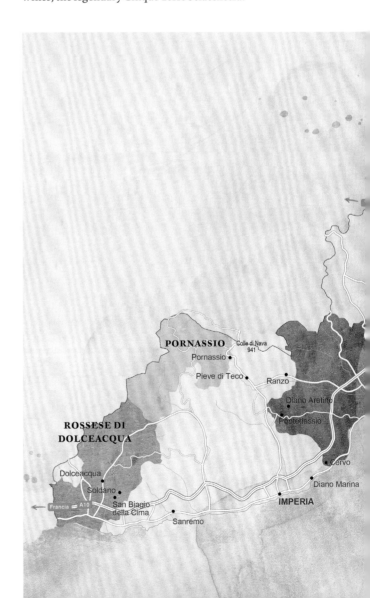

Bosco

The main grape variety of the Cinque Terre DOC in which it must be included at 40%, and a constituent grape of the Cinque Terre Sciacchetrà. In the wines, it contributes structure and persistence, but by tradition, it is almost never vinified in purity. It may originate from the woods of either the Cinque Terre or the Villa dei Marchesi in Genoa; in any case, it has been native to Liguria for centuries, clinging to the handkerchiefs of vines suspended between sky and sea in the Cinque Terre area. Several producers of Sciacchetrà still crush the grapes harvested in these vertical vines with their feet, after having dried them and dehusked them, berry by berry, by hand. Aging takes place in small wooden barrels made from local fruit trees, such as pear or cherry. The term Sciacchetrà derives from *sciacàa*, meaning "to crush," although it may have been a word invented by the Macchiaioli painter, Telemaco Signorini, who in the memoirs of his Ligurian summers described a *sciaccatras* wine, intoxicating insofar as strengthened by the drying of the grapes. The result is an amber-colored wine with mahogany hues, in which aromatic complexity, sweetness, acidity, and minerality are concentrated to the utmost and coexist in harmony.

Granaccia

→ Grenache in International Grape Varieties

Pigato

Biotype of → Vermentino

Rossese

DNA analyses have ascertained that Rossese is identical to Tibouren, one of the most widely cultivated grape varieties in Provence, where it is mainly used for rosé wines. It is a very ancient vine, cultivated in Mesopotamia twenty-five hundred years ago, which arrived in Liguria via Greece, through trade with Marseilles. In the extreme west of the Province of Imperia, in the Nervia and Verbone Valleys, between Ventimiglia, Vallecrosia, Dolceacqua, Camporosso, and Perinaldo, the vines are cultivated using the "alberello" system on steep terraces overlooking the sea. The vines are often very old and are deeply rooted in these marly soils, which are rather friable and rich in very fine gravel and clay, with a combination of *terroir* and vine variety that gives the wine a strong spicy and mineral character. It is a purplish-red with orange reflections—hence the name Rossese—and transmits strong Mediterranean sensations on the nose: white and yellow flowers, thyme, rosemary, wild strawberry, and dried rose, with hints of aromatic herbs.

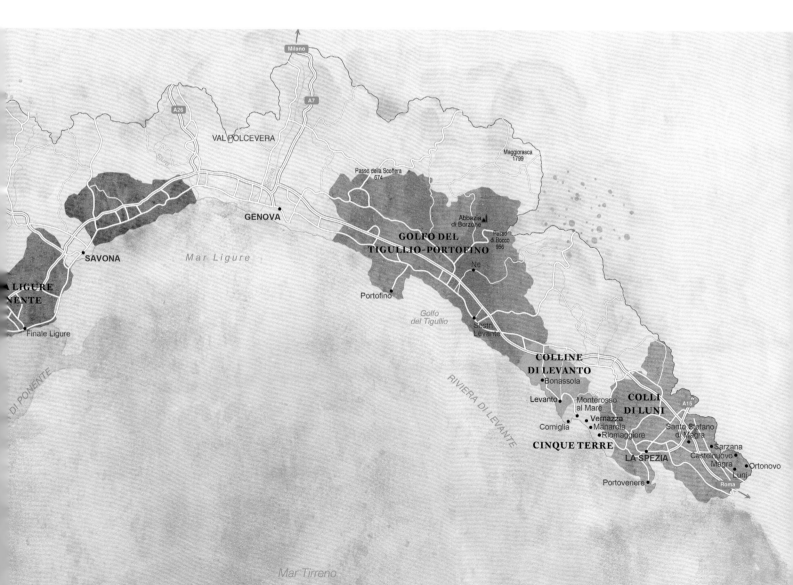

Vermentino

(→ also Sardinia)

Probably introduced to Sardinia and northern Italy from Corsica between the thirteenth and fourteenth centuries, it spread in Piedmont as a favorite and in Liguria as Pigato because of the "pighe," the pink spots that appear on ripe grapes, or else derived from the Latin "picatum," which indicates the ancient tradition of aromatizing wine with resins. It is cultivated at around 985 feet in areas with a wide temperature range that favor the development of aromas such as chamomile and honey, ripe peach and apricot, wildflowers and musk, with hints of pear, acacia, and melon. It also offers a marine note that in Sardinia is accompanied by an even warmer, tropical fruit bouquet, while in Liguria it maintains a lighter, herbaceous, slightly savory profile that can evolve toward flint, hazelnut, and hydrocarbons with aging. It is vinified on its own in the Riviera Ligure di Ponente DOC and is part of the Cinque Terre and Cinque Terre Sciacchetrà. The Colli di Luni Vermentino is also harmonious and floral, with a slightly bitter finish.

The DOCs

- Cinque Terre and Cinque Terre Sciacchetrà
- Colli di Luni
- Colline di Levanto
- Golfo del Tigullio-Portofino or Portofino
- Pornassio or Ormeasco di Pornassio
- Riviera Ligure di Ponente
- Rossese di Dolceacqua or Dolceacqua
- Val Polcèvera

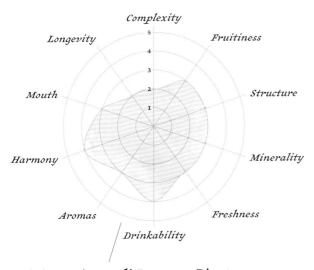

Riviera Ligure di Ponente Pigato

Riviera Ligure di Ponente DOC

This broad DOC mainly covers the province of Savona, with small encroachments into those areas closer to Genoa and Imperia. The most important grape, also in terms of quantity, is Pigato, but there are also excellent versions of Vermentino, which is genetically similar to Pigato and Granaccia, themselves synonymous with Grenache, Cannonau, Alicante, and Rossese. Yellow-fleshed fruit and balsamic hints are the most frequently used olfactory descriptions for Riviera Ligure di Ponente Vermentino, a wine as full-bodied as it is pleasantly saline: a harmonious wine, without excess, rarely refined in wood. Total annual production exceeds sixteen million bottles.

—

Producers and their trademark and signature wines:

1. Massimo ALESSANDRI, Ranzo
   Riviera Ligure di Ponente Pigato Vigne Vëggie ($)
   Riviera Ligure di Ponente Rossese Costa de Vigne ($)
2. Laura ASCHERO, Pontedassio
   Riviera Ligure di Ponente Pigato ($)
   Riviera Ligure di Ponente Vermentino ($)
3. Maria Donata BIANCHI, Diano Arentino
   Riviera Ligure di Ponente Pigato ($)
   Riviera Ligure di Ponente Vermentino ($)
4. BIOVIO, Albenga
   Riviera Ligure di Ponente Pigato Bon in da Bon ($)
   Riviera Ligure di Ponente Pigato MaRené ($)
5. BRUNA, Ranzo
   Riviera Ligure di Ponente Pigato U Baccan ($$)
   Riviera Ligure di Ponente Pigato Majé ($)
6. Luca CALVINI, Sanremo
   Riviera Ligure di Ponente Pigato ($)
7. CANTINE CALLERI, Albenga
   Riviera Ligure di Ponente Pigato di Albenga Saleasco ($)
   Riviera Ligure di Ponente Pigato di Albenga Il Calleri ($)
8. CASCINA DELLE TERRE ROSSE, Finale Ligure
   Riviera Ligure di Ponente Pigato ($)
   Riviera Ligure di Ponente Vermentino ($)
9. FONTANACOTA, Pornassio
   Riviera Ligure di Ponente Vermentino ($)
   Riviera Ligure di Ponente Pigato ($)
10. LA GINESTRAIA, Cervo
    Riviera Ligure di Ponente Pigato Le Marige ($)
11. LUPI, Pieve di Teco
    Riviera Ligure di Ponente Pigato Petraie ($)
12. PODERE GRECALE, Sanremo
    Riviera Ligure di Ponente Granaccia Beusi ($)
13. POGGIO DEI GORLERI, Diano Marina
    Riviera Ligure di Ponente Pigato Cycnus ($)
14. Innocenzo TURCO, Quiliano
    Riviera Ligure di Ponente Granaccia Cappuccini ($)
15. VISAMORIS, Imperia
    Riviera Ligure di Ponente Pigato Sogno ($)
    Riviera Ligure di Ponente Pigato Verum ($)

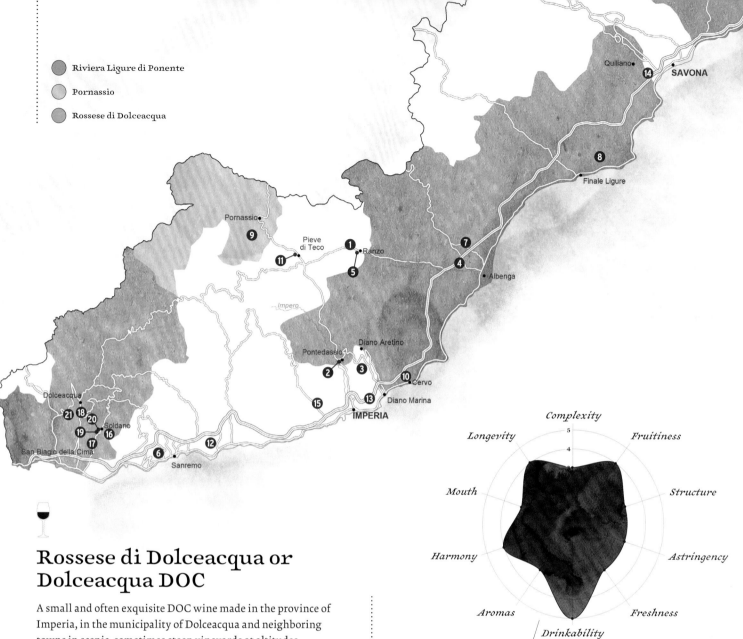

Rossese di Dolceacqua or Dolceacqua DOC

A small and often exquisite DOC wine made in the province of Imperia, in the municipality of Dolceacqua and neighboring towns in scenic, sometimes steep vineyards at altitudes varying between two hundred and five hundred and fifty metres, and at a distance from the sea ranging from a few hundred feet to 15 miles. The taste profile is certainly pleasant, thanks to notes ranging from small black fruits to spices, often with pleasant hints of talcum powder and wet earth in the background; the taste is not very tannic, just savory and closes on notes of almonds. Fewer than two hundred thousand bottles per year are produced, and need to be sought out.

—

Producers and their trademark and signature wines:

16. KA' MANCINÉ, Soldano
    Dolceacqua Beragna ($)
    Dolceacqua Galeae ($)
17. MACCARIO DRINGENBERG, San Biagio della Cima
    Dolceacqua Superiore Curli ($$)
    Dolceacqua Posaú ($)
    Dolceacqua Sette Cammini ($$)

18. MAIXEI, Dolceacqua
    Dolceacqua Superiore ($)
    Dolceacqua Superiore Barbadirame ($)
19. POGGI DELL'ELMO, Soldano
    Rossese di Dolceacqua ($)
20. TENUTA ANFOSSO, Soldano
    Dolceacqua Superiore Fulavin ($)
    Dolceacqua Superiore Poggio Pini ($)
21. TERRE BIANCHE, Dolceacqua
    Dolceacqua Bricco Arcagna ($$)
    Dolceacqua ($)

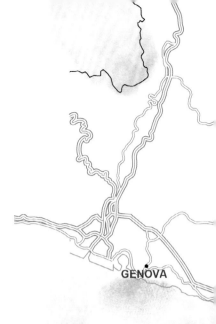

Cinque Terre and Cinque Terre Sciacchetrà DOC

A single DOC that originates in a splendid and world-famous scenic area, in the municipalities of Vernazza, Riomaggiore, and Monterosso, as well as in part of the provincial capital, La Spezia. The grapes are Il Bosco, up to at least 40%, possibly integrated by Albarola and Vermentino up to 40%, and any authorized grape varieties to no more than 20%. Also available is the Sciacchetrà type, mainly in the Passito and Riserva versions. The Cinque Terre has aromas of broom, Mediterranean scrub, citrus fruits, and herbs, followed by a rather taut and lively palate with refreshing tanginess. The rare Sciacchetrà, made from dried grapes (with a maximum grape/wine yield of 35%), calls to mind honey, nuts, and dried fruit, with a sweet but not undynamic note on the palate. Overall production is less than three hundred thousand bottles per year.

—

Producers and their trademark and signature wines:

1. CANTINA CINQUE TERRE, Riomaggiore
   Cinque Terre Vigne Alte ($)
2. Luciano CAPELLINI, Riomaggiore
   Cinque Terre ($)
3. CHEO, Vernazza
   Cinque Terre Sciacchetrà ($$)
4. POSSA, Riomaggiore
   Cinque Terre ($)
   Cinque Terre Sciacchetrà Riserva ($$$)

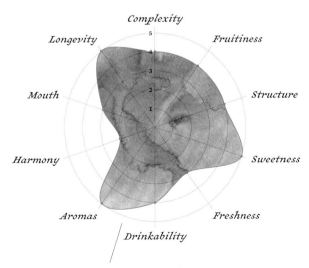

Cinque Terre Sciacchetrà

Colli di Luni DOC

An interregional designation covering the territory of fourteen municipalities in the province of La Spezia and three in the province of Massa Carrara, including Fosdinovo. There is also a red version at a minimum of 50% Sangiovese, but it is the grape called Vermentino that has proven to be best suited to this beautiful, hilly, and sometimes mountainous area. The aromas range between white flowers, sage, citrus, and brackish hints, while the taste is moderately acidic, soft but never too oily, and slightly saline. A total of 1.4 million bottles are produced annually.

—

Producers and their trademark and signature wines:

5. CANTINE LUNAE BOSONI, Castelnuovo Magra
   Colli di Luni Vermentino Numero Chiuso ($$)
6. GIACOMELLI, Castelnuovo Magra
   Colli di Luni Vermentino Boboli ($)
   Colli di Luni Vermentino Pianacce ($)
7. IL MONTICELLO, Sarzana
   Colli di Luni Vermentino Argille Rosse ($$)
8. LA BAIA DEL SOLE – Cantine Federici, Ortonovo
   Colli di Luni Vermentino Sarticola ($)
   Colli di Luni Vermentino Oro d'Isée ($)
9. LA PIETRA DEL FOCOLARE, Ortonovo
   Colli di Luni Vermentino Superiore Villa Linda ($)
   Colli di Luni Vermentino Superiore Solarancio ($)
10. Ottaviano LAMBRUSCHI, Castelnuovo Magra
    Colli di Luni Vermentino Superiore Il Maggiore ($)
    Colli di Luni Vermentino Costa Marina ($)
11. PODERE LAVANDARO, Fosdinovo (Tuscany)
    Colli di Luni Vermentino ($)
12. TERENZUOLA, Fosdinovo (Tuscany)
    Colli di Luni Vermentino Superiore Fosso di Corsano ($)
13. ZANGANI, Santo Stefano di Magra
    Colli di Luni Vermentino Superiore Boceda ($)

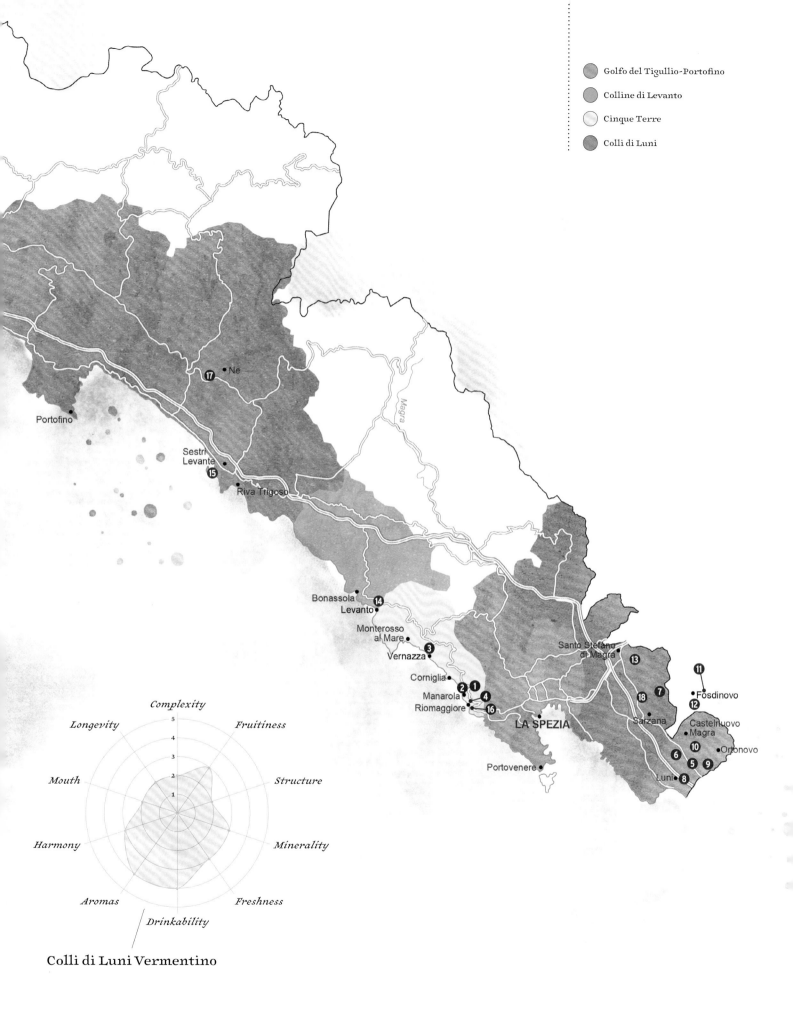

Golfo del Tigullio-Portofino
Colline di Levanto
Cinque Terre
Colli di Luni

Portofino

Ne

⑰

Sestri
Levante
⑮
Riva Trigoso

Magra

Bonassola
Levanto ⑭

Monterosso
al Mare
⑬

Vernazza

Corniglia
Manarola
Riomaggiore ⑯

② ①
④

Santo Stefano
di Magra

⑬

⑱

Sarzana

LA SPEZIA

Portovenere

Castelnuovo
Magra

Ortonovo

⑥
⑤ ⑨
⑩

Luni ⑧

⑪
Fosdinovo
⑫

⑦

Complexity
Fruitiness
Structure
Minerality
Freshness
Drinkability
Aromas
Harmony
Mouth
Longevity

5
4
3
2
1

Colli di Luni Vermentino

Colline di Levanto DOC

In a small area encompassing four municipalities, including Levanto, in the province of La Spezia, Vermentino—the most significant grape—is often grown in picturesque terraced vineyards. White flowers and good flavor are its main qualities. Fewer than one hundred thousand bottles are produced annually.

—

Producer and its trademark and signature wine:

14. CÀ DU FERRÀ, Bonassola
    Colline di Levanto Vermentino Luccicante ($)

Golfo del Tigullio-Portofino or Portofino DOC

A DOC wine of great appeal to tourists and little used by producers, relating to the province of Genoa, with different types, red and especially white, with grapes ranging from Ciliegiolo to Vermentino. Moscato must be made using 100% white grapes of the same name. Around two hundred sixty thousand bottles are produced annually.

—

Producer and its trademark and signature wine:

15. CANTINE BREGANTE, Sestri Levante
    Golfo del Tigullio-Portofino Moscato ($)

Recommended wines outside the DOC/DOCG designations:

- Massimo ALESSANDRI, Ranzo
  Ligustico (Granaccia, Syrah) ($$)
16. Walter DE BATTÈ, Riomaggiore
    Saladero (Bosco, Albarola, Vermentino) ($$)
17. LA RICOLLA, Ne
    Òua (Vermentino) ($$)
18. SANTA CATERINA, Sarzana
    Giuncàro (Friulano, Sauvignon Blanc) ($)
    Poggi al Bosco (Albarola) ($$)

OTTAVIANO LAMBRUSCHI
Via Olmarello 28
Castelnuovo Magra (SP)
ottavianolambruschisp.com
Year of establishment: 1975
Owner: the Lambruschi
family
Average number of bottles
produced per year: 34,000

The small winery inaugurated
by a very young Ottaviano
Lambruschi has always
dedicated itself to Vermentino,
reserving almost the entirety
of its 12 acres to this grape
and soon achieving notable
recognition. The strength
of these labels lies in their
immediate pleasantness, their
respect for the peculiarities of
the grape and the vineyard, and
an apparent simplicity rich in
flavor.

COLLI DI LUNI VERMENTINO
COSTA MARINA
First year of production: 1995
Average number of bottles produced
per year: 15,000
Grape variety: Vermentino

Matured in steel only, it is characterized by
flowers and white fruits, slightly enriched by
a hint of medicinal herbs and almond. The
palate has great immediacy and spontaneity,
a splendid smoothness dominated by acidity,
and an almost saline touch that enlivens a
finish in which the pear returns.
A prototype of refreshing drinkability.

MACCARIO
DRINGENBERG
Via Torre 3
San Biagio della Cima (IM)
Year of establishment: 2001
Owner: Giovanna
Maccario
Average number of bottles
produced per year: 25,000

There are just 12 acres under
vine and five different
vineyards facing mainly out to
sea, in that part of Liguria just
next to France where the red
wines have a robust structure
and remarkable longevity.
Here, Giovanna Maccario has
become a point of reference
for Dolceacqua wines that are
always dynamic, sometimes
even impetuous, always
tasty, offered in five labels to
respect the different origins
of the grapes. An admirable
interpretation of the Rossese
grape.

DOLCEACQUA POSAÚ
First year of production: 2000
Average number of bottles produced
per year: 7,500
Grape variety: Rossese

The pleasant floral range combines with
a refreshing balsamic touch, with subtle
hints of leather and wet earth bringing
character and complexity. The taste is
almost impetuous, assertive, full of vitality,
delicately astringent, and pleasantly acidic.
An apparently easy wine, highly satisfying
and capable of improving for a long time in
the bottle.

BRUNA
Via Umberto I 1
Ranzo (IM)
brunapigato.it
Year of establishment: 1970
Owner: Francesca Bruna
Average number of bottles
produced per year: 45,000

A winery that consistently
receives recognition and
awards every year, securing
its place at the top of
regional production, owing
in particular to the results
obtained with the Pigato
grape, from which three
productions originate from
different crus. The vineyards
have grown slowly over the
years to reach 22 organically
cultivated acres, also with
parcels of red grapes, in
particular Rossese and
Granaccia, which are of great
interest.

RIVIERA LIGURE DI PONENTE
PIGATO U BACCAN
First year of production: 1999
Average number of bottles produced
per year: 2,500
Grape variety: Pigato

It starts fermenting in steel and then
matures in casks, a process which in twenty
years has led to it becoming the standard-
bearer of the Riviera Ligure di Ponente
Pigato designation. The aromas tend toward
freshness, with hints that recall above all
herbs, Mediterranean scrub, sage, and
citrus fruits against a background of white
fruit and a hint of honey. The flavor is rich
and lively, with good sapidity, a delicately
almondy finish, and a balsamic touch. Every
year there's a great Pigato.

TERRE BIANCHE
Località Arcagna
Dolceacqua (IM)
terrebianche.com
Year of establishment: 1870
Owners: Filippo Rondelli,
Nicola Laconi
Average number of bottles
produced per year: 60,000

The company's one hundred
and fifty years of history have
made it possible, generation
after generation, to achieve
the deepest knowledge of the
cultivation and vinification
methods of the typical local
grapes, while also securing the
presence of precious plants
that are more than a century
old. The 22 organically farmed
acres yield both reds, with
three labels based exclusively
on Rossese grapes, and whites,
based on Vermentino and
Pigato. Wines that are always
clear and characteristic, of
exquisite workmanship.

DOLCEACQUA BRICCO ARCAGNA
First year of production: 1988
Average number of bottles produced
per year: 3,000
Grape variety: Rossese

From the vineyard of the same name at an
altitude of 1,300 feet above sea level, with
a view of Dolceacqua and the Ligurian Sea,
comes a Rossese of precise elegance, with
distinct hints of dark spices such as pepper
and an intense presence of ripe cherries. It is
set against an evocative background of fruit
in alcohol, also deriving from maturation in
small French wood barrels that are never too
fragrant. It tastes of good alcohol content,
pulpy, slightly astringent, and endowed
with lively savoriness. Bricco Arcagna
is endowed with tasty drinkability and
decades of bottle-aging capacity.

Tuscany

When it comes to winemaking, Tuscany is one of the most high-profile and popular regions in the world, basing its success on the heritage of hundreds of years of art, culture, and history, on taking care of the landscape, and on its ability to make tried-and-trusted favorites such as Chianti and Montalcino go hand in hand with wines of international repute. Along with Bolgheri and with the phenomenon of the Super Tuscans, these have succeeded in revolutionizing the image of Italian wine around the world.

Tuscany has become a universal synonym for beauty, goodness, and quality of life. With the exception of a few industrialized areas, in the collective imagination the gentle, poetic, and reassuring hilly landscapes, the artistic history of its towns and villages, and the ancient tradition of winegrowing make Tuscany an essential destination for anyone who wants to get to know Italian wine.

None of this happened spontaneously or by accident: except for some mountainous areas and nature reserves, the territory of this region has been shaped by the hand of man over the centuries. Beginning with the Etruscans, a hundred generations built cities such as Florence, Siena, Pisa, and Lucca, which vied for the greatest artists of the Renaissance and took care of forests, fields, rows of cypresses, olive groves, vineyards, and hills studded with villages, monasteries, and farms. Traveling through Tuscany, one of the key destinations on the Grand Tour, means immersing oneself in a harmonious composition and combination of nature and culture.

Here, native grape varieties such as Sangiovese and Vernaccia, but also Cabernet Sauvignon and Merlot, have found their natural homes, the result of entrepreneurial foresight, respect for the land, and human creativity.

The region is home to labels and names that have become famous and appreciated throughout the world. Yet only 5% of Italian wine is produced here. There are 150,000 acres of vineyards, distributed among 12,700 companies, with an annual production of just over two million hectoliters. That is down from previous years, and places the region at number seven in terms of production output in Italy. When analyzing the production structure in light of more recent developments, Tuscany's figures show why it is so successful. Four facts are important to understand why this is.

Firstly, the fifteen main wine cooperatives in the region harvest less than 20% of the production. Secondly, the average yield per acre is 165 hectoliters, compared to the Italian average of 270, which is also an indication of the general high quality of the wines. Thirdly, compared to the national average of 66%, in Tuscany almost the entire surface area under vine, or 96.4%, is regulated by 52 DOPs (*Denominazione di Origine Protetta*, or Protected Designation of Origin), of which 41 are DOCs (*Denominazione di Origine Controllata*, or Designation of Controlled Origin), 11 DOCGs (*Denominazione di Origine Controllata e Garantita*, or Designation of Controlled and Guaranteed Origin), plus 6 IGTs (*Indicazione Geografica Tipica*, or Typical Geographical Indication).

The increase of Tuscan wine sales in the world is constant, with sharp and rising growth in Australia and South Korea and consolidation in the United States, Canada, Germany, the United Kingdom, Switzerland, and France. Fourthly, the conversion to organic winemaking, which in Italy more than doubled between 2010 and 2020, is proceeding twice as fast in Tuscany as the national average: here, today, one vineyard out of three is organic or biodynamic.

More than half of all vineyards are planted with Sangiovese. Although its diffusion has practically halved, from 250,000 acres in the 1990s to 130,000 today, Sangiovese is still the most cultivated native vine in Italy and is the stalwart and lifeblood of the main Tuscan designations, from Chianti to Brunello di Montalcino, from Vino Nobile di Montepulciano and Morellino di Scansano to Carmignano.

The central Chianti area, with seven subzones and the heart of Chianti Classico, stretches over the hills between Florence and Siena. The wine produced in Chianti was served since the Middle Ages by the Vinattieri of Florence and, in 1716, the Grand Duke of Tuscany Cosimo III de' Medici established the boundaries of the Chianti Classico production area. The recipe for Chianti Classico was later codified by Bettino Ricasoli, the "Iron Baron." An agronomist and second President of the Council of the Kingdom of Italy after Cavour, he gave a strong push to the national economy and viticulture, won the gold medal for his wine at the 1867 International Exhibition in Paris, and in 1872 published the manifesto with guidelines for the production and aging of Chianti Classico.

In 1971, there came another revolution: Marquis Piero Antinori produced a wine in Chianti Classico based on Sangiovese, Cabernet Sauvignon, and Cabernet Franc, aiming to compete in complexity, structure, and elegance with the best wines in the world. Tignanello was born, the first Super Tuscan that overturned the perception of Tuscan wine internationally. In 1978 Solaia debuted, which was also the result of a collaboration between Antinori and Giacomo Tachis, the legendary Piedmontese oenologist and creator of Sassicaia. Then in 1985 came the arrival of Ornellaia. The race toward excellence moved from Chianti to Bolgheri, where Marquis Mario Incisa della Rocchetta had already, in 1944, overseen the production and growth of a wine based on Cabernet Sauvignon and Cabernet Franc, finding in this area climatic conditions similar to the Graves of Bordeaux. There were mild winters and hot, dry summers, with marine sediments and alluvial deposits of gravel, sand, and clay, ideal for draining water and retaining heat, shell fragments and a layer of silt rich in minerals and organic nutrients. In 1968, the first vintage of Sassicaia was marketed, with a definitive classification and

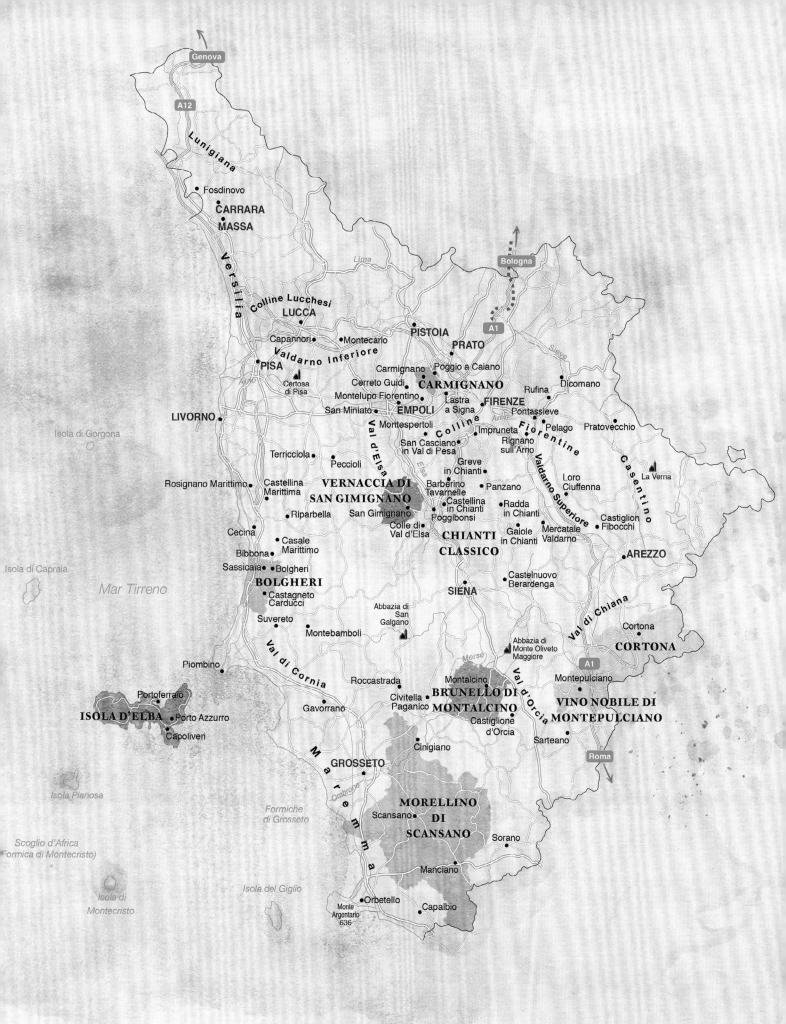

consecration in 1985, only five years after Brunello di Montalcino was awarded DOCG status.

In Montalcino, too, the history of oenology is intertwined with the Risorgimento: Garibaldi's Ferruccio Biondi-Santi inherited the company and the family tradition and on the outcrops and limestone of Montalcino created Brunello, today's Brunello di Montalcino, the only wine that can compete in complexity and longevity with Barolo. Less severe, softer, and spicier is the third Sangiovese-based wine; due to its value it was once reserved for the nobility, which is why it is called Vino Nobile di Montepulciano.

Just to the north, there is another magical place, where traces of viticulture date back 2,700 years, to the time of the Etruscans. At that time, an extraordinary grape variety, the Syrah, began the long journey that would take it from Persia to Europe, finding in Cortona a small DOC that is today a successful and original expression of it. The cultivation of Vernaccia di San Gimignano, which gave rise to the first DOC wine in Italy, in 1966, is also thousands of years old.

Among the sweet wines, there are the DOC Vin Santo, the result of delicate and long preparation, in which the grapes are left to dry on mats and are then refined in small oak, chestnut, and cherry casks, and at the same time there is also the DOCG Aleatico Passito dell'Elba.

The historic families, who do not remain too firmly stuck or anchored to the past, but continue to evolve their style in a search for more authentic and defined expressions of their *terroir*, are marching side by side with upcoming areas and new generations of growers, who are interpreting a sustainable and personal viticulture. From the nouvelle vague of the young winemakers of the Colline Lucchesi to the new Maremma, from the Apennines to the Argentario, there are many wines not to be missed, both within and outside the designations.

The DOCGs

- Brunello di Montalcino
- Carmignano
- Chianti
- Chianti Classico
- Elba Aleatico Passito / Aleatico Passito dell'Elba
- Montecucco Sangiovese
- Morellino di Scansano
- Suvereto
- Val di Cornia Rosso
- Vernaccia di San Gimignano
- Vino Nobile di Montepulciano

The DOCs

- Ansonica Costa dell'Argentario
- Barco Reale di Carmignano
- Bianco dell'Empolese
- Bianco di Pitigliano
- Bolgheri
- Bolgheri Sassicaia
- Candia dei Colli Apuani
- Capalbio
- Colli dell'Etruria Centrale
- Colli di Luni (→ Liguria)
- Colline Lucchesi
- Cortona
- Elba
- Grance Senesi
- Maremma Toscana
- Montecarlo
- Montecucco
- Monteregio di Massa Marittima
- Montescudaio
- Moscadello di Montalcino
- Orcia
- Parrina
- Pomino
- Rosso di Montalcino
- Rosso di Montepulciano
- San Gimignano
- San Torpé
- Sant'Antimo
- Sovana
- Terratico di Bibbona
- Terre di Casole
- Terre di Pisa
- Val d'Arbia
- Val d'Arno di Sopra or Valdarno di Sopra
- Val di Cornia
- Valdichiana Toscana
- Valdinievole
- Vin Santo del Chianti
- Vin Santo del Chianti Classico
- Vin Santo di Carmignano
- Vin Santo di Montepulciano

MAIN VINES GROWN IN THE REGION

Aleatico

A rare vine, similar to the black Muscatel, the Vernaccia di Pergola, and the Lacrima di Morro d'Alba, genetically identical to the Hungarian *halápi*, it does not have Greek origins as is commonly thought, given its sound affinity with the Greek *Liatiko* vine. Its name probably derives from July, the month in which its grapes ripen, producing the traditional, sweet, red passito of the Island of Elba. Small traces of it remain in Corsica, California, Kazakhstan, and the recent Pergola DOC from Ascoli Piceno.

Ansonica

Synonymous with Inzolia, in Tuscany the Sicilian grape variety retains its name of Norman origin, Ansonica. It is cultivated on the islands of Elba, Giglio, and Argentario and produces dry white wines of Mediterranean character, simple, with good flavor and notes of aromatic herbs and exotic fruit.

Canaiolo Nero, Ciliegiolo, Colorino

Three red grape varieties traditionally used as blending grapes together with Sangiovese, particularly in the Chianti area. Canaiolo brings softness and freshness thanks to its acidity and delicate tannins. It had already been mentioned in 1303 as *Canajuola* in Pietro de Crescenzi's *Opus Commodorum Ruralium*, praised in the seventeenth century as one of the best Tuscan varieties by the Florentine agronomist Soderini, and until the eighteenth century Canaiolo was more popular in Tuscany than Sangiovese, appreciated for its velvety structure and excellent drinkability.

Ciliegiolo, as its name suggests, lightens the palate to complement Sangiovese with an equally soft structure and light hints of cherry and raspberry.

Finally, there is Colorino or Colorino del Valdarno: a rare and almost dark blue grape, domesticated in ancient times from wild vines, it often appears in blends with Sangiovese. Its color intensity gives the wine a deep red color. More concentrated in tannins and aromas, it appears in smaller percentages than Ciliegiolo and Canaiolo.

Malvasia Nera

More widespread in Apulia but also present in Tuscany, especially in the province of Grosseto, and blended with Sangiovese in Carmignano, Chianti, and Vino Nobile di Montepulciano, to which it contributes good structure, softness, ripe fruit spices, and licorice notes, deriving from a cross between Malvasia Bianca Lunga and Negroamaro.

Pugnitello

A rare grape variety rediscovered in the 1980s, it owes its name to the shape of the bunches, similar to small bunched hands, or fists, with a good concentration of tannins and anthocyanins. It was authorized in the Tuscany IGT starting in 2022. Vinifiable in blends or on its own, it displays an intense character, with hints of cinnamon, black cherry, and cooked plum that may remind one of Tempranillo, but with a fresher texture and firmer tannins.

Sangiovese

Within the Italian designations, Sangiovese may be found together with other grape varieties, with the obligatory presence in Tuscany starting from a combination of a minimum of 50% in Carmignano to a minimum of 90% in Chianti Classico Gran Selezione.

The only *terroir* where, according to regulations, Sangiovese must be vinified in complete purity is Montalcino, so that it is only in Brunello di Montalcino that the full potential of this grape variety can be found. It reaches heights of complexity and refinement, evolving over time and becoming comparable only to the greatest Nebbiolo wines of Barolo and Barbaresco. Like Nebbiolo, it can be problematic when young—which is why it is marketed after five years of aging—severe, moody, austere, sometimes with haematic and almost wild streaks. Yet the best expressions of Sangiovese amaze with a mineral sequence reminiscent of the outcrops, limestone, and volcanic sediments of the Montalcino area, and a multitude of floral aromas reminiscent of the fields and woods of these areas, with their soil covered in foliage and acorns, with petals of geranium and violets wafting in the glass.

With the passage of time, some softness arrives and austerity is transformed into grace: the initial explosion of blackberries, black cherries, and plums gives way to dried flowers, tobacco, and coffee; the more balsamic crus converge as if on an apothecary's bench between eucalyptus, thyme, pink pepper, wild mint, and orange peel. The large quantity of terpenes that can be extracted from the skins determines the floral part, while the abundance of special aromatic compounds contained in the pulp gives notes of spices, candied fruit, camphor, and incense with age. Finally, the wood can round off with vanilla, cinnamon, and licorice, depending on the degree of roasting and the incidence of the barrique in the aging process.

Recent genetic studies have confirmed the Tuscan-Calabrian origin of the vine, a cross between Ciliegiolo and Calabrese di Montenuovo. Regarding the origin of the name, legend has it that the monks of Santarcangelo di Romagna, near Mount Jupiter, in response to a wayfarer who asked the name of the good wine they had offered him, simply stated: "the blood of Jupiter."

Trebbiano Toscano

Robust and versatile, capable of producing a simple, flowing white wine with good acidity and neutral character, from Tuscany it has spread throughout the world, even to India and to France, where it is known as Ugni Blanc and is the basis for Cognac and Armagnac. In Tuscany, Trebbiano produces the best results in the Vin Santo designations. These are dense and viscous oxidative wines, which, due to the particular process of drying the grapes and subsequent aging in wooden barrels, even very old ones, are dense with notes of dried fruit, walnut, almond, dried figs, caramel, and honey, accompanied by secondary aromas of sweet spices, jasmine, and orange peel.

Vernaccia di San Gimignano

Cultivated since antiquity, it is the source of fresh, light wines with a recognizable personality and the potential to develop complexity with age. In addition to the many floral notes of acacia, jasmine, and chamomile, and generally white and yellow flowers, we find hints of aromatic herbs and hay and an iodized mineral profile. The first mention of this grape variety in documents dates back to 1276, hence the name, which may derive from the Latin word *vernaculus*, meaning native or indigenous. Probably originating from Greece, via Spain and Liguria, it should not be confused with Vernaccia di Oristano, which is another vine, a relative of the Spanish Garnacha, nor with white Calabrian Guarnaccia, which is nothing more than white Foxtail or Falerno.

Bolgheri DOC

One of the most successful designations in recent decades, thanks to the famous Sassicaia but also thanks to the important investments made by a growing number of wineries that have seen in this land, close to the sea, well sunlit and rich in pebbles, the ideal place to plant vineyards that are mainly based on Bordeaux grapes. The climatic conditions favor wines that can be described as richer and more voluminous, as well as less vegetal, than the Bordeaux model, but the style varies from winery to winery. The Bolgheri DOC was established in 1994 and, through subsequent modifications, now proves that Bolgheri Rosso can be made from 100% Cabernet Sauvignon, Merlot, and Cabernet Franc, individually or in blends. Syrah and Sangiovese grapes are also permitted for no more than 50%, with the possible inclusion of a small amount of other grapes envisaged by the Region of Tuscany, at no more than 30%. Of lesser importance, but growing, is Bolgheri Bianco DOC, mainly based on Vermentino, Trebbiano Toscano, and Sauvignon. As is often the case in Tuscany, some major players, such as Masseto and Le Macchiole, prefer not to join the DOC, so they are listed at the end of the chapter. In addition to Rosso and Rosso Superiore, there are also Bianco, Sauvignon, Vermentino, and Rosato versions, from vineyards cultivated exclusively in the municipality of Castagneto Carducci. Total annual production, obtained from 3,200 acres under vine, is over seven million bottles, mainly dedicated to the red versions, with prices constantly increasing due to a strong demand on the international market.

—

Producers and their trademark and signature wines:

1. CA' MARCANDA, Castagneto Carducci
   Bolgheri Rosso Camarcanda ($$$$)
2. CAMPO ALLA SUGHERA, Castagneto Carducci
   Bolgheri Rosso Superiore Arnione ($$)
3. CASTELLO DI BOLGHERI, Castagneto Carducci
   Bolgheri Rosso Superiore Castello di Bolgheri
   ($$$)
4. Giovanni CHIAPPINI, Castagneto Carducci
   Bolgheri Rosso Superiore Guado de' Gemoli ($$$)
5. GRATTAMACCO, Castagneto Carducci
   Bolgheri Rosso Superiore Grattamacco ($$$)
6. GUADO AL MELO, Castagneto Carducci
   Bolgheri Bianco Criseo ($)
   Bolgheri Rosso Superiore Atis ($$)
7. I LUOGHI, Castagneto Carducci
   Bolgheri Rosso Superiore Campo al Fico ($$)
8. Fabio MOTTA, Castagneto Carducci
   Bolgheri Rosso Superiore Le Gonnare ($$)
9. ORNELLAIA, Castagneto Carducci
   Bolgheri Superiore Ornellaia ($$$$$)
10. PODERE SAPAIO, Castagneto Carducci
    Bolgheri Rosso Superiore Volpolo ($)
11. POGGIO AL TESORO, Castagneto Carducci
    Bolgheri Rosso Superiore Sondraia ($$$)
    Bolgheri Rosso Superiore Dedicato a Walter ($$$$)
12. Michele SATTA, Castagneto Carducci
    Bolgheri Rosso Superiore Marianova ($$$$)
13. TENUTA ARGENTIERA, Castagneto Carducci
    Bolgheri Rosso Superiore Argentiera ($$$)
14. TENUTA GUADO AL TASSO, Castagneto Carducci
    Bolgheri Rosso Superiore Guado al Tasso ($$$$)

Bolgheri Sassicaia DOC

It all began in the 1940s, when Mario Incisa della Rocchetta decided to emulate his esteemed friends in Bordeaux and plant the first Cabernet Sauvignon and Cabernet Franc vines using French vine shoots, limiting himself initially, between 1948 and 1967, to small, unmarketed productions. Success arrived as early as 1968, the first year of production, in a crescendo that led to international approval from the 1985 vintage. Between 1994, the year the designation was established, and 2012, Sassicaia was a subzone of the Bolgheri DOC, becoming an autonomous DOC in 2013. This was the only Italian case of a DOC established for a single owner. The winery's style tends not to be too rich and opulent, so it was decided to prefer the finesse of Cabernet to the richness of Merlot, with results that have led Sassicaia to become the most famous and award-winning Italian wine ever. The DOC envisages the use of at least 80% Cabernet Sauvignon in a delimited portion of the municipality of Castagneto Carducci, and annual production is around two hundred and fifty thousand bottles, sought after all over the world and quite expensive.

—

Sole producer:

15. TENUTA SAN GUIDO, Castagneto Carducci
    Bolgheri Sassicaia ($$$$$)

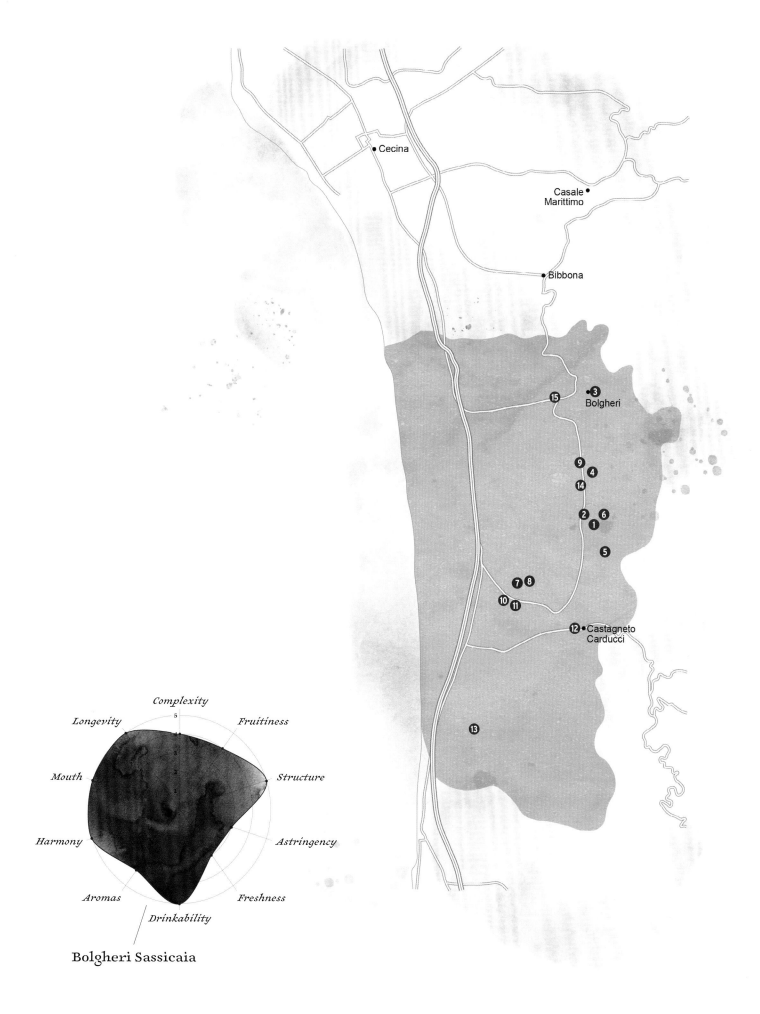

Complexity

Longevity

Fruitiness

Mouth

Structure

Harmony

Astringency

Aromas

Freshness

Drinkability

Bolgheri Sassicaia

• Cecina

Casale •
Marittimo

• Bibbona

15 • 3
Bolgheri

9
4

14

2 6
1

5

7 8

10
11

12 • Castagneto
Carducci

13

Brunello di Montalcino DOCG

The name Brunello di Montalcino originated in 1888, when Ferruccio Biondi Santi decided to name his Sangiovese "Brunello," which when aged in wood has garnered unwavering success. The reawakening of the area, however, took place gradually: in 1966, the year the Brunello di Montalcino DOC was instituted, there were only 160 acres involved and in 1980, the year the DOCG was established, there were only fifty-three farms that stated they produced Sangiovese grapes suitable for making Brunello wine. The regulations state that the wine must be put on the market no earlier than the fifth year after the harvest, must be aged in wood for at least two years, and must be made exclusively from Sangiovese grapes grown within the municipal territory of Montalcino, in the province of Siena. An area that may appear rather hot, but the good ventilation, the presence of forests, and the altitude of the vineyards, which can reach almost 2,000 feet, guarantee results that have allowed Brunello di Montalcino to be decreed one of the world's greatest red wines, also thanks to its ability to improve in the bottle for dozens of years. Montalcino is located 25 miles equidistant from both the Adriatic Sea and Siena, in an area bordered by the Orcia, Asso, and Ombrone Rivers. Within this vast municipal area—a good 120 square miles, compared to Florence's 39 and Siena's 45—vineyards are cultivated at altitudes ranging from a minimum of 395 to a maximum of 2,130 feet, as at Poggio Civitella. Three areas can be distinguished: the part to the north, facing the Val d'Orcia, produces a rather severe Brunello with good acidity; the part of the vineyards facing east is often referred to as the most harmonious and complex thanks to the perfect balance between tannins, acidity, and soft components linked to the presence of alcohol; and the area looking south toward the sea, in addition to being the largest, is the one that presents the most fruity and enveloping component in the wines, free of any harshness of acidity even in the early years. Today, just over two hundred wineries market their Brunello di Montalcino, made from a total area of 5,190 acres, with an annual production close to eleven million bottles.

Producers and their trademark and signature wines:

1. ALTESINO, Montalcino
   Brunello di Montalcino Montosoli ($$$)
2. ARGIANO, Montalcino
   Brunello di Montalcino ($$$)
   Brunello di Montalcino Vigna del Suolo ($$$$)
3. BANFI, Montalcino
   Brunello di Montalcino Riserva Poggio all'Oro ($$$$)
4. BARICCI, Montalcino
   Brunello di Montalcino Riserva Nello ($$$$)
   Brunello di Montalcino ($$$)
5. BIONDI-SANTI, Montalcino
   Brunello di Montalcino ($$$$$)
   Brunello di Montalcino Riserva ($$$$$)
6. Gianni BRUNELLI, Montalcino
   Brunello di Montalcino Riserva ($$$$)
7. CAMIGLIANO, Montalcino
   Brunello di Montalcino Riserva Gualto ($$$$)
8. CANALICCHIO DI SOPRA, Montalcino
   Brunello di Montalcino La Casaccia ($$$$)
   Brunello di Montalcino ($$$)
   Brunello di Montalcino Riserva ($$$$)
9. CAPANNA, Montalcino
   Brunello di Montalcino Riserva ($$$)
   Brunello di Montalcino ($$)
10. CAPARZO, Montalcino
    Brunello di Montalcino La Casa ($$)
11. CAPRILI, Montalcino
    Brunello di Montalcino ($$)
    Brunello di Montalcino Riserva Ad Alberto ($$$)
12. CASANOVA DI NERI, Montalcino
    Brunello di Montalcino Cerretalto ($$$$$)
    Brunello di Montalcino Tenuta Nuova ($$$)
    Brunello di Montalcino ($$$)

13. CASISANO, Montalcino
Brunello di Montalcino Riserva Colombaiolo ($$$)
14. CASTELLO ROMITORIO, Montalcino
Brunello di Montalcino Filo di Seta ($$$)
Brunello di Montalcino Riserva ($$$$)
15. CASTELLO TRICERCHI, Montalcino
Brunello di Montalcino A.D. 1441 ($$$)
16. CASTIGLION DEL BOSCO, Montalcino
Brunello di Montalcino ($$$)
Brunello di Montalcino Campo del Drago ($$$$)
17. CIACCI PICCOLOMINI D'ARAGONA, Montalcino
Brunello di Montalcino Riserva Vigna di Pianrosso
Santa Caterina d'Oro ($$$$)
Brunello di Montalcino Pianrosso ($$$)
18. Donatella CINELLI COLOMBINI, Montalcino
Brunello di Montalcino ($$)
19. COL D'ORCIA, Montalcino
Brunello di Montalcino Riserva Poggio al Vento ($$$$)
20. CORTE PAVONE, Montalcino
Brunello di Montalcino Fior di Vento ($$$)
21. COSTANTI, Montalcino
Brunello di Montalcino ($$$)
22. FATTOI, Montalcino
Brunello di Montalcino Riserva ($$$)
23. FATTORIA DEI BARBI, Montalcino
Brunello di Montalcino Riserva ($$$)
Brunello di Montalcino Vigna del Fiore ($$$)
24. FORNACINA, Montalcino
Brunello di Montalcino Riserva ($$$)
25. FULIGNI, Montalcino
Brunello di Montalcino ($$$)
Brunello di Montalcino Riserva ($$$$$)
26. GIODO, Montalcino
Brunello di Montalcino ($$$$$)
27. IL COLLE, Montalcino
Brunello di Montalcino ($$$$$)
28. IL MARRONETO, Montalcino
Brunello di Montalcino Madonna delle Grazie
($$$$$)
29. IL POGGIONE, Montalcino
Brunello di Montalcino Riserva Vigna Paganelli ($$$)
30. LA GERLA, Montalcino
Brunello di Montalcino Riserva Gli Angeli ($$$)
31. LA MAGIA, Montalcino
Brunello di Montalcino Ciliegio ($$$$)
32. LA RASINA, Montalcino
Brunello di Montalcino Persante ($$)
33. LE CHIUSE, Montalcino
Brunello di Montalcino Riserva Diecianni ($$$$)
34. LE RAGNAIE, Montalcino
Brunello di Montalcino Ragnaie V.V. ($$$)
35. LISINI, Montalcino
Brunello di Montalcino Ugolaia ($$$)
36. MASTROJANNI, Montalcino
Brunello di Montalcino Vigna Schiena
d'Asino ($$$$)

37. MOCALI, Montalcino
Brunello di Montalcino Riserva Vigna
delle Raunate ($$$)
38. Siro PACENTI, Montalcino
Brunello di Montalcino Riserva PS ($$$$)
Brunello di Montalcino Vecchie Vigne ($$$)
39. PADELLETTI, Montalcino
Brunello di Montalcino ($$)
40. PIAN DELLE QUERCI, Montalcino
Brunello di Montalcino ($$)
41. PIANCORNELLO, Montalcino
Brunello di Montalcino Riserva ($$$)
42. Agostina PIERI, Montalcino
Brunello di Montalcino ($$)
43. PIETROSO, Montalcino
Brunello di Montalcino ($$$)
Brunello di Montalcino Riserva ($$$$)
44. PIEVE SANTA RESTITUTA, Montalcino
Brunello di Montalcino Sugarille ($$$$)
45. POGGIO ANTICO, Montalcino
Brunello di Montalcino ($$$)
Brunello di Montalcino Riserva ($$$$)
46. POGGIO DI SOTTO, Montalcino
Brunello di Montalcino Riserva ($$$$$)
Brunello di Montalcino ($$$$)
47. RIDOLFI, Montalcino
Brunello di Montalcino ($$)
Brunello di Montalcino Riserva Mercatale ($$$)
48. SALVIONI – La Cerbaiola, Montalcino
Brunello di Montalcino ($$$$)
49. SAN FILIPPO, Montalcino
Brunello di Montalcino Le Lucére ($$$)
50. SANLORENZO, Montalcino
Brunello di Montalcino Bramante ($$)
51. SESTI - Castello di Argiano, Montalcino
Brunello di Montalcino ($$$)
52. TALENTI, Montalcino
Brunello di Montalcino Riserva Pian di Conte ($$$)
53. TENUTA DI SESTA, Montalcino
Brunello di Montalcino Riserva Duelecci Ovest ($$$)
54. TENUTA FANTI, Montalcino
Brunello di Montalcino ($$)
55. TENUTA LE POTAZZINE, Montalcino
Brunello di Montalcino ($$$)
56. TERRE NERE, Montalcino
Brunello di Montalcino ($$)
57. UCCELLIERA, Montalcino
Brunello di Montalcino Riserva ($$$$)
Brunello di Montalcino ($$$)
58. VAL DI SUGA, Montalcino
Brunello di Montalcino Vigna Spuntali ($$$)
59. VALDICAVA, Montalcino
Brunello di Montalcino Riserva Madonna del Piano
($$$$)
60. VILLA LE PRATA, Montalcino
Brunello di Montalcino Riserva Massimo ($$$$)

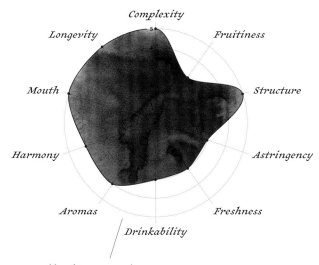

Brunello di Montalcino

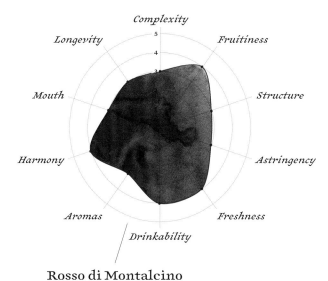

Rosso di Montalcino

Rosso di Montalcino DOC

Made exclusively from Sangiovese grapes, Rosso di Montalcino is mistakenly considered the "poor" relative—even in price—of Brunello, while more and more producers are dedicating adequate care to it both in the vineyard and in the cellar. It can be called a "spillover" DOC for Brunello di Montalcino, in that a producer can transform what was initially declared as Brunello DOCG into Rosso DOC—but not the other way around—which does not necessarily mean that it is a downgrading made necessary by unsuccessful harvests. The minimum aging required—only twelve months from the harvest—results in a wine that, compared to Brunello, is less complex and less suited to long maturation, fresher, and more immediate, but of great pleasure when made with skill and care. Annual production is close to three and a half million bottles, across 1,480 acres.

Producers and their trademark and signature wines:

4. BARICCI, Montalcino
   Rosso di Montalcino ($)
11. CAPRILI, Montalcino
   Rosso di Montalcino ($)
19. COL D'ORCIA, Montalcino
   Rosso di Montalcino Banditella ($)
61. COL DI LAMO, Montalcino
   Rosso di Montalcino ($)
28. IL MARRONETO, Montalcino
   Rosso di Montalcino Ignaccio ($$)
31. LA MAGIA, Montalcino
   Rosso di Montalcino ($)
33. LE CHIUSE, Montalcino
   Rosso di Montalcino ($)
39. Siro PACENTI, Montalcino
   Rosso di Montalcino ($$)
62. PIAN DELL'ORINO, Montalcino
   Rosso di Montalcino ($$)
46. POGGIO DI SOTTO, Montalcino
   Rosso di Montalcino Ciampoleto
   San Giorgio ($)
48. SALVIONI - La Cerbaiola, Montalcino
   Rosso di Montalcino ($$$)
63. STELLA DI CAMPALTO, Montalcino
   Rosso di Montalcino Podere S. Giuseppe ($$$)
57. UCCELLIERA, Montalcino
   Rosso di Montalcino ($)

Chianti DOCG

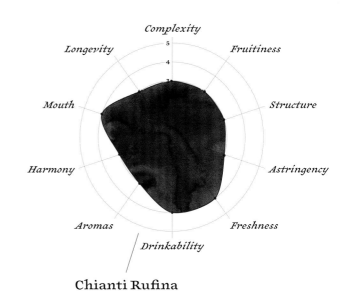

Chianti Rufina

On the strength of a prestigious centuries-old tradition, in which there have been changes in both the composition of the grapes and cellar techniques, Chianti must be produced with between 70 and 100% Sangiovese. Its longstanding commercial success was reinvigorated when, with the establishment of DOC status in 1967, the famous wine conquered the tables of half the world, starting with the increasingly popular Italian restaurants in the United States. The production area is vast, ranging from the vineyards north of Florence to those south of Siena, and has been subdivided by the regulations into seven subzones, which can be found on the label: Colli Aretini, Colli Fiorentini, Colli Senesi, Colline Pisane, Montalbano, Montespertoli, and Rufina. The taste characteristics are therefore also slightly different, ranging between the fresh, streamlined Chianti Rufina and the warmer, fruitier Chianti Colli Senesi. With the extra stylistic complexity due to the grapes that may potentially be added to Sangiovese, and besides the historic local varieties, the regulations state that Cabernet Franc and Cabernet Sauvignon may not exceed 15%, or 10% in the case of Colli Senesi. There are excellent expressions of Chianti with or without the indication of a subzone, but it is Chianti Rufina that has garnered the most recognition, so much so that discussions are underway regarding the possibility in the near future of its own autonomous DOCG. Annual production is around one hundred million bottles.

—

Producers and their trademark and signature wines:

Chianti Classico

1. CASTELLO DEL TREBBIO, Pontassieve
   Chianti Rufina Riserva Lastricato ($)
2. CORZANO E PATERNO, San Casciano in Val di Pesa
   Chianti Terre di Corzano ($)
3. FATTORIA SELVAPIANA, Rufina
   Chianti Rufina Riserva Vigneto Bucerchiale ($$)
4. FRASCOLE, Dicomano
   Chianti Rufina Riserva ($$)
5. FRESCOBALDI, Pelago
   Chianti Rúfina Riserva Nipozzano ($)
   Chianti Rúfina Nipozzano Riserva Vecchie Viti ($)
6. Guido GUALANDI, Montespertoli
   Chianti Colli Fiorentini Montebetti ($)
7. LA QUERCE, Impruneta
   Chianti Colli Fiorentini Riserva La Torretta ($)
8. Giacomo MORI, San Casciano dei Bagni
   Chianti ($)
9. POGGIOTONDO, Cerreto Guidi
   Chianti Superiore ($)
10. TENUTA SAN VITO, Montelupo Fiorentino
    Chianti Colli Fiorentini Riserva Madiere ($)
    Chianti Colli Fiorentini Darno ($)
11. TORRE A CONA, Rignano sull'Arno
    Chianti Colli Fiorentini Riserva Terre di Cino ($$)
    Chianti Colli Fiorentini Riserva Badia a Corte ($)

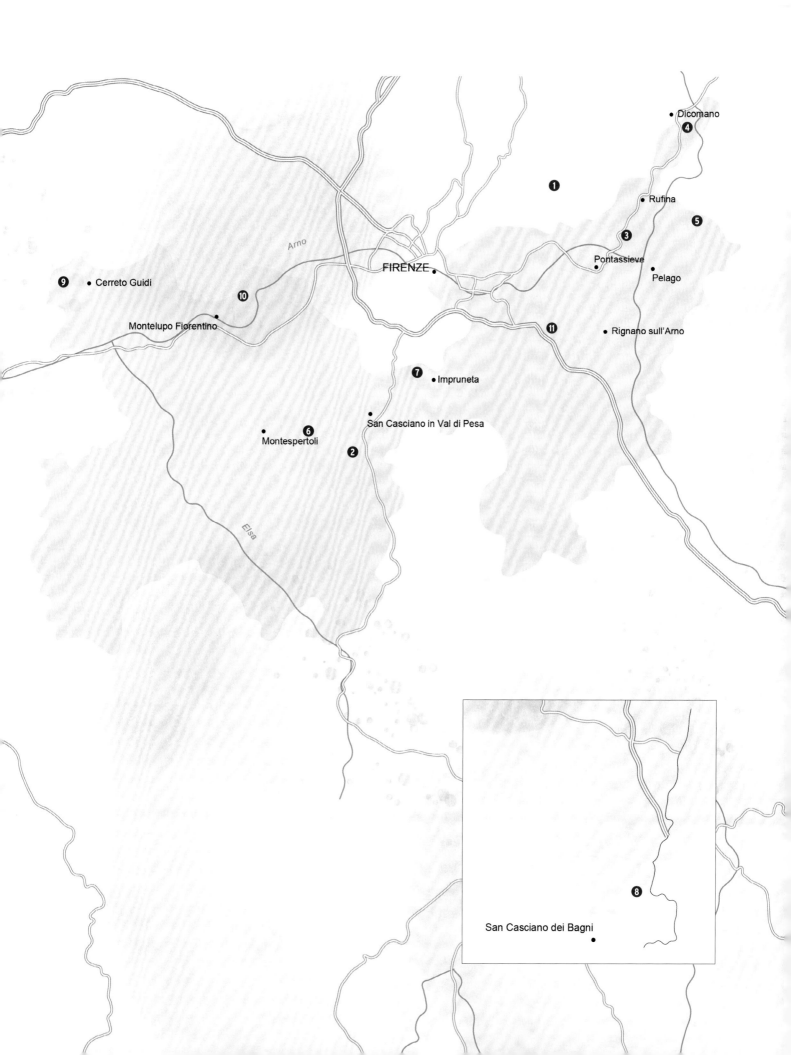

Dicomano
❹

❶

Rufina

❺

❸
Pontassieve

Pelago

❾ Cerreto Guidi

Arno

FIRENZE

❿

Montelupo Fiorentino

❶❶

Rignano sull'Arno

❼ Impruneta

San Casciano in Val di Pesa

❻
Montespertoli

❷

Elsa

❽

San Casciano dei Bagni

Chianti Classico DOCG

Chianti Classico comes from the soil of one of the world's most evocative winegrowing areas, with 17,000 acres spread across the provinces of Florence and Siena, where the ground was first cultivated by the Etruscans and Romans. The total surface area of Chianti Classico is 184,000 acres, and the wine was only given its own DOCG in 1996. The whole of the four Chianti districts of Greve, Castellina, Radda, and Gaiole are involved in viticulture, while parts of Castelnuovo Berardenga, Poggibonsi, San Casciano in Val di Pesa, and Barberino Tavarnelle are under cultivation as well. The production guidelines for Chianti Classico specify that Sangiovese grapes should be used for somewhere between 80% to 100%, with the possible addition of red grapes allowed, so long as they are from the Region of Tuscany. Since this production area is so vast, there are considerable variations both in the composition of the soil and the height of the land, which results in a certain variety of flavors, further influenced by the individual producers themselves. There are those who just use Sangiovese in its pure form, some who add small percentages of local Colorino and Canaiolo, and others who prefer a slight touch of Cabernet Sauvignon or Merlot; some use large Slavonian oak barrels, while others still favor casks. There are 350 wineries in the *Consorzio Chianti Classico* who produce wine and bottle it under their own labels, all with the distinctive black rooster logo, or Gallo Nero, which comes from the emblem of the Lega del Chianti, a political-military league founded in 1384. The producers' consortium has established a clearly defined project whose aim is to create and firmly maintain both the image of the region and the quality of wine coming from it, and these include modifications to the production. As of 2014, in addition to the two varieties called Chianti Classico and Chianti Classico Riserva, highlights of the label include the Gran Selezione, which is manufactured under careful and strict scrutiny, ensuring that the percentage of Sangiovese grapes used is at least 90%. Furthermore, since 2022 there are now the so-called *Unità Geografiche Aggiuntive* (UGA, or Additional Geographical Units), which are eleven place names so far reserved for the Gran Selezione. These names help to strengthen the close ties between Chianti Classico and the main areas where the grapes are grown. These are Castellina, Castelnuovo Berardenga, Gaiole, Greve, Lamole, Montefioralle, Panzano, Radda, San Casciano, San Donato in Poggio, and Vagliagli. This is different from what happens in Piedmont where the *Menzioni Geografiche Aggiuntive* (MGA, or Additional Geographical Indications) holds sway with the brands of Barbaresco, Barolo, and Roero, where under each MGA several dozen specific, award-winning vineyards are named. Chianti Classico is one of the great Italian wines, complex and whose signature is a characteristic freshness of flavor, not too astringent, with hits on the nose and palate that range from cherry to violet and from wild mint to leather, suitable for ten-year aging in the bottle. Compared to Brunello di Montalcino and to Vino Nobile di Montepulciano, the two celebrated Sangiovese-based *Denominazioni* that come from the more southern part of Tuscany, against which other wines are often measured, it can generally be said that here we come across a more streamlined yet incisive body, just a little less rounded on account of the slightly cooler climate. This commitment to quality by hundreds of vineyards has now been recognized worldwide, with American wine critics being among the first to give Chianti Classico products the renowned 100/100-point rating. The yearly production is around thirty-six million bottles.

—

Producers and their trademark and signature wines:

1. Maurizio ALONGI, Gaiole in Chianti
   Chianti Classico Vigna Barbischio ($$)
2. ARILLO IN TERRABIANCA, Radda in Chianti
   Chianti Classico Poggio Croce ($)
3. BADIA A COLTIBUONO, Gaiole in Chianti
   Chianti Classico Riserva Cultus ($)
   Chianti Classico ($)
4. BARONE RICASOLI, Gaiole in Chianti
   Chianti Classico Gran Selezione Ceni Primo ($$)
   Chianti Classico Gran Selezione Colledilà ($$$)
   Chianti Classico Gran Selezione Castello di Brolio ($$)
5. BRANCAIA, Radda in Chianti
   Chianti Classico Riserva ($$)
6. BUONDONNO - Casavecchia alla Piazza,
   Castellina in Chianti
   Chianti Classico ($)
7. CANDIALLE, Greve in Chianti
   Chianti Classico Riserva ($$)
8. CAPANNELLE, Gaiole in Chianti
   Chianti Classico Gran Selezione ($$)
9. CAPARSA, Radda in Chianti
   Chianti Classico Riserva Doccio a Matteo ($$)
   Chianti Classico ($)
10. CASTELL'IN VILLA, Castelnuovo Berardenga
    Chianti Classico Riserva ($$$$)
    Chianti Classico ($$)
11. CASTELLO DI ALBOLA, Radda in Chianti
    Chianti Classico Gran Selezione Il Solatio ($$)
    Chianti Classico Riserva ($)
12. CASTELLO DI AMA, Gaiole in Chianti
    Chianti Classico Gran Selezione La Casuccia ($$$$$)
    Chianti Classico Ama ($)
    Chianti Classico Gran Selezione San Lorenzo ($$)
13. CASTELLO DI CACCHIANO, Gaiole in Chianti
    Chianti Classico Gran Selezione Millennio ($$)
14. CASTELLO DI FONTERUTOLI, Castellina in Chianti
    Chianti Classico Gran Selezione Badiòla ($$$)
    Chianti Classico Gran Selezione Castello di
    Fonterutoli ($$)
15. CASTELLO DI MONSANTO, Barberino Tavarnelle
    Chianti Classico Gran Selezione Il Poggio ($$$)
    Chianti Classico Riserva ($)
16. CASTELLO DI QUERCETO, Greve in Chianti
    Chianti Classico Gran Selezione La Corte ($$)

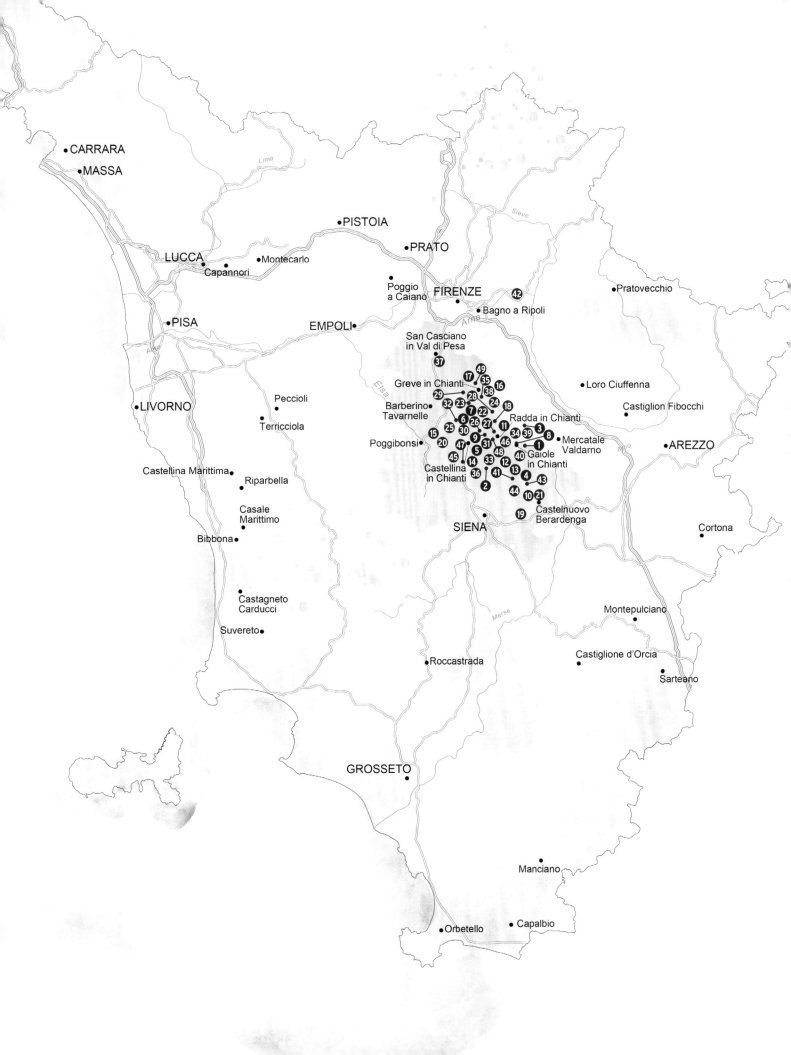

CARRARA

MASSA

PISTOIA

•PRATO

LUCCA   •Montecarlo
•Capannori

•Poggio
a Caiano   FIRENZE
•Bagno a Ripoli   ㊷   •Pratovecchio

•PISA   EMPOLI•

San Casciano
in Val di Pesa   •Loro Ciuffenna

㊲   •Castiglion Fibocchi

Peccioli   ㊾
㉟ ⑯
Greve in Chianti   ⑰   ㊳
⑯
•LIVORNO   ㉙   ㉘   ㉔
•Terricciola   Barberino   ㉜ ㉓ ㉒ ⑱
Tavarnelle   ⑥ ㉖ ㉗   Radda in Chianti
⑮ ㉕ ㉚ ⑨   ⑪ ㉞ ㊴ ③
⑳ ㊼   ⑤ ㉛ ㊻ ① ⑧   •AREZZO
Poggibonsi•   ⑨   ㊻   Mercatale
㊺ ⑭ ㉝ ⑫ ㊵   Valdarno
Castellina Marittima   ㊱ ④ ⑬ ④   Gaiole
in Chianti
Castellina   ②   ㊹ ㊸
•Riparbella   in Chianti   ⑩ ㉑   •Cortona
⑲   Castelnuovo
Casale   Berardenga
Marittimo

Bibbona•   SIENA

Montepulciano

Castagneto
Carducci   Castiglione d'Orcia

Suvereto•   •Sarteano

Roccastrada•

GROSSETO   Merse

Manciano

Orbetello•   •Capalbio

17. CASTELLO DI VERRAZZANO, Greve in Chianti
Chianti Classico Gran Selezione Valdonica ($$)
18. CASTELLO DI VOLPAIA, Radda in Chianti
Chianti Classico Gran Selezione Coltassala ($$)
Chianti Classico Riserva ($$)
Chianti Classico ($)
19. FATTORIA CARPINETA FONTALPINO,
Castelnuovo Berardenga
Chianti Classico Fontalpino ($)
Chianti Classico Montaperto ($$)
20. FATTORIA ORMANNI, Poggibonsi
Chianti Classico Riserva Borro del Diavolo ($)
21. FÈLSINA, Castelnuovo Berardenga
Chianti Classico Riserva Rancia ($$)
Chianti Classico Gran Selezione Colonia ($$$)
22. FONTODI, Greve in Chianti
Chianti Classico Gran Selezione Vigna del Sorbo ($$$)
23. GAGLIOLE, Greve in Chianti
Chianti Classico Riserva ($)
24. I FABBRI, Greve in Chianti
Chianti Classico Lamole ($)
25. ISOLE E OLENA, Barberino Tavarnelle
Chianti Classico ($)
26. ISTINE, Radda in Chianti
Chianti Classico Vigna Cavarchione ($$)
Chianti Classico Riserva Levigne ($$)
Chianti Classico Vigna Istine ($)
27. L'ERTA DI RADDA, Radda in Chianti
Chianti Classico ($)
28. LAMOLE DI LAMOLE, Greve in Chianti
Chianti Classico Gran Selezione Vigna Grospoli ($$)
29. LE CINCIOLE, Greve in Chianti
Chianti Classico Gran Selezione Aluigi Campo ai Peri ($$)
30. MONTE BERNARDI, Greve in Chianti
Chianti Classico Sa'etta ($$)
31. MONTERAPONI, Radda in Chianti
Chianti Classico Riserva Il Campitello ($$)
32. NITTARDI, Castellina in Chianti
Chianti Classico Vigna Doghessa ($$)
Chianti Classico Riserva ($$)
33. PODERE IL PALAZZINO, Gaiole in Chianti
Chianti Classico Argenina ($)
34. POGGERINO, Radda in Chianti
Chianti Classico Riserva Bugialla ($$)
35. POGGIO AL SOLE, Barberino Tavarnelle
Chianti Classico ($)
Chianti Classico Gran Selezione Casasilia ($$)
36. POMONA, Castellina in Chianti
Chianti Classico ($)
37. PRINCIPE CORSINI - Villa Le Corti,
San Casciano in Val di Pesa
Chianti Classico Gran Selezione Don Tommaso ($$)
38. QUERCIABELLA, Greve in Chianti
Chianti Classico Riserva ($$)
Chianti Classico ($)

39. RIECINE, Gaiole in Chianti
Chianti Classico Riserva ($$)
Chianti Classico ($)
40. ROCCA DI CASTAGNOLI, Gaiole in Chianti
Chianti Classico Riserva Capraia ($)
41. ROCCA DI MONTEGROSSI, Gaiole in Chianti
Chianti Classico Gran Selezione Vigneto San
Marcellino ($$)
42. RUFFINO, Bagno a Ripoli
Chianti Classico Riserva Ducale ($)
43. SAN FELICE, Castelnuovo Berardenga
Chianti Classico Gran Selezione Il Grigio ($)
44. SAN GIUSTO A RENTENNANO, Gaiole in Chianti
Chianti Classico Riserva Le Baroncole ($$)
Chianti Classico ($)
45. TENUTA DI BIBBIANO, Castellina in Chianti
Chianti Classico Gran Selezione Vigna del Capannino
($$)
46. TENUTA DI CARLEONE, Radda in Chianti
Chianti Classico ($)
47. TENUTA DI LILLIANO, Castellina in Chianti
Chianti Classico Gran Selezione ($$)
Chianti Classico Riserva ($)
48. VAL DELLE CORTI, Radda in Chianti
Chianti Classico Riserva ($$)
49. VILLA CALCINAIA, Greve in Chianti
Chianti Classico Gran Selezione Vigna Bastignano ($$$)

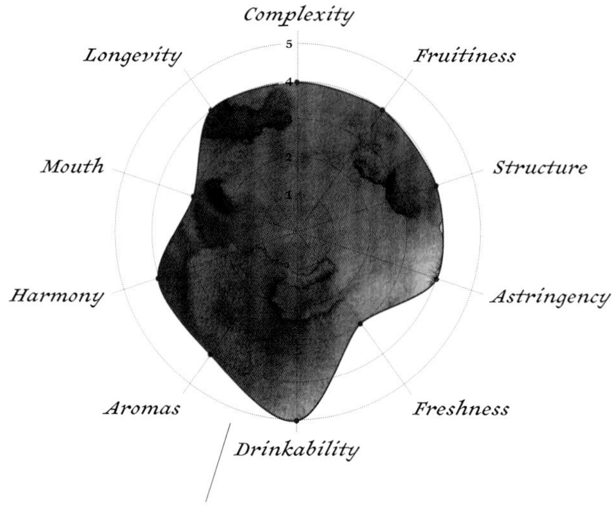

Vino Nobile di Montepulciano

Vino Nobile
di Montepulciano DOCG

It is produced exclusively in the hilly areas of the splendid municipality of Montepulciano and derives at least 70% from Sangiovese grapes, which are here called Prugnolo Gentile. There are possible permutations of additions of Canaiolo for no more than 20%, as well as other varieties to round it out. The rather clayey soils, combined with a slightly harsher and more continental climate than in Montalcino, create a robust and slightly tannic wine—according to some critics slightly more fruity and ripe than the best examples of Chianti Classico. It can be put on the market from January of the third year after the harvest, after mandatory aging in wood for at least twelve months. Montepulciano was already known at the time of the Etruscans for the quality of its wine, which took on the formal designation of Vino Nobile di Montepulciano from the eighteenth century onward, culminating in the recognition of DOC in 1966 and DOCG in 1980. A procedure set in place by the Consorzio del Vino Nobile is underway to enhance the various production territories through the recognition of twelve Additional Geographical Units, which will allow the wording "Pieve di . . ." to be placed before the DOCG name. Annual production, which is growing slightly, is close to eight million bottles, 70% of which are exported from 2,965 acres under vine.

Producers and their trademark and signature wines:

1. AVIGNONESI, Montepulciano
   Vino Nobile di Montepulciano ($)
2. BINDELLA, Montepulciano
   Vino Nobile di Montepulciano I Quadri ($$)
3. BOSCARELLI, Montepulciano
   Vino Nobile di Montepulciano Il Nocio ($$$)
   Vino Nobile di Montepulciano Costa Grande ($$$)
   Vino Nobile di Montepulciano ($)
4. CONTUCCI, Montepulciano
   Vino Nobile di Montepulciano Pietra Rossa ($)
5. DEI, Montepulciano
   Vino Nobile di Montepulciano Madonna della Querce ($$$)
   Vino Nobile di Montepulciano ($$)
6. LE BÈRNE, Montepulciano
   Vino Nobile di Montepulciano ($)
7. PODERI SANGUINETO I E II, Montepulciano
   Vino Nobile di Montepulciano ($$)
8. POLIZIANO, Montepulciano
   Vino Nobile di Montepulciano Asinone ($$)
   Vino Nobile di Montepulciano Le Caggiole ($$$)
9. SALCHETO, Montepulciano
   Vino Nobile di Montepulciano Vecchie Viti del Salco ($$$)
10. TENUTA TREROSE, Montepulciano
    Vino Nobile di Montepulciano Riserva Simposio ($$)
11. TENUTA VALDIPIATTA, Montepulciano
    Vino Nobile di Montepulciano Vigna d'Alfiero ($$)

Orcia DOC

Although the DOC provides for White, Rosé, and Vin Santo types, this valley nestled between Montalcino and Montepulciano is the kingdom of Sangiovese. It is an area in constant qualitative growth, thanks to the remarkable efforts of some twenty wine cellars, and here we mention the one that has won the most critical acclaim so far. Production is around five hundred thousand bottles per year, and growing steadily.

—

Producer and its trademark and signature wines:

12. PODERE FORTE, Castiglione d'Orcia
     Orcia Sangiovese Petrucci Melo ($$$$)
     Orcia Petruccino ($$$)

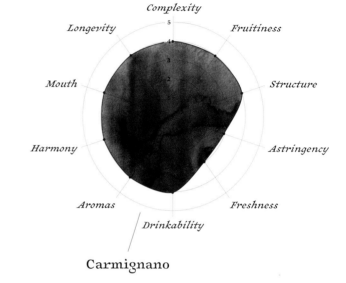

Carmignano

Carmignano DOCG

The Sangiovese grape remains the central one in this small DOCG in the province of Prato, where the regulations envisage a minimum presence of 50% of the grape, but it is worth noting that, together with other local grapes, the presence of Cabernet Sauvignon and/or Franc between 10 and 20% is mandatory. With its characteristic more vegetal and herbaceous nuances, it is a successful variant of Chianti Classico, which has earned its own DOCG thanks to the celebrity achieved over the centuries by the vineyards of this area, recognized for their excellence as early as the Renaissance. About six hundred thousand bottles are produced annually.

—

Producers and their trademark and signature wines:

1. ARTIMINO, Carmignano
    Carmignano Riserva Vigna Grumarello ($$)
2. CAPEZZANA, Carmignano
    Carmignano Villa di Capezzana ($$)
3. FATTORIA AMBRA, Carmignano
    Carmignano Santa Cristina in Pilli ($$)
4. FATTORIA DI BACCHERETO, Carmignano
    Carmignano Terre a Mano ($$)
5. PIAGGIA, Poggio a Caiano
    Carmignano Riserva Piaggia ($)
6. Fabrizio PRATESI, Carmignano
    Carmignano Riserva Il Circo Rosso ($)
7. TENUTA LE FARNETE, Carmignano
    Carmignano Riserva ($)

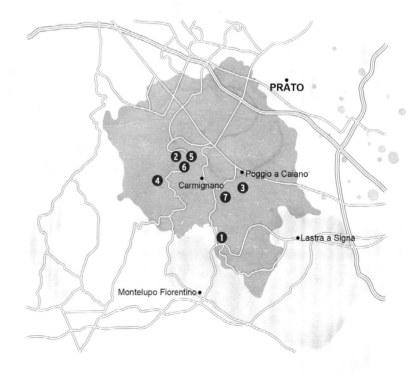

Cortona DOC

A DOC that exclusively includes the vineyards cultivated in the municipality of Cortona, in the province of Arezzo, with a total area of no less than 132 square miles. It lies in that part of the Val di Chiana not far from the border with the Umbria region and with Lake Trasimene, with a vast choice of white and red, local and international varieties. Viticulture, present since Etruscan times, began to take on importance only after impressive land reclamation work started in the sixteenth century by the Medici, but the real revolution did not begin until the 1980s, when the transition from traditional quantitative agriculture to agriculture based on high-density planting took place. Since then, Syrah cultivation has developed significantly, so much so that by now Cortona DOC has become synonymous with Cortona Syrah. The most commonly encountered aromas are those of blackberry, raspberry, and olive, while the flavor is always dense, with nonaggressive tannicity and acidity. The Tenimenti D'Alessandro, founded in 1967, remain excellent interpreters of the grape variety, even though they have chosen not to use the DOC designation. Overall annual production is close to one million bottles.

—

Producers and their trademark and signature wines:

1. Stefano AMERIGHI, Cortona
   Cortona Syrah ($$)
2. Fabrizio DIONISIO, Cortona
   Cortona Syrah Il Castagno ($)
3. TREVISAN, Cortona
   Cortona Syrah Candito ($$)

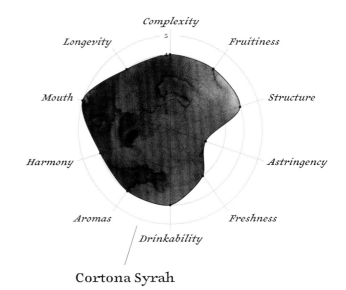

Cortona Syrah

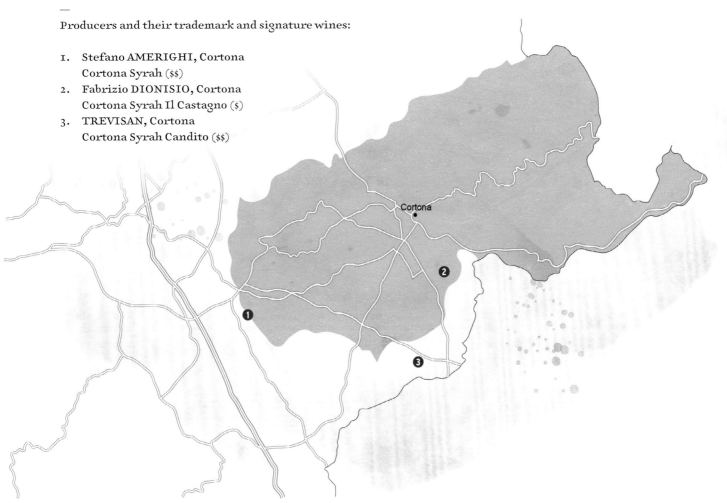

Vernaccia
di San Gimignano DOCG

Tuscany's best known and most consumed DOCG white wine originates exclusively in the municipality of San Gimignano, in the province of Siena, from the Vernaccia grapes of the same name. It should be noted that Vernaccia di San Gimignano was, in 1966, the first Italian wine to obtain DOC status, later becoming a DOCG in 1993. It has been praised by writers and artists since the Middle Ages. It is a wine as delicate as it is rich in olfactory nuances, ranging from citrus to resin to white fruits, with interesting saline and iodine notes during aging. On the palate it always offers a good savory bite and pleasant freshness, without excessive alcoholicity. Annual production exceeds five million bottles, more than 50% of which are exported.

—

Producers and their trademark
and signature wines:

1. CAPPELLASANTANDREA, San Gimignano
    Vernaccia di San Gimignano Rialto ($)
2. CASA ALLE VACCHE, San Gimignano
    Vernaccia di San Gimignano Riserva Crocus ($)
3. CESANI, San Gimignano
    Vernaccia di San Gimignano Riserva Sanice ($)
4. FONTALEONI, San Gimignano
    Vernaccia di San Gimignano ($)
5. IL COLOMBAIO DI SANTA CHIARA, San
    Gimignano
    Vernaccia di San Gimignano Riserva
    L'Albereta ($$)
    Vernaccia di San Gimignano Campo della
    Pieve ($)
6. IL PALAGIONE, San Gimignano
    Vernaccia di San Gimignano Riserva Ori ($)
7. LA LASTRA, San Gimignano
    Vernaccia di San Gimignano Riserva ($)
8. MONTENIDOLI, San Gimignano
    Vernaccia di San Gimignano Carato ($$)
    Vernaccia di San Gimignano Tradizionale ($)
9. PANIZZI, San Gimignano
    Vernaccia di San Gimignano Riserva ($)
    Vernaccia di San Gimignano Vigna Santa
    Margherita ($)
10. TENUTA LE CALCINAIE, San Gimignano
    Vernaccia di San Gimignano Riserva Vigna
    ai Sassi ($)

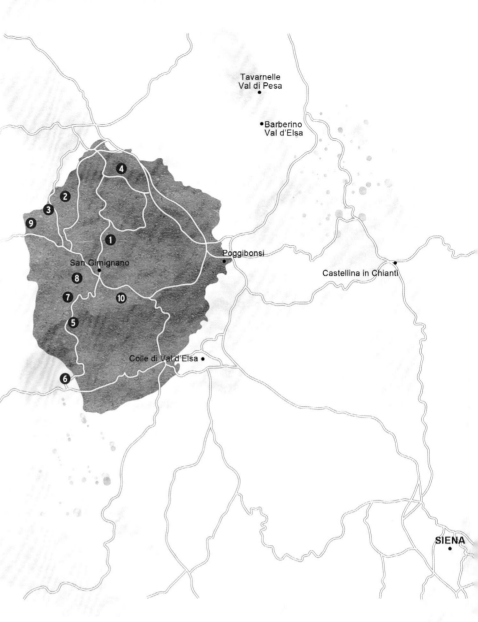

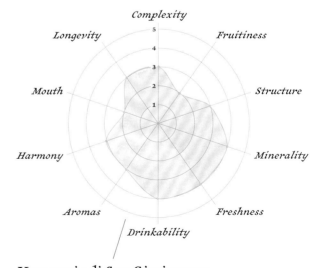

Vernaccia di San Gimignano

Terre di Pisa DOC

A DOC encompassing seventeen municipalities in
the province of Pisa, dedicated only to red wines and
recognized in 2011, and which mainly uses Sangiovese.
But there is also the Terre di Pisa Rosso type, in which
Bordeaux and Syrah grapes are widely used. There are
clear similarities between a Terre di Pisa Sangiovese
and a good Chianti. Annual production is limited to
less than three hundred thousand bottles.

—

Producers and their trademark
and signature wines:

1. BADIA DI MORRONA, Terricciola
   Terre di Pisa Sangiovese VignaAlta ($)
2. TENUTADIGHIZZANO-VenerosiPesciolini,
   Peccioli
   Terre di Pisa Sangiovese Mimesi ($$)

Colline Lucchesi DOC

A small DOC, which is relative only to the municipalities
of Lucca, Capannori, and Porcari, which includes
numerous types: the most relevant and positive results
are obtained from Sangiovese grapes, present in the
Rosso between 45 and 70%, to which both traditional and
international varieties are blended. Annual production
does not exceed three hundred thousand bottles.

—

Producer and its trademark
and signature wines:

3. TENUTA DI VALGIANO, Capannori
   Colline Lucchesi Rosso Tenuta di Valgiano
   (sangiovese; syrah, merlot) ($$$)
   Colline Lucchesi Rosso Palistorti di Valgiano
   (sangiovese; merlot, syrah) ($)

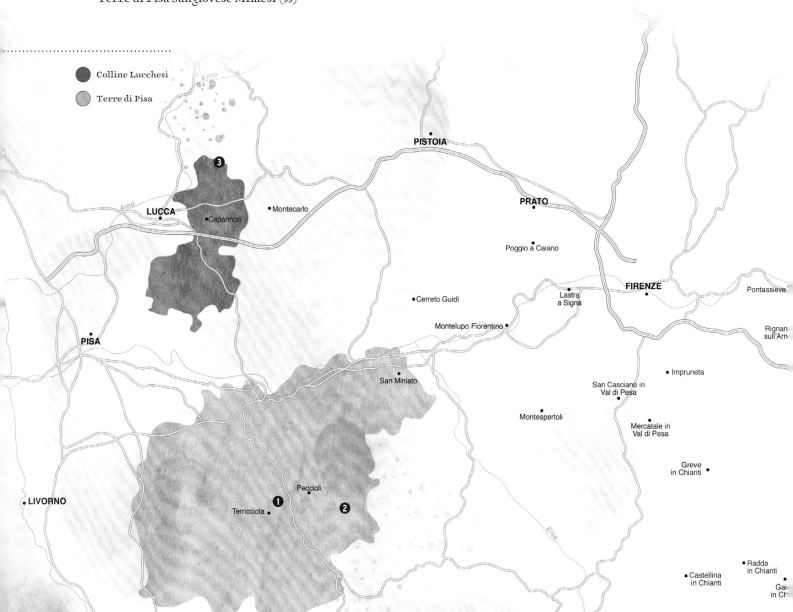

Colline Lucchesi
Terre di Pisa

Val d'Arno di Sopra
or Valdarno di Sopra DOC

In this area in the province of Arezzo, both classic Sangiovese and red grapes from the South of France have performed well, without forgetting small quantities of traditional white or Burgundy grapes. Fewer than thirty wineries currently use this DOC, clearly aiming high however, for a total annual production close to five hundred thousand bottles, and growing.

—

Producers and their trademark and signature wines:

1. IL BORRO, Loro Ciuffenna
    Valdarno di Sopra Sangiovese
    Vigna Polissena ($$)
2. PETROLO, Bucine
    Val d'Arno di Sopra Merlot
    Vigna Galatrona ($$$$)
    Val d'Arno di Sopra Sangiovese (dal 2019) Riserva
    Bòggina C ($$$)
3. TENUTA SETTE PONTI, Castiglion Fibocchi
    Valdarno di Sopra Sangiovese
    Vigna dell'Impero ($$$)

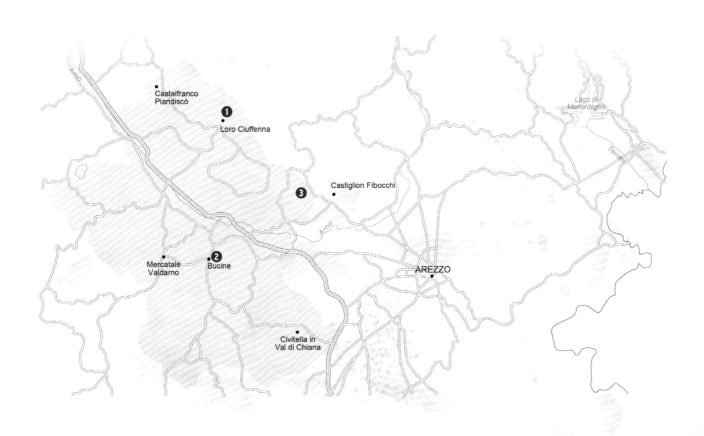

Ansonica Costa dell'Argentario DOC

The white Inzolia grape variety, of Sicilian origin, has also spread to Tuscany, particularly in the southern area of the province of Grosseto and the islands of Giglio and Argentario, where it has taken on the name Ansonica. The aromas are reminiscent of white fruits and herbs, while the palate always maintains a discreet acidic freshness to guarantee pleasant drinkability. Production is less than one hundred thousand bottles per year.

—

Producer and its trademark and signature wine:

1. ANTICA FATTORIA LA PARRINA, Orbetello
    Ansonica Costa dell'Argentario ($)

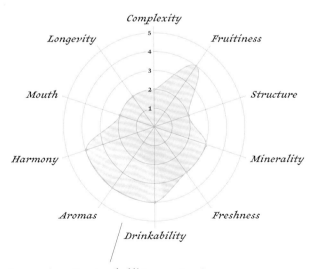

Ansonica Costa dell'Argentario

Bianco di Pitigliano DOC

A simple and straightforward white wine, lively and fresh, certainly pleasant when well vinified, usually aged only in steel and put on the market a few months after the harvest. The most important grape is Trebbiano, which must be present for at least 40%, to which Grechetto, Malvasia, and other white grapes are added. About 1.3 million bottles are produced annually in four municipalities in the province of Grosseto, including Pitigliano.

—

Producer and its trademark and signature wine:

2. SASSOTONDO, Sorano
    Bianco di Pitigliano Superiore Isolina ($)

Maremma Toscana DOC

Established relatively recently, in 2011, this DOC includes the entire territory of the province of Grosseto, thus the southernmost and warmest area of Tuscany. The traditional grape varieties of the area—Alicante and Ciliegiolo among the reds, Vermentino among the whites—are accompanied with interesting results by productions from Bordeaux, such as Cabernet Sauvignon, Merlot, and Cabernet Franc, and from the Rhone with Syrah. Annual production exceeds eleven million bottles.

—

Producers and their trademark and signature wines:

3. BRUNI, Orbetello
    Maremma Toscana Alicante Oltreconfine ($)
4. Antonio CAMILLO, Manciano
    Maremma Toscana Ciliegiolo
    Vigna Vallerana Alta ($$)
5. LE SODE DI SANT'ANGELO, Montebamboli
    Maremma Toscana Vermentino
    Le Gessaie ($)
6. ROCCA DI FRASSINELLO, Gavorrano
    Maremma Toscana Merlot Baffonero ($$$$)
7. ROCCA DI MONTEMASSI, Roccastrada
    Maremma Toscana Rosso
    Rocca di Montemassi ($$)
2. SASSOTONDO, Sorano
    Maremma Toscana Ciliegiolo
    San Lorenzo ($$)

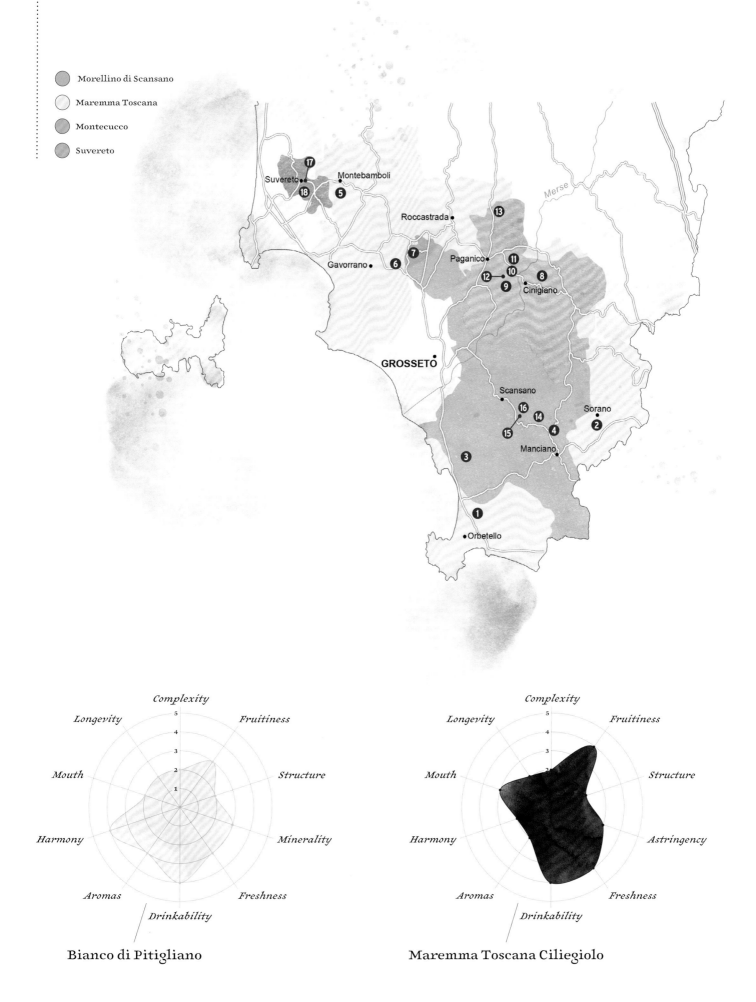

Legend

- Morellino di Scansano
- Maremma Toscana
- Montecucco
- Suvereto

Map labels

17
Suvereto
18
Montebamboli
5
Roccastrada
7
Paganico
6
Gavorrano
13
11
12 10
9
8
Cinigiano
GROSSETO
Scansano
16
14
Sorano
15
4
2
Manciano
3
1
Orbetello
Merse

Bianco di Pitigliano

Complexity
Longevity
Fruitiness
Mouth
Structure
Harmony
Minerality
Aromas
Freshness
Drinkability

Maremma Toscana Ciliegiolo

Complexity
Longevity
Fruitiness
Mouth
Structure
Harmony
Astringency
Aromas
Freshness
Drinkability

Montecucco Sangiovese DOCG and Montecucco DOC

A small area within the province of Grosseto, with the DOCG dedicated to Sangiovese, which must make up at least 90% of grape content, while the DOC also includes the presence of the Bianco, Vermentino, Rosato, and Vin Santo types, as well as a Rosso in which Sangiovese is required for at least 60%. Being a rather warm area, the Sangiovese-based wines produced have a slightly lower acidity and a more evident red fruit component than in the neighboring Chianti Classico zone. Annual production is around seven hundred thousand bottles for DOC and just over one million for DOCG.

—

Producers and their trademark and signature wines:

8. BASILE, Cinigiano
   Montecucco Sangiovese Riserva Ad Agio ($$)
9. COLLEMASSARI, Cinigiano
   Montecucco Sangiovese Riserva Poggio Lombrone ($$)
   Montecucco Rosso Riserva ($)
10. LE CALLE, Cinigiano
    Montecucco Sangiovese Riserva Poggio d'Oro ($)
11. PIANIROSSI, Cinigiano
    Montecucco Rosso Sidus ($)
12. SALUSTRI, Cinigiano
    Montecucco Sangiovese Grotte Rosse ($$)
13. TENUTA L'IMPOSTINO, Paganico
    Montecucco Sangiovese Riserva Viandante ($)

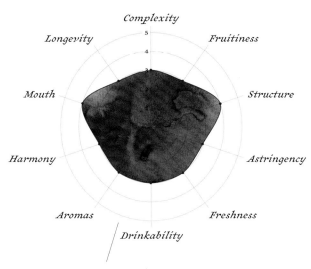

Montecucco Sangiovese

Morellino di Scansano DOCG

Morellino is the name given locally to Sangiovese, at least 85% of which is present in this DOCG that has seen continuous growth in recent years. The production area is made up of a stretch of hillside that runs from the provincial capital, Grosseto. The result is wines that are rather easy and straightforward when aged exclusively in steel, while the Riserva version, for which at least one year's maturation in wood is required, often has the characteristics of complexity typical of the Sangiovese grape. It differs from Chianti Classico, as this is a warmer area, by its slightly more intense color and a palate more characterized by ripe notes. Approximately ten million bottles are produced annually.

—

Producers and their trademark and signature wines:

14. Erik BANTI, Scansano
    Morellino di Scansano Ciabatta ($)
3. BRUNI, Orbetello
   Morellino di Scansano Riserva Laire ($)
15. ROCCAPESTA, Scansano
    Morellino di Scansano Riserva Calestaia ($$)
16. TERENZI, Scansano
    Morellino di Scansano Riserva Madrechiesa ($$)

Morellino di Scansano

Suvereto DOCG

This small and recent DOCG covers a small part of the territory of the municipality of Suvereto, which itself covers a total of 36 square miles, and mainly involves the use of classic Bordeaux vines, although there are also Sangiovese-based blends. On the splendid hills that rise from the Cornia River, 19 miles from Bolgheri, there are already about twenty active wineries, although some do not use the DOCG, such as Tua Rita. In 2021, the Consorzio di Tutela Suvereto e Val di Cornia was established, with twenty-seven member wineries. Annual production is around three hundred thousand bottles, with a marked increase.

—

Producers and their trademark
and signature wines:

17. BULICHELLA, Suvereto
    Suvereto Montecristo ($$$)
    Suvereto Coldipietrerosse ($$)
18. GUALDO DEL RE, Suvereto
    Suvereto Merlot I' Rennero ($$)

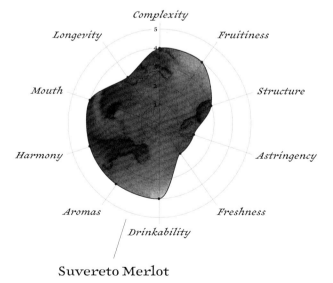

Suvereto Merlot

Vin Santo
– del Chianti DOC
– del Chianti Classico DOC
– di Carmignano DOC
– di Montepulciano DOC

Trebbiano Toscano and Malvasia Bianca, which at one time also formed part of the composition of the various types of Chianti wine, are the basis of the famous Tuscan Vin Santo. The dried grapes are aged for years in small barrels called *caratelli*, and then slightly drained when, at the end of fermentation, the wine is rather alcoholic, golden, and rich in aromas of walnuts, dried figs, and apricots, with a dense and still rather sweet taste thanks to the residual sugars. Using the same process, but starting mainly from Sangiovese grapes, the prized Vin Santo Occhio di Pernice is obtained. While not as popular with consumers as it once was, when the custom of ending the meal with a sweet wine was widespread, it is particularly suited to accompanying biscuits or dry sweets or as a nightcap. The total annual production is around seven hundred and fifty thousand bottles, mostly of small format.

—

Producers and their trademark and signature wines:

1. AVIGNONESI, Montepulciano
   Vin Santo di Montepulciano Occhio di Pernice ($$$$$)
2. BARONE RICASOLI, Gaiole in Chianti
   Vin Santo del Chianti Classico Castello di Brolio ($$)
3. Pietro BECONCINI, San Miniato
   Vin Santo del Chianti Occhio di Pernice Aria ($$)

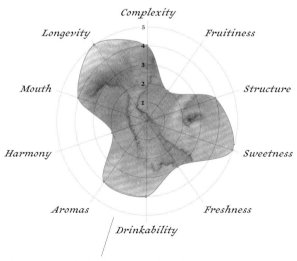

Vin Santo del Chianti Classico

4. BOSCARELLI, Montepulciano
   Vin Santo di Montepulciano Familiae ($$)
5. CAPEZZANA, Carmignano
   Vin Santo di Carmignano Riserva ($$$)
6. FATTORIA SELVAPIANA, Rufina
   Vin Santo del Chianti Rufina ($$)
7. FRASCOLE, Dicomano
   Vin Santo del Chianti Rufina ($$$)
8. I VERONI, Pontassieve
   Vin Santo del Chianti Rufina ($$)
9. ROCCA DI MONTEGROSSI, Gaiole in Chianti
   Vin Santo del Chianti Classico ($$$)

....

Elba Aleatico Passito or Aleatico Passito dell'Elba DOCG

The Aleatico grapes, cultivated exclusively on the island of Elba, are dried in the sun on racks, resulting in a wine with a good alcohol content, around 13.5%, still rich in sugar and therefore persuasively sweet. After aging in stainless steel or in barrels, it is particularly appreciated for its rich aromas of red fruits and spices and for its soft, lovable envelopment on the palate. Recommended for consumption with chocolate. Annual production is limited to a few thousand 37.5-centiliter bottles.

—

Producers and their trademark and signature wines:

10. ACQUABONA, Portoferraio
    Elba Aleatico Passito ($$)
11. ARRIGHI, Porto Azzurro
    Elba Aleatico Passito Silosò ($$)
12. CHIESINA DI LACONA, Capoliveri
    Aleatico Passito dell'Elba Chiesina di Lacona ($$)
13. TENUTA DELLE RIPALTE, Capoliveri
    Aleatico Passito dell'Elba Alea Ludendo ($$)

Moscadello di Montalcino DOC

Rather widespread in past centuries, the presence of the Muscat grape in Montalcino almost disappeared after the arrival of phylloxera and is now almost symbolic, occupying less than 25 acres of cultivation. The still, sweet wine made from it is a pleasant accompaniment to biscuits and dry sweets and, more generally, after dinner, thanks to its seductive aromatic richness. The annual number of bottles is close to forty thousand.

—

Producer and its trademark and signature wine:

14. CAPANNA, Montalcino
    Moscadello di Montalcino Vendemmia Tardiva ($)

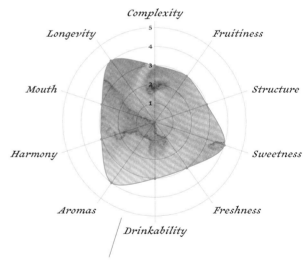

Elba Aleatico Passito

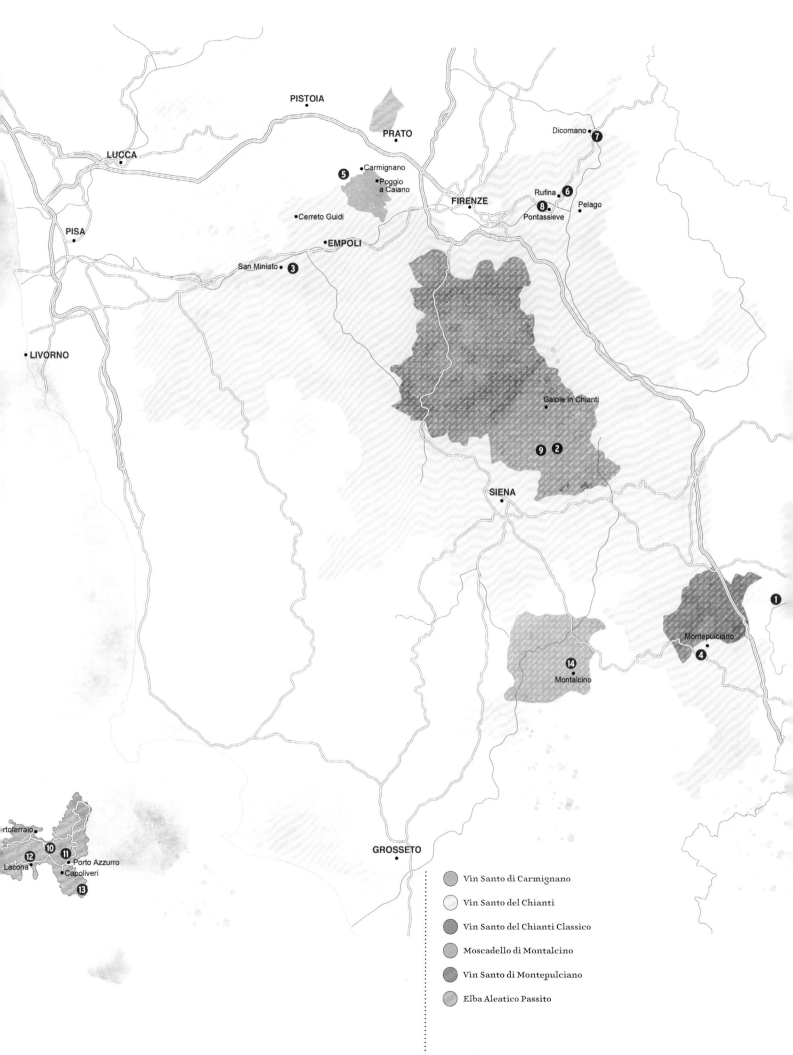

PISTOIA

PRATO

LUCCA

Dicomano • ❼

Carmignano ❺
• Poggio
  a Caiano

FIRENZE

Rufina • ❻
❽ • Pelago
• Pontassieve

PISA

• Cerreto Guidi

EMPOLI

San Miniato • ❸

LIVORNO

Gaiole in Chianti •

❾ ❷

SIENA

❶

Montepulciano •
❹

❿ ⓫
Lacona
• Porto Azzurro
Capoliveri
⓭

rtoferraio •

⓬

⓮
Montalcino •

GROSSETO

◯ Vin Santo di Carmignano

◯ Vin Santo del Chianti

◯ Vin Santo del Chianti Classico

◯ Moscadello di Montalcino

◯ Vin Santo di Montepulciano

◯ Elba Aleatico Passito

The Super Tuscans and recommended wines outside the DOC/DOCG designations

The phenomenon of the Super Tuscans was born and developed in the late 1960s and early 1980s in the Chianti Classico region. Many producers were dissatisfied with the Chianti production regulations—the autonomous Chianti Classico DOCG was only established in 1996, while before that "Classico" was only a geographical specification included in the all-encompassing "Chianti"—which imposed the exclusive use of the area's typical grapes, including white ones, to the detriment of both the worth of pure Sangiovese grapes and the possibility of experimenting with innovative blends thanks to the inclusion of international vines. Hence the choice, initiated in 1968 by Vigorello of the San Felice winery, of an ever-increasing number of companies to produce wines outside of the Chianti DOC, with a consequent and immediate split. Some decided to make reds based exclusively on Sangiovese while others favored the use of international vines, either on their own or blended with Sangiovese in varying percentages. For these reasons, Super Tuscans will be characterized by the use of the Toscana IGT, without adhering to the DOC and DOCG specifications.

Among the wines that have brought this category to international success, and led to the creation of the name "Super Tuscan," or "SuperTuscan," the most famous are:
- Tignanello di Antinori (since 1971, based on Sangiovese, Cabernet Franc, and Cabernet Sauvignon);
- Fabrizio Bianchi Sangioveto Grosso del Castello di Monsanto (since 1974, Sangiovese);
- Le Pergole Torte di Montevertine (since 1977, Sangiovese);
- I Sodi di San Niccolò di Castellare di Castellina (since 1979, Sangiovese and Malvasia Nera);
- Cepparello di Isole e Olena (since 1980, Sangiovese);
- Sammarco del Castello dei Rampolla (since 1980, Cabernet Sauvignon joined and blended with Sangiovese and Merlot);
- Sangioveto di Badia a Coltibuono (since 1980, Sangiovese);
- Camartina di Querciabella (since 1981, Cabernet Sauvignon and Sangiovese);
- Flaccianello di Fontodi (since 1981, Sangiovese);
- Fontalloro di Fèlsina (since 1983, Sangiovese);
- L'Apparita del Castello di Ama (since 1985, Merlot);
- Il Blu di Brancaia (since 1988, Merlot blended with Sangiovese and Cabernet Sauvignon).

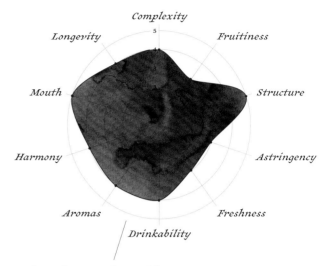

Sangiovese SuperTuscan

Over the years, many have tended to make the term "Super Tuscans" synonymous with quality red wines produced throughout the region, with Bolgheri in the forefront, an area that established its own DOC in 1984, followed in 1994 by another DOC dedicated exclusively to Bolgheri Sassicaia. It seems more correct to limit the use of the term to the Chianti Classico area, something which has been underlined by the statute of the Historical Super Tuscans Committee, established in 2021 by the collaboration of sixteen producers: it is open to new applicants and members and recognizes Piero Antinori as its "Honorary Founder."

—

Producers and their trademark and signature wines:

1. AMPELEIA, Roccastrada
   Ampeleia (Cabernet Franc) ($$)
2. AVIGNONESI, Montepulciano
   Grandi Annate (Sangiovese) ($$$)
3. AVIGNONESI - CAPANNELLE, Montepulciano
   50 & 50 (Sangiovese, Merlot) ($$$)
4. BERTINGA, Gaiole in Chianti
   Volta di Bertinga (Merlot) ($$$)
   Bertinga (Sangiovese, Merlot) ($$$)
5. BRANCAIA, Radda in Chianti
   Il Blu (Merlot; Sangiovese, Cabernet Sauvignon) ($$$)
6. CAIAROSSA, Riparbella
   Caiarossa (Merlot, Cabernet Franc, Cabernet Sauvignon, Syrah, Sangiovese, Alicante) ($$$)
7. Antonio CAMILLO, Manciano
   Ciliegiolo ($)

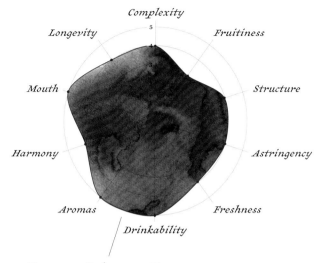

Toscana Cabernet Franc

(radar chart axes: Complexity, Fruitiness, Structure, Astringency, Freshness, Drinkability, Aromas, Harmony, Mouth, Longevity)

8. CASTELL'IN VILLA, Castelnuovo Berardenga
Santacroce (Sangiovese, Cabernet Sauvignon) ($$$)

9. CASTELLARE DI CASTELLINA, Castellina in Chianti
I Sodi di S. Niccolò (Sangiovese, Malvasia Nera) ($$$)

10. CASTELLO DEI RAMPOLLA, Greve in Chianti
D'Alceo (Cabernet Sauvignon, Petit Verdot) ($$$$)
Sammarco (Cabernet Sauvignon, Sangiovese, Merlot) ($$$)
Liù (Merlot) ($$)

11. CASTELLO DEL TERRICCIO, Castellina Marittima
Lupicaia (Cabernet Sauvignon; Petit Verdot) ($$$$)
Castello del Terriccio (Syrah) ($$$)
Tassinaia (Cabernet Sauvignon, Merlot) ($$$$$)

12. CASTELLO DI AMA, Gaiole in Chianti
L'Apparita (Merlot) ($$$$$)

13. CASTELLO DI FONTERUTOLI, Castellina in Chianti
Siepi (Sangiovese, Merlot) ($$$)

14. CASTELLO DI MONSANTO, Barberino Tavarnelle
Fabrizio Bianchi Sangioveto Grosso (Sangiovese) ($$)

15. CASTELLO VICCHIOMAGGIO, Greve in Chianti
Ripa delle More (Sangiovese, Cabernet Sauvignon, Merlot) ($)

16. CASTELVECCHIO, San Casciano in Val di Pesa
Il Brecciolino (Merlot; Petit Verdot, Sangiovese) ($$)

17. CORZANO E PATERNO, San Casciano in Val di Pesa
Il Corzano (Sangiovese, Cabernet Sauvignon, Merlot) ($$)
I Tre Borri (Sangiovese) ($$)

18. DUEMANI, Castellina Marittima
Duemani (Cabernet Franc) ($$$$)
Suisassi (Syrah) ($$$$)
Altrovino (Cabernet Franc, Merlot) ($$)

19. FATTORIA CARPINETA FONTALPINO, Castelnuovo Berardenga
Do Ut Des (Merlot, Petit Verdot, Cabernet Sauvignon) ($$)

20. FATTORIA LE PUPILLE, Grosseto
Saffredi (Cabernet Sauvignon, Merlot, Petit Verdot) ($$$)

21. FATTORIA LE SPIGHE, Orbetello
Giragira (Ansonica) ($)

22. FÈLSINA, Castelnuovo Berardenga
Fontalloro (Sangiovese) ($$)

23. FONTODI, Greve in Chianti
Flaccianello della Pieve (Sangiovese) ($$$$)

24. IL BORRO, Loro Ciuffenna
Il Borro (Merlot, Cabernet Sauvignon, Syrah) ($$)

25. ISOLE E OLENA, Barberino Tavarnelle
Cepparello (Sangiovese) ($$$)
Chardonnay Collezione Privata ($$$)

26. LA REGOLA, Riparbella
La Regola (Cabernet Franc) ($$)

27. LA SPINETTA CASANOVA, Terricciola
Il Nero di Casanova (Sangiovese) ($)

28. LE MACCHIOLE, Castagneto Carducci
Paleo (Cabernet Franc) ($$$)
Messorio (Merlot) ($$$$)
Scrio (Syrah) ($$$)

29. MALGIACCA, Capannori
Malgiacca (Sangiovese; Canaiolo, Ciliegiolo, Malvasia Nera, Syrah...) ($)

30. MARCHESI ANTINORI, San Casciano in Val di Pesa
Solaia (Cabernet Sauvignon, Cabernet Franc, Sangiovese) ($$$$$)
Tignanello (Sangiovese, Cabernet Sauvignon, Cabernet Franc) ($$$$)

31. MASSETO, Castagneto Carducci
Masseto (Merlot) ($$$$$)

32. MONTERAPONI, Radda in Chianti
Baron'Ugo (formerly Chianti Classico: Sangiovese; Canaiolo, Colorino) ($$)

33. MONTEVERRO, Capalbio
Monteverro (Cabernet Sauvignon, Cabernet Franc, Merlot, Petit Verdot) ($$$$)
Monteverro Chardonnay ($$$)

34. MONTEVERTINE, Radda in Chianti
Le Pergole Torte (Sangiovese) ($$$$$)
Montevertine (Sangiovese; Colorino, Canaiolo) ($$$)

35. PACINA, Castelnuovo Berardenga
Pacina (Sangiovese; Canaiolo, Ciliegiolo) ($)

36. PAGANI DE MARCHI, Casale Marittimo
Principe Guerriero (formerly Sangiovese, since 2019 Merlot, Cabernet Sauvignon) ($)

37. PAKRAVAN - PAPI, Riparbella
Cancellaia (Cabernet Sauvignon, Cabernet Franc) ($$)
38. PETRA, Suvereto
Petra (Cabernet Sauvignon, Merlot) ($$)
39. PIAGGIA, Poggio a Caiano
Poggio de' Colli (Cabernet Franc) ($$)
40. PODERE DELLA CIVETTAJA, Pratovecchio
Pinot Nero ($$)
41. PODERE FORTE, Castiglione d'Orcia
Guardiavigna (Cabernet Franc) ($$$$)
42. PODERE IL CARNASCIALE, Mercatale Valdarno
Il Caberlot (cross between Cabernet Franc
and Merlot) ($$$$)
Carnasciale (cross between Cabernet Franc
and Merlot) ($$$)
43. PODERE IL CASTELLACCIO, Castagneto Carducci
Somatico (Pugnitello) ($$)
44. PODERE POGGIO SCALETTE, Greve in Chianti
Il Carbonaione (Sangiovese) ($$)
45. PODERE SAPAIO, Castagneto Carducci
Sapaio (Cabernet Sauvignon; Cabernet Franc,
Petit Verdot) ($$$)
46. QUERCIABELLA, Greve in Chianti
Batàr (Chardonnay, Pinot Grigio) ($$$)
Camartina (Cabernet Sauvignon, Sangiovese) ($$$)
47. RIECINE, Gaiole in Chianti
Riecine di Riecine (Sangiovese) ($$$)
La Gioia (Sangiovese) ($$$)
48. SAN FELICE, Castelnuovo Berardenga
Vigorello (Pugnitello, Cabernet Sauvignon,
Merlot, Petit Verdot) ($$)
49. SAN GIUSTO A RENTENNANO, Gaiole in Chianti
Percarlo (Sangiovese) ($$$)
La Ricolma (Merlot) ($$$$)
50. TENIMENTI D'ALESSANDRO, Cortona
Bosco ($)
Migliara Syrah ($$)
51. TENUTA CASADEI, Suvereto
Filare 18 (Cabernet Franc) ($$)
52. TENUTA DEL BUONAMICO, Montecarlo
Il Fortino (Syrah) ($)
Vasario (Pinot Bianco) ($)
53. TENUTA DI BISERNO, Bibbona
Biserno (Cabernet Franc, Cabernet Sauvignon,
Merlot) ($$$$)
54. TENUTA DI CARLEONE, Radda in Chianti
Uno (Sangiovese) ($$$)
55. TENUTA DI GHIZZANO - Venerosi Pesciolini,
Peccioli
Nambrot (Merlot, Cabernet Franc, Petit Verdot) ($$)
56. TENUTA DI TRINORO, Sarteano
Tenuta di Trinoro (Cabernet Franc, Merlot,
Cabernet Sauvignon, Petit Verdot) ($$$$$)
Palazzi (Merlot) ($$$$$)
Campo di Magnacosta (Cabernet Franc) ($$$)

57. TENUTA LUCE, Montalcino
Luce (Sangiovese, Merlot) ($$$)
58. TENUTA SETTE PONTI, Castiglion Fibocchi
Oreno (Merlot, Cabernet Sauvignon, Petit
Verdot) ($$$)
Orma (Merlot, Cabernet Sauvignon, Cabernet
Franc) ($$$)
59. TENUTE AMBROGIO E GIOVANNI FOLONARI,
Greve in Chianti
Tenuta di Nozzole Il Pareto (Cabernet
Sauvignon) ($$)
Tenute del Cabreo Il Borgo (Cabernet Sauvignon,
Merlot, Sangiovese) ($$)
60. TUA RITA, Suvereto
Redigaffi (Merlot) ($$$$$)
Giusto di Notri (Cabernet Sauvignon, Merlot,
Cabernet Franc) ($$$)
Per Sempre (Syrah) ($$$$)
61. VALLE DEL SOLE, Lucca
Ébrius (Sangiovese) ($)

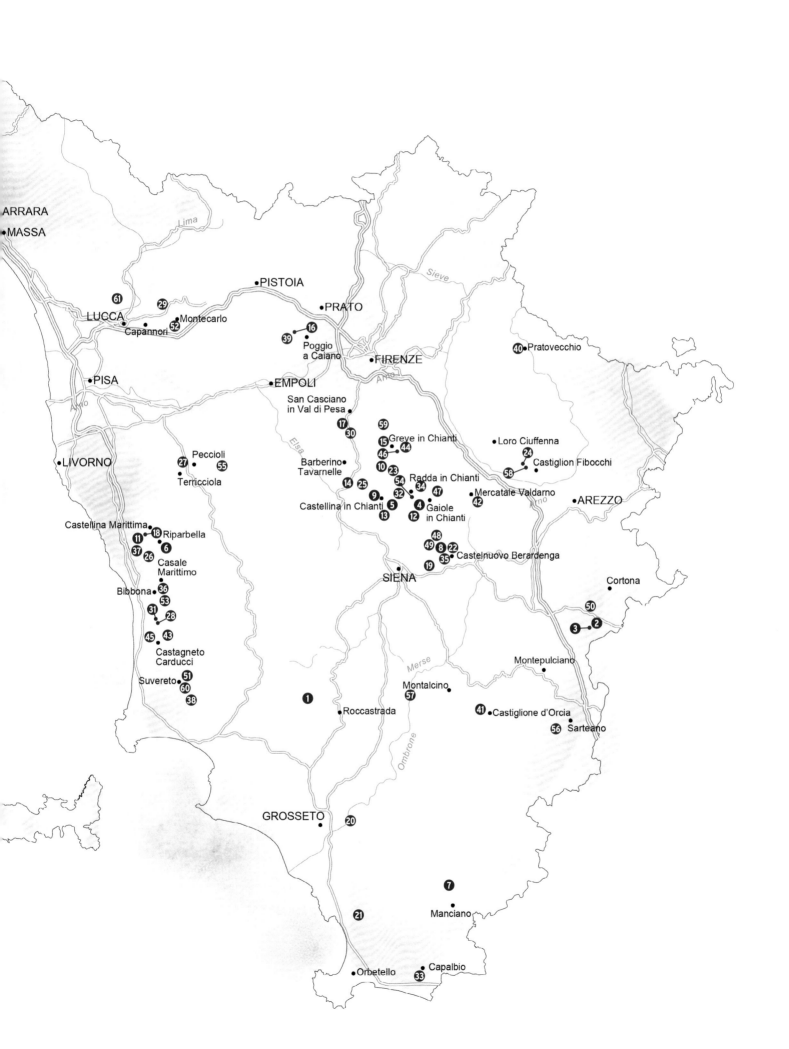

CARRARA

•MASSA

PISTOIA

•PRATO

61 29
LUCCA• •Montecarlo
•Capannori 52

•PISA

16
39 •Poggio
a Caiano

FIRENZE

•EMPOLI

San Casciano
in Val di Pesa•

17
30 59 Greve in Chianti
15 44 •Loro Ciuffenna
46 24
Barberino• 10 23 Castiglion Fibocchi
Tavarnelle 54 Radda in Chianti 58
14 25 34 47
9 32 •Mercatale Valdarno
Castellina in Chianti 5 4 42 •AREZZO
13 12 Gaiole
in Chianti

•LIVORNO

Peccioli
27 • 55
•Terricciola

Castellina Marittima• 48
18•Riparbella 49 8 22
11 6 35 •Castelnuovo Berardenga
37 26 19
Casale SIENA
Marittimo
Bibbona• 36 Cortona
53 50
31 3 2
28
45 43 Montepulciano
Castagneto
Carducci Montalcino
Suvereto• 51 57
60 41 •Castiglione d'Orcia
38 1 56 •Sarteano
•Roccastrada

GROSSETO
20

7

21

•Manciano

•Orbetello •Capalbio
33

Pratovecchio
40

CASTELLO DI BOLGHERI

Località Bolgheri, Via Lauretta 7
Castagneto Carducci (LI)
castellodibolgheri.com
Year of establishment: 1986
Owner: Federico Zileri Dal Verme
Average number of bottles produced per year: 100,000

The 135 acres under vine are located next to the famous, and much-photographed, avenue of poplars leading to the center of Bolgheri, while the cooperative itself is in the underground rooms of the castle, built in 1796. For the time being, the company is dedicated to only two labels, the Bolgheri Rosso Superiore Castello di Bolgheri and the slightly fresher and more youthful Bolgheri Rosso Varvàra, derived from a very similar grape blend. Clean, elegant wines with fine fruit integrity.

BOLGHERI ROSSO SUPERIORE CASTELLO DI BOLGHERI

First year of production: 2001
Average number of bottles produced per year: 30,000
Grape varieties: Cabernet Sauvignon, Merlot, Cabernet Franc, Petit Verdot

The percentage of the different grapes varies from vintage to vintage in order to achieve the fresh, vivid complexity that remains the winery's goal. The aromas are characterized by small black fruits and refined hints of incense, while the contribution of the French wood in which it ages for twenty months is barely perceptible. The palate is of rare harmony and elegance, with delicate tannins and a hint of savoriness lending vitality and volume.

ORNELLAIA

Località Ornellaia 191
Frazione Bolgheri
Castagneto Carducci (LI)
ornellaia.it
Year of establishment: 1981
Owner: the Frescobaldi family
Average number of bottles produced per year: 800,000

An ever-expanding winery, to whose growth the most celebrated international oenologists have contributed, with the sole aim of obtaining wines that speak to fine dining and gourmands of the world. In addition to the world-famous Ornellaia, the 247 acres of property produce other labels that aim for high quality, from Ornellaia Bianco (based on Sauvignon and Viognier) to Le Volte dell'Ornellaia (in which Bordeaux vines are joined to Sangiovese) to Bolgheri Rosso Le Serre Nuove dell'Ornellaia (with the same blend as its elder brother) to the Sauvignon Poggio alle Gazze.

BOLGHERI SUPERIORE ORNELLAIA

First year of production: 1985
Average number of bottles produced per year: 170,000
Grape varieties: Cabernet Sauvignon, Cabernet Franc, Merlot, Petit Verdot

Matured in barriques for about eighteen months, it offers aromas of fine elegance in which notes of eucalyptus, spices, and small black fruits are discernible; the flavor is dense, multifaceted, and progressive, very long and endowed with a fresh and enchanting acid component. An exceptional wine, with a price commensurate with its deserved fame.

GRATTAMACCO

Località Lungagnano 129
Castagneto Carducci (LI)
collemassari.it
Year of establishment: 1977
Owner: the Tipa family
Average number of bottles produced per year: 95,000

Brought to fame by Giorgio Meletti Cavallari, who founded it in 1977, the winery has, since 2001, together with Castello ColleMassari, Tenuta San Giorgio, and Poggio di Sotto, been part of the winemaking group led by Claudio Tipa. The 72 acres under vine are organically farmed and, as the area requires, produces only red Bordeaux grapes, with Cabernet Sauvignon in the lead and a small portion of white grapes, from which Bolgheri Vermentino is made. There are four labels on offer, all of outstanding quality.

BOLGHERI ROSSO SUPERIORE GRATTAMACCO

First year of production: 1982
Average number of bottles produced per year: 50,000
Grape varieties: Cabernet Sauvignon (65%), Merlot (20%), Sangiovese (15%)

A lively spiciness combines with Mediterranean scrub and small black fruits to create an articulate aroma dominated by freshness. The taste is powerful and harmoniously rounded, soft in its velvety tannins, barely enlivened by seductive hints of medicinal herbs, with excellent balance. One of the most celebrated and awarded names in the Bolgheri designation.

TENUTA GUADO AL TASSO

Via Bolgherese km 3.9
Castagneto Carducci (LI)
guadoaltasso.it
Year of establishment: 1934
Owner: the Antinori family
Average number of bottles produced per year: 1,900,000

Almost a century ago, the historic Della Gherardesca family crossed paths with the Florentine Antinori family, bringing as its dowry this estate, today with 790 acres under vine. The vines are those typical of the Bolgherese area and are used both in purity, as is the case with the Merlot of Cont'Ugo or the Cabernet Franc of Matarocchio, and in blends, as in the award-winning Guado al Tasso.

BOLGHERI ROSSO SUPERIORE GUADO AL TASSO

First year of production: 1990
Average number of bottles produced per year: 160,000
Grape varieties: Cabernet Sauvignon, Merlot, Cabernet Franc, sometimes Petit Verdot

Elegance and harmony at the highest level: very complex aromas, highlighting small red and black fruits, smoky hints, and touches of eucalyptus, which is followed by an important and dense palate with excellent smoothness, devoid of harshness and with great personality, long and sinuous. The contribution of small French wood, in which Guado al Tasso ages for eighteen months, lends exceptional delicacy and refinement.

TENUTA SAN GUIDO
Frazione Bolgheri,
Località Le Capanne 27
Castagneto Carducci (LI)
tenutasanguido.com
Year of establishment: 1940
Owner: the Incisa della
Rocchetta family
Average number of
bottles produced per year:
1,100,000

Mario Incisa della Rocchetta's intuition about the potential of Bordeaux vines in Bolgheri, combined with the most careful agronomic and oenological choices, has led to the creation of a winery that, with 285 acres currently under vine, has become an international model. The wine-legend Sassicaia tends to overshadow the rest of the offering, but the well-articulated Guidalberto, based on Cabernet Sauvignon and Merlot, and the Le Difese, in which 30% Sangiovese is blended with Cabernet Sauvignon, are also of certain value and more accessible.

BOLGHERI SASSICAIA
First year of production: 1968
Average number of bottles produced
per year: 260,000
Grape varieties: Cabernet Sauvignon
(85%), Cabernet Franc (15%)

Aged for twenty-four months in barriques, this is a champion of complexity, persuasiveness, and pleasantness, enjoyable and always very articulate, with an aromatic range that contains blackberry and blackcurrant, Mediterranean scrub and delicate sweet spices. The palate is silky and smooth, rich and of unparalleled harmony, with hints of tannins and enchanting balsamic freshness: an example of elegance on an absolute level.

BIONDI-SANTI
Villa Greppo 183
Montalcino (SI)
biondisanti.it
Year of establishment: 1888
Owner: the Descourt family
Average number of bottles
produced per year: 84,000

The acquisition by the EPI group of the Descourt family business, which took place in 2016, does not seem destined to change the winery's qualitative structure; on the contrary, research is being conducted into the peculiarities of each individual vineyard parcel present on the 57 acres of property. A now legendary name that, with the primogeniture of Brunello di Montalcino that accompanied the creation of the first bottle in 1888, has conquered the world of connoisseurs with austere, long-lived wines, always endowed with energetic personality. It is the name that started the history of Brunello.

BRUNELLO DI MONTALCINO
First year of production: 1888
Average number of bottles produced
per year: 48,000
Grape variety: Sangiovese

The style is dictated by the centuries-old history of this name, whose objective is the representation of absolute classicism. The large wood helps in this sense to express the purest Sangiovese aromas through youthful red fruits and officinal herbs, with measured intensity and articulated complexity. The taste is of measured strength, with good acidity and astringency that softens year after year, with a balsamic hint on the finish: the splendid continuity of the timeless Brunello.

TENIMENTI D'ALESSANDRO
Via Manzano 15
Cortona (AR)
tenimentidalessandro.it
Year of establishment: 1967
Owner: the Calabresi
family
Average number of bottles
produced per year: 100,000

Filippo Calabresi guides the entire production process, and has done so since 2013, when his family acquired a company that had already become famous thanks to its Syrah-based offerings. The company's standard-bearer is the Bosco, which is described opposite, but the small Migliara selection, also based on Syrah, enjoys similar critical acclaim. This is the winery that, thanks to its 94 organically cultivated acres, has made Cortona known throughout the world.

BOSCO
First year of production: 1992
Average number of bottles produced
per year: 15,000
Grape variety: Syrah

Many of the grapes are fermented in whole bunches, followed by two years of aging in wood: thus was born this now-famous Syrah, rich in aromas of spices and small black fruits that overhang a delicate nuance of eucalyptus. The taste is refined and austere, never too astringent, always endowed with good dynamism, long and harmonious, and splendidly drinkable.

CAPANNA
Località Capanna 333
Montalcino (SI)
capannamontalcino.com
Year of establishment: 1957
Owner: the Cencioni family
Average number of bottles
produced per year: 95,000

Patrizio Cencioni has set his production line on the classicism and longevity of Brunello di Montalcino, using only large Slavonian oak barrels and leaving free expression to a certain tannic astringency that in the first few years in the bottle achieves a convincing and pleasant austerity of taste. The Riserva is joined by an always award-winning Brunello di Montalcino, a fragrant Rosso di Montalcino, and a small production of Moscadello di Montalcino Vendemmia Tardiva. There is careful processing and continuous experimentation on the 62 acres of vineyards, which have just been converted to organic farming.

BRUNELLO DI MONTALCINO RISERVA
First year of production: 1970
Average number of bottles produced
per year: 15,000
Grape variety: Sangiovese

The most complete expression of the winery's style, with no appreciable contribution of wood, characterized by notes of rhubarb and undergrowth against a rich fruity and delicately spicy background, with a hint of captivating licorice; the taste is solid, long, slightly severe thanks to the impressive acid-tannic component, accompanied by the soft presence of alcohol until the finish in which notes of blackberry and mint stand out.

CASANOVA DI NERI
Podere Fiesole
Montalcino (SI)
casanovadineri.com
Year of establishment: 1971
Owner: Giacomo Neri
Average number of bottles
produced per year: 310,000

A winery that in recent decades
has come to the forefront of
international attention thanks
to meticulous care in the
vineyard and in the cellar, and
that has succeeded in bringing
out a style of its own that has
enchanted those who taste the
wine. Everything comes from
185 acres of property divided
into seven vineyards, with
wines matured in barrels of
different origins and sizes.
They are "modern wines," if
by this we mean the purity
of the fruit, the use of new
wood, and superfine elegance.
"Classic," if we refer to the
power of taste, the broad
olfactory expressiveness, and
the blending of grapes from
different vineyards for other
labels.

BRUNELLO DI MONTALCINO CERRETALTO
First year of production: 1981
Average number of bottles produced
per year: 9,000
Grape variety: Sangiovese

The fruit of the vineyard of the same name
and thirty-six months of aging in wood leads
to this wine that first brought the Neri family
estate to world fame. It bewitches for its
olfactory precision, clear and deep, in which
hints of black fruits—from blackberry to
cherry—and variegated spicy nuances prevail
against a background of violet petals. The
palate is important and dense, with the wine
flowing slowly, offering a hint of graceful
tannicity until the crisp finish in which sour
cherries and licorice are added. When it
comes to prizes, it is among the most highly
awarded wines in the world.

IL MARRONETO
Località Madonna delle
Grazie 307
Montalcino (SI)
ilmarroneto.it
Year of establishment: 1974
Owner: Alessandro Mori
Average number of bottles
produced per year: 28,000

At the beginning and at the
heart of the great success
of this small winery is the
passion of Alessandro Mori,
who has worked hard to
achieve the goal of maximum
quality, itself understood
as a pure expression of the
complexity and vitality
that traditional Brunello
di Montalcino can possess.
This does not mean that only
large, untreated Slavonian
barrels are used in the cellar
and that fine French oak is
not also used in the maturing
process, but rather that the
wood must never overwhelm
the pure and varied aromas
of the Sangiovese grapes, to
which the estate's 17 acres of
vineyards are dedicated.

BRUNELLO DI MONTALCINO MADONNA DELLE GRAZIE
First year of production: 1980
Average number of bottles produced
per year: 8,500
Grape variety: Sangiovese

Red flowers and small black fruits blend in
harmony, creating an elegance that is well
refined during the long aging in wood. It is
the quintessence of balance, with a hint of
tannic astringency and a touch of savoriness
to add freshness and dynamism. A jewel, it is
expensive and sought-after throughout the
world, and has few equals.

COL D'ORCIA
Frazione Sant'Angelo in
Colle, Via Giuncheti
Montalcino (SI)
coldorcia.it
Year of establishment: 1890
Owner: the Marone
Cinzano family
Average number of bottles
produced per year: 800,000

The farm's history is centuries
old, but it was only in 1973
that the Cinzano family began
the process of improving the
quality and quantity that
today places it at the forefront
of the Ilcinese area, with 370
acres under vine, using organic
and biodynamic methods. The
oenological project includes
numerous labels in which
there are international grapes
that play a small role, but the
production pivot is centered
on the Brunello offer and a
reliable Rosso di Montalcino.

BRUNELLO DI MONTALCINO RISERVA POGGIO AL VENTO
First year of production: 1982
Average number of bottles produced
per year: 25,000
Grape variety: Sangiovese

Fruity notes with cherry and blackberry
in evidence, then hints of spices and
subsequent fresh hints of eucalyptus: these
are found with every vintage in the complex
and fascinating aromas offered by the
Poggio al Vento vineyard. The taste texture
includes important but never aggressive
tannins, something that is also the result
of the many years that separate harvesting
from marketing. There is a very impressive,
tasty, and persuasive overall structure,
leading up to a finish in which violets
emerge.

LE RAGNAIE
Località Le Ragnaie
Montalcino (SI)
leragnaie.com
Year of establishment: 1996
Owner: the Campinoti family
Average number of bottles
produced per year: 90,000

A winery dedicated to
high quality from the
very beginning, and with
the purchase by Riccardo
Campinoti in 2002 there was
a slight stylistic change, in
which more space is left to
the purity of the grapes and
less to the contribution of
wood. The 49 acres under
vine, cultivated organically,
are entirely dedicated to the
Sangiovese grape and give
rise to five labels of Brunello
based on the different estate
vineyards, in addition to Rosso
di Montalcino and Troncone.
An essential reference point in
the world of Brunello.

BRUNELLO DI MONTALCINO RAGNAIE V.V.
First year of production: 2007
Average number of bottles produced
per year: 4,000
Grape variety: Sangiovese

The result of delicate aging in large oak
barrels for thirty-six months, the aroma is
a kaleidoscope of fruits and flowers, with
a delicate background of spices: cherry,
balsamic herbs, citrus fruits, and roses are
all perceptible. In the mouth it amazes
and fascinates with the harmony of a well-
structured body in which the silkiness of
the tannins leaves room for stimulating
freshness and an energetic, long, and
balanced progression.

POGGIO DI SOTTO

Località Castelnuovo
Abate
Montalcino (SI)
collemassariwines.it
Year of establishment: 1989
Owner: Claudio Tipa
Average number of bottles
produced per year: 110,000

In 2011, Claudio Tipa's
ColleMassari group acquired
the estate that once belonged
to Piero Palmucci. This was
immediately followed by an
expansion of the vineyard
areas, which now include
the organic cultivation of no
less than 119 acres. The well-
deserved celebrity of Poggio
di Sotto has been guaranteed
by maintaining high levels
of quality together with
an increase in production
capacity, relative not only to
the Riserva that we describe
here but also to a Brunello and
a Rosso di Montalcino that
are always at the top of their
respective categories.

BRUNELLO DI MONTALCINO RISERVA

First year of production: 1991
Average number of bottles produced
per year: 8,000
Grape variety: Sangiovese

Persuasive red petals and bewitching
hints of incense accompany the red fruit
component in this Riserva sought after
by aficionados everywhere, thus making
it expensive. The palate is the archetype
of complexity combined with joyful ease
of drinking, with power, freshness, and
intensity, making it one of the world's great
wines.

QUERCIABELLA

Via di Barbiano 17
Greve in Chianti (FI)
querciabella.com
Year of establishment: 1974
Owner: the Cossia
Castiglioni family
Average number of bottles
produced per year: 300,000

Always committed to
sustainable agriculture,
Querciabella first switched
to certified organic and then
to biodynamic farming on its
255 acres of property, 82 of
which are on the Maremma
estate. Today it is committed
to reducing carbon emissions
and self-producing the energy
needed in its new winemaking
cellar. The entire range of
products is well known, from
Camartina to the white Batàr
to the Chianti Classico labels.
A point of reference in Tuscan
oenology.

CAMARTINA

First year of production: 1981
Average number of bottles produced
per year: 11,000
Grape varieties: Cabernet Sauvignon
(70%), Sangiovese (30%)

A famous example of the Super Tuscans,
Camartina combines the typical vegetal and
black fruit notes of Cabernet Sauvignon
with the fruity and floral component of
Sangiovese, and the contribution of the
eighteen-month barrique passage that adds
refined spicy notes. The palate is structured,
finely tannic, long, and well articulated.

VAL DI SUGA

Località Val di Cava
Montalcino (SI)
valdisuga.it
Year of establishment: 1969
Owner: Bertani Domains
Average number of bottles
produced per year: 270,000

Only Sangiovese grapes are
used for this winery that has
been part of the Bertani group
since 2014. In addition to the
basic and Riserva versions,
there are three crus reserved
for Brunello di Montalcino:
Vigna Spuntali, which matures
first in barriques and then in
Slavonian oak, Vigna del Lago,
made from oval barrels and
cement vats, and the more
recent Poggio al Granchio, in
which large wood is used. The
result is different exposures
and styles united by an
impeccable elegance, born in
Montalcino on 128 acres of
vineyards, 101 of which are
dedicated to Brunello.

BRUNELLO DI MONTALCINO VIGNA SPUNTALI

First year of production: 1988
Average number of bottles produced
per year: 10,000
Grape variety: Sangiovese

Due to its location on the southwest
side of Montalcino, and the considerable
presence of sand, the Spuntali vineyard
offers intense and enveloping aromas, in
which yellow-fleshed fruits, blackberries,
and cherries combine on a citrusy and fine
vanilla background. In the mouth it is soft,
not very astringent, and of refined balance,
with a sweet finish reminiscent of cocoa.
An enchanting modern interpretation of
Brunello.

PIAGGIA

Località Poggetto, Via
Cegoli 47
Poggio a Caiano (PO)
piaggia.com
Year of establishment: 1990
Owner: the Vannucci family
Average number of bottles
produced per year: 95,000

The vineyards, acquired in
the 1970s, now cover a total
of 49 acres and are able to
provide particularly rich
and concentrated grapes,
with results that place this
winery at the top of regional
oenology. The famous Riserva
Piaggia is joined by a limited
offering in which the spicy
and powerful Poggio de' Colli,
from Cabernet Franc grapes,
and the fresh and enjoyable
Carmignano Il Sasso stand
out.

CARMIGNANO RISERVA PIAGGIA

First year of production: 1991
Average number of bottles produced
per year: 36,000
Grape varieties: Sangiovese (70%),
Cabernet Sauvignon and Cabernet
Franc (20%), Merlot (10%)

Being kept in barriques for eighteen
months adds elegance to the purity of the
grapes, creating a blend of small red fruits
interspersed with spices and citrus hints.
The taste is very lively, with remarkable
freshness and a slight astringency, with
refined pleasantness. A demonstration of the
greatness of Carmignano.

ISOLE E OLENA

Località Isole 1
Barberino Tavarnelle (FI)
office@isoleolena.it
Year of establishment: 1956
Owner: the De Marchi family
Average number of bottles
produced per year: 230,000

Paolo De Marchi from
Piedmont took over the family
estate in 1976, immediately
beginning a complex and farsighted research project on
clones and soils that involved
all 138 acres of the property.
The results are of the highest
level, both on the non-DOP
labels—from Cepparello to
Syrah to the Chardonnay of
the Private Collection—and on
Chianti Classico, constantly a
reference point in the area. A
world-famous name thanks
to outstanding production
quality in every vintage.

CEPPARELLO

First year of production: 1980
Average number of bottles produced
per year: 5,000
Grape variety: Sangiovese

One of the most famous Super Tuscans,
always a clear expression of the pure
Sangiovese grape, characterized by cherry
and violet aromas that then open up to hints
of medicinal herbs and fine smokiness from
the French oak. The palate is persistent
and responsive, with good freshness and
moderate tannic astringency; it's very
enjoyable to drink. A milestone in Chianti
wine quality.

FRESCOBALDI

Pelago (FI)
frescobaldi.com
Year of establishment: 1300
Owner: the Frescobaldi
family
Average number of
bottles produced per year:
7,500,000

In seven centuries of history,
the Frescobaldi family has
built an oenological empire
with 2,350 acres under vine
and eight production sectors
in the most significant areas
of Tuscan wine, to which must
be added the Attems winery
in Collio and Ornellaia (➔)
and Masseto (➔) in Bolgheri;
separate entries are dedicated
to those. The most historic and
famous production center is
in Nipozzano, with its castle
in Chianti Rufina, with a wine
mission that ranges from
Chianti Classico to Morellino
di Scansano, from Brunello
di Montalcino to Maremma
Toscana. Mainly Sangiovese,
but prestigious labels are also
obtained from international
varieties.

CHIANTI RÚFINA RISERVA NIPOZZANO VECCHIE VITI

First year of production: 2011
Average number of bottles produced
per year: 90,000
Grape varieties: Sangiovese (90%);
Malvasia Nera, Canaiolo, Colorino

This interpretation of Chianti Rufina is as
much linked to its *terroir*, through the use of
the area's historic vines, as it is modern in its
olfactory clarity and harmony of taste. The
aromas are reminiscent of red flowers and
small black fruits against a background of light
spice; the palate is soft and persuasive, tasty
but not acidic, masterfully refreshed by a final
balsamic note. Elegance in classicism.

FATTORIA SELVAPIANA

Località Selvapiana 43
Rufina (FI)
selvapiana.it
Year of establishment: 1826
Owner: the Giuntini family
Average number of bottles
produced per year: 250,000

The history of Villa
Selvapiana took on the
current characteristics of
a winegrowing center a
century ago, proceeding in
gradual stages along a path
of development that has led it
to be recognized today as an
ambassador of Chianti Rufina
around world. The 148 acres
under vine are organically
farmed and predominantly
planted with Sangiovese
grapes, which are joined by
historic local varieties such
as Colorino and Malvasia
Nera, along with a splash of
Cabernet Sauvignon, Merlot,
and Syrah.

CHIANTI RUFINA RISERVA VIGNETO BUCERCHIALE

First year of production: 1979
Average number of bottles produced
per year: 36,000
Grape variety: Sangiovese

The classic acidic freshness of Sangiovese is
combined with the savory and almost saline
touch that characterizes the Chianti Rufina
area, creating a lively and youthful taste
sensation that is flavorful and captivatingly
drinkable. The aromas are richly fruity, pure,
and crisp, with a touch of wilted violets that
over the years combines with spicy notes of
refined classicism.

BADIA A COLTIBUONO

Località Badia a
Coltibuono
Gaiole in Chianti (SI)
coltibuono.com
Year of establishment: 1846
Owner: the Stucchi
Prinetti family
Average number of bottles
produced per year: 250,000

An enchanting thousand-
year-old abbey is home to the
headquarters of the Badia a
Coltibuono, a winery. These
has earned international
renown for its wines of stellar
classicism, where the star is
Sangiovese, organically and
biodynamically cultivated
on the 155 acres of the estate,
joined by small parcels with
the area's historic vines
such as Colorino, Ciliegiolo,
Mammolo, Pugnitello, and
Malvasia Nera. In addition
to the more recent Riserva
Cultus, the range includes
Chianti Classico and Chianti
Classico Riserva of precious
purity of taste, capable
of evolving positively for
decades, where the strength
lies in balance and harmony,
never in wood or in power.

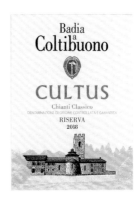

CHIANTI CLASSICO RISERVA CULTUS

First year of production: 2011
Average number of bottles produced
per year: 12,000
Grape varieties: Sangiovese (80%);
Canaiolo, Colorino, Ciliegiolo

Long aging—between eighteen and twenty-
four months—in wood of different sizes,
and the presence of the now rare varieties
that have made the history of Chianti,
build a very complex aroma, in which violet
and cherry are highlighted together with
fresh balsamic notes. The palate is warm
and impressive, vital and progressive, with
a savory touch that creates harmonious
drinkability.

BARONE RICASOLI

Located in Madonna a Brolio, Castello di Brolio Gaiole in Chianti (SI)
ricasoli.com
Year of establishment: 1141
Owner: the Ricasoli family
Average number of bottles produced per year: 1,300,000

In 2008, Francesco Ricasoli began the impressive redevelopment of this winery, which for centuries has been the emblem of quality in the classic Sangiovese region. The wines offered, which are increasingly praised by critics worldwide, originate from no less than 593 acres of estate vineyards found primarily in the fantastic Castello di Brolio. The Chianti Classico Gran Selezione Castello di Brolio is accompanied by other Chianti Classico Gran Selezione projects that faithfully respect the vineyards of origin, with well-deserved success among consumers: Ceni Primo, Colledilà, Roncicone.

CHIANTI CLASSICO GRAN SELEZIONE CASTELLO DI BROLIO

First year of production: 1934
Average number of bottles produced per year: 40,000
Grape varieties: Sangiovese (95%); Merlot, Cabernet Sauvignon

While open and expansive on the nose, with hints of ripe red fruit and citrus nuances against a slightly smoky and vanilla background, in the mouth it is taut and decisive, with measured tannins and impressive, almost savory freshness, incisive right up to the refined, spicy finish. A taste that speaks of centuries of oenological history.

CASTELLO DI MONSANTO

Via Monsanto 8
Barberino Tavarnelle (FI)
castellodimonsanto.it
Year of establishment: 1961
Owner: the Bianchi family
Average number of bottles produced per year: 450,000

A winery that has become synonymous with Chianti Classico and has enjoyed great prestige since its beginnings, when Fabrizio Bianchi acquired the first 12 acres of vines, which have now grown to 178. One of the strengths of Castello di Monsanto lies in its decades-long ability to develop wine in stored bottles, as underlined by the one hundred thousand bottles resting in the winery's enchanting cellars. The Gran Selezione Il Poggio is accompanied by the vintage Chianti Classico and Riserva labels, along with the prestigious Sangioveto Grosso Fabrizio Bianchi, and small Cabernet Sauvignon-based productions, Nemo, from 1982, and Chardonnay Collezione, from 1990.

CHIANTI CLASSICO GRAN SELEZIONE IL POGGIO

First year of production: 1962
Average number of bottles produced per year: 18,000
Grape varieties: Sangiovese (90%); Canaiolo and Colorino (10%)

A wine of great personality: it ages in wood for twenty months and offers spicy aromas that combine with fruity hints of cherry and floral hints of violets. The taste is one of perfect harmony, substantial but lean thanks to the slight astringency and stimulating acid freshness: the emblem of the Chianti Classico renaissance.

CASTELL'IN VILLA

Località Castell'in Villa
Castelnuovo Berardenga (SI)
castellinvilla.com
Year of establishment: 1971
Owner: Coralia Pignatelli della Leonessa
Average number of bottles produced per year: 120,000

The terms with which this winery is described speak of classicism, purity, and tradition, but what must also be included is the extraordinary length of time invested in a production made only from Sangiovese grapes. These improve and enrich themselves in the bottle for at least twenty or thirty years, the result of the 125 acres of property that use organic methods. The Chianti Classico Riserva is accompanied by two other celebrated Riserva selections, Poggio delle Rose and IN, along with an exquisite and more immediate Chianti Classico and a small production of Santacroce, a Super Tuscan in which Cabernet Sauvignon is present.

CHIANTI CLASSICO RISERVA

First year of production: 1971
Average number of bottles produced per year: 15,000
Grape variety: Sangiovese

Matured for forty months in large casks, it displays delicate, unadulterated fruit and spicy qualities, followed by a taste that is both structured and fresh, crisp and direct, with a hint of savoriness that makes it particularly persuasive and tasty. Consistently one of the greatest interpretations of the Chianti *terroir*.

CASTELLO DI VOLPAIA

Località Volpaia, Via Pier Capponi 2
Radda in Chianti (SI)
volpaia.com
Year of establishment: 1966
Owner: the Mascheroni Stianti family
Average number of bottles produced per year: 220,000

The medieval walls of the village conceal the cellar, which is a fascinating destination and a must for wine tourists. The vocation of the winery, of which 111 acres are certified organic, is mainly for Chianti Classico, especially in the Riserva and Gran Selezione versions, where Il Puro Casanova, made from the oldest vines, also stands out. Labels from the estates in Maremma and Pantelleria make things even better.

CHIANTI CLASSICO GRAN SELEZIONE COLTASSALA

First year of production: 1980
Average number of bottles produced per year: 8,000
Grape varieties: Sangiovese (95%), Mammolo (5%)

Born outside the official designations with the simple name of Coltassala, it has become an appreciated Super Tuscan and, after the institution of the Gran Selezione in 2014, joined the Chianti Classico DOCG. Matured in small French barrels that lend a gentle, spicy touch, it displays the classic Sangiovese aromas, with violets and small berries in the foreground followed by a refreshing hint of orange. The taste is of rare balance, with a multifaceted, vigorous, and refined elegance.

FÈLSINA

Via del Chianti 103
Castelnuovo Berardenga
(SI)
felsina.it
Year of establishment: 1966
Owner: Giovanni Poggiali
Average number of bottles
produced per year: 550,000

A winery that is in a constant
state of change and flux,
thanks to the presence of
several generations of the
Poggiali family, both in
vinification techniques and
agronomic management,
which also includes a variety
of oil productions.The
emblematic Rancia came
out in the same year, 1983,
as the first release of the
company's celebrated Super
Tuscan, Fontalloro, followed
by several Chianti Classico
offerings, including today's
Gran Selezione Colonia, which
originate from the 222 acres of
estate vineyards.

CHIANTI CLASSICO RISERVA RANCIA

First year of production: 1983
Average number of bottles produced
per year: 48,000
Grape variety: Sangiovese

Aged for eighteen months in small French
oak barrels, the wine offers ripe red fruits
and spices against a stimulating mineral
background of damp earth. In the mouth it
is rich in pulp and has good tannicity that
gives character and volume; in addition, it
lingers and is elegant thanks to the smoky
hints of oak that embellish the finish. A
modern interpretation of the great Chianti
Classico.

ISTINE

Località Istine 28/A
Radda in Chianti (SI)
istine.it
Year of establishment: 2009
Owner: the Fronti family
Average number of bottles
produced per year: 90,000

Angela Fronti, an oenologist
with experience in various
Tuscan wine cellars, decided to
devote herself to the 57 acres of
her family's vineyards, which
are organically cultivated. She
makes wines that are most of
all the pure expression of the
different personalities of her
three different crus: Vigna
Cavarchione, Vigna Istine,
Vigna Casanova dell'Aia. The
results were immediately
brilliant, succeeding in
palpably expressing purity,
freshness, and classicism,
which can also be attributed
to the use of cement and
Slavonian oak barrels in the
cellar processes. An important
novelty in the rich world of
Chianti Classico.

CHIANTI CLASSICO VIGNA CAVARCHIONE

First year of production: 2013
Average number of bottles produced
per year: 3,000
Grape variety: Sangiovese

From young vines grown in Gaiole comes
this fresh and lively selection, in which
the classic nuances of violet and cherry
are joined by intense notes of eucalyptus
and medicinal herbs. The flavor is incisive,
almost pawing, of excellent substance,
persistent, and enchantingly drinkable. The
energetic complexity of Sangiovese at the
highest level.

TENUTA DI VALGIANO

Via di Valgiano 7
Capannori (LU)
valgiano.it
Year of establishment: 1993
Owner: Moreno Petrini
Average number of bottles
produced per year: 65,000

The biodynamic approach
desired by Moreno Petrini was
implemented from the very
beginning with the help of a
well-known oenologist and
promoter of this agronomic
theory, Saverio Petrilli. The
result can be appreciated
both in 40 acres of scenic
vineyards interspersed with
forests and cultivations of
olive trees and grains, and in
wines of impeccable quality
and increasing fame. This is
a winery that has revitalized
an entire winegrowing area
by demonstrating, through
the elegance and vitality
of its wines, the validity of
environmentally sustainable
viticulture.

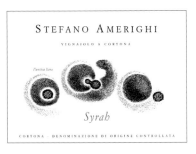

COLLINE LUCCHESI ROSSO TENUTA DI VALGIANO

First year of production: 1999
Average number of bottles produced
per year: 7,500
Grape varieties: Sangiovese (60%),
Merlot (20%), Syrah (20%)

To the natural taste nuances of the basic
grape varieties is added the contribution,
perceptible in the first few years in the
bottle, of the French oak, creating a refined
blend of fruity, spicy, and balsamic notes.
The palate is an ode to finesse and balance,
long and persuasive, delicately astringent,
with an enchanting licorice finish. A taste
that is hard to forget.

STEFANO AMERIGHI

Località Poggiobello di
Farneta
Cortona (AR)
stefanoamerighi.it
Year of establishment: 2000
Owner: Stefano Amerighi
Average number of bottles
produced per year: 40,000

A natural approach is
taken here, with the 27
biodynamically certified
acres under vine being the
start of a process whereby the
stalk crusher is replaced by
people's feet or whole cluster
vinification, with no use of
chemicals throughout the
production process. After
aging in stoneware, cement,
and used wood, the wines are
lively and crisp, very enjoyable,
the exact expression of a *terroir*
that has well demonstrated
its predilection for the Syrah
grape. The goodness all comes
from the vineyard and the
sensitivity of the producer.

Cortona Syrah

First year of production: 2006
Average number of bottles produced
per year: 22,000
Grape variety: Syrah

The result of separate vinifications of thirty
different plots, blended from year to year
according to seasonal trends, this is a Syrah
rich in personality, dynamic, endowed
with spicy scents and black fruits ranging
from pepper to olive to ink. On the palate,
it is dense, free of slackness, with tasty
drinkability and excellent freshness; it is
vibrant and sharp right through to the
licorice finish. The complexity is equal to the
pleasantness.

FONTODI

Località Panzano, Via San Leolino 89
Greve in Chianti (FI)
fontodi.com
Year of establishment: 1968
Owner: Giovanni Manetti
Average number of bottles produced per year: 350,000

The Conca d'Oro in Panzano is known as the home of great Sangiovese grapes, and it is here that Giovanni Manetti owns the most prestigious vineyards: 227 acres in total, organically cultivated in an environment that is as natural as it is fascinating and full of vitality. Sangiovese gives rise to Flaccianello and three Chianti Classico offerings, among which the Gran Selezione Vigna del Sorbo stands out, while Syrah, Pinot Noir, and Sauvignon grapes create other small, prized labels.

FLACCIANELLO DELLA PIEVE

First year of production: 1981
Average number of bottles produced per year: 60,000
Grape variety: Sangiovese

The style is rich and multifaceted, characterized by ample aromas of red fruits combined with cocoa, balsamic notes, and spices also deriving from two years of aging in French barriques. The taste structure is persistent, characterized by velvety tannins and a backbone of beautiful freshness. A fine interpretation of pure Sangiovese, a great Super Tuscan.

PODERE IL CARNASCIALE

Località Podere Il Carnasciale
Mercatale Valdarno (AR)
caberlot.eu
Year of establishment: 1988
Owner: the Rogosky family
Average number of bottles produced per year: 20,000

A small winery that deserves to be known thanks to the commitment that the Rogosky family has put into creating a business devoted to quality, and based on just 12 acres that are organically farmed. From the same crossbreed of Cabernet Franc and Merlot from which Il Caberlot is made comes the Carnasciale, which is slightly more fruity and delicate. While this might have seemed like a game at first, over time it has become a workable and valid reality.

IL CABERLOT

First year of production: 1988
Average number of bottles produced per year: 3,500 magnums
Grape variety: Caberlot (cross between Cabernet Franc and Merlot)

A wine with strong taste energy, attractive and fascinating thanks to an intense and persistent spiciness reminiscent of black pepper, combined with small black fruits and fine mineral hints such as graphite and ink. The flavor is impressive and dynamic, never very tannic and enriched by a harmonizing contribution from the barrique. A wine with a rich personality, rare and costly, of superlative pleasantness.

IL BORRO

Frazione San Giustino Valdarno, Località Borro 1
Loro Ciuffenna (AR)
ilborro.it
Year of establishment: 1993
Owner: the Ferragamo family
Average number of bottles produced per year: 160,000

Valdarno has long proven to be an area in which not only Sangiovese but also vines of French origin produce excellent results. This is the consideration that the Ferragamo family made, thirty years ago, when they began the complex renovation of the splendid medieval village and vineyards, giving rise to labels with different personalities, united by the finesse and naturalness with which they are worked, first using organic methods on the 111 acres of land and then in the spectacular cellars. The critical acclaim of Il Borro label is equal to that of Valdarno di Sopra Sangiovese Vigna Polissena.

IL BORRO

First year of production: 1999
Average number of bottles produced per year: 45,000
Grape varieties: Merlot (50%), Cabernet Sauvignon (35%), Syrah (15%)

Plums and blueberries open a refined bouquet rich in spices, medicinal herbs, and balsamic hints. The palate is powerful and of excellent harmony thanks to delicate tannins and tonic freshness, with a fascinating, slightly peppery, smoky finish. Masterful use of wood, never aggressive.

CASTELLO DI AMA

Frazione Lecchi, Località Ama
Gaiole in Chianti (SI)
castellodiama.com
Year of establishment: 1972
Owners: the Sebasti, Carini, and Tradico families
Average number of bottles produced per year: 320,000

The first thing Marco Pallanti and Lorenza Sebaste did was to achieve oenological excellence and then make it known to the world, receiving deserved recognition. L'Apparita is probably the most famous of their wines, but it should be emphasized that the Chianti Classico San Lorenzo, Bellavista, and La Casuccia are also of the highest level, pivotal to the revolution that began in the 1970s. The winery is set in a splendid hamlet rich in works of art, surrounded by forests and 198 acres of vineyards.

L'APPARITA

First year of production: 1985
Average number of bottles produced per year: 8,000
Grape variety: Merlot

Matured for over a year in French barriques, the nose is refined, penetrating, and intensely endowed with spices and small berries, with a refreshing touch of eucalyptus in the background. The palate is splendid, always dense, rich, and powerful but never soft or tired, possessing delicate tannins and an acidic backbone that makes it irresistibly drinkable: one of the world's great Merlots.

MONTEVERTINE

Località Montevertine
Radda in Chianti (SI)
montevertine.it
Year of establishment: 1967
Owner: Martino Manetti
Average number of bottles
produced per year: 80,000

The winery founded by Sergio Manetti immediately stood out for the finesse with which it makes its wines, in which Sangiovese is always delicate, almost whispered, never too woody or concentrated or alcoholic. From the 47 acres of the property come the famous Super Tuscan Le Pergole Torte, and also, without the use of the Chianti Classico DOCG but with the intervention of small doses of Canaiolo and Colorino grapes, the multi-award-winning Montevertine and the more youthful Pian del Ciampolo. An essential reference point for getting to know Sangiovese.

LE PERGOLE TORTE
2019

LE PERGOLE TORTE

First year of production: 1977
Average number of bottles produced
per year: 29,000
Grape variety: Sangiovese

The purity of the typical Sangiovese aromas, with violets, cherries, field herbs, spices, and citrus hints, precede a sip of excellent structure, fresh and slightly savory, lively, long, delicately astringent, with a finish that evokes red flowers. Deservedly famous, it is a great expression of quintessential Tuscany.

MASSETO

Località Ornellaia 191
Frazione Bolgheri
Castagneto Carducci (LI)
masseto.com
Year of establishment: 1981
Owner: the Frescobaldi
family
Average number of bottles
produced per year: 32,000

The continuous challenge of the pursuit of excellence led the Frescobaldi family to the decision to endow Masseto with its own cellar and its own vineyards, making it productively independent from Ornellaia. It was the famous oenologist André Tchelistcheff who recommended dedicating a specific portion of the estate's 27 acres to the Merlot grape and making a single wine from it, with worldwide successes following each year since 1987. Since 2017, there has also been Massetino, itself highly sought-after and small only in name, in whose blend there is a share of Cabernet Franc.

MASSETO

First year of production: 1987
Average number of bottles produced
per year: 32,000
Grape variety: Merlot

One of the most famous wines on the planet, and very expensive, beloved by collectors and the star at many auctions in bottles of all sizes: proof that from the Merlot grape one can obtain wines that are as rich as they are complex, as structured as they are dynamic, as spicy as they are fresh and incisive. Many have tried to recreate it, but it remains inimitable.

CASTELLO DEL TERRICCIO

Località Terriccio, Via Bagnoli 16
Castellina Marittima (PI)
terriccio.com
Year of establishment: 1921
Owner: Vittorio Piozzo di Rosignano
Average number of bottles produced per year: 200,000

The 160 acres of vineyards are located on a hilly estate rich in olive groves and woods, where grapes of French origin have found ideal terrain. This gives rise to qualified international style labels that include, in addition to Lupicaia, the powerful Castello del Terriccio—in which Syrah is also present—and the cooler Tassinaia, joined by the white Con Vento, from Viognier and Sauvignon grapes.

Lupicaia
2010
G.A. ROSSI DI MEDELANA
CASTELLINA M.MA (PI) - ITALIA

LUPICAIA

First year of production: 1993
Average number of bottles produced
per year: 30,000
Grape varieties: Cabernet Sauvignon
(90%); Merlot, Petit Verdot

Always made avoiding excessive concentration and heaviness, it offers an admirable expression of freshness and vitality, with balsamic notes ranging from eucalyptus to rosemary and pine resin to incense. The flavor is robust and energetic, lean and well fruited, ample and endowed with a delicate but snappy tannin, very enjoyable even with its smoky finish. It has become a classic of the new oenological Tuscany.

COLLEMASSARI

Località Poggi del Sasso
Cinigiano (GR)
collemassari.it
Year of establishment: 1998
Owners: Claudio Tipa and Maria Iris Bertarelli
Average number of bottles produced per year: 500,000

This wine shows the best of the upper Maremma region, thanks to 297 acres of organically grown vineyards from which seven labels are born. In addition to Poggio Lombrone there is Montecucco Rosso Riserva ColleMassari, in which the predominant Sangiovese is joined by 10% Ciliegiolo and as much Cabernet Sauvignon, which is particularly prized. Castello ColleMassari is part of Claudio Tipa's group of wineries along with Grattamacco, San Giorgio, and Poggio di Sotto.

CASTELLO COLLEMASSARI
ColleMassari
POGGIO LOMBRONE
MONTECUCCO
Denominazione di Origine Controllata e Garantita
SANGIOVESE RISERVA
2017

MONTECUCCO SANGIOVESE RISERVA POGGIO LOMBRONE

First year of production: 2004
Average number of bottles produced
per year: 15,000
Grape variety: Sangiovese

Matured for thirty months in large oak, it offers nuances of well-ripened red fruits with essential notes of spice and refreshing, refined pine resin. The taste is imposing, characterized more by the enveloping pulp than by acidity, with delicate astringency and an elegant finish that ranges from citrus to cocoa. This is the wine that ennobles the Montecucco Sangiovese DOCG to the highest level.

TENUTA SETTE PONTI

Via Sette Ponti 71
Castiglion Fibocchi (AR)
tenutasetteponti.it
Year of establishment: 1998
Owner: the Moretti Cuseri
family
Average number of bottles
produced per year: 250,000

The company immediately
attracted international
attention thanks to Oreno and
Orma, wines of rare elegance
and personality. Although it
should not be forgotten that
the estate's 148 organically
farmed acres include plots
of Sangiovese grapes, from
which the winery's first
label, Crognolo, was born in
1998. This was followed by
the always award-winning
Valdarno di Sopra Sangiovese
Vigna dell'Impero and two
Chianti.

ORENO

First year of production: 1999
Average number of bottles produced
per year: 48,000
Grape varieties: Merlot (50%),
Cabernet Sauvignon (40%), Petit
Verdot (10%)

Matured for eighteen months in small
barrels, it offers fine notes of small black
fruits and plum tarts against a background
of eucalyptus. The palate is quite
straightforward and almost severe, with the
soft, enveloping touch of Merlot perfectly
contrasted by the texture and dynamism of
Cabernet Sauvignon. An excellent Bordeaux
interpretation that is now found in Tuscany.

SAN GIUSTO A RENTENNANO

Località San Giusto a
Rentennano
Gaiole in Chianti (SI)
fattoriasangiusto.it
Year of establishment: 1914
Owner: the Martini di Cigala
family
Average number of bottles
produced per year: 90,000

Even today the evocative cellars
of the ancient monastery contain
the barrels dedicated to aging
Sangiovese, offered in the fine
versions of Chianti Classico and
Riserva Le Baròncole, as well
as Percarlo. An ever-successful
Merlot, La Ricolma, and the very
rich Vin San Giusto Passito, aged
for six years in classic Tuscan
caratelli, or kegs, complete the
range. Everything comes from 77
acres of vines, organically farmed,
in a company with a century-long
history that looks to the future by
increasing the ecological aspects of
production and adopting tools to
safeguard the environment, from
photovoltaics to water recycling.
All the wines are of impeccable
workmanship, consistently
winning international awards.

PERCARLO

First year of production: 1983
Average number of bottles produced
per year: 14,000
Grape variety: Sangiovese

For forty years one of the best expressions
of the pure Sangiovese grape, rich in red
fruits and violets against a background
of field grass and eucalyptus, with a
powerful and decisive flavor, always with
good freshness and invigorating tannicity,
delicately smoked by the long stay in oak
in the very long finish. A splendid example
of a Super Tuscan from Sangiovese grapes.

LE MACCHIOLE

Via Bolgherese 189/A
Castagneto Carducci (LI)
lemacchiole.it
Year of establishment: 1983
Owner: Cinzia Merli
Average number of bottles
produced per year: 190,000

Eugenio Campolmi and
Cinzia Merli were among
the architects of the success
of the wines in this area and,
although they use the Bolgheri
Rosso DOC on only one label,
they express its deepest and
most genuine soul. Grapes
and wood of French origin
give rise to options in addition
to Paleo, world famous and
absolutely refined, based on
Merlot (Messorio) as well
as Syrah (Scrio), with space
dedicated to white grapes
in Paleo Bianco, based on
Chardonnay with a touch of
Sauvignon. The winery makes
wine with the utmost care
from grapes grown on 69 acres
of organically cultivated land.

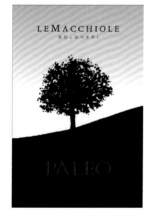

PALEO

First year of production: 1989
Average number of bottles produced
per year: 25,000
Grape variety: Cabernet Franc

Fascinating, with refined aromas that
range from small berries to medicinal
herbs, against a background in which the
oak is barely present to give complexity
and elegance. The palate is decidedly solid
and rich in texture, with velvety tannins
and a long plum finish against a balsamic
background.

TUA RITA

Località Notri 81
Suvereto (LI)
tuarita.it
Year of establishment: 1984
Owners: the Bisti and
Frascolla families
Average number of bottles
produced per year: 330,000

Virgilio Bisti and Rita Tua
began making wine for fun
and out of passion, having
only 5 acres of vines at their
disposal, which has now turned
into 138, all cultivated with
the utmost respect for nature,
in this evocative area of the
Colline Metallifere that has its
reference point in Suvereto.
Together with the sought-after
and expensive Redigaffi, the
winery offers ten other quality
labels, in which the Giusto di
Notri (Cabernet Sauvignon),
Lodano Rosso (Petit Verdot
and Merlot), Per Sempre
(Syrah), and the two Perlatos,
Rosso (Sangiovese) and Bianco
(Vermentino), stand out. A
winery that has brought the Val
di Cornia into the ranks of the
great Tuscan wine region.

REDIGAFFI

First year of production: 1994
Average number of bottles produced
per year: 15,000
Grape variety: Merlot

The first production was limited to two
experimental barriques, which led to
consistent success over the years, including
Redigaffi in its own right into the small
circle of the world's great Merlots. Matured
in barriques, it is a wine of rare finesse, rich
in the nose of small berries and red flowers
in a delicate smoky setting; in the mouth it
is broad and dense, with great balance due
to the gentle contribution of acidity.

RIECINE

Riecine, Gaiole in Chianti (SI)
riecine.it
Year of establishment: 1971
Owner: Lana Frank
Average number of bottles
produced per year: 80,000

The Frank family took over the
ownership of the winery created
by John Dunkley in 2011 and it
soon became well-known for the
very high quality of its output.
The current production line,
based on 40 acres of organically
cultivated land, tends to
emphasize classicism and
freshness, as the award-winning
Chianti Classico Gran Selezione
Vigna Gittori and Chianti
Classico Riserva demonstrate,
without in any way renouncing
the enhancement of the Super
Tuscan that has made the
winery famous, La Gioia.

RIECINE DI RIECINE

First year of production: 2010
Average number of bottles produced
per year: 3,000
Grape variety: Sangiovese

It ferments in wood and ages for thirty
months in cement, offering rich citrus scents
that combine with small red and black fruits
such as currants and blackberries. The palate
is lively, dynamic, harmoniously progressive,
never too concentrated, of persuasive
and fresh drinkability: the multifaceted
complexity of Sangiovese.

CASTELLO DI FONTERUTOLI

Via Ottone III di Sassonia 5
Castellina in Chianti (SI)
mazzei.it
Year of establishment: 1435
Owner: the Mazzei family
Average number of bottles
produced per year: 750,000

Siepi's fame should not
overshadow the Mazzei
family's commitment to
Chianti Classico, which is
also offered in three award-
winning Gran Selezione
versions: Badiòla, Vicoregio,
and Castello Fonterutoli. The
272 acres cultivated in the
Chianti region are flanked by
the Tenuta Belguardo, with
84 acres in Maremma, and the
Tenuta Zisola, with 52 acres in
Sicily. It is a story that began
in the Middle Ages and has
evolved through the study
of the peculiarities of each
vineyard and strict respect for
the environment.

SIEPI

First year of production: 1992
Average number of bottles produced
per year: 35,000
Grape varieties: Sangiovese (50%),
Merlot (50%)

It starts out on 35 dedicated acres and is
then matured in new wood for eighteen
months, giving the nose both the plummy
and vegetal notes of Merlot and the floral
freshness of Sangiovese, as well as the
spiciness of oak, in a combination of assured
complexity and elegance. The taste is soft,
with barely noticeable tannin, while the
acidity achieves a precise and balanced
overall harmony.

CASTELLO DEI RAMPOLLA

Località Panzano, Via Case
Sparse 22
Greve in Chianti (FI)
castellodeirampolla.it
Year of establishment: 1965
Owner: the Di Napoli
Rampolla family
Average number of bottles
produced per year: 80,000

The first choice of this winery
was to make sure that as much
of the production process
adhered to a natural way of
doing things, starting, albeit
without official certification,
with the biodynamic approach
on the 79 acres of cultivated
land. The second was to use all
the grape varieties that grow
best in this part of Panzano—
not only Sangiovese, but also
typical Bordeaux varieties—so
much so that the winery's
most famous label, along with
Sammarco, is D'Alceo, from
Cabernet Sauvignon and Petit
Verdot grapes.

SAMMARCO

First year of production: 1980
Average number of bottles produced
per year: 25,000
Grape varieties: Cabernet Sauvignon;
Sangiovese, Merlot

The complex aromas are characterized
by small black fruits and mineral hints of
cinchona, with an overall expression of
crisp vegetal freshness favored by the use of
delicate, lightly roasted French wood. The
palate is built on a solid tannic base and a
great fruity texture that characterizes the
lingering finish. A Super Tuscan as rich as it
is elegant.

DUEMANI

Via del Commercio 80
Castellina Marittima (PI)
duemani.eu
Year of establishment: 2002
Owners: Elena Celli and
Luca D'Attoma
Average number of bottles
produced per year: 40,000

Thanks to his work as an
oenological consultant, Luca
D'Attoma was convinced of the
winegrowing potential of this
area, and his partnership with
Elena Celli was important to
deciding to operate his own
company. The grape varieties
that best express themselves
in this fascinating but little-
known area close to the sea are
the classic French ones, from
Cabernet Franc to Syrah, from
Grenache to Merlot, cultivated
biodynamically on 27 acres
of property. This gives rise to
world-famous labels, among
which the Cabernet Franc-
based Duemani and Suisassi
stand out.

SUISASSI

First year of production: 2004
Average number of bottles produced
per year: 3,000
Grape variety: Syrah

Aged in barriques, it offers aromas that
open on notes of spices and undergrowth
fruits, with a vegetal hint of olive to lend
complexity. The taste is dense, enveloping,
and well-articulated, with a fine tannic mass
that adds volume to the fruity component.
Rich, energetic, elegant.

TENUTA DI TRINORO
Via Val d'Orcia 15
Sarteano (SI)
vinifranchetti.com
Year of establishment: 1995
Owner: the Franchetti
family
Average number of bottles
produced per year: 90,000

Andrea Franchetti has always
been passionate about the
wines of Bordeaux and
wanted to rework them in a
Tuscan way, on his 62 acres
of vineyards set in the Val
d'Orcia region. The same grape
varieties are there—Cabernet
Franc, Cabernet Sauvignon,
Merlot, and Petit Verdot—but
with different soils and a
personal style of vinification,
with cement tanks built
especially for his cellar in
addition to classic barriques.
The highly celebrated Tenuta
di Trinoro is accompanied by
the few qualified labels among
which the younger brother Le
Cupole (from the same vines),
the powerful Palazzi (Merlot),
and Campo di Magnacosta
(Cabernet Franc) stand out.

TENUTA DI TRINORO
First year of production: 1997
Average number of bottles produced
per year: 9,500
Grape varieties: Cabernet Franc,
Merlot; Cabernet Sauvignon, Petit
Verdot

Small black fruits, tart plums, blueberries,
blackberries, and dark spices create an
elegant and intense bouquet not lacking
in refreshing medicinal herbs. The taste
enthuses with richness and a mass of flavor,
with more than velvety tannins and rare
vitality. A world-famous and esteemed label,
and therefore expensive, characterized by
complexity, power, and refinement at the
highest level.

PETROLO
Via Petrolo 30
Bucine (AR)
petrolo.it
Year of establishment: 1947
Owner: Luca Sanjust di
Teulada
Average number of bottles
produced per year: 90,000

The company's mission is
"not to make basic wines."
In each of the seven different
labels they produce wines
that are the best possible
outcome from the 77 acres of
estate vineyards, organically
cultivated with particularly
low yields. In an area already
described as valuable by
Grand Duke Cosimo III in
1716, Sangiovese is cultivated,
with the offers of Bòggina
A and C, as well as Merlot
(Galatrona) and Cabernet
Sauvignon (Campo Lusso),
with limited space dedicated
to white Trebbiano (Bòggina
B). Wines of great personality
and elegance.

VAL D'ARNO DI SOPRA MERLOT
VIGNA GALATRONA
First year of production: 1994
Average number of bottles produced
per year: 30,000
Grape variety: Merlot

Produced from 25 acres where fifty thousand
Bordeaux Merlot vines are grown, one-third
of which are aged for eighteen months in
new barriques. The classic ripe blackberry
and plum tart is joined by a fragrant
balsamic whiff against a delicately smoky
background. It has a slight astringency
in the mouth, a backbone with a touch of
acidity, a rich structure of fruity flesh, and a
toasty finish rich in herbs. One of the most
celebrated Tuscan wines, at the top of the
so-called "international style," it has been in
the Val d'Arno di Sopra DOC since 2013.

MARCHESI ANTINORI
Via Cassia per Siena 133,
Località Bargino
San Casciano in Val di Pesa
(FI)
antinori.it
Year of establishment: 1385
Owner: the Antinori family
Average number of
bottles produced per year:
18,000,000

The nerve center today is
in the winery inaugurated
in 2012, but there are many
estates from which the
variegated Antinori product
comes. From Tignanello,
Badia a Passignano, and
Pèppoli in Chianti Classico to
Guado al Tasso in Bolgheri,
from Pian delle Vigne in
Montalcino to La Braccesca in
Montepulciano, while outside
the region the most famous are
Castello della Sala in Umbria,
Montenisa in Lombardy,
Tormaresca in Apulia, and
Prunotto in Piedmont, for a
total surface area close to 5,930
acres under vine.

TIGNANELLO
First year of production: 1971
Average number of bottles produced
per year: 345,000
Grape varieties: Sangiovese (80%);
Cabernet Sauvignon, Cabernet Franc

Fifty years of growing success for a wine that
has best demonstrated how complexity and
tasty drinkability can form an inseparable
pair. Born as "Chianti Classico Riserva
Vigneto Tignanello," it has been a celebrated
Super Tuscan since 1971, took the exclusive
name of Tignanello in 1975, and today is
the fruit of 141 dedicated acres. Power and
finesse, silky tannicity and refreshing acidity,
barrique aging and constant elegance make
it a wine loved the world over.

IL COLOMBAIO DI SANTA
CHIARA
Località San Donato 1
San Gimignano (SI)
colombaiosantachiara.it
Year of establishment: 2001
Owner: the Logi family
Average number of bottles
produced per year: 100,000

Theirs is a classic family
history in which several
generations are united by the
desire to develop their winery
in terms of both vineyards
and quality. The results have
brought Il Colombaio di Santa
Chiara into the top echelons
of the designation, thanks
to three top Vernaccia di San
Gimignano offerings, joined
by fine Sangiovese-based
labels. The vineyard area has
reached 52 acres, managed
organically, while careful
vinification uses cement, steel,
and wood.

VERNACCIA DI SAN GIMIGNANO
RISERVA L'ALBERETA
First year of production: 2008
Average number of bottles produced
per year: 7,000
Grape variety: Vernaccia di San
Gimignano

The only selection of white wine in which
oak is used, handled sparingly to add a
little creaminess and softness to the taste's
freshness, which is typical of the variety.
White flowers and yellow-fleshed fruits
characterize the aromas, in which there is no
shortage of suggestive spicy and balsamic
hints. There is excellent capacity for
development and maturing in bottles.

MONTENIDOLI

Località Montenidoli
San Gimignano (SI)
montenidoli.com
Year of establishment: 1965
Owner: Elisabetta Fagiuoli
Average number of bottles
produced per year: 110,000

Montenidoli is an oenological
project based on total respect
for nature, set in one of the
most fascinating winegrowing
landscapes in the world,
where, amid woods and
olive groves, the 67 acres of
vineyards are cultivated using
organic and biodynamic
methods on land where
shells and sand recall the
ancient presence of the sea.
Production is centered around
Vernaccia di San Gimignano,
in the Fiore and Tradizionale
versions as well as in Carato,
but there is also output based
on Sangiovese and historical
local vines, from Colorino to
Trebbiano.

VERNACCIA DI SAN GIMIGNANO
CARATO

First year of production: 1989
Average number of bottles produced
per year: 6,000
Grape variety: Vernaccia di San
Gimignano

The aroma is fresh, with hints ranging from
citrus to mint to aniseed, sweetened by a
slight buttery notes deriving from aging in
wood. The taste is decisive and lively, rich in
flavor and freshness, persistent and balanced
until the long finish in which a return of
almond emerges. A version of Vernaccia di
San Gimignano that is as complex as it is
easy and pleasant to drink.

BOSCARELLI

Via di Montenero 28
Montepulciano (SI)
poderiboscarelli.com
Year of establishment: 1962
Owner: the De Ferrari
Corradi family
Average number of bottles
produced per year: 100,000

A family-run business, brought
to international fame and
appreciation by Paola De
Ferrari Corradi—daughter of
Egidio Corradi, the founder
of Boscarelli—whose stylistic
approach is also successfully
followed by her sons Luca
and Niccolò De Ferrari. A style
made of Sangiovese grapes
processed and selected on 52
acres of property, of refinement
combined with good warmth
of flavor, of clean and never
intrusive woods. The famous
Il Nocio is flanked by four
other productions of Vino
Nobile di Montepulciano, with
the Riserva Costa Grande—
produced in small quantities—
increasingly appreciated by
wine critics.

VINO NOBILE DI MONTEPULCIANO
IL NOCIO

First year of production: 1991
Average number of bottles produced
per year: 5,000
Grape variety: Sangiovese

A wine that is reminiscent of the squaring of
the circle: always important and never too
concentrated, tannins present but velvety,
unobtrusive freshness but vital, firm on the
palate and well faceted.

CAPEZZANA

Via di Capezzana 100
Carmignano (PO)
capezzana.it
Year of establishment: 1920
Owner: the Contini
Bonacossi family
Average number of bottles
produced per year: 350,000

Sisters Beatrice and Benedetta
lead an estate that became
the property of the Bonacossi
family a century ago, in an
area where vines have been
growing since the early Middle
Ages. The 198 acres under vine
are organically farmed and
predominantly Sangiovese,
the main grape in both the
structured Carmignano DOCG
and the fresh Barco Reale
di Carmignano DOC. This
grape is joined by Trebbiano,
from which the Vin Santo we
present is also made, as well as
the French varieties Cabernet
Sauvignon, Merlot, and Syrah,
which give rise to the famous
Ghiaie della Furba.

VIN SANTO DI CARMIGNANO
RISERVA

First year of production: 1925
Average number of bottles produced per
year: 5,500 (375 ml)
Grape varieties: Trebbiano (90%), San
Colombano (10%)

After the harvest, the grapes are dried for a
few months, during which time they attain
a high sugar concentration; what follows
is the six-year period dedicated to aging in
hundred-liter casks. The result is a Vin Santo
di Carmignano Riserva rich in aromas of
dried citrus fruits and dried fruit, followed
by a warm and captivating taste, with a
good alcohol content—around 13.5 %—and
persuasive sweetness, made harmonious by
an important backbone endowed with lively
acidity.

POLIZIANO

Via Fontago 1
Montepulciano (SI)
carlettipoliziano.com
Year of establishment: 1961
Owner: Federico Carletti
Average number of bottles
produced per year: 800,000

With 371 acres under vine,
Federico Carletti's cellar has
contributed to making the
wines of this Tuscan region
famous, also enhancing the
cru concept through Asinone
and, more recently, with the
highly successful Le Caggiole.
It is of reliable quality, in
which there is also an elegant
Bordeaux-inspired offering, Le
Stanze, made from Cabernet
Sauvignon and a small
percentage of Merlot. The
winery's style is modern and
focuses on crisp elegance of
taste above all.

VINO NOBILE DI MONTEPULCIANO
ASINONE

First year of production: 1983
Average number of bottles produced
per year: 30,000
Grape variety: Sangiovese (90 to
100%); possible Colorino and Canaiolo
(max. 10%)

No less than 30 acres of vineyards are
dedicated to the production of Asinone,
which matures for eighteen months in
tonneaux, acquiring a felicitous spiciness that
blends with the floral and fruity character of
Sangiovese. The palate is full and compact,
firm, with rather soft tannins and a clear
finish of violets and ripe cherries. A very
successful expression of a great Tuscan wine
region.

Umbria

A region admired worldwide for its artistic and scenic treasures and that is admirably renewing the image of its wines. The red Sagrantino di Montefalco proves that power can translate into balance, and Orvieto, the fruit of a commercial past based on large numbers, is entering—together with Grechetto di Todi—the circle of the most typical and pleasant Italian whites.

In a country with 4,720 miles of coastline, Umbria is landlocked: an immense garden in the heart of Italy. Expanses of woods, meadows, olive groves, orchards, and vineyards designed by the patience and care of generations of farmers over the centuries, building villages and towns such as Assisi, Orvieto, Perugia, Gubbio, Spoleto, and Todi, large enough to hold the dreams of incredulous visitors stunned by so much beauty, but not so large as to upset the harmony between nature and civilization.

Moving southward from the north, one encounters viticulture still rather tied to Tuscan tradition, with a strong presence of both white Trebbiano and red Sangiovese. Moving slightly westward, the most significant designation is found in the Colli del Trasimeno, influenced by the warm waters of the similarly named lake, where a well-established tradition has elected Gamay as the most characteristic grape variety.

Just south of Perugia is the municipality of Torgiano, endowed with its own DOC mainly dedicated to whites and, even more so, with a prized and long-lived DOCG based on Sangiovese, the Torgiano Rosso Riserva.

A little farther down is the area reserved for the region's most famous red wine, Montefalco Sagrantino, once presented as a sweet wine due to its considerable residual sugar, later becoming a symbol of the more astringent tannicity in its dry version and, finally, in recent decades, a fine representative of the union of character, power, and elegance.

Beyond the western border of this DOCG lies the Colli Martani area, a territory where the Grechetto grape gives its best thanks to a solid and enveloping taste structure. Toward the border with Lazio, on the other hand, is the area dedicated to Orvieto, which is increasingly appreciated in its dry version but also capable of making passito and muffato wines of rare quality. Still in the province of Terni, the Colli Amerini area is becoming more interesting every year, highlighting fine results based on Grechetto and Ciliegiolo grapes.

From 30,900 acres under vine, nearly 16 million gallons of wine are produced annually, the fruit of grapes from fourteen thousand often very small farms and the work of eleven cooperative wineries that vinify one-third of the total harvest. The altimetric distribution of the vineyards is 80% hills and 20% plains.

MAIN VINES GROWN IN THE REGION

Ciliegiolo
→ Tuscany

Gamay del Trasimeno
→ Grenache in International Grape Varieties

Grechetto

There are two main clones of Grechetto used in Umbria. The first is clone G109, Grechetto di Orvieto or simply Grechetto, grown in the Orvieto DOC area—where it is grown alongside Trebbiano—and Grechetto di Todi, or Grechetto Gentile, clone G5, in the Todi DOC area, which is genetically identical to Pignoletto. In the vineyards, the plants can still be mixed, because in the Orvietano there are still old strains of Grechetto di Todi, which means there are wines of each of the two varieties in purity, wines in which they are found together, and wines in which they are found with other white cultivars.

A common profile can be identified, linked to the *terroir*, in which this family of vines of Greek origin—probably brought to Italy from the colonies of Magna Graecia—expresses a regional identity linked to an idea of a white wine in which considerable structure is able to coexist with general harmony, olfactory breadth, and drinkability.

The fruit is more evident in the Grechetto di Todi, while the aromas in the Grechetto di Orvieto can almost recall a Sauvignon Blanc: pineapple, passion fruit, lemon, lychee, apple and boxwood, aromatic herbs, especially thyme and rosemary, with sulfurous notes on the finish and a fresh, mineral flavor with a soft, persistent finish.

Grechetto di Todi
→ Pignoletto in Emilia-Romagna

Sagrantino

Of uncertain origin, it has been spoken of since the nineteenth century, but its production area, Montefalco, was already known to the Romans in the first century as an area suited to viticulture, and both Martial and Pliny the Elder extol a wine made from Hirtiola grapes, which could be the ancestor

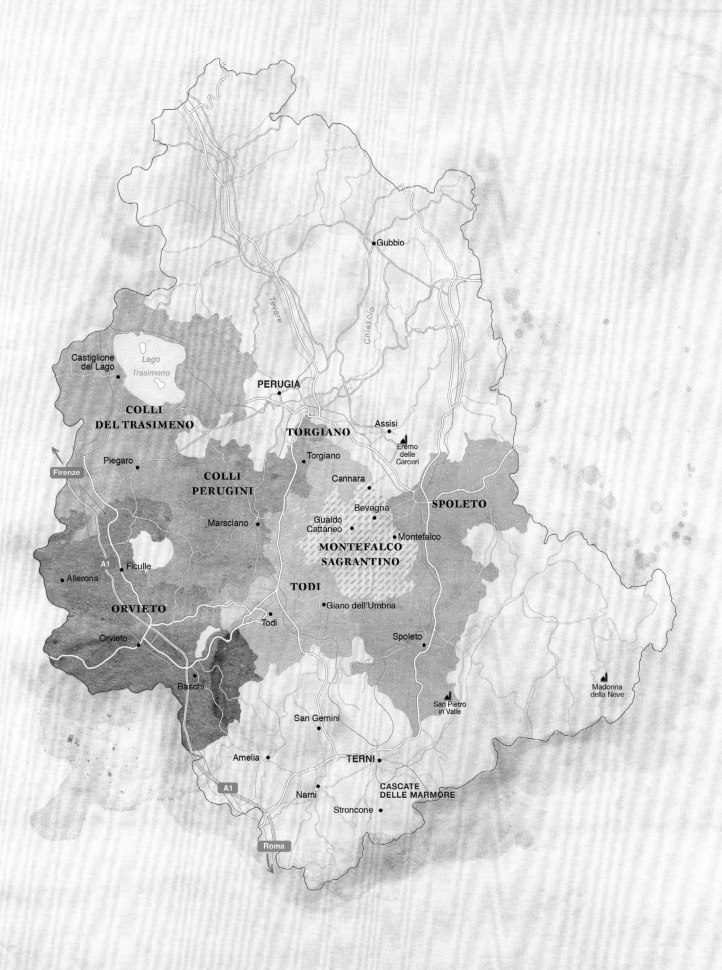

Gubbio

Tevere

Chiascio

Castiglione
del Lago

*Lago
Trasimeno*

PERUGIA

**COLLI
DEL TRASIMENO**

Assisi

TORGIANO

Eremo
delle
Carceri

Piegaro

Torgiano

Firenze

**COLLI
PERUGINI**

Cannara

Bevagna

SPOLETO

Marsciano

Gualdo
Cattaneo

Montefalco

A1

Ficulle

**MONTEFALCO
SAGRANTINO**

Allerona

TODI

Giano dell'Umbria

ORVIETO

Todi

Spoleto

Orvieto

Madonna
della Neve

Baschi

San Pietro
in Valle

San Gemini

Amelia

TERNI

A1

Narni

**CASCATE
DELLE MARMORE**

Stroncone

Roma

of Sagrantino. Other hypotheses have it arriving from Asia Minor by Franciscan monks, or from Greece through trade with Byzantium. After the Second World War, Sagrantino had become almost extinct, but thanks to the Caprai winery, which relaunched it in the 1960s, it has become the symbol of Umbrian wine worldwide. A dark and complex grape variety from which to extract a very structured and tannic violet wine, capable of developing a broad and intense range of red and black fruits including plum, blackberry, and raspberry, with a marked spiciness of pepper, cinnamon, and star anise, a balsamic note of eucalyptus, pine resin, and wild mint, sometimes with a roast of coffee and cocoa. With age, further balsamic notes and a vintage touch of camphor appear.

Trebbiano Spoletino

Recognized as an independent vine variety and listed in the National Catalog of Vine Varieties since 1970, it is a cultivar of the Trebbiano family dedicated to the small Spoleto DOC. The wines mature for a few months—usually in steel but there are interesting experiments in amphora and wood—before being bottled, and are remarkably fresh, delicate, and smooth, with notes of hawthorn, grapefruit, turmeric and lychee, peach and elderflower.

The DOCGs

- Montefalco Sagrantino
- Torgiano Rosso Riserva

The DOCs

- Amelia
- Assisi
- Colli Altotiberini
- Colli del Trasimeno / Trasimeno
- Colli Martani
- Colli Perugini
- Lago di Corbara
- Montefalco
- Orvieto
- Rosso Orvietano / Orvietano Rosso
- Spoleto
- Todi
- Torgiano

Montefalco Sagrantino DOCG

The small area from which this DOCG originates is located both in the hills of Montefalco as well as in four other municipalities in the central part of the region in the province of Perugia, at altitudes varying between 720 and 1,550 feet. There we find ourselves in one of the few cases in which the grapes must be entirely derived, at 100%, from a single variety, in this case, Sagrantino. While thirty years ago, all experts tended to emphasize the astringency of the taste due to an incisive presence of tannin, today it can be affirmed that when sipping it, Sagrantino di Montefalco is endowed with great dynamics. The charm owes more to the freshness and long finish than any severity or strictness of the notes; no less valuable is the olfactory expression, where it passes from small berries of undergrowth to sweet spices. An important wine, among the great Italian classics, whose presence has been documented since at least the sixteenth century. Approximately 1.6 million bottles are produced annually.

—

Producers and their trademark and signature wines:

1. ADANTI, Bevagna
    Montefalco Sagrantino Arquata ($)
    Montefalco Sagrantino Il Domenico ($$)
2. ANTONELLI SAN MARCO, Montefalco
    Montefalco Sagrantino Molino dell'Attone ($$)
    Montefalco Sagrantino ($)
3. BOCALE, Montefalco
    Montefalco Sagrantino Ennio ($$)
    Montefalco Sagrantino ($$)
4. CANTINA FRATELLI PARDI, Montefalco
    Montefalco Sagrantino Sacrantino ($$)
5. Arnaldo CAPRAI, Montefalco
    Montefalco Sagrantino 25 Anni ($$$)
    Montefalco Sagrantino Collepiano ($)
6. COLLE CIOCCO, Montefalco
    Montefalco Sagrantino ($$)
7. PERTICAIA, Montefalco
    Montefalco Sagrantino ($)
8. RAÍNA, Montefalco
    Montefalco Sagrantino Campo di Raína ($$)
9. ROMANELLI, Montefalco
    Montefalco Sagrantino Terra Cupa ($$)
10. TABARRINI, Montefalco
    Montefalco Sagrantino Campo alla Cerqua ($$$)
    Montefalco Sagrantino Colle alle Macchie ($$)
11. TENUTA BELLAFONTE, Bevagna
    Montefalco Sagrantino Collenottolo ($$)
12. TENUTA CASTELBUONO – Lunelli, Bevagna
    Montefalco Sagrantino Carapace Lunga Attesa ($$$)

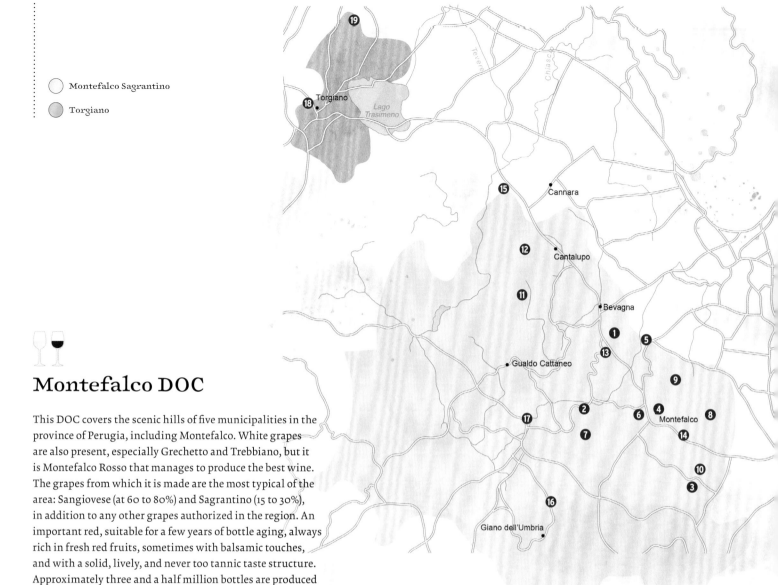

Montefalco Sagrantino
Torgiano

Montefalco DOC

This DOC covers the scenic hills of five municipalities in the province of Perugia, including Montefalco. White grapes are also present, especially Grechetto and Trebbiano, but it is Montefalco Rosso that manages to produce the best wine. The grapes from which it is made are the most typical of the area: Sangiovese (at 60 to 80%) and Sagrantino (15 to 30%), in addition to any other grapes authorized in the region. An important red, suitable for a few years of bottle aging, always rich in fresh red fruits, sometimes with balsamic touches, and with a solid, lively, and never too tannic taste structure. Approximately three and a half million bottles are produced each year from a total of 1,210 acres.

—

Producers and their trademark and signature wines:

1. ADANTI, Bevagna
   Montefalco Rosso Riserva ($)
2. ANTONELLI SAN MARCO, Montefalco
   Montefalco Rosso Riserva ($)
13. BRIZIARELLI, Bevagna
   Montefalco Rosso ($)
4. CANTINA FRATELLI PARDI, Montefalco
   Montefalco Rosso Riserva ($)
14. Ilaria COCCO, Montefalco
   Montefalco Rosso Camorata ($)
15. DI FILIPPO, Cannara
   Montefalco Rosso ($)
16. Omero MORETTI, Giano dell'Umbria
   Montefalco Rosso Riserva Faccia Tosta ($)
12. TENUTA CASTELBUONO – Lunelli, Bevagna
   Montefalco Rosso Ziggurat ($)
   Montefalco Rosso Riserva Lampante ($)
17. TERRE DE LA CUSTODIA, Gualdo Cattaneo
   Montefalco Rosso ($)

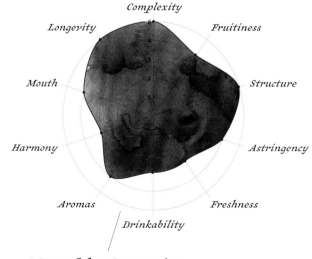

Montefalco Sagrantino

Torgiano DOC

A DOC that refers only to the municipality of Torgiano, where a visit to the interesting and rich Wine Museum is recommended. There are numerous types in white and red, but the most prestigious is Bianco di Torgiano, made from 20–70% Trebbiano grapes: there's white fruit, almonds, and wildflowers on the nose, good volume, and a touch of savoriness in the mouth. Annual production is close to one million bottles.

—

Producers and their trademark and signature wines:

18. LUNGAROTTI, Torgiano
    Bianco di Torgiano Torre di Giano Vigna Il Pino ($)
19. TERRE MARGARITELLI, Torgiano
    Bianco di Torgiano Costellato ($)

Torgiano Rosso Riserva DOCG

There are 70% to 100% Sangiovese grapes in this small, prestigious DOCG made famous by the Lungarotti family. A very lively and fruity wine, complex, rich, and dynamic, capable of improving for decades in the bottle. Sixty thousand bottles are produced per year.

—

Producers and their trademark and signature wines:

18. LUNGAROTTI, Torgiano
    Torgiano Rosso Riserva Rubesco Vigna Monticchio ($$)
19. TERRE MARGARITELLI, Torgiano
    Torgiano Rosso Riserva Freccia degli Scacchi ($$)

Orvieto DOC

A vast DOC spread across southwestern Umbria and upper Lazio that, in addition to thirteen municipalities in the province of Terni, also includes five towns in the province of Viterbo. The production terrain is quite varied, including some almost flat areas, as well as hilly areas of considerable steepness: the advice for wine tourists is to admire the panorama of vineyards from the Rocca di Orvieto, a hill that arose three hundred thousand years ago from a volcanic eruption. The regulations require an overall content of at least 60% Trebbiano Toscano (also known as Procanico) and Grechetto, and the tendency of producers is not to use other complementary varieties but rather to increase the presence of Grechetto. The aromas turn toward white fruit and field grasses, not infrequently with a fine balsamic touch, while the taste is always rich and enveloping, soft on the entry, and then more savory and snappy on the finish. Quality wineries here are on the rise. The total production of the two regions, from 5,190 acres under vine, exceeds eleven million bottles per year, 75% of which are exported.

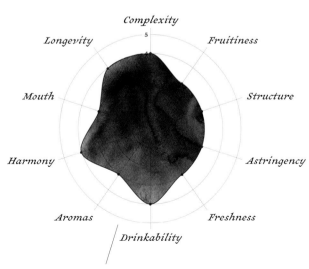

Torgiano Rosso Riserva

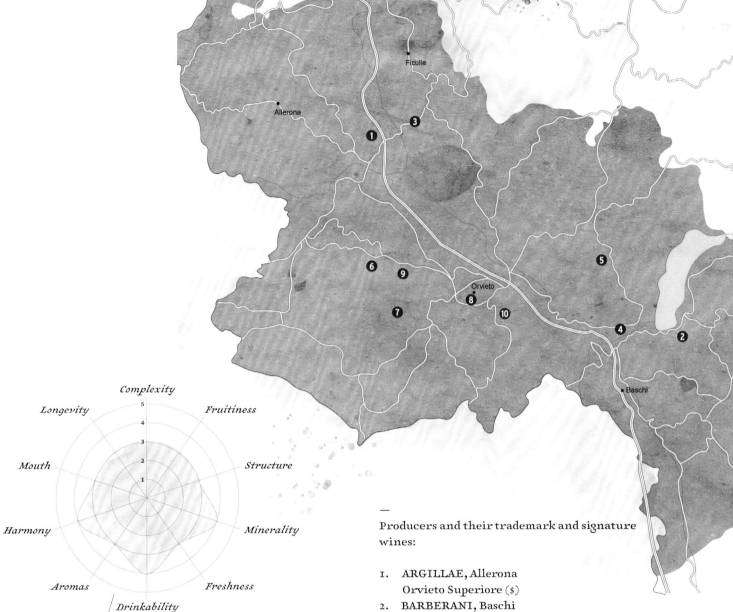

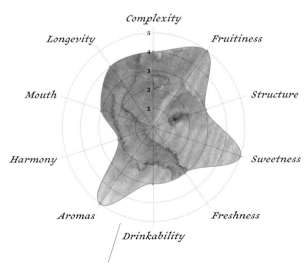

Orvieto Classico Superiore

Orvieto Classico Superiore Muffa Nobile

—
Producers and their trademark and signature wines:

1. ARGILLAE, Allerona
    Orvieto Superiore ($)
2. BARBERANI, Baschi
    Orvieto Classico Superiore Luigi e Giovanna ($$)
    Orvieto Classico Superiore Muffa Nobile Calcaia ($$)
3. CASTELLO DELLA SALA, Ficulle
    Orvieto Classico Superiore San Giovanni della Sala ($)
4. CASTELLO DI CORBARA, Orvieto
    Orvieto Classico Superiore ($)
5. DECUGNANO DEI BARBI, Orvieto
    Orvieto Classico Superiore Mare Antico ($)
    Orvieto Classico Superiore Pourriture Noble ($$)
6. LAPONE, Orvieto
    Orvieto Classico Superiore L'Escluso ($)
7. MADONNA DEL LATTE, Orvieto
    Orvieto Classico Superiore ($)
8. Enrico NERI, Orvieto
    Orvieto Classico Superiore Ca' Viti ($)
9. PALAZZONE, Orvieto
    Orvieto Classico Superiore Vendemmia Tardiva ($)
    Orvieto Classico Superiore Campo del Guardiano ($)
10. TENUTA LE VELETTE, Orvieto
    Orvieto Classico Superiore Lunato ($)

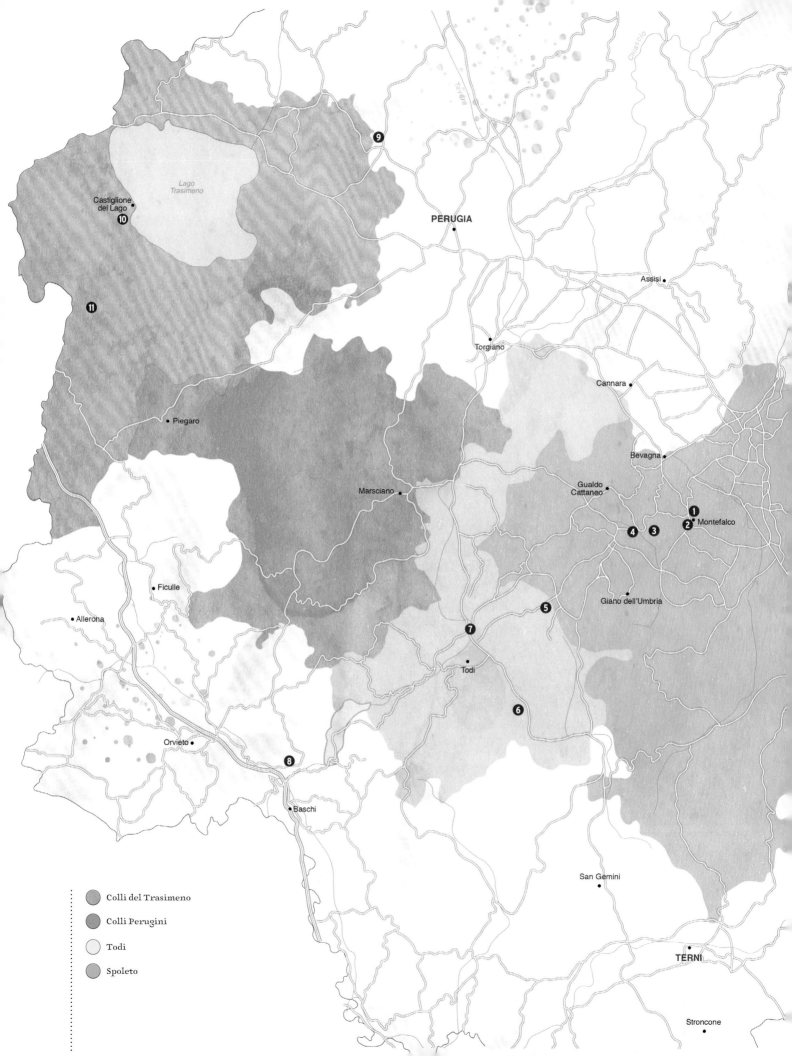

Lago
Trasimeno

Castiglione
del Lago
⑩

⑪

PERUGIA

Assisi

Torgiano

Cannara

Bevagna

Gualdo
Cattaneo

① Montefalco
②

④ ③

Giano dell'Umbria

Piegaro

Marsciano

⑤

⑦

Ficulle

Todi

Allerona

⑥

Orvieto

⑧

Baschi

San Gemini

TERNI

Stroncone

Colli del Trasimeno

Colli Perugini

Todi

Spoleto

Spoleto DOC

A small DOC dedicated exclusively to white wine, covering the territory of Spoleto and five other municipalities in the province of Perugia. The main grape variety is Trebbiano Spoletino, a type that comes from the large Trebbiano family and is endowed with particular acidity, making it pleasantly and smoothly drinkable; herbs and wildflowers characterize an aroma that is not very intense but certainly pleasant. Almost two hundred thousand bottles are produced per year.

—

Producers and their trademark and signature wines:

1. CANTINA FRATELLI PARDI, Montefalco
   Spoleto Trebbiano Spoletino ($)
2. COLLE CIOCCO, Montefalco
   Spoleto Trebbiano Spoletino Tempestivo ($)
3. PERTICAIA, Montefalco
   Spoleto Trebbiano Spoletino ($)
4. SCACCIADIAVOLI, Montefalco
   Spoleto Trebbiano Spoletino ($)

Todi DOC

The small Todi DOC area includes four municipalities in the province of Perugia and is mainly dedicated to the cultivation of white Grechetto and red Sangiovese. The Todi Grechetto (or Grechetto di Todi) has pleasant citrus notes on the nose and a nice fresh dynamism in the mouth; the Todi Sangiovese (or Sangiovese di Todi) is smooth and lively, with small red fruits in evidence. About five hundred thousand bottles are produced annually.

—

Producers and their trademark and signature wines:

5. PEPPUCCI, Todi
   Todi Grechetto Superiore I Rovi ($)
6. TODINI, Todi
   Todi Sangiovese ($)
7. TUDERNUM, Todi
   Todi Grechetto Superiore Colle Nobile ($)

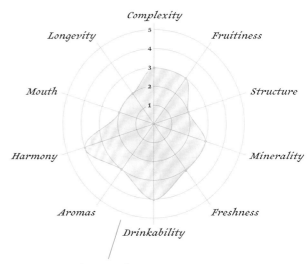

Todi Grechetto

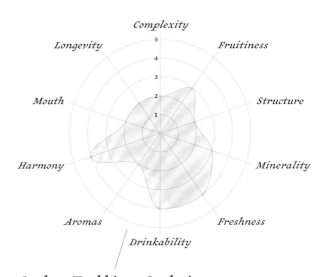

Spoleto Trebbiano Spoletino

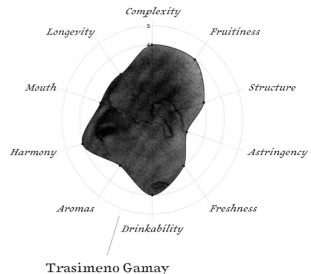

Trasimeno Gamay

Lago di Corbara DOC

The small territory of this DOC is limited to the municipalities of Baschi and Orvieto, with vineyards dedicated above all to red grapes, among which Sangiovese and Bordeaux varieties dominate. Over 99 acres of vines yield about two hundred thousand bottles per year, three thousand of which are of the recommended wine.

—

Producer and its trademark and signature wine:

8. CASTELLO DI CORBARA, Orvieto
   Lago di Corbara Sangiovese Calistri ($)

....

Colli del Trasimeno or Trasimeno DOC

The grape variety which elsewhere is called Cannonao, Grenache, Garnacha, or Tai Rosso, is called the Gamay del Trasimeno in the province of Perugia. It always produces wines with tasty and not too demanding drinkability, intriguing spiciness on the nose, and good balance in the mouth. The DOC spans ten municipalities in the province of Perugia and includes numerous types, but recommendations are limited to Trasimeno Gamay. Overall, just under one million bottles are produced per year.

—

Producers and their trademark and signature wines:

9. COLDIBETTO, Perugia
   Trasimeno Gamay Etrusco ($)
10. DUCA DELLA CORGNA, Castiglione del Lago
    Trasimeno Gamay Riserva Poggio Petroso ($)
    Trasimeno Gamay Riserva Divina Villa ($)
11. MADREVITE, Castiglione del Lago
    Trasimeno Gamay Riserva C'Osa ($$)

Colli Martani DOC

A variegated DOC covering thirteen municipalities in the province of Perugia, which in addition to the area's classic grape varieties (from Grechetto, which remains the most widespread, to Sangiovese) also includes the use of international varieties, such as a couple originating in Bordeaux: Cabernet Sauvignon and Merlot. And it is from one of these that the recommended wine originates. The DOC total is close to 1.1 million bottles per year.

—

Producer and its trademark and signature wine:

1. TERRE DE LA CUSTODIA, Gualdo Cattaneo
   Colli Martani Merlot Riserva Vigna San Martino ($$)

....

Amelia DOC

A vast DOC spread across fourteen municipalities in the province of Terni, where traditional local white and red varieties are mainly used. The recommended wine is made from dried Trebbiano and Malvasia grapes, followed by three years of aging in small, drained barrels. Total production is close to three hundred thousand bottles per year.

—

Producer and its trademark and signature wine:

2. LA PALAZZOLA, Stroncone
   Amelia Vinsanto Occhio di Pernice ($)

Recommended wines outside the DOC/DOCG designations:

3. Leonardo BUSSOLETTI, San Gemini
   Ràmici (Ciliegiolo) ($)
   Colleozio (Grechetto) ($)
   Brecciaro (Ciliegiolo) ($)
4. CANTINA CENCI, Marsciano
   Piantata (Sangiovese) ($)
5. CASTELLO DELLA SALA, Ficulle
   Cervaro della Sala (Chardonnay, Grechetto) ($$$)
   Muffato della Sala (Sauvignon Blanc, Traminer,
   Riesling, Grechetto, Sémillon) ($$)
2. LA PALAZZOLA, Stroncone
   Brut Gran Cuvée (Pinot Nero, Chardonnay) ($)
6. MADONNA DEL LATTE, Orvieto
   Viognier ($)
7. POMARIO, Piegaro
   Sariano (Sangiovese) ($)
8. ROCCAFIORE, Todi
   Fiorfiore (Grechetto) ($)
9. ROMANELLI, Montefalco
   Le Tese (Trebbiano Spoletino) ($)
10. TABARRINI, Montefalco
    Adarmando (Trebbiano Spoletino) ($)
11. TODINI, Todi
    Laudato (Grechetto, Chardonnay, Altri) ($)
12. VILLA MONGALLI, Bevagna
    Calicanto (Trebbiano Spoletino) ($)

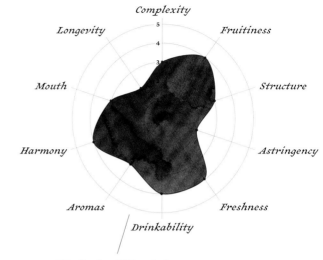

Umbria Ciliegiolo

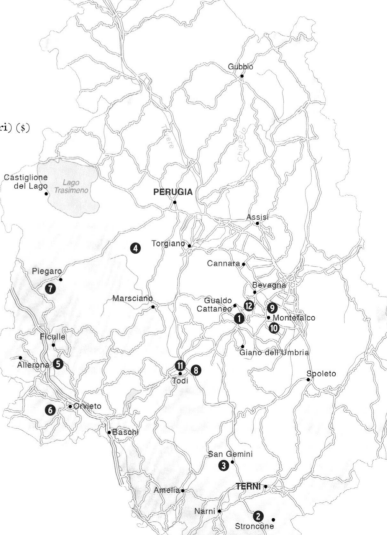

CASTELLO DELLA SALA

Località Sala
Ficulle (TR)
antinori.it
Year of establishment: 1940
Owner: the Antinori family
Average number of
bottles produced per year:
1,000,000

The Antinori family chose
this area specifically for
its ability to produce great
whites. In addition to the
typical local grapes (Grechetto
and Procanico, as the Tuscan
Trebbiano is called here), many
international grape varieties
have been added to the estate's
420 acres over time, from
Chardonnay to Traminer,
from Sauvignon to Riesling,
offered in a varied and
increasingly successful line. An
international interpretation of
Umbria in white.

CERVARO DELLA SALA

First year of production: 1985
Average number of bottles produced
per year: 130,000
Grape varieties: Chardonnay,
Grechetto

A wine that enchanted from its very first
release, thanks to intense aromas in which
barrique-ripened Chardonnay combines
with the freshness of Grechetto. A felicitous
olfactory fusion in which hazelnuts and
citrus fruits, smoky tones, and sweet spices
are perceived. The flavor is important, with
considerable volume, round and persuasive,
slightly savory, and with a rich finish of
yellow fruit. A classic among the great
Italian whites.

ARNALDO CAPRAI

Località Torre 1
Montefalco (PG)
arnaldocaprai.it
Year of establishment: 1971
Owner: the Caprai family
Average number of
bottles produced per year:
1,000,000

Started out of passion by
Arnaldo Caprai with only 7.5
acres under vine, the winery
has undergone relentless
development and since grown
to its current size of 420 acres.
The style of the wines can
be defined as modern, in the
sense that aromas derived
from French wood are also
welcome and the tannin of
the Sagrantino is molded
on the palate in a persuasive
and nonaggressive manner.
The Montefalco Sagrantino
25 Anni is accompanied by
twenty-one other labels,
in which Sagrantino and
Grechetto-based wines
predominate. The winery
that relaunched Montefalco
Sagrantino at an international
level.

MONTEFALCO SAGRANTINO 25 ANNI

First year of production: 1993
Average number of bottles produced
per year: 21,000
Grape variety: Sagrantino

Highly varied aromas, sumptuous taste
development. Spicy hints predominate,
favored by a twenty-four-month stay in
small barrels, accompanied by a substratum
of red fruit and balsamic appeal. The
structure is powerful, as important as it is
gentle in the astringent articulation of the
tannins, up to a savory finish in which the
fresh component given by the acidity is also
well perceived. A milestone.

ANTONELLI SAN MARCO

Località San Marco 60
Montefalco (PG)
antonellisanmarco.it
Year of establishment: 1881
Owner: the Antonelli
family
Average number of bottles
produced per year: 350,000

The 128 acres under vine,
organically cultivated,
are dedicated to the area's
historic vines: Sagrantino
and Sangiovese for the reds,
Grechetto and Trebbiano
Spoletino for the whites. The
result is eleven labels, headed
by productions of Montefalco
Sagrantino, which have made
the history of this area, with the
Chiusa di Pannone selection—
proposed since 2003—
garnering the most recognition
until Molino dell'Attone
appeared, to which the label
is dedicated. A production
line characterized by refined
classicism.

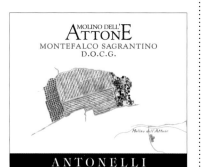

MONTEFALCO SAGRANTINO MOLINO DELL'ATTONE

First year of production: 2015
Average number of bottles produced
per year: 3,000
Grape variety: Sagrantino

High praise and international kudos for the
first release of this new label, made from just
1.2 acres of the similarly named vineyard at
an altitude of 1,312 feet, with an east-facing
exposure guaranteeing more freshness than
power. Maturation in barrels adds smoky
notes to a rich bouquet based on wilted red
petals, ripe red fruits, and field herbs. The
palate is rich, expansive, slightly astringent,
and savory, with an elegant licorice finish.

BARBERANI

Località Cerreto
Baschi (TR)
barberani.it
Year of establishment: 1961
Owner: the Barberani
family
Average number of bottles
produced per year: 330,000

A winery that expresses its
white wine vocation through
numerous productions whose
protagonists are the historic
local grape varieties, Grechetto
and Procanico (as the Tuscan
Trebbiano is called here), in
148 organically cultivated acres
with preparations that refer to
biodynamics. The particular
climatic conditions of this area
near Lake Bolsena often allow
the development of noble rot,
not only in the Calcaia but
also in the Orvieto Classico
dedicated to Luigi and
Giovanna. Also of interest are
the fresher and more youthful
productions, among which the
Castagnolo selection stands
out.

ORVIETO CLASSICO SUPERIORE MUFFA NOBILE CALCAIA

First year of production: 1986
Average number of bottles produced
per year: 30,000 (50 cl)
Grape varieties: Grechetto (80%),
Procanico (20%)

The noble rot (botrytis cinerea) slowly
develops on the grapes between October
and December, causing the bunches to be
harvested in multiple grape-picking stages
once they have already lost much of their
weight due to water evaporation. This is
how Calcaia was born, intense in its hints of
dehydrated peach and candied orange, with
a whiff of dried aromatic herbs. The flavor is
voluminous and sweet, balanced by a good
acidic tension, and very long. As difficult to
make as it is enchanting after a meal.

DECUGNANO DEI BARBI
Località Fossatello 50
Orvieto (TR)
decugnanodeibarbi.com
Year of establishment: 1973
Owner: the Barbi family
Average number of bottles
produced per year: 110,000

Splendid is the area that hosts
the 82 acres under vine, part
of which is biodynamically
managed, splendid is the
winery's headquarters, splendid
the interpretation of Grechetto.
In addition to Mare Antico, the
wines on offer include the multi-
award-winning Muffa Nobile,
which also features botrytized
Sauvignon and Sémillon, and
A.D. 1212, a red wine that in turn
combines transalpine vines with
minority parts of Montepulciano.
For fifty years, it has been the
flagship name of the Orvietano
area.

ORVIETO CLASSICO SUPERIORE
MARE ANTICO
First year of production: 1994
Average number of bottles produced
per year: 30,000
Grape varieties: Grechetto (55%),
Vermentino (20%), Chardonnay
(20%), Procanico (5%)

Known simply as Il Bianco until 2018, it
enchants with its aromas of flowers and
field grasses; the flavor is rich and engaging,
delicately saline, long, and slightly spicy
thanks to the aging in wood of 5% of the
must. It also stands out for its low cost and
is best appreciated after a few years in the
bottle. A white wine of distinct taste and
pleasantness.

LUNGAROTTI
Viale G. Lungarotti 2
Torgiano (PG)
lungarotti.it
Year of establishment: 1962
Owner: the Lungarotti
family
Average number of
bottles produced per year:
2,500,000

The most famous name in
the region, among the great
wine cellars of Italy, thanks to
a quality that is well spread
throughout the production.
The project was pursued with
determination by founder
Giorgio Lungarotti and
is continued today by the
family, with an agronomic
commitment that reaches
618 acres under vine. The
famous label presented here is
accompanied by an extensive
series of wines, including
the increasingly acclaimed
Bianco di Torgiano Torre di
Giano Vigna il Pino, made
from Trebbiano, Vermentino,
and Grechetto grapes, joined
by Sagrantino di Montefalco,
the fruit of a more recent
acquisition.

TORGIANO ROSSO RISERVA
RUBESCO VIGNA MONTICCHIO
First year of production: 1964
Average number of bottles produced
per year: 42,000
Grape variety: Sangiovese

Put on the market only after long
maturation, first in wood and then in the
bottle, it has the merits of the Sangiovese
grape at the highest level. On the nose, a
sweet spicy vein is complemented by hints
of strawberry and violet, in an ensemble of
refined elegance. The palate is multifaceted
and displays both good power and lively
freshness, with a touch of astringency that
gives volume to the flavor.

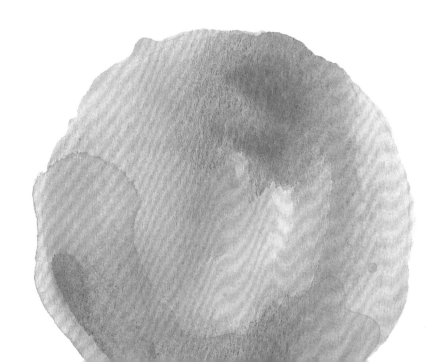

Marche

An oenological region with a human face, still rather far from the spotlight and little frequented by wine tourists but able to offer excellent wines in a hospitable environment, amidst marvelous landscapes, in the ancient villages scattered among the hills as well as along the beaches of the Adriatic Sea. This is the realm of Verdicchio, certainly among the greatest Italian white wines, and of Montepulciano, capable here of expressing complexity combined with elegance.

Descending from the Romagna border, one enters the Colli Pesaresi, where the similarities with the neighboring region are still evident, especially due to the strong presence of the same grape varieties: white Trebbiano and red Sangiovese. This area is also home to Bianchello del Metauro, always fresh and easy to drink, which comes from Bianchello grapes, a likely biotype of Trebbiano.

Moving farther south and entering the province of Ancona, we reach the productive heart of the region in the beautiful valleys that descend toward the sea. Here, after difficult years in which it was considered a commercial, simple, and cheap white wine, Verdicchio dei Castelli di Jesi DOC, together with Castelli di Jesi Verdicchio Riserva DOCG, is finally conquering the palates of connoisseurs. In the neighboring Macerata area, and to a lesser extent in the Ancona area, further inland where the Adriatic influences are less strong, Verdicchio di Matelica and its Riserva are endowed with greater freshness and a valuable capacity to evolve over the years.

The panorama of whites is completed by two types that are enjoying growing market success: wines made from the easy and straightforward Passerina grape and those made from the more articulate and richer Pecorino.

Moving on to the reds, the enchanting Conero area produces refined versions based mainly on Montepulciano grapes, in which today several producers are choosing olfactory richness and gustative finesse over opulence and fruity concentrations. Two strongly aromatic productions endowed with distinct and singular personalities, are Lacrima di Morro d'Alba and Vernaccia di Serrapetrona.

The picture of regional production can be summarized as 43,240 acres under vine and an average annual wine production of more than 18.5 million gallons, made from the grapes harvested by forty-three hundred farms. There are eleven active cooperative wine cellars that produce just 16% of the total wine production. The vineyards are classified as 82% hilly, 15% lowland, and 3% mountain.

MAIN VINES GROWN IN THE REGION

Biancame
A variety for fresh, delicate, and floral wines, Bianchello del Metauro was first mentioned in the De Naturali Vinorum Historia of the physician and ampelographer Andrea Bacci, from Sant'Elpidio al Mare, in 1596. Appreciated by artists and statesmen such as Piero della Francesca and Winston Churchill, it was even more appreciated by the Carthaginian army commanded by Hannibal's brother Hasdrubal, who on the banks of the Metauro River—as legend has it—lost an important battle against Rome because his army was clouded by too much Bianchello.

Lacrima
So called because of the tears of grape juice that seep from the skins of its ripe grapes, it is vinified, in dry or passito versions, in the Morro d'Alba area, hence the small DOC in the province of Ancona, and is recognizable by its pleasant scents of violets and red berries and by its astringent but nonaggressive, dry, and balsamic palate.

Montepulciano (→ also Abruzzo)
Not to be confused with Vino Nobile di Montepulciano, which is Sangiovese-based, the Montepulciano grape variety originates in Abruzzo, in the Torre de' Passeri area. An extraordinary grape with explosive potential, in Conero DOCG, Rosso Conero, and Rosso Piceno DOC it produces succulent wines that can be refined when the producer remembers that Montepulciano should not only be cultivated but also tamed. The color is dense and impenetrable, the aroma intense and wild. With due refinement, it rounds out on ripe red and black berry fruit, orange peel, and licorice. The flavor is always warm, long, and enveloping.

Passerina
An ancient Adriatic grape variety appreciated for its good resistance to weather and disease. Today widespread in the province of Ascoli Piceno and mentioned here in the Offida DOCG, it generates medium-intensity wines that smell of hawthorn, pineapple, and plum. Also known locally as Scacciadebiti and Uva d'Oro.

MONTEFELTRO

Bologna

PESARO

A14

Fano

VAL TIBERINA

URBINO

Cartoceto

San Costanzo

BIANCHELLO
DEL METAURO

Mare Adriatico

Fossombrone

Terre Roveresche

Barchi

LACRIMA
DI
MORRO D'ALBA

Fratte Rosa

Castelleone di Suasa

Ostra
Vetere

Morro d'Alba

ANCONA

COLLI PESARESI

Barbara

San Marcello

A14

Serra de' Conti

Montecarotto

Camerano

Monastero
di Fonte Avellana

Poggio San Marcello

Jesi

CONERO

Numana

Castelplanio

Osimo

Maiolati Spontini

San Paolo di Jesi

Castelfidardo

Loreto

Cupramontana

Staffolo

VERDICCHIO DEI
CASTELLI DI JESI

Montefano

Recanati

Fabriano

Apiro

Cingoli

VERDICCHIO
DI
MATELICA

COLLI MACERATESI

Civitanova
Marche

MACERATA

Matelica

Basilica di
Santa Maria
a Pié di Chienti

Castelraimondo

Tolentino

Abbazia
Chiaravalle
di Fiastra

Monte Urano

Serrapetrona

Camerino

FERMO

San Giusto

A14

Pedaso

Servigliano

Carassai

Cupra Marittima

OFFIDA

Cossignano

Ripatransone

Grottammare

Castignano

Offida

MONTI
SIBILLINI

Monsanpolo del Tronto

Monteprandone

Castorano

Taranto

Monte
Vettore
2470

ASCOLI PICENO

Tronto

Pecorino

Originally from the Sibillini Mountains, it was first mentioned in a document from 1526 in the Norcia area of Umbria and is now cultivated in the Marche and Abruzzo regions. Here it is the protagonist in Offida DOCG, in which it reveals a surprising aromatic intensity, with field essences and white and yellow flowers combined with tropical and herbaceous hints. The flavor is played on the fine relationship between savory and balsamic sensations.

Ribona (Maceratino)

A rare white berry cultivar native to the province of Macerata, vigorous and sensitive to frost, it has the Colli Maceratesi as its reference DOC and produces wines similar to Verdicchio, with which it is closely related.

Sangiovese (→ Tuscany)

Valuable expressions of Sangiovese, either in purity in the Colli Pesaresi or in blends with Montepulciano in Rosso Piceno, make its presence relevant also in the Marche. The Marche hills highlight its typicality compared to Tuscany or Romagna, enhancing its earthy and woody traits, with violet and dried flowers in the opening and a pleasant impact of blackberry, currant, plum, and blueberry in the center of the mouth, closing on wet earth, leather, and licorice.

Trebbiano

This vine is widespread in much of Italy as it produces wines with a good structure but a somewhat neutral character; in reality, it is a very ancient family of vines and, in the best processes, has a personality that can be identified depending on the area. Here in the Marche, it is found in the Colli Pesaresi, in Falerio, and in some fine bottles noted outside the designations, thanks to its perfumes of exotic fruits, chamomile, and honey, with toasted and mineral hints. Soft but also savory on the palate.

Verdicchio

An emblem of elective affinity between *terroir* and vine, Verdicchio is one of Italy's most prized native white wines. It is produced in the Jesi area, closer to the sea, and in Matelica, higher up. The results are similar but, with the same pleasantness and character, Verdicchio dei Castelli di Jesi is softer and more structured than Verdicchio di Matelica, which is fresher and stronger. The wine is recognizable for its intense aromas of white flowers and aromatic herbs and its typical almondy and persistent finish. Vibrant and citrusy, when tasted young it awakens memories of lime, peach, and almond, while with time, notes of chamomile, lime, broom, and wildflower honey are added.

Vernaccia Nera

Already listed in 1877 as one of the best grapes in the Marche by the famous ampelographer Giuseppe Di Rovasenda, it appears in the unusual red sparkling wine Vernaccia di Serrapetrona DOCG, in which it combines effervescence with pleasant hints of berries and a peppery accent.

The DOCGs

- Castelli di Jesi Verdicchio Riserva
- Conero
- Offida
- Verdicchio di Matelica Riserva
- Vernaccia di Serrapetrona

The DOCs

- Bianchello del Metauro
- Colli Maceratesi
- Colli Pesaresi
- Esino
- Falerio
- I Terreni di San Severino
- Lacrima di Morro d'Alba
- Pergola
- Rosso Conero
- Rosso Piceno / Piceno
- San Ginesio
- Serrapetrona
- Terre di Offida
- Verdicchio dei Castelli di Jesi
- Verdicchio di Matelica

Verdicchio di Matelica DOC and Verdicchio di Matelica Riserva DOCG

The small production area covers two municipalities in the province of Ancona and five in the province of Macerata. Verdicchio di Matelica is not very different from that of Castelli di Jesi, though in the first years in the bottle it can be a little more acidic and decisive in the mouth, while the aromas turn toward citrus, spice, and, over time, mineral sensations of flint. Here as well, refining in steel is preferred, but there is no shortage of aging in wood, often only of a part of the final wine. Close to three million bottles of the DOC are produced each year, around two hundred thousand being those of the DOCG.

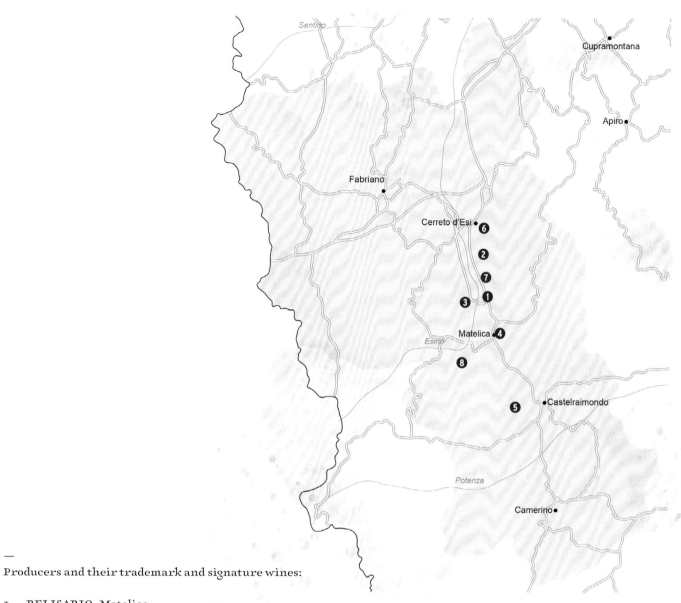

—

Producers and their trademark and signature wines:

1. BELISARIO, Matelica
   Verdicchio di Matelica Riserva Cambrugiano ($)
   Verdicchio di Matelica Meridia ($)
   Verdicchio di Matelica Del Cerro ($)
   Verdicchio di Matelica Animologico ($)

2. BISCI, Matelica
   Verdicchio di Matelica Vigneto Fogliano ($)
   Verdicchio di Matelica Riserva Senex ($$)
   Verdicchio di Matelica ($)

3. BORGO PAGLIANETTO, Matelica
   Verdicchio di Matelica Vertis ($)
   Verdicchio di Matelica Terravignata ($)
   Verdicchio di Matelica Ergon ($)

4. CAVALIERI, Matelica
   Verdicchio di Matelica Cavalieri ($)

5. COLLESTEFANO, Castelraimondo
   Verdicchio di Matelica ($)

6. Marco GATTI, Cerreto d'Esi
   Verdicchio di Matelica Villa Marilla ($)

7. LA MONACESCA, Matelica
   Verdicchio di Matelica Riserva Mirum ($$)

8. TENUTA GRIMALDI, Matelica
   Verdicchio di Matelica ($)

Verdicchio di Matelica

Verdicchio dei Castelli di Jesi DOC and Castelli di Jesi Verdicchio Riserva DOCG

One of the great Italian whites, which has not yet been fully recognized by consumers due to an old reputation it no longer deserves as being a wine of little value. There are many producers currently making prestigious whites from this valuable indigenous Marche grape. Since 2011, what was once the Riserva version of Verdicchio dei Castelli di Jesi DOC has been transformed into an autonomous DOCG, putting Castelli di Jesi before the name of the grape and providing for an aging period in the cellar of at least eighteen months before marketing. The aromas are characterized by notes of white fruits, often peach, to which lively hints of almond and, at times, aniseed are added; the flavor is of good volume, often with an alcohol content of around 14% by volume, but always with perceptible freshness and savoriness. The capacity for development in the bottle is excellent, often even beyond ten years. It is usually refined in steel or cement, more rarely in wood. The prices of most of the productions are rather friendly on the pocket. The annual bottles of DOC are over twenty million while those of DOCG are around one million.

—

Producers and their trademark and signature wines:

1. BUCCI, Ostra Vetere
Castelli di Jesi Verdicchio Riserva Classico Villa Bucci ($$$)
Verdicchio dei Castelli di Jesi Classico Superiore ($)

2. CA' LIPTRA, Cupramontana
Castelli di Jesi Verdicchio Riserva Classico S. Michele ($)

3. CASALFARNETO, Serra de' Conti
Verdicchio dei Castelli di Jesi Classico Superiore Grancasale ($)
Verdicchio dei Castelli di Jesi Classico Superiore Fontevecchia ($)

4. Luca CIMARELLI, Staffolo
Castelli di Jesi Verdicchio Riserva Classico Selezione Cimarelli ($)

5. COL DI CORTE, Montecarotto
Verdicchio dei Castelli di Jesi Classico Superiore Vigneto di Tobia ($)

6. COLÓGNOLA – Tenuta Musone, Cingoli
Verdicchio dei Castelli di Jesi Classico Superiore Ghiffa ($)

7. COLONNARA, Cupramontana
Verdicchio dei Castelli di Jesi Classico Superiore Cuprese ($)
Verdicchio dei Castelli di Jesi Brut M. Cl. Ubaldo Rosi ($$)

8. FATTORIA CORONCINO, Staffolo
Verdicchio dei Castelli di Jesi Classico Superiore Gaiospino ($)

9. FATTORIA NANNÌ, Apiro
Verdicchio dei Castelli di Jesi Classico Superiore Origini ($)
Verdicchio dei Castelli di Jesi Classico Superiore Arsicci ($)

10. FAZI BATTAGLIA – Tenute San Sisto, Castelplanio
Castelli di Jesi Verdicchio Riserva Classico San Sisto ($)
Verdicchio dei Castelli di Jesi Classico Superiore Massaccio ($)

11. Andrea FELICI, Apiro
Verdicchio dei Castelli di Jesi Classico Superiore ($)
Castelli di Jesi Verdicchio Riserva Classico Vigna Il Cantico della Figura ($$$)

12. FILODIVINO, San Marcello
Verdicchio dei Castelli di Jesi Classico Superiore Matto ($)

13. Gioacchino GAROFOLI, Castelfidardo
Verdicchio dei Castelli di Jesi Classico Superiore Podium ($)

14. LA MARCA DI SAN MICHELE, Cupramontana
Verdicchio dei Castelli di Jesi Classico Superiore Capovolto ($)

15. LA STAFFA, Staffolo
Castelli di Jesi Verdicchio Riserva Classico Rincrocca ($$)

16. MANCINI, Maiolati Spontini
Verdicchio dei Castelli di Jesi Classico Superiore Talliano ($)

17. MAROTTI CAMPI, Morro d'Alba
Castelli di Jesi Verdicchio Riserva Classico Salmariano ($)
Verdicchio dei Castelli di Jesi Classico Superiore Luzano ($)

18. MONTE SCHIAVO – Tenute Pieralisi, Maiolati Spontini
Verdicchio dei Castelli di Jesi Classico Superiore Pallio di San Floriano ($)

19. MONTECAPPONE – Mirizzi, Jesi
Castelli di Jesi Verdicchio Riserva Classico Utopia ($$)
Verdicchio dei Castelli di Jesi Classico Superiore Ergo Mirizzi ($$)
Verdicchio dei Castelli di Jesi Classico Superiore Cogito A. Mirizzi ($)

20. PIEVALTA, Maiolati Spontini
Verdicchio dei Castelli di Jesi Classico Superiore Dominè Chiesa del Pozzo ($)
Verdicchio dei Castelli di Jesi Classico Superiore Tre Ripe ($)
Castelli di Jesi Verdicchio Riserva Classico San Paolo ($$)

21. PODERI MATTIOLI, Serra de' Conti
Castelli di Jesi Verdicchio Riserva Classico Lauro ($)
Verdicchio dei Castelli di Jesi Classico Superiore Ylice ($)

22. SANTA BARBARA, Barbara
Castelli di Jesi Verdicchio Riserva Classico Tardivo Ma Non Tardo ($$)
Verdicchio dei Castelli di Jesi Classico Superiore Stefano Antonucci ($)

23. SARTARELLI, Poggio San Marcello
Verdicchio dei Castelli di Jesi Classico Superiore Balciana ($$)

24. SPARAPANI – Frati Bianchi, Cupramontana
Verdicchio dei Castelli di Jesi Classico Superiore Il Priore ($)
25. TENUTA DELL'UGOLINO, Castelplanio
Verdicchio dei Castelli di Jesi Classico Superiore Vigneto
del Balluccio ($)
26. TENUTA DI FRA', Morro d'Alba
Castelli di Jesi Verdicchio Riserva Classico Franz ($$)
27. TENUTA DI TAVIGNANO, Cingoli
Castelli di Jesi Verdicchio Riserva Classico Misco ($$)
Verdicchio dei Castelli di Jesi Classico Superiore Misco ($)
28. TERRE CORTESI MONCARO, Montecarotto
Castelli di Jesi Verdicchio Riserva Classico Vigna Novali ($)
Verdicchio dei Castelli di Jesi Classico Superiore Verde Ca'
Ruptae ($)
29. UMANI RONCHI, Osimo
Castelli di Jesi Verdicchio Riserva Classico Plenio ($)
Verdicchio dei Castelli di Jesi Classico Superiore Vecchie
Vigne ($)
Verdicchio dei Castelli di Jesi Classico Superiore Vecchie
Vigne Historical ($$$)
30. Roberto VENTURI, Castelleone di Suasa
Verdicchio dei Castelli di Jesi Classico Superiore Qudì ($)
31. VIGNAMATO, San Paolo di Jesi
Castelli di Jesi Verdicchio Riserva Classico Ambrosia ($)

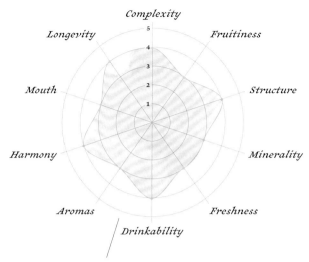

Verdicchio dei Castelli di Jesi

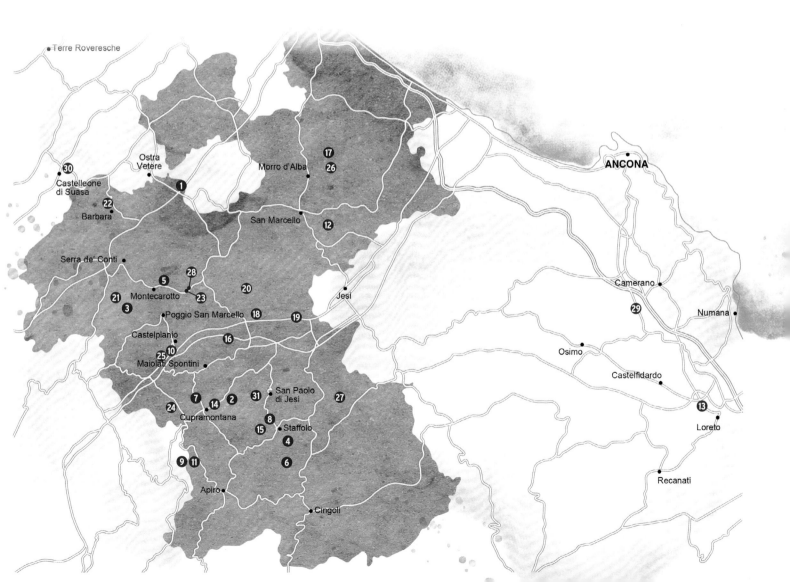

Offida DOCG

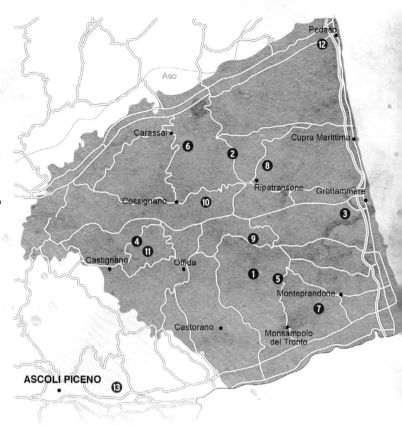

A rather young DOCG that has been in existence only since 2011 and covers several municipalities in the province of Ascoli Piceno and a small portion of the province of Fermo. Contrary to what is usually the case with DOCGs, it includes both white versions, with Pecorino and Passerina, and a red, based on Montepulciano grapes. Success has come especially thanks to Pecorino, a white wine that recalls fresh herbs on the nose, sometimes even aniseed and mint, and has a distinct savoriness in the mouth; it is usually aged in steel or cement, rather rarely in wood. Total production is over three and a half million bottles per year, and growing.

—

Producers and their trademark and signature wines:

1. AURORA, Offida
   Offida Pecorino Fiobbo ($)
   Offida Rosso Barricadiero ($)
2. CANTINA DEI COLLI RIPANI, Ripatransone
   Offida Pecorino Mercantino ($)
3. CARMINUCCI, Grottammare
   Offida Pecorino Belato ($)
4. CASTIGNANO, Castignano
   Offida Pecorino Montemisio ($)
5. COLLEVITE, Monsampolo del Tronto
   Offida Pecorino Villa Piatti ($)
6. Emanuele DIANETTI, Carassai
   Offida Pecorino Vignagiulia ($)
7. IL CONTE VILLA PRANDONE, Monteprandone
   Offida Pecorino Navicchio ($)
8. LE CANIETTE, Ripatransone
   Offida Pecorino Io Sono Gaia Non Sono Lucrezia ($)

9. TENUTA COCCI GRIFONI, Ripatransone
   Offida Pecorino Colle Vecchio ($)
10. TENUTA SANTORI, Ripatransone
    Offida Pecorino ($)
    Offida Passerina ($)
11. TENUTA SPINELLI, Castignano
    Offida Pecorino Artemisia ($)
12. TERRA FAGETO, Pedaso
    Offida Pecorino Fenèsia ($)
13. VELENOSI, Ascoli Piceno
    Offida Pecorino Rêve ($)

Offida Pecorino

Falerio DOC

This is an exclusively white wine designation, which envisages a Falerio made within the geographical confines of the province of Ascoli Piceno. It is made with Trebbiano Toscano, Passerina, and Pecorino, along with a Falerio Pecorino in which the grape of the same name must be present in quantities of at least 85%. In this case, bearing in mind that processing almost always takes place in steel only, there are therefore intense sensations of white fruits and citrus fruits on the nose, followed by considerable acidity and beautiful vitality in the mouth. Annual production is around four million bottles.

—

Producer and its trademark and signature wine:

14. PANTALEONE, Ascoli Piceno
    Falerio Pecorino Onirocep ($)

Bianchello del Metauro DOC

Produced in seventeen municipalities in the province of Pesaro-Urbino from the Bianchello grape variety of the same name—also called Biancame—this white wine is fresh both in its aromas of white flowers and in its richly acidic palate, never becoming too alcoholic. The Superiore version offers more fruity richness, a slight spiciness, and good grip on the palate, although vinification usually takes place only in steel. Approximately 1.7 million bottles are produced per annum, at quite reasonable prices.

—

Producers and their trademark and signature wines:

1. BRUSCIA, San Costanzo
   Bianchello del Metauro Superiore Lubác ($)
2. DI SANTE, Fano
   Bianchello del Metauro Superiore Giglio ($)
3. FIORINI, Barchi
   Bianchello del Metauro Superiore Andy ($)
4. Roberto LUCARELLI, Cartoceto
   Bianchello del Metauro Superiore Rocho ($)
5. TERRACRUDA, Fratte Rosa
   Bianchello del Metauro Superiore Campodarchi Argento ($)

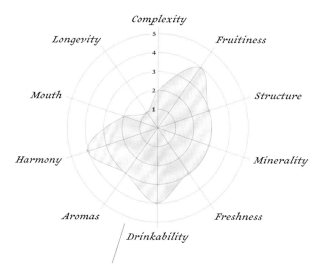

Bianchello del Metauro

Colli Pesaresi DOC

This DOC, covering the territory of thirty-six municipalities in the province of Pesaro-Urbino, uses numerous grape varieties: both local grapes—mainly Trebbiano, Verdicchio, and Bianchello for the whites, and Sangiovese for the reds—and imported ones, from Chardonnay to Sauvignon, and from Pinot Noir to Cabernet Sauvignon. But the real protagonist is Sangiovese, which alone accounts for two-thirds of the overall production, close to 1.3 million bottles per year.

—

Producers and their trademark and signature wines:

6. CIGNANO, Fossombrone
   Colli Pesaresi Sangiovese Sottovento ($)
3. FIORINI, Barchi
   Colli Pesaresi Sangiovese Riserva Luigi Fiorini ($$)

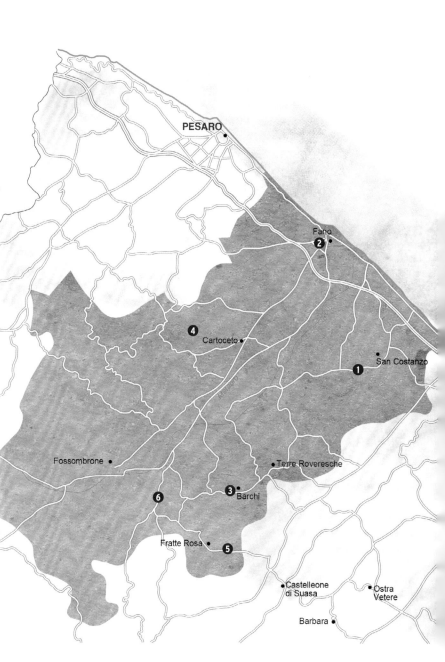

Lacrima di Morro d'Alba DOC

A small DOC that covers six municipalities in the province of Ancona, including Morro d'Alba. There is the fruit of the *lacrima* vine of the same name, which stands out above all for its delicately aromatic aromas that are rarely found in still red wines. They range from dog rose to violets, from currants to balsamic herbs, and are often blended with the notes of the wood in which it is aged. The palate is always fairly fresh, with rather restrained tannicity. About two million bottles per year are produced.

—

Producers and their trademark and signature wines:

1. FILODIVINO, San Marcello
   Lacrima di Morro d'Alba Diana ($)
2. Mario LUCCHETTI, Morro d'Alba
   Lacrima di Morro d'Alba Superiore Guardengo ($)
3. Stefano MANCINELLI, Morro d'Alba
   Lacrima di Morro d'Alba Passito Re Sole ($)
   Lacrima di Morro d'Alba Superiore ($)
4. MAROTTI CAMPI, Morro d'Alba
   Lacrima di Morro d'Alba Superiore Orgiolo ($)
5. VICARI, Morro d'Alba
   Lacrima di Morro d'Alba Superiore Del Pozzo Buono ($)

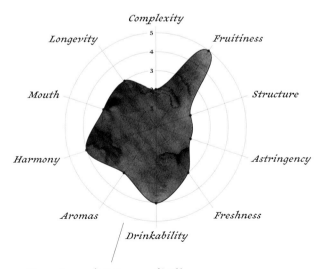

Lacrima di Morro d'Alba

Colli Maceratesi DOC

A vast DOC, covering the entire province of Macerata, with a small stretch of land in the Ancona province of Loreto. For the white it mainly uses the ancient Maceratino grape, which is also known as Ribona, as demonstrated in the wines suggested. Meanwhile it is Sangiovese that prevails in the red. Maceratino bears many similarities to Verdicchio, hence delicate aromas of fresh herbs and a palate of considerable acidity. Annual production is around one million bottles.

—

Producers and their trademark and signature wines:

6. COLLESTEFANO, Castelraimondo
   Colli Maceratesi Ribona ($)
7. CONTI DEGLI AZZONI, Montefano
   Colli Maceratesi Ribona ($)
8. FONTEZOPPA, Civitanova Marche
   Colli Maceratesi Ribona Asola ($$$)

Vernaccia di Serrapetrona DOCG

This rare and extravagant example of red sparkling wine, made both dry and sweet, comes from the black Vernaccia grape in the municipality of the same name of Serrapetrona, and in part of the municipalities of Belforte del Chienti and San Severino Marche, lying in the province of Macerata. The first alcoholic fermentation is followed by a second one, carried out by adding a part of dried grapes for a few weeks; the wine is then transferred to an autoclave and enriched with sugars and yeasts, undergoing a new fermentation and reaching a pressure not exceeding 5 atmospheres. The aromas of wild strawberries, raspberries, fresh plums, and pepper are intense; the palate is more or less soft but never very tannic, fragrant, or sparkling. The production is about one hundred thousand bottles per year.

—

Producer and its trademark and signature wines:

9. Alberto QUACQUARINI, Serrapetrona
   Vernaccia di Serrapetrona Secco ($)
   Vernaccia di Serrapetrona Dolce ($)

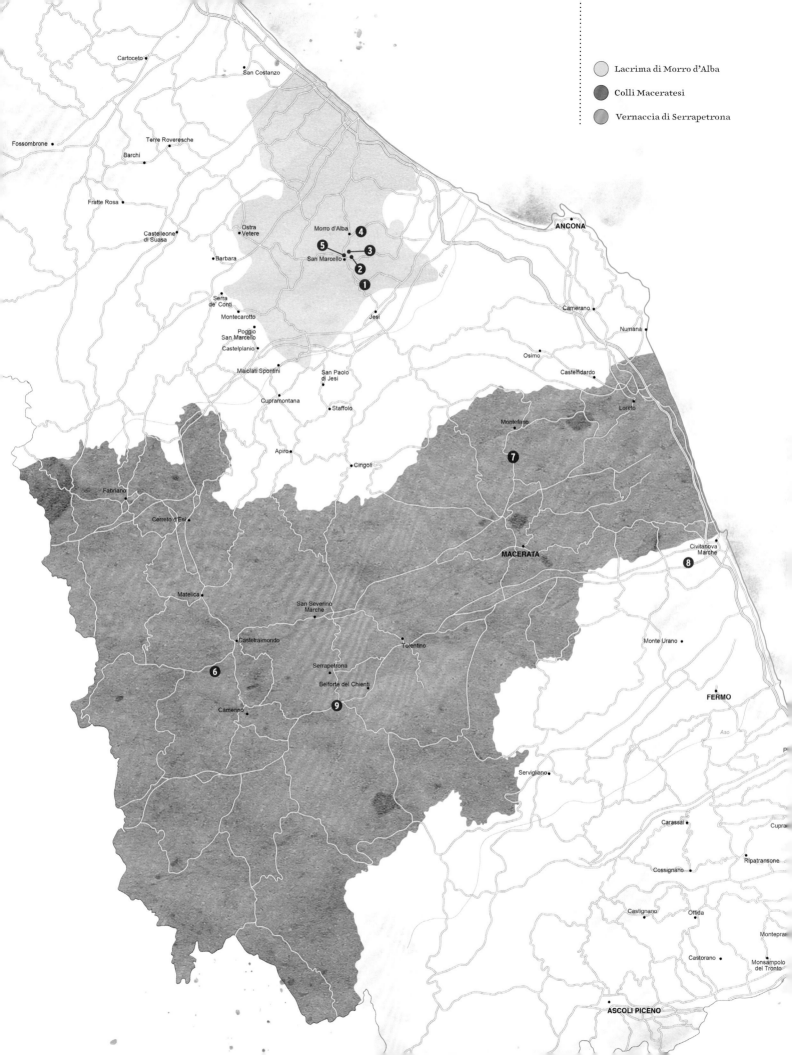

Lacrima di Morro d'Alba

Colli Maceratesi

Vernaccia di Serrapetrona

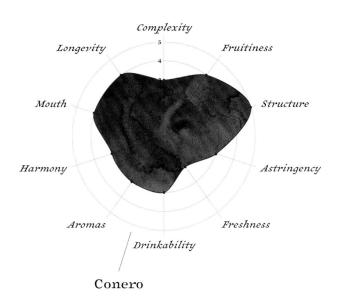

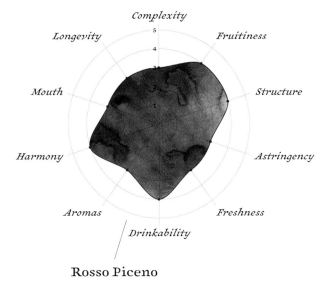

Rosso Piceno or Piceno DOC

A vast DOC, embracing most of the provinces of Ancona, Macerata, Fermo, and Ascoli Piceno, in which, in addition to the prevalent Montepulciano grape, a portion of Sangiovese is always present. Thanks to widespread aging in wood, this wine is never too impetuous or overwhelming, and aspires to elegance and balance. More than ten million bottles per year are produced, with good market success.

—

Producers and their trademark and signature wines:

1. BOCCADIGABBIA, Civitanova Marche
   Rosso Piceno ($)
2. BUCCI, Ostra Vetere
   Rosso Piceno Villa Bucci ($$)
3. LE CANIETTE, Ripatransone
   Piceno Superiore Nero di Vite ($$)
   Piceno Superiore Morellone ($)
4. TENUTA SANTORI, Ripatransone
   Rosso Piceno Superiore ($)
5. VELENOSI, Ascoli Piceno
   Rosso Piceno Superiore Roggio del Filare ($$)

Rosso Piceno

Conero DOCG and Rosso Conero DOC

What was once the Riserva of Rosso Conero DOC has, since 2004, been promoted to Conero DOCG and originates in a beautiful area of the province of Ancona recommended for wine tourists. In both types, the protagonist is Montepulciano, expected to be at least 85%. With greater or lesser concentration depending on the production style, here wines are made that are very rich in fruit that ranges from raspberry to plum. They are present on the nose and tannic on the palate, where a good alcoholic content is also often noticeable. The total annual bottles are eight hundred thousand for Conero DOCG and seventeen hundred thousand for Rosso Conero DOC.

—

Producers and their trademark and signature wines:

6. CONTE LEOPARDI DITTAJUTI, Numana
   Conero Riserva Pigmento ($$)
7. FATTORIA LE TERRAZZE, Numana
   Conero Riserva Sassi Neri ($)
   Rosso Conero Le Terrazze ($)
   Conero Riserva Visions of J. ($$)
8. Gioacchino GAROFOLI, Castelfidardo
   Conero Riserva Grosso Agontano ($)
9. MARCHETTI, Ancona
   Conero Riserva Villa Bonomi ($)
10. MORODER, Ancona
    Conero Riserva Dorico ($$)
11. Silvano STROLOGO, Camerano
    Conero Riserva Decebalo ($$)
12. TERRE CORTESI MONCARO, Montecarotto
    Conero Riserva Nerone ($$)
13. UMANI RONCHI, Osimo
    Conero Riserva Cumaro ($)

Conero

Conero

Rosso Piceno

Barchi

Terre Roveresche

Rosa

Castelleone
di Suasa

Ostra
Vetere ②

Barbara

Morro d'Alba

San Marcello

ANCONA

⑨   ⑩

Serra
de' Conti   ⑫
Montecarotto

Poggio
San Marcello

Jesi

Camerano

⑬   ⑪

Numana

Castelplanio

Maiolati Spontini

San Paolo
di Jesi

Osimo

⑥
⑦

Cupramontana

Staffolo

Castelfidardo

⑧

Apiro

Loreto

Montefano

Cingoli

Fabriano

Cerreto d'Esi

MACERATA

①

Matelica

Civitanova
Marche

Castelraimondo

Tolentino

Monte Urano

Serrapetrona

Camerino

FERMO

Pedaso

Servigliano

Carassai

Cupra Marittima

③

Cossignano   ④

Ripatransone

Grottammare

Castignano

Offida

Monteprandone

Castorano

Monsampolo
del Tronto

⑤

ASCOLI PICENO

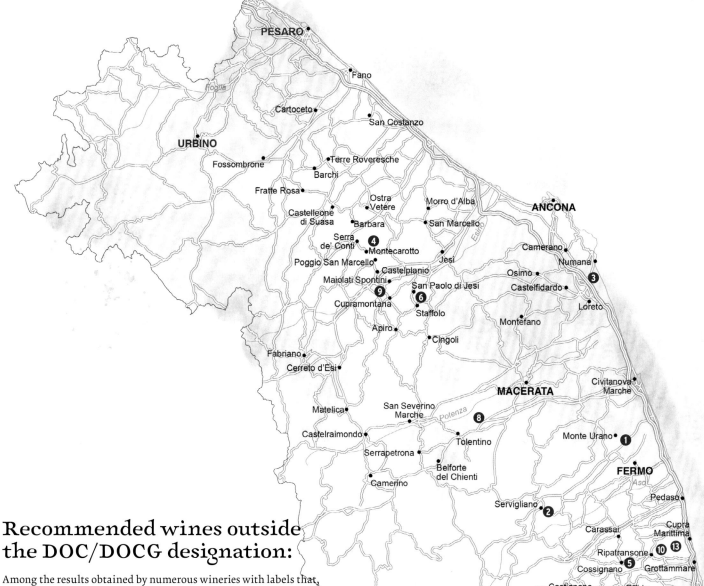

Recommended wines outside the DOC/DOCG designation:

Among the results obtained by numerous wineries with labels that, for various reasons, do not use the PDO (Protected Designation of Origin) designations, we mention the revolutionary role played in the region by Oasi degli Angeli since 1997.

1. Maria Pia CASTELLI, Monte Urano
   Erasmo Castelli (Montepulciano) ($$)
2. FATTORIA DEZI, Servigliano
   Regina del Bosco (Montepulciano) ($$)
3. FATTORIA LE TERRAZZE, Numana
   Chaos (Montepulciano, Merlot, Syrah) ($)
4. FATTORIA SAN LORENZO, Montecarotto
   Il San Lorenzo Bianco (Verdicchio) ($$$)
   Le Oche (Verdicchio) ($)
   Il San Lorenzo Rosso (Syrah) ($$$)
5. FIORANO, Cossignano
   Giulia Erminia (Pecorino) ($$)
6. Esther HAUSER, Staffolo
   Il Ceppo (Montepulciano, Sangiovese, Cabernet) ($)
7. IL CONTE VILLA PRANDONE, Monteprandone
   Lu Kont (Montepulciano) ($$)
8. IL POLLENZA, Tolentino
   Il Pollenza (Cabernet Sauvignon, Merlot, Cabernet Franc, Petit Verdot) ($$$)

9. LA DISTESA, Cupramontana
   Gli Eremi (Verdicchio) ($$)
   Terre Silvate (Verdicchio, Trebbiano) ($)
10. LE CANIETTE, Ripatransone
    Cinabro (Grenache) ($$$)
11. Clara MARCELLI, Castorano
    K'un (Montepulciano) ($)
12. Valter MATTONI, Castorano
    Arshura (Montepulciano) ($$)
    Trebbien (Trebbiano) ($)
13. OASI DEGLI ANGELI, Cupra Marittima
    Kupra (Grenache) ($$$$$)
    Kurni (Montepulciano) ($$$$)
14. PANTALEONE, Ascoli Piceno
    Boccascena (Montepulciano, Sangiovese, Grenache) ($$)
    La Ribalta (Grenache) ($$$)

MORODER

Frazione Montacuto 112
Ancona
moroder.wine
Year of establishment: 1984
Owner: the Moroder
family
Average number of bottles
produced per year: 150,000

Organically grown since 2008
on the 94 acres managed by
brothers Marco and Mattia
Moroder, with a predilection
for the region's main red grape
variety, Montepulciano. The
Dorico is thus flanked by
three other DOC or DOCG
productions of this grape in
purity, while the fruity Rosso
Conero Aiòn is blended with
15% Sangiovese grapes. The
location of the vineyards, in
the evocative and multifaceted
Conero Natural Park, deserves
special mention. Wines rich in
personality and flavor with a
distinct drinkability.

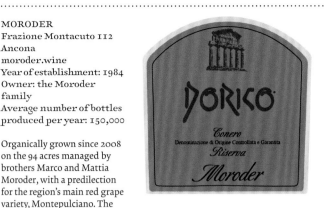

CONERO RISERVA DORICO

First year of production: 1985
Average number of bottles produced
per year: 13,000
Grape variety: Montepulciano

After thirty months of maturation in wood,
it first presents itself with ripe red and
black fruits that come to resemble jam,
followed by refreshing vegetal hints that
give complexity and harmony. The palate
is enveloping and soft, not without a touch
of tannin that gives more robustness than
astringency, with pleasant smoothness to
the finish where violets and blackberries are
appreciated. The Conero story spells high
quality.

IL POLLENZA

Contrada Casone 4
Tolentino (MC)
ilpollenza.it
Year of establishment: 2000
Owner: the Brachetti
Peretti family
Average number of bottles
produced per year: 200,000

Aldo Brachetti Peretti began
his new professional life as
an agricultural entrepreneur
by immediately aiming
for excellence, starting off
by establishing a team of
agronomists and oenologists
with proven skills. He oversaw
the renovation of the splendid
premises, where grapes from
the 148 acres of property,
including both French and
indigenous vines, arrive in
the evocative barrique cellar.
Elegance comes first.

IL POLLENZA

First year of production: 2001
Average number of bottles produced
per year: 20,000
Grape varieties: Cabernet Sauvignon
(90%), Cabernet Franc, Petit Verdot

The long sojourn in French oak barrels adds
spicy, smoky, and balsamic notes to the
important vegetal and fruity base inherent
to the grapes. In the mouth, it achieves
excellent tension and perfect balance thanks
to a persistent acid base accompanying a
remarkable body and velvety tannins.

OASI DEGLI ANGELI

Contrada Sant'Egidio 50
Cupra Marittima (AP)
kurni.it
Year of establishment: 1997
Owners: Eleonora Rossi
and Marco Casolanetti
Average number of bottles
produced per year: 7,500

Marco Casolanetti's revolution
began in his 40 acres of
vineyards, notable for the
very high density of the
plants, treated only with
natural products and from
which sulfur and copper
have also been banned. The
style of the cellar is rather
noninterventionist, where
the cornerstones are limited
to choosing excellent woods
and letting the wine freely
express its own personality,
which is different with every
harvest. In addition to Kurni, a
tiny, expensive, and not easily
available quantity of Kupra,
made from Grenache grapes, is
produced.

KURNI

First year of production: 1997
Average number of bottles produced
per year: 7,000
Grape variety: Montepulciano

The color is almost impenetrable and the
aromas are very intense, with red and
black fruit in evidence combined with an
important and refined spicy component.
The flavor is powerful and soft, enveloped
in evident but not drying tannins, always
endowed with a tasty smoothness: a true
tasting experience, as original as it is
fascinating.

LE CANIETTE

Contrada Canali 23
Ripatransone (AP)
lecaniette.it
Year of establishment: 1897
Owner: the Vagnoni
family
Average number of bottles
produced per year: 130,000

The Vagnoni brothers'
winery is growing in quality,
being an interpreter of the
main local grape varieties:
Montepulciano and
Sangiovese for reds, Pecorino
and Passerina for whites. With
one exception produced in
small quantities and highly
sought by the public, Cinabro,
made from Grenache, a grape
that has long been present in
the Marche region. In addition
to the Offida Pecorino we
present, the winery's success
has for years been linked to the
Piceno Superiore Morellone,
which is also produced on the
40 acres of organically farmed
land.

OFFIDA PECORINO IO SONO GAIA
NON SONO LUCREZIA

First year of production: 2001
Average number of bottles produced
per year: 5,500
Grape variety: Pecorino

The nose has pleasant notes of white
flowers, yellow fruit, and herbs, vague
mineral hints of hydrocarbons, and a soft,
almost buttery touch resulting from aging
in wood. The taste is also enveloping and
rich in matter, lively, and captivating thanks
to the lovely finish that recalls citrus fruits. A
rich and fine version of Pecorino.

VELENOSI

Via dei Biancospini 11
Ascoli Piceno
velenosivini.com
Year of establishment: 1984
Owners: the Velenosi
family, Paolo Garbini
Average number of
bottles produced per year:
2,500,000

One of Italy's most dynamic
wineries, with quality evenly
distributed throughout its
range, as evidenced by the
awards numerous labels have
received from international
critics. The famous Roggio del
Filare is flanked by the success
of Rosso Piceno Superiore
Brecciarolo and Offida Rosso
Ludi, while among the whites,
the Pecorino Rêve and Villa
Angela shine, and the Metodo
Classico sparkling wines
are led by Gran Cuvée Gold.
Everything stems from 400
acres of vines, partially in
organic cultivation, joined
by grapes from historic
vine growers with a good
dose of passion and marked
entrepreneurial ability.

ROSSO PICENO SUPERIORE ROGGIO DEL FILARE

First year of production: 1993
Average number of bottles produced
per year: 50,000
Grape varieties: Montepulciano
(70%), Sangiovese (30%)

The power of Montepulciano is united with
the fresh personality of Sangiovese, creating
a rich, multifaceted wine with lots of red
fruit on the nose and a rounded pulpiness
on the palate, in a framework finely enriched
by the spiciness of the new oak in which
Roggio del Filare matures for eighteen
months. A great representative of Marche
quality.

ANDREA FELICI

Contrada S. Isidoro 28
Apiro (MC)
andreafelici.it
Year of establishment: 1978
Owner: the Felici family
Average number of bottles
produced per year: 75,000

Leo Felici has shown that he
has clear ideas: he uses only
Verdicchio grapes from his
own 30 organically cultivated
acres, vineyards in the highest
areas of the designation to
obtain acidity and vitality, and
no wood to avoid aromas not
derived from the grapes. With
these prerequisites, he has
managed to achieve notoriety,
adding nothing more than
technical expertise to the
production of the two house
labels, also pursued through
skilled collaborators. The
classicality of Verdicchio dei
Castelli at the highest level.

CASTELLI DI JESI VERDICCHIO RISERVA CLASSICO VIGNA IL CANTICO DELLA FIGURA

First year of production: 2003
Average number of bottles produced
per year: 10,000
Grape variety: Verdicchio

In its youth, it offers fresh aromas in the
foreground, from white flowers to aniseed
to sage, accompanied by some citrus hints; it
then combines mineral hints such as iodine,
which are very useful in giving complexity
and further elegance while maintaining the
vital profile that characterizes Il Cantico.
The taste tends to create sensations of good
gustative tension thanks to the savory call
that enlivens the important structure and
great finesse.

BUCCI

Via Cona 30
Ostra Vetere (AN)
villabucci.com
Year of establishment: 1983
Owner: the Bucci family
Average number of bottles
produced per year: 130,000

Ampelio Bucci created
a winery synonymous
throughout the world
with a Verdicchio endowed
with grace and lightness,
infinite whispering nuances,
and finesse, never with
opulence, woodiness, or
muscular displays. A style
that he perfected with the
collaboration of Giorgio Grai,
then-famous as Italy's best
taster, and never abandoned
again, so much so that it has
become an absolute point
of reference for the Castelli
di Jesi. Accompanying the
Riserva Villa Bucci is a more
economical Verdicchio
Classico Superiore, similarly
remarkable, and two Rosso
Piceno productions emerging
from the 77 acres of organically
cultivated land.

CASTELLI DI JESI VERDICCHIO RISERVA CLASSICO VILLA BUCCI

First year of production: 1983
Average number of bottles produced
per year: 24,000
Grape variety: Verdicchio

Fresh scents prevail in its youth, from
wildflowers to celery to aniseed, then
delicate mineral notes of hydrocarbons and
flint appear. The taste has good consistency
and cohesion, favored by the long passage
in unroasted barrels, always remaining
sinuous and varied, invigorated by a touch
of savoriness. A wine of rare balance.

GAROFOLI

Località Villa Musone, Via
C. Marx 123
Castelfidardo (AN)
garofolivini.it
Year of establishment: 1901
Owner: the Garofoli
family
Average number of
bottles produced per year:
1,400,000

Significant dimensions for
a winery that has made the
history not only of Verdicchio
dei Castelli di Jesi but also
of Conero and Piceno, both
through the grapes from its
124 acres of property and
through the contribution
of trusted suppliers. In
addition to Podium, it is often
the Conero Riserva Grosso
Agontano that stands out
in the critics' assessments,
but the reliability of quality
is spread over many labels,
from the Verdicchio Classico
Superiore Macrina to the
Rosso Conero Piancarda to the
Verdicchio Spumante Brut.

VERDICCHIO DEI CASTELLI DI JESI CLASSICO SUPERIORE PODIUM

First year of production: 1991
Average number of bottles produced
per year: 45,000
Grape variety: Verdicchio

Only steel for the maturation of Podium,
which best embodies the two characteristics
of Verdicchio dei Castelli di Jesi: a rich
and fresh component of flowers and white
fruits on the nose, joined here by medicinal
herbs and a hint of citrus, and an important
gustative structure on the palate, where one
also perceives a fine savoriness and a final
almond call. Timeless classicism.

MONTECAPPONE
Via Colle Olivo 2
Jesi (AN)
montecappone.com
Year of establishment: 1968
Owner: the Mirizzi family
Average number of bottles
produced per year: 180,000

Gianluca Mirizzi began
by recovering his
grandparents' land, which
was then expanded to allow
a quantitatively suitable
production for the dynamic
and innovative winery he
had in mind. The project
was successful and today
Montecappone is one of the
most interesting names in
the Verdicchio di Jesi area.
The estate's vineyards have
now reached 111 acres and the
winery has made more room
for cement vats, which are
joined by wood in the Riserva
Utopia. The year 2015 saw the
birth of the Mirizzi brand,
which uses organically grown
vineyards in Cupramontana,
with outstanding results
thanks to the Verdicchio Ergo
and Ergo Sum selections.

CASTELLI DI JESI VERDICCHIO
RISERVA CLASSICO UTOPIA
First year of production: 2006
Average number of bottles produced
per year: 6,000
Grape variety: Verdicchio

Maturing in wood for a few months does
not soften a personality based above all on
dynamism, taste tension, and freshness.
Thus, from a specially dedicated vineyard
in the municipality of Staffolo, comes a
utopia that smells of field grass and plum,
elder and citrus, with an almost balsamic
background reminiscent of aniseed. The
palate is rich in matter and elegant, with
a very pleasant savoriness that achieves a
persistent balance.

BELISARIO
Via A. Merloni 12
Matelica (MC)
belisario.it
Year of establishment: 1971
Owner: Cooperative of the
Cantina Sociale Belisario
Average number of
bottles produced per year:
1,200,000

Belisario has made the most of
Verdicchio di Matelica, relying
on 741 acres of vineyards,
partially organic, from which
seven different labels have
been produced since 1988 by
the capable oenologist Roberto
Potentini. This well-deserving
community wine cellar, made
up of one hundred and fifty
growers who confer their
own grapes, is a flagship of
oenology in the Marche region
and nationally.

VERDICCHIO DI MATELICA
RISERVA CAMBRUGIANO
First year of production: 1988
Average number of bottles produced
per year: 80,000
Grape variety: Verdicchio

A particularly pleasant wine, which also has
the advantage of being able to improve for
many years in the bottle, over time passing
from the typical aromas of anise, mint, and
white fruit to more complex mineral hints
of hydrocarbons. The palate is taut and
vital, rich in flesh, and enveloping thanks
to the passage of a small part of the wine in
wood, but never too soft thanks to a vein of
savoriness. A great expression of Matelica.

UMANI RONCHI
Via Adriatica 12
Osimo (AN)
umanironchi.it
Year of establishment: 1957
Owner: the Bernetti
Bianchi family
Average number of
bottles produced per year:
2,900,000

On the strength of a farsighted
vision that has led to the
distribution of quality across
all the labels made, Umani
Ronchi has become the world
ambassador of the Conero
and Castelli di Jesi, and
subsequently also of Abruzzo,
with 74 acres in organic
cultivation just below the
Gran Sasso massif. The Plenio
is not the only one to shine,
accompanied as it is by two
selections of Conero Riserva
DOCG, the elegant Cúmaro
and the powerful Campo San
Giorgio, the international
Pelago, and the Verdicchio
Vecchie Vigne. Entrepreneurial
skill combined with the search
for quality and respect for the
environment.

CASTELLI DI JESI VERDICCHIO
RISERVA CLASSICO PLENIO
First year of production: 1995
Average number of bottles produced
per year: 17,000
Grape variety: Verdicchio

A faithful interpretation of the Verdicchio
grape combined with a quest for complexity
and elegance. Lovely fresh notes of herbs,
citrus fruits, and a whiff of aniseed combine
with tropical fruit and spice from the partial
aging in wood. The taste is important and
absolutely balanced, creamy and delicately
acidic, with a persuasive smoky touch on the
finish. A refined expression of the Castelli
di Jesi.

COLLESTEFANO
Località Colle Stefano 3
Castelraimondo (MC)
collestefano.com
Year of establishment: 1978
Owner: Fabio Marchionni
Average number of bottles
produced per year: 120,000

Fabio Marchionni's wine
cellar has become a sure point
of reference in the Matelica
area thanks to a production
style centered on the purest
expression of the Verdicchio
grape, organically grown in
twelve vineyards totaling
just over 49 acres. Only noninvasive processing in the field
and only steel in the cellar,
to avoid unwanted aromatic
overloads. The preponderant
production of Verdicchio di
Matelica is joined by valid
Spumante offers, similarly
based on Verdicchio, and the
fragrant Colli Maceratesi
Ribona.

VERDICCHIO DI MATELICA
First year of production: 1998
Average number of bottles produced
per year: 110,000
Grape variety: Verdicchio

A lively and fresh white, elegant and
endowed with almond, citrus, and balsamic
scents that make it immediately pleasing;
the body is quite robust and perfectly
balanced thanks to an always enjoyable
acidulous and savory component giving it
energy. A fine Verdicchio, moreover offered
at an affordable price.

Lazio

A region favored by climate, light, hills, lakes, and the sea, in which winegrowing is not yet fully expressing the potential of the many suitable areas. Among the whites, the quality of Frascati is growing, the rich personality of the Grechetto grape is confirmed, and productions based on French grapes such as Chardonnay and Viognier are increasing. The reds are driven by the qualitative growth of the various Cesanese-based productions, increasingly accompanied by the once unthinkable results of international grapes, from Cabernet Sauvignon to Syrah.

The journey through Lazio begins with the famous Castelli Romani and Frascati, which in its Superiore DOCG version is revealing the excellent qualities of the different types of Malvasia. It is worth noting how the aromatic elements typical of this grape are softened and attenuated here compared to other areas, which, combined with always refreshing acidity, makes Frascati a pleasant and easy pairing with food.

To the north is the vast Viterbese area, where the influence of neighboring Tuscany in the use of vines such as Sangiovese and Trebbiano is still evident. And it is mainly from Tuscan Trebbiano that comes Tuscia's most famous wine, Est! Est!!! Est!!! from Montefiascone, in a high hilly area positively influenced by the presence of the vast Lake Bolsena. A simple, immediate wine that finds its best qualities in its lively, fresh aromas.

Moving south inland, we find an area particularly suited to the Cesanese grape, both in the Piglio and Olevano Romano versions. The resulting red wines have the greatest merits in aromatic intensity, rich in red flowers and small black fruits, while the palate is rather docile and harmonious, just enlivened by a touch of astringency.

The journey becomes more jagged and uneven when facing the geography of the many wines that do not use Designations of Controlled Origin: a whimsical and original world in which Lazio producers experiment on-site, often with considerable critical success, with the potential of Cabernet and Merlot, Petit Verdot and Grenache, Syrah and Viognier, but also the traditional Grechetto, Biancolella, and Bellone.

The distribution of vineyards is 71% hilly, 20% flat, and 9% mountainous, with a total of 44,500 acres under vine producing 31.7 million gallons of wine, 75% of which is dedicated to whites. The production sector is made up of four thousand farms, which also supply grapes to the seven community wine cellars that are active today and which alone produce 40% of Lazio's wine.

MAIN VINES GROWN IN THE REGION

Abbuoto, Serpe
Very rare red berry cultivars found exclusively in the area between Itri, Fondi, and Sperlonga, in the province of Frosinone. They were used two thousand years ago for Cæcubum, the Caecubus wine of ancient Rome, which is deep ruby red in color, with spicy hints of pepper and licorice that are grafted onto a classic fruity background of cherry and plum.

Bellone
A white grape with the curious synonyms of Pampanaro, Cacchione, Zinnavacca, and Arciprete, it traditionally descended from the Pantastica grape described by Pliny the Elder in his Naturalis Historia. Today, it has been rediscovered and is mentioned here in the savory and citrusy Cori DOC and in some notable versions outside the designations.

Biancolella
→ Campania

Cesanese Comune, Cesanese di Affile

Historic black berry cultivars of the Roman hills. Cesanese Comune yields wines that are generally less long-lived than Cesanese di Affile. The wines of the relative designations, Cesanese del Piglio and Cesanese di Olevano Romano, are fruity and dry, of discreet complexity and, depending on the style of production, more or less structured, with a finish tending toward balsamic.

Grechetto
→ Umbria

TUSCIA

Castiglione in Tiberina

Civitella d'Aliano

Firenze

Montefiascone

Lago di Bolsena

VITERBO

Amone

Marta

Lago di Vico

Lago Lungo

Monte Terminillo
2213

Lago
Ripa Sottile

Convento
la Foresta

ROMA

Farfa

Lago del
Salto

Abbazia
di Farfa

Farfa

Lago di
Turano

A1

Lago di Bracciano

Madonna
di Bracciano

COLLI
DELLA
SABINA

L'Aquila

Cerveteri

A24

A24

ROMA

Tivoli

Serrone

Colonna

Monteporzio Catone

Olevano
Romano

Piglio

FRASCATI

Frascati

Labico

CESANESE
DEL PIGLIO

Abbazia
di Casamari

A90

ROMA

Anagni

Alviro

Marino

Lago di Nemi

Velletri

ATINA

COLLI
LANUVINI

Cori

FROSINONE

Àtina

COLLI
ALBANI

Arce

Abbazia
di Montecassino

Mar Tirreno

Cassino

LATINA

A1

Abbazia
di Fossanova

Napoli

Liri

TERRACINA

Madonna
della Civita

Monte Petrella
1535

PARCO
NAZIONALE
DEL CIRCEO

Lago di
Fondi

Terracina

Itri

Circeo
541

Isola Palmarola

Isola Zannone

Isola di Ponza

Isola di Ventotene

Malvasia Bianca di Candia, Malvasia del Lazio

Malvasia Bianca di Candia originates from the island of Crete and is widespread in central Italy, particularly in Lazio. It is closely related to Garganega, from which Soave is made in Veneto, and to other white varieties such as Albana in Emilia-Romagna, Catarratto in Sicily, Montonico, and Trebbiano Toscano. In the Frascati area, it is used to produce pleasant and immediate wines with citrus characteristics and good intensity of flavor.

Malvasia del Lazio, also known as Malvasia Puntinata, originates from a cross between Moscato di Alessandria and Schiava Grossa. The pure wines are characterized by floral and exotic aromas of white fruits and are best consumed rather young.

Montepulciano
→ Abruzzo and Marche

Procanico
→ Trebbiano Toscano in Tuscany

....

The DOCGs
- Cannellino di Frascati
- Cesanese del Piglio / Piglio
- Frascati Superiore

The DOCs
- Aleatico di Gradoli
- Aprilia
- Atina
- Bianco Capena
- Castelli Romani
- Cerveteri
- Cesanese di Affile / Affile
- Cesanese di Olevano Romano / Olevano Romano
- Circeo
- Colli Albani
- Colli della Sabina
- Colli Etruschi Viterbesi / Tuscia
- Colli Lanuvini
- Cori
- Est! Est!! Est!!! di Montefiascone
- Frascati
- Genazzano
- Marino
- Montecompatri Colonna / Montecompatri / Colonna
- Nettuno
- Orvieto (→ Umbria)
- Roma
- Tarquinia
- Terracina / Moscato di Terracina
- Velletri
- Vignanello
- Zagarolo

Cannellino di Frascati DOCG

The vineyards are located in five municipalities in the province of Rome, and the grapes used are Malvasia Bianca di Candia, and/or Malvasia del Lazio up to at least 70%, with possible inclusion of local white grapes. It is a sweet wine with a long tradition, which comes from drying bunches of grapes in the vineyard until November, so as to obtain a remarkable aromatic and sugar concentration. About fifty thousand bottles are produced annually.

—

Producer and its trademark and signature wine:

1. VILLA SIMONE, Monte Porzio Catone
    Cannellino di Frascati ($)

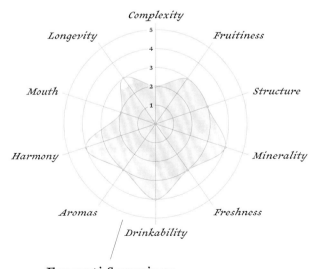

Frascati Superiore

Frascati DOC

Produced in five municipalities in the Rome area, including some vineyards within the territory of Rome itself, it is made from Malvasia Bianca di Candia and/or Malvasia del Lazio, at a minimum of 70%, with possible additions of other local white grapes, not used in the suggested wine. Notes of white fruits and flowers emerge with finesse, as well as the classic almond aroma typical of Malvasia, in a taste of good, overall vitality. Over six million bottles a year are produced, of varying quality and fame, so much so that many wineries have preferred to dedicate themselves to the Superiore DOCG version alone.

—

Producer and its trademark and signature wine:

2. VITUS VINI, Roma
    Frascati Auranova ($)

Frascati Superiore DOCG

The wines from this area of the Colli Albani, characterized by the residues resulting from the activity of a volcano that disappeared some twenty-five thousand years ago, were already appreciated in Roman times. The vine-growing area and vines are the same as those of Frascati, but in the Superiore version, and even more so in the Riserva, concentration and robust flavor are more often desired, without in any way affecting the freshness of this product, which is due to the citrus notes. Around 1.5 million bottles are produced annually.

—

Producers and their trademark and signature wines:

3. CASALE VALLECHIESA, Frascati
    Frascati Superiore Riserva Heredio ($$)
4. CASTEL DE PAOLIS, Grottaferrata
    Frascati Superiore ($)
5. DE SANCTIS, Frascati
    Frascati Superiore Abelos ($)
6. FONTANA CANDIDA, Monte Porzio Catone
    Frascati Superiore Riserva Luna Mater ($)
7. L'OLIVELLA, Frascati
    Frascati Superiore Racemo ($)
8. Gabriele MAGNO, Grottaferrata
    Frascati Superiore ($)
9. MERUMALIA, Frascati
    Frascati Superiore Riserva Primo ($)
10. POGGIO LE VOLPI, Monte Porzio Catone
    Frascati Superiore Epos ($)
11. PRINCIPE PALLAVICINI, Colonna
    Frascati Superiore Poggio Verde ($)
1. VILLA SIMONE, Monte Porzio Catone
    Frascati Superiore Riserva Vigneto Filonardi ($)

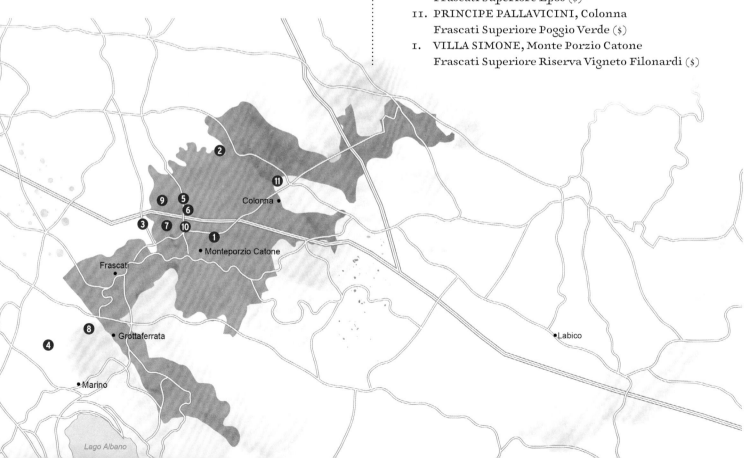

Cesanese del Piglio or Piglio DOCG

It is made from Cesanese di Affile and Cesanese Comune grapes—two biotypes, or variants, of the same vine—in five municipalities in the province of Frosinone. The main merit of this red wine lies in its bouquet, appreciable also in the finish in the mouth, ranging from violets to citrus fruits, from blackberry to black cherry and to damp soil. There is always a certain tannicity, not without notable freshness. Annual production is close to seven hundred thousand bottles.

—

Producers and their trademark and signature wines:

1. CASALE DELLA IORIA, Anagni
   Cesanese del Piglio Superiore Riserva Torre del Piano ($)
2. COLETTI CONTI, Anagni
   Cesanese del Piglio Superiore Romanico ($)
   Cesanese del Piglio Superiore Hernicus ($)
3. Marcella GIULIANI, Anagni
   Cesanese del Piglio Superiore Dives ($)
4. LA VISCIOLA, Piglio
   Cesanese del Piglio Priore Vignali ($$)
5. Mario MACCIOCCA, Piglio
   Cesanese del Piglio Civitella ($)
6. Carlo NORO, Labico
   Cesanese del Piglio Foretano ($)
7. Giovanni TERENZI, Serrone
   Cesanese del Piglio Superiore Colle Forma ($)

Cesanese di Olevano Romano or Olevano Romano DOC

Produced only in the vineyards of the municipalities of Olevano Romano and Genazzano, in the province of Rome, and from the same grapes as Piglio, it also includes the Amabile and Dolce types, but it is from the dry versions that the best results are achieved. A greater overall freshness, based on currants, wild strawberries, and balsamic hints, is sometimes noted when compared to Cesanese del Piglio, but much depends on the style of the producers. About two hundred and thirty thousand bottles are made annually.

—

Producers and their trademark and signature wines:

8. Damiano CIOLLI, Olevano Romano
   Olevano Romano Cesanese Riserva Cirsium ($$)
   Olevano Romano Cesanese Silene ($)
9. RICCARDI REALE VITICOLTORI, Olevano Romano
   Olevano Romano Neccio ($$)

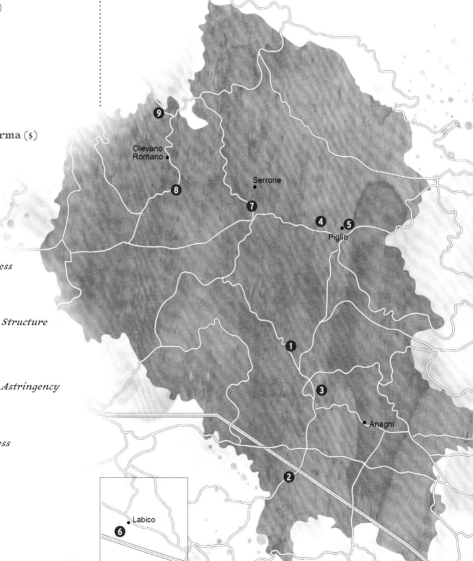

Cesanese del Piglio Superiore

[Radar chart with axes: Complexity, Fruitiness, Structure, Astringency, Freshness, Drinkability, Aromas, Harmony, Mouth, Longevity]

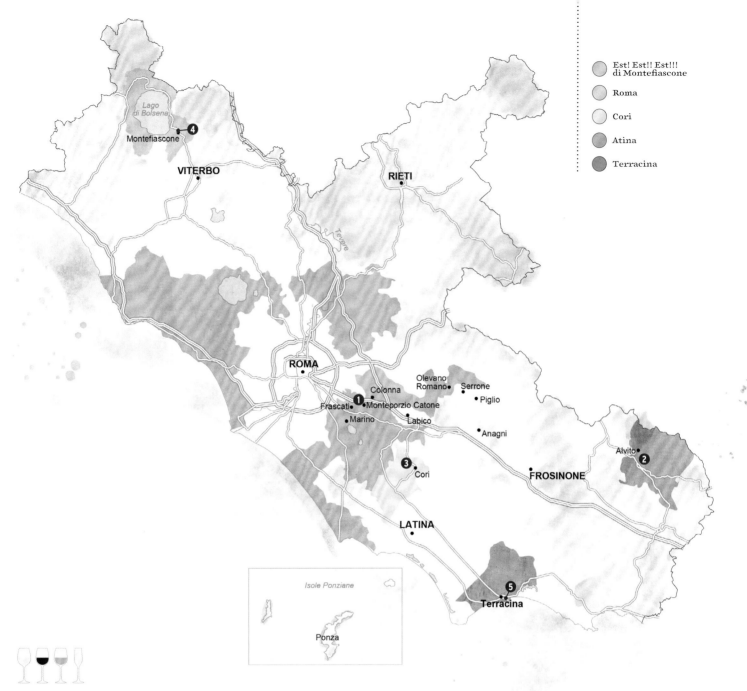

Legend:
- Est! Est!! Est!!! di Montefiascone
- Roma
- Cori
- Atina
- Terracina

Roma DOC

Produced almost everywhere in the province of Rome, it is a DOC designed in 2011 above all as a tourist attraction, and includes numerous types based on the most widespread and typical grapes of the Lazio region, but also includes others. The Rosso is made from at least 50% Montepulciano. In the recommended wine, Cesanese and Syrah are blended. Production is close to two million bottles per year.

—

Producer and its trademark and signature wines:

1. **POGGIO LE VOLPI**, Monte Porzio Catone
   Roma Malvasia Puntinata ($)
   Roma Rosso Edizione Limitata ($$)

Atina DOC

Produced in twelve municipalities in the province of Frosinone, it is a DOC wine with a French soul, providing for the priority use of Cabernet Sauvignon and Franc, Syrah, and Merlot while leaving a small space for white Atina Sémillon. Just over one hundred thousand bottles are produced each year.

—

Producer and its trademark and signature wine:

2. **COMINIUM**, Alvito
   Atina Cabernet Satur ($)

Cori DOC

A DOC, relating to the municipality of Cori and partly to that of Cisterna, where among the white grapes the little-known Bellone dominates almost unchallenged. The resulting wine is of great delicacy and elegance, never too rich or full-bodied, with a seductive saltiness. The different types total three hundred and thirty thousand bottles per year.
—
Producer and its trademark and signature wine:

3. Marco CARPINETI, Cori
    Cori Bellone Collesanti ($)

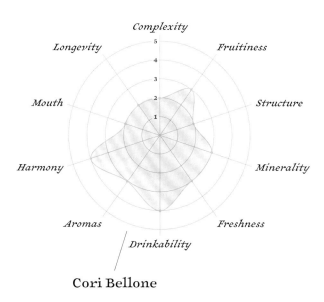

Cori Bellone

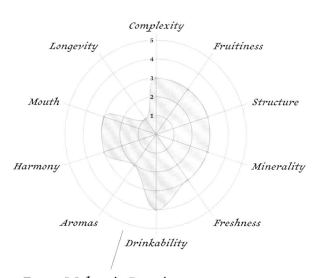

Roma Malvasia Puntinata

Est! Est!! Est!!! di Montefiascone DOC

Produced in six municipalities, in addition to Montefiascone, in the province of Viterbo, it is made from 50 to 65% Trebbiano Toscano grapes, which here are called Procanico. There are variable additions of Trebbiano Giallo and Malvasia. It has known moments of glory in past centuries, thanks to its aroma of field grass and white flowers followed by a delicate taste of good freshness and crispness. Over three million bottles per year are produced.
—
Producer and its trademark and signature wine:

4. ANTICA CANTINA LEONARDI, Montefiascone
    Est! Est!! Est!!! di Montefiascone Poggio del Cardinale ($)

Terracina or Moscato di Terracina DOC

The mysterious Terracina Muscat, perhaps a relative of the Muscat of Alexandria of Egypt, originates in three municipalities in the province of Latina. Production is insignificant, but it is worth taking note of a rather dry version of this wine with its seductive aroma. Fewer than a hundred thousand bottles are produced each year.
—
Producer and its trademark and signature wine:

5. SANT'ANDREA, Terracina
    Moscato di Terracina Hum ($)

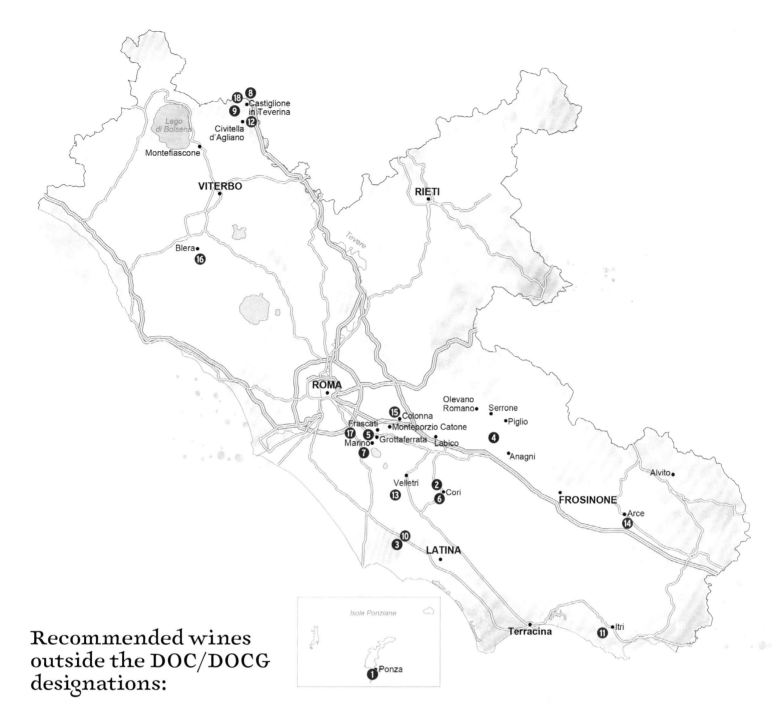

Recommended wines outside the DOC/DOCG designations:

1. ANTICHE CANTINE MIGLIACCIO, Ponza
   Fieno di Ponza Bianco (Biancolella...) ($$)
2. Marco CARPINETI, Cori
   Nzù (Bellone) ($$)
   Capolemole Rosso (Nero Buono, Montepulciano, Cesanese) ($)
3. CASALE DEL GIGLIO, Latina
   Anthium Bellone ($)
   Faro della Guardia Biancolella ($$)
   Mater Matuta (Syrah, Petit Verdot) ($$)
4. CASALE DELLA IORIA, Anagni
   Espero (Olivella Nera) ($)
5. CASTEL DE PAOLIS, Grottaferrata
   Donna Adriana (Viognier, Malvasia del Lazio) ($)
   I Quattro Mori (Syrah, Cabernet Sauvignon, Merlot, Petit Verdot) ($$)

6. CINCINNATO, Cori
   Enyo Bellone ($)
7. COLLE PICCHIONI, Marino
   Il Vassallo (Merlot, Cabernet Sauvignon, Cabernet Franc) ($)
   Le Vignole (Malvasia Puntinata, Sauvignon) ($)
8. COTARELLA, Montefiascone
   Montiano (Merlot) ($$$)
   Soente (Viognier) ($)
9. Paolo e Noemia D'AMICO, Castiglione in Teverina
   Notturno dei Calanchi (Pinot Noir) ($$)
   Atlante (Cabernet Franc) ($$)
10. Donato GIANGIROLAMI, Latina
    Propizio (Grechetto) ($)
11. MONTI CECUBI, Itri
    Caecubum Rosso (Abbuoto, Uva Spina) ($)
12. Sergio MOTTURA, Civitella d'Agliano
    Poggio della Costa (Grechetto) ($)
    Latour a Civitella (Grechetto) ($)

13. ÔMINA ROMANA, Velletri
    Ars Magna Merlot ($$$)
    Ars Magna Chardonnay ($$$)
14. PALAZZO TRONCONI, Arce
    Zi'tore (Lecinaro) ($)
15. PRINCIPE PALLAVICINI, Colonna
    Casa Romana (Petit Verdot, Cabernet Sauvignon) ($)
16. SAN GIOVENALE, Blera
    Habemus Etichetta Bianca (Grenache, Carignano, Syrah, Tempranillo) ($$$)
    Habemus (Cabernet Franc) ($$$$)
17. TENUTA DI FIORANO, Roma
    Fiorano Rosso (Cabernet Sauvignon, Merlot) ($$)
    Fiorano Bianco (Grechetto, Viognier) ($$)
18. TENUTA LA PAZZAGLIA, Castiglione in Teverina
    Poggio Triale (Grechetto) ($)

TENUTA DI FIORANO

Via di Fioranello 19
Rome
tenutadifiorano.it
Year of establishment: 1940
Owner: Alessandrojacopo
Boncompagni Ludovisi
Average number of bottles
produced per year: 32,000

Alessandrojacopo
Boncompagni Ludovisi
has resumed the activity
that was begun, and then
abandoned, by the winery's
founder, Alberico, and has
chosen to use the Bordeaux
red grape varieties that had
already proved their worth in
past decades. For the award-
winning Fiorano Bianco,
however, he relied on a
good blend of Grechetto and
Viognier. It is surprising to
discover how such important
and expressive wines can come
out of 30 organically cultivated
acres in Rome's Appia Antica
Park. A successful rebirth.

FIORANO ROSSO

First year of production: 1956
Average number of bottles produced
per year: 13,000
Grape varieties: Cabernet Sauvignon
(65%), Merlot (35%)

Bordeaux varietals but traditional and
long maturation in Slavonian oak barrels
for this very refined Fiorano Rosso, with
aromas of herbs and Mediterranean scrub
that combine with ripe cherries and an inky
mineral touch. The palate is bewitching
for its richness and pulp, sinuous, slow,
and always velvety right up to the finish
with hints of black pepper and smoke. The
excellent fruit of successful intuition.

CASTEL DE PAOLIS

Via Val De Paolis
Grottaferrata (RM)
casteldepaolis.com
Year of establishment: 1985
Owner: the Santarelli
family
Average number of bottles
produced per year: 85,000

Giulio Santarelli had one
certainty: that his volcanic
soils could yield great wines.
Thus, he began a research
project forty years ago that,
with the collaboration of
Attilio Scienza, involved
twenty grape varieties, both
local and international.
The results have been more
than positive and today the
oenological production stems
from 35 acres of vineyards,
combining labels of French
origin, such as the award-
winning I Quattro Mori, or
purely from Lazio, such as the
Frascati Superiore we present,
or the result of blends, such
as Donna Adriana in which
the predominant Viognier
is combined with Malvasia
Puntinata.

FRASCATI SUPERIORE

First year of production: 1993
Average number of bottles produced
per year: 12,000
Grape varieties: Malvasia Puntinata
(70%); Trebbiano Giallo, Bombino,
Bellone (30%)

Matured in stainless steel only, it offers
intense aromas of citrus and exotic fruits
joined by hints of almost minty herbs. The
mouth is fresh and of excellent density, with
a whirlwind of final aromas in which spices
such as saffron and turmeric are appreciated
together with hints of white flowers. A
perfect example of the potential of Frascati
Superiore.

SAN GIOVENALE

Località La Macchia
Blera (VT)
sangiovenale.it
Year of establishment: 2006
Owner: Emanuele
Pangrazi
Average number of bottles
produced per year: 9,000

Emanuele Pangrazi has made a
courageous choice in deciding
to reproduce a glimpse of the
Rhône in Tuscia, planting
predominantly Grenache,
Carignan, and Syrah, joined
by small parcels of Cabernet
Franc and Tempranillo. The
wine presented is joined
by a tiny, award-winning
production of Habemus
Etichetta Rossa, from pure
Cabernet Franc. Only 25 acres
are currently planted with
vines, with certified organic
cultivation, but the results
are so successful that the
wine world is already paying
high praise to this visionary
production.

HABEMUS

First year of production: 2010
Average number of bottles produced
per year: 8,000
Grape varieties: Grenache, Carignan,
Syrah, Tempranillo

The toastiness of the barriques in which
the wine has stayed for twenty months is
not imposing, merely adding spicy notes
on an aroma of prestigious complexity in
which black olives, small red fruits, incense,
and eucalyptus are perceived. The flavor is
particularly dynamic and agile, just warmed
by good alcohol and dense with fruity pulp,
ending with elegant balsamic returns. A
more than brilliant result, also achieved
thanks to the oenological advice of Marco
Casolanetti of Oasi degli Angeli.

SERGIO MOTTURA

Località Poggio della
Costa 1
Civitella d'Agliano (VT)
sergiomottura.com
Year of establishment: 1933
Owner: Sergio Mottura
Average number of bottles
produced per year: 93,000

Sergio Mottura and his
son Giuseppe's winery is
by now recognized as an
extraordinary interpreter of
the Grechetto grape, which
grows on the estate's 91
organically cultivated acres
and is the protagonist of six
of the house's eleven labels.
These include, in addition to
Latour a Civitella, the citrusy
Poggio della Costa, the savory
Orvieto Tragugnano, and the
Muffo, made by exploiting the
excellent drying capacity of
this cultivar. This is the winery
that has revitalized Latium
Grechetto.

LATOUR A CIVITELLA

First year of production: 1994
Average number of bottles produced
per year: 14,000
Grape variety: Grechetto

It ferments and matures in woods that do
not yield excessive aromatic contributions,
presenting itself rich in medicinal herbs and
yellow fruits on a floral base reminiscent
of orange blossom; the palate is dry, full,
never very acidic but lively and stimulating,
flavorsome.

Abruzzo

In terms of landscape, Abruzzo is one of the most genuine and best-preserved regions in Italy, rich in forests, mountains, ancient villages, and vine-covered hillsides. The oenological situation is finally showing signs of improvement in a production that until a few decades ago was bought at low prices by bottlers from the North. There is no doubt that Montepulciano d'Abruzzo is one of Italy's great reds and that Trebbiano can have considerable weight in the world of whites.

The size of the four main designations (Montepulciano, Trebbiano, Cerasuolo d'Abruzzo, in addition to the Abruzzo DOC itself) has somewhat stifled the emergence of specific territorial expressions, tending to give the region a unitary and compact image that little corresponds to a production reality based on different soils, a varied influence of the sea and mountains, and very jagged altitudes. A positive sign that we hope will be grasped comes from the only two regional DOCGs: the larger Colline Teramane Montepulciano d'Abruzzo and the tiny Tullum.

The oenological panorama is evolving rapidly, thanks in part to several producers who are pandering to the growing consumer demand for young, immediate, happening wines. Both the relatively newly created Cerasuolo d'Abruzzo DOC and the expansion of the areas cultivated with Pecorino and Passerina grapes are heading in this direction. And it is precisely Abruzzo Pecorino DOC that is gaining ground thanks to its freshness and drinkability, while it is increasingly clear that the other great local white, Trebbiano d'Abruzzo, is at its best after a few years of aging when tertiary aromas with a definite mineral imprint manage to join the always valid structure. Also encouraging are the results obtained by the few wineries that have undertaken to propose the white Cococciola vine, traditionally combined with Trebbiano, in purity. An articulated and still contradictory situation, where alongside world-renowned names are grapes bought at derisory prices from winegrowers.

About 79 million gallons of wine are produced annually from 81,500 acres of vineyards, 97% of which are located in hilly terrain, the vast majority of which are reds and rosés. The fifteen thousand wineries, two hundred and fifty of which are present on the market with their own brand names, are accompanied by the strong presence of cooperative wine cellars, which alone produce 80% of Abruzzo wine: a national record.

MAIN VINES GROWN IN THE REGION

Montepulciano (→ also Marche)

Vinified in Abruzzo, it becomes a fruit "bomb" that strikes with a decisive impact of red fruit jam, cherry, and dehydrated plum, to the point where it is difficult to imagine a wine that adheres more eloquently to these wild, ancestral lands. Never cloying or grumpy, because the tannins are soft and the acidity supports the alcohol component well. With time come spices and tertiary aromas from black pepper, cinnamon, and nutmeg to licorice, tobacco, leather, and toasted bitter almond. In the rosé version, this exciting grape variety with inexhaustible potential translates into the delicate and joyful Cerasuolo d'Abruzzo DOC.

Trebbiano d'Abruzzo

An Abruzzese variant of the Trebbiano family, it is grown exclusively in the region and is included in the similarly named DOC, either on its own or in a blend with Trebbiano Toscano, Bombino Bianco, Passerina, or Malvasia Bianca. Juicy and sometimes savory on the palate, its citrus and mineral aromas may recall orange, rennet apple, white peach, field herbs, and bay leaf, arriving with aging at musk, flint, and hydrocarbons.

The DOCGs
- Colline Teramane Montepulciano d'Abruzzo
- Terre Tollesi / Tullum

The DOCs
- Abruzzo
- Cerasuolo d'Abruzzo
- Controguerra
- Montepulciano d'Abruzzo
- Ortona
- Trebbiano d'Abruzzo
- Villamagna

CONTROGUERRA
• Controguerra
Torano Nuovo •
• Tortoreto
• Sant'Omero

COLLINE
TERAMANE
Corno Grande   TERAMO
2914
• Notaresco   • Roseto degli Abruzzi
San Clemente
al Vomano   • Pineto
• Atri
• Castilenti

Lago di
Campotosto

Montereale
1283
San Giovanni   • Città Sant'Angelo
al Mavone   • Caparrone
Corno Grande   • Spoltore
2914   Loreto Aprutino   PESCARA
                                        • Francavilla al Mare
                    TERRE
                    DEI VESTINI   San Giovanni
                                    Teatino   ORTONA
L'AQUILA   CHIETI   TULLUM
                    • Ofena   • Ortona
                                        Tollo
                    ALTO TIRINO   • Nocciano   Villamagna
                    • Cugnoli   VILLAMAGNA
A24   • Alanno   • Ari
                                        • Rocca San Giovanni
                    Abbazia di
                    San Clemente   CASAURIA   • Orsogna
Aterno   CASAURIA   • Bolognano
Santa Maria in
Valle Porclaneta
                    • Popoli   • Casoli   TEATE
A25
Roma   TERRE
                    DEI PELIGNI   Lago   A14   • Vasto
                    • Prezza • Sulmona   di Bomba   Taranto

Liri
                    Lago di
                    Scanno
            Passo
            del Diavolo
            1391
            Monte Marsicano
            2242   Sangro
            Lago
            di Barrea

Mar Adriatico

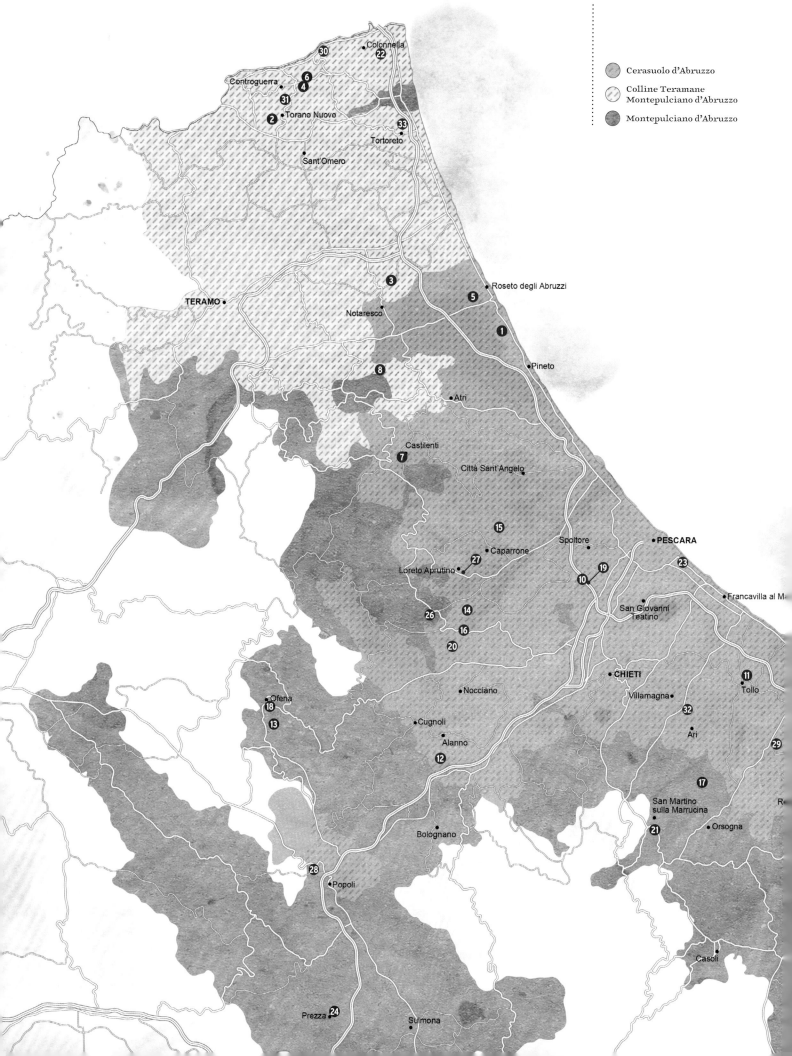

Cerasuolo d'Abruzzo

Colline Teramane
Montepulciano d'Abruzzo

Montepulciano d'Abruzzo

Colonnella
30
22
6
4
Controguerra
31
2
Torano Nuovo
33
Tortoreto
Sant'Omero

3
TERAMO
Roseto degli Abruzzi
5
Notaresco
1
Pineto
8
Atri
Castilenti
7
Città Sant'Angelo
15
Spoltore
PESCARA
27
Caparrone
19
Loreto Aprutino
10
23
26
14
Francavilla al M
16
San Giovanni
Teatino
20
CHIETI
11
Nocciano
Tollo
Ofena
Villamagna
18
32
13
Ari
Cugnoli
29
Alanno
12
17
San Martino
sulla Marrucina
21
Orsogna
Bolognano
Casoli
28
Popoli

Prezza
24
Sulmona

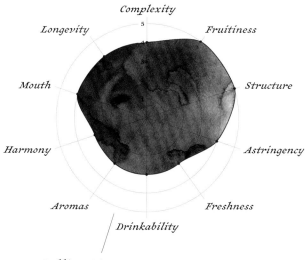

Complexity
Longevity
Fruitiness
Mouth
Structure
Harmony
Astringency
Aromas
Freshness
Drinkability

**Colline Teramane
Montepulciano d'Abruzzo**

ni•

25

Vasto

Colline Teramane Montepulciano d'Abruzzo DOCG

The hilly area in the province of Teramo has been known for the quality of its red wines since Roman times, and it was here that this DOCG was born in 2003, extending across some thirty territories. Montepulciano grapes make up 90% of it. In 2015, the name Montepulciano d'Abruzzo Colline Teramane was changed to Colline Teramane Montepulciano d'Abruzzo. There are two types: the basic one, with at least one year of aging, and the Riserva, with three years of aging in cellars, of which at least one is in wood. The regular version is fruity, from cherry to plum, and has an instantaneous taste. Often aged in steel or cement, more spicy, powerful, concentrated, and not very astringent, the Riserva maintains an enjoyable balsamic-oriented freshness of flavor. Over five hundred thousand bottles a year are produced.

—

Producers and their trademark and signature wines:

1. BARBA, Pineto
   Colline Teramane Montepulciano d'Abruzzo Yang ($)
2. BARONE CORNACCHIA, Torano Nuovo
   Colline Teramane Montepulciano d'Abruzzo Riserva Vizzarro ($$)
3. FATTORIA NICODEMI, Notaresco
   Colline Teramane Montepulciano d'Abruzzo Notàri ($)
4. ILLUMINATI, Controguerra
   Colline Teramane Montepulciano d'Abruzzo Riserva Zanna ($)
   Colline Teramane Montepulciano d'Abruzzo Riserva Pieluni ($$)
5. ORLANDI CONTUCCI PONNO, Roseto degli Abruzzi
   Colline Teramane Montepulciano d'Abruzzo Riserva ($)
6. PROPE, Controguerra
   Colline Teramane Montepulciano d'Abruzzo Verso Sera ($$)
7. SAN LORENZO, Castilenti
   Colline Teramane Montepulciano d'Abruzzo Riserva Escol ($$)
8. VILLA MEDORO, Atri
   Colline Teramane Montepulciano d'Abruzzo Adrano ($)

Montepulciano d'Abruzzo DOC

It can be made in all the hilly areas that are cultivated in the region, at an altitude not exceeding 1,900 feet, with Montepulciano grapes accounting for at least 85%, possibly accompanied by other authorized red cultivars as the remainder. The production regulations are less strict than those for Colline Teramane, as they provide for a higher grape production per acre and less aging for the Riserva. This allows the production of a wine that is more suitable for immediate consumption and not too demanding. This also allows an annual production that covers over 70% of the regional total and exceeds one hundred million bottles. In reality, there are many producers who are committed to making Montepulciano d'Abruzzo DOC a great Italian red—tasty and hearty. The new DOCG Casauria, or Terre di Casauria, is in the process of being established in the hills of the Pescara Valley that surround the splendid abbey of San Clemente.

—

Producers and their trademark and signature wines:

9. AGRIVERDE, Ortona
Montepulciano d'Abruzzo Solàrea ($)
1. BARBA, Pineto
Montepulciano d'Abruzzo I Vasari ($)
2. BARONE CORNACCHIA, Torano Nuovo
Montepulciano d'Abruzzo Riserva Vigna Le Coste ($)
10. BINOMIO, Spoltore
Montepulciano d'Abruzzo Riserva Binomio ($$)
11. CANTINA TOLLO, Tollo
Montepulciano d'Abruzzo Riserva Mo ($)
Montepulciano d'Abruzzo Riserva Cagiòlo ($)
12. CASTORANI, Alanno
Montepulciano d'Abruzzo Casauria Riserva ($$)
13. CATALDI MADONNA, Ofena
Montepulciano d'Abruzzo Tonì ($$)
14. CIAVOLICH, Loreto Aprutino
Montepulciano d'Abruzzo Fosso Cancelli ($$)
15. CONTESA, Caparrone
Montepulciano d'Abruzzo Terre dei Vestini Riserva Chiedi alla Polvere ($)
16. DE FERMO, Loreto Aprutino
Montepulciano d'Abruzzo Prologo ($$)
17. ILFEUDUCCIODISANTAMARIAD'ORNI, Orsogna
Montepulciano d'Abruzzo Ursonia ($)
Montepulciano d'Abruzzo Margae ($$)
4. ILLUMINATI, Controguerra
Montepulciano d'Abruzzo Ilico ($)
18. INALTO, Ofena
Montepulciano d'Abruzzo Campo Affamato ($$)

19. Fattoria LA VALENTINA, Spoltore
Montepulciano d'Abruzzo Terre dei Vestini Riserva Bellovedere ($$)
Montepulciano d'Abruzzo Riserva Spelt ($)
20. MARCHESI DE' CORDANO, Loreto Aprutino
Montepulciano d'Abruzzo Terre dei Vestini Riserva Santinumi ($$)
21. MASCIARELLI, San Martino sulla Marrucina
Montepulciano d'Abruzzo Riserva Iskra Marina Cvetic ($$)
Montepulciano d'Abruzzo Riserva Villa Gemma ($$$$)
22. Francesco MASSETTI, Colonnella
Montepulciano d'Abruzzo Quaranta Cinque ($$)
23. PASETTI, Francavilla al Mare
Montepulciano d'Abruzzo Harimann ($$)
24. PRAESIDIUM, Prezza
Montepulciano d'Abruzzo Riserva ($$)
25. TIBERIO, Cugnoli
Montepulciano d'Abruzzo ($)
26. TORRE DEI BEATI, Loreto Aprutino
Montepulciano d'Abruzzo Mazzamurello ($$)
Montepulciano d'Abruzzo Cocciapazza ($)
27. VALENTINI, Loreto Aprutino
Montepulciano d'Abruzzo ($$$$$)
28. VALLE REALE, Popoli
Montepulciano d'Abruzzo San Calisto ($$$)
Montepulciano d'Abruzzo Vigneto Sant'Eusanio ($$)
Montepulciano d'Abruzzo ($)
29. VIGNAMADRE, Ortona
Montepulciano d'Abruzzo Capo Le Vigne ($)
8. VILLA MEDORO, Atri
Montepulciano d'Abruzzo ($)

Cerasuolo d'Abruzzo DOC

This was the first Italian rosé to obtain its own independent DOC in 2010, and its composition is at least 85% Montepulciano d'Abruzzo grapes, and so can count on vineyards scattered throughout the region. It opens on the nose with hints of raspberry, citrus, and at times a whiff of mint. The taste is important but light, dynamic, almost saline, and closes with notes of fresh red fruit. A commercial success, with an annual production of more than seven million bottles.

—

Producers and their trademark and signature wines:

13. CATALDI MADONNA, Ofena
    Cerasuolo d'Abruzzo Piè delle Vigne ($$)
15. CONTESA, Caparrone
    Cerasuolo d'Abruzzo ($)
19. Fattoria LA VALENTINA, Spoltore
    Cerasuolo d'Abruzzo Superiore Spelt ($)
30. Camillo MONTORI, Controguerra
    Cerasuolo d'Abruzzo Fonte Cupa ($)
31. Emidio PEPE, Torano Nuovo
    Cerasuolo d'Abruzzo ($$)
32. TENUTA I FAURI, Ari
    Cerasuolo d'Abruzzo Baldovino ($)
33. TERRAVIVA, Tortoreto
    Cerasuolo d'Abruzzo Giusi ($)
25. TIBERIO, Cugnoli
    Cerasuolo d'Abruzzo ($)

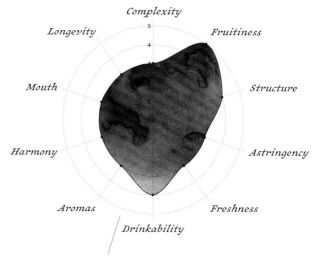

Montepulciano d'Abruzzo

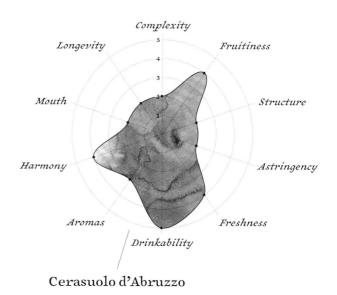

Cerasuolo d'Abruzzo

Trebbiano d'Abruzzo DOC

It is produced in a vast area of the region, in which the province of Chieti stands out. Due to the difficulties encountered in identifying the genetic differences between these vines, it is made from Trebbiano Abruzzese and/or Bombino Bianco and/or Trebbiano Toscano grapes, despite the fact that since 1994 the Abruzzese variety's autonomy has been recognized and included in the National Register of Vine Varieties. In general, it is a simple white, not very expressive in its aromas and easy on the palate, where the acidity is usually quite low, not particularly suitable for aging. In actual fact, there are numerous examples of producers who, starting from selected grapes and adopting careful vinification and aging methods, from cement to wood, succeed in producing Trebbiano d'Abruzzo with individual flavors. These are citrusy and, over time, almost like flint, in its rock smoke aroma, with iodine on an almond background. Left in the bottle, it will improve over decades. Over thirteen million bottles a year are produced.

—

Producers and their trademark and signature wines:

1. AMOROTTI, Loreto Aprutino
   Trebbiano d'Abruzzo ($$)
2. AUSONIA, Atri
   Trebbiano d'Abruzzo Apollo ($)
3. BOSSANOVA, Controguerra
   Trebbiano d'Abruzzo ($)
4. CANTINA RAPINO, Francavilla al Mare
   Trebbiano d'Abruzzo Gira ($)
5. CHIUSA GRANDE, Nocciano
   Trebbiano d'Abruzzo In Petra ($)
6. Francesco CIRELLI, Atri
   Trebbiano d'Abruzzo Anfora ($$)
7. DE ANGELIS CORVI, Controguerra
   Trebbiano d'Abruzzo Superiore Fonte Raviliano ($)
8. FATTORIA NICODEMI, Notaresco
   Trebbiano d'Abruzzo Superiore Notàri ($)
   Trebbiano d'Abruzzo Cocciopesto ($)
9. INALTO, Ofena
   Trebbiano d'Abruzzo Superiore ($)
10. MASCIARELLI, Loreto Aprutino
    Trebbiano d'Abruzzo Superiore Castello di Semivicoli ($)
    Trebbiano d'Abruzzo Riserva La Botte di Gianni ($$$)
11. ORLANDI CONTUCCI PONNO, Roseto degli Abruzzi
    Trebbiano d'Abruzzo Superiore Podere Colle della Corte ($)
12. Emidio PEPE, Torano Nuovo
    Trebbiano d'Abruzzo ($$$)
13. RABOTTINI, San Giovanni Teatino
    Trebbiano d'Abruzzo Per Iniziare ($)
14. TERRAVIVA, Tortoreto
    Trebbiano d'Abruzzo Superiore Mario's 47 ($)
15. TIBERIO, Cugnoli
    Trebbiano d'Abruzzo ($)
16. TORRE DEI BEATI, Loreto Aprutino
    Trebbiano d'Abruzzo Bianchi Grilli per la Testa ($)
17. VALENTINI, Loreto Aprutino
    Trebbiano d'Abruzzo ($$$$)
18. VALLE REALE, Popoli
    Trebbiano d'Abruzzo Vigna del Convento di Capestrano ($$)
    Trebbiano d'Abruzzo ($)
19. ZACCAGNINI, Bolognano
    Trebbiano d'Abruzzo Chronicon ($)

Terre Tollesi or Tullum DOCG

A DOCG created in 2019 after carefully studying the soil, relating only to the territory of the municipality of Tollo, and for the moment used by only a handful of producers. The types are Rosso (also Riserva), Passerina, and Pecorino: it is this type that is intriguing, thanks to a lively presence of citrus fruits and a discreet contribution of balsamic notes, even on the final taste. A total of one hundred forty thousand bottles per year are produced.

—

Producer and its trademark and signature wine:

20. FEUDO ANTICO, Tollo
    Tullum Pecorino ($)

Abruzzo DOC

Being a regional DOC, it includes territories planted with vines in the provinces of Chieti, L'Aquila, Teramo, and Pescara, with a variety of different types of white grapes that can be used, such as Trebbiano, and red grapes, such as Montepulciano. However, in recent years it is the Abruzzo Pecorino that has attracted the most interest, from both producers and consumers, with remarkable results in terms of quality. The aromas, usually developed during aging in steel or cement, are fresh and range from citrus to medicinal herbs, like those sold in old apothecary shops, sometimes playing against a mineral background reminiscent of flint. There is no complexity on the nose, just dynamism and joyful acidity. A total of over three million bottles are produced annually.

—

Producers and their trademark and signature wines:

1. CANTINA FRENTANA, Rocca San Giovanni
    Abruzzo Cococciola Costa del Mulino ($)
2. CANTINA TOLLO, Tollo
    Abruzzo Pecorino ($)
3. CASTORANI, Alanno
    Abruzzo Pecorino Superiore Amorino ($)
4. CODICE VINO, Ortona
    Abruzzo Pecorino Superiore Tegèo ($)
5. D'ALESIO, Città Sant'Angelo
    Abruzzo Pecorino Superiore ($)
6. Tommaso MASCIANTONIO, Casoli
    Abruzzo Pecorino Jernare ($)
    Abruzzo Pecorino Superiore Mantica Vigna di Caprafico ($)
7. MASCIARELLI, Loreto Aprutino
    Abruzzo Pecorino Castello di Semivicoli ($)
8. TENUTA I FAURI, Ari
    Abruzzo Pecorino ($)
9. TERRAVIVA, Tortoreto
    Abruzzo Pecorino Èkwo ($)
10. TORRE DEI BEATI, Loreto Aprutino
    Abruzzo Pecorino Bianchi Grilli per la Testa ($)
    Abruzzo Pecorino Giocheremo con i Fiori ($)
11. VALORI, Sant'Omero
    Abruzzo Pecorino Octava Dies ($)
12. ZACCAGNINI, Bolognano
    Abruzzo Pecorino Chronicon ($)

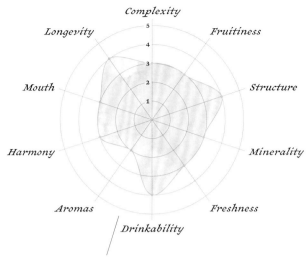

Trebbiano d'Abruzzo

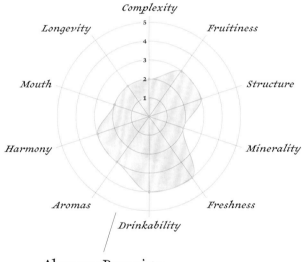

Abruzzo Pecorino

Recommended wines outside the DOC/DOCG designations:

13. FEUDO ANTICO, Tollo
    Casadonna (Pecorino) ($$)
14. PRAESIDIUM, Prezza
    Lucì (Trebbiano) ($$)
15. TIBERIO, Cugnoli
    Pecorino ($)
16. VIGNAMADRE, Ortona
    Pecorino Becco Reale ($)
17. VILLA MEDORO, Atri
    8 ½ Pecorino ($)
12. ZACCAGNINI, Bolognano
    Clematis Rosso Passito (blackberry grapes) ($$)

TORRE DEI BEATI

Contrada Poggioragone 56
Loreto Aprutino (PE)
torredeibeati.it
Year of establishment: 1999
Owners: Adriana Galasso,
Fausto Albanesi
Average number of bottles
produced per year: 100,000

A small and recent
undertaking that immediately
distinguished itself for
the exclusive attention
afforded to the area's three
most classic grape varieties:
Montepulciano, Trebbiano,
and, more recently, Pecorino.
The overall project, therefore,
tends to represent, albeit with
different nuances depending
on the soil and winemaking
methods, the perfect
adherence between grapes and
territory, starting from the 49
organically cultivated acres.
Together with the Pecorino we
present, the Montepulciano
d'Abruzzo Cocciapazza and
the Trebbiano d'Abruzzo
Bianchi Grilli are always in the
spotlight.

ABRUZZO PECORINO BIANCHI GRILLI PER LA TESTA

First year of production: 2010
Average number of bottles produced
per year: 100,000
Grape variety: Pecorino

It best expresses the characteristics of the
grape variety based on aromas of exotic
fruit—such as pineapple—and local
ones—such as apple and plum—against a
background of fresh notes, such as mint,
and riper ones, such as almond. The delicate
passage in wood ensures a soft and rich taste
despite the inherent acidity of this grape,
featuring a finish with a mineral touch of
flint after a few years in the bottle. A fine
example of Pecorino's taste capacity, at an
affordable price.

ILLUMINATI

Contrada San Biagio 18
Controguerra (TE)
illuminativini.it
Year of establishment: 1890
Owner: the Illuminati family
Average number of bottles
produced per year: 950,000

This is a more than century-old
farm that started bottling wine
after the Second World War,
with increasingly appreciated
qualitative results. The most
significant part of the vineyards
is located within the Teramane
Hills, in a panoramic position
from which one can enjoy
views of the Adriatic Sea
and the fresh influences of
the Gran Sasso, the highest
massif in the Apennines.
The considerable size of the
company is backed by 321
acres of vineyards, allowing
it to range across seventeen
labels including whites, reds,
and rosés based on the area's
various traditional grapes, such
as Pecorino and Passerina, but
the most essential remains
Montepulciano d'Abruzzo,
declined in various types but
among which the famous
Riserva Zanna stands out.

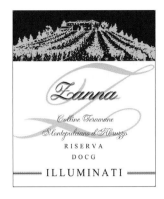

COLLINE TERAMANE MONTEPULCIANO D'ABRUZZO RISERVA ZANNA

First year of production: 1985
Average number of bottles produced
per year: 60,000
Grape variety: Montepulciano

A rich and multifaceted red, endowed with
ample fruity hints ranging from blackberry
to plum, with mineral nuances in the cooler
vintages leading toward wet earth and flint;
more austere and with hints of cocoa, tannic
and robust in the warmer vintages. Every
year, a very enjoyable—and economical—
rendition of a great Montepulciano
d'Abruzzo.

CATALDI MADONNA

Località Madonna del
Piano
Ofena (AQ)
cataldimadonna.com
Year of establishment: 1920
Owner: the Cataldi
Madonna family
Average number of bottles
produced per year: 230,000

In thirty years of work,
Luigi Cataldi Madonna has
succeeded in revitalizing
an entire winegrowing area
through the validation of its
traditional grape varieties,
especially Montepulciano and
Pecorino. The vineyards, 74
acres of certified organic land,
are located in the Ofena basin,
between the provinces of
Pescara and L'Aquila, a plateau
in the shadow of the Gran
Sasso where the grapes best
display their aromas due to the
area's significant temperature
fluctuations. Among the seven
labels proposed, in addition to
the Cerasuolo Piè delle Vigne,
the Montepulciano d'Abruzzo
Tonì and the Pecorino
Supergiulia stand out and
receive the highest praise from
wine critics.

CERASUOLO D'ABRUZZO PIÈ DELLE VIGNE

First year of production: 1997
Average number of bottles produced
per year: 3,000
Grape variety: Montepulciano

Matured in steel only, on the nose it is
fragrant, lively, and rich in fresh scents
reminiscent of cherries; on the palate,
it offers good alcoholic warmth and
marked acidity combined with an almost
saline touch, while on the finish it offers
captivating hints of red fruit and spices
typical of the Montepulciano grape. An
interpretation that demonstrates the taste
qualities of Cerasuolo d'Abruzzo at the
highest level.

FATTORIA LA VALENTINA

Via Torretta 52
Spoltore (PE)
lavalentina.it
Year of establishment: 1990
Owner: the Di Properzio
family
Average number of bottles
produced per year: 350,000

The winery's cornerstone
is strict adherence to the
peculiarities of the land.
Hence the decision to use only
indigenous vines, to cultivate
the 99-acre property with
organic methods, and to avoid
oenological "forcing," limiting
cellar care to obtaining long-
lasting products of great
elegance. In addition to the
Bellovedere, the very typical
Montepulciano d'Abruzzo
Riserva Spelt, the fresh and
fruity Cerasuolo d'Abruzzo
Superiore Spelt, and the more
straightforward Pecorino also
regularly enjoy international
acclaim. Also of interest is the
Montepulciano d'Abruzzo
Riserva Binomio, made by
Sabatino di Properzio in a
company specially created in
2000 with his friend Stefano
Inama from Veneto.

MONTEPULCIANO D'ABRUZZO TERRE DEI VESTINI RISERVA BELLOVEDERE

First year of production: 2000
Average number of bottles produced
per year: 7,000
Grape variety: Montepulciano

Hints of blackberries and well-ripened
blueberries are joined by a refreshing vegetal
touch reminiscent of the Mediterranean
scrub; the taste is structured and important,
endowed with splendid tannin that
reinforces the volume without being
astringent, all the way to a crisp finish with
red flowers and delicate spices. An excellent
demonstration of the qualities of the great
Montepulciano d'Abruzzo.

MASCIARELLI
Via Gamberale 2
San Martino sulla
Marrucina (CH)
masciarelli.it
Year of establishment: 1981
Owner: Marina Cvetic
Average number of
bottles produced per year:
2,500,000

Modern Abruzzo owes much to the winery founded by Gianni Masciarelli, an entrepreneur as volcanic and visionary as he is capable and enterprising. The immediate success of these modern, crisp, and fragrant wines, a little woody in their first years in the bottle but endowed with great longevity, revealed a way forward and gave rise to a company that, thanks to the farsighted and tireless work of Marina Cvetic, continues to grow and evolve. Today, it boasts 790 acres of vineyards and three vinification centers, with twenty-two labels endowed with a sensory quality of rare precision.

MONTEPULCIANO D'ABRUZZO RISERVA VILLA GEMMA
First year of production: 1984
Average number of bottles produced per year: 18,000
Grape variety: Montepulciano

Plum and blackberry are the most evident fruity scents, against a bewitching balsamic backdrop that lends vitality and elegance; the palate reveals a firm, full-bodied structure with good alcohol content but not lacking in freshness, with smoothness and drinkability aided by a delicate contribution of tannin, all the way to an elegantly licorice-like finish. The perfect expression of the harmony that can come from Montepulciano d'Abruzzo.

EMIDIO PEPE
Via Chiesi 10
Torano Nuovo (TE)
emidiopepe.com
Year of establishment: 1964
Owner: the Pepe family
Average number of bottles produced per year: 80,000

Emidio Pepe's production philosophy has always been marked by an almost organic and natural approach both in the vineyard and in the cellar: no chemical pesticides, no industrial yeasts, and much respect for the expressive and evolutionary capacities of the Trebbiano, Pecorino, and Montepulciano grapes. The winery has also become famous for its traditional foot treading of the grapes, vinification in cement tanks, and the long aging of the bottles before being released on the market. The 49 acres of vineyards are run under a certified biodynamic system and concrete tanks are used for vinification. A hymn to winemaking purity.

TREBBIANO D'ABRUZZO
First year of production: 1964
Average number of bottles produced per year: 45,000
Grape variety: Trebbiano

A wine that best expresses the often-overlooked aging capabilities of Trebbiano d'Abruzzo. After two years of fermentation in cement, it is endowed with articulate olfactory scents that move between aromatic herbs and citrus fruits, to which hints of flint and almond notes are joined with age. The flavor is both powerful and fresh, rich and dynamic, with a finish in which savoriness and hints of white fruit come together.

VALLE REALE
Località San Calisto
Popoli (PE)
vallereale.it
Year of establishment: 1999
Owner: Leonardo Pizzolo
Average number of bottles produced per year: 130,000

Leonardo Pizzolo sought to set up his own company in a secluded and unpolluted location so that he could practice organic and biodynamic farming without external interference and influences. His 114 acres are therefore located between Gran Sasso Park and Majella Park, divided into vineyards from which the respective labels are born. The grapes are exclusively the classic local ones and thus give rise to Montepulciano, Trebbiano, and Cerasuolo d'Abruzzo: all wines endowed with great expressiveness and character, consistently praised by wine critics.

MONTEPULCIANO D'ABRUZZO VIGNETO SANT'EUSANIO
First year of production: 2009
Average number of bottles produced per year: 14,000
Grape variety: Montepulciano

An admirable result, obtained without the aid of wood maturation but relying solely on steel to preserve the characteristics that are born in the tall, cool Vigneto Sant'Eusanio. The aromas include red petals, currants, a touch of mentholated herbs, and a subtle backdrop of damp earth; the flavor is solid and direct, incisive, rich in well-ripened fruity flesh, delicately acidic, and of rare balance. An admirable execution of Montepulciano in purity.

VALENTINI
Via del Baio 2
Loreto Aprutino (PE)
info@agricolavalentini.it
Year of establishment: 1860
Owner: Francesco Paolo Valentini
Average number of bottles produced per year: 50,000

A name that has achieved international renown thanks to the quality and surprising longevity of his wines, not only Montepulciano but also Trebbiano d'Abruzzo. This is mainly owing to Edoardo Valentini's choice, today confirmed by his son Francesco Paolo, to use only first-choice grapes for bottling, reducing quantities and avoiding entering the market when the quality of a vintage is uncertain. As a result, the property's 173 acres produce wines that are sold more in demijohns than in bottles. There's no website and the cellar isn't open to the public. These are not simple wines and must be calmly waited for over time.

TREBBIANO D'ABRUZZO
First year of production: 1958
Average number of bottles produced per year: 23,000
Grape variety: Trebbiano

The archetypal Trebbiano d'Abruzzo in all its complexity provided one has the patience to wait a few years before tasting it. White fruit, such as apple, and aromatic herbs, joined over time by flint, precede a substantial and lively flavor, at times with a touch of freshness that is almost saline, authoritative, and savory. A rare oenological pearl.

Molise

Molise produces more wine than Valle d'Aosta, Liguria, and Basilicata,
but struggles to make a name for itself due to the few wineries active on the international
market and the scarce use of DOCs. The winegrowing bases are there, however, thanks to the
presence of famous grapes such as Montepulciano, Aglianico, and Falanghina, joined by the
increasingly appreciated Tintilia, a symbol of regional originality.

A millennial wine history that can be experienced by visiting the archaeological site in Arcora, in the municipality of Campomarino, with wine vases dating back to at least the ninth century BC. Molise's image, however, has long been overshadowed by its secular merger with Abruzzo, from which it only formally broke away—becoming an autonomous region—in 1963.

The most intense vine-growing area is in the province of Campobasso, where there is also a significant production of white wines based on Bombino Bianco, Falanghina, Greco, and Trebbiano, while the more mountainous province of Isernia is beginning to make its mark on the markets with small quantities of its own Pentro DOC.

The good news is the increase in the area under vines, which in recent years has allowed a quantitative development that, initially around 5.3 million gallons per year, will lead to almost 13.2 million within a few years. The most common grape remains Montepulciano, which, however, does not give rise to specific DOCs, often aided by Aglianico in the production of important and structured reds.

The brilliant success of Tintilia del Molise, to which more than thirty wineries are now dedicated, must not overshadow the complexity and finesse that Montepulciano and hillside Aglianico can achieve, as is already well demonstrated by a still small number of wineries.

There is a strong red wine vocation in Molise's small production, averaging around 13.2 million gallons per year, on land that is 65% hilly, 30% flat, and 5% mountainous. Around one thousand five hundred farms are dedicated to cultivating the 13,100 acres under vine, which also supply grapes to the three cooperative wine cellars holding 45% of the local wine market.

MAIN VINES GROWN IN THE REGION

Aglianico, Falanghina, Fiano
(→ Campania)

Montepulciano
(→ Marche and Abruzzo)

Tintilia
The only native vine cultivated almost exclusively in Molise and probably imported by the Spanish in the eighteenth century, it owes its name to the word *tinto*, meaning red. The name *tintilia* appears for the first time in 1820, in a register of the Agricultural Society of Campobasso. Abandoned after the Second World War because of its low yields, it was rediscovered in the 1990s thanks to a few intrepid producers who were able to bring out its younger, more dynamic characteristics, while others sought more structure and complexity. The nose is herbaceous and vegetal, reminiscent of artichoke and asparagus, with tones of ripe black fruit, particularly blackberry, blueberry, and plum, and a balsamic note on the finish. The color is an impenetrable dark purple; the flavor is silky and enveloping.

The DOCs
- Biferno
- Molise / del Molise
- Pentro d'Isernia / Pentro
- Tintilia del Molise

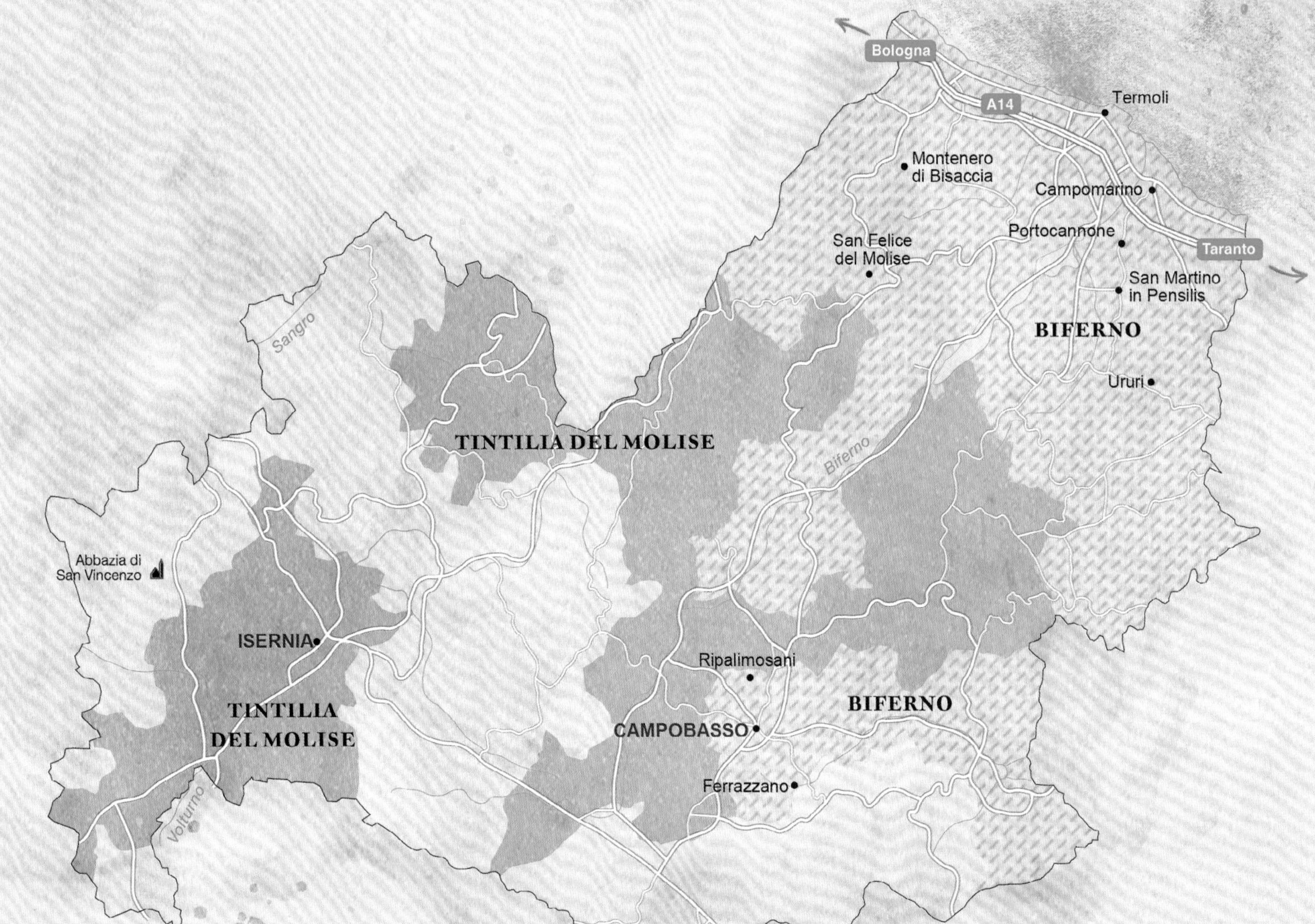

Mare Adriatico

Bologna

A14

Termoli

Montenero
di Bisaccia

Campomarino

Portocannone

San Felice
del Molise

Taranto

San Martino
in Pensilis

BIFERNO

Sangro

Ururi

TINTILIA DEL MOLISE

Biferno

Abbazia di
San Vincenzo

Ripalimosani

ISERNIA

CAMPOBASSO

BIFERNO

TINTILIA
DEL MOLISE

Ferrazzano

Volturno

Tintilia del Molise DOC

Tintilia del Molise has only been a DOC since 2011, even if it has been cultivated here for centuries. It is the revelation wine of the new millennium, so much so that it has refocused the spotlight on a region considered not very lively as far as winemaking is concerned. Produced mostly in the provinces of Campobasso and Isernia, only in the red and in small quantities of the rosé versions, it is a rather soft ruby red wine, never too concentrated or astringent, always floral and well spiced, suitable for medium aging. The production area covers a large part of the province of Campobasso and a small part of that of Isernia. Four hundred thousand bottles are produced annually, and growing.

—

Producers and their trademark and signature wines:

1. AGRICOLAVINICA, Ripalimolisani
   Tintilia del Molise Rosso Riserva Lame del Sorbo ($)
2. CANTINA HERERO, Campobasso
   Tintilia del Molise Rosso Herero.16 ($$)
3. CANTINA SAN ZENONE, Montenero di Bisaccia
   Tintilia del Molise Rosso ($)
4. CANTINE SALVATORE, Ururi
   Tintilia del Molise Rosso Rutilia ($)
5. CATABBO Cantine, San Martino in Pensilis
   Tintilia del Molise Rosso Riserva Vincè ($)
   Tintilia del Molise Rosso S ($)
6. Claudio CIPRESSI, San Felice del Molise
   Tintilia del Molise Rosso Macchiarossa ($)
7. LA CANTINA DI REMO, Ferrazzano
   Tintilia del Molise Rosso Riserva Uvanera ($)
8. TENIMENTI GRIECO, Portocannone
   Tintilia del Molise Rosso 200 Metri ($)
9. TENUTE MARTAROSA, Campomarino
   Tintilia del Molise Rosso ($)
10. TERRESACRE, Montenero di Bisaccia
    Tintilia del Molise Rosso ($$)

Biferno DOC

This DOC may be produced in the vineyards of forty-one municipalities in the province of Campobasso and includes Rosso, Rosato, and Bianco types. The Rosso, mainly made from Montepulciano, at 70 to 80%, and Aglianico, at 10 to 20%, makes up the most particular type, thanks to red fruit aromas amalgamated with a decisive spicy component that often closes on hints of cocoa. The taste is very rich and enveloping, with little astringency. Total annual production is close to five hundred thousand bottles.

—

Producers and their trademark and signature wines:

11. BORGO DI COLLOREDO, Campomarino
    Biferno Rosso Riserva Gironia ($)
12. DI MAJO NORANTE, Campomarino
    Biferno Rosso Ramitello ($)

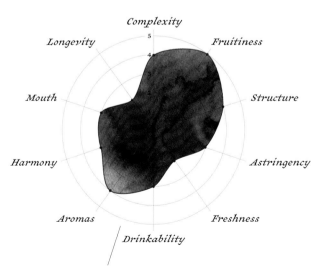

Tintilia del Molise

Molise or del Molise DOC

An immense DOC both in terms of breadth—the territory of dozens and dozens of municipalities in the provinces of Campobasso and Isernia—and in terms of types. There are eighteen, often with further specifications, based on Italian and international vines. The best results come from the typical grapes of Central and Southern Italy, such as Falanghina, Fiano, and Trebbiano. But there is no shortage of Moscato for the whites, with Montepulciano, present to at least 85% in Molise Rosso, and Aglianico for the reds. The annual production exceeds one million five hundred thousand bottles.

—

Producers and their trademark and signature wines:

6. Claudio CIPRESSI, San Felice del Molise
   Trebbiano del Molise Le Scoste ($)
12. DI MAJO NORANTE, Campomarino
   Molise Rosso Riserva Don Luigi ($$)
   Molise Aglianico Riserva Contado ($)
   Molise Moscato Apianae ($)
9. TENUTE MARTAROSA, Campomarino
   Molise Fiano ($)

DI MAJO NORANTE
Via Vino Ramitello 4
Campomarino (CB)
Year of establishment: 1968
Owner: Alessio Di Majo Norante
Average number of bottles produced per year: 800,000

The vast vineyards, organically cultivated, have reached 346 acres and enjoy the beneficial sea breezes of the not-too-distant Adriatic Sea. Production is focused on the Montepulciano grape, with more than good results with Aglianico and Fiano as well. In addition to Don Luigi, two Reserves stand out in the vast production: the recent and already award-winning Aglianico del Molise Sassius and the mature Contado.

MOLISE ROSSO RISERVA DON LUIGI
First year of production: 1998
Average number of bottles produced per year: 34,000
Grape varieties: Montepulciano (90%), Aglianico (10%)

Persuasive notes of cocoa and vanilla are enlivened by a hint of lavender and pine resin; the palate is rich, warm, dense, and enveloping, made even more robust by a notable tannic presence. The pleasant power of Montepulciano at the highest level.

Campania

Already rich in oenological fame at the time of the ancient Romans, when it was called Campania Felix, the region's strength lay and lies in the development of a very high number of indigenous grape varieties, from Aglianico to Fiano, from Piedirosso to Greco. Merit also goes to a wealth of soils, biodiversity, and vineyard landscapes that embrace splendid islands and coastlines, Apennine hills, and the Vesuvius volcano.

Campania encapsulates many of the elements most typically associated with the popular image of Italy throughout the world and has its heart in the vibrant, sun-drenched city of Naples, which has been able to express great creative and artistic energy in recent years. The region reflects and multiplies the contrasts of Naples: between Pompeii, Caserta, Paestum, Scampia, and Casal di Principe lies the history of Italy and the South, from which Italy cannot prescind.

A large part of the territory lies within an ancient volcanic theater that has contributed to the creation of a variety of soils ranging from the pyroclastic and basaltic rocks of the north, to the quartz and limestone-rich sands and sandstones of the south, to the clays and sands of Irpinia, which is rainier and cooler than the dry heat of the coasts. Viticulture is widely developed in all the provinces. The cultivation of Aglianico and Falanghina grapes begins on the border with Lazio, where it gave rise to the Galluccio and Falerno del Massico DOCs, but can be found in much of the region, as is already evident in the Campi Flegrei area, where Falanghina is accompanied by an important Campanian red grape variety, the savory Piedirosso.

Looking toward the sea, the small productions of two of the world's most famous islands stand out: the unmissable Ischia is characterized by the fragrant and juicy Biancolella, while the touristic Capri has its strong point in Piedirosso.

Continuing southward, one enters the province of Salerno and finds another of the peninsula's most evocative landscapes, the Amalfi Coast, characterized by a rich variety of rare local grapes that grow clinging to the rock.

Inland, in the province of Avellino, lies Irpinia, Campania's most famous winegrowing area. In the highest area, white grapes are particularly developed, giving rise to the Fiano di Avellino and Greco di Tufo DOCGs, while on the hills bordering the Calore River, Aglianico grapes—and the Taurasi DOCG they produce—find their highest expression.

Just a little farther north is Sannio, important both for the quantities produced and the widespread quality achieved by using all the region's main grape varieties, with particular emphasis on Falanghina, which enjoys its own independent designation. Also in the province of Benevento, the persuasive Aglianico del Taburno has obtained recognition as an autonomous DOCG.

The three community wine cellars utilize just 18% of the grapes produced on 69,200 acres by almost forty thousand farms, most of which have very small holdings averaging close to 1.3 acres. The vineyards, 79% hilly, 17% mountainous, and 4% flat, allow an annual production of close to 37 million gallons.

The DOCGs

- Aglianico del Taburno
- Fiano di Avellino
- Greco di Tufo
- Taurasi

The DOCs

- Aversa
- Campi Flegrei
- Capri
- Casavecchia di Pontelatone
- Castel San Lorenzo
- Cilento
- Costa d'Amalfi
- Falanghina del Sannio
- Falerno del Massico
- Galluccio
- Irpinia
- Ischia
- Penisola Sorrentina
- Sannio
- Vesuvio

Roma
A1
Galluccio
Santa Maria
dei Lattani
Conca della
Campania
Sessa Aurunca
Teano
**FALERNO DEL
MASSICO**
Cellole
Falciano
del Massico

Volturno
Lago del
Mateso

Guardia
Sanframondi
Castelvenere
Solopaca
Pontelatone

Casalduni

Torrecuso

SANNIO

Tammaro

TABURNO

Sant'Agata
de' Goti
Bonea
Montesarchio

BENEVENTO

Calore

CASERTA

Aversa
Carinaro
Lusciano

Torrioni
Montefusco
Santa Paolina
GRECO DI TUFO
Tufo
Taurasi

Mirabella Eclano
A16

Montemiletto

Montefredane
Lapio
Montefalcione
Summonte
TAURASI

IRPINIA

Santuario
di Monte Vergine

AVELLINO
Atripalda
**FIANO DI
AVELLINO**
Sorbo
Serpico
Montemarano

Castelfranci

**CAMPI
FLEGREI**
Pozzuoli
NAPOLI

VESUVIO
Vulcano
Vesuvio
Terzigno

Solofra

Bacoli
Monte
di Procida

Ercolano
Trecase
Boscotrecase
Pompei

Monte
Cervialto
1809

Sele

Lacco Ameno
Ischia
Forio **ISCHIA**

Golfo di Napoli

**COSTA
D'AMALFI**
Tramonti
**PENISOLA
SORRENTINA**
Ravello
Vico Equense
Amalfi

San Cipriano Picentino
SALERNO
Montecorvino Rovella

CAPRI

Furore

Golfo di Salerno

Sele

Monte
Alburno
1742

Calore

Mar Tirreno

Giungano

Monte Cervati
1899

A2

CILENTO

Reggio Calabria

Bari

MAIN VINES GROWN IN THE REGION

Aglianico (→ also Basilicata)

A southern red of great power, difficult to domesticate: originating in Greece and thus called Hellenicum, in Campania it was harvested in the ancient Roman era to obtain Falerno, the most prized wine of the time. Today, it is present in Aglianico del Taburno DOCG, Cilento DOC, Falerno del Massico DOC, and in Taurasi DOCG, the area where it shows the best affinity between vine and *terroir*. It requires patient aging to impress with a full and harmonious body, due to the high sugar—and consequently alcohol—content and the considerable presence of tannin, which is well suited to the clayey soils favored by the variety. The aromatic range is complex and multifaceted and is articulated between floral, fruity, and spicy notes: rose and violet, blueberry, currant, wild blackberry and ripe plum, pepper and nutmeg, and, with time, medicinal herbs, ginger, cinchona and licorice, incense, leather, and tobacco.

Asprinio

A grape that is also elaborated in a sparkling version, traditionally bred with the help of tall trees, elms, or poplars, between which a vegetal barrier is created that can exceed 65 feet in height. Therefore, the dangerous grape harvest is carried out by hand, climbing wooden ladders with a basket. Aversa DOC is vinified in a sparkling version to bring out the best of its marked acidity.

Biancolella

Brought to the island of Ischia by the Euboeans in 770 BC—according to legend—it is the island's indigenous white wine. In purity, it is fragrant, agile, and fruity. A fresh white from a warm area, with a typical almondy finish. The vineyards clinging to steep cliffs require enormous care, and the harvest is done by hand using racks—another example of the heroic viticulture characterizing Italian wine.

Coda di Volpe

Already cultivated in Roman times, it is found exclusively in Campania. Vinified on its own in the DOCs Irpinia Coda di Volpe, Taburno Coda di Volpe, and Sannio Coda di Volpe, it is part of the Vesuvio DOC and can also be found in coupage with Fiano and Greco. In purity, it is reminiscent of field grasses and is citrusy and fresh, with good flavor.

Falanghina

Wines made from the Falanghina grape are always recognizable: they are fresh, smell of lemon blossom and pine needles, and taste of apple, banana, eucalyptus, and saltiness. It is the most widespread white grape variety in the region: the hilly ones are more floral and balsamic, the coastal ones more citrusy and marine. It is widely reported in the dedicated Falanghina del Sannio DOC but also in the Falerno del Massico, Irpinia, and Campi Flegrei designations.

Fenile, Ginestra, and Ripoli

Used together in Costa d'Amalfi whites, subzone Furore. The color of the Fenile is reminiscent of hay in the fields: it is grown using the pergola method from the freestanding vines still present along the Amalfi Coast. Due to its late ripening, it is able to provide considerable structure and alcohol. The scent of broom characterizes Ginestra, which contributes acidity to the wines above all, as it has less alcohol. Finally, the Ripoli, described by Giuseppe di Rovasenda, which contributes softness and exotic suggestions. Brought to overripeness and blended, they create a rare wine, evocative in its aromas of Moselle Rieslings.

Fiano

The famous Fiano is the protagonist of the Fiano di Avellino DOC, where it expresses a singular olfactory complexity, played on medicinal plants, white flowers, and smoky hints, to which aging adds a more common hint of hazelnut, while more precise and recognizable typical descriptors of the cultivar are apple, pear, moss, fern, mint, thyme, lime, and chamomile. Finally, on the ancient extinct volcanoes of Irpinia, the plants extract a notable mineral component to complete the rich bouquet.

Greco

Campania's second-best-known and most appreciated white variety after Fiano, but for some critics first in terms of structure and aromatic breadth. Deep and refined, it is recognizable by its intense golden color and on the nose by its orange blossoms tossed over a basket of ripe fruit: peaches, apricots, quinces, candied citrus, with a light spiciness of ginger and cinnamon, and traces of mint. It is also grown in the province of Avellino, in the similarly named DOCG but higher up than Fiano, which can translate into greater freshness on the palate.

Piedirosso

An indigenous red wine from Campania, one of the rare free-range varieties to have resisted phylloxera, it is the most widespread after Aglianico, with which, interestingly, it is often found in blends, bringing good acidity and less astringent tannins that make the wine softer and more accessible, even when young. It is found throughout the region, especially in the Campi Flegrei, Capri, Ischia, Falerno del Massico, and Galluccio designations; outside Campania it is only authorized in the province of Bari. It is an ancient cultivar, already known in Pliny the Elder's time as Columbina, which sixteenth-century agronomists Gabriel Alonso d'Herrera and Giovan Vettorio Soderini linked to the Campania black Palombina, today known as Piedirosso. In purity, hints of violets and berries, geranium and cherry, plum and Mediterranean herbs come from the glass, accompanying a crisp, juicy flavor.

Sciascinoso

An unusual variety from Campania, also called Olivella Nera, due to its slender structure it is often blended with Piedirosso and Aglianico. In purity, it tends to be rather light, so that more acidity and fruit can be extracted with carbonic maceration.

Greco di Tufo DOCG

Produced in a small area in the province of Avellino from the Greco grape of the same name, it is one of Italy's most famous white wines. With its rich bouquet, fresh notes of citrus and sage can be detected and, with aging, mineral nuances reminiscent of smoke and hydrocarbons. The palate is always vibrant, with good freshness and equal softness. From 2020, and aged at the site of the producer for at least one year, the Riserva type can also be manufactured. Production is close to five million bottles per year.

—

Producers and their trademark and signature wines:

1. BAMBINUTO, Santa Paolina
   Greco di Tufo Picoli ($)
2. CANTINE DELL'ANGELO, Tufo
   Greco di Tufo Miniere ($)
3. CANTINE DI MARZO, Tufo
   Greco di Tufo Riserva Vigna Laure ($)
   Greco di Tufo ($)
4. COLLI DI LAPIO, Lapio
   Greco di Tufo Alèxandros ($)
5. DI MEO, Salza Irpina
   Greco di Tufo Riserva Vittorio ($$$)
   Greco di Tufo ($)

6. DONNACHIARA, Montefalcione
   Greco di Tufo Riserva Aletheia ($)
7. Benito FERRARA, Tufo
   Greco di Tufo Vigna Cicogna ($)
8. FEUDI DI SAN GREGORIO, Sorbo Serpico
   Greco di Tufo Cutizzi ($)
9. FONZONE, Paternopoli
   Greco di Tufo ($)
10. Salvatore MOLETTIERI, Montemarano
    Greco di Tufo ($)
11. PASSO DELLE TORTORE, Pietradefusi
    Greco di Tufo Le Arcaie ($)
12. QUINTODECIMO, Mirabella Eclano
    Greco di Tufo Giallo d'Arles ($$)
13. SANPAOLO di Claudio Quarta, Torrioni
    Greco di Tufo Claudio Quarta ($)
    Greco di Tufo ($)
14. TENUTA SCUOTTO, Lapio
    Greco di Tufo ($)
15. TERREDORA DI PAOLO, Montefusco
    Greco di Tufo Loggia della Serra ($)
16. TRAERTE, Solofra
    Greco di Tufo Tornante ($$)

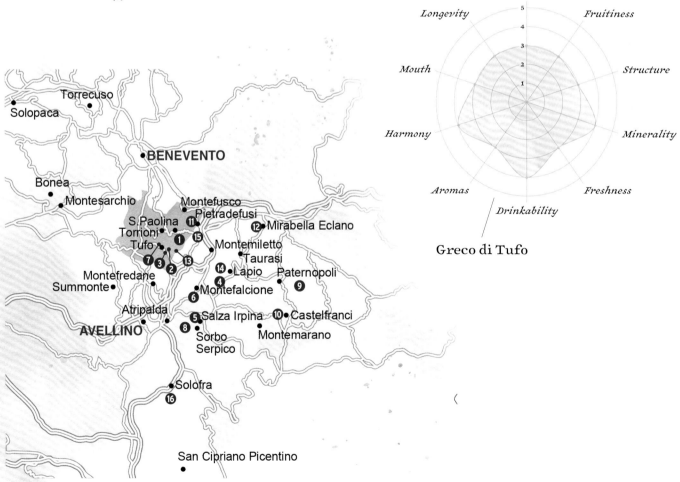

Greco di Tufo

Fiano di Avellino DOCG

One of Italy's best-known whites, made from at least 85% Fiano grapes, appreciated for thousands of years for its intense bouquet of white fruit, almonds, field grass, and honey, followed by a taut, lively, fresh, and long palate, with hints of hazelnut. In 2020, the Riserva type was introduced, underlining the excellent evolutionary capability of this DOCG. Almost three and a half million bottles a year are produced in twenty-six municipalities in the province of Avellino, exported all over the world.

—

Producers and their trademark and signature wines:

1. Antonio CAGGIANO, Taurasi
   Fiano di Avellino Béchar ($)
2. COLLI DI LAPIO, Lapio
   Fiano di Avellino ($)
3. DI MEO, Salza Irpina
   Fiano di Avellino ($)
   Fiano di Avellino Riserva Alessandra ($$$)
4. FEUDI DI SAN GREGORIO, Sorbo Serpico
   Fiano di Avellino Pietracalda ($)
5. FONZONE, Paternopoli
   Fiano di Avellino ($)
6. JOAQUIN, Lapio
   Fiano di Avellino Vino della Stella ($$)
7. Guido MARSELLA, Summonte
   Fiano di Avellino ($)
8. PASSO DELLE TORTORE, Pietradefusi
   Fiano di Avellino Bacio delle Tortore ($)
9. Ciro PICARIELLO, Summonte
   Fiano di Avellino Ciro 906 ($$)
   Fiano di Avellino ($)
10. QUINTODECIMO, Mirabella Eclano
    Fiano di Avellino Exultet ($$)
11. ROCCA DEL PRINCIPE, Lapio
    Fiano di Avellino Riserva Tognano ($)
    Fiano di Avellino Riserva Neviera di Sopra ($$)
    Fiano di Avellino ($)
12. TENUTA DEL MERIGGIO, Montemiletto
    Fiano di Avellino ($)
13. TENUTA SARNO 1860, Avellino
    Fiano di Avellino ($)
14. TENUTA SCUOTTO, Lapio
    Fiano di Avellino ($)
15. TORRICINO, Tufo
    Fiano di Avellino Riserva Serrapiano ($)
16. VILLA DIAMANTE, Montefredane
    Fiano di Avellino Vigna della Congregazione ($$)
17. VILLA MATILDE AVALLONE, Cellole
    Fiano di Avellino Montelapio ($)
18. VILLA RAIANO, San Michele di Serino
    Fiano di Avellino Alimata ($)
    Fiano di Avellino Ventidue ($)

Fiano di Avellino

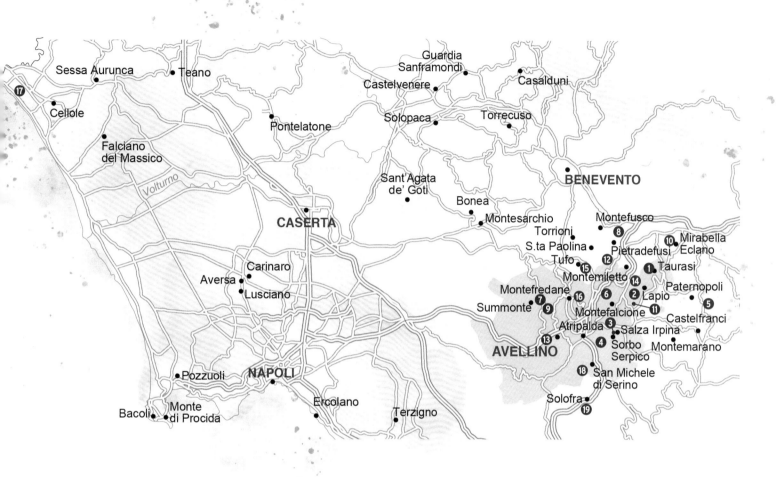

Irpinia DOC

In the huge territory that is the province of Avellino, there is also ongoing experimentation with wine production based on less famous grape varieties, or made from blends. In these the classic grapes of Fiano, Falanghina, Coda di Volpe, and Greco remain dominant among the whites, and Aglianico among the reds. There are not many varieties of Irpinia Coda di Volpe, entirely made from the grape of the same name, which is a citrusy and fresh white reminiscent of field grass, with good flavor, mostly vinified in steel only. About three million bottles per year are produced in total.

Producers and their trademark and signature wines:

10. QUINTODECIMO, Mirabella Eclano
    Irpinia Bianco Grande Cuvée Luigi Moio ($$$)
    Irpinia Falanghina Via del Campo ($$)
19. TRAERTE, Solofra
    Irpinia Coda di Volpe Torama ($)

Falerno del Massico DOC

The composition of grapes in the white version of this DOC wine, from the Alto Casertano area, is at least 85% Falanghina and results in citrusy and floral notes against a background of iodine reminiscent of a sea breeze. Total annual production is close to six hundred thousand bottles, including the Primitivo and Rosso versions, based on Aglianico and Piedirosso.

—

Producers and their trademark and signature wines:

1. MASSERIA FELICIA, Sessa Aurunca
   Falerno del Massico Rosso Etichetta Bronzo ($$)
2. Gennaro PAPA, Falciano del Massico
   Falerno del Massico Primitivo Campantuono ($$)
3. VILLA MATILDE AVALLONE, Cellole
   Falerno del Massico Bianco Vigna Caracci ($$)

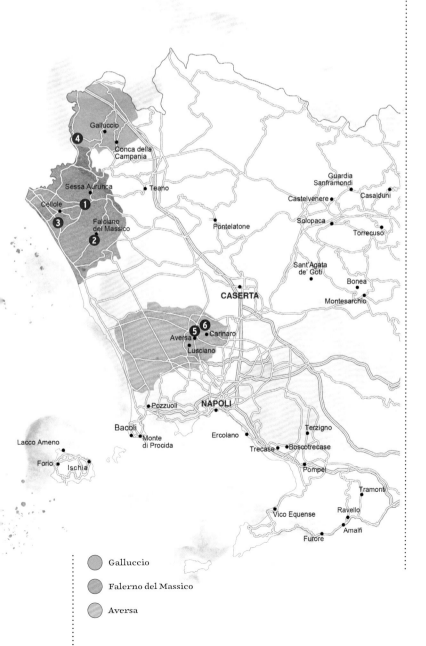

Galluccio

Falerno del Massico

Aversa

Galluccio DOC

A small but noteworthy production in six municipalities—including Galluccio—in the province of Caserta that includes, in addition to a white and a rosé version, a red wine based mainly on Aglianico grapes, which is rich and quite robust. Total annual production is close to three hundred thousand bottles.

—

Producer and its trademark and signature wine:

4. PORTO DI MOLA, Galluccio
   Galluccio Rosso Riserva Contra del Duca ($)

Aversa DOC

Just under two hundred thousand bottles per year are produced of this DOC, which covers nineteen municipalities in the province of Caserta and three in the province of Naples, and which includes only two types: the non-sparkling Asprinio and Asprinio Spumante. As the name of the grape Asprinio suggests, this is a wine of excellent acidity, and is well regarded thanks to its moderate alcohol content and its citrusy and almost saline taste, making it suitable for processing with the Metodo Classico as well.

—

Producers and their trademark and signature wines:

5. I BORBONI, Lusciano
   Asprinio di Aversa Vite Maritata ($)
6. TENUTA FONTANA, Carinaro
   Asprinio di Aversa Vigneti ad Alberata ($$)

Asprinio di Aversa

Falanghina del Sannio DOC

With a remarkable freshness of aroma, ranging from citrus fruits to sage and white flowers, and with good acidity on the palate, often with an almost saline note, is this DOC from the province of Benevento. It is consequently popular with drinkers, so much so that over nine million bottles are consumed each year.

—

Producers and their trademark and signature wines:

1. AIA DEI COLOMBI, Guardia Sanframondi
   Falanghina del Sannio Guardia Sanframondi Vignasuprema ($)
2. CANTINA DI SOLOPACA, Solopaca
   Falanghina del Sannio Identitas ($)
3. FATTORIA LA RIVOLTA, Torrecuso
   Falanghina del Sannio Taburno ($)
4. FONTANAVECCHIA, Torrecuso
   Falanghina del Sannio Taburno ($)
5. FOSSO DEGLI ANGELI, Casalduni
   Falanghina del Sannio Cese ($)
6. LA GUARDIENSE, Guardia Sanframondi
   Falanghina del Sannio Janare Anima Lavica ($)
   Falanghina del Sannio Janare Senete ($)
7. MASSERIA FRATTASI, Bonea
   Falanghina del Sannio Taburno Bonea ($)
8. MUSTILLI, Sant'Agata de' Goti
   Falanghina del Sannio Sant'Agata dei Goti Vigna Segreta ($)
9. TERRE STREGATE, Guardia Sanframondi
   Falanghina del Sannio Svelato ($)
10. VIGNE SANNITE, Castelvenere
    Falanghina del Sannio Lazzarella ($)

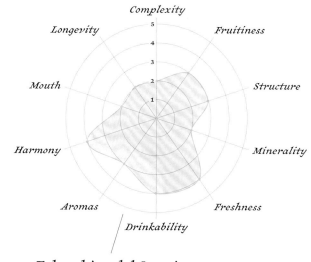

Falanghina del Sannio

....

◯ Sannio

◉ Aglianico del Taburno

Sannio DOC

This DOC embraces the entire province of Benevento and uses the most classic Campania grapes, from Fiano to Greco to Falanghina for the whites, and from Piedirosso to Aglianico for the reds, to which northern grapes, such as Sangiovese and Barbera, are typically added. From over 2,700 acres under the vine, around six and a half million liters of the different types are produced annually.

—

Producers and their trademark and signature wines:

8. MUSTILLI, Sant'Agata de' Goti
   Sannio Sant'Agata dei Goti Piedirosso Artus ($)
9. TERRE STREGATE, Guardia Sanframondi
   Sannio Fiano Genius Loci ($)

Aglianico del Taburno DOCG

In Sannio, in the province of Benevento, there is an area that has proven it can achieve excellent results from the most typical Campania grape varieties, both white and red. Among these is Aglianico, whose name seems to derive from the ancient attribute of "Hellenic grape." Taburno is one of the three most widespread biotypes of the Aglianico grape—along with those of Taurasi and Vulture—and has slightly softer taste characteristics than the other areas. Almost six hundred thousand bottles are produced annually.

—

Producer and its trademark and signature wine:

3. FATTORIA LA RIVOLTA, Torrecuso
   Aglianico del Taburno ($)

Campi Flegrei DOC

This picturesque area in the province of Naples is the almost uncontested realm of Falanghina and Piedirosso. Even when they have not been aged in wood, the Falanghina-based wines always display woody, spicy, and citrusy aromas, good flavor, and moderate alcohol content. Those with a Piedirosso base have good fruitiness, a small, balanced structure, and moderate alcohol content. Each year about eight hundred thousand bottles, mostly Falanghina, are produced.

—

Producers and their trademark and signature wines:

1. AGNANUM, Napoli
   Campi Flegrei Falanghina ($)
   Campi Flegrei Piedirosso ($)
2. CANTINE ASTRONI, Napoli
   Campi Flegrei Falanghina Vigna Astroni ($)
   Campi Flegrei Falanghina Colle Imperatrice ($)
   Campi Flegrei Piedirosso Riserva Tenuta Camaldoli ($$)
3. CANTINE BABBO, Bacoli
   Campi Flegrei Piedirosso Terracalda ($)
4. CANTINE DEL MARE, Monte di Procida
   Campi Flegrei Falanghina ($)
5. CONTRADA SALANDRA, Pozzuoli
   Campi Flegrei Falanghina ($)
   Campi Flegrei Piedirosso ($)
6. LA SIBILLA, Bacoli
   Campi Flegrei Piedirosso Vigna Madre ($$)
   Campi Flegrei Falanghina Cruna deLago ($$)

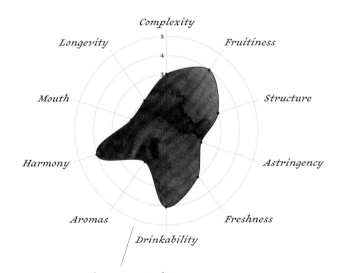

Campi Flegrei Piedirosso

Ischia DOC

Not everyone knows that on this volcanic island in the Gulf of Naples there are also about 250 acres, around what was once a volcano, that are dedicated to vineyards. They are cultivated mainly with the white grapes called Forastera and Biancolella, as well as the red Piedirosso, also known as *per' e palummo* or "an act of palmistry." These are isolated vineyards, whose grapes can only be transported by sea, on the shoulder, or by monorail. Ischia Biancolella is best known for its rich aromas, ranging from aromatic herbs to citrus fruits. The island's production is around seven hundred thousand bottles per year.

—

Producers and their trademark and signature wines:

7. CASA D'AMBRA, Forio
   Ischia Biancolella Tenuta Frassitelli ($)
8. Antonio MAZZELLA, Ischia
   Ischia Biancolella Vigna del Lume ($$)
9. TOMMASONE, Lacco Ameno
   Ischia Biancolella ($)

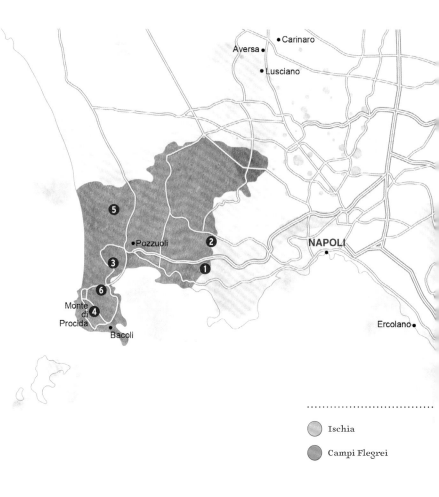

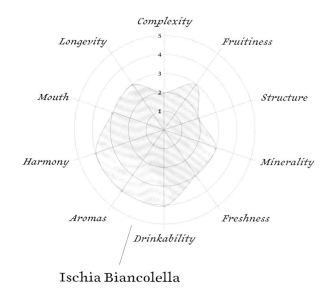

Ischia Biancolella

Costa d'Amalfi DOC

The grapes grown along this stunning coastline are diverse, including both the most popular Campanian varieties such as Falanghina and Aglianico, and lesser-known varieties such as Piedirosso, Sciascinoso, Fenile, and Ripoli. Decidedly floral, often mentholated and of saline freshness are the main notes of the Costa d'Amalfi Bianco, while its counterpart, the Rosso, is not very full-bodied, balsamic, and without much astringency. Regulations also allow for the three best-known subzones: Ravello, Furore, and Tramonti. Annual production is around five hundred thousand bottles, and growing.

—

Producers and their trademark and signature wines:

1. Giuseppe APICELLA, Tramonti
   Costa d'Amalfi Tramonti Rosso Riserva A' Scippata ($$)
   Costa d'Amalfi Tramonti Bianco Colle Santa Marina ($)
2. Marisa CUOMO, Furore
   Costa d'Amalfi Furore Bianco Fiorduva ($$$)
   Costa d'Amalfi Ravello Bianco ($)
   Costa d'Amalfi Furore Rosso Riserva ($$)
3. REALE, Tramonti
   Costa d'Amalfi Tramonti Rosso Cardamone ($)
4. Ettore SAMMARCO, Ravello
   Costa d'Amalfi Ravello Bianco Selva delle Monache ($)
   Costa d'Amalfi Ravello Bianco Vigna Grotta Piana ($$)
5. TENUTA SAN FRANCESCO, Tramonti
   Costa d'Amalfi Bianco Per Eva ($$)
   Costa d'Amalfi Rosso Riserva 4 Spine ($$)

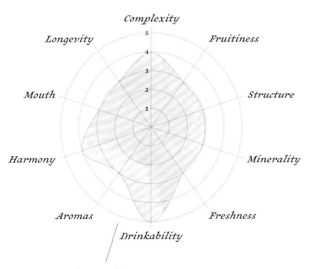

Costa d'Amalfi Bianco

Vesuvio DOC

Fifteen municipalities in the province of Naples are involved in the Volcano DOC. The whites are mainly made from foxtail or *caprettone* grapes, at 35%, and Verdeca at a maximum of 45%. The reds, meanwhile, see a prevalence of Piedirosso, with a minimum of 50%, and Sciascinoso, at a maximum of 45%. There is yellow-pulp fruit, smoky notes, and field grasses in the aromas of the savory Vesuvio Bianco, flowers and small red fruits in the vigorous and multifaceted Vesuvio Rosso as well as in the Lacryma Christi version. The name seems to be derived from thousands of years of popular legends of the blood-red tears of Christ. Around 1.2 million bottles are produced annually.

—

Producers and their trademark and signature wines:

6. CANTINE MATRONE, Boscotrecase
   Lacryma Christi del Vesuvio Rosso Territorio de' Matroni ($)
7. CASA SETARO, Trecase
   Vesuvio Bianco Contradae 61·37 Bosco del Monaco ($$)
   Vesuvio Piedirosso Fuocoallegro ($)
8. SORRENTINO, Boscotrecase
   Lacryma Christi del Vesuvio Rosso Superiore Vigna Lapillo ($)
9. VILLA DORA, Terzigno
   Lacryma Christi del Vesuvio Rosso Gelsonero ($)

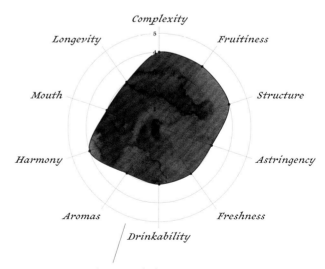

Lacryma Christi del Vesuvio Rosso

Capri DOC

A very small DOC, producing just over five thousand bottles per year, in which one can find the Bianco version, based on Falanghina and Greco, and Rosso, which is based on at least 80% Piedirosso. This results in more soft and delicate sensations than the robust Aglianico, with which it is often compared. Reportedly, it is as difficult to find as it is worth tasting.

—

Producer and its trademark and signature wine:

10. MASSERIA FRATTASI, Bonea
    Capri Rosso ($$$$)

Cilento DOC

This area in the southern part of Campania, in the province of Salerno, is mainly cultivated with Fiano and Aglianico grapes. Here a particularly spicy and citrusy white wine called Cilento Fiano Pietraincatenata, which boasts remarkable finesse and drinkability, is well worthy of note. Total DOC production is close to four hundred thousand bottles per year.

—

Producer and its trademark and signature wine:

• Luigi MAFFINI, Giungano
  Cilento Fiano Pietraincatenata ($$)

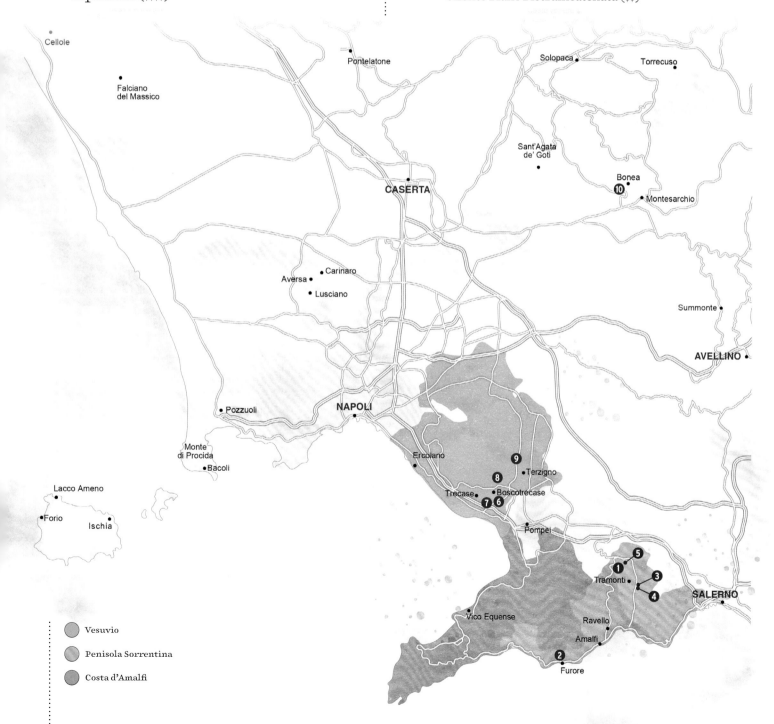

Taurasi DOCG

Sometimes incorrectly referred to as "the Barolo of the South,"
Taurasi is a great Italian wine and has its own rich and
multifaceted personality, with aromas of well-ripened red
fruit, sweet spices, and at times spearmint, which precede a
prominent and harmonious body with good dynamism, in
which the tannin is not intrusive. It is produced in vineyards
in seventeen municipalities in the province of Avellino and
is put on the market at least three years after the harvest,
of which no less than twelve months is spent in wood, or
four years and eighteen months in the case of the Riserva. A
suggestive production area of around 990 acres yields just over
two million bottles annually.

—

Producers and their trademark and signature wines:

1. Antonio CAGGIANO, Taurasi
    Taurasi Vigna Macchia dei Goti ($$)
2. CANTINA MITO, Nusco
    Taurasi Amato ($$)
3. CONTRADE DI TAURASI, Taurasi
    Taurasi Coste ($$)
4. DONNACHIARA, Montefalcione
    Taurasi Riserva ($$)
5. FEUDI DI SAN GREGORIO, Sorbo Serpico
    Taurasi Riserva Piano di Montevergine ($$)
6. FIORENTINO, Paternopoli
    Taurasi Riserva ($$)
7. MASTROBERARDINO, Atripalda
    Taurasi Riserva Radici ($$)
8. Salvatore MOLETTIERI, Montemarano
    Taurasi Renonno ($$)
    Taurasi Vigna Cinque Querce ($$)
9. PERILLO, Castelfranci
    Taurasi Riserva ($$$)
10. QUINTODECIMO, Mirabella Eclano
    Taurasi Riserva Vigna Grande Cerzito ($$$$)
11. Luigi TECCE, Paternopoli
    Taurasi Riserva Poliphemo ($$$)
12. TENUTA CAVALIER PEPE, Sant'Angelo all'Esca
    Taurasi Riserva La Loggia del Cavaliere ($$)
13. TENUTA SCUOTTO, Lapio
    Taurasi ($$)
14. TERREDORA DI PAOLO, Montefusco
    Taurasi Fatica Contadina ($)

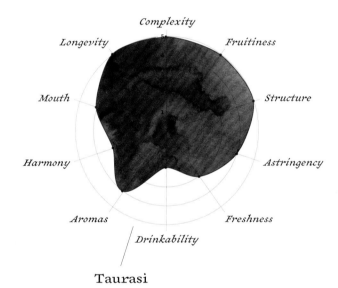

Taurasi

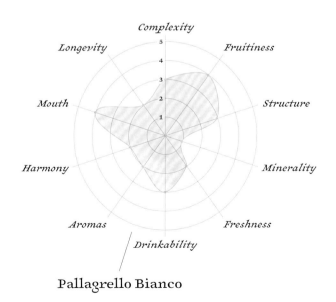

Pallagrello Bianco

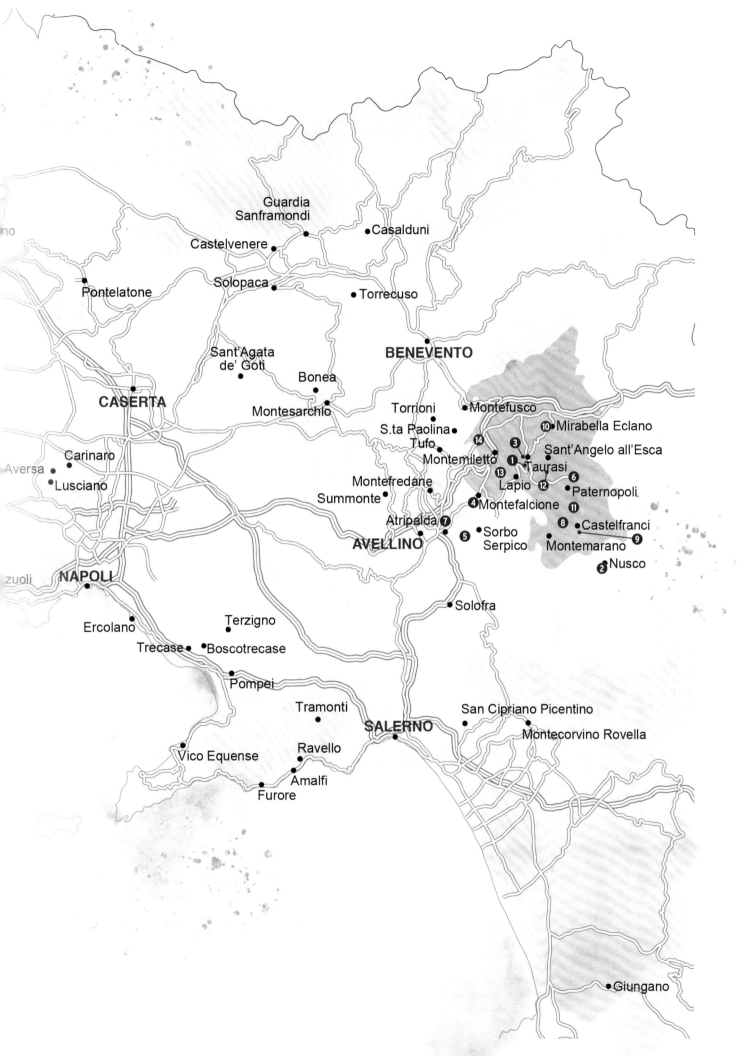

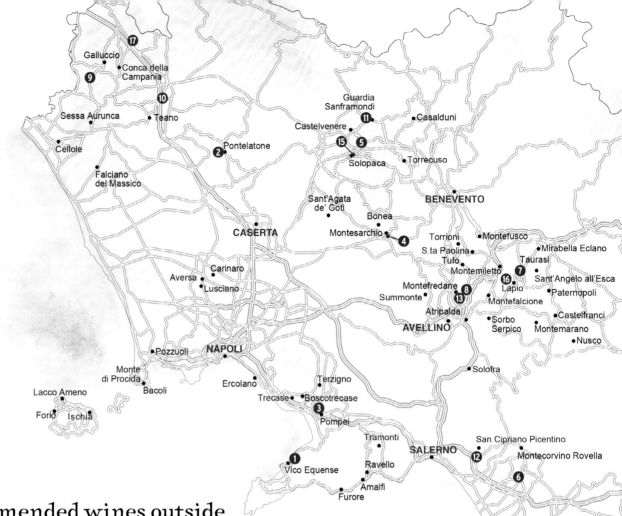

Recommended wines outside the DOC/DOCG designations:

In addition to the recommended wineries, the reputation of Campania's non-DOP wines is headed internationally by the award-winning Montevetrano and Galardi, with its traditional and refined Terre di Lavoro.

1. ABBAZIA DI CRAPOLLA, Vico Equense
   Sireo (Falanghina, Fiano) ($)
2. ALOIS, Pontelatone
   Morrone Pallagrello Bianco ($$)
   Caiatì Pallagrello Bianco ($)
3. BOSCO DE' MEDICI, Pompei
   Pompeii Bianco (Caprettone) ($$)
4. CANTINA DEL BARONE, Montesarchio
   Particella 928 Fiano ($)
5. CAPOLINO PERLINGIERI, Castelvenere
   Preta (Falanghina) ($)
6. CASA DI BAAL, Montecorvino Rovella
   Aglianico di Baal ($)
7. CONTRADE DI TAURASI, Taurasi
   Grecomusc' (Roviello Bianco) ($)
8. DRYAS, Montefredane
   Dosaggio Zero M. Cl. (Fiano) ($$)
9. GALARDI, Sessa Aurunca
   Terra di Lavoro (Aglianico, Piedirosso) ($$)
10. I CACCIAGALLI, Teano
    Zagreo (Fiano) ($)

11. Giovanni IANNUCCI, Guardia Sanframondi
    Campo di Mandrie (Falanghina) ($)
12. MONTEVETRANO, San Cipriano Picentino
    Montevetrano (Cabernet Sauvignon, Merlot, Aglianico) ($$$)
    Core Bianco (Fiano, Greco) ($)
13. PIETRACUPA, Montefredane
    Greco ($)
    Fiano ($)
    Cupo (Fiano) ($$)
14. SAN SALVATORE 1988, Giungano
    Pian di Stio (Fiano) ($$)
    Trentanare (Fiano) ($)
15. TENUTA SANT'AGOSTINO, Solopaca
    Ventiventi (Trebbiano Toscano) ($)
16. TENUTA SCUOTTO, Lapio
    Oi Nì (Fiano) ($$)
17. VESTINI CAMPAGNANO, Conca della Campania
    Pallagrello Bianco ($)

MARISA CUOMO
Via G.B. Lama 16
Furore (SA)
marisacuomo.com
Year of establishment: 1980
Owners: Marisa Cuomo
and Andrea Ferraioli
Average number of bottles
produced per year: 200,000

A famous name, a symbol of
the enhancement of an area as
fascinating as it is difficult to
cultivate, with small, terraced
vineyards overlooking the sea,
where ancient local varieties
are cared for exclusively by
hand. The product of the 35-
acre property is added to the
fruit of small winegrowers on
the Amalfi Coast, allowing the
production of nine labels in
which white grapes prevail,
from Biancolella to Falanghina
to almost extinct types, but
also reds based on Piedirosso
and Aglianico. Great respect
for the local viticultural
history and prestigious skills
in the cellar.

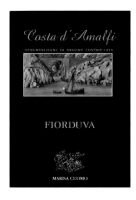

COSTA D'AMALFI FURORE BIANCO FIORDUVA
First year of production: 1990
Average number of bottles produced
per year: 20,000
Grape varieties: Ripoli (40%), Fenile
(30%), Ginestra (30%)

The power of phenyl and the softness of
Ripoli combine with the remarkable acidity
of the Ginestra grape to create a white wine
of rare charm, which is made from well-
ripened grapes and matured for several
months in small oak barrels. The aromas
are centered on hints of dried apricot, citrus
peel, and Mediterranean scrub; the palate is
securely balanced thanks to the density of
the flesh and the harmonious contribution
of an almost saline freshness.

CIRO PICARIELLO
Via Marroni 18/A
Summonte (AV)
ciropicariello.it
Year of establishment: 2002
Owner: Ciro Picariello
Average number of bottles
produced per year: 75,000

In twenty years, Ciro Picariello
has established himself as an
emblematic representative of
Fiano di Avellino, above all for
having best demonstrated the
aging capacity of this DOCG
wine capable of improving
in the bottle for more than
ten years after the harvest.
Its labels are sought by those
who love a multifaceted
Fiano, complex and open, of
seductive maturity. From the
Fiano grapes of his 30 acres of
vineyards come four offerings,
including the Brut Contadino
sparkling wine, in addition
to small productions deriving
from the area's other typical
grapes: Greco, Falanghina, and
Aglianico.

FIANO DI AVELLINO CIRO 906
First year of production: 2012
Average number of bottles produced
per year: 3,500
Grape variety: Fiano

The aromas unite several olfactory families:
white fruit and Mediterranean herbs stand
out against a background of citrus peel
and, more or less intensely depending on
the years of aging in glass, hydrocarbons.
Maturation in steel serves to maintain
good freshness, with an important but
never opulent, always graceful structure.
An essential point of reference in Fiano di
Avellino.

ROCCA DEL PRINCIPE
Contrada Arianiello 9
Lapio (AV)
roccadelprincipe.it
Year of establishment: 2004
Owners: the Zarrella and
Fabrizio family
Average number of bottles
produced per year: 40,000

The 17 acres of vineyards are
located in the upper part
of Lapio, one of the most
historically famous areas for
the cultivation of Fiano, at
an altitude of between 1,640
and 1,970 feet. At the center
of the company's production
are three labels of Fiano
di Avellino, accompanied
by a few thousand bottles
dedicated to the area's other
most typical grapes: Aglianico
del Vulture and Greco. The
oenological line is aimed
at the clarity of vision and
clear expression of the grape
varieties, for which wood is
used only for the maturation
of the reds.

FIANO DI AVELLINO RISERVA TOGNANO
First year of production: 2014
Average number of bottles produced
per year: 4,000
Grape variety: Fiano

Although vinified in steel only, over the
years it combines a fine note of smoke
with classic flint and chalk, in an olfactory
complex that nonetheless sees citrus fruits
and white pulp fruit at the forefront. The
palate is decisive, voluminous, never too
hot, and indeed well refreshed by a saline
touch, with a finish in which hints of iodine
and Mediterranean herbs are added. A
masterpiece of its kind.

PIETRACUPA
Contrada Vadiaperti 17
Montefredane (AV)
Year of establishment: 1992
Owner: Sabino Loffredo
Average number of bottles
produced per year: 40,000

Sabino Loffredo embodies
the concept of artistic
craftsmanship: on the one
hand, small productions
from just 22 acres of vines,
and on the other, a style and
personality that make his
wines true benchmarks in
the Fiano and Greco varieties,
and also Taurasi, which since
2008 has only been offered in
the best vintages. Wine critics
are unanimous in considering
these labels worthy of
inclusion at the top of Italian
oenology.

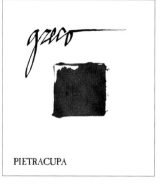

GRECO
First year of production: 1992
Average number of bottles produced
per year: 15,000
Grape variety: Greco

It no longer makes use of the Greco di Tufo
DOCG but possesses the characteristics
of the vine in purity at the highest level:
mineral scents reminiscent of iodine
combine with white fruit against a barely
smoky background. The flavor is incisive,
direct, easy to drink despite being rich in
pulp, and irresistible until the finish in
which elegant hints of medicinal herbs
appear. One of Irpinia's most interesting
whites, offered at an affordable price.

DI MEO

Contrada Coccovoni I
Salza Irpina (AV)
dimeo.it
Year of establishment: 1986
Owners: the Di Meo
brothers
Average number of bottles
produced per year: 360,000

Production is based on two lines, Tradition and Time. The latter includes productions, such as the Riserva Vittorio, that mature for years in the cellar before release on the market, while the former is dedicated to wines released only a few months after the harvest. The younger wines come across as neither predictable nor simple, to the extent that they even win awards from wine guides. The varied offer stems from 94 acres of vines, as well as from grapes produced by small vine growers, and is of outstanding reliability.

GRECO DI TUFO RISERVA VITTORIO
First year of production: 2007
Average number of bottles produced
per year: 10,000
Grape variety: Greco

To propose a Greco di Tufo matured in steel for twelve years is a courageous choice. The results, however, are profound, as the aromas are developed to perfection and include not only notes of citrus and white fruits but also almonds and spices, with a splendid complexity enriched by hints of flint. The flavor is harmonious, sinuous, and closes on refined hints of hydrocarbons.

MONTEVETRANO

Via Montevetrano 3
San Cipriano Picentino (SA)
montevetrano.it
Year of establishment: 1991
Owner: the Imparato
family
Average number of bottles
produced per year: 84,000

To build her own prestigious winery, Silvia Imparato chose a historic building dating back to the Bourbons in a picturesque area of the Salerno hills. The results obtained from 12 acres of vines, joined by grapes from trustworthy growers, were brilliant right from the start, and Montevetrano, the only wine offered for twenty years, has become an international symbol of the new winemaking Campania. This was followed by the two versions of Core: the already award-winning Bianco, made from Fiano and Greco grapes, and the robust Rosso, from Aglianico grapes.

MONTEVETRANO
First year of production: 1993
Average number of bottles produced
per year: 30,000
Grape varieties: Cabernet Sauvignon
(50%), Aglianico (30%), Merlot (20%)

Born from Cabernet Sauvignon grapes along with a small addition of Aglianico, it then evolved with the union of Merlot, always expressing a sunny Mediterranean character without heaviness, indeed of flowing elegance. It matures for a year in small oak barrels and expresses very classic aromas of sweet spices, medicinal herbs, and wild berries; the flavor is responsive and almost savory, enveloping but without excess concentration, with a gentle and persuasive tannicity.

BENITO FERRARA

Frazione San Paolo 14/A
Tufo (AV)
benitoferrara.it
Year of establishment: 1860
Owners: Gabriella Ferrara
and Sergio Ambrosino
Average number of bottles
produced per year: 80,000

A winery that has become the emblem of quality Greco di Tufo, proposed in various versions, without forgetting that Fiano and Taurasi also enjoy an excellent reputation. The company's long history has seen a gradual expansion of the vineyard, which has now reached 62 acres, guaranteeing ample opportunities to expand the number of bottles marketed. The production line is aimed at proposing pure and essential whites, which mature in steel only, while oak is reserved for productions from Aglianico grapes. The qualitative constancy is remarkable.

GRECO DI TUFO VIGNA CICOGNA
First year of production: 1997
Average number of bottles produced
per year: 24,000
Grape variety: Greco

The aromas move between soft scents such as peach, lime, and chamomile, and lively hints reminiscent of orange and lemon peel, to which fine notes of hydrocarbons are added as the wine ages in the glass. The palate has good tension due to the acidity and sapidity, in a context in which the pulp and alcohol guarantee roundness and harmony, right through to the crisp finish rich in Mediterranean herbs. A great Italian white, offered at an affordable price.

ANTONIO CAGGIANO

Contrada Sala
Taurasi (AV)
cantinecaggiano.it
Year of establishment: 1990
Owner: Antonio and
Giuseppe Caggiano
Average number of bottles
produced per year: 160,000

In thirty years, the Caggiano family winery has become a celebrated interpreter of Taurasi at an international level, but respectable results also come from the other more typical wines of this area, in particular Greco di Tufo and Fiano di Avellino. The beautiful wine cellar, which is enriched by works of art and utensils that make up a small, delightful museum of winemaking culture, is immediately characterized both by the resolute use of traditional local vines and by the stylistic elegance of the entire production line, articulated in ten labels deriving from 79 acres of vines.

TAURASI VIGNA MACCHIA DEI GOTI
First year of production: 1994
Average number of bottles produced
per year: 13,000
Grape variety: Aglianico

Standing out among the acres of owned vines is the historic Macchia dei Goti vineyard, from which the similarly named Taurasi is made. The style is refined, obtained due to long maturation in small French barriques; notes of black fruits, red petals, and spices emerge, not without a persuasive balsamic hint. The taste is always quite fresh, lively, and savory, with important but not aggressive tannins. A fine point of reference for the Taurasi DOCG.

FEUDI DI SAN GREGORIO
Località Cerza Grossa
Sorbo Serpico (AV)
feudi.it
Year of establishment: 1986
Owner: the Capaldo family
Average number of bottles produced per year: 3,500,000

A solid company that produces all the Irpinia designations, obtained from a vineyard area that has reached 741 acres, vinified in separate parcels under the guidance of renowned agronomist Pierpaolo Sirch. The Taurasi presented is accompanied by labels of Fiano d'Avellino and Greco di Tufo, at moderate prices, which constantly garner acclaim. A winery as important in numbers as it is in oenological quality.

TAURASI RISERVA PIANO DI MONTEVERGINE
First year of production: 1996
Average number of bottles produced per year: 12,000
Grape variety: Aglianico

The long maturation in French oak expresses itself in evident spicy hints and elegant balsamic notes, to which the Aglianico from this historic vineyard adds important notes of red fruits and undergrowth. The palate is powerful without being aggressive thanks to soft tannins and a delicate freshness; the long finish adds a complex note of leather and damp earth.

MASTROBERARDINO
Via Manfredi 75
Atripalda (AV)
mastroberardino.com
Year of establishment: 1878
Owner: Piero Mastroberardino
Average number of bottles produced per year: 1,700,000

A winery with a viticultural history that began in the eighteenth century and was officially born one hundred years later, when the bottling and export of wines began. The traditional purchase of grapes by small vine growers has gradually been reduced in favor of the purchase of vineyards, which today total 642 acres, partially organically cultivated. Production tends to emphasize, with increasing determination, also through the articulated Stilèma project, the use of the Irpinian territory's most representative grapes: Aglianico, Fiano, and Greco. This gives rise to a few labels, all award-winning, marked by an elegant classicism.

TAURASI RISERVA RADICI
First year of production: 1986
Average number of bottles produced per year: 15,000
Grape variety: Aglianico

Matured in wood for two years, it offers clear and articulate aromas of cherries, mint, licorice, and cinchona, in an almost severe ensemble of bewitching complexity. The flavor is important and compelling, rich in pulp and a gentle astringency, with a persistent finish full of nuances, from cocoa to field herbs, from cherry to plum.

QUINTODECIMO
Via San Leonardo 27
Mirabella Eclano (AV)
quintodecimo.it
Year of establishment: 2001
Owner: Laura Di Marzo and Luigi Moio
Average number of bottles produced per year: 90,000

Luigi Moio, with a strong oenological background acquired through years of research and study between Italy and France, has aimed for excellence, building a wine production, based on 74 acres under vine, of three whites and three reds that has amazed the critics. Not only the Vigna Grande Cerzito but also the Taurasi from the Quintodecimo vineyard, and the slightly more immediate Irpinia Aglianico Terra d'Eclano. The white Greco di Tufo Giallo d'Arles, the Fiano di Avellino Exultet, and the Irpinia Falanghina Via del Campo, all fermented in wood, are arousing just as much interest.

TAURASI RISERVA VIGNA GRANDE CERZITO
First year of production: 2009
Average number of bottles produced per year: 5,000
Grape variety: Aglianico

The long maturation in French barriques enhances the complexity and finesse of the grapes that grow from the five thousand Aglianico vines cultivated in the Granze Cerzito vineyard: the aromas range from blackberry to cocoa and from incense to blueberry, while the flavor is solid and enveloping but always delicate thanks to the fine tannins and the contribution of acidity.

GALARDI
Frazione San Carlo,
Strada Provinciale Sessa Aurunca-Mignano Monte Lungo km 8
Sessa Aurunca (CE)
terradilavoro.com
Year of establishment: 1991
Owner: Arturo Celentano
Average number of bottles produced per year: 30,000

Right from the outset, the objective was the highest quality, achieved from the first release on the market with a single wine named after the ancient province that the Romans called Campania Felix, which has presented itself to the world as an ambassador of the region's finest winemaking elegance. In the 25 acres of the organically cultivated property, the Terra di Rosso has also been produced from pure Piedirosso grapes since 2017, and already highly praised by critics. An outstanding name among the great producers of Campania and Italy. In 2023, the winery was bought by the Tenute Capaldo (Feudi di San Gregorio).

TERRA DI LAVORO
First year of production: 1994
Average number of bottles produced per year: 25,000
Grape varieties: Aglianico (80%), Piedirosso (20%)

Born on the slopes of the extinct Roccamonfina volcano overlooking the sea in the Gulf of Gaeta, it offers the typical power of Aglianico barely diluted by the contribution of the softer Piedirosso, with a result of admirable balance. The nose reveals complex hints of blackberries, mint, and black pepper, against a background reminiscent of leather and damp earth; the palate is voluminous, endowed with excellent pulp and calibrated acidity, leading to a sinuous licorice finish. A great expression of Campania's indigenous grape varieties.

Apulia

The Apulia "of wine" is going through a period of productive ferment, with its great reds based on Primitivo, Negroamaro, and Uva di Troia relying increasingly on finesse rather than power. Wineries too are picking up on the growing demand for rosé wines, offering successful versions thanks to the good structure of the underlying grape varieties, especially Bombino Nero and Negroamaro. The world of whites is also growing, with productions based on the Fiano, Malvasia Bianca, and Verdeca grape varieties.

The southeastern region forming the heel of the Italian boot is an increasingly popular destination: from white beaches to cliffs overlooking crystal-clear waters, from Salento gastronomy to Lecce Baroque to monumental complexes such as Alberobello or Castel del Monte, Apulia knows how to promote a kind of tourism that combines quality of life and Mediterranean style with historical, artistic, and landscape heritage.

The northern area of the region is characterized by the presence of the Troia grape (often called Nero di Troia), which begins to make its mark in the Cacc'e Mmitte di Lucera and then enters more securely into the large Castel del Monte DOC. There are many complementary grapes, from Montepulciano to Aglianico, so the results differ depending on the producers' choices; however, it can be said that the Troia grape gives rise to wines of good richness, slightly less powerful and fresher than those from the southern part of the region. Also worth noting is how the Castel Monte Bombino Nero DOCG is dedicated exclusively to rosé wines, and also the increasing success of sparkling wines, especially those based on the acidulous Bombino Bianco.

Moving farther south we enter the lands dedicated to Primitivo, often accompanied by Montepulciano and Negroamaro, with the Gioia del Colle DOC offering numerous examples of richness and complexity when managed with careful oenological finesse. Approaching the cities of Brindisi and Lecce on the Adriatic Sea is Salento, a famous tourist area and the acknowledged home of splendid versions of the powerful, spicy, bush-grown Negroamaro grapes, in both red and rosé varieties. Good results also come to the Salento Peninsula from whites, often made from grapes of French origin such as Chardonnay and Pinot Blanc.

On the opposite side of the region, we turn instead to the Ionian Sea and Apulia's most famous and productive DOC, Primitivo di Manduria, here slightly more impetuous, rich, and powerful—and sometimes even a little wilder—than the wine that originates on the Gioia del Colle plateau.

Apulian wine production touches the 264-million-gallon mark, putting the region firmly in second place nationally after Veneto. The almost 223,000 acres, 70% of which lie on flat land, 25% on hilly land, and 5% on mountainous land, are cultivated by over forty thousand farms, six hundred of which make and also market wine.

MAIN VINES GROWN IN THE REGION

Malvasia Nera

It belongs to the large Malvasia family, and in Apulia is mainly used to add an alcoholic touch and softness to Negroamaro, in the Copertino and Gioia del Colle DOCs, and to Troia grapes in Cacc'e Mmitte di Lucera. The rare pure versions are characterized by a ruby red color, a spicy but never very aromatic nose with notes of licorice and a soft palate, in a balance of astringency and savoriness.

Negroamaro

A symbol of Apulia together with the even more imposing Primitivo, probably of Greek origin, reported here in many designations such as Salice Salentino, Copertino and Lizzano, Nardò Rosso and Rosato, and in blends in Gioia del Colle. Its wines are dark with violet hues, velvety and with a strong impact on the palate, warm and intense in their aromas of spices, black cherries, red and black fruit jam, leather and pepper. In the rosé versions, with a beautiful onion skin color, freshness and floral notes prevail.

Ottavianello (Cinsault)

A Mediterranean grape variety, also widespread in the south of France, particularly in Corsica, here in Apulia it is used exclusively in winemaking, usually in blends with Negroamaro, Malvasia, and Primitivo. The very rare pure varietals have a soft ruby color and a marked note of cherry, dried fruit, black pepper, and mint, with slightly aromatic traits and a soft taste that leaves a fresh, lingering memory of blood orange.

Primitivo (Zinfandel, Tribidrag)

A concentrate of flavor is extracted from this indigenous Apulian cultivar, identified by a genetic study at the University of Davis in California in 2001 as Tribidrag, a Croatian vine native to Dalmatia. Its spread in Apulia is

Ancona

Lago di Lesina
Lago del Varano
A14
• Vieste

San Severo •

GARGANO

Santa Maria
di Siponto

DAUNIA
S. Leonardo

Candelaro

Mare Adriatico

Lucera •

**CACC'E MMITTE
DI LUCERA**

• **FOGGIA**

TAVOLIERE DELLE PUGLIE

Tressanti •

Stornarella •

• Cerignola

A16

Lago
di Capacciotti

Napoli

BARLETTA

TRANI •

ANDRIA

Corato •

Minervino
Murge

CASTEL DEL MONTE

• **BARI**

Castel
del Monte

MURGE

San Felice
in Balsignano

Casamassima

Monopoli •

Gravina di Puglia •

Cassano alle Murgie •

GIOIA DEL COLLE

• Turi

Acquaviva
delle Fonti

Sammichele
di Bari

• Castellana Grotte

Santerano del Colle •

Gioia del Colle

Castellaneta •

VALLE D'ITRIA

• Ostuni

Lato

Massafra •

Bradano

BRINDISI

San Marzano
di San Giuseppe

**PRIMITIVO
DI MANDURIA**

**SALICE
SALENTINO**

• Torchiarolo

TARANTO

LIZZANO

Erchie •

Cellino San Marco •

Leporano •

Lizzano •

Manduria

San Donaci •

Guagnano •

Torricella •

Salice Salentino •

LECCE

• Monteroni di Lecce

Leverano •

COPERTINO

Mare Ionio

NARDÒ

• Copertino

SALENTO

Nardò •

Otranto •

Tuglie •

• Scorrano

Gallipoli •

Cutrofiano •

Alezio •

Capo Santa Maria di Leuca

attributed to the canon and amateur agronomist Don Filippo Francesco Indellicati, who, noticing the early ripening of the vine, christened it Primativo—from the Latin *primitivus*, "first"—and began cultivating it in 1799, in Liponti, a village near Gioia del Colle. Prior to this date, the vine was known as Zagarese, a possible reference to the city of Zagreb, or the Apulian name "Zaga." Like our migrant ancestors, the Primitivo traveled to the Californian hills, where it was successfully planted to such an extent that it has long since become the standard-bearer for Californian natives under the name Zinfandel. Primitivo grapes yield wines of intense color and flavor, with an exciting bouquet of black cherry, currants, blueberries, sultanas, wild strawberries, and cooked plums, along with nuances of tobacco and licorice. Robust and velvety in the mouth, they are made pure in the Primitivo di Manduria and in a blend in the Gioia del Colle, but also in a sweet version, in the Primitivo di Manduria Dolce Naturale.

Susumaniello

Typical of the province of Brindisi, Susumaniello is rarely vinified in purity but brings much color and pleasant nuances of sweet spices and ripe fruit to its wines. A dark red, with marked acidity bordering on austerity, in purity it brings out essences of cedar, black currant, blackberry, cinnamon, and nutmeg; vinified in the rosé version, it gives way to peony, rose, strawberry, and raspberry, with a marine touch and a beautiful coppery-orange color.

Uva di Troia or Nero di Troia

Legend has it that this vine came from the distant Homeric city of Asia Minor via the Mycenaeans, but its name more likely derives from Troia in the province of Foggia. Traditional to the plains of the Tavoliere delle Puglie, less powerful than Primitivo but more balanced, it is included in significant percentages in Cacc'e Mmitte di Lucera and Castel del Monte. Wines made from pure Nero di Troia are an intense red color with violet hues, a nose reminiscent of black cherry compote, plums in alcohol but also figs, cocoa, and licorice, with hints of pepper, cinnamon, juniper, and cloves. Full-bodied, dry, and enveloping on the palate, with softness prevailing over acidity.

The DOCGs
- Castel del Monte Bombino Nero
- Castel del Monte Nero di Troia Riserva
- Castel del Monte Rosso Riserva
- Primitivo di Manduria Dolce Naturale

The DOCs
- Aleatico di Puglia
- Alezio
- Barletta
- Brindisi
- Cacc'e Mmitte di Lucera
- Castel del Monte
- Colline Joniche Tarantine
- Copertino
- Galatina
- Gioia del Colle
- Gravina
- Leverano
- Lizzano
- Locorotondo
- Martina / Martina Franca
- Matino
- Moscato di Trani
- Nardò
- Negroamaro di Terra d'Otranto
- Orta Nova
- Ostuni
- Primitivo di Manduria
- Rosso di Cerignola
- Salice Salentino
- San Severo
- Squinzano
- Tavoliere delle Puglie / Tavoliere
- Terra d'Otranto

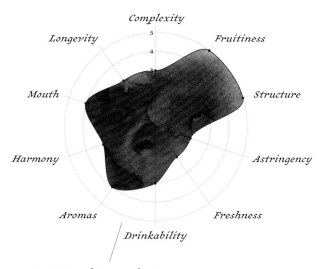

Primitivo di Manduria

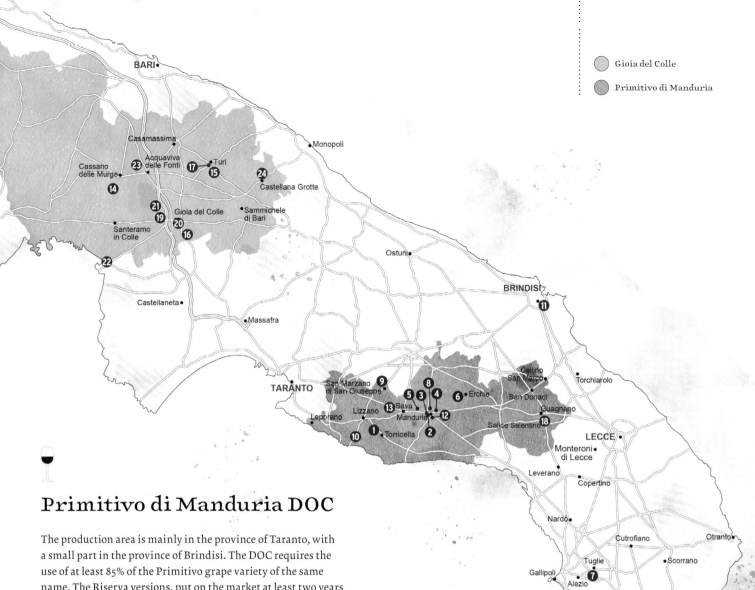

Gioia del Colle

Primitivo di Manduria

Primitivo di Manduria DOC

The production area is mainly in the province of Taranto, with a small part in the province of Brindisi. The DOC requires the use of at least 85% of the Primitivo grape variety of the same name. The Riserva versions, put on the market at least two years after the harvest and aged in wood for no less than nine months, are particularly rich and structured, endowed with scents of spices, plums, and ripe cherries, with an alcoholic, powerful yet delicate taste, never too astringent. The same characteristics of depth and vigor are found, slightly attenuated, in wines without the Riserva indication. A heated debate is underway among producers on whether to apply for DOCG status, as has already happened for the Dolce Naturale version. Gianfranco Fino's famous winery has decided to stop using the DOC designation, so it is on the region's final list. About thirty million bottles per year are produced.

—

Producers and their trademark and signature wines:

1. ANTICA MASSERIA JORCHE, Torricella
Primitivo di Manduria Riserva ($)
2. ANTICO PALMENTO, Manduria
Primitivo di Manduria Riserva Acini Spargoli ($$)
3. ATTANASIO, Manduria
Primitivo di Manduria ($$)
4. CANTOLIO, Manduria
Primitivo di Manduria Riserva Tema ($$)

5. FELLINE, Manduria
Primitivo di Manduria Sinfarosa Zinfandel ($)
Primitivo di Manduria Felline ($)
Primitivo di Manduria Dunico ($$)
6. MASCA DEL TACCO, Erchie
Primitivo di Manduria Riserva Piano Chiuso 26 27 63 ($)
7. MOTTURA, Tuglie
Primitivo di Manduria Villa Mottura ($)
8. PRODUTTORI DI MANDURIA, Manduria
Primitivo di Manduria Lirica ($)
Primitivo di Manduria Memoria ($)
9. SAN MARZANO, San Marzano di San Giuseppe
Primitivo di Manduria Sessantanni ($)
Primitivo di Manduria Riserva Anniversario 62 ($$)
10. TENUTE EMÉRA di Claudio Quarta, Lizzano
Primitivo di Manduria Oro di Eméra ($)
Primitivo di Manduria Anima di Primitivo ($)
11. TENUTE RUBINO, Brindisi
Primitivo di Manduria Palombara ($)
12. VIGNE MONACHE, Manduria
Primitivo di Manduria Assiade ($)

Primitivo di Manduria Dolce Naturale DOCG

In the same area as Primitivo di Manduria DOC, this DOCG is made exclusively from Primitivo grapes dried on the vine or on mats, with a minimum alcohol content of 13% and a residual sugar content of no less than 50 g/l. Dried fruit, dried red flowers, and jam on the nose, persuasive and soft sweetness on the palate, with a hint of freshness on the finish. About two hundred thousand bottles per year are produced.

—

Producers and their trademark and signature wines:

1. ANTICA MASSERIA JORCHE, Torricella
   Primitivo di Manduria Dolce Naturale Lo Apu ($)
3. ATTANASIO, Manduria
   Primitivo di Manduria Dolce Naturale ($$)
8. PRODUTTORI DI MANDURIA, Manduria
   Primitivo di Manduria Dolce Naturale Madrigale ($)
13. VINICOLA SAVESE, Sava
   Primitivo di Manduria Dolce Naturale Il Sava ($)

Gioia del Colle DOC

Produced in sixteen municipalities in the province of Bari, it has two versions, Rosso and Rosato, which are made from Primitivo grapes at 50 to 60%, Montepulciano and/or Sangiovese and/or Negroamaro at 40 to 50%, with a possible addition of Malvasia Nera for no more than 10%. However, the Gioia del Colle Primitivo DOC must be made from 100% of the grape of the same name. The result is a wine with an intense ruby color and refined aromas in which plums and cherries are often detected, not without a fresh vein of licorice that also emerges in the long, slightly tannic finish. In addition to visiting the winery, the Norman-Swabian Castle of Gioia del Colle is also worth seeing. Six hundred fifty thousand bottles are produced each year.

—

Producers and their trademark and signature wines:

14. CANTINE TRE PINI, Cassano delle Murge
    Gioia del Colle Primitivo Riserva ($)
15. COPPI, Turi
    Gioia del Colle Primitivo Senatore ($$)
16. FATALONE, Gioia del Colle
    Gioia del Colle Primitivo ($)
    Gioia del Colle Primitivo Riserva ($)
17. GIULIANI, Turi
    Gioia del Colle Primitivo Riserva Baronaggio ($$)
18. LEONE DE CASTRIS, Salice Salentino
    Gioia del Colle Primitivo Colpo di Zappa ($$)
19. PIETRAVENTOSA, Gioia del Colle
    Gioia del Colle Primitivo Riserva ($$)
20. PLANTAMURA, Gioia del Colle
    Gioia del Colle Primitivo Riserva ($)
    Gioia del Colle Primitivo Contrada San Pietro ($)
21. POLVANERA, Gioia del Colle
    Gioia del Colle Primitivo 17 Vigneto
    Montevella ($$)
    Gioia del Colle Primitivo 16 Vigneto San
    Benedetto ($)
    Gioia del Colle Primitivo 14 Vigneto
    Marchesana ($)
22. TENUTA VIGLIONE, Santeramo in Colle
    Gioia del Colle Primitivo Riserva Marpione ($)
    Gioia del Colle Primitivo Sellato ($)
23. TENUTE CHIAROMONTE, Acquaviva delle Fonti
    Gioia del Colle Primitivo Muro Sant'Angelo
    Contrada Barbatto ($$)
    Gioia del Colle Primitivo Riserva
    Chiaromonte ($$$)
24. TERRECARSICHE 1939, Castellana Grotte
    Gioia del Colle Primitivo Fanova ($)

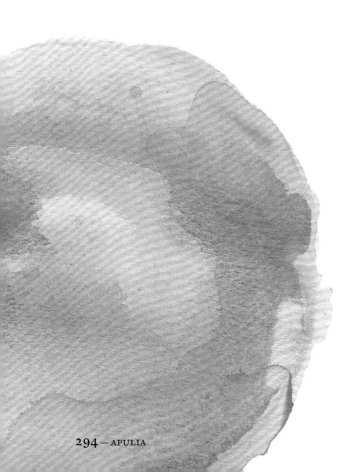

Salice Salentino DOC

Produced in an area that includes four municipalities, including Salice Salentino, in the province of Lecce and three in the province of Brindisi, this DOC allows for the production of several types, including still and sparkling whites, with Negroamaro predominating, present in the Rosso, Rosato, and Riserva for at least 75%. The reds are powerful, warm, and soft despite the presence of tannins, reminiscent of cherries and jam with a hint of Mediterranean scrub and pepper. The rosé is fresh and floral, as well as rich in flavor substance. Over eleven million bottles are produced annually.

—

Producers and their trademark and signature wines:

1. Francesco CANDIDO, San Donaci
    Salice Salentino Riserva La Carta ($)
    Salice Salentino Rosato Le Pozzelle ($)
2. CANTINE DUE PALME, Cellino San Marco
    Salice Salentino Rosso Riserva Selvarossa ($)
3. CASTELLO MONACI, Salice Salentino
    Salice Salentino Riserva Aiace ($)
4. FEUDI DI GUAGNANO, Guagnano
    Salice Salentino Rosarò ($)
5. MASSERIA LI VELI, Cellino San Marco
    Salice Salentino Riserva Pezzo Morgana ($)
6. MOTTURA, Tuglie
    Salice Salentino Le Pitre ($)
7. VIGNETI REALE, Lecce
    Salice Salentino Riserva Santa Croce ($)

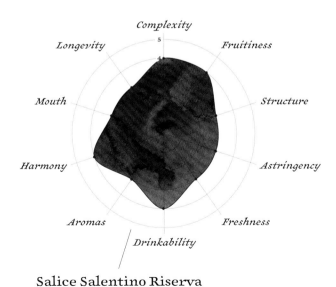

Salice Salentino Riserva

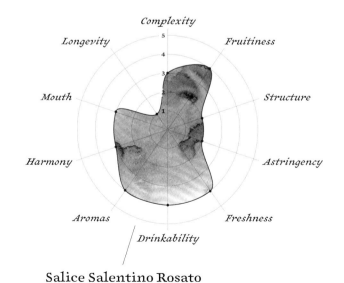

Salice Salentino Rosato

Castel del Monte DOC and Castel del Monte Nero di Troia Riserva DOCG and Castel del Monte Rosso Riserva DOCG

It includes vineyards in seven municipalities in the province of Bari and two in the province of Barletta-Andria-Trani, in the so-called Central Murgia, where the Nero di Troia grape grows best. The regulations provide for ten different types, in which other red grapes (such as Aglianico and Montepulciano) also stand out and can form the basis of Castel del Monte Rosso. Both this typology and the Castel del Monte Nero di Troia have an intense ruby color, aromas of both small fresh fruit and spices, and an intense and robust flavor but one which always has a harmonious and gentle smoothness. Three new DOCGs were established in this same area in 2011: Castel del Monte Bombino Nero, Castel del Monte Nero di Troia Riserva, and Castel del Monte Rosso Riserva. About three and a half million liters per year are produced from the DOC.

—

Producers and their trademark and signature wines:

1. CANTINE CARPENTIERE, Corato
   Castel del Monte Nero di Troia Pietra dei Lupi ($)
2. Giancarlo CECI, Andria
   Castel del Monte Nero di Troia Parco Marano ($)
3. CONTE SPAGNOLETTI ZEULI, Andria
   Castel del Monte Rosso Riserva Terranera ($)
4. RIVERA, Andria
   Castel del Monte Nero di Troia Riserva Puer Apuliae ($)
   Castel del Monte Rosso Riserva Il Falcone ($)
5. TORREVENTO, Corato
   Castel del Monte Rosso Riserva Vigna Pedale ($)

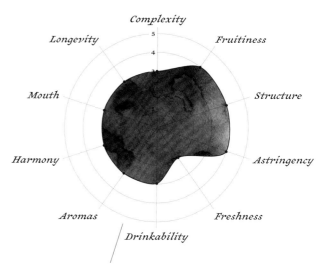

Castel del Monte Nero di Troia

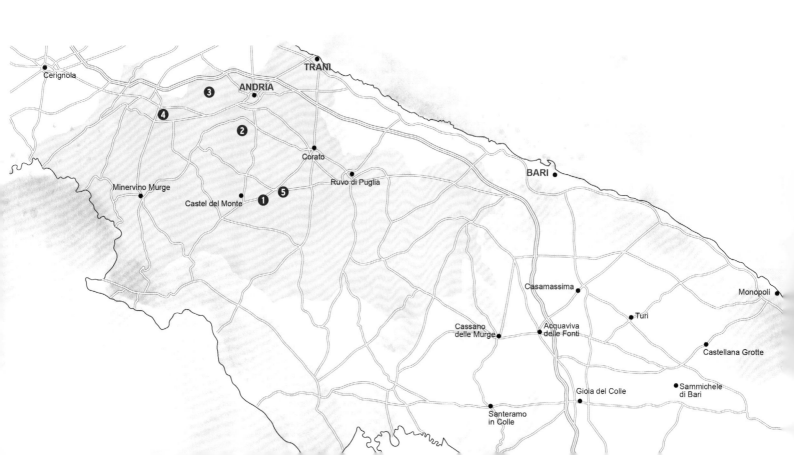

Brindisi DOC

A small DOC limited to the municipalities of Brindisi and Mesagne, initially conceived for red and rosé wines, mainly based on Negroamaro grapes but now also open to the contribution of white grapes, from Fiano to Chardonnay. Brindisi Susumaniello is made from at least 85% of the Susumaniello grape of the same name: deep ruby red; fresh aromas of small red fruits; smooth, undemanding, and joyfully drinkable on the palate. Overall DOC production exceeds 1.6 million bottles per year.

—

Producer and its trademark and signature wine:

1.   TENUTE RUBINO, Brindisi
     Brindisi Rosso Susumaniello Oltremé ($)

Copertino DOC

Produced in six municipalities in the province of Lecce, including Copertino, it is mainly made from Negroamaro grapes, at a minimum of 70%, designed only for the Rosso and Rosato typologies, and in which no more than 30% of Malvasia Nera and/or Sangiovese and/or Montepulciano may be blended. The aromas tend to be ripe and include red fruits and spices reminiscent of cocoa; the flavor is dense, not very astringent, and not very acidic. Three hundred fifty thousand bottles are produced annually.

—

Producer and its trademark and signature wine:

2.   APOLLONIO, Monteroni di Lecce
     Copertino Rosso Riserva Divoto ($$)

Lizzano DOC

A few plots of land in the municipalities of Lizzano and Fagiano, as well as a small portion in the municipality of Taranto, yield three hundred thousand bottles per year of different types, with a prevalence of Negroamaro grapes. The Lizzano Negroamaro DOC version calls for the presence of this grape from 40 to 60%, with Montepulciano and/or Sangiovese and/or Bombino Nero and/or Pinot Nero for the remainder. Very intense ruby color, very rich aromas of black cherries, with a dense but also fresh taste.

—

Producer and its trademark and signature wine:

3.   CANTINE LIZZANO, Lizzano
     Lizzano Negroamaro Manorossa ($$)

Nardò DOC

A small DOC, originating in the vineyards of Nardò and Porto Cesareo, which until 1975 was just a hamlet of the latter. It is dedicated only to types deriving from the Negroamaro grape at a minimum of 80%, hence Rosso and Rosato. The latter is made after steeping the skins for a few hours and displays a pale cherry color, followed by hints of fresh red flowers and herbs and characterized by tasty savoriness. Just over one hundred fifty thousand bottles per year in total are produced.

—

Producer and its trademark and signature wine:

4.   Alessandro BONSEGNA, Nardò
     Nardò Rosato Danze della Contessa ($)

Cacc'e Mmitte di Lucera DOC

Produced in just three municipalities, including Lucera, in the province of Foggia, it has a curious ampelographic composition: Troia grapes at 35 to 60%, Montepulciano and/or Sangiovese and/or black Malvasia at 25 to 35%, and white grapes such as Trebbiano Toscano and/or Bombino Bianco and/or Malvasia at 15 to 30%. Notes of aromatic herbs emerge on the nose and in the finish. The taste is fresh, not very astringent, of limited complexity, and enjoyable. Fifty thousand bottles per year are produced.

—

Producer and its trademark and signature wine:

*   Paolo PETRILLI, Lucera
    Cacc'e Mmitte di Lucera Motta del Lupo ($)

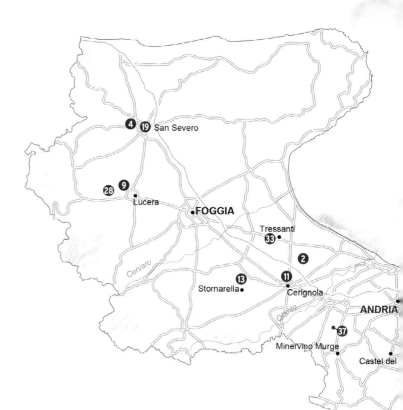

....

Recommended wines outside the DOC/DOCG designations:

1. AMASTUOLA, Massafra
    Aglianico ($)
2. ANTICA ENOTRIA, Cerignola
    Il Sale della Terra (Uva di Troia) ($)
3. APOLLONIO, Monteroni di Lecce
    Primitivo Terragnolo ($)
4. ARIANO – Terra & Famiglia, San Severo
    Sogno di Volpe Rosato (Uva di Troia) ($)
5. BOTROMAGNO, Gravina in Puglia
    Dedicato a Franco e Lucia (Primitivo) ($$)
6. Michele CALÒ & Figli, Tuglie
    Cerasa (Negroamaro) ($)
7. Francesco CANDIDO, San Donaci
    Duca D'Aragona (Negroamaro, Montepulciano) ($)
8. CANTELE, Guagnano
    Rohesia Susumaniello ($)
    Teresa Manara Negroamaro ($)
9. CANTINA LA MARCHESA, Lucera
    Il Nerone della Marchesa (Uva di Troia) ($)
10. CANTINE DUE PALME, Cellino San Marco
    1943 del Presidente (Primitivo, Aglianico) ($$)
11. CANTINE PARADISO, Cerignola
    Angelo Primo Nero di Troia ($)
12. CARVINEA, Casamassima
    Negroamaro ($)
    Otto (Ottavianello) ($)
13. CASA PRIMIS, Stornarella
    Crusta (Uva di Troia) ($)

14. CASTEL DI SALVE, Tricase
    Armécolo (Negroamaro, Malvasia Nera) ($)
15. CASTELLO MONACI, Salice Salentino
    Artas (Primitivo) ($$)
16. CONTI ZECCA, Leverano
    Nero (Negroamaro, Cabernet Sauvignon) ($$)
17. COPPI, Turi
    Don Antonio Primitivo ($)
18. CUPERTINUMANTICACANTINADELSALENTO,
    Copertino
    Spinello dei Falconi Rosato (Negroamaro) ($)
19. D'ARAPRÌ, San Severo
    RN Riserva Nobile Brut M. Cl.
    (Bombino Bianco) ($$)
    Gran Cuvée XXI Secolo (Bombino Bianco 60%),
    (Pinot Nero 25%), (Montepulciano 15%) ($$)
20. DUCA CARLO GUARINI, Scorrano
    Malvasia Nera 900 ($$)
    Negroamaro 900 ($$)
21. FELLINE, Manduria
    Edmond Dantes Pas Dosé M. Cl. (Vermentino,
    Chardonnay) ($$)
    Alberello (Primitivo, Negroamaro) ($)
22. Gianfranco FINO, Manduria
    Es (former Primitivo di Manduria Es) ($$$)
    Simona Natale Rosé Dosaggio Zero M. Cl.
    (Negroamaro) ($$)
23. GAROFANO, Copertino
    Le Braci (Negroamaro) ($$)
24. HISO TELARAY – Libera Terra Puglia, Torchiarolo
    Filari de Sant'Antoni (Negroamaro) ($)

25. L'ARCHETIPO, Castellaneta
    Fiano ($)
26. L'ASTORE MASSERIA, Cutrofiano
    Massaro Rosa (Negroamaro) ($)
27. LEONE DE CASTRIS, Salice Salentino
    Five Roses (Negroamaro, Malvasia Nera) ($)
    Primitivo Per Lui ($$)
28. Alberto LONGO, Lucera
    Montepeloso Aglianico ($)
29. MASSERIA LI VELI, Cellino San Marco
    Askos Verdeca ($)
    Askos Susumaniello ($)

30. MORELLA, Manduria
    Old Vines Primitivo ($$)
31. PALAMÀ, Cutrofiano
    Metiusco Rosso (Negroamaro, Malvasia Nera,
    Primitivo) ($)
    Metiusco Rosato (Negroamaro) ($)
32. PIETRAVENTOSA, Gioia del Colle
    Est Rosa (Primitivo) ($)
33. PODERE 29, Tressanti
    Gelso d'Oro Nero di Troia ($)
34. ROSA DEL GOLFO, Alezio
    Rosa del Golfo (Negroamaro) ($)
35. Cosimo TAURINO, Guagnano
    Notarpanaro (Negroamaro) ($)
    Patriglione (Negroamaro) ($$$)
36. TERRE DEI VAAZ, Sammichele di Bari
    Ipnotico (Primitivo) ($$$$)
    Onirico (Primitivo) ($$)
37. TORMARESCA, Minervino Murge
    Masseria Maìme Negroamaro ($)
    Torcicoda Primitivo ($)
38. VALLONE, Lecce
    Graticciaia (Negroamaro) ($$)
    Castel Serranova (Negroamaro, Susumaniello) ($)
39. VARVAGLIONE 1921, Leporano
    Cosimo Varvaglione Old Vines Negroamaro
    Collezione Privata ($$)
    Idea Rosa di Primitivo ($)

RIVERA

Strada Provinciale 231 km 60,5
Andria (BT)
rivera.it
Year of establishment: 1950
Owner: the De Corato family
Average number of bottles produced per year: 1,050,000

Now a historic and famous name at the vanguard of Apulian oenology, it is a model of how to use traditional local grapes and at the same time carefully use the most up-to-date cellar technology. The company's vineyard area has reached 185 acres and allows for a wide range of labels, including the standout Puer Apuliae but also the famous Il Falcone, made mainly from black Troia grapes, the robust Aglianico Cappellaccio, and the fresh Pungirosa, a rosé made from black Bombino grapes boasting the recent DOCG.

CASTEL DEL MONTE NERO DI TROIA RISERVA PUER APULIAE

First year of production: 1991
Average number of bottles produced per year: 12,000
Grape variety: Nero di Troia

It shows, at its highest level, the power and richness that can come from the pure Nero di Troia grape, combining an almost balsamic freshness and harmonious elegance to which the maturation in small French barrels contributes. It also has an excellent capacity to improve with bottle aging, which can happily continue for several years. A point of reference in the panorama of the best Apulian wine.

TORREVENTO

Strada Statale 234 km 10,600
Corato (BA)
torrevento.it
Year of establishment: 1948
Owner: Francesco and Gianrocco Liantonio, Alessandra Tedone
Average number of bottles produced per year: 4,000,000

Taking into account the vastness of the available vineyards, which total 1,235 acres, partly organically managed, the company's objective was to demonstrate that it was possible to make millions of bottles that faithfully represent the territory of the Bari Murgia and that could be sold at very reasonable prices. The goal was met, noting also the cleanliness and oenological precision of all the products across the board, not just the top ones. These include, in addition to Vigna Pedale, the persuasive and complex Castel del Monte Rosso Riserva Ottagono and the more direct and immediate Castel del Monte Bolonero.

CASTEL DEL MONTE ROSSO RISERVA VIGNA PEDALE

First year of production: 1993
Average number of bottles produced per year: 700,000
Grape variety: Nero di Troia

After maturing in the cellar, first in steel and then in large wood for a year, it is the red fruit aromas that dominate, accompanied by a slight undertone of spices and a fine smoky note. The fruity pulp is also the protagonist on the powerful palate, together with an important, slightly astringent tannic mass. A model of splendid and articulate drinkability.

GIANFRANCO FINO

Via Piave 12
Manduria (TA)
gianfrancofino.it
Year of establishment: 2004
Owner: the Fino family
Average number of bottles produced per year: 26,000

The fascinating bush-trained vines reach a century in age, guaranteeing a high concentration of substances within the berries and thus particularly structured wines. The oenological production of Gianfranco Fino, a great expert in both vineyards and winemaking, originates from 57 acres of vines and is centered on the Primitivo grape, elaborated in four versions with the highest levels of personality and pleasantness. Also enjoying well-deserved success is the Negroamaro fruit, made in the taut and fresh still version of Jo, as well as in the Metodo Classico Rosé dedicated to Fino's wife, Simona Natale.

ES

First year of production: 2004
Average number of bottles produced per year: 15,000
Grape variety: Primitivo

The most award-winning version of the Primitivo grape in terms of purity, thanks to the harmony and balance that accompany the entire tasting. The nose is rich in well-ripened red fruits and dried flowers, always enlivened by hints of medicinal herbs and spices; the flavor is dense and alcoholic, made persuasive and very inviting by a persistent fresh component enriched by a touch of savoriness.

POLVANERA

Strada Vicinale Lamie-Marchesana 601
Gioia del Colle (BA)
cantinepolvanera.it
Year of establishment: 2003
Owner: Filippo Cassano
Average number of bottles produced per year: 750,000

In twenty years, Filippo Cassano has taken his winery to the top of regional oenology, making a decisive contribution to the promotion of the Primitivo grape on the international scene. Five versions are made from this on the 297 organically cultivated acres, while from the local white grapes, two Metodo Classico sparkling wines and five still wines of great interest are also produced.

GIOIA DEL COLLE PRIMITIVO 17 VIGNETO MONTEVELLA

First year of production: 2005
Average number of bottles produced per year: 20,000
Grape variety: Primitivo

The long aging takes place in steel to bring out the aromatic qualities of the Primitivo grape to the full. The low yields in the vineyard result in a very concentrated and powerful red that remains refined and flowing, joyfully drinkable thanks to the rich bouquet, which moves between ripe black berries, medicinal herbs, and a refreshing balsamic appeal. A perfect example of the potential of this grape and this area.

TENUTE CHIAROMONTE

Contrada Scappagrano
Acquaviva delle Fonti (BA)
tenutechiaromonte.com
Year of establishment: 1826
Owners: Nicola
Chiaromonte, Paolo
Montanaro
Average number of bottles
produced per year: 300,000

Nicola Chiaromonte has been at the helm of the company since 1998 and has never stopped researching in the vineyards and in the cellar, giving his wines a distinct and original personality. The production is surprising at times, some for power and alcohol content, as in the Primitivo Reserve, others for the originality of the blend, as in the Metodo Classico Rosé based on Pinot Noir with an addition of Primitivo. From 173 acres of vineyards come unforgettable productions.

GIOIA DEL COLLE PRIMITIVO MURO SANT'ANGELO CONTRADA BARBATTO

First year of production: 2007
Average number of bottles produced per year: 10,000
Grape variety: Primitivo

It matures in steel only and offers a deep and intense fruitiness with cherries and black currants in evidence, followed by medicinal herbs and hot spices; the palate is powerful and ample, with an unexpected freshness that harmonizes well with the alcohol, creating an irresistible drinkability all the way to the crisp finish in which a delicate cocoa memory emerges. The authentic character of Primitivo.

VALLONE

Via XXV Luglio 7
Lecce
agricolevallone.it
Year of establishment: 1934
Owner: the Vallone family
Average number of bottles
produced per year: 500,000

The various estates encompass 420 acres under vine and are headed up by the splendid headquarters in the Castello di Serranova, representing the important role played by the Vallone family in the development of viticulture in Salento. The main grape variety is Negroamaro, offered in various types, but prestigious results are also obtained with the white Fiano and the traditional red Susumaniello, from which a fine rosé is also made. Elegant wines, faithful representatives of the territory.

GRATICCIAIA

First year of production: 1986
Average number of bottles produced per year: 18,000
Grape variety: Negroamaro

A wine that has become famous for its combination of power, also derived from the delicate drying of Negroamaro grapes on racks, with incisive fresh and vital notes. Matured for a year in French oak, it offers a rich spiciness and hints of small berries; the flavor is pleasant and enveloping, harmonious and rounded, with a superlative finish in which citrus and mentholated hints are to be savored.

COSIMO TAURINO

Strada Provinciale 365 km 1,400
Guagnano (LE)
taurinovini.it
Year of establishment: 1970
Owner: Rosanna Taurino and Antonio Bello
Average number of bottles produced per year: 900,000

Cosimo Taurino set up one of the wineries that most successfully promoted the Negroamaro grape and quality Apulian wine. Commercial and critical success quickly followed, thanks to the collaboration of one of the most appreciated oenologists of the time, Severino Garofano, who contributed to the creation of Patriglione and the entire subsequent production line. There are now twelve labels from 235 acres of vines, among which—in addition to Patriglione—Notarpanaro, from Negroamaro grapes, also excels. It is also characterized by its low price. An architect of the Apulian renaissance.

PATRIGLIONE

First year of production: 1975
Average number of bottles produced per year: 36,000
Grape variety: Negroamaro

It is made from grapes lightly dried on the vine, followed by a year's maturation in French barriques of varying ages, and then a long period of bottle aging before release. On the nose, ripe red fruit combines with a hint of eucalyptus to create not only pleasantness but also articulation and complexity. The taste is confident and dense, deep, very clean, and never too alcoholic, with a fine acid component. One of the best-known symbols of the great oenological South.

FELLINE

Strada Comunale Santo Stasi Primo 42
Manduria (TA)
agricolafelline.it
Year of establishment: 1996
Owner: Gregory Perrucci
Average number of bottles produced per year: 800,000

The history of Felline is closely linked to the Accademia dei Racemi, the project set up by Gregory Perrucci to enhance Apulia's historical grape varieties and erase their negative image, which was convenient for the large bottling companies in northern Italy and southern France insofar as the wines could be bought at low prices. The 264 acres under organic cultivation are distinguished by a clear prevalence of Primitivo, with Susumaniello, Negroamaro, and Fiano also offering progressively interesting results. Excellent products, great ideas, constant research.

PRIMITIVO DI MANDURIA FELLINE

First year of production: 1996
Average number of bottles produced per year: 6,000
Grape variety: Primitivo

Italian and American critics evenly distribute their awards among the various selections of Primitivo di Manduria—Dunico, Giravolta, Zinfandel Sinfarosa—but it is Felline that stands out for the precision and immediacy with which it expresses the grape's most significant characters. The intense red-purple color is followed by clear aromas of small red fruits, cherries, plums, and Mediterranean herbs with a refreshing balsamic touch; a fine balance on the palate, where the coexistence of alcoholic warmth and acidity achieves a tasty, soft harmony.

Basilicata

Small quantities in a region now famous not only for its Sassi di Matera but also its Aglianico del Vulture, cultivated in an evocative volcanic area that offers grapes rich in vigor and personality. Meanwhile, other vine-growing areas are being revitalized, using both local and international grapes, with already excellent results obtained from the white Greco as well as the Red Cabernet Sauvignon, Merlot, and Pinot Noir.

The area in which the grapes for Aglianico del Vulture are grown includes vineyards that reach 2,300 feet in altitude, and presents an interesting ethnic and cultural diversity, so much so that in the municipalities of Maschito, Ginestra, and Barile there are communities of Albanian origin that settled here over six hundred years ago. The Aglianico del Vulture DOC and its Superiore DOCG version are characterized by a notable presence of red fruits on the nose and great alcoholic and tannic power on the palate, which is why, in the past, many producers tended to adopt long maturation periods before marketing, with results often characterized by oxidative notes. Today, the tendency to use barrels that are never too old for shorter periods of time guarantees elements of refined elegance that were once unimaginable and allows for faster marketing, with pleasant results that are increasingly appreciated by consumers.

The more recent Grottino di Roccanova and Terre d'Alta Val d'Agri DOCs are still a bit sleepy, while the DOC reserved for the province of Matera is showing good signs of vitality, with careful use of French grape varieties and some significant white productions, especially based on Malvasia and Greco. There are less than 9,900 acres under vine in the region, 47% of which are mountainous, 45% hilly, and 8% flat, managed by two hundred and eighty farms, which also supply the three community wine cellars producing 30% of the local wine. The hundred companies on the market with their own labels produce a total of just under 2.7 million gallons per year.

MAIN VINES GROWN IN THE REGION

Aglianico (→ also Campania)

The first mention of the name Aglianico dates back to 1520, in a document certifying the ownership of Aglian vines by the Count of Conversano, Giulio Antonio Acquaviva of Aragon. Toward the end of the sixteenth century, the Neapolitan Giambattista della Porta put forward the hypothesis of the vine's Greek origin, equating the Helvola grape mentioned by Pliny the Elder with a Hellenic grape from Greece. Linguists dispute this hypothesis since the adjective used in antiquity was *graecus*, while Aglianico is thought to be derived from the Spanish *llano*, or "flat," which during Hispanic domination would have indicated a fine wine from the plains cultivated with Aglianico in Campania. Viticulture was already practiced here 2,600 years ago and in the sixteenth century, there were hundreds of cellars dug into the rock in Lucania. To date, DNA analyses are unable to confirm or deny with certainty the Greek origins of the vine. As a result, beyond questions of ampelographic archeology, when concentrating on the glass, one discovers the protagonist of one of Italy's most exciting wines due to the complexity and richness of the sensations it is able to extract from the volcanic rocks of Vulture. The mild Mediterranean climate favors the ripening of the grapes, which in this area express all their intensity and aromatic variety: from violets to Morello cherries, from black currants to rosemary, with a long, spicy finish that fades to tobacco, cocoa, and dried flowers.

Cabernet Sauvignon, Merlot
→ International Grape Varieties

Greco
→ Campania

Primitivo
→ Apulia

Sangiovese
→ Tuscany

....

The DOCG
- Aglianico del Vulture Superiore

The DOCs
- Aglianico del Vulture
- Grottino di Roccanova
- Matera
- Terre dell'Alta Val d'Agri

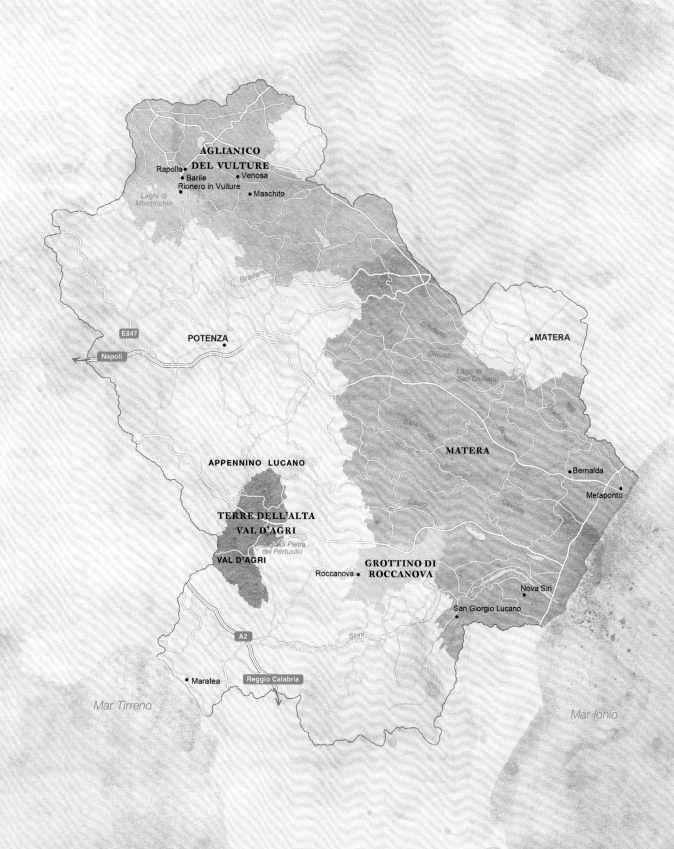

AGLIANICO DEL VULTURE

Rapolla
Barile • Venosa
Rionero in Vulture • Maschito

Laghi di Monticchio

Bradano

POTENZA

E847

Napoli

MATERA

MATERA

Bernalda

Metaponto

APPENNINO LUCANO

TERRE DELL'ALTA VAL D'AGRI

Lago di Pietra del Pertusillo

VAL D'AGRI

GROTTINO DI ROCCANOVA

Roccanova •

Nova Siri

San Giorgio Lucano

A2

Maratea

Reggio Calabria

Mar Tirreno

Mar Ionio

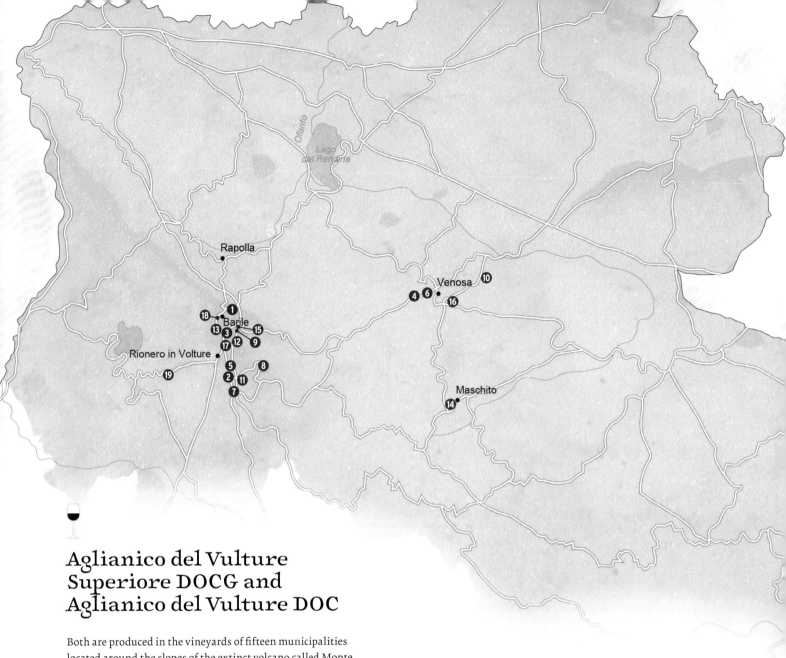

Aglianico del Vulture Superiore DOCG and Aglianico del Vulture DOC

Both are produced in the vineyards of fifteen municipalities located around the slopes of the extinct volcano called Monte Vulture, in the province of Potenza, where wine tourists should not miss the small lakes of Monticchio. They are among the most outstanding reds, not only of the South but of the entire Italian peninsula. They are made from the Aglianico vine of the same name and have different times for marketing: one year from the harvest for Aglianico del Vulture DOC, three for Aglianico del Vulture Superiore DOCG, five for Aglianico del Vulture Superiore Riserva DOCG. The regulations also provide for the possibility of indicating on the label one of seventy additional geographical indications, relating to districts or hamlets where the grapes are grown. Excellent products can be found in both DOC and DOCG, often without significant differences. The vineyards are located between 650 and 2,300 feet above sea level and the harvest is late, between October and November. The wines are robust, rich, and muscular, with a high tannicity but always with an acidic vein that facilitates drinking, with aromas of violets and cherries often combined with a spicy background that can range from pepper to licorice. Annual production is three million two hundred thousand DOC and four hundred thousand DOCG bottles.

Aglianico del Vulture

Producers and their trademark and signature wines:

1. BASILISCO, Barile
   Aglianico del Vulture Superiore Storico ($$$)
2. CANTINA DEL VULTURE, Rionero in Vulture
   Aglianico del Vulture Il Toppo del Brigante ($)
3. CANTINA DI BARILE, Barile
   Aglianico del Vulture Vetusto ($)
4. CANTINA DI VENOSA, Venosa
   Aglianico del Vulture Superiore Carato Venusio ($)
5. CANTINE DEL NOTAIO, Rionero in Vulture
   Aglianico del Vulture La Firma ($$)
   Aglianico del Vulture Il Sigillo ($$)
   Aglianico del Vulture Il Repertorio ($)
6. CANTINE MADONNA DELLE GRAZIE, Venosa
   Aglianico del Vulture Liscone ($)
7. Donato D'ANGELO, Rionero in Vulture
   Aglianico del Vulture Calice ($)
   Aglianico del Vulture Donato D'Angelo ($)
8. EUBEA, Rionero in Vulture
   Aglianico del Vulture Ròinos ($$)
9. Elena FUCCI, Barile
   Aglianico del Vulture Titolo ($$)
   Aglianico del Vulture Sceg ($)
10. GRIFALCO, Venosa
    Aglianico del Vulture Gricos ($)
    Aglianico del Vulture Superiore DaMaschito ($$)
    Aglianico del Vulture Superiore DaGinestra ($$)
11. MACARICO, Rionero in Vulture
    Aglianico del Vulture Macarico ($)
12. MARTINO, Rionero in Vulture
    Aglianico del Vulture Pretoriano ($)
    Aglianico del Vulture Superiore Riserva ($$)
13. MASTRODOMENICO, Barile
    Aglianico del Vulture Première Likos
    Etichetta Blu ($$)
14. MUSTO CARMELITANO, Maschito
    Aglianico del Vulture Serra del Prete ($)
15. PATERNOSTER, Barile
    Aglianico del Vulture Superiore Don
    Anselmo ($$)
    Aglianico del Vulture Rotondo ($)
16. RE MANFREDI, Venosa
    Aglianico del Vulture Re Manfredi ($)
    Aglianico del Vulture Superiore Serpara ($$)
17. TENUTA DEL PORTALE, Rionero in Vulture
    Aglianico del Vulture Riserva Palmenti ($$)
18. TENUTA LE QUERCE, Barile
    Aglianico del Vulture Vigna della Corona ($$$)
19. TERRA DEI RE, Rionero in Vulture
    Aglianico del Vulture Nocte ($)

Matera DOC

It encompasses the entire territory of the province of Matera, with the use of both indigenous grapes such as Primitivo, Sangiovese, and Greco, and Bordeaux, both Cabernet Sauvignon and Merlot. There are different elaborations, from Passito to Spumante. Matera Moro is made from Cabernet Sauvignon with ratios of a minimum of 60%, then 20% Primitivo and 10% minimum Merlot. About three hundred eighty thousand bottles per year are produced.

—

Producers and their trademark and signature wines:

1. BATTIFARANO, Nova Siri
   Matera Moro Riserva Curaffanni ($$)
   Matera Moro Terra Bollita ($)
2. MASSERIA CARDILLO, Bernalda
   Matera Moro Malandrina ($)
3. TENUTA MARINO, San Giorgio Lucano
   Matera Greco Terra Aspra ($)
4. TENUTA PARCO DEI MONACI, Matera
   Matera Moro Spaccasassi ($)

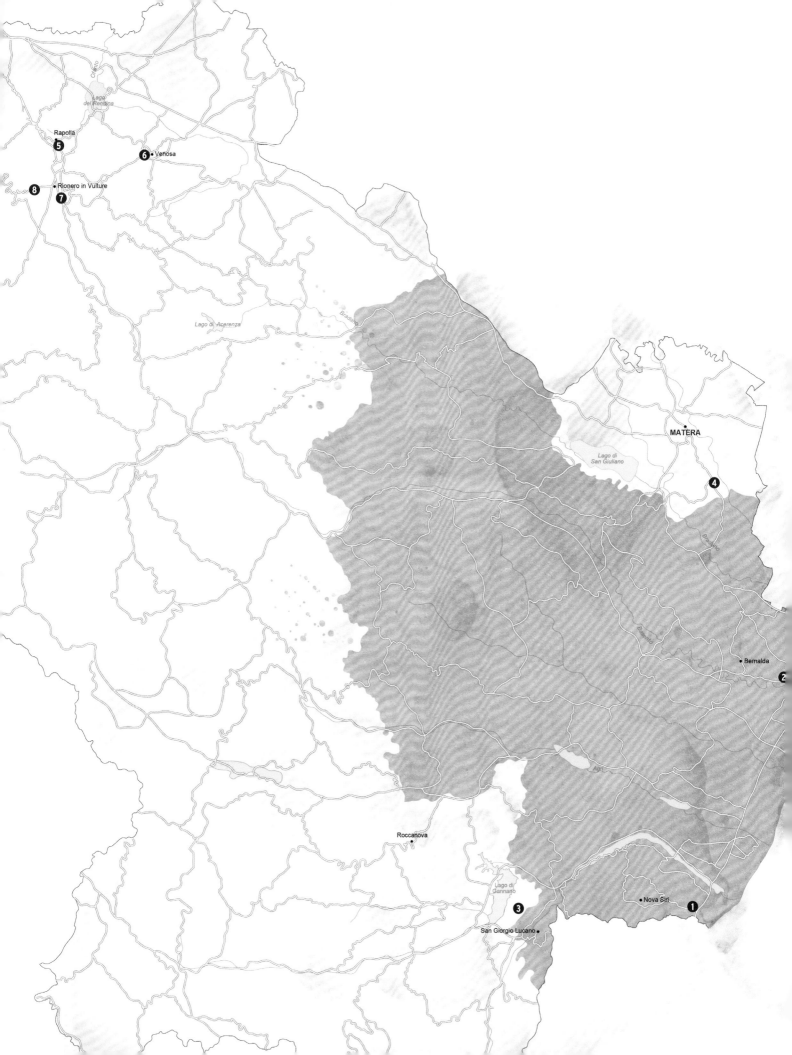

Recommended wines outside the DOC/DOCG designations:

5. CAMERLENGO, Rapolla
   Camerlengo (Aglianico) ($)
6. CANTINA DI VENOSA, Venosa
   Matematico (Merlot, Aglianico) ($$)
7. Donato D'ANGELO, Rionero in Vulture
   Balconara (Aglianico, Cabernet Sauvignon) ($)
3. TENUTA MARINO, San Giorgio Lucano
   Merlot Terra Aspra ($)
8. TERRA DEI RE, Rionero in Vulture
   Vulcano 800 (Pinot Nero) ($$)

ELENA FUCCI
Contrada Solagna del
Titolo
Barile (PZ)
elenafuccivini.com
Year of establishment: 2000
Owner: Elena Fucci
Average number of bottles
produced per year: 30,000

Good technical training
from the University of Pisa,
with great determination to
best represent the qualities
of her territory through
her chosen grape variety,
Aglianico. That is how Elena
Fucci has built growing and
lasting success. From her 17
organically cultivated acres
comes an offering that for
years was limited to Titolo,
which was then gradually
joined by Aglianico del Vulture
SCEG and two tiny, delicious
productions, a Titolo aged in
amphora and a Titolo in pink,
the Pink Edition.

AGLIANICO DEL VULTURE TITOLO
First year of production: 2000
Average number of bottles produced
per year: 33,000
Grape variety: Aglianico

Lots of red fruit and refined fresh notes
reminiscent of basil and spearmint
are the two points of reference for the
aromatic component, in which there is a
slight undertone of roasting for overall
complexity; the taste is quite fresh, almost
savory, not very astringent, and very pleasant
to drink. A clear and enjoyable expression
of Vulture.

CANTINE DEL NOTAIO
Via Roma 159
Rionero in Vulture (PZ)
cantinedelnotaio.it
Year of establishment: 1998
Owner: Gerardo
Giuratrabocchetti
Average number of bottles
produced per year: 480,000

A project studied in every
detail, combining modern
technology and maturation in
"tufa" caves, respect for nature,
and new French woods. The
results are of certain value,
with several labels enjoying
regular accolades, among
which the five Aglianico del
Vulture productions—born
from 129 acres of property
on predominantly volcanic
soils—consistently stand out.
It is a matter of taste, richness,
and elegance above all else.

AGLIANICO DEL VULTURE
LA FIRMA
First year of production: 1998
Average number of bottles produced
per year: 20,000
Grape variety: Aglianico

Black cherries, blackberries, and plums are
in evidence against a spicy, lightly toasted
background. The palate is robust, fresh, and
lively but without obvious acidity, with well-
presented tannins embedded in the softness
provided by the alcohol and fruity flesh. A
great expression of pure Aglianico.

PATERNOSTER
Contrada Valle del Titolo
Barile (PZ)
paternosterwine.it
Year of establishment: 1925
Owner: the Tommasi
family
Average number of bottles
produced per year: 150,000

The acquisition of the majority
shareholding by the Veneto-
based Tommasi Family Estates
group took place in 2016, and
guarantees secure qualitative
continuity for one of the most
celebrated names in southern
oenology, repeatedly awarded
prizes by international
magazines. The predominant
grape in the 49 acres of
organically cultivated property
is Aglianico, from which four
productions are born that
differ slightly in their stylistic
approach and aging woods,
but which are always and in
any case of great classicism.

AGLIANICO DEL VULTURE
SUPERIORE DON ANSELMO
First year of production: before 1985
Average number of bottles produced
per year: 11,000
Grape variety: Aglianico

Since 2017, it has held the Aglianico del
Vulture Superiore DOCG. The aromas are
characterized by black cherry, small berries,
and dried rose, not without fresh balsamic
hints against a delicately spiced background.
The flavor is rather austere even if with
good alcohol content, slow in its progression
thanks to an important tannic component.
Valuable classicism in a wine that is an
emblem of the region.

Calabria

This is a splendid region not lacking in signs of a quest for oenological quality, even if overall production continues to shrink, mainly due to the difficulties encountered in cultivating steep hilly terrain. However, young and motivated wineries are springing up, with more interesting results every year, and various indigenous grape varieties are showing their potential: from Gaglioppo to Magliocco Canino to Nerello among the reds, from Guarnaccia to Malvasia and Greco among the whites.

Calabria is a mystery suspended between utopia and apocalypse. A region of terrific beauty, it is the antipodes of Tuscany, which for centuries has succeeded in presenting itself to the world just as the world dreams and desires it. Calabria, by contrast, does not put on a show but is always itself in the roughest, most brutal, and authentic sense of an identity that includes elements of ancient Greece, South American rainforest-covered mountains, Mexican desert landscapes, and Middle Eastern urban vistas, with towns that seem either bombed out, from the Middle Ages, from 1950, half-built, or so ancient and remote that they have merged with the mountains. Calabria is one of the last outposts of an unexplored world where anyone who wants to understand what Italy is must venture at least once. One of the few regions in the world whose forests still conceal unknown vines.

Looking northward, on the border with Basilicata, is the Cosentino area, a vast expanse encompassing the entire territory of the province of Cosenza and comprising seven subzones that can be labeled, with the Pollino area increasingly on the rise. It is here that the Magliocco Canino is giving its best performance, together with the fragrant white Guarnaccia and Malvasia cultivated up to 2,620 feet above sea level. At the foot of the suggestive Pollino Natural Park, we also find the few vines destined for the Moscato Passito di Saracena, a type that deserves to be known and offered on the market in more suitable quantities. Moving southward, we encounter the Lamezia and Savuto DOCs, where the main Calabrian grape variety, Gaglioppo, joins other local grapes and begins to dictate the physiognomy of small quantities of fine red wines.

Moving to the east coast, beyond the Sila massif acting as a watershed between the vineyards facing the Tyrrhenian Sea and those facing the Ionian Sea, we find the region's most important designation, Cirò Rosso, a triumph of the Gaglioppo grape, often used in purity and appreciated since the time of Greek colonization.

Lastly, approaching the Strait of Messina, one encounters several small production enterprises, among which, still on the Ionian side, an intoxicating sweet wine emerges. It is the almost unobtainable Greco di Bianco, the fruit of grapes, often dried in the sun for a few weeks, that offers unparalleled aromas in terms of seduction and suavity. Relying on 27,200 acres of vineyards and the work of 1,300 mostly small farms, Calabria produces an average of 7.9 million gallons of wine per year.

MAIN VINES GROWN IN THE REGION

Gaglioppo
The largest indigenous Calabrian vine, suitable for aging, also known as Aglianico di Cassano, Paesano, Galaffa, Lancianese, Montonico Nero, or Galloppo, is said to originate from a cross between Sangiovese and a yet unidentified variety, while its kinship with the Sicilian Nerello Mascalese and Frappato is certified. Its origins are ancient, since its reference DOC, Cirò, once called Cremissa, was one of the main colonies of Magna Graecia, together with Crotone and Sibari, the latter being the center of wine trade for the entire area. Vinified, it presents itself in the glass with a pale, almost brick-red color; well-balanced when young, it rounds off with time, and underbrush, herbaceous, and spicy notes emerge. It is grown on high ground and harvested early to avoid overripening at the expense of freshness and good acidity. It is also indicated here in the Lamezia and Savuto designations.

Greco Bianco
Different from the Campania Greco, it is grown exclusively in the provinces of Catanzaro and Reggio Calabria. In dry form, it has no particular personality, but in the municipality of Bianco and Casignana it is used to make Greco di Bianco DOC wine, a passito whose concentration reveals softness on the palate and persistent notes of orange blossom, honey, and dried fruit.

Greco Nero
Cultivated in Calabria since the times of Magna Graecia, it is usually found in blends with other reds. A pale red color, fruity and harmonious nose, full-bodied and intriguing, it is also appreciable in the rosé version where it is more snappy and vinous.

Guarnaccia, Malvasia Bianca di Candia, Moscatello Selvatico, Odoacra
A white grape variety, a constituent of the Moscato al Governo di Saracena. Guarnaccia is none other than Coda di Volpe Bianca

Roma

A2

Saracena •

POLLINO

Altomonte •

**TERRE
DI COSENZA**

Abbazia della
Sambucina

Lago
di Cecita

Rovito •

Mar Tirreno

COSENZA •   Celico •

Monte
Botte Donato
1925

SILA

CIRÒ
Cirò •

Cirò Marina •

Melissa •

Strongoli •

MELISSA

Marzi •

SAVUTO

Cleto •

Savuto •

Monte
Cariglione
1765

Lago
di Lorica

Crati

CROTONE •

**SANT'ANNA
DI ISOLA
CAPO RIZZUTO**

Lamezia Terme •

LAMEZIA

Amato

CATANZARO •

• Isola di Capo Rizzuto

Francavilla Angitola •

VIBO VALENTIA •

Nicotera •

Bivongi •

BIVONGI

Riace •

Gerace •

ASPROMONTE

Mar Ionio

Montalto
1955

RÉGGIO CALABRIA •

**GRECO
DI BIANCO**

Bianco •

Stretto di Messina

(→ Campania), a grape variety originating from Campania that prefers blends since it is loaded with alcohol but lacks acidity and fragrance.

Malvasia Bianca di Candia (→ Lazio) is a cultivar originating from the island of Crete, where the town of Chania derives its name from *al-khandaq*—"the moat": it should be drunk young and prefers blends, in which it brings a good load of color and a dry, savory body.

Moscatello Selvatico is a cultivar of the Muscat family and is mainly found in Apulia, between Barletta and Monopoli, and can also be found in smaller percentages in Moscadello di Montalcino.

Odoacra, or Duraca or Addoraca, is another white variety whose name means fragrant and is only grown in Saracena. These varieties, in varying percentages, go into making wine using a very ancient procedure whereby Odoacra and Moscatello are harvested first and dried on shaded racks so that the sugars and aromas are delicately concentrated in the dehydrated berries; Guarnaccia and Malvasia are harvested a month later and the must obtained is boiled until it is reduced by two-thirds. The Muscatel and Odoacra grapes are then selected one by one and pressed by hand, finally immersed in the concentrated must and left to ferment naturally. After about six months of maceration, the result is an amber-colored wine, dense and perfumed with resinous and aromatic notes, combined with sumptuous hints of dried figs, dates, and honey, balanced between sweetness and freshness, with a lingering almondy finish.

Magliocco Canino

An indigenous red vine, in purity it knows how to be balanced and harmonious, with good sapidity, dry and medium tannicity. Spicy on the nose, with pepper, licorice, and clove, it opens on plum, myrtle, and Morello cherry. It is also capable of providing good structure in blends, where it complements and rounds off other varieties. It is found in the Terre di Cosenza and Lamezia DOC.

Pecorello

An indigenous Calabrian white, not to be confused with the Pecorino vine of Central Italy that has conquered the scene in recent years, being appreciated in purity for its bright straw color, intense aromas of apple, pineapple, peach, and lychee, on which citrus and balsamic notes of mandarin, mint, and lavender emerge, closing on salty and iodine tones.

The DOCG

- Cirò Rosso Classico Superiore

The DOCs

- Bivongi
- Cirò
- Greco di Bianco
- Lamezia
- Melissa
- S. Anna di Isola Capo Rizzuto
- Savuto
- Scavigna
- Terre di Cosenza

Cirò DOC and Cirò Rosso Classico Superiore DOCG

It is the most famous Calabrian *denominazione* in Italy and abroad, with a vineyard area that occupies 75% of all the region's DOCs, even though there are only four municipalities involved, of which Cirò and Cirò Marina qualify as Classico. There are Rosso, Rosato, and Bianco typologies: the first two are made up of Gaglioppo grapes at a minimum of 80%, and the third, from Greco Bianco grapes, also in the same percentage. This area, which is located in the province of Crotone between the Ionian coast and the slopes of the Sila plateau, has been known for millennia for the quality of its grapes, thanks to the colonization of the Greeks who offered this wine to the winners of the Olympics. Of all the versions, the Cirò Rosso Classico Superiore stands out. It offers ripe red fruits to the nose, ranging from blueberries to plums, often accompanied by refreshing notes from licorice toward the balsamic. The palate is characterized by restrained tannicity and a savory freshness that builds a pleasant drinkability. This type has recently obtained the DOCG designation. Three and a half million bottles are produced annually.

—

Producers and their trademark and signature wines:

1. 'A VITA, Cirò Marina
   Cirò Rosso Classico Superiore Riserva ($$)
2. Sergio ARCURI, Cirò Marina
   Cirò Rosso Classico Superiore Aris ($$)
3. Cataldo CALABRETTA, Cirò Marina
   Cirò Rosso Classico Superiore ($)
4. CAPARRA & SICILIANI, Cirò Marina
   Cirò Rosso Classico Superiore Riserva Volvito ($)
5. COTE DI FRANZE, Cirò Marina
   Cirò Rosso Classico Superiore Riserva ($)
6. IPPOLITO 1845, Cirò Marina
   Cirò Rosso Classico Superiore Riserva Ripe del
   Falco ($$)
   Cirò Rosato Mabilia ($)
7. LIBRANDI, Cirò Marina
   Cirò Rosso Classico Superiore Riserva Duca San
   Felice ($)
8. SANTA VENERE, Cirò Marina
   Cirò Rosso Classico Superiore Riserva Federico
   Scala ($)
9. TENUTA DEL CONTE, Cirò Marina
   Cirò Rosso Classico Superiore Riserva Dalla
   Terra ($)
10. VIGNETI VUMBACA, Cirò Marina
    Cirò Rosso Classico Superiore ($)

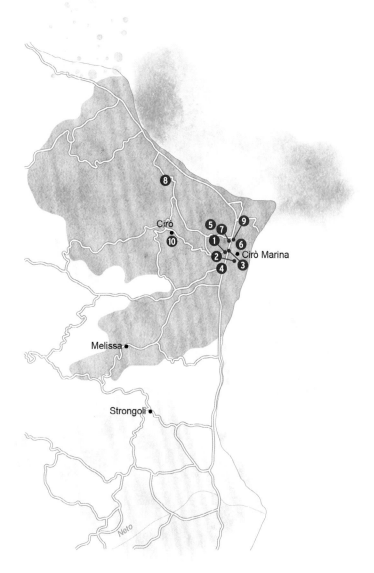

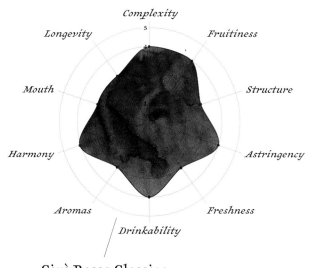

Cirò Rosso Classico

Terre di Cosenza DOC

A vast DOC that embraces the entire province of Cosenza, allowing the use of all local grapes and a few international varieties to make white, red, rosé, passito, and sparkling wines. For the Rosso, the use of 60 to 100% Magliocco is envisaged, and aging can be in wood (as in the second wine suggested) or steel. Particularly in the case of the Riserva, which is released at least twenty-four months after the harvest, aging may continue in the bottle for several years. These are wines with considerable fruitiness, fresh both on the nose and in the mouth thanks to balsamic hints, and always softly drinkable. Total annual production of around seven hundred thousand bottles.

—

Producers and their trademark and signature wines:

1. Giuseppe CALABRESE, Saracena
   Terre di Cosenza Pollino Rosso ($)
2. MASSERIA FALVO 1727, Saracena
   Terre di Cosenza Pollino Rosso
   Riserva Don Rosario ($)

Savuto DOC

The DOC covers numerous municipalities in the provinces of Cosenza—where the Rosso and Rosato can carry the appellation Classico—and Catanzaro, and also includes the Bianco type. Savuto Rosso is mainly based on Gaglioppo, at up to 45%, and Aglianico, up to 45% as well, with Greco Nero and/or Nerello Cappuccio up to 10%. There are other grapes included up to 45%. The Rosso is very fruity, well-balanced on the palate, rather dry, and appetizingly drinkable. Production is about fifty thousand bottles per year in total.

—

Producer and its trademark and signature wine:

3. ANTICHE VIGNE, Marzì
   Savuto Rosso Classico ($)

Terre di Cosenza Pollino Rosso

Lamezia DOC

Produced in nine municipalities in the province of Catanzaro, the Lamezia DOC includes different types of white and red, mainly based on classic local grapes. For the Rosso there is a blend of Gaglioppo and or Magliocco at 25 to 45%, with Greco Nero and or Marsigliana at 25 to 45%, with other authorized red grapes being included at up to 40%. In the case of the Riserva, after twenty-four months of aging, at least twelve of which are in wood, a wine suitable for medium aging is born, rich in red fruits and flowers against a spicy background, with good acidity and medium tannic astringency. A total of almost one hundred thousand bottles per year are produced.

—

Producer and its trademark and signature wine:

4. CANTINE LENTO, Lamezia Terme
    Lamezia Rosso Riserva ($)

Melissa DOC

A small designation, relating to fifteen municipalities in the province of Crotone, including Melissa, which provides two types. There is Bianco, based on Greco Bianco for 80 to 95%, and Rosso, from Gaglioppo grapes between 75 and 95%, with small additions of other local grapes as well. The Rosso is rich in aromas of medicinal herbs and has a slender, flowing structure, with a barely noticeable astringency and a pleasant hint of cherry on the finish. Annual production is just over one hundred thousand bottles.

—

Producer and its trademark and signature wine:

5. LA PIZZUTA DEL PRINCIPE, Strongoli
    Melissa Rosso Superiore Jacca Ventu ($)

Greco di Bianco DOC

As small in numbers as it is enchanting in the glass, Greco di Bianco is made only in the municipalities of Bianco and Casignana, in the province of Reggio Calabria, from the grapes of the same name. They are dried so as to obtain a wine with a somewhat higher percentage proof of least 14% by volume, capable of retaining good residual sugar content. Aromas range from rose to apricot to oily dried fruit, the taste being enveloping but not without a pleasant acidic appeal. In all, about one hundred thousand bottles per year are produced.

—

Producer and its trademark and signature wine:

•   CERATTI, Casignana
    Greco di Bianco Passito Etichetta Nera ($)

Greco di Bianco Passito

Recommended wines outside the DOC/DOCG designations:

1. BARONE G.R. MACRÌ, Gerace
   Centocamere Greco Passito ($)
2. CANTINE BENVENUTO, Francavilla Angitola
   Benvenuto (Zibibbo) ($)
3. CANTINE VIOLA, Saracena
   Moscato Passito di Saracena (Guarnaccia, Malvasia, Moscatello, Adduroca) ($$)
   Rosso Viola (Magliocco) ($)
4. CASA COMERCI, Nicotera
   Granàtu Rosato (Magliocco Canino) ($)
5. CERAUDO, Strongoli
   Grisara Pecorello ($)
   Petelia (Greco, Mantonico) ($)
   Grayasusi Argento (Gaglioppo) ($)
6. FEUDO DEI SANSEVERINO, Saracena
   Moscato Passito al Governo di Saracena ($$)
7. IPPOLITO 1845, Cirò Marina
   Pecorello ($)
8. LIBRANDI, Cirò Marina
   Gravello (Gaglioppo, Cabernet Sauvignon) ($)
   Megonio (Magliocco) ($)
9. Antonella LOMBARDO, Bianco
   Cheiras (Greco di Bianco) ($$)
   Pi Greco (Greco di Bianco) ($)
10. RUSSO & LONGO, Strongoli
    Ois Pecorello ($)
11. SPIRITI EBBRI, Celico
    Neostòs Bianco (Pecorello) ($)
    Neostòs Rosso (Greco Nero, Guarnaccia, Merlot) ($)
    See... Rosso (Magliocco Dolce, Magliocco Canino, Greco Nero, Gaglioppo...) ($$)
12. STATTI, Lamezia Terme
    Mantonico ($)
13. TENUTA DEL TRAVALE, Rovito
    Esmén Tetra (Nerello Mascalese, Nerello Cappuccio) ($$)
    Eleuteria (Nerello Mascalese) ($$$)
14. TERRE DI BALBIA, Altomonte
    Blandus (Merlot) ($)

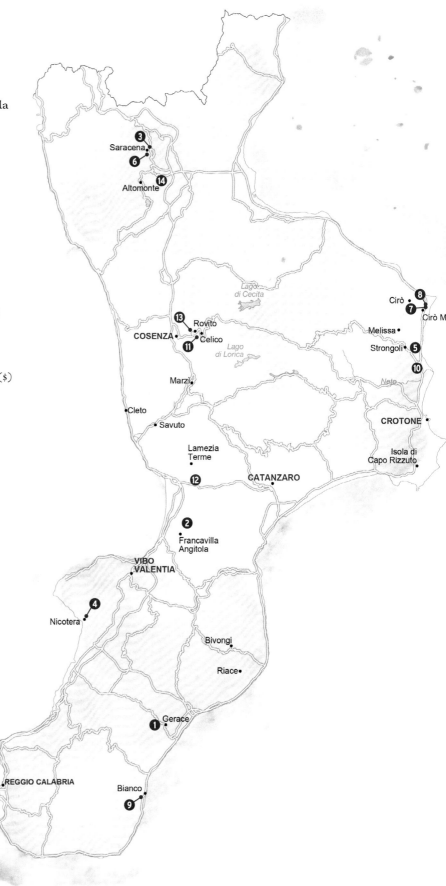

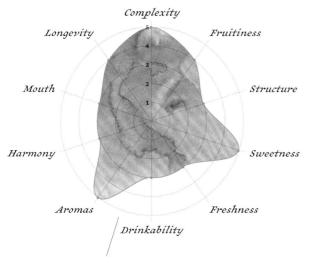

Moscato Passito di Saracena

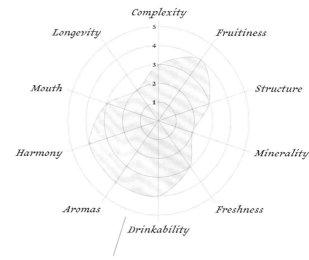

Calabria Pecorello

'A VITA
Strada Statale 106 km
279.8
Cirò Marina (KR)
avitavini.it
Year of establishment: 2008
Owner: Francesco De
Franco and Laura Violino
Average number of bottles
produced per year: 25,000

A small and valid enterprise
that has set itself the goal of
making wines born from clean
agriculture and spontaneous
fermentation, using only the
most typical grapes of the
Cirò Marina area: Gaglioppo,
Magliocco, Mantonico, and
Greco Bianco. From the 20
organically farmed acres
come four strongly territorial
labels, all very established and
worth tasting, from the white
Leukò to the rosé, from Il
Rosso to the Riserva. A model
of environmental respect and
quality.

CIRÒ ROSSO CLASSICO
SUPERIORE RISERVA
First year of production: 2008
Average number of bottles produced
per year: 3,000
Grape variety: Gaglioppo

It is matured in wood and for a long
time in glass before greeting the outside
world, presenting itself well, openly and
expansively on tasting, with prevalent notes
of ripe red fruit and a fine spiciness. The
palate is compelling, very structured, with
pleasant tannicity and refreshing acidity,
with an elegant and long finish on hints of
licorice. An excellent expression of the great
Cirò.

LIBRANDI
Strada Statale 106,
Contrada San Gennaro
Cirò Marina (KR)
librandi.it
Year of establishment: 1953
Owner: the Librandi
family
Average number of
bottles produced per year:
2,400,000

A family history characterized
by strong entrepreneurial
skill and a constant desire to
grow. This is how, in seventy
years, Librandi has become
synonymous with quality and
large numbers, with 573 acres
of property and a modern
wine cellar. It is from here that
internationally appreciated
labels are produced, including
Duca San Felice but also
Megonio, from Magliocco
grapes, and Gravello, from
Gaglioppo and Cabernet
Sauvignon grapes. A great
name in Italian wine.

CIRÒ ROSSO CLASSICO SUPERIORE
RISERVA DUCA SAN FELICE
First year of production: 1983
Average number of bottles produced
per year: 90,000
Grape variety: Gaglioppo

A careful selection of grapes from alberello
vines and an aging process involving only
steel and cement give a very fruity and
straightforward wine, in which strawberries,
currants, and Scotch pine dominate the clear
nose. The palate is agile and supple, with
good tannicity and plenty of fresh fruity
flesh. A wine suitable for long bottle aging.

Sicily

Over the last forty years, Sicilian winegrowing has revolutionized its image, going from being a reservoir of bulk wines destined for bottlers in northern Italy to a producer of a wide range of high-quality wines. The Nero d'Avola, Nerello Mascalese, and Grillo grapes dominate the scene, in a healthy, multifaceted, and rich production that also includes passito wines that are among the best in the world.

Sicily competes with Emilia-Romagna for third place among the most productive regions in Italy, after Veneto and Apulia. But rather than quantity, journalists in the sector are attentive to the ever-increasing quality on offer, not just from indigenous grapes but also all the main varieties of French origin.

Traveling clockwise around the island, starting from the province of Messina in the northeastern tip, is the small and prestigious Faro DOC, heralding the reign of Nerello Mascalese and Nerello Cappuccio grapes on the slopes of Etna. Here a laborious recovery of centuries-old vineyards—never attacked by phylloxera—continues, with results of aromatic complexity and taste finesse that are winning over the palates of wine lovers everywhere. The Etna DOC itself also provides for a white version, mainly made from the Carricante grape, with results that are already very convincing.

Heading south to the provinces of Siracusa and Ragusa, the most widely used grape variety is Nero d'Avola, which yields its most successful fruit in the Eloro DOC area; it is blended with Frappato in the only regional DOCG, Cerasuolo di Vittoria. But it is a grape that also emerges with a distinct personality in the central and western parts of the island. In the latter, there is an articulated series of designations, among which we should point out those relating to the most famous Sicilian white wine, Alcamo, and those dedicated to two of the most representative Sicilian companies: Contea di Sclafani for Tasca D'Almerita and Contessa Entellina for Donnafugata. In this area, in the province of Trapani, comes the most famous—and often weakened by industrial-style production—fortified wine in Italy, Marsala, capable of attractive complexity and endowed with an unmistakable personality.

The journey concludes with the caressing sweet wines produced in the smaller islands: Malvasia delle Lipari and Passito di Pantelleria, offered in small quantities and considered by experts to be among the most involving and intoxicating wines on the planet.

The region's production is characterized by the strong activity of its sixty wine cooperatives, which process 60% of the total grapes, provided by most of the 6,300 wineries. The 158.5 million gallons per year are produced from roughly 247,000 acres of vineyards, 65% of which are hilly, 30% flat, and 5% mountainous.

MAIN VINES GROWN IN THE REGION

Carricante

A historic Sicilian cultivar, whose birthplace was Varanni - Viagrande, near Catania in the Etna area. It is at its best in white Etna, where it is cultivated up to an altitude of 3,280 feet, a height that guarantees surprising finesse and longevity for a southern white: up there, the volcanic rocks, the strong temperature fluctuations, and the influence of the sea contribute to freshness and minerality. In purity, the wines are crisp and sinuous, with distinctive traits of orange and lemon blossom, apple, bergamot, white peach, and yellow plum, with strong Mediterranean hints of oregano, tomato leaf, caper flower and sage, elderflower and chamomile.

Catarratto

Already widespread in the eighteenth century, particularly in the provinces of Trapani, Palermo, and Agrigento, together with Grillo and Inzolia it can be used in Marsala but is also used in Alcamo Bianco Classico, Monreale, and Etna Bianco, where together with Carricante it contributes to wines of great charm and marked personality. In purity or blending, it brings warmth, fruit, and complexity, in particular aromas of broom and jasmine, white peach, elderflower, freshly cut grass, and citrus fruits. Of the approximately 247,000 acres under vine in Sicily, one-third are of Catarratto.

Frappato

Widespread in the Ragusano area and registered in the Vittoria area since the seventeenth century, it complements Nero d'Avola in the Cerasuolo di Vittoria DOCG and is also included in the Vittoria DOC and Eloro, together with Perricone. On its own, the wine is cherry-colored, fruity, intense, and spicy; the aromas are those of a bright, multifaceted red: raspberry, blackberry, myrtle, red rose, violet, bramble, blueberry, and medicinal herbs. The palate is juicy, sanguine, and drinkable.

Stromboli
I. Stromboli

I. Basiluzzo

I. Panarea
I. Filicudi
Malfa
I. Salina S. Marina Salina
I. Alicudi
MALVASIA *I. Lipari* Lipari
DELLE LIPARI
I. Vulcano

Ustica
I. Ustica

San Vito lo Capo
Isola
delle
Femmine *Golfo*
di Palermo Salina **FARO** Faro Superiore
Golfo Grotte
PALERMO **MESSINA**
di Castellammare San Martino
I. di Levanzo San Martino delle Scale Monreale
ERICE Monreale **PELORITANI**
TRAPANI Partinico
Favignana Paceco **ALCAMO** Santa Cristina Gela **E90**
Isola Alcamo San Cipirello Randazzo Castiglione
Favignana Segesta **MONREALE** di Sicilia
Marsala Camporeale *Santuario* *Santuario* Linguaglossa **E45**
DELIA Madonna di Tagliavia di Gibilmanna Bronte
NIVOLELLI **N E B R O D I** Milo
Mazara **MARSALA** Contessa Entellina Sclafani **MADONIE** **ETNA**
del Vallo Bagni Trecastagni Viagrande
Menfi **CONTEA** **E90**
MENFI Cammarata **DI SCLAFANI** **CATANIA**
ENNA **A19**
Grotte **CALTANISSETTA** *Golfo*
AGRIGENTO *di Catania*
VALLE DEI Campobello Caltagirone **MONTI IBLEI**
TEMPLI di Licata **E45**
Butera **SIRACUSA**
Mar Mediterraneo Niscemi **CERASUOLO** **SIRACUSA**
DI VITTORIA Chiaramonte
Acate Gulfi **NOTO**
E45 **RAGUSA** Noto
Vittoria
Modica
PANTELLERIA Scicli Ispica
ELORO
Pantelleria Pachino
I. di Pantelleria

Grillo

Much less widespread than Catarratto, of which it is a natural cross with Zibibbo, it is cultivated on 16,000 acres and found mostly in the Trapani area. A base for Marsala, in the pure versions it brings out floral aromas and dried herbs such as hay and green tea, framed by citrus peel and hints of saffron and cloves.

Inzolia (Ansonica)

A semi-aromatic, traditional cultivar in Sicily, Sardinia, and in Tuscany on the islands of Giglio and Elba. Here it is present in Menfi DOC, and above all in the Palermo area and in the provinces of Agrigento and Caltanissetta. Purity-wise, it does not lack structure and roundness, with a rather low acidity that nevertheless does not preclude intense aromas of unripe fruit and herbaceous and floral notes of thyme, broom, and chamomile flowers, with a good salinity that compensates for the high sugar content of the must.

Malvasia delle Lipari

Another case of heroic viticulture for a grape variety cultivated here on the steep slopes of volcanic terrain, overlooking the sea of the Aeolian or Lipari islands. The cultivar is genetically identical to Malvasia di Sardegna, Greco Bianco di Gerace, Spanish Malvasia de Sitges, and Malvasia Cândida di Madeira. In Sicily it performs best in the passito version: the wine, a distillate of sun and sea, has an amber color and aromas of honey, tamarind, and dehydrated fruit, with exceptional olfactory complexity and longevity.

Moscato Bianco

Used in the Siracusa DOC.

→ Piedmont

Nerello Cappuccio

The least widespread and most velvety of the Sicilian Nerellos, typical of Etna and Faro, it is used as a blending grape except in very rare cases, often in combination with Nerello Mascalese to mitigate its excessive acidity with softness and complete its aromas, with a complement of ripe red fruit and a full, harmonious flavor.

Nerello Mascalese

Native to the Mascali plain, it can be found in the Capo di Faro and Messina areas, but finds its *terroir* of choice on the volcanic rock slopes of Etna, to which it clings between 1,300 and 3,280 feet, where temperature fluctuations guarantee its freshness and aromatic integrity. A genetic pedigree—a cross between Sangiovese and white Mantonico, making it a sibling of the Calabrian Gaglioppo—as well as microclimatic conditions, late ripening, and careful selection work in the vineyard make it the Sicilian Pinot Noir by way of the refinement and aromatic complexity it can express. When pure, it results in wines characterized by a bright ruby color and a fine, sumptuous bouquet of violets and wild red berries, cherries and raspberries, fern, undergrowth and licorice, with a hint of burnt sugar.

Nero d'Avola (Calabrese)

An iconic Sicilian vine, ironically registered in the National Catalog of Vine Varieties under the name "Calabrese," it was used in the past as a blending grape due to its power and versatility. Today it occupies more than 37,000 acres under vine and is a symbol of quality Sicilian viticulture; it is often vinified in purity, both in young wines of great freshness and drinkability and in wines for aging. It has a remarkable structural intensity and a fruity, balsamic, enveloping nose reminiscent of strawberry, raspberry, cherry and currant, blackberry and black mulberry, juniper, myrtle, thyme and cinnamon, dehydrated plum, carob, incense, and tobacco. It is the protagonist—together with Frappato—of Cerasuolo di Vittoria DOCG, and is also found in Vittoria DOC, Contea di Sclafani, Sicilia DOC, and in memorable interpretations in other Sicilian areas.

Nocera

A minor indigenous variety, widespread between Sicily and Calabria, here it is part of the Faro DOC, where it contributes a notable chromatic, acid, and alcoholic content.

Perricone (Pignatello)

Widespread in eastern Sicily, it is blended with Nero d'Avola and other varieties in Eloro and Contea di Sclafani. In purity, it is dry, warm, vinous, and fruity, with predominantly ripe rose and violet aromas.

Zibibbo (Moscato d'Alessandria)

Moscato di Pantelleria is an aromatic variety of the great Muscat family, and on these rocks in the heart of the Mediterranean finds a unique *terroir* in which to express itself in the famous Passito da Meditazione. Dense, viscous, astonishing for the patience and poetry with which the vine and vine-grower extract such lively and concentrated contents, capable of producing in the memory endless suggestions of white and yellow flowers, fruit tarts, peaches in syrup, dehydrated apricots, and honey. There are dates, candied citrus fruits, dried figs, jams, and marmalades, in a jubilation to which one cannot help but abandon oneself, like being shipwrecked in an exotic and distant place.

The DOCG
- Cerasuolo di Vittoria

The DOCs
- Alcamo
- Contea di Sclafani / Valledolmo-Contea di Sclafani
- Contessa Entellina
- Delia Nivolelli
- Eloro
- Erice
- Etna
- Faro
- Malvasia delle Lipari
- Mamertino / Mamertino di Milazzo
- Marsala
- Menfi
- Monreale
- Noto
- Pantelleria
- Riesi
- Salaparuta
- Sambuca di Sicilia
- Santa Margherita di Belice
- Sciacca
- Sicilia
- Siracusa
- Vittoria

Etna DOC

A designation that covers twenty municipalities on the slopes of the Etna volcano and which, on the strength of a thirty-century-long viticultural history, has achieved great success in recent years. This is thanks to two wines. The first is Etna Bianco, made from at least 60% Carricante grapes with Catarratto making up the remainder, and even more so, Etna Rosso, made from at least 80% Nerello Mascalese and possibly Nerello Cappuccio. It is not just the soil that is volcanic in this area. There have been tumultuous developments of late, bearing in mind that dozens of quality entrepreneurs have arrived recently. They are mostly Sicilians but Angelo Gaja, Oscar Farinetti, and Davide Rosso, to give a few examples, have already arrived from Piedmont. They have created new cellars, refurbished ancient vineyards, and restructured terraces on the slopes of Etna, where the bush vine thrives up to 3,280 feet above sea level, with its roots in the lava and the snow that often whitens the rows. Moreover, in the last fifteen years, the number of active wineries has risen from twenty-five to one hundred sixty-six, with three hundred ninety wineries working a total of 2,940 acres, divided up into one hundred forty-two Contrade, which are similar to the MGA and UGA. The aromas of Etna Bianco range from Mediterranean scrub to citrus fruits, leaving room for persuasive minerality as the years go by, while the flavor is rich and lively, rather acidic, and often pleasantly saline. The Etna Rosso opens on small red berries from the undergrowth, with spices and vegetal hints sometimes reminiscent of mushrooms to which a pleasantly balsamic touch can be added. The tannins are dense but soft, never too astringent, the finish rather long and fresh, with good dynamism. Similarities with Pinot Noir and Nebbiolo have been attempted, but Etna Rosso does not need them. The process of creating the new Etna DOCG has recently begun. Including the small quantities of Etna Rosato and Etna Spumante, it produces 5.5 million bottles per year, and growing.

—

Producers and their trademark and signature wines:

1. ALTA MORA – CUSUMANO, Castiglione di Sicilia
   Etna Rosso Guardiola ($$)
   Etna Bianco ($)
   Etna Rosso Feudo di Mezzo ($$)
2. BARONE DI VILLAGRANDE, Milo
   Etna Bianco Superiore Contrada Villagrande ($$)
3. BENANTI, Viagrande
   Etna Bianco Superiore Contrada Rinazzo ($$)
   Etna Rosso Riserva Rovittello Particella No. 341 ($$$)
4. Ciro BIONDI, Trecastagni
   Etna Bianco Pianta ($$)
5. Alice BONACCORSI – ValCerasa, Randazzo
   Etna Bianco ValCerasa ($)

Scafani Bagni

㉒

⑱

① ㉖
Randazzo ㉓ ⑩ ⑭ ⑫
⑪ ⑤ ⑦ ⑮ ㉕ Castiglione di Sicilia
⑲ ㉔ ⑥
㉑ ⑳
⑬ Linguaglossa

Bronte

ETNA

Milo ⑰
⑯ ②

④
Trecastagni
⑨ ③
Viagrande

CATANIA ⑧

6. Pietro CACIORGNA, Castiglione di Sicilia
   Etna Rosso N'Anticchia ($$$)
7. CALCAGNO, Castiglione di Sicilia
   Etna Rosso Arcuria ($$)
8. CANTINE DI NESSUNO, Catania
   Etna Bianco Milice ($$)
9. CANTINE NICOSIA, Trecastagni
   Etna Rosso Contrada Monte Gorna Riserva
   Vecchie Viti ($$)
10. COTTANERA, Castiglione di Sicilia
    Etna Rosso Riserva Zottorinoto ($$$)
    Etna Bianco Calderara ($)
    Etna Rosso Feudo di Mezzo ($$)
11. DONNAFUGATA, Randazzo
    Etna Rosso Contrada Marchesa ($$$)

12. FIRRIATO, Castiglione di Sicilia
    Etna Bianco Cavanera Ripa di Scorciavacca ($)
    Etna Rosso Cavanera Rovo delle Coturnie ($)
13. GENERAZIONE ALESSANDRO, Linguaglossa
    Etna Rosso Croceferro ($)
    Etna Bianco Trainara ($)
14. GRACI, Castiglione di Sicilia
    Etna Rosso Arcurìa ($$)
    Etna Bianco Arcurìa ($$)
15. ICUSTODIDELLEVIGNEDELL'ETNA, Castiglione
    di Sicilia
    Etna Bianco Ante ($$)
16. I VIGNERI, Milo
    Etna Bianco Superiore Vigna di Milo ($$)
    Etna Rosso Vinupetra ($$)
17. MAUGERI, Milo
    Etna Bianco Superiore Contrada Volpare
    Frontebosco ($$)
18. MONTELEONE, Castiglione di Sicilia
    Etna Bianco Anthemis ($$$)
    Etna Rosso Qubba ($$$)
19. PALMENTO COSTANZO, Castiglione di Sicilia
    Etna Rosso Prefillossera ($$$)
    Etna Rosso Contrada Santo Spirito Particella 468
    ($$)
20. PIETRADOLCE, Castiglione di Sicilia
    Etna Rosso Barbagalli ($$$$)
    Etna Rosso Contrada Rampante ($$)
21. Girolamo RUSSO, Castiglione di Sicilia
    Etna Rosso Feudo di Mezzo ($$$)
    Etna Bianco Nerina ($$)
    Etna Rosso San Lorenzo ($$$)
22. TASCA D'ALMERITA, Sclafani Bagni
    Etna Rosso Tenuta Tascante Contrada
    Sciaranuova VV ($$$)
23. TENUTA DELLE TERRE NERE, Randazzo
    Etna Rosso San Lorenzo ($$$)
    Etna Rosso Guardiola ($$$)
    Etna Bianco Cuvée delle Vigne Niche ($$)
24. TENUTA DI FESSINA, Castiglione di Sicilia
    Etna Bianco A' Puddara ($$)
25. TENUTE BOSCO, Castiglione di Sicilia
    Etna Rosso Vico Prephylloxera ($$)
26. Francesco TORNATORE, Castiglione di Sicilia
    Etna Bianco Zottorinotto ($$)
    Etna Bianco Pietrarizzo ($)
    Etna Rosso Calderara ($$$)

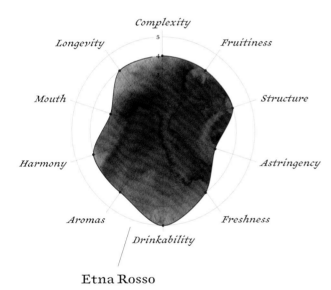

Etna Rosso

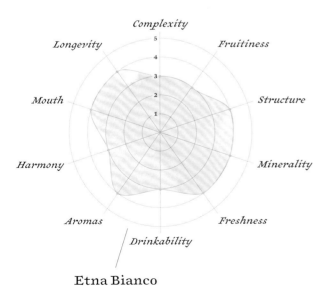

Etna Bianco

Faro DOC

As small as it is idiosyncratic, this red DOC comes from vineyards located exclusively in the municipality of Messina. The wines are mainly based on Nerello Mascalese at 45 to 60%, Nerello Cappuccio at 15 to 30%, and Nocera at 5 to 10%. On the terraced vineyards cultivated with sapling vines on the steep hills overlooking the Strait of Messina, a harmonious and velvety wine is born, with a particularly complex nose that ranges from red flowers to wet earth, from smoky to spicy. Just seventy thousand bottles are produced per year.

—

Producers and their trademark and signature wines:

1. BONAVITA, Messina
   Faro ($$)
2. LE CASEMATTE, Messina
   Faro ($)
3. PALARI, Messina
   Faro Palari ($$)

Mamertino or Mamertino di Milazzo DOC

The production area includes thirty-one municipalities in the province of Messina, with a vineyard area of only 124 acres distributed between the Tyrrhenian Sea and the Nebrodi Mountains. The most interesting results come from the Rosso, made from Nero d'Avola, Nocera, and Nerello Mascalese grapes, as is well demonstrated by the robust wines we recommend, rich in aromas of small black fruits and Mediterranean herbs. The Consorzio di Tutela was set up in 2022 and is aiming for a decisive increase in production, currently at just over one hundred thousand bottles per year.

—

Producers and their trademark and signature wines:

4. CAMBRIA, Furnari
   Mamertino Rosso Giulio Cesare ($$)
5. VIGNA NICA, Barcellona Pozzo di Gotto
   Mamertino Rosso ($)

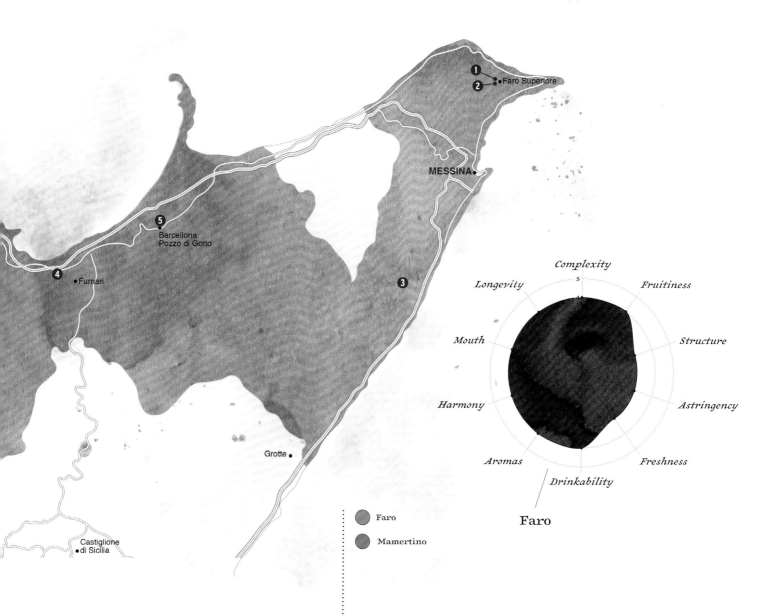

Faro

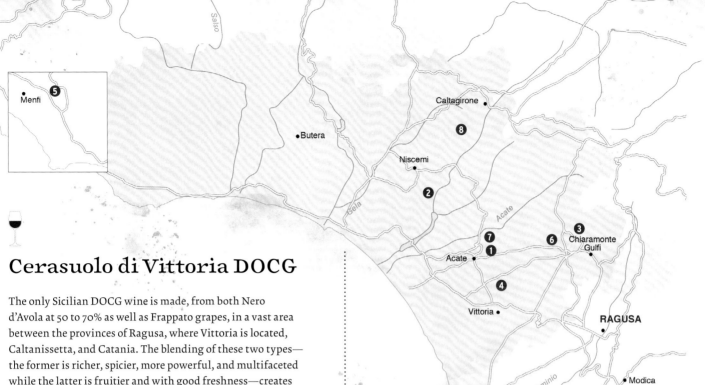

Cerasuolo di Vittoria DOCG

The only Sicilian DOCG wine is made, from both Nero d'Avola at 50 to 70% as well as Frappato grapes, in a vast area between the provinces of Ragusa, where Vittoria is located, Caltanissetta, and Catania. The blending of these two types—the former is richer, spicier, more powerful, and multifaceted while the latter is fruitier and with good freshness—creates a complex wine, dominated on the nose by notes of ripe red fruits such as plum and cherry. Meanwhile the palate is rounded, enveloping, soft, and at times endowed with pleasant savoriness. Nearly one million bottles are produced each year.

—

Producers and their trademark and signature wines:

1. COS, Vittoria
   Cerasuolo di Vittoria Classico ($)
2. FEUDI DEL PISCIOTTO, Niscemi
   Cerasuolo di Vittoria Giambattista Valli ($)
3. GULFI, Chiaramonte Gulfi
   Cerasuolo di Vittoria ($)
4. Arianna OCCHIPINTI, Vittoria
   Cerasuolo di Vittoria Classico Grotte Alte ($ $ $)

5. PLANETA, Menfi
   Cerasuolo di Vittoria Classico Dorilli ($)
6. POGGIO DI BORTOLONE, Chiaramonte Gulfi
   Cerasuolo di Vittoria Il Para Para ($)
7. VALLE DELL'ACATE, Acate
   Cerasuolo di Vittoria Classico Iri da Iri ($$)
   Cerasuolo di Vittoria Classico ($)

Cerasuolo di Vittoria

Vittoria DOC

It is said to be the secondary DOC of Cerasuolo di Vittoria DOCG, for which the most widely used grape varieties and from which the most notable results are obtained are from Nero d'Avola and Frappato. Annual production is just over six hundred thousand bottles.

—

Producers and their trademark and signature wines:

8. JUDEKA, Caltagirone
   Vittoria Nero d'Avola ($)
7. VALLE DELL'ACATE, Acate
   Vittoria Frappato ($)

Eloro DOC

We are between the provinces of Siracusa and Ragusa, in the realm of the Nero d'Avola grape, to which Frappato and Pignatello—or Perricone, as it is called here—can be added. This DOC only covers reds and rosés, and produces wines with distinct fruity notes on the nose and fresh savoriness on the palate. Two hundred eighty thousand bottles are produced each year.

—

Producers and their trademark and signature wines:

1. CURTO, Ispica
    Eloro Nero d'Avola Fontanelle ($)
2. RIOFAVARA, Ispica
    Eloro Nero d'Avola Spaccaforno ($)

Siracusa DOC

A small and cohesive DOC, relating only to the territory of the municipality of Siracusa and with less than 49 acres from which almost thirty thousand bottles are produced annually, where the most particular results are obtained from the white Muscat grape. The grapes are lightly dried, so the aromas lead to honey and dried figs, while the flavor is delicately sweet.

—

Producers and their trademark and signature wines:

3. CANTINE GULINO, Siracusa
    Siracusa Moscato Don Nuzzo ($)
4. PUPILLO, Siracusa
    Siracusa Moscato Pollio ($)

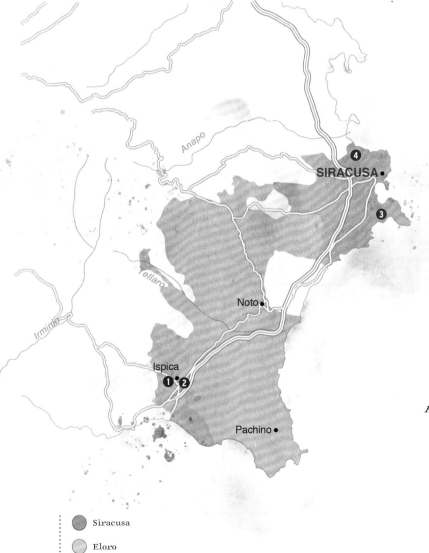

Siracusa

Eloro

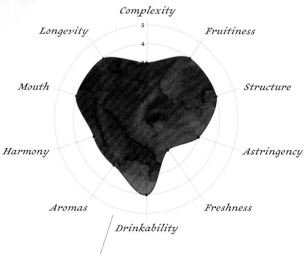

Eloro Nero d'Avola

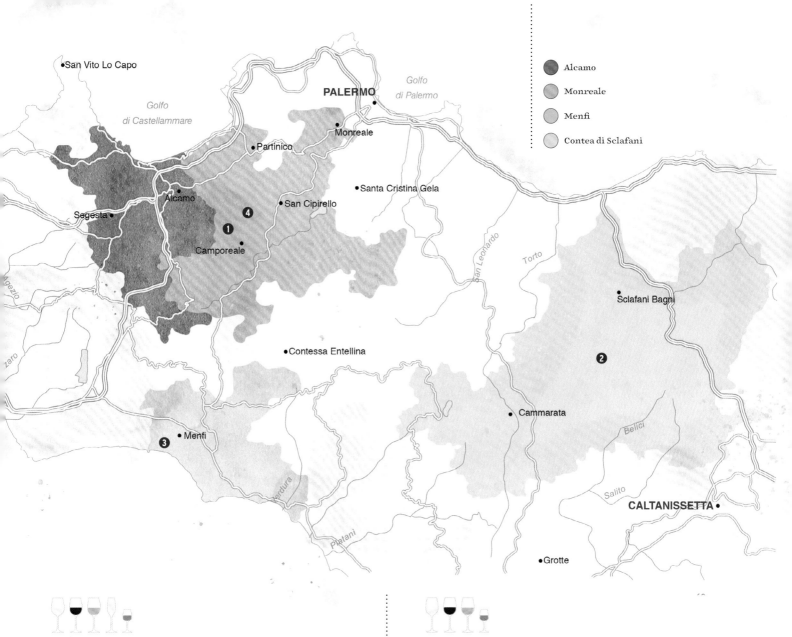

Alcamo DOC

A growing DOC, which is gradually shedding its former reputation in which this area was simply seen as a supplier of grapes and wines for the wineries of Northern Italy. The production area covers ten municipalities, including Alcamo, between the provinces of Trapani and Palermo. There are various versions, in white and red, but the outstanding type is the Alcamo Bianco Classico, from Catarratto grapes, in this case delicately aged in wood. Flowers and white fruits combine with notes of citrus, followed by a decisive and rich taste, not lacking in freshness. Total annual production is 1.5 million bottles.

—

Producer and its trademark and signature wine:

1. TENUTA RAPITALÀ, Camporeale
    Alcamo Bianco Classico Vigna Casalj ($)

Contea di Sclafani or Valledolmo-Contea di Sclafani DOC

A little-used designation, it originates from vineyards in the provinces of Palermo, where Sclafani Bagni is located, as well as Caltanissetta and Agrigento. The DOC permits the use of numerous varieties, including international ones, but the most outstanding result in terms of quality and quantity comes from the Rosso type, made from Perricone and Nero d'Avola grapes. There is joyful freshness of black fruits and spices on the nose, and remarkable harmony in the mouth, despite the imposing body. Overall production is one hundred twenty thousand bottles per year.

—

Producer and its trademark and signature wine:

2. TASCA D'ALMERITA, Sclafani Bagni
    Contea di Sclafani Rosso Riserva del Conte ($$$$)

Menfi DOC

A complex DOC located between the provinces of Agrigento and Trapani. Local and international grapes are grown on an area of less than 494 acres under vine, producing about 1.1 million bottles a year. Our recommendation is for a fruity white wine with a good palate, aged in steel only from Inzolia grapes, also known as Ansonica.

—

Producer and its trademark and signature wine:

3. BARBERA, Menfi
   Menfi Inzolia Dietro le Case ($)

....

Monreale DOC

A composite DOC, covering the territory of eight municipalities in the province of Palermo, where both local and international grapes can be grown. Our preference goes to a rather citrusy Catarratto with a gratifying savoriness. An average of two hundred thousand bottles per year are produced from 94 acres of vineyards.

—

Producer and its trademark and signature wine:

4. FEUDO DISISA, Monreale
   Monreale Catarratto Lu Bancu ($)

Marsala DOC

It is said that the history of Marsala was born in 1774, when merchant John Woodhouse began exporting this wine to London, adding a bit of alcohol to ensure the best possible preservation. It immediately achieved considerable success and encouraged the birth of numerous new cellars. These days, Marsala does not enjoy the fortunes of past centuries, due to changing tastes and a production that often favors quantity over quality. The DOC covers almost the entire province of Trapani and is quite varied, due to the grapes used, the method of enrichment, and the different residual sugar content; this gives rise to very different types. The recommended versions, from a vast selection based on an annual production that approaches seven million bottles, come from white grapes—Grillo above all—with a limited residual sugar content and long barrel aging. To allow the DOC wine to be relaunched, the Consorzio per la Tutela del Vino Marsala was reconstituted in 2022, with sixteen producers joining.

—

Producers and their trademark and signature wines:

1. Marco DE BARTOLI, Marsala
   Marsala Superiore Semisecco Riserva Oro Vigna La Miccia ($$)
2. FLORIO, Marsala
   Marsala Superiore Semisecco Riserva Ambra Donna Franca ($$)
   Marsala Vergine Secco Riserva Terre Arse ($)
3. HERITAGE – Francesco Intorcia, Marsala
   Marsala Vergine Secco Millesimato ($$)
   Marsala Superiore Semisecco Riserva Ambra ($$)

....

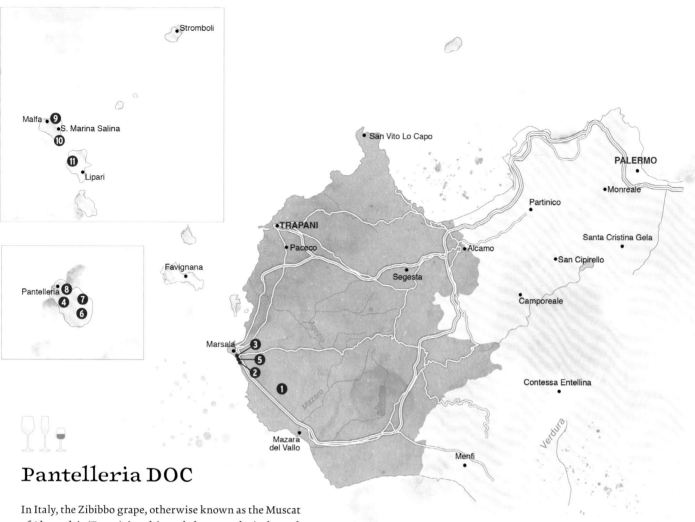

Pantelleria DOC

In Italy, the Zibibbo grape, otherwise known as the Muscat of Alexandria (Egypt), is cultivated almost exclusively on the island of Pantelleria, where it gives rise to this DOC, which includes several types, the most distinctive and well known of which is Passito. The grapes are laid out to dry in the sun and thus attain a considerable concentration of sugars, which give rise to both a good alcohol content—around 14% by volume—and a consistent sweet residue that makes the palate particularly persuasive. The aromas are very intense and mainly conjure honey and citrus fruits. Over 1.1 million bottles are produced annually.

—

Producers and their trademark and signature wines:

4. Marco DE BARTOLI, Pantelleria
    Passito di Pantelleria Bukkuram Sole d'Agosto ($$)
5. DONNAFUGATA, Marsala
    Passito di Pantelleria Ben Ryé ($$)
6. FERRANDES, Pantelleria
    Passito di Pantelleria ($$)
7. Salvatore MURANA, Pantelleria
    Passito di Pantelleria Martingana ($$$)
    Passito di Pantelleria Mueggen ($$)
8. SOLIDEA, Pantelleria
    Passito di Pantelleria ($$)

Malvasia delle Lipari DOC

Less than 25 acres are dedicated to this wine on the various islands that make up the Lipari archipelago. The aromas are persuasive and put dry apricot in the foreground, while on the palate the sweetness is contrasted by marked salinity: it is one of the world's great sweet wines. A total of around thirty thousand liters per year are produced, mostly offered in small bottles.

—

Producers and their trademark and signature wines:

9. CARAVAGLIO, Malfa
    Malvasia delle Lipari Passito ($$)
10. HAUNER, Santa Marina Salina
    Malvasia delle Lipari Passito Selezione Carlo
    Hauner ($$)
11. TENUTA DI CASTELLARO, Lipari
    Malvasia delle Lipari ($$)

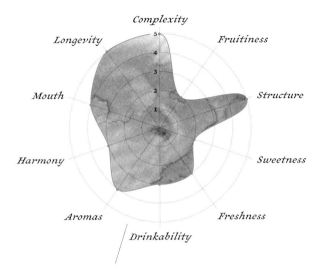

Marsala Vergine Secco

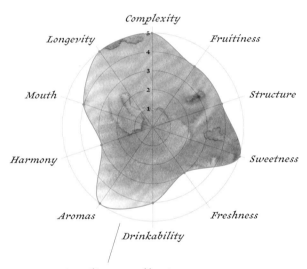

Passito di Pantelleria

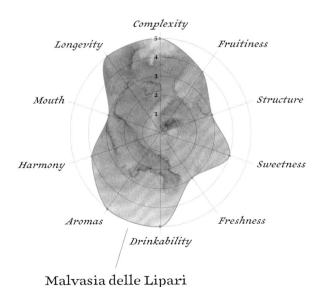

Malvasia delle Lipari

Sicilia DOC

The Sicilian region is undergoing a vast reorganization of its DOCs, since, as the 2011 regulations specify, the designation "Sicilia" may be used as the largest geographical unit for DOC/DOCG wines of the Sicilian region, provided that the use is expressly factored into the respective production specifications. Each individual DOC may therefore be included in the all-encompassing DOC Sicilia, such as Sicilia Contessa Entellina Chardonnay. Meanwhile, producers may choose to limit themselves to the use of DOC Sicilia without further specification, by highlighting only the type or grape variety, such as Sicilia Bianco or Sicilia Nero d'Avola, in a regulatory process that has been constantly evolving in recent years. Production has exceeded ninety-six million bottles in 2021, with good prospects for substantial growth thanks to the market's favorable reception of DOC Sicilia.

—

Producers and their trademark and signature wines:

1. ALESSANDRO DI CAMPOREALE, Camporeale
   Sicilia Syrah Kaid ($)
   Sicilia Catarratto Vigna di Mandranova ($)
2. ASSULI, Mazara del Vallo
   Sicilia Perricone Furioso ($)
   Sicilia Nero d'Avola Lorlando ($)
3. BAGLIO DEL CRISTO DEL CAMPOBELLO, Campobello di Licata
   Sicilia Nero d'Avola Lu Patri ($)
   Sicilia Grillo Lalùci ($)
4. BARRACO, Marsala
   Sicilia Grillo ($)
5. CASTELLUCCI MIANO, Valledolmo
   Sicilia Valledolmo-Contea di Sclafani Shiarà ($)
6. CENTOPASSI, San Cipirello
   Sicilia Catarratto Terre Rosse di Giabbascio ($)
7. CUSUMANO, Partinico
   Sicilia Nero d'Avola Sagana ($$)
8. DONNAFUGATA, Marsala
   Sicilia Rosso Mille e Una Notte (Nero d'Avola...) ($$$)
   Sicilia Contessa Entellina Chardonnay Chiarandà ($$)
9. DUCA DI SALAPARUTA, Casteldaccia
   Sicilia Nero d'Avola Duca Enrico ($$$)
10. FEUDI DEL PISCIOTTO, Niscemi
    Sicilia Nero d'Avola Versace ($)
11. FEUDO DISISA, Monreale
    Sicilia Chardonnay ($)
12. FEUDO MACCARI, Noto
    Sicilia Nero d'Avola Saia ($)
13. FEUDO MONTONI, Cammarata
    Sicilia Nero d'Avola Vrucara ($$)

14. FIRRIATO, Paceco
    Sicilia Harmonium (Nero d'Avola) ($$)
15. FONDO ANTICO, Trapani
    Sicilia Grillo Parlante ($)
16. GIODO, Castiglione di Sicilia
    Sicilia Nerello Mascalese Alberelli di Giodo ($$$)
17. GULFI, Chiaramonte Gulfi
    Sicilia Rosso NeroBufaleffj (Nero d'Avola) ($$)
    Sicilia Rosso NeroMaccarj (Nero d'Avola) ($$)
18. MANDRAROSSA – Cantine Settesoli, Menfi
    Sicilia Cartagho (Nero d'Avola) ($)
19. MORGANTE, Grotte
    Sicilia Nero d'Avola Riserva Don Antonio ($$)
20. Arianna OCCHIPINTI, Vittoria
    Sicilia Il Frappato ($$)
21. PLANETA, Menfi
    Sicilia Menfi Chardonnay Didacus ($$$)
    Sicilia Noto Santa Cecilia (Nero d'Avola) ($$)
    Sicilia Menfi Cometa (Fiano) ($)
22. PRINCIPI DI BUTERA, Butera
    Sicilia Nero d'Avola Deliella ($$)
23. RALLO, Marsala
    Sicilia Grillo Bianco Maggiore ($)
    Sicilia Zibibbo Al Qasar ($)
24. TASCA D'ALMERITA, Sclafani Bagni
    Sicilia Chardonnay Vigna San Francesco ($$)
    Sicilia Cabernet Sauvignon Vigna San Francesco
    ($$)
    Sicilia Contea di Sclafani Rosso del Conte ($$)
    Sicilia Grillo Mozia ($)
25. TENUTA GORGHI TONDI, Mazara del Vallo
    Sicilia Grillo Kheiré ($)
    Sicilia Rajah (Zibibbo) ($)
    Sicilia Segreante (Syrah) ($)
26. TENUTA RAPITALÀ, Camporeale
    Sicilia Hugonis (Nero d'Avola, Cabernet
    Sauvignon) ($)
27. VALDIBELLA, Camporeale
    Sicilia Nero d'Avola Kerasos ($)

Sicilia Grillo

Sicilia Catarratto

Recommended wines outside the DOC/DOCG designations:

28. BAGLIO DI PIANETTO, Santa Cristina Gela
    Shymer (Syrah, Merlot) ($)
4. BARRACO, Marsala
    Altomare (Grillo) ($$)
29. Mirella BUSCEMI, Bronte
    Tartaraci (Nerello Mascalese) ($$)
6. CENTOPASSI, San Cipirello
    Argille di Tagghia Via di Sutta (Nero d'Avola) ($)
30. Frank CORNELISSEN, Castiglione di Sicilia
    Munjebel Rosso BB (Nerello Mascalese) ($$$$)
7. CUSUMANO, Partinico
    Salealto Tenuta Ficuzza
    (Grillo, Inzolia, Zibibbo) ($$)
31. Marco DE BARTOLI, Marsala
    Vecchio Samperi Perpetuo Quarantennale
    (Inzolia, Catarratto, Grillo) ($$$$$)
32. DEI PRINCIPI DI SPADAFORA, Monreale
    Siriki Rosso (Syrah) ($$)
33. GUCCIONE, San Cipirello
    C (Catarratto) ($)
34. HIBISCUS, Ustica
    Grotta dell'Oro (Zibibbo) ($)
    Zhabib Zibibbo Passito ($$)
35. MANENTI, Scicli
    Frappato ($)
36. MARABINO, Noto
    Rosso di Contrada Parrino (Nero d'Avola) ($)
    Moscato della Torre ($)
37. PALARI, Messina
    Rosso del Soprano (Nerello Mascalese, Nerello
    Cappuccio, Nocera) ($)
38. PASSOPISCIARO, Castiglione di Sicilia
    Contrada R (Nerello Mascalese) ($$)
    Contrada C (Nerello Mascalese) ($$)
    Contrada G (Nerello Mascalese) ($$)
21. PLANETA, Menfi
    Riesling Eruzione 1614 ($$)
39. VITE AD OVEST, Marsala
    Ghammi (Nero d'Avola) ($)

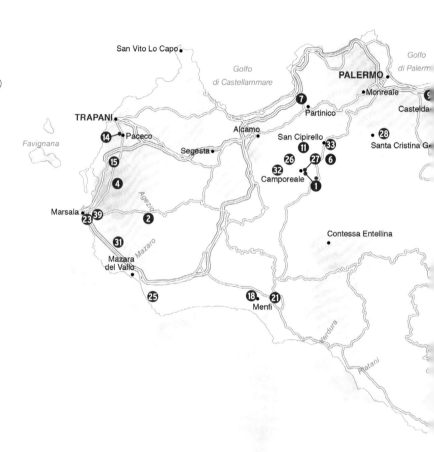

Pecorini Malfa Lipari

Faro Superiore

MESSINA

Barcellona
Pozzo di Gotto

Furnari

(37)

Grotte

Castiglione
di Sicilia

Randazzo (8) (30)

(29)

Linguaglossa

(16) (38)

Bronte

ETNA

Milo

Sclafani Bagni

Valledolmo (5)

(24)

(13)

Curo

Belici

Saliso

Salito

Trecastagni Viagrande

CALTANISSETTA

Simeto

CATANIA

Gornalunga

Grotte

(9)

Salso

Campobello
di Licata

(3) (22)

Butera

Caltagirone

Gela

Niscemi

(10)

Acate

(17)

Anapo

SIRACUSA

Acate

(35)

(20)

Chiaramonte
Gulfi

Vittoria

RAGUSA

Tellaro

Modica

Irminio

Noto

Scicli

Ispica

(36) (12)

Pachino

TASCA D'ALMERITA
Contrada Regaleali
Sclafani Bagni (PA)
tascadalmerita.it
Year of establishment: 1830
Owner: the Tasca
d'Almerita family
Average number of
bottles produced per year:
2,600,000

A prestigious company
steeped in history, deservedly
famous for offering great
interpretations of traditional
as well as international
grape varieties, in particular
through the always
impeccable Chardonnay
and Cabernet Sauvignon
Vigna San Francesco. The
vineyards extend over 1,160
acres in several estates: the
historic Regaleali in Sclafani
Bagni, Sallier de La Tour in
Camporeale, Capofaro in
Salina, Whitaker in Mozia,
and Tascante on Etna.

CONTEA DI SCLAFANI ROSSO
RISERVA DEL CONTE

First year of production: 1970
Average number of bottles produced
per year: 30,000
Grape varieties: Nero d'Avola (60%),
Perricone, other local varieties

A demonstration of the complexity and
longevity of the Nero d'Avola grape, capable
of improving for decades in the bottle.
The nose is particularly fruity due to the
presence of Perricone; it is also rich in
fresh notes reminiscent of eucalyptus. The
palate is dense and warm, well enlivened
by balsamic memories in the long finish. A
happy interpretation, in any vintage.

ALTA MORA - CUSUMANO
Contrada Verzella
Castiglione di Sicilia (CT)
altamora.it
Year of establishment: 2013
Owner: the Cusumano
family
Average number of bottles
produced per year: 100,000

Alta Mora constitutes an
autonomous project within
the Cusumano winery and
is aimed exclusively at the
establishment of Etna's main
historical vines, Nerello
Mascalese and Carricante.
The futuristic, largely
underground cellar, built
according to environmentally
friendly criteria, is already in
operation, while the 109 acres
acquired in various districts
are gradually increasing
production. The qualitative
results achieved in these
few years are already very
important, with wine critics
convincingly rewarding both
Etna Rosso and Etna Bianco.

ETNA ROSSO GUARDIOLA

First year of production: 2013
Average number of bottles produced
per year: 5,500
Grape variety: Nerello Mascalese

It originates from old vines grown as small
trees in a charming, terraced vineyard at an
altitude of between 2,625 and 3,280 feet. The
initial aromas tend toward berries and red
fruits such as black currants and blueberries,
followed by both citrus and finely vegetal
tones. The palate is characterized by a
restrained astringency, soft flesh, and refined
acidity that provides joyful drinkability. A
precise example of the elegance that can be
found on Etna.

PASSOPISCIARO
Contrada Guardiola
Castiglione di Sicilia (CT)
vinifranchetti.com/it/
passopisciaro
Year of establishment: 2000
Owner: the Franchetti
family
Average number of bottles
produced per year: 100,000

Andrea Franchetti has made
a decisive contribution to
the establishment of Nerello
Mascalese and Etna wines,
also developing knowledge
of the peculiarities of each
individual vine-growing area
through the indication of
the "Contrade," geographical
specifications that are now the
focus of an important annual
event. Thus, from 64 acres
of very old vines, six labels
dedicated to the company's
various plots of land have been
created, flanked by a "super-
Etna" that is as unthinkable
as it is successful, made from
Petit Verdot and Cesanese
d'Affile grapes. The only red
production to use Etna DOC
is Passorosso, the result of a
blend derived from different
Contrade.

CONTRADA R

First year of production: 2008
Average number of bottles produced
per year: 3,000
Grape variety: Nerello Mascalese

The grapes come from the estate's highest
vineyard, in the Rampante district at an
altitude of around 3,280 feet, and are
characterized by a particularly rich nose
and a soft, fresh palate. Matured in large
wood, it has refined hints of small red and
black fruits that give way to a dynamic and
harmonious flavor, never very astringent
and enlivened by a touch of savoriness. A
rare expression of Etna's potential.

BENANTI
Via G. Garibaldi 361
Viagrande (CT)
benanti.it
Year of establishment: 1988
Owner: the Benanti family
Average number of bottles
produced per year: 170,000

Giuseppe Benanti was, until
his death in 2023, one of
the earliest proponents of
the great potential not only
of Etna's reds but also of its
whites, demonstrating, in
particular, their excellent
ability to evolve in the bottle.
From the 74 acres of vineyards,
organically farmed on the
typical terraces with dry-
stone walls, fourteen labels
are produced, in which, in
addition to the Etna Bianco
Superiore Contrada Rinazzo,
the Etna Rosso Riserva
Rovittello, the Etna Rosso
Contrada Cavaliere, and the
famous Etna Bianco Superiore
Pietra Marina stand out with
regularity. A winery that, over
thirty-five years, has played a
decisive role in the creation of
Etna's new oenological history.

ETNA BIANCO SUPERIORE
CONTRADA RINAZZO

First year of production: 2018
Average number of bottles produced
per year: 4,000
Grape variety: Carricante

Enchanting and typical aromas of white
flowers, citrus fruits, and medicinal herbs
anticipate a taste of great acidic freshness,
rich in pulp and low in alcohol, in which
savory saline notes move through to a
finish of great purity with hints of the
Mediterranean scrub. Matured in steel
only, it best represents the greatness of the
Carricante grape.

COTTANERA

Strada Provinciale 89,
Contrada Iannazzo
Castiglione di Sicilia (CT)
cottanera.it
Year of establishment: 1990
Owner: the Cambria
family
Average number of bottles
produced per year: 300,000

A winery that, despite
having 136 acres under vine,
remains strictly family-run,
with a shared commitment
to continuing research into
the winery's viticultural
potential, starting with the
separate vinification of each
parcel in order to identify its
peculiarities. Production is
centered on Etna, with results
consistently rewarded by
critics not only for Zottorinoto
but also for Rosso Feudo di
Mezzo and Bianco Calderara.

ETNA ROSSO RISERVA ZOTTORINOTO

First year of production: 2011
Average number of bottles produced
per year: 2,000
Grape variety: Nerello Mascalese

It is born in the similarly named district at
an altitude of around 2,628 feet and, after
two years in the barrel, reveals delicate
and very articulate aromas, in which red
fruit and herbs prevail over notes of sweet
spices. The palate is of considerable matter,
pleasantly warm, particularly elegant in its
hint of tannicity, and enticing thanks to its
savoriness. Few bottles, many merits.

PIETRADOLCE

Contrada Rampante
Castiglione di Sicilia (CT)
pietradolce.it
Year of establishment: 2005
Owner: the Faro family
Average number of bottles
produced per year: 80,000

The grapes from 74 acres of
these vineyards are dedicated
predominantly to Nerello
Mascalese, with the oldest
saplings reaching up to a
century in age. They arrive in
the extraordinary wine cellar,
along a pathway full of works
of art. The winery's style is
aimed at confident elegance,
achieved with the help of
expert oenological consultants
and some small French wood.
The success of the Etna Rosso
does not slow down the
commitment to the Carricante
grape, from which the already
award-winning Sant'Andrea
and Etna Bianco Archineri are
made.

ETNA ROSSO BARBAGALLI

First year of production: 2010
Average number of bottles produced
per year: 2,000
Grape variety: Nerello Mascalese

After twenty months in small French oak
barrels, it announces and declares itself with
notes of pepper and smoke on a good base
of red fruits and rose petals, in an articulate
and refined whole; the taste is well marked
by a persistent tannicity in the background,
while the pleasant acidic freshness
emerges clearly until the elegant finish
with red flowers and incense. The complex
refinement of Etna.

GRACI

Località Passopisciaro,
Contrada Arcuria
Castiglione di Sicilia (CT)
graci.eu
Year of establishment: 2004
Owner: the Aiello Graci
family
Average number of bottles
produced per year: 95,000

The 74 acres of organically
cultivated vineyards are
located in various districts in
the Passopisciaro area, known
throughout history for the
high quality of its grapes.
Alberto Aiello interprets his
vineyards with painstaking
faithfulness, using only local
vines planted with high
density and very low yields,
avoiding the use of invasive
wood during the maturation
process in the cellar. In
addition to the Arcuria,
presented with the label, the
superselection Arcuria Sopra
il Pozzo and the Etna Rosso
Feudo di Mezzo now enjoy
particular praise. In 2016, the
Idda project, a winery founded
together with Angelo Gaja
from Piedmont, was born.

ETNA ROSSO ARCURÌA

First year of production: 2011
Average number of bottles produced
per year: 6,000
Grape variety: Nerello Mascalese

The nose expresses a rare and delicate
complexity that ranges from spices to
Mediterranean herbs to small red fruits,
with suggestions of black pepper, oregano,
and currants. The palate is gently rounded
by the long passage in large wood,
pleasantly fresh and harmonious, sinuous
and barely astringent, enthralling all the
way to the finish that recalls citrus fruits as
well as a more severe and reviving hint of
rhubarb.

GIROLAMO RUSSO

Frazione Passopisciaro,
Via Regina Margherita 78
Castiglione di Sicilia (CT)
girolamorusso.it
Year of establishment: 2005
Owner: Giuseppe Russo
Average number of bottles
produced per year: 90,000

Giuseppe Russo has made a
name for himself in recent
years as one of the most
attentive interpreters of
Etna's red wines, all of which
share a precise respect for
each vineyard's individual
personality and noninvasive
cellar techniques. Hence the
decision to offer numerous
labels, in addition to the one
presented here, based on
Nerello Mascalese. It ranges
from the more immediate
'A Rina to the unobtainable
Piano delle Colombe, from the
fragrant Feudo di Mezzo to
the fruity Calderara Sottana,
all preferring used wood and
spontaneous fermentation.
The property's 49 acres are
organically managed.

ETNA ROSSO SAN LORENZO

First year of production: 2005
Average number of bottles produced
per year: 4,500
Grape varieties: Nerello Mascalese,
Nerello Cappuccio

Quite intense aromas in which berries
and spices dominate, with a fine note of
rosemary to give olfactory vivacity. An
important and structured taste in which the
presence of acidity plays a perfect balancing
role, ensuring harmony. Nice finish with
hints of medicinal herbs to give freshness
and elegance.

TENUTA DELLE TERRE NERE

Contrada Calderara
Randazzo (CT)
tenutaterrenere.com
Year of establishment: 2001
Owner: the De Grazia family
Average number of bottles produced per year: 290,000

Marc De Grazia, thanks to his work as a wine importer, has always been a careful explorer of the relationship between wine and *terroir*. In his cellar on Etna, he is even more meticulous, studying the potential of each plot and its adaptability to the historical local grape varieties, both red and white. The 109 organically cultivated acres thus give rise to numerous labels that, like San Lorenzo, are a model of fidelity to the individual vineyard and regularly receive prestigious ratings, from the Etna Rosso Feudo di Mezzo Il Quadro delle Rose to the Calderara Sottana to the Etna Bianco Montalto, from Carricante grapes. The winery that has relaunched Etna at the summit of world oenology.

ETNA ROSSO SAN LORENZO

First year of production: 2015
Average number of bottles produced per year: 9,000
Grape variety: Nerello Mascalese

It originates from 20 dedicated acres on the north slope of the volcano and offers a rich range of aromas in which wilted roses, violets, and cherries are joined by the fine contribution of French oak bringing smoky and spicy notes. The palate is both structured and furrowed by fresh tannins, with a superb finish in which citrus notes and a touch of vanilla appear.

TENUTA DI FESSINA

Frazione Rovittello, via Nazionale 22
Castiglione di Sicilia (CT)
tenutadifessina.com
Year of establishment: 2007
Owner: Lavinia Silva
Average number of bottles produced per year: 65,000

The winery built with skill and determination by Silvia Maestrelli is now run by her daughter Lavinia, who manages 35 acres of vines as well as a splendid and well-structured company headquarters. The most important cultivated area is around the winery in Rovittello, on the northern slope of the volcano, but there are also vineyards in Milo, facing east, and in Biancavilla, facing south. This gives rise to six labels including the Etna Bianco A' Puddara and the Etna Musmeci, both white and red, which are particularly marked out for awards.

ETNA BIANCO A' PUDDARA

First year of production: 2009
Average number of bottles produced per year: 9,000
Grape variety: Carricante

It is matured in large French oak barrels and brings out, above all, the hints of citrus and medicinal herbs typical of Carricante. In the mouth, it is soft at first and then increasingly fresh and acidulous, closing with refined hints of tropical fruit. Always one of the most successful expressions of Etna Bianco.

PALARI

Frazione Santo Stefano Briga, Contrada Barna
Messina
palari.it
Year of establishment: 1990
Owner: Salvatore Geraci
Average number of bottles produced per year: 36,000

The many varieties of indigenous grapes grow on 17 terraced acres, cultivated with the alberello system, overlooking the Strait of Messina, in a position as scenic as it is difficult to work due to the steep slopes. It is here that Salvatore Geraci, an expert connoisseur of great wines from all over the world, decided to create his ideal wine, Palari. This now famous label is joined by Rosso del Soprano, similar in approach and slightly less concentrated, and the elegant Etna Bianco Rocca Coeli. Small numbers, big wines.

FARO PALARI

First year of production: 1995
Average number of bottles produced per year: 12,000
Grape varieties: Nerello Mascalese (50%), Nerello Cappuccio (40%), Nocera (10%)

The fruity, floral, and spicy aromas typical of the two types of Nerello are enriched by the contribution of the French oak, which brings memories of smoke and roasting without altering the composite personality of the grape. The flavor is of good warmth and splendid balance, refined, with a finish of tasty hints of red berries and citrus fruits. Elegance and complexity.

CARAVAGLIO

Via Provinciale 33
Malfa di Salina (ME)
caravaglio.it
Year of establishment: 1989
Owner: Antonino Caravaglio
Average number of bottles produced per year: 65,000

Antonino Caravaglio continues to passionately explore the Aeolian Islands in search of old vineyards to bring back to life with renewed productivity, each cultivated with the grapes that have historically proved best suited to that specific *terroir*. He has thus recently added to the 27 organically cultivated acres in Salina, Lipari, and Stromboli with vineyards in Panarea; the vines range from Malvasia di Lipari to Catarratto, from Nerello Mascalese to Corinto Nero. Wines of great expressiveness and purity.

MALVASIA DELLE LIPARI PASSITO

First year of production: 1989
Average number of bottles produced per year: 5,500 (50 cl) (17 fl oz)
Grape varieties: Malvasia di Lipari (95%), Corinto Nero (5%)

The grapes are laid out in the sun to dry immediately after the harvest, then the wine is matured partly in steel and partly in wood. The aromas are as deep and compelling as imaginable, with walnuts, sultanas, and figs in clear evidence against a background of aromatic herbs. The palate offers a remarkable sweetness that rests on a refreshing acidic framework, at times savory, guaranteeing harmonious pleasantness.

MARCO DE BARTOLI
Contrada Bukkuram 9
Pantelleria (TP)
marcodebartoli.com
Year of establishment: 1978
Owner: the De Bartoli
family
Average number of bottles
produced per year: 150,000

Marco De Bartoli has been
a faithful interpreter of the
local winemaking tradition,
to which he has added that
touch of experimentation
rewarded by his curiosity
and passion. He has thus
created prestigious versions
of Marsala wines with even
decades of aging and, from
the 12 acres he owns on
Pantelleria, a small offering
in which two versions of
Bukkuram—the Sole d'Agosto
and the Padre della Vigna—
stand out.

PASSITO DI PANTELLERIA BUKKURAM SOLE D'AGOSTO
First year of production: 1984
Average number of bottles produced
per year: 13,000
Grape variety: Zibibbo

The inviting, luminous amber color is
followed by enchanting aromas of withered
fruits, from figs to grapes, joined by
memories of custard and, above it all, a fresh
breath of sea air: this is rare complexity.
The taste is sweet and very soft, thanks to
a residual sugar content close to 130 g/l (4.3
oz/qt), marked by an acidic backbone that
enlivens and ensures exciting drinkability,
facilitated by a low dose of sulfur dioxide.

DUCA DI SALAPARUTA
Strada Statale 113, Via
Nazionale
Casteldaccia (PA)
duca.it
Year of establishment: 1824
Owner: Illva Saronno, and
the Reina family
Average number of
bottles produced per year:
9,500,000

The Casteldaccia wine cellar
winds its way through steel
vats along a route that can
be cycled, given the many
grapes brought here from the
various estates the cellar owns,
joined by those of numerous
established vintners. Already
known in the nineteenth
century due to the work
of Giuseppe Alliata, today
it operates on 3,830 acres
through two main production
lines, the one labeled Corvo
and the Duca di Salaparuta,
as well as with Florio, the
famous name for Marsala.
A winery that has chosen to
focus more and more on the
territorial identity of its wines,
as evidenced by the new Suòlo
line.

SICILIA NERO D'AVOLA DUCA ENRICO
First year of production: 1984
Average number of bottles produced
per year: 15,000
Grape variety: Nero d'Avola

For forty years, this has been classic Nero
d'Avola at the highest level, the fruit of
carefully selected grapes and an eighteen-
month maturation in French oak. The fruity
component is enriched by a fine spiciness
and stimulating herbal reminder, while the
taste is particularly powerful, with a soft
velvet resting on a gentle layer of tannins,
very long and persuasive. Of well-deserved
international success, it has joined the Sicilia
DOC as of the 2018 vintage.

DONNAFUGATA
Via S. Lipari 18
Marsala (TP)
donnafugata.it
Year of establishment: 1983
Owner: the Rallo family
Average number of
bottles produced per year:
2,700,000

Giacomo Rallo, endowed
with a profound passion for
the world of wine and a rare
entrepreneurial ability, has
built up a world-famous, first-
class winery that has been run
with equal commitment by
his family since 2016. The vast
estates, with 1,013 acres under
vine, comprise four different
winegrowing areas, the main
labels of which are Contessa
Entellina (Mille e Una Notte,
Chiarandà Chardonnay),
Pantelleria (Passito di
Pantelleria Ben Ryé), Acate
(Cerasuolo di Vittoria
Floramundi), and Randazzo
(Etna Rosso Contrada
Marchesa), while Marsala
is home to the enchanting
historic cellars. One of the
most brilliant examples of
modern quality wine in Sicily.

PASSITO DI PANTELLERIA BEN RYÉ
First year of production: 1983
Average number of bottles produced
per year: 70,000
Grape variety: Zibibbo

Made from partially dried grapes vinified
in steel, it has intense aromas ranging
from dried fruit—dates, apricots, almonds,
grapes, figs—to incense and Mediterranean
herbs. The taste has the dual virtues of
sweetness and freshness, in a perfect balance
that builds an enveloping and very long,
stimulating, and fascinating taste. Sunny
and Mediterranean, it is one of the world's
finest sweet wines, born in one of the
world's most evocative natural settings.

FEUDO MONTONI
Contrada Montoni Vecchi
Cammarata (AG)
feudomontoni.it
Year of establishment: 1469
Owner: Fabio Sireci
Average number of bottles
produced per year: 250,000

The splendid old "baglio" has
been renovated over the last
century by the Sireci family,
who have made it functional
for vinifying grapes from their
99 acres, which are organically
cultivated. The winery's
protagonist is the Nero
d'Avola, but the company's ten
labels have also been widely
awarded for wines made from
Grillo, Catarratto, Inzolia, and
Nerello Mascalese. The winery
is committed to the recovery
of ancient local varieties and
the peculiarities of the genetic
heritage of old vines through
the use of mass selection.
These wines are a true
expression of the territory's
history.

SICILIA NERO D'AVOLA VRUCARA
First year of production: 1980
Average number of bottles produced
per year: 5,000
Grape Variety: Nero d'Avola

It originates from sapling plants derived
from an ancient Nero d'Avola biotype,
hence the wine is presented with the
appellation "prephylloxera." At the end of
the long maturation process, which lasts
for more than four years mostly in cement,
harmonious aromas are to be found,
especially of red fruits and flowers, citrus
fruits and spices. The palate is reminiscent
of velvet and silk, thanks to the presence of
particularly soft tannins, while the finish is
of precise elegance and rich in licorice hints.
It has a strong personality.

GULFI
Contrada Patria
Chiaramonte Gulfi (RG)
gulfi.it
Year of establishment: 1996
Owner: the Catania family
Average number of bottles
produced per year: 200,000

Three production centers in
different areas of the island
allow for a wide range of
output, all with a precise
territorial imprint in the
various vineyards making up
the 148 acres, all organically
cultivated, of the company's
estate. The winery successfully
founded by Vito Catania
immediately made a name for
itself thanks to the various
productions of Nero d'Avola,
cultivated around Pachino,
but solid and firm results have
already been consolidated
with Cerasuolo di Vittoria and,
more recently, on Etna, where
not only Nerello Mascalese but
also Pinot Noir is cultivated.
These are interpretations of
Nero d'Avola at the highest
level.

SICILIA ROSSO NEROBUFALEFFJ
First year of production: 2000
Average number of bottles produced
per year: 7,000
Grape variety: Nero d'Avola

Matured for two years in oak, it combines
the typical red fruit component with hints
of the freshness of Mediterranean herbs and
orange peel. The taste has a splendid vigor,
with a touch of acidity and the pressure
of the tannins cloaking a consistent fruity
flesh, creating a tasty harmony. The rich
personality of Nero d'Avola in purity.

PLANETA
Contrada Dispensa
Menfi (AG)
planeta.it
Year of establishment: 1995
Owner: the Planeta family
Average number of
bottles produced per year:
2,400,000

A company that has made
a decisive contribution to
the relaunch of oenological
Sicily, creating in a quarter
of a century a splendid
establishment based on 964
acres of property. The cellars
are located in Menfi, Noto,
Vittoria, on Mount Etna,
in the Syracuse area, and
at Capo Milazzo on the sea
in the province of Messina.
From these come increasingly
famous labels such as Sicilia
Nerello Mascalese Eruzione
1614 and Sicilia Carricante
Eruzione 1614, Sicilia Menfi
Chardonnay and Sicilia
Menfi Burdese, Noto Santa
Cecilia, Vittoria Frappato, and
Cerasuolo di Vittoria Classico
Dorilli. The level of quality is
very high, making it difficult
to pick out the label that has
received the most awards from
international wine critics.

SICILIA NOTO SANTA CECILIA
First year of production: 1997
Average number of bottles produced
per year: 90,000
Grape variety: Nero d'Avola

Matured for fourteen months in small oak
barrels, it elegantly offers both the typical
spiciness of toasted oak and the rich fruit
component typical of the grape variety,
from plum to blood orange; taste-wise, in
the mouth it has good muscle and excellent
balance, with barely perceptible tannins and
valid freshness. A great expression of a great
grape variety, the Nero d'Avola.

Sardinia

There is a three-thousand-year-old oenological history, the sea that has favored the arrival of vines from France and Spain, 1,865 miles of splendid coastline that guarantees a flowing consumption of wine by millions of tourists, new enterprises that are emerging after a few decades of stagnation, and historical brands that are renewing themselves to enter international markets. There is a very multifaceted production that is capable of growing, especially thanks to modern interpretations of historical vines such as Cannonau and Vermentino.

Following the territories of the different DOCs is of little use because the most important ones—the red ones dedicated to Cannonau and Monica, the white ones to Vermentino and Moscato—cover the entire region and do not give due prominence to the peculiarities of individual *terroirs*. It is a bit like if Tuscany were to have a single DOC for Sangiovese grapes and Piedmont a single DOC for Nebbiolo. Help in finding one's bearings comes from the island's only DOCG, Vermentino di Gallura, indicating the area of choice for the Vermentino grape, which is also successfully cultivated in other areas. A timid attempt to indicate particularly suitable areas also comes from Cannonau, whose label can indicate one of the three subzones set out in the production regulations: Oliena, Jerzu, and Capo Ferrato.

It is therefore worth relying on the oenological chronicles of those who have traveled in this region, which is often referred to as the "island-continent" for its unique quirks that are not found elsewhere. In the northeastern part is the area of Alghero, which has earned a good reputation thanks to the presence of the most important private Sardinian winery, Sella&Mosca. Moving eastward is Gallura, on whose granite soils the Vermentino grape springs forth, giving rise to heavily fragrant grape clusters.

Moving toward the central-western part we find two oxidative whites as equally famous as they are (now) off the routes of mass consumption: the dry Vernaccia di Oristano and the softer Malvasia di Bosa, both more than worth tasting. To the east, we then find the area most suited to Cannonau, with the Barbagia and Ogliastra areas demonstrating the true potential of this grape, destined to keep building its international reputation.

The southern Sardinian scene sees the presence of many and often good local grapes but is still firmly occupied by Carignano del Sulcis, which also grows on sandier soils close to the sea, enhancing its aromatic qualities, and further inland, where it is more robust and astringent.

In terms of vineyard location, rather flat areas prevail at 68%, followed by hilly areas at 26%, and mountainous areas at 6%, for a total cultivated surface area of 66,720 acres, slightly decreasing in recent years, and an annual production of 17.2 million gallons. There is a strong presence of community wine cellars, which in their twenty-one production facilities process

55% of total regional production. The number of wineries is decidedly high, at thirty-eight thousand, with an average property area of less than 2.5 acres.

....

MAIN VINES GROWN IN THE REGION

Bovale, Cagnulari

While in the past, the Cagnulari was thought to be a clone of the Sardinian Bovale, recent genetic profiling has confirmed that these ancient indigenous reds, reported here in Alghero DOC, Mandrolisai, and outside the designations, are in fact exactly the same vine, identical to the Spanish Graciano, Parraleta, and Tintilla de Rota. Moreover, Bovale Grande is also genetically identical to Carignano, which in Spain is called Mazuelo: all signs of the Spanish imprint on Sardinian viticulture. They are often used in blends to which they bring structure, tannin, and good alcohol content, as well as a strong flavor of ripe red fruit.

Cannonau

(→ also Grenache, International Grape Varieties)
It is the most cultivated grape in Sardinia: it withstands the heat and leads to powerful wines with an alcohol content that rises even above 15% by volume. Its origin is still shrouded in mystery: DNA analysis confirms an 82% sharing of genetic heritage between Cannonau and Garnacha, a grape variety originating in Aragon. Sardinia was Spanish from 1479 to 1720—when it passed to the House of Savoy—but Sardinian settlements in Spain existed as far back as 800 BC, in Nuragic times, because of flourishing trade with the Phoenicians. So it could be that Grenache derives from Cannonau and not vice versa, and that Cannonau has become ampelographically distinct from Grenache in recent centuries. In any case, it is a great grape variety that represents the essence of the Mediterranean: in addition to Sardinia and Spain, where it is the most widespread after the Tempranillo, it has acclimatized in

Isola di Budelli
Isola S.Maria
Isola Maddalena
Isola Caprera

VERMENTINO DI GALLURA

Luogosanto
Arzachena

Costa Smeralda

Isola Asinara

Golfo dell'Asinara

Liscia

GALLURA

Luras
Telti
OLBIA
Golfo di Olbia
Loiri Porto San Paolo

MOSCATO DI SORSO - SENNORI

ROMANGIA

Sorso
Sennori
S. Pietro di Simbranos

TEMPIO PAUSANIA

Monte Limbara 1162

Monti

Isola Molara

SASSARI

Lago del Coghinas

ALGHERO

Alghero

S.S. Trinità di Saccargia

LOGUDORO

Santuario di Valverde

San Pietro di Sorres

Tirso

BARONIE

Monte Albo 1127

Mar Mediterraneo

San Nicolò di Trullas

MALVASIA DI BOSA

PLANARGIA

Bosa

Abbazia di S. Maria di Corte

NUORO
Dorgali
Oliena
Mamoiada
Golfo di Orosei

Monte Ferru 1050

VERNACCIA DI ORISTANO

Lago Omodeo

Taloro

CANNONAU DI SARDEGNA CLASSICO

Neoneli

Isola di Mal di Ventre

Tramatza
Zeddiani
Cabras
ORISTANO

Sorgono
MANDROLISAI
Atzara

BARBAGIA

Monti del Gennargentu 1834

OGLIASTRA

Baunei

Flumendosa

Golfo di Oristano

Arborea

ARBOREA

GENNARGENTU

TORTOLÌ

Mar Tirreno

LANUSEI

Jerzu

Mannu

Gergei

TERRALBA

MEDIO CAMPIDANO

SANLURI

Lago Mulargia

TREXENTA

VILLACIDRO

CAGLIARI

IGLESIAS

Serdiana
Dolianova

Isola di S. Pietro

CARBONIA

Settimo San Pietro

Calasetta

IGLESIENTE

Giba
Santadi

CAGLIARI

Sant'Antioco

CARIGNANO DEL SULCIS

Sant'Anna Arresi

Golfo di Palmas

Isola di S. Antioco

Golfo di Cagliari

Isola dei Cavoli

Châteauneuf-du-Pape and Provence, as well as in Croatia, Cyprus, Malta, Turkey, Morocco, Algeria, and Israel, before its latest travels, which have taken it to Australia. Traditionally associated with the idea of very full-bodied and alcoholic wines, in recent years, thanks to scrupulous vinification, it also manages to express a pleasant freshness and structural harmony. On the nose, a variegated bouquet of ripe fruit emerges, particularly black currant and plum, Mediterranean herbs, eucalyptus, capers, and juniper, all wrapped in souvenirs of orange peel, rose, and dried violets, with spicy hints of pepper, cinnamon, and cloves. The finish is dry and balsamic unless it is vinified overripe, which adds a distinctive trait of berry jam and caramel.

Carignano

Having found its genius loci in the Sulcis lands, this delicate and difficult cultivar gives refined and pleasant wines of great harmony. Brilliant ruby red with violet reflections, fresh vinous perfume, blackberries, plums, currants, and blueberries, with herbaceous notes of laurel and juniper. Taut and snappy on the palate, with soft tannins, and an enveloping and persistent taste. It has been improved in Sardinia by Piedmont-born oenologist Giacomo Tachis, the man behind some of Italy's most celebrated wines, such as Sassicaia, Solaia, Tignanello, San Leonardo, Pelago, Mille e una Notte, and Turriga.

Malvasia di Sardegna

It grows on the white Planargia limestone, rich in marine fossils, and undergoes a long oxidative and concentration process to become the inimitable Malvasia di Bosa: a velvety, warm, heady wine with amber reflections and characteristic scents of toasted almond and hazelnut, helichrysum, and bergamot, with a dry and saline flavor, moderately sweet, defined by its producers as a "conversation wine."

Monica

Planted on the island by the Camaldolese monks a thousand years ago, and the protagonist of the similarly named DOC, it yields a dark, soft, and pleasant red wine, rich in vinous and earthy tones that are rounded off with proper aging. Consumed young, it is snappy and enjoyable for its sensations of fresh fruit such as currants, cherries, and pomegranate, accompanied by scents of bramble roses, cyclamen, and lilac, and a balsamic note of mint and cardamom.

Nasco

An indigenous white variety cultivated on thirty-odd acres, it is vinified on its own in the similarly named DOC area near Cagliari, or in blends in the production of sweet or liqueur wines in which it contributes good acidity and a range of aromas. These are of dried apricot and candied orange peel, honey, and saffron, with a recognizable hint of musk—*muscus* in Latin—from which it derives its name.

Pascale

Introduced by the Spanish and first identified in 1780 by agronomist Andrea Manca Dell'Arca in his treatise Agricoltura di Sardegna, it occupies one-fifth of the vineyards in the province of Sassari. In the experimental pure versions, it is bright red in color and evokes aromas of blackberry, black cherry, myrtle, and white pepper. The flavor is tannic, balsamic, and spicy.

Torbato

An indigenous white grape genetically identical to Malvasia de Roussillon or Malvasia dei Pirenei Orientali, it prefers limestone and clay soils with a warm, dry climate. In Alghero, Torbato DOC produces wines of a luminous straw-yellow color, with a wide range of Mediterranean scents, on which helichrysum, thistle, pear, and chamomile stand out, followed by a decisive, fresh, and marine flavor.

Vermentino (→ also Liguria)

Of all the *terroirs* in which it has taken root, it is on the arid granites of Gallura that it gives its best results, becoming one of the symbols of Sardinian viticulture: strong aromatic intensity, recognizable character, and great drinkability, with a wide range of aromas that recall apple and yellow melon, on nuances of Mediterranean scrub. A careful olfactory analysis reveals jasmine flowers, mimosa, and magnolia. The flavor is full and balanced between brilliant acidity and a fine iodine note reminiscent of saltiness and fresh sea breezes.

Vernaccia

An ancient cultivar for a mythological wine, Vernaccia di Oristano, capable of remaining as is, has been intact for more than a century. The first Vernaccia seeds date back three thousand years and were found in a nuraghe. Today, it is cultivated in the Tirso valley, between the highlands, called Gregori, and the lowlands, called Bennaxi. The wines have an oxidative character due to the long aging in drained barrels that goes on for years. The result is an extreme wine, dense and structured, difficult to decipher, with characteristic aromas of almond blossom. A wine for meditation.

The DOCG
- Vermentino di Gallura

The DOCs
- Alghero
- Arborea
- Cagliari
- Campidano di Terralba / Terralba
- Cannonau di Sardegna
- Carignano del Sulcis
- Girò di Cagliari
- Malvasia di Bosa
- Mandrolisai
- Monica di Sardegna
- Moscato di Sardegna
- Moscato di Sorso-Sennori / Moscato di Sorso or Moscato di Sennori
- Nasco di Cagliari
- Nuragus di Cagliari
- Sardegna Semidano
- Vermentino di Sardegna
- Vernaccia di Oristano

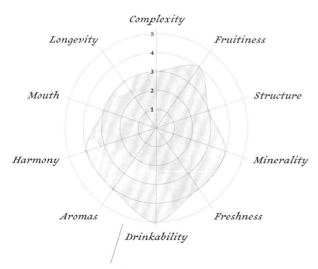

Vermentino di Gallura

Vermentino di Gallura DOCG and Vermentino di Sardegna DOC

Gallura has deserved DOCG status as home to the region's most significant Vermentino champions, at times endowed with an appealing salty note and always rich in personality, while worthy producers achieve impressive results in several areas. In the mouth, a delicate savoriness consistently prevails that well supports an acidity that is never excessive, while the aromas range from white flowers to a touch of pine resin, from citrus to white fruits and wisteria. Around six million bottles of Gallura DOCG are produced annually, and more than double that for Sardegna DOC.

—

Producers and their trademark and signature wines:

1. CANTINA GALLURA, Tempio Pausania
   Vermentino di Gallura Canayli Vendemmia Tardiva ($)
   Vermentino di Gallura Piras ($)
2. CANTINA PEDRES, Olbia
   Vermentino di Gallura Superiore Thilibas ($)
3. Giovanni Maria CHERCHI, Usini
   Vermentino di Sardegna Tuvaoes ($)
4. Antonella CORDA, Serdiana
   Vermentino di Sardegna ($)
5. Ferruccio DEIANA, Settimo San Pietro
   Vermentino di Sardegna Arvali ($)
6. LA CONTRALTA, Loiri Porto San Paolo
   Vermentino di Gallura Superiore Fiore del Sasso ($$)
7. LEDDA, Bonnanaro
   Vermentino di Gallura Superiore Soliànu Tenuta Matteu ($)
8. MASONE MANNU, Monti
   Vermentino di Gallura Petrizza ($)
   Vermentino di Gallura Superiore Costarenas ($)
9. MURA, Loiri Porto San Paolo
   Vermentino di Gallura Superiore Sienda ($)
10. PALA, Serdiana
    Vermentino di Sardegna Stellato ($)
11. SA RAJA, Telti
    Vermentino di Gallura Superiore ($)
12. SIDDÙRA, Luogosanto
    Vermentino di Gallura Superiore Maìa ($)
    Vermentino di Gallura Spèra ($)
13. SURRAU, Arzachena
    Vermentino di Gallura Superiore Sciala ($)
14. TENUTA ASINARA, Sorso
    Vermentino di Sardegna Indolente Vintage Grazia ($)

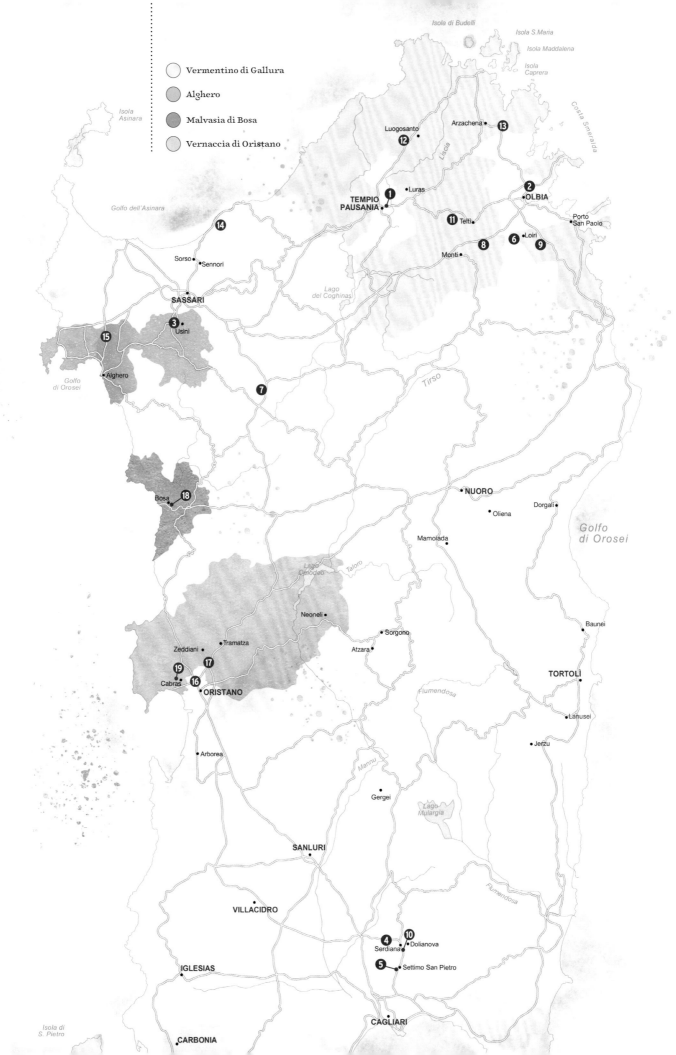

Vermentino di Gallura

Alghero

Malvasia di Bosa

Vernaccia di Oristano

Isola di Budelli
Isola S.Maria
Isola Maddalena
Isola Caprera

Costa Smeralda

Isola Asinara

Golfo dell'Asinara

Luogosanto
Arzachena
13

12

2
•OLBIA

Luras
1
TEMPIO PAUSANIA•

Telti
11

Porto San Paolo

8
6 Loiri
9
Monti•

Sorso• •Sennori

SASSARI•

Lago del Coghinas

3
•Usini

15

•Alghero

Golfo di Orosei

7

Tirso

NUORO

Dorgali•
Oliena•

Golfo di Orosei

Bosa• **18**

Mamoiada•

Neoneli•

Lago Omodeo
Taloro

Baunei•

Zeddiani• •Tramatza
19 **17**
Cabras• **16**
•ORISTANO

Sorgono•
Atzara•

TORTOLÌ

•Lanusei

•Arborea

Mannu

•Jerzu

•Gergei

Lago Mulargia

SANLURI
•

VILLACIDRO

10
4 •Dolianova
Serdiana•
5 •Settimo San Pietro

Flumendosa

IGLESIAS

Isola di S. Pietro

CARBONIA

CAGLIARI

Alghero DOC

An appellation that covers eight municipalities in the province of Sassari and is now close to two million bottles per year, made famous primarily by the Cabernet Marchese di Villamarina. The permitted grapes are Chardonnay, Sauvignon, Torbato, and Vermentino for the whites; Cabernet, Cagnulari, Merlot, and Sangiovese for the reds. The most significant results are being achieved, in addition to the aforementioned Cabernet, with the peat grape, which creates sophisticated herbaceous and mineral nuances followed by a taste that is always very fresh and never too opulent.

—

Producer and its trademark and signature wines:

15. SELLA&MOSCA, Alghero
    Alghero Cabernet Riserva Marchese di Villamarina ($$)
    Alghero Torbato Catore ($)
    Alghero Torbato Terre Bianche Cuvée 161 ($)

Malvasia di Bosa DOC and Vernaccia di Oristano DOC

There is a diversity of grape varieties and production areas—Malvasia di Bosa is cultivated mainly in the province of Nuoro while Vernaccia di Oristano is produced in the adjacent province of Oristano—but these rare wines are equally charming, made from dried grapes and an oxidative style that leads to aromas of walnut husk, spices, honey, and almonds. They are wines with a good natural alcohol content, around 15% by volume, not easy to pair with food but rich in vitality, capable of evolving for decades: softer, more lovable, and savory is the Malvasia, drier and more enveloping the Vernaccia, aged for a long time in drained barrels. Several tens of thousands of liters per year for both DOC wines, often offered in 50 or 37.5 centiliter formats.

—

Producers and their trademark and signature wines:

16. CANTINA DELLA VERNACCIA, Oristano
    Vernaccia di Oristano Riserva Judikes ($$)
17. Silvio CARTA, Zeddiani
    Vernaccia di Oristano Riserva ($)
18. G. Battista COLUMBU, Bosa
    Malvasia di Bosa Riserva ($$)
19. Attilio CONTINI, Cabras
    Vernaccia di Oristano Riserva Antico Gregori ($$$)
    Vernaccia di Oristano Riserva ($$)
    Vernaccia di Oristano Flor ($)

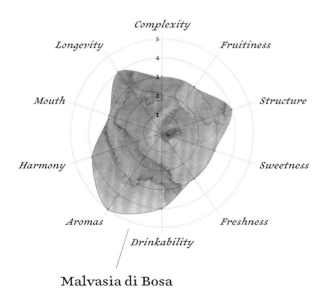

Malvasia di Bosa

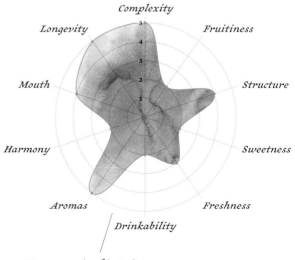

Vernaccia di Oristano

Carignano del Sulcis DOC

The production area comprises seventeen municipalities in the southwest of the island, in the provinces of Cagliari and Carbonia-Iglesias. It is an outstanding wine both in its aromas, always rich in Mediterranean herbs and spices, and on the palate, where delicate tannins and good freshness guarantee satisfying drinkability. The DOC has become increasingly famous since 1984, when Cantina Santadi first produced Terre Brune, thanks to the advice of the most famous Italian oenologist of the time, Giacomo Tachis. Annual production is around two million bottles.

—

Producers and their trademark and signature wines:

1. CANTINA DI CALASETTA, Calasetta
   Carignano del Sulcis Riserva Bricco delle Piane ($)
   Carignano del Sulcis Piede Franco ($)
2. CANTINA GIBA, Giba
   Carignano del Sulcis Riserva 6Mura ($$)
3. CANTINA MESA, Sant'Anna Arresi
   Carignano del Sulcis Riserva Buio Buio ($$)
4. CANTINA SANTADI, Santadi
   Carignano del Sulcis Superiore Terre Brune ($$)
   Carignano del Sulcis Riserva Rocca Rubia ($$)
5. Enrico ESU, Carbonia
   Carignano del Sulcis Nero Miniera ($)
6. SARDUS PATER, Sant'Antioco
   Carignano del Sulcis Riserva Is Arenas ($)
   Carignano del Sulcis Superiore Arruga ($$)

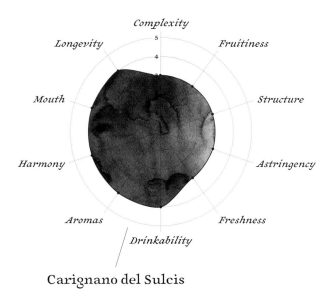

Carignano del Sulcis

Cagliari DOC

The vast territory of this DOC is mainly cultivated with Malvasia, Monica, and Vermentino grapes. Of particular interest is the Cagliari Malvasia, which is delicately scented of flowers and white fruits, with an almost saline palate that fades into finely aromatic memories. Overall annual production is around five hundred thousand bottles.

—

Producer and its trademark and signature wine:

1. AUDARYA, Serdiana
   Cagliari Malvasia Estissa ($)

Mandrolisai DOC

A small DOC, made in the center of Sardinia in seven municipalities between the provinces of Nuoro and Oristano. The wine is made from a blend of Bovale grapes, at no less than 35%, Monica at 20 to 35%, and Cannonau at 20 to 35%. The grapes are grown on small trees, capable of displaying good elegance and finesse as soon as the initial tannic component amalgamates. About two hundred thousand bottles are produced annually.

—

Producers and their trademark and signature wines:

2. CANTINA DEL MANDROLISAI, Sorgono
    Mandrolisai Rosso Superiore 100/Kent'Annos ($)
3. FRADILES, Atzara
    Mandrolisai Rosso Superiore Antiogu ($)

....

Monica di Sardegna DOC

This rather straightforward red wine, never too full-bodied, mostly refined in steel only, with a tasty and fragrant drinkability, can be produced throughout the region from the Monica grape of the same name. The aromas often include notes of Mediterranean scrub and delicate spices. More than 1.6 million bottles are sold annually.

—

Producers and their trademark and signature wines:

1. AUDARYA, Serdiana
    Monica di Sardegna ($)
4. Ferruccio DEIANA, Settimo San Pietro
    Monica di Sardegna Karel ($)
5. I GARAGISTI DI SORGONO, Sorgono
    Monica di Sardegna Murru ($)

Mandrolisai

Cagliari

Monica di Sardegna

Cannonau di Sardegna DOC

Nearly ten million bottles per year are produced of a DOC that embraces the entire regional territory, foreseeing that production in the provinces of Nuoro and Ogliastra can be qualified as Classico. The three main subzones are also sometimes indicated on the label: Nepente di Oliena, Capo Ferrato, and Jerzu. Once thought to be particularly alcoholic and robust, Cannonau di Sardegna is now showing, thanks to targeted vinification, valuable qualities of finesse, lightness, and drinkability, so much so that on the palate it may remind one of Pinot Noir.

—

Producers and their trademark and signature wines:

1. ANTICHI PODERI JERZU, Jerzu
   Cannonau di Sardegna Riserva Josto Miglior ($)
2. ARGIOLAS, Serdiana
   Cannonau di Sardegna Passito Antonio Argiolas 100 ($$)
3. ATHA RUJA, Dorgali
   Cannonau di Sardegna Riserva Kuéntu ($$)
4. BERRITTA, Dorgali
   Cannonau di Sardegna Thurcalesu ($)
5. Francesco CADINU, Mamoiada
   Cannonau di Sardegna Perdas Longas ($)
6. CANTINA DORGALI, Dorgali
   Cannonau di Sardegna Classico D53 ($)
   Cannonau di Sardegna Riserva Vinìola ($)
7. CANTINA GUNGUI, Mamoiada
   Cannonau di Sardegna Berteru ($$)
8. CANTINA SANNAS, Mamoiada
   Cannonau di Sardegna Bobotti ($$)
9. CANTINE DI NEONELI, Neoneli
   Cannonau di Sardegna Omèstica ($$)
10. Antonella CORDA, Serdiana
    Cannonau di Sardegna ($)
11. GABBAS, Nuoro
    Cannonau di Sardegna Classico Dule ($)
    Cannonau di Sardegna Riserva Arbòre ($$)
12. LA CONTRALTA, Loiri Porto San Paolo
    Cannonau di Sardegna L'Ora Grande ($$)
13. Giovanni MONTISCI, Mamoiada
    Cannonau di Sardegna Barrosu Riserva Franzisca ($$$)
14. OLIANAS, Gergei
    Cannonau di Sardegna Le Anfore ($)
15. PALA, Serdiana
    Cannonau di Sardegna Riserva ($)
16. PODERI PARPINELLO, Sassari
    Cannonau di Sardegna Riserva ($)
17. Fratelli PUDDU, Oliena
    Cannonau di Sardegna Nepente di Oliena Riserva Pro Vois ($$)
18. Giuliana PULIGHEDDU, Oliena
    Cannonau di Sardegna Classico Cupanera ($$)
19. QUARTOMORO DI SARDEGNA, Arborea
    Cannonau di Sardegna Òrriu ($)
20. Giuseppe SEDILESU, Mamoiada
    Cannonau di Sardegna Mamuthone ($)
    Cannonau di Sardegna Riserva Carnevale ($$)
21. SU'ENTU, Sanluri
    Cannonau di Sardegna Su'Anima ($)
22. SURRAU, Arzachena
    Cannonau di Sardegna Sincaru ($)
23. VIKEVIKE, Mamoiada
    Cannonau di Sardegna Ghirada Gurguruó ($$)

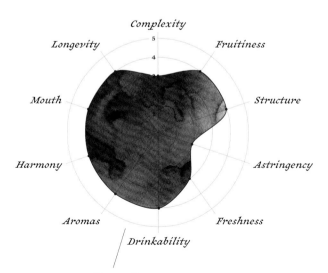

Cannonau di Sardegna

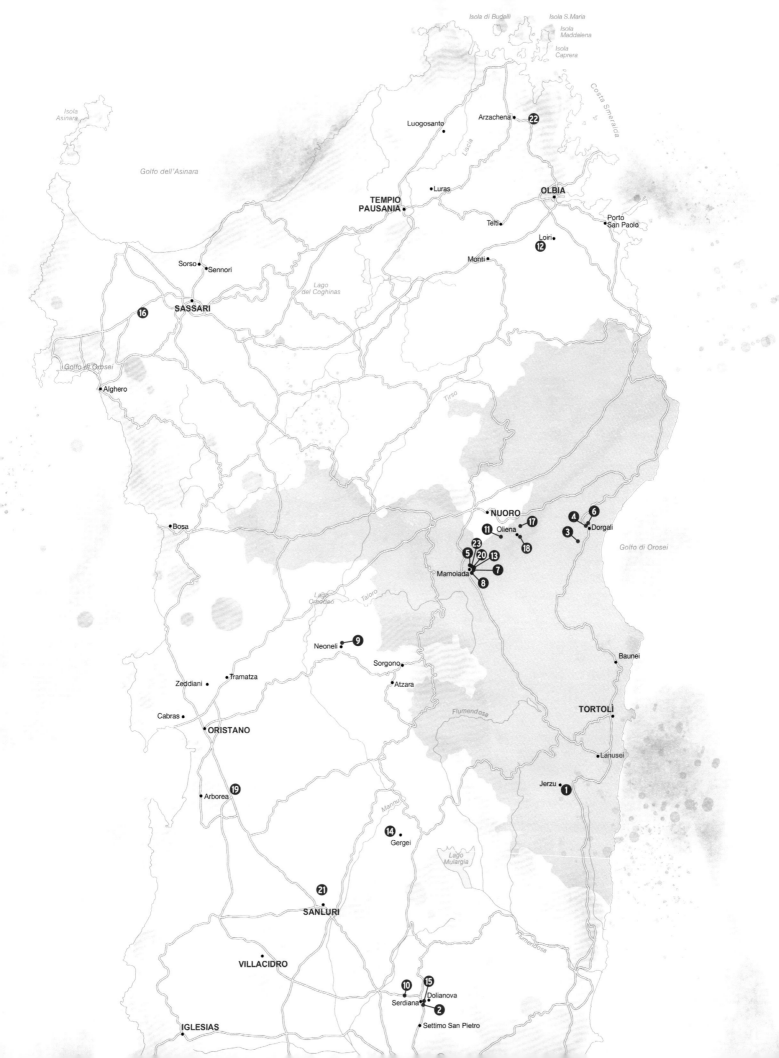

Recommended wines outside the DOC/DOCG designations:

1. **AGRIPUNICA**, Santadi
   Barrua (Carignano, Cabernet Sauvignon, Merlot) ($$)
2. **ANTICHI VIGNETI MANCA**, Sorso
   Li Sureddi Rosso (Cannonau) ($$)
3. **ARGIOLAS**, Serdiana
   Turriga (Cannonau, Carignano, Bovale, Malvasia Nera) ($$$)
   Angialis da uve stramature (Nasco) ($$)
   Korem (Bovale, Carignano, Cannonau) ($$)
4. **AUDARYA**, Serdiana
   Nuracada (Bovale) ($$)
5. **BENTU LUNA**, Neoneli
   Sobi (Cannonau, Bovale, Monica...) ($$)
   Susu (Cannonau) ($$$)
6. **CANTINADELLAVERNACCIA**, Oristano
   Corbesa (Vernaccia) ($)
7. **CANTINE DI DOLIANOVA**, Dolianova
   Terresicci (Barbera Sarda) ($$)
8. **CANTINE DI NEONELI**, Neoneli
   Canàles (Pascale, Muristello, Monica, Cannonau...) ($$)
9. **CAPICHERA**, Arzachena
   VT (Vermentino) ($$$)
   Capichera (Vermentino) ($$)
   Santigàini (Vermentino) ($$$$)
10. Attilio **CONTINI**, Cabras
    Barrile Nieddera ($$)
11. **DEPPERU**, Luras
    Ruinas (Vermentino) ($)
12. **FAMIGLIA ORRO**, Tramatza
    Crannatza (Vernaccia) ($)
13. **NURAGHE CRABIONI**, Sorso
    Sussinku Bianco (Vermentino) ($)
    Sussinku Rosso (Cagnulari) ($)
14. **OLIANAS**, Gergei
    Perdixi (Bovale, Carignano) ($)
15. Lorenzo **PUSOLE**, Baunei
    Pusole Bianco (Vermentino) ($)
16. **SU'ENTU**, Sanluri
    Su'Nico Bovale ($)
17. **TENUTE DETTORI**, Sennori
    Tenores (Cannonau) ($$)
    Chimbanta (Monica) ($$)
    Ottomarzo (Pascale) ($$)

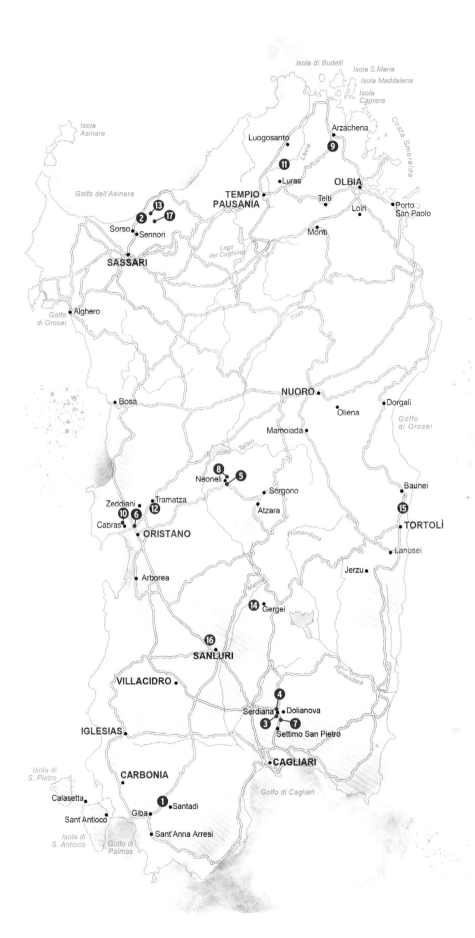

SELLA&MOSCA
Località I Piani
Alghero (SS)
sellaemosca.com
Year of establishment: 1899
Owner: Terra Moretti
Average number of
bottles produced per year:
6,000,000

Founded more than a century
ago by two Piedmontese
entrepreneurs (Sella, an
engineer, and Mosca, a lawyer),
the Sardinian production
giant became part of the Terra
Moretti Holding in 2016, after
having undergone a period of
production and commercial
relaunch by the Campari
Group, which had acquired it
in 2002. There are 1,360 acres
under vine, most of them
organically managed around
the production plant, allowing
the production not only of the
famous Alghero Marchese di
Villamarina but also a wide
range in which white wines,
including the Metodo Classico,
are increasingly important,
headed by Alghero Torbato
Terre Bianche Cuvée 161.

**ALGHERO CABERNET RISERVA
MARCHESE DI VILLAMARINA**
First year of production: 1989
Average number of bottles produced
per year: 23,000
Grape variety: Cabernet Sauvignon

A splendid Mediterranean expression of
Cabernet Sauvignon, with a profusion of
typical Bordeaux grape aromas accompanied
by the warmth and richness of these
luminous bush-trained vineyards. Notes of
cherries and ripe black berries are joined by
hints of spices and cinchona, against a broad
and intense background of aromatic herbs.
The flavor is rich and full, with remarkable
density, just fresh, very long, and with a
finish of assured elegance. A great Cabernet
that manages to combine power and
refinement at its best.

GIUSEPPE SEDILESU
Via Vittorio Emanuele
II 64
Mamoiada (NU)
giuseppesedilesu.com
Year of establishment: 2000
Owner: Salvatore Sedilesu
Average number of bottles
produced per year: 100,000

This winery has helped
relaunch the name of
Barbagia oenology thanks
to 54 acres of vineyards
up to a hundred years old,
organically cultivated with
alberello vines, at an altitude
that can exceed 1,970 feet. In
addition to Mamuthone, the
winery offers six other labels
of Cannonau di Sardegna
DOC, in which the Gràssia
and Carnevale Reserves stand
out in particular, as well
as the one named after the
founder, Giuseppe Sedilesu.
Also noteworthy is the small
production of whites, the fruit
of the indigenous Granazza
grape, made with different
vinification styles.

**CANNONAU DI SARDEGNA
MAMUTHONE**
First year of production: 2000
Average number of bottles produced
per year: 70,000
Grape variety: Cannonau

This Mamuthone is delicately matured first
in 132-gallon oak barrels and then in cement,
splendid in its personality of red fruits,
citrus fruits, and spices, with a robust and
warm but always energetic and vital taste,
of constant acidity and long persistence.
A great example of typical Cannonau, a
paradigm of the type.

GABBAS
Via Trieste 59
Nuoro
gabbas.it
Year of establishment: 1974
Owner: Giuseppe Gabbas
Average number of bottles
produced per year: 75,000

In the heart of Barbagia, 50
acres of vineyards breathe
in the cool winds of the
Gennargentu massif on one
side and the sea breezes
of the Gulf of Orosei on
the other. Here, Giuseppe
Gabbas has committed to
the enhancement of the
Cannonau grape, relying on
low grape yields per plant in
the vineyard and small French
woods in the cellar. The three
Cannonau-based productions
are joined by bottles of the
fresh Vermentino di Sardegna
Manzanile.

**CANNONAU DI SARDEGNA
CLASSICO DULE**
First year of production: 1994
Average number of bottles produced
per year: 20,000
Grape variety: Cannonau

Dule is well suited to dispel the belief that
Cannonau is a wine characterized only by
power, structure, and immediate fruitiness.
This is a multifaceted and elegant red, not
lacking in substance but even richer in
personality, with notes of cherries against
a citrus background. This is followed by
a palate that expresses a softness resting
on a refreshing acidic and slightly tannic
backbone. The authentic character of great
Cannonau.

CANTINA SANTADI
Via Giacomo Tachis 14
Santadi (SU)
cantinadisantadi.it
Year of establishment: 1960
Owner: the 200 cellar
cooperatives of Santadi
Average number of
bottles produced per year:
1,700,000

Three key elements have led
this flagship winery of Sulcis
to success: the determination
of the partners in striving
for the area's oenological
redemption, an excellent grape
variety such as Carignano,
and the collaboration, starting
in the 1980s, with Italy's
most successful oenologist,
Giacomo Tachis. Production
is therefore centered on
the Carignano del Sulcis
DOC, but the production is
completed by a rich offering
made predominantly from
Cannonau grapes for the
reds and Vermentino for the
whites. A fine cooperative
winery with 1,600 acres under
vine.

**CARIGNANO DEL SULCIS
SUPERIORE TERRE BRUNE**
First year of production: 1984
Average number of bottles produced
per year: 80,000
Grape varieties: Carignano (95%),
Bovaleddu (5%)

A wine that shows Sulcis's vocation for the
Carignano grape at its highest level. It is
born in suggestive vineyards cultivated with
the alberello system and matures for a long
time in French wood, giving fruity and spicy
aromas harmonized by an elegant touch of
oak. The palate is rich and important, long,
with intense but flowing tannins, dense
without being opulent, with moderate
acidity. A great, internationally renowned
wine.

G. BATTISTA COLUMBU
Via Carmine 104
Bosa (OR)
malvasiacolumbu.com
Year of establishment: 1972
Owner: the Columbu family
Average number of bottles
produced per year: 8,000

Giovanni Battista Columbu has received awards from all over the world and was chosen by American director Jonathan Nossiter to testify to his role as "guardian of tradition" in the film *Mondovino*. The property, now run by his sons with the same philosophy, has 8.5 acres in front of the sea, dedicated exclusively to Malvasia. There are two labels on offer, both oxidative in style: the simpler, sweeter Malvasia di Bosa Alvaréga version and the monumental Riserva.

MALVASIA DI BOSA RISERVA
First year of production: 1992
Average number of bottles produced per year: 3,500 (500 ml) (17 fl oz)
Grape variety: Malvasia di Sardegna

It matures in small, drained chestnut barrels for three or four years and thus acquires distinct aromas of dried fruit, almond in particular, together with sunny herbs and a hint of marine iodine. The structure in the mouth is rich, with a long, slow progression in which the soft part given by the 16 to 17% by volume of alcohol is made tauter and drier by the savoriness and continuous nutty returns. Impressive for its incisiveness and persistence.

AUDARYA
Strada Statale 466 km 10,1
Serdiana (SU)
audarya.it
Year of foundation : 2014
Owner: the Pala family
Average number of bottles
produced per year: 350,000

The Pala brothers have clear ideas and are demonstrating this with precision: utmost care of the 101 acres of property cultivated with the alberello system, putting local vines at the fore, and modern technology in winemaking operations. In addition to Nuracada, the result is emblematic labels such as the fruity Monica di Sardegna, the savory Vermentino di Sardegna, the mineral Nasco, and the floral Nuragus di Cagliari. Excellent overall quality and wines rich in personality.

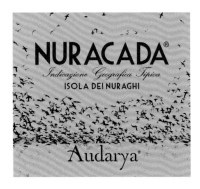

NURACADA
First year of production: 2014
Average number of bottles produced per year: 5,000
Grape variety: Bovale

From a grape variety little known on international markets comes a pleasant red wine, easy to drink, not for lack of complexity but for its harmonious balance of taste. Delicately matured in wood for a year, it has aromas of ripe currants and sweet spices, with a lively note of Mediterranean scrub. The palate is rich, lush, and snappy thanks to the fine tannic component, with a hint of tar on the finish.

TENUTE DETTORI
Località Badde Nigolosu
Sennori (SS)
tenutedettori.it
Year of establishment: 1981
Owner: the Dettori family
Average number of bottles
produced per year: 90,000

The elements that lead to the transformation of grapes into wine are already present in nature, says Alessandro Dettori, who uncompromisingly pursues the realization of his ideal wine, made both in the vineyard and the cellar in the most natural way possible, without the use of chemical pesticides and also by renouncing sulfites, yeasts, and barrels. His 72 biodynamically certified acres—planted with Cannonau, Vermentino, Muscat, Monica, and Pascale—reflect the dazzling light of the Romangia Sea, opposite the island of Asinara. Wines that are sometimes difficult, yet so rich in overflowing personality.

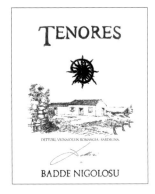

TENORES
First year of production: 2000
Average number of bottles produced per year: 6,000
Grape variety: Cannonau

Produced only in the best vintages, it is the fruit of the Retagliadu Nieddu grape, an ancient biotype of Cannonau. It matures for over four years in cement and has rich, penetrating aromas in which blackberry, dark cherry, spice, and Mediterranean herbs emerge. The palate is characterized by power, to which a dense and nonaggressive tannic mass also contributes, elegance, and the vitality of the fruity pulp.

ARGIOLAS
Via Roma 18
Serdiana (SU)
argiolas.it
Year of establishment: 1938
Owner: the Argiolas family
Average number of bottles produced per year: 2,500,000

A winery that has quickly conquered the world's markets thanks to the precise interpretation given to each grape variety present in the 568 acres of property, to which are added grapes from trusted suppliers. Thus, in addition to Turriga, fine labels such as Cannonau di Sardegna Riserva Senes and Carignano del Sulcis Cardanera are also produced, while in the whites, Vermentino di Sardegna Is Argiolas and Nasco di Cagliari Iselis excel. A quality that also stems from research, with field experimentation involving no less than five hundred different clones of local grape varieties.

TURRIGA
First year of production: 1988
Average number of bottles produced per year: 50,000
Grape varieties: Cannonau (85%), Carignano, Bovale, Malvasia Nera

Matured in small, not very aromatic French woods, it reveals well on the nose both the fresh vein of Mediterranean herbs and the complex facets of sweet spices, in a combination of intense pleasantness. The palate combines the fruity fullness typical of Cannonau with a good acidic and refreshing backbone.

SURRAU

Strada Provinciale
Arzachena-Porto Cervo
km 0,5
Arzachena (SS)
vignesurrau.it
Year of establishment: 2004
Owner: the Demuro family
Average number of bottles
produced per year: 460,000

A dynamic enterprise, always
intent on experiments that
lead to harvesting beautiful
grapes while increasing
respect for the ecosystem.
Production, from 148 acres of
property, is centered on the
Vermentino grape, from which
also comes the recent and
already famous Vermentino di
Gallura Vendemmia Tardiva
Montimidola. There is no
lack of labels from red grapes,
among which the Cannonau di
Sardegna Sincaru stands out,
also in the Riserva version.

VERMENTINO DI GALLURA SUPERIORE SCIALA

First year of production: 2006
Average number of bottles produced
per year: 75,000
Grape variety: Vermentino

Matured in steel only, it is rich in tropical
fruit, from pineapple to grapefruit, joined by
orange blossom and Mediterranean scrub;
bottle aging creates refined mineral hints of
flint. The palate is fresh and lively, endowed
with a pleasant savoriness that goes well
with the density of the flesh. A faithful
and vital interpretation of Vermentino di
Gallura.

CAPICHERA

Strada per Sant'Antonio di
Gallura km 4
Arzachena (SS)
capichera.it
Year of establishment: 1975
Owner: the Ragnedda
family
Average number of bottles
produced per year: 280,000

The winery that has
relaunched Sardinia's
Vermentino on an
international level, offering
versions in different styles
but always with a precise
territorial imprint. VT is joined
by the historic Capichera, the
rich Vermentino di Gallura
Vign'Angena, the youthful
Lintóri, and the rare and
mature Santigaìni. The estate's
124 acres of vineyards also
allow for outstanding results
with the reds, led by Assajé,
from Carignano grapes with
a touch of Syrah. A name that
has become famous thanks to
its prestigious constancy in
quality.

VT

First year of production: 1990
Average number of bottles produced
per year: 12,000
Grape variety: Vermentino

It expresses the potential and quality of the
Vermentino grape at its highest level: it is
rich in fresh notes that combine balsamic
hints with mint, yellow fruit, and a mineral
hint of flint. The palate is ample and well-
structured, full of fresh sapidity, elegant
harmony, and a long finish in which sweet
spices and marine scents appear.

CONTINI

Via Genova 48
Cabras (OR)
vinicontini.com
Year of establishment: 1898
Owner: the Contini family
Average number of
bottles produced per year:
1,800,000

In more than a century of
activity, the winery has
enjoyed considerable success
with its sought-after Vernaccia
di Oristano, which has allowed
for a gradual but consistent
expansion of the area under
vine, having now reached 544
acres, partially organically
worked. Production also
embraces types based
on historical Sardinian
grapes, from Vermentino
to Cannonau, without
prejudice to the predilection
for Vernaccia, of which the
Antico Gregori version is also
famous. Wines with a strong
personality and great charm.

VERNACCIA DI ORISTANO RISERVA

First year of production: 1964
Average number of bottles produced
per year: 3,500 (375 ml) (12.7 fl oz)
Grape variety: Vernaccia

It matures in chestnut and oak casks for
about twenty years, during which time it
develops a rich veil of yeast called "flor."
This gives rise to aromas reminiscent of pan
brioche and fresh pastries together with
almonds, spices, and hints of sea breeze. The
flavor is powerful, warm, and structured but
at the same time endowed with good acidity,
with a pleasantly drying finish. A wine that
involves and conquers with every taste.

The Most Widely Used International Grape Varieties in Italy

Cabernet Franc

It originated in the Basque Country, where it was known as achéria, or fox, while the name Cabernet comes from the Latin *carbon*, referring to the black color of the berries. It spread in the Middle Ages, first to Brittany, where the climate was milder at the time, and then to the Loire Valley, particularly to the excellent designations of Chinon, Saumur-Champigny, and Bourgueil. In the Libournais, and the Bordeaux region in general, it is used on its own or in classic Bordeaux blends, together with Cabernet Sauvignon and Merlot. Since the seventeenth century, it has spread to the rest of the world, and today it is cultivated with the best results in Napa Valley in California, Mendoza in Argentina, as well as Maipo Valley and Colchagua in Chile. In Italy, it is mostly found in Tuscany and the historic Triveneto area.

The main recurring aromas in Cabernet Franc wines refer to wild strawberry, raspberry, plum, violet, rosemary, green pepper, and pepper.

Cabernet Sauvignon

Originating in the Gironde, the department of New Aquitaine that embraces the estuary of the Dordogne and Garonne rivers, downstream from Bordeaux, it is the most widespread red grape variety in the world, due to its ability to adapt to the most diverse *terroirs*. It is a cross between Cabernet Franc and Sauvignon Blanc, and as well as in Bordeaux, it also produces brilliant results—on its own or in blends—in Napa and Sonoma Valley in California, Maipo Valley in Chile, Coonawarra in Australia, and in Ningxia and Xinjiang in China. In Italy, the best results are found in Tuscany, Veneto, Friuli-Venezia Giulia, Sicily, and Sardinia.

The main recurring aromas in Cabernet Sauvignon–based wines refer to black berries, cherry, pepper, cassis, cedar, thyme, eucalyptus, mint, tobacco leaf, and licorice.

Carmenère

An ancient French variety first mentioned in 1783 in Bergerac, Dordogne, it is a descendant of Cabernet Franc, and before the scourge of phylloxera was widely used throughout the southwest of France. Abandoned and then rediscovered, it is now cultivated from the Americas to China, where it has been present since the end of the nineteenth century, while in Italy it is mainly widespread in the northeast.

The main recurring aromas in Carmenère-based wines refer to small black berries—blueberry, blackberry, black cherry—as well as mint, licorice, and undergrowth.

Chardonnay

A spontaneous cross of Pinot and Gouais Blanc, it can be traced back to the late Middle Ages in Saône-et-Loire, Burgundy, of which it is the white grape variety par excellence. It is also the most widely used white wine grape in the world, as it does not have strong aromatic characteristics but adapts to the most diverse climates, *terroirs*, and winemaking styles, with results ranging from mediocrity to splendor. These range from France (Chablis, Côte de Beaune, Côte de Nuits, Jura) to Australia (Yarra Valley, Adelaide Hills, McLaren Vale, Hunter Valley), from the United States (California and Oregon) to Chile (Valle de Casablanca and Valle de Limarì), and to South Africa (Stellenbosch and Franschhoek). Then there is New Zealand (Marlborough and Central Otago), Germany (Baden and Rheingau), Austria (Wachau), and Canada (Ontario and British Columbia). It is also cultivated everywhere in Italy, with particular diffusion in the northeast, Maremma, and Langhe, and as a base for sparkling wines in Alta Langa, Trentino, Veneto, and Franciacorta. The main recurring aromas in Chardonnay-based wines refer to peach blossom, tropical fruit, apple, butter, lime, hazelnut, and toast.

Gamay

An ancient red variety from Burgundy, mainly used for young and refreshing wines such as Beaujolais, it belongs to the Noirien ampelographic family, the natural progeny of Pinot and Gouais Blanc, and is also widespread in Germany in Hesse and the Palatinate, in the Valais Canton in Switzerland, and in the New World. Here, it is widely found in California, Ontario (Niagara Peninsula), and Brazil (Serra Gaúcha) with often lively and characteristic results. In Italy, it can be found in new and experimental forms in Oltrepò Pavese, the province of Asti, and Piacenza.

The main recurring aromas in Gamay-based wines refer to strawberry, banana, elderflower, cherry, and undergrowth.

Grenache or Garnacha

Known and cultivated for centuries in Sardinia, under the name of Cannonau, but also in the Trasimeno area, where it is known as Gamay, the Garnacha grape was first mentioned in 1513 by the Spanish agronomist Gabriel Alonso de Herrera in his treatise on general agriculture, and in 1678 by the historian Estevan de Corbera in his book *Cataluña Illustrada*, which attests to its origins in Catalonia and Aragon. Spread widely over the centuries in the Mediterranean and the New World following colonization, migration, and trade by the Spanish, it has settled today in the Rhône Valley in France where it is one of the main vines used in Châteauneuf-du-Pape. It is also found especially in Languedoc-Roussillon and Provence, in Greece, in central Macedonia, in Naoussa, in Portugal, in Vidigueira and the Alentejo, and in Arizona and Texas. In American Upper California it is found in Santa Barbara County and Paso Robles, and in Mexican Lower California in Valle de Guadalupe. Then there is the Barossa Valley, Australia, the Western Cape region of South Africa, and to a lesser extent also North Africa, particularly in the foothills of the Atlas Mountains. In Morocco, it is present in the Meknes and Beni-Mellal regions, and in Tunisia, in Cap Bon and on the island of Djerba.

The main recurring aromas in the usually intense, full-bodied, and smooth Grenache-based wines are reminiscent of laurel, Mediterranean scrub, ripe strawberry and red cherry, plum, lavender, musk, pepper, and licorice.

Grüner Veltliner

So named for the golden-green color of its berries, it comes from the Wachau region in Austria. This is its homeland and the place in which it is the most representative white, and it has spread to the surrounding countries and to South Tyrol in Italy.

The main recurring aromas in Grüner Veltliner wines refer to apple, pear, tropical fruit, and flint with an accent of white pepper.

Merlot

First mentioned in 1784 in Libourne, Gironde, it is a fleshy, dark grape, like the feathers of the blackbirds from which it takes its name, widely used both in Bordeaux blends and in single-varietal wines. A cross between Cabernet Franc and Magdeleine Noire des Charentes, an ancient grape variety from Brittany, it has successfully taken root all over the world, in the most varied *terroirs*, thanks to its resistance and early ripening. Of the approximately 1.7 million acres of global vineyards, 277,000 are in France, 32,000 in Spain, followed by smaller extensions in Germany, Switzerland, and other European countries. It is found throughout the New World: in the United States it is the fourth most planted red variety and the second in New Zealand, after Pinot Noir. In Italy, there are 62,000 acres distributed between Friuli, Maremma, Veneto, Alto Adige, and Umbria.

The main recurring aromas in Merlot-based wines refer to violet and iris flowers, plum and black berries, cherries, prunes, sultanas, black tea, undergrowth, and dark chocolate.

Moscato Bianco / Muscat à Petit Grains

Originally from Greece, it was brought to Italy by the ancient Romans and has since spread throughout the Mediterranean, first appearing under the Latin name Muscatellus in 1304, in Ruralium Commodorum Libri XII, by the agronomist and ampelographer Pietro de Crescenzi. Today, it is one of the world's most characteristic and intoxicating banquets, especially in sparkling and passito versions, particularly in France, Spain, Portugal, Greece, Hungary, Israel, South Africa, California, and Australia. In Italy, the most significant productions are concentrated in the province of Asti, in Piedmont, and in the South, particularly Calabria and Sicily.

The main recurring aromas in white Muscat wines refer to sage, jasmine, peach, apricot, orange peel, and honey.

Müller-Thurgau

A very prolific grape forming the basis of soft, semi-aromatic white wines, originating in the Rheingau region of Germany, it is the result of a cross between Riesling and Madeleine Royale. It was developed by the botanist and oenologist Hermann Müller, who was born in the Swiss canton of Thurgau, hence the name of the variety. Cultivated in the German and Slavic areas of Europe, with small experiments also in New Zealand, Russia, and Japan, it produces the best results in the high *terroirs* of South Tyrol.

The main recurring aromas in Müller-Thurgau-based wines refer to white flowers, lemon, apricot, and nutmeg.

Petit Verdot

A traditional blending grape originating in the extreme southwest of France—now the Pyrénées Atlantiques department—where it is thought to have been domesticated from wild vines. Used since the eighteenth century in Bordeaux, it has spread to Tuscany since the 1960s to add color, character, and spice to classic blends of Cabernet Sauvignon, Cabernet Franc, and Merlot, while in other areas, such as Languedoc and Spain, it is also vinified as a single varietal. Due to its late ripening, it prefers warm areas and is enjoying renewed popularity in this era of global warming. Small plots are also found in Portugal, Turkey, Israel, California, Washington, Virginia, Argentina, and Chile, and these are rapidly growing in Uruguay, Peru, Australia, and South Africa.

The main recurring aromas in wines made from Petit Verdot refer to currants, blackberries, violets, pepper and cloves, leather, licorice, and cocoa.

Pinot Bianco / Pinot Blanc

Originally from Burgundy and cultivated mainly in Alsace, Austria, Germany, Switzerland, and Hungary, in Italy it is found in monovarietal editions in Alto Adige, while in Collio Friulano it is often associated with other grape varieties, to which it brings freshness and complexity.

The main recurring aromas in Pinot Blanc–based wines refer to apple blossom and jasmine, pear, white peach, fresh grass, anise, white pepper, and almond.

Pinot Grigio / Pinot Gris

A Pinot Noir mutation that has been established throughout the Alps since the Middle Ages, in France, Switzerland, Piedmont, and Valle d'Aosta it is also known as Malvoisie and produces often exciting white wines. In Hungary, Cistercian monks in the retinue of Emperor Charles IV planted it on the Badacsony hill on the northern shore of Lake Balaton in 1375. Also of note are the Slovenian Pinot Gris wines from Primorska, the Czech ones from Moravia, and the Romanian ones from Transylvania. In Germany, the most suitable *terroirs* are in the Palatinate and Baden, in France in Alsace, in Switzerland in Canton Ticino, in Italy in South Tyrol, Collio, and Karst.

The main recurring aromas in Pinot Gris wines refer to freshly cut hay, apple, apricot, kiwi and lime, wet stone, almond, ginger, and honey.

Pinot Meunier

A classic red grape that is vinified white to bring fruit and liveliness to Champagne, it is also used in Germany, Italy, and the New World to make high-quality sparkling wines due to its good resistance to cold and its ability to mature more quickly than Pinot Noir.

The main recurring aromas in Pinot Meunier–based sparkling wines are reminiscent of wildflowers, apple, plum, freshly baked bread, leavened dough, and nuts: walnuts, almonds, and hazelnuts.

Pinot Nero / Pinot Noir

The Pinot family is one of the most varied and articulate, although its origins are uncertain. Known and cultivated since the time of the ancient Romans, and probably domesticated from wild vines and called as such because of its pine cone–shaped bunches. Along with the historical region of Burgundy—with the unmatched Grand Crus of the Côte de Nuits, such as La Romanée-Conti, La Tâche, Richebourg, Musigny, and Chambertin—it thrives only within delicate equations of climate and *terroir*. These are preferably cool, high areas with a continental climate, such as the Jura, South Tyrol, Canada (Niagara Peninsula and British Columbia), or Moldova (Valul lui Traian), and Hungary (the Eiger and Lake Balaton Kékfrankos). Also suitable are coastal areas cooled by the sea or more extreme latitudes such as Oregon (Willamette Valley), the Sonoma Coast and Russian River Valley, Carneros, Monterey in the United States, New Zealand (Central Otago in the South Island), Tasmania, Patagonia, and South Africa (Walker Bay and Hemel-en-Aarde).

In Germany, it is cultivated under the name Spätburgunder along the banks of the Ahr River, while in the Austrian Steiermark—Styria—and South Tyrol, it is known as Blauburgunder. In the rest of Northern Italy, it produces the best red versions in Oltrepò Pavese and Valle d'Aosta, and sparkling wines in Franciacorta, Alta Langa, and Trentino, where it is traditionally vinified together with Chardonnay and Pinot Meunier.

The main recurring aromas in Pinot Noir–based wines are reminiscent of rose petals, violets, red cherries, strawberries, raspberries, currants, dried plums, white pepper, black tea, mushrooms, moss, and chicken. In Pinot Noir–based sparkling wines, on the other hand, the aromas refer to apple, white peach, orange peel, small red fruits, and bread crust.

Riesling

An extraordinary German white grape variety, capable of expressing the widest range of geographical, human, and sensory expressions, extracting the soul and ancestral complexity of each *terroir* in which it grows. When treated with due respect and vinified with wisdom and style, it produces wines that are eternal and unforgettable. The most astonishing results are to be found along the winding banks of the Moselle, the summit of heroic viticulture and scenic beauty, where vine cultivation was introduced by the ancient Romans who built the first terraces here.

Other bright and mineral Rieslings are produced in Alsace and Austria, in Wachau, Kamptal, and Kremstal; more citrusy, dry, and aromatic Rieslings in the Clare Valley and Eden Valley in South Australia; simpler and fruitier Rieslings in the Columbia Valley in Washington State, while in New Zealand, Riesling is mainly cultivated in Central Otago, Marlborough, and Canterbury in the South Island, with remarkably fresh results. In Italy, cultivation is mainly in Trentino, Alto Adige, Friuli, Valle d'Aosta, and in Lombardy, on the shores of Lake Garda.

The main recurring aromas in Riesling-based wines refer to acacia flowers, jasmine, apple and peach blossom, citrus fruits—lime, grapefruit, orange—papaya and cinnamon, hydrocarbons, herbs, honey, and flint.

Sauvignon Blanc

Among the most characteristic and popular white grape varieties in the world, Sauvignon has been cultivated in the Loire, and particularly in Sancerre, since ancient times: the French word *sauvage*, from which the name is derived, describes its vigorous and wild nature.

From the Loire, it took root in Bordeaux and today is one of the most widely cultivated vines in Chile, the Casablanca Valley, Napa, and Sonoma Valley in California, as well as South Africa and New Zealand. In Italy, it is found throughout the North, with the best productions concentrated in Collio, Carso, and Alto Adige.

The main recurring aromas in Sauvignon-based wines refer to tomato leaf and peel, cut grass, grapefruit, melon, mango, chalk, almond, and elderberry.

Savagnin (Gewürztraminer)

Known in Alto Adige as Traminer, or wine from Termeno, it is a very distinctive aromatic white wine, originating in the Jura where it is used in the traditional Vin Jaune, but is also cultivated in Switzerland, where it is known as Heida. It is known in Western Australia, in the Swan Valley, as Verdelho, in the Czech Republic as Prynč, but also in Slovenia, in Lower Styria, in Bulgaria, where it is one of the most popular whites, and in Argentina, in the far northwest of the country, around the city of Salta.

The main recurring aromas in Sauvignon-based wines refer to rose, jasmine, lychee, pineapple, lemon, and ginger with, in some cases, a final note of resin and honey.

Sylvaner

A German white with a rather neutral profile and just slightly aromatic but good body, popular in Germany and Alsace. It is a natural cross between Savagnin and Osterreichisch Weiss, first mentioned in 1655 by the Cistercian abbot of Ebrach in southern Germany. In Italy, there is a small, valid production concentrated mainly in the Isarco Valley in South Tyrol.

The main recurring aromas in Sylvaner-based wines refer to citrus fruits, green apple, aromatic herbs—thyme, mint—chalk, and wet stone.

Syrah

One of the most fascinating and cosmopolitan red grape varieties in the world, characterized by an intense and spicy personality. Its land of origin is the Rhône Valley in France, and DNA analysis confirms that it is a cross between Dureza, a vine from Ardèche, and Mondeuse Blanc, a vine from Savoie, making it a half-brother of Viognier, and one of the great-grandchildren of Pinot Noir. Large extensions of Syrah are found in Spain, Portugal, the United States, Chile, and Argentina, but it is in Australia, at the antipodes of France, that it has enjoyed the most success under the name of Shiraz. Since 1843, nearly 99,000 acres have been planted with it, corresponding to just under a third of Australia's total production. In Italy, it has found its fortune in Sicily, Veneto, and Tuscany, particularly in Cortona, where it has a dedicated DOC.

The main recurring aromas in Syrah-based wines refer to violets and herbs, blueberry, blackberry, black currant, plum, pepper, cinnamon, smoked meat, earth, pipe tobacco, licorice, leather, and cocoa.

Viognier

Originally from the Rhône Valley in France, a close relative of Syrah, it produces structured and complex whites with a recognizable aromatic profile. Almost extinct at the end of the 1960s, it has been rediscovered and exploited primarily in the south of France, and with small extensions in Spain, Portugal, and Argentina. In the United States, it has found adopted *terroirs* in California, Oregon, and Virginia. In Italy, there are scattered productions in Valle d'Aosta, Piedmont, Friuli, and Tuscany, in blends or in purity.

The main recurring aromas in Viognier-based wines refer to peach blossom, apricot, mandarin, exotic notes, acacia honey, orange peel, and toasted hazelnut.

Glossary

ACESCENCE
Caused by acetic bacteria, it is the transformation of alcohol into acetic acid. The risk of acescence is greater in wines with a low alcohol content, a weak body, and in the event of premature fermentation and excessive exposure to air.

ACID
One of the five flavors. In wine, it is mainly from citric, malic, tartaric, acetic, lactic, and succinic acids. It brings a feeling of freshness, which is particularly noticeable in wines made from Sauvignon, Riesling, Barbera, and Sangiovese grapes.

AERATION
A process that can take place in the glass, carafe, or decanter, and is useful in allowing the wine to reach the optimal level of olfactory expressiveness.

ALBERELLO
An Italian method of training vines, mainly in hot areas, that does not require wood or concrete supports and allows the grapes to ripen well; since it is difficult to coordinate logistically, it is not widely used.

ALCOHOL
An organic compound, obtained from the fermentation of sugars naturally present in grapes. The main alcohol present in wine is ethyl alcohol. For wine, the final concentration of ethyl alcohol is usually less than 16% by volume, with higher percentages in the case of fortified or liqueur wines.

ALCOHOLIC CONTENT or PERCENT PROOF
Also called alcoholic strength, it is one of the mandatory indications that must be on the label. Alcoholic strength is expressed as a percentage of ethyl alcohol by volume.

ALCOHOLIC FERMENTATION
Metabolic process involving the transformation by yeasts of the sugars in the must into alcohol, with the production also of carbon dioxide and a significant rise in temperature.

AMPELOGRAPHY
A discipline that describes the different grape varieties and classifies them according to specific systematic criteria, through the external morphological study primarily of buds, leaves, and bunches. The identification of grape varieties through DNA analysis falls under molecular ampelography.

ANTHOCYANINS
Of the polyphenol family, they are pigments found mainly in the skin of red grapes and are responsible for the color of wine.

AROMATIC AROMA
This is typical of terpene-rich grape varieties such as Muscat, Malvasia, Traminer, and Brachetto, whereby the same aromas can be perceived in the wine as when the grapes are tasted at harvest. In contrast, Aleatico, Müller-Thurgau, Sauvignon Blanc, Riesling, and Sylvaner are considered semi-aromatic.

ASTRINGENCY
Sensation of dryness, also known as *allappamento*, felt in the mouth and throat, caused mainly by tannins.

AUTOCLAVE
A steel container used in the production of sparkling and semi-sparkling wines. Of considerable size (up to twenty-six-thousand gallons), thanks to its hermetic closure and the fact that it can be thermoregulated, it tolerates the considerable internal pressure caused by fermentation.

BALANCE
The balanced relationship, both on the nose and in the mouth, between the components, without the clear dominance of any one element.

BALSAMIC
Hints and notes reminiscent of mint, eucalyptus, resin, and pine, typical in some red wines but occasionally also brought about by aging in wood.

BARRIQUE
Type of small barrel (usually 225 liters, or 60 gallons), usually in oak, but also chestnut or cherry, mainly from France, Eastern Europe, and the United States. For smaller capacity barrels, the Italian word used is *caratelli*—such as those used for aging Vin Santo—while barrels with volumes of around 500 liters (130 gallons) are called tonneaux. The use and spread of barriques dates back to the time of the Gauls, who abandoned terracotta amphorae in favor of wooden barrels, which were less fragile and more suitable for transporting wine.

BÂTONNAGE
The action of moving and circulating the lees deposited at the bottom of a barrel. Traditionally carried out with the aid of a stick, or *bâton*, this operation is typically used with white wines in order to increase their smoothness and plumpness.

BIODYNAMIC
Biodynamic agriculture and viticulture originated from the concepts of Austrian theosophist Rudolf Steiner in the early 1900s, interpreted by German agronomist Ehrenfried Pfeiffer. The diffusion of the biodynamic approach is constantly increasing, and its practice is based on the observation of celestial bodies and their influence on the plant and wine cycle, on the balance between the anthropological world and nature, and on preserving and restoring the microbiodiversity of the soil and its mineral components. Biodynamic wines are always also certified as organic.

BIODYNAMIC WINE
Wine made from grapes and cellar practices that meet the requirements of biodynamics. In Italy, biodynamic certification is issued by the Demeter company.

BIOLOGICAL WINE
This term is used to define wines that follow the EU rules approved by the Standing Committee on Organic Production in 2012. The regulation sets out the oenological practices and substances that may be used in the production of these products.

BIOTYPE
Within a grape variety, a type is understood to have different morphological or oenological characteristics due to its evolution or adaptation to different environments.

BITTER
Flavor contributed mainly by the presence and quality of tannins. The more balanced the wine, the more the bitterness will be hidden by other components, such as alcohol and sugars. The clear perception of bitterness during tasting is always to be considered a defect.

BLANC DE BLANCS
A type of Metodo Classico Spumante obtained solely from white grapes.

BLANC DE NOIRS
Metodo Classico Spumante obtained from only red grapes.

BLEND
see **COMPOSITION**

BLENDING OF WINES
Also known by the nouns blend and cuvée. With respect to blending, it indicates the operation by which wines of different grapes, or wines of the same variety but from several vineyards or from harvests at different times, are actually blended.

BODY
A characteristic that indicates the structure of a wine, i.e., its capacity for tannins, acidity, alcohol, and other extracts. The richer a wine is in all or some of these elements, the more full-bodied it can be described.

BOISÉ
A French term for woody, it refers to the hints given to the wine by the barrique, which can be traced back to toast, vanilla, or smoke.

BORDEAUX BLEND
A typical blend of wines from the Bordeaux area composed of Cabernet Franc, Cabernet Sauvignon, Merlot, and also Petit Verdot.

BOTRYTIS CINEREA
This is so-called "Noble Rot," or *Muffa Nobile* in Italian, or *Pourriture Noble* in French: it is caused by fungal parasites which, by drying out the berry, concentrate the sugars and aromas. This makes it possible to obtain grapes suitable for the production of passito wines, also known as *Muffati*, with aromas of dried fruit and honey. The same fungus can also cause a serious alteration, gray rot, which makes winemaking impossible.

BOTTLING COMPANY
A term for an industrial-type company that cans, kegs, or bottles wines bought from those who originally produced them, mostly wineries but also private individuals. Bottlers sometimes package the wine without intervention; in other cases they adjust the color, alcohol content, and acidity to produce a product—mostly simple white, red, or rosé wine, but also DOC and DOCG—that the consumer will find to be consistently the same over time. The main commercial outlet for these products, which are usually very cheap, are supermarkets and so-called "house wines."

BOUQUET
Term defining the complex of olfactory sensations perceived during tasting.

CARATELLO
A small barrel with limited capacity, 50 to 100 liters (13.25 to 26.5 gallons), often made of oak, but also chestnut, mulberry, or cherry wood. Traditionally used for aging Vin Santo.

CARBON DIOXIDE
A gaseous component that develops through the action of yeasts during alcoholic fermentation.

CARBONIC MACERATION
An operation that allows fermentation within the whole grapes, without crushing and in a CO_2-saturated environment. Using this method, it is possible to maximize the quantity of fruity aromas and obtain a more intense olfactory profile. It is typical of Vini Novelli, which are also expressly provided for in numerous designations.

CHARMAT METHOD
A sparkling winemaking method involving fermentation in autoclaves, with a time span ranging from a few days to a few months, and very low cost compared to the Metodo Classico.

CLONE
A type that is part of a group of elements derived from a single matrix and identical on a genetic level, but carrying slightly different characteristics, in order to achieve different production results. In Sangiovese, for example, one hundred and fourteen clones are encoded.

COMPOSITION
The different components and ingredients that make up a particular wine; also called its "makeup."

COMPOST
A soil-improving product obtained from the decomposition and rotting of organic substances, such as certain food waste, pruning and gardening waste, slurry and manure.

COUPAGE
In Metodo Classico sparkling wines, it indicates the moment when all the wine masses are united and made homogeneous before bottling and subsequent frothing.

CROSSOVER
Resulting from the crossing of different existing grape varieties. In Italy, it is not uncommon to find crosses even between the most widespread regional grape varieties, such as Cabernet Sauvignon (Cabernet Franc and Sauvignon Blanc) and Manzoni crosses (Rhine Riesling and Pinot Blanc).

CRU
A French word used throughout the world to indicate a vineyard whose sensory and qualitative uniqueness is recognized, and whose limits have been precisely defined. The word means "growth."

CRYOMACERATION
Used in the production of white wines, this technique requires the must to remain in contact with the skins at low temperatures, generally for twelve to thirty-six hours, in order to extract the greatest number of substances, particularly aromatic ones.

CULTIVAR
See **GRAPE VARIETY**

CUVÉE
See **COMPOSITION**

DEMISEC
It means "half-dry" and is a characteristic of a wine that tends toward sweetness with a residual sugar content of between 12 and 45 g/l (0.39 and 1.49 oz/qt).

DESTEMMING
Carried out using destemming machines, this operation separates the stalks from the grapes in order to eliminate plant substances with a strong astringent power, which in excessive quantities could compromise the harmony of the wine.

DISGORGEMENT
The process by which wine producers remove the dead yeast cells, or lees, from the neck of a bottle.

DOC/DOCG
They stand for *Denominazione di Origine Controllata* (Designation of Controlled Origin), and *Denominazione di Origine Controllata e Garantita* (Designation of Controlled and Guaranteed Origin) respectively. They were established in 1963 and have been fully operational since 1980. The purpose of these designations is to protect chains of particular products of excellence, codified by detailed Disciplinary Regulations. For the wine, this means that the geographical area of production, its extension, the methods and techniques of viticulture, and the main cellar activities, such as vinification and aging, as well as sensory and physical parameters such as alcohol and acidity, are indicated.

DOP
The acronym for *Denominazione di Origine Protetta* (Protected Designation of Origin, PDO in Europe), a categorization awarded by the European Union to protect specific quality products. For Italian wine, it includes both DOC and DOCG and may be used in place of these.

DOWNY MILDEW
A vine disease caused by Plasmopara Viticola, a parasite that causes the necrotization of shoots and leaves and their subsequent fall, as well as extensive damage to shoots and bunches, leading to drastic reductions in production. Native to America, it arrived in Europe at the end of the nineteenth century. It is counteracted using chemical products and/or a mixture of water with copper sulfate and calcium, also known as the Bordeaux mixture.

DRY EXTRACT
Residue obtained from the evaporation of water and volatile substances in wine. It constitutes the unit of measurement of the concentration of a wine, and is expressed in grams per liter (g/l), a parameter present in the production regulations that stipulate minimum quantities according to the type of product. It is mainly made up of tannins, sugars, salts, acids, and glycerin.

EFFERVESCENCE
Characteristic of wines that have a concentration of carbon dioxide that can be perceived by the senses during tasting. Based on the quantity in grams per liter of CO_2, the wine can be defined in ascending order of "sparkle."

ETHEREAL
Descriptor relating to olfactory examination. A wine with this characteristic is usually well-matured, very pleasant, and balanced in terms of the fusion of aromatic and alcoholic scents. It is often used to indicate delicacy, purity, and refined complexity.

FIXED ACIDITY
Measured in grams of tartaric acid per liter, it represents the set of fixed acids—such as tartaric, citric, and malic acid, naturally present in grapes—and lactic and succinic acids—formed during fermentation. Together with volatile acidity, it gives rise to the total acidity of a wine, which is defined in its minimum threshold by each particular production regulation.

FLOATING ACIDITY
Arising from volatile acids, such as acetic acid, formed during and after the alcoholic fermentation processes. It is measured as the amount of acetic acid present in a wine expressed in grams per liter (g/l). Its perception varies depending on the structure of the wine and personal sensitivities, but it can be said that if it exceeds 0.7 g/l (0.024 oz/qt), it is considered too much.

FORTIFICATION, FORTIFIED
A characteristic denoting that alcohol has been added to a wine.

FULL-BODIED
Descriptor indicating a pleasant saline sensation.

FULLING
This is the phase that involves breaking the cap of the solid mass of skins that emerges during alcoholic fermentation: it takes place inside the tanks, either mechanically or manually, in order to maximize the extraction of the grape's aromatic and coloring substances.

FUMÉE
A characteristic that denotes hints of smoke and roasting, deriving from the *terroir* or from the wood of the barrique used for aging.

GLYCERIN
Organic compound that occurs as a trivalent alcohol, i.e., consisting of three carbon atoms bonded to three -OH groups. Its presence in wine is natural; in the EU, it is forbidden to increase its levels artificially. It amplifies tactile sensations during tasting as it gives roundness and smoothness.

GOUDRON / TAR
French expression indicating a scent related to the pleasant and complex tarry sensations on the nose and in the mouth, particularly in aged reds.

GRAPE PHYLLOXERA
A parasitic insect native to North America that attacks vine roots. The arrival of the pest in Europe at the end of the nineteenth century caused the destruction of a large part of its vineyards, devastation that was stopped by the use of American rootstocks, which are resistant to the insect's attack.

GRAPE VARIETY
Also called a cultivar or variety, it indicates each individual type of cultivated grape. It is estimated that there are over ten thousand different grape varieties in the world.

HYBRID
A mix of different grape varieties or grapes in one vineyard or *terroir*.

IGP
An acronym for *Indicazione Geografica Protetta* (Protected Geographical Indication, PGI in Europe), it is a designation established by the EU that mainly stipulates that at least one of the production steps must take place in a specific area.

IGT
An acronym for *Indicazione Geografica Tipica* (Typical Geographical Indication), it falls under the PGI mark established by the EU and always has specific production rules, with less stringent limits than DOC and DOCG. There are 118 in Italy. In some cases, such as Toscana IGT, they enjoy considerable prestige, while in the Piedmont region, they have been abolished.

INDIGENOUS
When used in regard to a grape variety, it indicates that it is native or indigenous to the area in which it is cultivated, thus not having been imported from other areas, and that its presence and diffusion in that area has often been recorded for centuries.

INITIAL AROMAS
Also called varietals, they are volatile mixes produced by aromatic molecules, already perceptible in the grape before fermentation and typical of each grape variety.

INTERNATIONAL TASTE
An expression that has taken on a negative connotation, defining what could be the genre or even the archetype of wine in which planning and construction in the cellar have often been more relevant than work in the vineyard. In these types of products, it is difficult to pick out particular nuances of the grape varieties or *terroir* during tasting, also due to the use of blends of international grapes and time spent in new wood. On a sensory level, the result is an opulent, structured, at times pandering, easy wine whose drinkability can even be cloying.

LABEL
One of the components of the bottle design, the label is the medium containing all the main and compulsory information of a wine, also depending on the designation to which it belongs. It includes the vintage, indications on the origin and place of production, the name and logo of the winery, information on the composition and type of wine, the production batch, the percentage of alcohol by volume, any logos related to certifications (e.g. organic, biodynamic), and warnings addressed to specific groups of individuals (e.g. pregnant women). In addition to the label, information may also be present on the back label. A wine label can be compared to a book cover; it is the element that, even before the contents and other information, attracts the interest of consumers. It is not only a means of recognizing the wine, but it can also evoke particular imagery for the wine-buying public. Over time, many wineries have relied on artists and designers to create labels considered objects of great interest to collectors.

LABELING & PRESENTATION
How the bottle is visually presented, with a label on the front, label on the back, cork, wrapper, and bezel.

LIQUEUR DE TIRAGE
A mixture of wine, sugar, yeast, and must used in all types of Metodo Classico sparkling wines, both Italian and foreign, to enable the essential frothing of the base wine.

LIQUEUR D'EXPÉDITION
A French term for a mixture of wine, sugar, and possibly distillates that can be added to Metodo Classico sparkling wines after disgorgement to refill the bottle. Every winery has its own secret recipe.

MACERATION
The stage during which, by coming into contact, the solid parts such as skins, grape seeds, and possibly also stalks, yield coloring substances, aromas, and tannins to the must. The duration of this operation is at the discretion of the winery and the winemaker, and is essential for red wines and orange wines, while it is rare in whites.

MALOLACTIC FERMENTATION
Metabolic process involving the transformation of malic acid into lactic acid by bacteria, following the alcoholic fermentation phase. This reduces fixed acidity, perceptions of hardness, and aggressive acidity such as that of unripe fruit, making the wine softer and more pleasant. Malolactic fermentation is typical of red wines or long-lived whites, while it does not occur in wines that are to be consumed young, so as to preserve their acidity and freshness.

METODO CLASSICO
Also known in the past as *méthode champenoise* (a term that can no longer be used), this is the sparkling winemaking method in which refermentation takes place in the bottle, through the addition of yeast and sugar—*liqueur de tirage*—for minimum periods established by the various Disciplinary regulations. This can be from a few months to a few years. After this phase, disgorgement takes place to eliminate the residual lees deposited, then to add any liqueur d'expédition, and to proceed with the final corking.

MINERAL
In white wines, the complex hints are reminiscent of flint, rubbed matchstick, and hydrocarbons. The term is also sometimes used in descriptions of red wines to indicate hints of earth or roots.

MODERN
A term often used to define wines that envisage the use of specific methods and techniques in the vineyard and cellar and that, on a sensory level, present particular characteristics deriving from the contribution of wood. In particular, this can be defined as a wine that involves thinning out the grapes and aging in barriques.

MONOVARIETAL
Also called "monovine," it indicates a wine that is made from a single type of vine and, therefore, is not the result of a combination or assembly of different varieties.

MUST
Juice, possibly with residual skins, obtained from crushing grapes, with a good sugar content and almost zero alcohol content. The moment the alcoholic fermentation process starts, the transformation of must into wine begins.

MUST CONCENTRATE
As the name suggests, the product obtained by the concentration of must, in particular by removal of water, which can be used in Italy to increase sugars and thus alcohol content, in musts and wines.

NOBLE ROT
See **BOTRYTIS CINEREA**

OFF-DRY
The presence of a slightly sweet taste, from residual sugars in quantities of between 4 and 12 g/l (0.13 and 0.39 oz/qt).

ORGANIC, OR NATURAL WINE
This defines all those wines that use environmentally sustainable viticulture practices in the vineyard, such as organic and biodynamic ones, with almost no chemical substances or invasive actions.

In the cellar, ancient techniques can be used to support the natural evolution of the wine through the spontaneous fermentation of the must without the addition of selected yeasts and other substances, except for small quantities of sulfur dioxide. All this with the aim of producing a product that reflects the *terroir* without adulteration or corrections. Although the term "natural" is not allowed by current legislation, several associations have their own processing protocols that are adhered to by numerous producers: these include Vinnatur, Triple A, and Renaissance des Appellations.

OXIDIZATION
Process in which the action of oxygen causes a change in the wine. Whether intentional or accidental, this alteration occurs naturally, resulting in a decay that is also perceptible on a sensory level. Oxidation is a peculiar and positive characteristic of certain products, achieved thanks to their acidity or alcohol content, as in the case of certain sweet wines.

OXIDIZED
An adjective indicating an effect caused by oxidation, which is perceived on a sensory level when the wine is reminiscent of Marsala or Madeira. It may be intentional, but in other cases it is a defect caused by poor storage or being aged for too long.

PASSITO
A sweet wine made from grapes that have been partially dried, or raisined.

PERFUME, NOSE
The totality of all odorous substances present in wine, perceived first through the nostrils and then retronasally.

PERLAGE
Typical of sparkling wines, it is a French term defining the emergence of CO2 bubbles. A fine, dense, and long-lasting perlage is an indication of quality.

PHENOLS
Organic compounds from which polyphenols are derived. They are present in must and wine. They can be volatile, imparting animal scents and, in white wines, if oxidized, give a coloring tending toward deep yellow.

PHYTOPHARMACEUTICALS
Pesticide substances used in agriculture and viticulture to protect, prevent, and treat plants from developing diseases.

POLYMERIZATION
A chemical process in which anthocyanins and tannins, thanks to oxygen, aggregate to create larger molecules. This softens the wine, decreasing its astringency in the mouth.

POLYPHENOLS
Organic compounds derived from phenols, including anthocyanins, natural coloring substances, and tannins, which have an antioxidant effect in wine and reduce their effect with age.

PRODUCTION GUIDELINES
Issued by the Ministry of Agriculture, these specifications represent the set of production, commercial, and sensory standards and requirements for a specific product.

PROLONGED FINISH
The durability and maintenance of the wine's characteristics over time once swallowing has been completed and the sensory examination concluded.

PRUINA
Latin term meaning frost; a thin whitish waxy layer that protects the skin of the grapes.

REDUCTION
The result of a low oxygen content in a wine leading to unpleasant closed, cellar, and stale air sensations. It sometimes compromises the overall tasting of the wine; in the case of very old vintages, it may be reduced by favoring oxygenation in the glass or decanter.

REFINEMENT
The period of time during which the wine matures in different storage materials, such as steel, wood, terracotta, and cement, but also in glass bottles. The aging period can vary from a few months to tens of years. Although there is no unanimous convention, the term maturation is generally used to indicate the evolution of the wine at the winery, while refinement is more often used in relation to its "stay" in the bottle.

RESIDUAL SUGARS
Sugars that have not undergone transformation into alcohol. Absent or almost absent in dry wines, they can reach concentrations of 300 g/l (9.95 oz/qt) or more in sweet, passito, muffato, and liqueur wines (e.g. around 100 g/l or 3.31 oz/qt in Vin Santo del Chianti, 140 g/l or 4.64 oz/qt in Moscato d'Asti, and 200 g/l or 6.63 oz/qt in Passito di Pantelleria).

RESIDUAL TASTE
Tasting phase indicating the sensations that remain even after swallowing, their intensity, complexity, and length.

RIM
It indicates the upper edge of the wine that is created when tilting the goblet. The faded crescent created by the loss of coloring substances can help identify the age of a wine or even assess its aging.

RIPASSO or REPASSED
A technique involving the addition of wet skins to the base wine in order to trigger a second fermentation, with a subsequent increase in alcohol content and the extraction of substances. In Italy, for example, companies producing Chianti Ripasso and Valpolicella Ripasso use this technique.

SALASSO or BLEEDING
Stage at the start of fermentation in which a liquid part of the red must is removed to increase the percentage of skins and intensify color and extracts. The removed must may continue fermentation, giving rise mainly to rosé wines.

SALTY
One of the fundamental flavors; in wine, critics and sommeliers use this descriptor when the strongly perceived saltiness is not pleasant.

SATÈN
Exclusive designation of the Franciacorta appellation, registered by its Consortium, to indicate a specific type of Franciacorta Brut with a pressure not exceeding 4.5 atmospheres.

SECOND FERMENTATION FOR SPARKLING WINES
In sparkling wines, the phase in which refermentation takes place after the addition of *liqueur de tirage* to the base wine.

SECONDARY AROMAS
Volatile compounds given by aromatic molecules perceptible through the sense of smell, which are formed during winemaking, particularly in alcoholic fermentation.

SENSORY
Of a product, a characteristic that can be perceived through the senses.

SINGLE VARIETAL
Indicates a wine that is produced from only one type of grape variety and is therefore not the result of blending different varieties.

SOLERAS
This method consists of arranging small barrels in overlapping rows. The young wine is only added to the top ones, while the older wine is only taken from the lower ones and then bottled. Historically used in the production of Madeira and Sherry, but also Marsala since 1812.

SPUMANTE or SPARKLING
A wine characterized by a high concentration of dissolved carbon dioxide, responsible for considerable effervescence and the formation of froth, the pressure of which must be greater than 3.5 atmospheres. Sparkling wines can be classified according to the amount of residual sugar present. From 3 to 5 g/l (0.09 to 0.17 oz/qt) of sugar can be defined as extra brut, up to 12 g/l (0.38 oz/qt) as brut, between 12 and 17 g/l (0.38 and 0.56 oz/qt) as extra sec or extra dry. Up to 32 g/l (1.06 oz/qt) we have dry or sec; further increasing the amount of sugar up to 50 g/l (1.66 oz/qt) we have medium dry or demi-sec, and finally doux for amounts of sugar above 50 g/l (1.66 oz/qt).

STALKS and SEEDS
The solid parts of the grape cluster, such as skins, seeds, and stems, that emerge during the alcoholic fermentation of red wines. During fulling, the grapes are sunk and sprayed to prevent rotting and acescence.

SUGARS
Simple carbohydrates, mainly glucose and fructose, are naturally present in grapes and form the basis of alcoholic fermentation. Only specific types of products, such as sparkling wines, Barolo Chinato, and Vermouth, may involve the addition of sucrose.

SULFUR DIOXIDE
A chemical compound containing tetravalent sulfur (SO_2) added to wine for its antioxidant and antiseptic action in order to improve its preservation.

SUPER TUSCANS
A term introduced during the 1980s, it identifies wines produced in Tuscany that do not fall under DOC and DOCG, as they do not follow the traditional rules laid down in the Disciplinary regulations. These wines are often called Bordeaux blends, since they are made from Cabernet Sauvignon, Merlot, and/or other international vines, but can also be made from local grapes, especially Sangiovese (→ Tuscany).

SWEET
One of the fundamental flavors, it indicates the sensation of sweetness given by residual sugars, which can be amplified by other factors such as the percentage of alcohol and glycerin, or particular serving methods such as temperature, while being dampened by acid and bitter components present in the wine.

TANNINS
Polyphenolic compounds, naturally occurring as plant protection. During the production process, skins, seeds, and stems transfer their tannins to the must. The wood used for aging can also contribute to increasing the amount of tannins. On a sensory level, these compounds are perceived through the sensation of astringency they create during tasting. Tannin when too young or excessive is unpleasant; on the contrary, if balanced and mature, it can be a quality of a great wine.

TARTRATES
White, crystalline tartaric acid salts naturally present in wine. If the wine undergoes changes in temperature or during aging, precipitation of these compounds may occur. Although the deposit of tartrates at the bottom of the bottle is a natural phenomenon, and although it does not give rise to sensory changes, it is considered a defect, so producers tend to check that the tartrate precipitation has fully taken place in the cellar before bottling.

TERPENES
Groups of unsaturated hydrocarbons produced by plants; these chemical compounds are found mainly in aromatic and semi-aromatic grapes, which define certain olfactory and tasting characteristics. They are particularly responsible for the aromas of menthol, rose, geranium, and lemongrass.

TERROIR
A complex set of factors relating to the soil, climate, and environment of a specific area, and the action of man in the vineyard and cellar, which define an inseparable link between the wine and its territory of origin.

TERTIARY AROMAS
Volatile compounds, given by aromatic molecules perceptible through the sense of smell, which are formed during aging.

THE PROCESS OF DRYING GRAPES
The process of gradually dehydrating grapes in order to increase their sugar concentration and produce passito wines. The grapes can be dried on the vine, on racks, and mats, in special drying lofts, or by direct exposure to the sun after harvest.

TONNEAU
A barrel-shaped wooden container, usually with a capacity of 350/600 liters (92/159 gallons), but never more than 1,000 liters (264 gallons). The micro-oxygenation of the wine is slower, more delicate, and aromatically less invasive than in the barrique.

TYPICALITY
Ability of a wine to be recognized and traced to others made from the same grape variety, in the same territory, and using the same production method.

UMAMI
A Japanese term meaning tasty, it is the flavor related to the presence of glutamates and nucleosides. Typical in foods such as mature cheeses, well-ripened tomatoes, mushrooms, meat, and fermented products.

VARIETAL
See **MONOVARIETAL**

VINE SHOOT
Young vine, often reproduced in nurseries, which has its "beard," i.e., roots, and is ready to be planted in the vineyard.

VINIFICATION
The set of processes and actions following the grape harvest, in which the alcoholic fermentation and transformation of the must into wine takes place.

VINIFICATION "IN BIANCO"
Set of processes involving the fermentation of the must in the absence of the skins, in order to avoid the release of the coloring substances they contain. This makes it possible, particularly in the case of sparkling wines made from Pinot Noir, to use red grapes to make white wines.

VINTAGE
It indicates the year in which the grapes were harvested and turned into wine. "Vintage" indicates the last marketed vintage of a wine.

VINTAGE DATE
Synonymous with vintage, year, and harvest. It is a mandatory indication in almost all DOC wines and, in Metodo Classico sparkling wines, often indicates the exclusive use of grapes from a high-quality harvest.

WINE
Defined at the EU level as "the product obtained exclusively from the total or partial alcoholic fermentation of fresh grapes, whether or not crushed, or of grape must."

WINE CRITICISM
The group of professionals dedicated to the description and, often, the evaluation of wines through the publication of volumes and/or texts in guides, specialized periodicals, columns in generalist magazines, blogs, and websites, whether free or paid. The most famous international wine critics who also deal with Italian wines include Robert Parker, Jancis Robinson, Antonio Galloni, James Suckling, and Hugh Johnson, along with the Frenchmen Olivier Poussier and Michel Bettane. For Italy, mention should be made of the forerunner Luigi Veronelli and, today, Daniele Cernilli.

WINEMAKING
The sum total of all methods, techniques, and activities related to the cultivation and care of vines, carried out throughout the year and throughout their life.

YEAST
Single-celled microorganisms of the fungus family responsible for the alcoholic fermentation of wine, i.e., the transformation of sugars into alcohol, but also for specific sensory characteristics due to the contribution of certain aromatic components. In oenology, only about ten species are used, naturally present on grapes, including Saccharomyces Bayanus and Saccharomyces Cerevisiae.

Some Useful Books, Magazines, and Websites, in English and Italian, to Get to Know Italian Wine

BOOKS

Atlante dei territori del vino Italiano. Pisa: Pacini, 2014.

Boroli, *Enciclopedia del vino.* Milan: 2004.

Calò, Antonio, Scienza, Attilio, and Costacurta, Angelo, *Vitigni d'Italia.* Bologna: Edagricole, 2001.

Cernilli, Daniele, *I racconti (e i consigli) di Doctor Wine.* Turin: Einaudi, 2014.

Cernilli, Daniele, *Memorie di un assaggiatore di vini.* Turin: Einaudi, 2006.

D'Agata, Ian, *Native Wine Grapes of Italy.* Oakland: University of California Press, 2014.

Della Rosa, Paolo, ed, *Enciclopedia del vino.* Milan: Garzanti, 2009.

Giavedoni, Fabio and Gily, Maurizio, ed, *Guida ai vitigni d'Italia.* Bra: Slow Food, 2016.

Goode, Jamie, *Il vino perfetto.* Casarano: Ampelos, 2021.

Grandi cru d'Italia. Milan: Mondadori Electa, 2008.

Guerini, Eleonora, *Il grande libro illustrato del vino italiano.* Turin: Edt, 2019.

Italian Michelin, *Itinerari tra i vigneti.* Pero: 2015.

Johnson, Hugh, *Il vino: storia, tradizioni, cultura.* Rome: Franco Muzzio, 2011.

Johnson, Hugh and Robinson, Jancis, *Atlante mondiale dei vini.* Milan: Mondadori, 2020.

Marescalchi, Arturo and Dalmasso, Giovanni, *Storia della vite e del vino in Italia.* Milan: Unione Italiana Vini, 1979.

Masnaghetti, Alessandro, *Barbaresco MGA.* Monza: Enogea, 2021.

Masnaghetti, Alessandro, *Barolo MGA.* 2 vol. Monza: Enogea, 2015–2018.

Masnaghetti, Alessandro and De Cristofaro, Paolo, *Chianti Classico: l'atlante dei vigneti e delle UGA.* Monza: Enogea, 2022.

Moio, Luigi, *Il respiro del vino.* Milan: Mondadori, 2016.

Monelli, Paolo, *O.P. ossia Il vero bevitore.* Milan: Longanesi, 1963.

Officina Enoica, ed, *Guida al vino critico.* Milan: Altra Economia, 2014.

Racca, Roberto, ed, *Il vino: istruzioni per l'uso.* Florence: CinqueSensi, 2015.

Rastelli, Pierpaolo, *Guida ai vini d'Italia bio.* Milan: Tecniche Nuove, 2012.

Robinson, Jancis, ed, *The Oxford Companion to Wine.* Oxford: Oxford University Press, 2015.

Robinson, Jancis, Harding, Julia, and Vouillamoz, José, *Wine Grapes.* London: Penguin Books, 2012.

Rossi, Antonio, ed, *Codice della vite e del vino.* Milan: Unione Italiana Vini, 2021.

Rossi, Antonio, ed, *Codice denominazioni di origine dei vini.* Milan: Unione Italiana Vini, 2018.

Sangiorgi, Sandro, *L'invenzione della gioia.* Rome: Porthos, 2010.

Scienza, Attilio, ed, et al. *Atlante geologico dei vini d'Italia.* Florence: Giunti, 2015.

Scienza, Attilio and Imazio, Serena, *La stirpe del vino.* Milan: Sperling & Kupfer, 2018.

Sicheri, Giuseppe, *Il libro completo del vino.* Novara: De Agostini, 2021.

Soldati, Mario, *Vino al vino.* Milan: Bompiani, 2020.

Stara, Pietro, *Il discorso del vino.* Milan: Zero in condotta, 2012.

Supp, Eckhard, ed, *Enciclopedia del vino italiano.* Offenbach: Weincongress, 1995.

The Art of Italian Wine. Bra: Slow Food, 2010.

Unwin, Tim, *Storia del vino.* Rome: Donzelli, 1993.

Veronelli, Luigi, *Catalogo Veronelli dei vini D.O.C. & D.O.C.G.* Bergamo: 1994.

Veronelli, Luigi, *I vini d'Italia.* Rome: Canesi, 1961.

Veronelli, Luigi, *Repertorio Veronelli dei vini italiani.* Bergamo: 2005.

Veronelli, Luigi, ed, *Catalogo Bolaffi dei vini bianchi d'Italia.* Turin: Bolaffi, 1979.

Veronelli, Luigi, ed, *Catalogo Bolaffi dei vini rossi d'Italia.* Turin: Bolaffi, 1980.

Veronelli, Luigi, ed, *Le cantine di Veronelli.* Milan: Giorgio Mondadori, 1987.

Wasserman, Sheldon and Pauline, *Italy's Noble Red Wines.* Piscataway (NJ): New Century Publishers, 1985.

MAGAZINES AND OTHER PUBLICATIONS

Decanter, London (monthly magazine).

Guida essenziale ai vini d'Italia, Doctor Wine, Rome (annual publication).

I vini di Veronelli, Permanent Seminar by Luigi Veronelli, Bergamo (annual publication).

Slow Wine, Slow Food Editore, Bra (annual publication).

Vini d'Italia, Gambero Rosso, Rome (annual publication).

Vitae, Associazione Italiana Sommelier, Milan (annual publication).

Wine Spectator, New York (monthly publication).

WEBSITES

civiltadelbere.com

diwinetaste.com

doctorwine.it

intravino.com

inumeridelvino.it

lavinium.it

quattrocalici.it

slowfood.it/slowine

vinoinrete.it

winenews.it/it

winesurf.it

The History and Images of Italian Wine in 275 Famous Labels

Region and Wine	Producer						Page
Piedmont							
Alta Langa Pas Dosé Blanc de Noirs For England	Contratto				•		47
Alta Langa Pas Dosé Blanc de Noirs Riserva Zero	Enrico Serafino				•		47
Barbaresco Albesani Borgese	Piero Busso		•				47
Barbaresco Asili	Ceretto		•				48
Barbaresco Currà	Sottimano		•				50
Barbaresco Martinenga Riserva Camp Gros	Marchesi di Grésy		•				49
Barbaresco Ovello Vigna Loreto	Albino Rocca		•				49
Barbaresco Pora	Ca' del Baio		•				47
Barbaresco Rabajà	Bruno Rocca		•				50
Barbaresco Rabajà	Giuseppe Cortese		•				48
Barbaresco Riserva Asili	Bruno Giacosa		•				48
Barbaresco Riserva Ovello	Produttori del Barbaresco		•				49
Barbaresco Rombone	Fiorenzo Nada		•				49
Barbaresco Sorì Tildin	Gaja		•				48
Barbera d'Alba Bric du Luv	Ca' Viola		•				50
Barbera d'Alba Vittoria	Gianfranco Alessandria		•				50
Barolo	Bartolo Mascarello		•				54
Barolo Aleste	Luciano Sandrone		•				55
Barolo Bric dël Fiasc	Paolo Scavino		•				55
Barolo Bricco Boschis Riserva Vigna San Giuseppe	Cavallotto – Tenuta Bricco Boschis		•				52
Barolo Brunate	Mario Marengo		•				54
Barolo Ginestra Casa Maté	Elio Grasso		•				53
Barolo Ginestra Ciabot Mentin	Domenico Clerico		•				52
Barolo Monprivato	Giuseppe Mascarello e Figlio		•				54
Barolo Monvigliero	Comm. G.B. Burlotto		•				52
Barolo Ravera Bricco Pernice	Elvio Cogno		•				52
Barolo Riserva	Giacomo Borgogno & Figli		•				51
Barolo Riserva Lazzarito	Ettore Germano		•				53
Barolo Riserva Monfortino	Giacomo Conterno		•				53
Barolo Riserva Vigna Rionda	Massolino		•				54
Barolo Riserva Vignarionda	Oddero Poderi e Cantine		•				55
Barolo Riserva Villero	Vietti		•				56
Barolo Rocche dell'Annunziata	Renato Corino		•				53
Barolo San Rocco	Azelia		•				51
Barolo Sarmassa Riserva Vigna Bricco	Giacomo Brezza e Figli		•				51
Barolo Vignarionda Ester Canale Rosso	Giovanni Rosso		•				55
Barolo Villero	Brovia		•				51
Derthona Costa del Vento	Vigneti Massa	•					56
Dogliani Papà Celso	Marziano Abbona		•				56
Erbaluce di Caluso Tredicimesi	Favaro	•					56
Gattinara Riserva	Giancarlo Travaglini		•				57
Gattinara Riserva Osso San Grato	Antoniolo		•				57
Gavi del comune di Gavi Monterotondo	Villa Sparina	•					57
Gavi del comune di Gavi Rovereto Minaia	Nicola Bergaglio	•					57
Langhe Rosso Larigi	Elio Altare		•				58
Moscato d'Asti Canelli Sant'Ilario	Ca' d' Gal				•	•	58
Moscato d'Asti La Galeisa	Caudrina				•	•	58
Nizza Riserva Bauda	Olim Bauda		•				59
Nizza Riserva La Court	Michele Chiarlo		•				58
Roero Arneis Le Rive del Bricco delle Ciliegie	Giovanni Almondo	•					59
Roero Riserva Renesio Incisa	Monchiero Carbone	•					59

Region and Wine	Producer					Page
Valle d'Aosta						
Sopraquota 900	Rosset Terroir	•				65
Valle d'Aosta Chardonnay Cuvée Bois	Les Crêtes	•				65
Vallée d'Aoste Chardonnay Mains et Coeur	Anselmet	•				65
Vallée d'Aoste Pinot Gris	Lo Triolet	•				65
Lombardy						
Franciacorta Dosage Zéro Riserva Annamaria Clementi	Ca' del Bosco			•		81
Franciacorta Dosaggio Zero Riserva 33	Ferghettina			•		81
Franciacorta Extra Brut Comarì del Salem	Uberti			•		82
Franciacorta Extra Brut Pas Operé	Bellavista			•		81
Franciacorta Satèn Brut	Mosnel			•		81
Nature M. Cl.	Monsupello			•		83
Pinot Nero dell'Oltrepò Pavese Giorgio Odero	Frecciarossa		•			82
Pinot Nero dell'Oltrepò Pavese Pernice	Conte Vistarino		•			82
Sforzato di Valtellina Sfursat 5 Stelle	Nino Negri		•			83
Valtellina Superiore Grumello Riserva	Rainoldi		•			83
Valtellina Superiore Sassella Riserva Rocce Rosse	Ar.Pe.Pe		•			83
Veneto						
Amarone della Valpolicella Campo dei Gigli	Tenuta Sant'Antonio		•			107
Amarone della Valpolicella Classico	Allegrini		•			106
Amarone della Valpolicella Classico	Bertani		•			106
Amarone della Valpolicella Classico	Giuseppe Quintarelli		•			106
Amarone della Valpolicella Classico Riserva Fumetto	Secondo Marco		•			107
Amarone della Valpolicella Classico Riserva La Mattonara	Zýmē		•			108
Amarone della Valpolicella Classico Sant'Urbano	Speri		•			107
Amarone della Valpolicella Riserva Maternigo	Tedeschi		•			107
Amarone della Valpolicella Vigneto di Monte Lodoletta	Romano Dal Forno		•			106
Colli Euganei Fior d'Arancio Passito Donna Daria	Conte Emo Capodilista – La Montecchia				•	108
Colli Euganei Rosso Gemola	Vignalta		•			108
Custoza Superiore Cà del Magro	Monte del Frà	•				108
Fratta	Maculan		•			109
Grave di Stecca	Nino Franco			•		109
Lugana Riserva Sergio Zenato	Zenato	•				82
Montello – Colli Asolani Il Rosso dell'Abazia	Serafini & Vidotto		•			109
Soave Classico Calvarino	Pieropan	•				110
Soave Classico Contrada Salvarenza Vecchie Vigne	Gini	•				110
Soave Classico Foscarino I Palchi Grande Cuvée	Inama	•				110
Soave Classico Monte Carbonare	Suavia	•				111
Soave Classico Monte Fiorentine	Ca' Rugate	•				109
Soave Classico Monte Grande	Prà	•				110
Valdobbiadene Prosecco Superiore Extra Dry Millesimato Giustino B.	Ruggeri			•		111
Valpolicella Classico Superiore San Giorgio Alto	Monte dall'Ora		•			111
Valpolicella Superiore	Roccolo Grassi		•			111
Trentino-Alto Adige						
Alto Adige Cabernet Sauvignon Riserva Freienfeld	Cantina Kurtatsch		•			127
Alto Adige Chardonnay Löwengang	Alois Lageder	•				128
Alto Adige Gewürztraminer Nussbaumer	Cantina Tramin	•				128
Alto Adige Lagrein Riserva Vigna Klosteranger	Cantina Convento Muri-Gries		•			127
Alto Adige Müller Thurgau Feldmarschall von Fenner	Tiefenbrunner – Schlosskellerei Turmhof	•				128
Alto Adige Sauvignon Lafóa	Cantina Colterenzio	•				127
Alto Adige Sauvignon Sanct Valentin	Cantina St. Michael Eppan	•				127
Alto Adige Terlano Pinot Bianco Riserva Vorberg	Cantina Terlano	•				129
Alto Adige Terlano Sauvignon Tannenberg	Manincor	•				130
Alto Adige Val Venosta Riesling Windbichel	Castel Juval – Unterortl	•				130
Alto Adige Valle Isarco Riesling Kaiton	Kuenhof – Peter Pliger	•				129
Alto Adige Valle Isarco Riesling Praepositus	Abbazia di Novacella	•				129

Region and Wine	Producer	🍷	🍷	🍷	🍷	🍷	Page
Alto Adige Valle Isarco Sylvaner Riserva	Köfererhof – Günther Kerschbaumer	•					129
Alto Adige Weissburgunder Riserva Renaissance	Gumphof – Markus Prackwieser	•					128
Granato	Foradori		•				130
San Leonardo	San Leonardo		•				130
Teroldego Rotaliano Riserva Diedri	Dorigati		•				131
Trento Dosaggio Zero Riserva	Letrari				•		131
Trento Extra Brut Riserva del Fondatore Giulio Ferrari	Ferrari				•		131
Friuli-Venezia Giulia							
Carso Vitovska	Kante	•					144
Collio Bianco	Edi Keber	•					144
Collio Bianco Fosarin	Ronco dei Tassi	•					145
Collio Friulano	Franco Toros	•					145
Collio Friulano Vigna del Rolat	Raccaro	•					144
Collio Merlot Graf de La Tour	Villa Russiz		•				145
Collio Pinot Bianco	Doro Princic	•					144
Collio Sauvignon Ronco delle Mele	Venica & Venica	•					145
Friuli Colli Orientali Bianco Biancosesto	Tunella	•					146
Friuli Colli Orientali Bianco Sacrisassi	Le Due Terre	•					146
Friuli Colli Orientali Chardonnay Ronco delle Acacie	Le Vigne di Zamò	•					146
Friuli Isonzo Bianco Lis	Lis Neris	•					146
Friuli Isonzo Sauvignon Blanc Piere	Vie di Romans	•					147
Ribolla	Gravner	•					147
Rosazzo Terre Alte	Livio Felluga	•					147
Vintage Tunina	Jermann	•					147
Emilia-Romagna							
Gutturnio Superiore Vignamorello	La Tosa		•				162
Lambrusco di Sorbara del Fondatore	Cleto Chiarli		•		•		162
Lambrusco di Sorbara Leclisse	Paltrinieri		•		•		162
Lambrusco di Sorbara Spumante Brut Rosé M. Cl.	Cantina della Volta			•	•		162
Romagna Albana Passito Scacco Matto	Fattoria Zerbina					•	163
Romagna Albana Secco Vitalba	Tre Monti	•					163
Romagna Sangiovese Riserva Modigliana Vigna Probi	Villa Papiano		•				163
Romagna Sangiovese Superiore Predappio di Predappio Riserva Vigna del Generale	Fattoria Nicolucci		•				163
Liguria							
Colli di Luni Vermentino Costa Marina	Ottaviano Lambruschi	•					171
Dolceacqua Bricco Arcagna	Terre Bianche		•				171
Dolceacqua Posaú	Maccario Dringenberg		•				171
Riviera Ligure di Ponente Pigato U Baccan	Bruna	•					171
Tuscany							
Bolgheri Rosso Superiore Castello di Bolgheri	Castello di Bolgheri		•				204
Bolgheri Rosso Superiore Grattamacco	Grattamacco		•				204
Bolgheri Rosso Superiore Guado al Tasso	Tenuta Guado al Tasso		•				204
Bolgheri Sassicaia	Tenuta San Guido		•				205
Bolgheri Superiore Ornellaia	Ornellaia		•				204
Bosco	Tenimenti D'Alessandro		•				205
Brunello di Montalcino	Biondi-Santi		•				205
Brunello di Montalcino Cerretalto	Casanova di Neri		•				206
Brunello di Montalcino Madonna delle Grazie	Il Marroneto		•				206
Brunello di Montalcino Ragnaie V.V.	Le Ragnaie		•				206
Brunello di Montalcino Riserva	Capanna		•				205
Brunello di Montalcino Riserva	Poggio di Sotto		•				207
Brunello di Montalcino Riserva Poggio al Vento	Col d'Orcia		•				206
Brunello di Montalcino Vigna Spuntali	Val di Suga		•				207
Camartina	Querciabella		•				207
Carmignano Riserva Piaggia	Piaggia		•				207
Cepparello	Isole e Olena		•				208

Region and Wine	Producer						Page
Chianti Classico Gran Selezione Castello di Brolio	Barone Ricasoli		•				209
Chianti Classico Gran Selezione Coltassala	Castello di Volpaia		•				209
Chianti Classico Gran Selezione Il Poggio	Castello di Monsanto		•				209
Chianti Classico Riserva	Castell'in Villa		•				209
Chianti Classico Riserva Cultus	Badia a Coltibuono		•				208
Chianti Classico Riserva Rancia	Fèlsina		•				210
Chianti Classico Vigna Cavarchione	Istine		•				210
Chianti Rufina Riserva Nipozzano Vecchie Viti	Frescobaldi		•				208
Chianti Rufina Riserva Vigneto Bucerchiale	Fattoria Selvapiana		•				208
Colline Lucchesi Rosso Tenuta di Valgiano	Tenuta di Valgiano		•				210
Cortona Syrah	Stefano Amerighi		•				210
Flaccianello della Pieve	Fontodi		•				211
Il Borro	Il Borro		•				211
Il Caberlot	Podere Il Carnasciale		•				211
L'Apparita	Castello di Ama		•				211
Le Pergole Torte	Montevertine		•				212
Lupicaia	Castello del Terriccio		•				212
Masseto	Masseto		•				212
Montecucco Sangiovese Riserva Poggio Lombrone	ColleMassari		•				212
Oreno	Tenuta Sette Ponti		•				213
Paleo	Le Macchiole		•				213
Percarlo	San Giusto a Rentennano		•				213
Redigaffi	Tua Rita		•				213
Riecine di Riecine	Riecine		•				214
Sammarco	Castello dei Rampolla		•				214
Siepi	Castello di Fonterutoli		•				214
Suisassi	Duemani		•				214
Tenuta di Trinoro	Tenuta di Trinoro		•				215
Tignanello	Marchesi Antinori		•				215
Val d'Arno di Sopra Merlot Vigna Galatrona	Petrolo		•				215
Vernaccia di San Gimignano Carato	Montenidoli	•					216
Vernaccia di San Gimignano Riserva L'Albereta	Il Colombaio di Santa Chiara	•					215
Vin Santo di Carmignano Riserva	Capezzana					•	216
Vino Nobile di Montepulciano Asinone	Poliziano		•				216
Vino Nobile di Montepulciano Il Nocio	Boscarelli		•				216
Umbria							
Cervaro della Sala	Castello della Sala	•					228
Montefalco Sagrantino 25 Anni	Arnaldo Caprai		•				228
Montefalco Sagrantino Molino dell'Attone	Antonelli San Marco		•				228
Orvieto Classico Superiore Mare Antico	Decugnano dei Barbi	•					229
Orvieto Classico Superiore Muffa Nobile Calcaia	Barberani					•	228
Torgiano Rosso Riserva Rubesco Vigna Monticchio	Lungarotti		•				229
Marche							
Castelli di Jesi Verdicchio Riserva Classico Plenio	Umani Ronchi	•					245
Castelli di Jesi Verdicchio Riserva Classico Utopia	Montecappone	•					245
Castelli di Jesi Verdicchio Riserva Classico Vigna Il Cantico della Figura	Andrea Felici	•					244
Castelli di Jesi Verdicchio Riserva Classico Villa Bucci	Bucci	•					244
Conero Riserva Dorico	Moroder		•				243
Il Pollenza	Il Pollenza		•				243
Kurni	Oasi degli Angeli		•				243
Offida Pecorino Io Sono Gaia Non Sono Lucrezia	Le Caniette	•					243
Rosso Piceno Superiore Roggio del Filare	Velenosi		•				244
Verdicchio dei Castelli di Jesi Classico Superiore Podium	Garofoli	•					244
Verdicchio di Matelica	ColleStefano	•					245
Verdicchio di Matelica Riserva Cambrugiano	Belisario	•					245

Region and Wine	Producer						Page
Lazio							
Fiorano Rosso	Tenuta di Fiorano		•				255
Frascati Superiore	Castel De Paolis	•					255
Habemus	San Giovenale		•				255
Latour a Civitella	Sergio Mottura	•					255
Abruzzo							
Abruzzo Pecorino Bianchi Grilli per la Testa	Torre dei Beati	•					266
Cerasuolo d'Abruzzo Piè delle Vigne	Cataldi Madonna			•			266
Colline Teramane Montepulciano d'Abruzzo Riserva Zanna	Illuminati		•				266
Montepulciano d'Abruzzo Riserva Villa Gemma	Masciarelli		•				267
Montepulciano d'Abruzzo Terre dei Vestini Riserva Bellovedere	Fattoria La Valentina		•				266
Montepulciano d'Abruzzo Vigneto Sant'Eusanio	Valle Reale		•				267
Trebbiano d'Abruzzo	Emidio Pepe	•					267
Trebbiano d'Abruzzo	Valentini	•					267
Molise							
Molise Rosso Riserva Don Luigi	Di Majo Norante		•				271
Campania							
Costa d'Amalfi Furore Bianco Fiorduva	Marisa Cuomo	•					287
Fiano di Avellino Ciro 906	Ciro Picariello	•					287
Fiano di Avellino Riserva Tognano	Rocca del Principe	•					287
Greco	Pietracupa	•					287
Greco di Tufo Riserva Vittorio	Di Meo	•					288
Greco di Tufo Vigna Cicogna	Benito Ferrara	•					288
Montevetrano	Montevetrano		•				288
Taurasi Riserva Piano di Montevergine	Feudi di San Gregorio		•				289
Taurasi Riserva Radici	Mastroberardino		•				289
Taurasi Riserva Vigna Grande Cerzito	Quintodecimo		•				289
Taurasi Vigna Macchia dei Goti	Antonio Caggiano		•				288
Terra di Lavoro	Galardi		•				289
Apulia							
Castel del Monte Nero di Troia Riserva Puer Apuliae	Rivera		•				300
Castel del Monte Rosso Riserva Vigna Pedale	Torrevento		•				300
Es	Gianfranco Fino		•				300
Gioia del Colle Primitivo 17 Vigneto Montevella	Polvanera		•				300
Gioia del Colle Primitivo Muro Sant'Angelo Contrada Barbatto	Tenute Chiaromonte		•				301
Graticciaia	Vallone		•				301
Patriglione	Cosimo Taurino		•				301
Primitivo di Manduria Felline	Felline		•				301
Basilicata							
Aglianico del Vulture La Firma	Cantine del Notaio		•				307
Aglianico del Vulture Superiore Don Anselmo	Paternoster		•				307
Aglianico del Vulture Titolo	Elena Fucci		•				307
Calabria							
Cirò Rosso Classico Superiore Riserva	'A Vita		•				315
Cirò Rosso Classico Superiore Riserva Duca San Felice	Librandi		•				315
Sicily							
Contea di Sclafani Rosso Riserva del Conte	Tasca d'Almerita		•				332
Contrada R	Passopisciaro		•				332
Etna Bianco A' Puddara	Tenuta di Fessina	•					334
Etna Bianco Superiore Contrada Rinazzo	Benanti	•					332
Etna Rosso Arcurìa	Graci		•				333
Etna Rosso Barbagalli	Pietradolce		•				333
Etna Rosso Guardiola	Alta Mora – Cusumano		•				332
Etna Rosso Riserva Zottorinoto	Cottanera		•				333
Etna Rosso San Lorenzo	Girolamo Russo		•				333
Etna Rosso San Lorenzo	Tenuta delle Terre Nere		•				334

Region and Wine	Producer	🍷	🍷	🍷	🍷	🍷	Page
Faro Palari	Palari		•				334
Malvasia delle Lipari Passito	Caravaglio					•	334
Passito di Pantelleria Ben Ryé	Donnafugata					•	335
Passito di Pantelleria Bukkuram Sole d'Agosto	Marco De Bartoli					•	335
Sicilia Nero d'Avola Duca Enrico	Duca di Salaparuta		•				335
Sicilia Nero d'Avola Vrucara	Feudo Montoni		•				335
Sicilia Noto Santa Cecilia	Planeta		•				336
Sicilia Rosso NeroBufaleffj	Gulfi		•				336
Sardinia							
Alghero Cabernet Riserva Marchese di Villamarina	Sella&Mosca		•				349
Cannonau di Sardegna Classico Dule	Gabbas		•				349
Cannonau di Sardegna Mamuthone	Giuseppe Sedilesu		•				349
Carignano del Sulcis Superiore Terre Brune	Cantina Santadi		•				349
Malvasia di Bosa Riserva	G. Battista Columbu					•	350
Nuracada	Audarya		•				350
Tenores	Tenute Dettori		•				350
Turriga	Argiolas		•				350
Vermentino di Gallura Superiore Sciala	Surrau	•					351
Vernaccia di Oristano Riserva	Contini					•	351
VT	Capichera	•					351

Recommended Producers, Region by Region

374

A Selection of Quality Wines that, Based on the Choice of the Producers, Do Not Have a DOC or DOCG

(A • separates each wine from the winery that produces it; a – separates the wines within the same region)

Wines from indigenous white vines without DOP (PDO)

FIANO
Apulia: Fiano • L'Archetipo
Campania: Particella 928 Fiano • Cantina del Barone — Zagreo • I Cacciagalli — Campo di Mandrie • Iannucci, Giovanni — Fiano, Cupo • Pietracupa — Pian di Stio, Trentanare • San Salvatore 1988 — Oi Nì • Tenuta Scuotto

FRIULANO
Friuli: Nekaj • Podversic, Damijan — Jakot • Radikon

GARGANEGA
Veneto: Capitel Croce, I Capitelli, Capitel Foscarino • Anselmi — Pico • La Biancara

GLERA
Veneto: Frizzante a Rifermentazione Spontanea in Bottiglia • Ca' dei Zago — Grave di Stecca • Franco, Nino

• GRECHETTO
Lazio: Propizio • Giangirolami, Donato — Poggio della Costa, Latour a Civitella • Mottura, Sergio — Poggio Triale • Tenuta La Pazzaglia
Umbria: Colleozio • Bussoletti, Leonardo — Fiorfiore • Roccafiore

NOSIOLA
Trentino: Largiller • Cantina Toblino — Nosiola Fontanasanta • Foradori — Nosiola • Pojer & Sandri — L'Ora • Pravis

PECORINO
Abruzzo: Casadonna • Feudo Antico — Pecorino • Tiberio — Pecorino Becco Reale • VignaMadre — 8 ½ Pecorino • Villa Medoro
Marche: Giulia Erminia • Fiorano

RIBOLLA
Friuli: Ribolla Gialla • Gravner — Ribolla Gialla • Il Carpino — Ribolla Gialla • Podversic, Damijan — Ribolla • Radikon — Ribolla Gialla • Terpin, Franco

TIMORASSO
Piedmont: Derthona Costa del Vento, Derthona Montecitorio, Derthona Sterpi • Vigneti Massa

TREBBIANO
Abruzzo: Lucì • Praesidium
Campania: Ventiventi • Tenuta Sant'Agostino
Marche: Trebbien • Mattoni, Valter
Umbria: Adarmando • Tabarrini — Le Tese • Romanelli — Calicanto • Villa Mongalli

VERDICCHIO
Marche: Il San Lorenzo Bianco, Le Oche • Fattoria San Lorenzo — Gli Eremi • La Distesa

VERMENTINO
Liguria: Òua • La Ricolla
Sardinia: VT, Capichera, Santigaìni • Capichera — Ruinas • Depperu — Sussinku Bianco • Nuraghe Crabioni — Pusole Bianco • Pusole, Lorenzo

VITOVSKA
Friuli: Vitovska • Kante — Vitovska • Skerk — Solo MM, Vitovska • Vodopivec — V. Vitovska Collection • Zidarich

BLENDS OF LOCAL WHITE GRAPES
Calabria: Petelia • Ceraudo, Roberto
Campania: Sireo • Abbazia di Crapolla — Core Bianco • Montevetrano — Pian di Stio • San Salvatore 1988
Emilia: Il Nativo Ancestrale • TerraQuilia
Friuli: Capo Martino • Jermann
Liguria: Saladero • De Battè, Walter
Marche: Terre Silvate • La Distesa
Sicily: Salealto Tenuta Ficuzza • Cusumano — Vecchio Samperi Perpetuo Quarantennale • De Bartoli, Marco
Veneto: Studio • Ca' Rugate

Wines from indigenous red vines without DOP (PDO)

AGLIANICO
Apulia: Aglianico • Amastuola
Basilicata: Camerlengo • Camerlengo
Campania: Aglianico di Baal • Casa di Baal

BARBERA
Lombardy: Roncolongo • Roncolongo
Piedmont: Barabba • Iuli

CANNONAU
Sardinia: Li Sureddi Rosso • Antichi Vigneti Manca — Susu • Bentu Luna — Tenores • Tenute Dettori

CILIEGIOLO
Tuscany: Ciliegiolo • Camillo, Antonio
Umbria: Ràmici, Brecciaro • Bussoletti, Leonardo

CORVINA
Veneto: La Poja • Allegrini — Hurlo • Garbole

MONTEPULCIANO
Marche: Erasmo Castelli • Castelli, Maria Pia — Regina del Bosco • Fattoria Dezi — Lu Kont • Il Conte Villa Prandone — K'un • Marcelli, Clara — Arshura • Mattoni, Valter — Kurni • Oasi degli Angeli

NERELLO MASCALESE
Calabria: Eleuteria • Tenuta del Travale
Sicily: Tartaraci • Buscemi, Mirella — Munjebel Rosso BB • Cornelissen, Frank — Contrada R, Contrada C, Contrada G • Passopisciaro

NEGROAMARO
Apulia: Cerasa • Calò, Michele & Figli — Teresa Manara Negroamaro — Cantele — Negroamaro • Carvinea — Negroamaro 900 • Duca Carlo Guarini — Le Braci • Garofano — Filari de Sant'Antonī • Hiso Telaray — Notarpanaro, Patriglione • Taurino, Cosimo — Masseria Maìme Negroamaro • Tormaresca — Graticciaia • Vallone — Cosimo Varvaglione Old Vines Negroamaro Collezione Privata • Varvaglione 1921

NERO D'AVOLA
Sicily: Argille di Tagghia Via di Sutta • Centopassi — Rosso di Contrada Parrino • Marabino — Ghammi • Vite ad Ovest

PRIMITIVO
Apulia: Primitivo Terragnolo • Apollonio — Dedicato a Franco e Lucia • Botromagno — Artas • Castello Monaci — Don Antonio Primitivo • Coppi — Es • Fino, Gianfranco — Primitivo Per Lui • Leone De Castris — Old Vines Primitivo • Morella — Ipnotico, Onirico • Terre dei Vaaz — Torcicoda Primitivo • Tormaresca

SANGIOVESE
Romagna: Poggio Tura • Vigne dei Boschi
Tuscany: Grandi Annate • Avignonesi — Fabrizio Bianchi Sangioveto Grosso • Castello di Monsanto — I Tre Borri • Corzano e Paterno — Fontalloro • Fèlsina — Flaccianello della Pieve

• Fontodi — Cepparello • Isole e Olena — Il Nero di Casanova • La Spinetta Casanova — Le Pergole Torte • Montevertine — Il Carbonaione • Podere Poggio Scalette — Riecine di Riecine • Roecine — Percarlo • San Giusto a Rentennano — Uno • Tenuta di Carleone — Ébrius • Valle del Sole
Umbria: Piantata • Cantina Cenci — Sariano • Pomario

UVA DI TROIA
Apulia: Il Sale della Terra • Antica Enotria — Il Nerone della Marchesa • Cantina La Marchesa — Angelo Primo Nero di Troia • Cantine Paradiso — Crusta • Casa Primis — Gelso d'Oro Nero di Troia • Podere 29

BLENDS OF LOCAL RED GRAPES
Apulia: Duca D'Aragona • Candido, Francesco — 1943 del Presidente • Cantine Due Palme — Armécolo • Castel di Salve — Alberello • Felline — Metiusco Rosso • Palamà — Castel Serranova • Vallone
Calabria: Esmén Tetra • Tenuta del Travale — See... Rosso • Spiriti Ebbri
Campania: Terra di Lavoro • Galardi
Sardinia: Turriga, Korem • Argiolas — Sobi • Bentu Luna — Canàles • Cantine di Neoneli — Perdixi • Olianas
Sicily: Rosso del Soprano • Palari
Tuscany: I Sodi di S. Niccolò • Castellare di Castellina — Malgiacca • Malgiacca — Baron'Ugo • Monteraponi — Montevertine • Montevertine — Pācina • Pācina

Wines from international white vines without DOP (PDO)

CHARDONNAY
Friuli-Venezia Giulia: W... Dreams • Jermann — La Bora di Kante, Chardonnay • Kante
Lazio: Ars Magna Chardonnay • Ômina Romana
Tuscany: Chardonnay Collezione Privata • Isole e Olena — Monteverro Chardonnay • Monteverro — Batàr • Querciabella
Umbria: Cervaro della Sala • Castello della Sala

RIESLING
Lombardy: Mat • Cantina Concarena
Sicily: Riesling Eruzione 1614 • Planeta
Veneto: Riesling Renano Collezione di Famiglia • Roeno

SAUVIGNON
Friuli-Venezia Giulia: Eclisse • La Roncaia
Valle d'Aosta: Ferox • La Plantze

VIOGNIER
Lazio: Donna Adriana • Castel de Paolis — Soente • Cotarella — Fiorano Bianco • Tenuta di Fiorano
Umbria: Viognier • Madonna del Latte

BLENDS OF INTERNATIONAL WHITE GRAPES
Alto Adige: Manna • Franz Haas
Friuli-Venezia Giulia: Arnis Blanc • Borgo San Daniele — Bianco Breg • Gravner — Vintage Tunina • Jermann — Braide Alte • Livon — Desiderium I Ferretti • Tenuta Luisa — Dut'Un • Vie di Romans
Veneto: Hora Prima • Mosole — Olivar • Cesconi

Wines from international red vines without DOP (PDO)

CABERNET SAUVIGNON
Calabria: Balconara • Donato D'Angelo
Tuscany: D'Alceo • Castello dei Rampolla — Lupicaia • Castello del Terriccio — Camartina • Querciabella
Veneto: Fratta • Maculan

CABERNET FRANC
Lazio: Atlante • D'Amico, Paolo e Noemia — Habemus Etichetta Rossa • San Giovenale
Romagna: Luna Nuova • San Valentino
Tuscany: Ampeleia • Ampeleia — Duemani • Duemani — La Regola • La Regola — Paleo Rosso • Le Macchiole — Poggio de' Colli • Piaggia — Guardiavigna • Podere Forte — La Regola • Podere La Regola — Filare 18 • Tenuta Casadei
Veneto: Frank! • Barollo

GRENACHE
Marche: Cinabro • Le Caniette — Kupra • Oasi degli Angeli — La Ribalta • Pantaleone

MERLOT
Basilicata: Matematico • Cantina di Venosa
Calabria: Blandus • Terre di Balbia
Friuli-Venezia Giulia: Merlot Vistorta • Vistorta — Ruje • Zidarich
Lazio: Montiano • Cotarella — Ars Magna Merlot • Ômina Romana
Lombardy: Serìz • La Costa — Rebaioli Cavalier Enrico • Togni Rebaioli, Enrico
Tuscany: Volta di Bertinga• Bertinga — Il Blu • Brancaia — Liù • Castello dei Rampolla — L'Apparita • Castello di Ama — Siepi • Castello di Fonterutoli — Il Brecciolino • Castelvecchio — Messorio • Le Macchiole — Masseto • Masseto — La Ricolma • San Giusto a Rentennano — Palazzi • Tenuta di Trinoro — Luce • Tenuta Luce — Redigaffi • Tua Rita

Veneto: Crosara • Maculan — Campo Sella • Sutto

PINOT NERO
Alto Adige: Abraham Art Pinot Noir • Tenuta Abraham — Pinot Nero • Tenuta Dornach
Calabria: Vulcano 800 • Terra dei Re
Lazio: Notturno dei Calanchi • D'Amico, Paolo e Noemia
Lombardy: San Giobbe • La Costa — Arfena • Picchioni, Andrea
Tuscany: Pinot Nero • Podere della Civettaja

SYRAH
Lazio: Mater Matuta • Casale del Giglio
Marche: Il San Lorenzo Rosso • Fattoria San Lorenzo
Sicily: Siriki Rosso • Dei Principi di Spadafora
Tuscany: Castello del Terriccio • Castello del Terriccio — Suisassi • Duemani — Scrio • Le Macchiole — Bosco, Migliara • Tenimenti D'Alessandro — Il Fortino • Tenuta del Buonamico — Per Sempre • Tua Rita

BLENDS OF INTERNATIONAL RED GRAPES
Campania: Montevetrano • Montevetrano
Lazio: I Quattro Mori • Castel de Paolis — Il Vassallo • Colle Picchioni — Casa Romana • Principe Pallavicini — Habemus Etichetta Bianca • San Giovenale — Fiorano Rosso • Tenuta di Fiorano
Lombardy: Le Zalte • Sincette
Marche: Chaos • Fattoria Le Terrazze — Il Pollenza • Il Pollenza
Sicily: Shymer • Baglio di Pianetto
Trentino: Rosso Faye • Pojer & Sandri — San Leonardo, Villa Gresti di San Leonardo • Tenuta San Leonardo
Tuscany: Caiarossa • Caiarossa — Sammarco • Castello dei Rampolla — Gian Annibale • Castello del Terriccio — Ripa delle More • Castello Vicchiomaggio — Duemani • Altrovino — Do Ut Des • Fattoria Carpineta Fontalpino — Saffredi • Fattoria Le Pupille — Il Borro • Il Borro — Solaia • Marchesi Antinori — Monteverro • Monteverro — Principe Guerriero • Pagani De Marchi — Petra • Petra — Caberlot, Carnasciale • Podere Il Carnasciale — Sapaio • Podere Sapaio — Vigorello • San Felice — Biserno • Tenuta di Biserno — Nambrot • Tenuta di Ghizzano — Tenuta di Trinoro • Tenuta di Trinoro — Oreno, Orma • Tenuta Sette Ponti — Il Pareto, Il Borgo • Tenute Ambrogio e Giovanni Folonari — Giusto di Notri • Tua Rita
Veneto: Zuàn • Borin Vini e Vigne — Relógio • Ca' Orologio — Baòn • Conte Emo Capodilista — Masari • Masari

Index

387

389

397

Photo credits
Cover illustration: © Adobe Stock
p. 23: Codegoni Daniele/Shutterstock
p. 64: Co-Enfer - Cooperative de l'Enfer soc. coop
p. 66: Claudio Giovanni Colombo/Shutterstock
p. 114: StevanZZ/Shutterstock
p. 170: Gaspar Janos/Shutterstock
p. 188: Taiga/Shutterstock
p. 217: Kishivan/Shutterstock
p. 254: Stefano Carocci Ph/Shutterstock
p. 310: Giambattista Lazazzera
p. 337: robertonencini/Shutterstock

Art Direction and Graphic Design
Heartfelt.it

Translation by
Christian Jennings

Maps
Marco Zanella
Cristiano Lissoni

Maps on pp. 15 and 19
Francesco Guaita

Hypercritic editorial team
Clara Gastaldi

© 2023 Mondadori Libri S.p.A.
Distributed in English throughout the World
by Rizzoli International Publications Inc.
300 Park Avenue South
New York, NY 10010, USA

ISBN: 978-88-918385-5-1

2024 2025 2026 2027 / 10 9 8 7 6 5 4 3 2 1

First edition: March 2024

This volume was printed at L.E.G.O. S.p.A., Vicenza
Printed in Italy

Visit us online:
Facebook.com/RizzoliNewYork
Twitter: @Rizzoli_Books
Instagram.com/RizzoliBooks
Pinterest.com/RizzoliBooks
Youtube.com/user/RizzoliNY
Issuu.com/Rizzoli